Supervision in Social Work

Supervision in Social Work

SECOND EDITION

ALFRED KADUSHIN

New York   Columbia University Press

Library of Congress Cataloging in Publication Data

Kadushin, Alfred.
Supervision in social work.

Bibliography p.　.
Includes index.
1. Supervision of social work.　I. Title.
HV41.K23 1985　361.3'068'3　84-21397
ISBN 0-231-06008-4

Columbia University Press
New York　Guildford, Surrey

PRINTED IN THE UNITED STATES OF AMERICA

c 10 9 8 7 6 5 4 3

To the good people of Wisconsin who, over a third of a century, have paid me for doing what I would choose to do even if I did not have to do it for a living—teaching, researching, and writing.

CONTENTS

PREFACE TO THE FIRST EDITION

I N TEACHING COURSES in social work supervision in a graduate school and leading supervision workshops and institutes, I became keenly aware of the need for an updated basic text on the subject. This book was written in an effort to meet this need. It provides an overview of the state of the art of social work supervision. It is addressed to supervisors and those preparing to do supervision, whatever their formal educational background. It is also useful to social work supervisees, students and workers, in enabling them to make more productive use of supervision.

The book is designed to help the reader understand the place of supervision in the social agency, the functions it performs, the process of supervision, and the problems with which it is currently concerned. While no book can directly further the development of skills, it provides the knowledge base which is a necessary prerequisite to learning how to do supervision. The book frees the course instructor from the burden of presenting the general background content of supervision so that more time can be devoted to consideration of clinical material and controversial points of view.

An effort has been made to remain eclectic and neutral in presenting a comprehensive, systematic review of social work supervision. While this is generally the orientation of the text, it is pro-supervision. The stance is frankly somewhat conservative, based on my conviction that social work supervision makes a significant contribution to ensuring effective and efficient service to the client. I recognize that such an orientation runs somewhat against the Zeitgeist. However, this may be an advantage. A particular, clearly articulated point of view against which the reader can react, positively or negatively, provides the basis for a dialogue and may help the reader define her, or his, own point of view.

I have made a studied effort to be generic in the presentation. Alas, it ends up heavily weighted in the direction of casework. In soliciting absolution I plead *ex nihilo, nihil fit*—out of nothing, nothing can be made. The experience of the profession and, consequently, the available literature is most heavily weighted in the direction of casework supervision. There is little recent material on supervision in group work and almost nothing on supervision in community organization.

Pronouns are a source of trouble throughout the text. At one time it would suffice to note that all supervisors would be designated "she" and all supervisees "he." We are beyond the point where such conventional designations are acceptable. Consequently, I have randomized the use of pronouns. "He," "she," "her," and "his" are scattered throughout the text in no particular pattern except to equalize the frequency with which they are used.

The book was written during the year that I was a fellow at the Center for Advanced Study in the Behavioral Sciences, Palo Alto, California. My very warm thanks and sincere appreciation to the Center for the opportunity the fellowship provided. The Center not only offered financial support but also a stimulating, supportive context. During the year at the Center I was a member of a fellows seminar on organizational theory. The seminar discussions were relevant to the problems of social work supervision, and I am indebted to other members of the seminar for helping me clarify my ideas—Michael Crozier, Herbert Jacobs, Martin Krieger, James March, Eugene Pusic, Daniel Shimshoni, Judith Tendler, Julian Wolpert.

My thanks to John D. Moore of Columbia University Press for editorial encouragement. My further thanks to Anna Tower who patiently deciphered my handwritten hieroglyphics and conscientiously typed many more pages than appear here.

To Sylvia, severest critic and most compassionate friend, my deepest love for constant help, support, and comfort, as well as to Goldie and Raphael, formerly children, now my friends.

                                                                          A. K.

PREFACE TO THE SECOND EDITION

WHAT JUSTIFIES a second edition of the book at this time? One traditional justification for the second edition of any text is applicable here. The first edition was published in 1976, and in the ten years which have elapsed much additional research and expository material on social work supervision has become available.

Since 1976 eleven books concerned with social work supervision have been published. Five principal social work journals—*Social Work; Social Casework; Social Service Review; Administration in Social Work;* and *The Journal of Social Work Education*—have published, in aggregate, more than fifty articles on social work supervision between 1975 and 1985. Continuing interest in social work supervision is validated by the publication of a new journal directed toward this interest—*The Journal of Clinical Supervision*. In addition, during the past ten years the list of books concerned with social work supervision has expanded rapidly.

Changes in public social welfare policy during the past ten years have intensified concern with social work supervision, particularly its administrative responsibilities. At the time the first edition of the book was published, we had already seen a growing concern with agency accountability to clients and the community. More recently other concerns—for efficiency and productivity—have been added to the continuing concern for accountability. Tax and spending limitations at all levels of government, and growing budgetary stringency reflecting the more sluggish economy have resulted in reduction of financial support for social service agency programs. The current situation is characterized by reduction in staff, retrenchment in programming, and limitations in resources available to agencies.

Social agencies are labor intensive operations. The current political context, which now provides less financial support for social services than at any time in the immediate past, calls for doing more with less. One possible if difficult solution is to increase the productivity of each worker. Increasing productivity requires greater managerial efficiency and more imaginative agency management.

Organizational survival may hinge on the ability of administrative supervision to fine tune agency performance, increase efficiency, and deploy limited staff more effectively. As Miringoff (1980) says, "The development of human services in the coming decade will come not through major increases in funds but through more effective and efficient use of current resources" (p. 3). And supervisory personnel are the crucial element in dealing with worker efficiency and productivity, as they were in meeting the earlier demands for increased agency accountability.

More limited resources and the demands associated with taxpayer revolts have made issues of accountability a matter of much greater concern than ever before. Since agency accountability starts with the supervisor's review and evaluation of the work of the direct service staff, such issues intensify the visibility and importance of supervision.

Increasing dependence of agencies on governmental funding, third-party payments, and legislative mandates have all resulted in the increasing external regulation of agencies. The need for documentation of agency activities through periodic reports further increases the need for administrative supervision to insure that such information is available. Compliance with external regulatory requirements of funding sources such as medicaid, medicare, and Title XX put a premium on the need for supervisory personnel.

Some regulatory changes during the past ten years have once again increased the importance and significance of social work supervision. Third-party insurance payments often require that the worker be receiving formal supervision as an eligibility condition for payment. Licensing and registration legislation adopted by now in some 31 states often requires that the worker licensed or registered have formal access to supervision.

Reduction in services and resources available to the social worker has resulted in a greater need to prioritize work and to prioritize decisions regarding the allocation of scarce supplies. Now more than ever before the worker is faced with the necessity of making difficult decisions regarding what gets done, what is ignored, who is provided service, and who is denied service. Many triage, lifeboat decisions which are more frequent now require, if not the help, at least the shared responsibility of a representative of management. Such situations increase the need for supervisory personnel.

Supervision and in-service training and staff development share responsibility for helping the worker learn what he needs to know in order to effectively do his job. Cuts in agency budgets have frequently required cuts in in-service training and staff development programs. Agencies have increasing difficulty in funding worker attendance at workshops or institutes and national meetings. As a consequence, supervision becomes increasingly more important as a source of training and often is the only resource available to help workers enhance their skills.

A review of the major modifications made by administrators of social service programs in response to funding cuts noted that "less qualified people are being hired by state and local agencies in order to reduce the average staff salary" and "staff training is being postponed or eliminated" (Gutowski and Koshel, 1982, p. 327). Both changes place an increasing burden on supervisors for training the newly hired untrained worker.

Recognition of the need for supervision has been formalized, in that candidates for the title of certified social worker (ACSW) are required to have been supervised for a minimum of two years following the MSW. Similarly other specialized professional organizations that enlist social workers require some minimum hours of supervised practice for licensing or registration. This includes organizations such as The American Association of Marriage and Family Therapists and The National Commission for Credentialing of Alcoholism Counselors.

The ascendence of a political orientation that seeks to curtail the development of social programs and limit access to resources increases the importance of supervision for preserving the commitment of social work to a political orientation that is more humanistic. An orientation antagonistic to the objectives and values of social work has been made evident not only in legislative changes but in attempts at imposing business management technologies on social agencies. The increasing tendency to appoint business managers to administer social agencies has been encouraged by the proliferation of business administration graduates who are actively seeking such positions.

If social work, in defense of its own values, hopes to resist such impositions, it needs to be concerned with increasing the effectiveness of its own managerial practices. Concern by social agencies with improving the practice of supervision is one approach to contesting the imposition by outsiders of managerial practices which might conflict with the values, ethics, and philosophy of social work. "We" rather than "they" would formulate and implement the changes in managerial practice. In doing so we would increase the certainty that social agency administration reflects social work ideology.

Not only do social agencies depend on the community for continuing support and for their very existence, but the nature of this support is tenuous and ambivalent. The public attitude toward social agencies and their clientele has never been enthusiastically positive. Most often the attitude toward the support of social agencies has been begrudgingly hesitant. Consequently agencies are constantly mindful of public relations and the need to carefully monitor the basis for their continuing social and political support. Any action on the part of agency personnel which might threaten the legitimacy of the agencies' claim for public support is a matter of serious concern. This is particularly true during a period of political reaction and conservatism, a time when embarrassing decisions can be more effectively exploited to reduce agency support. The vulnerable position of social agencies indicates the need for supervisors who have the responsibility and the authority to reduce the probability of such incidents.

Changes in the relationship between human service organizations and the courts during the last ten years have also increased the significance of supervisory personnel. The past decade has been characterized by increases in the frequency of legal challenges to human service programs as courts more actively inquire into areas previously left to the discretion of agencies.

With increased attention to clients' rights and malpractice suits, many ethical and professional issues have been transformed into legal issues. The increased possibility of legal action against agencies by clients and community groups highlights the need for supervision to prevent damaging challenges from developing.

Since the publication of the first edition of this book, another previously unexplored problem—the problem of worker burn-out—was "discovered" and given considerable attention in the literature.

The relevance to supervision of this new development lies in the fact that the research on burn-out has come to the consensual conclusion that supportive supervision is a key prophylactic and palliative for burn-out. The lack of any discussion of burn-out in the first edition has been compensated for in the second.

Though the calls for more supervision predominate, there are admittedly some changes that reduce the need for supervision. The tightened job market has reduced turnover and increased time in the position; experienced workers need less supervision than beginners; and there is a tendency to reduce agency managerial costs by eliminating layers of supervision as part of a general trend toward debureaucratizing agencies. On balance, however, recent changes would tend to suggest a heightened concern with social agency supervision.

All of these various changes and developments justify a second edition. It is also prompted by the fact that widespread use of the book in courses, workshops, and institutes has clearly identified some of the strengths and weaknesses of the first edition. Based on the feedback from supervisors and supervisees, students and instructors, a second edition permits the opportunity to give increased space, emphasis, and priority to the strengths and to eliminate some of the shortcomings of the first edition.

Because of the addition of considerable new material and the necessity of keeping the book to a manageable size, we have deleted a chapter on "Supervision of Paraprofessonals" which appeared in the first edition. We have, however, updated this chapter and would be glad to provide a copy to any reader who is especially interested in this subject. You can obtain such a copy by writing to me at the School of Social Work, 425 Henry Mall, University of Wisconsin, Madison, Wisconsin 53706.

Completion of this second edition was assisted by summer salary support provided by funds from the Julia C. Lathrop Distinguished Professorship Award to the author from the University of Wisconsin. My very sincere thanks to the University for this help.

My sincere appreciation and thanks to Carol Betts, an indefatigable secretary, who patiently and accurately typed revisions to revisions of revisions.

A. K.

CHAPTER ONE
Introduction, History, and Definition

THE QUALITY of supervision is a significant factor in professional socialization, social-work job satisfaction, and job turnover. In a study of the process through which therapists are educated to perform their roles, Henry, Sims, and Spray (1971) obtained detailed material from some 1,100 psychiatric social workers. They note that "among the various specific experiences considered important by mental health professionals, supervision stands out as the single most important experience—even among mental health professionals who have received psychotherapy, supervision is most often considered the single most important socialization experience" (pp. 150–52).

A nationwide study of 1,600 workers in 31 social welfare and rehabilitation agencies states that "the data are conclusive. High agency scores on the supervision variable were accompanied by greater satisfaction, better individual performance, less absenteeism, better agency performance and higher agency competence" (Olmstead and Christensen 1973, p. 304).

Similar findings are noted in studies of supervision in related service professions. Aiken, Smits, and Lollar (1972) studied the job satisfaction of workers in state rehabilitation agencies. Employing a series of psychological and attitudinal scales with 360 counselors, they found that

> the most important aspect of employment in state rehabilitation agencies, as far as counselors are concerned, is the interpersonal behavior in which the supervisor and counselor engage. How the supervisior treats the counselor seems to be far more important than working conditions or the reward system of the agency. The importance of the supervisor-counselor relationship is consistent with the attractability and the role demands of the counselor's position . . . . A major component of their role demands is the ability to establish rapport with their clients. It is not suprising that these same people look to their supervisors for help via an interpersonal modality. (p. 5)

The *Local Child Welfare Services Self-Assessment Manual* (1978) distributed by the Children's Bureau states that "effective supervision is one of the most important means of improving staff morale and performance and reducing costly turnover" (p. VIII–64). *The NASW Standards for Social Service Manpower* (1973) requires supervision of the worker at four of the levels of practice cited—"social service aide; social service technician; baccalaureate degree social worker; graduate masters degree social worker." Only the "Certified Social Worker" is regarded as fully "capable of autonomous self directed practice."

By 1982, twenty-three states had some kind of law regulating the licensing and/or registration of social workers. Such legislation often mandates varying amounts of experience under supervision as a requirement for licensing and registration. State licensing law often requires two years of supervised practice after attaining the MSW in order to obtain independent licensed status.

Supervision is of increasing significance to the professionally trained social worker. With more explicit recognition, by both the National Association of Social Workers and the Council of Social Work Education, of the Bachelor of Social Work (BSW) as a first professional degree for entry-level positions, greater emphasis is being placed on MSW training as preparation for supervisory, consultative, administrative, and planning tasks.

Studies of the activities of Bachelor's Degree and Master's Degree social workers in the same agencies pointed out that BSWs were more likely to be providing direct service, whereas the MSWs were more involved in supervision of, and/or consultation with, BSW workers (Barker 1972, p. 92). A survey of 205 graduates (1971–76) of the University of Texas School of Social Work found that "Middle management kinds of skills are called into play rather early in the careers of many MSW social workers" (Sherwood and Daley 1979, p. 71).

An examination of the process of supervision is thus significant not only to social workers generally but to professionally trained social workers in particular. These workers are very likely to be faced with the responsibility of acting in the role of supervisor early in their professional careers.

Historical Development

There are few and scattered references to social work supervision before 1920. Many of the references listed under supervision in the index of the *Proceedings of Conferences on Charities and Correction* or in older social work journals refer, in fact, to quite a different process from the supervision we talk about today. Such references are usually concerned with administrative supervision of agencies by some licensing authority or governmental board to which the agencies were accountable for public funds spent and for their service to the client. Supervision referred to the control and coordinating function of a State Board of Supervisors, a State Board of Charities, or a State Board of Control. The term "supervision" applied to the inspection and review of programs and institutions rather than to supervision of individual workers within the program.

The first social work text that used the word "supervision" in the title, *Supervision and Education in Charity* by Jeffrey R. Brackett (1904), was concerned with supervision of welfare agencies and institutions by public boards and commissions. Sidney Eisenberg, who has written a short history of supervision in social work, notes that Mary Richmond, "one of the most original contributors to the development of social work, made no mention of supervision in her published works" (1956a, p. 1).

With publication of *The Family* (now *Social Casework*) by the Family Welfare Organizing Association of America, beginning in 1920, there are increasingly frequent references to supervision as we know it today, that is, supervision of the individual social worker.

Mary Burns (1958) comments that while components of the supervisory process were described in the literature as early as 1880 and 1890, the entity with which we are concerned in this book was not clearly recognized and explicitly identified until much later. It "was not included in the index of *Family* until 1925 and not until after 1930 in the *Proceedings of the National Conference of Social Work*" (1958, p. 8).

Supervision as we know it today had its origins in the Charity Organization Society movement in the nineteenth century. A concern for the possible consequences of indiscriminate almsgiving led to organization of charity on a rational basis. Starting in Buffalo, New York, in 1878, Charity Organization societies soon were developed in most of the large eastern cities. The agencies granted financial assistance after a rigorous investigation, but such help was regarded as only one aspect of the service offered. The more important component of help was offered by "friendly visitors," volunteers who were assigned to families to offer personal support and to influence behavior in a socially desirable direction. "Not alms, but a friend" was the watchword of the Charity Organization movement.

"Visitors" were the direct service workers, the foot soldiers, of the Charity Organization agencies. As volunteers they were generally assigned to a limited number of families (Gurteen 1882). Limited caseloads coupled with high turnover of volunteers meant that the agencies faced a continuous problem of recruiting, training, and directing new visitors. These tasks were primarily the responsibility of a limited number of "paid agents" employed by the Charity Organization societies. The paid agents were the early predecessors of the modern supervisor. Each agent-supervisor was responsible for a sizable number of visitors. The few statistics we have available testify to the fact that the principal burden of contact with the client was covered by visitors under the direction of a limited number of paid agents. Burns (1958) indicates that "by 1890 there were 78 charity organization societies with 174 paid workers and 2,017 volunteer friendly visitors" (p. 16).

Initially the paid agent shared responsibility for supervision of the visitor with the district committee. The district committee was in effect the local executive committee of the Charity Organization district office. The committee generally consisted of lay people and representatives of local charitable agencies.

When a family requested help the initial study was done by the agent, who then reported the findings at a weekly district committee conference. The committee discussed the case and decided its disposition. The fact that cases were brought directly to the district committee for determination of action meant that, initially, the paid agent-supervisor had relatively little managerial autonomy. He and the visitor both were "agents" of the district committee. Generally, however, district committees became more policy- and general-administration-oriented. Gradually over time, responsibility for decision-making on individual cases was given to the paid agent-supervisor. The visitors, and the paid workers who subsequently replaced them, discussed their cases with the agent-supervisor, who was responsible for the decision and its subsequent implementation by the visitor or worker. The agent-supervisor thus became the administrative-managerial representative of the organization who was most immediately responsible for the work of the direct service worker.

The agent provided a dependable administrative point of contact for the visitor, gave continuity to the work, and acted as a channel of communication. "The agent is always to be found at certain hours and, giving all this time, naturally becomes the center of district work, receiving both from visitors and [the District] Committee information and advice to be transmitted one to the other" (Smith 1884, p. 70). As Fields says in one of the earliest social work texts, *How to Help the Poor* (1885), "The agent becomes the connecting link for the volunteer visitors who come daily for advice and assistance" (p. 18). The agent-supervisor, acting as a channel of communication, needed to be "careful to represent the Committee faithfully to the visitors and the visitors faithfully to the Committee" (Smith 1887, p. 161).

All the significant components of current supervisory procedures can be discerned in descriptions of the activities of the paid agent-supervisors. Zilpha Smith, general secretary of the Boston Associated Charities and later director of the Smith College Training School of Psychiatric Social Work, was one of the first to write on supervision and training of visitors. She exhorted the district agent to "look over the records of the visited families frequently to see if the work is satisfactory or if any suggestions can make it so" (Smith 1901b, p. 46). Here the administrative requirement of ensuring that the "work is satisfactory" is coupled with the educational task of supervision.

According to a Boston Associated Charities report of 1881, the agent was charged with the responsibility of "investigation and preparation of cases for the volunteer visitors and advising and aiding the visitors in their work. . . . The visitors . . . consult with the agent regarding the families they have befriended. Investigation by the agent precedes the appointment of a visitor in every case. This is necessary for the purpose of getting accurate and thorough knowledge; and when we know the family we can select the visitors whom we think most likely to perservere and be of greatest benefit" (Burns 1958, p. 24). Here the administrative task of differential case assignment is coupled with the educational task of "advising and aiding."

The paid agent or district secretary had to deal with the feeling responses of visitors to their work. On meeting the family to which she had been assigned, a "visitor returned immediately to say that those children must be taken away, the home was too dreadful.

Then she was persuaded to try to make the home fit for them to stay in. As in this instance the new visitor often needs another's steady hand and head to guide her through the first shocks of finding conditions so strange to his experience that he cannot judge them rightly" (Smith 1892, p. 53).

Since visitors were always difficult to recruit, easy to lose, and often frustrated and disappointed, they needed such supportive supervision from the agent-supervisor in addition to administrative direction and training.

In a report written in 1889, the Boston Associated Charities stated that "a large part of the agent's day consists of consultation with visitors . . . and there is opportunity for much tact and personal power in helping new visitors to understand what aid will benefit and what aid would harm their families, and in inspiring those who become discouraged to keep on until things look brighter again." Here the supervisor's responsibility for "consultation with visitors" in furthering the visitor's "understanding" is supplemented by the need to offer support and inspiration for discouraged workers. One way of showing support in times of discouragement was to commend the worker for progress with families to whom they had been assigned:

> A lady who had shown herself a good visitor came to the office one day and said, "I think I may as well give up the Browns, I cannot see that I do any good there." But the agent said: "Think over last week. Do you remember what you said then?" "No." "You said those children's faces were never clean; they were clean before. That surely shows a little improvement. Do go once more." (Smith 1892, p. 57)

The early literature points to many principles of supervision that are still accepted and desirable. For instance, the paid agents assigned work to visitors with a sensitive contemporary-sounding regard for the visitor's needs.

> A visitor showed ingenuity and force of character but the first hint of responsibility frightened her. The Agent asked her to take a message to a serving woman, later to take another, then when she was calling on a family near by, would she not slip in and see how she was getting on and after three or four times, the agent said, "Now I am going to put you down as a visitor to Mrs. B." She has been drawn in such a way into visiting seven families in all, more than we usually think wise for one visitor but she can give her whole time, is interested and enthusi-

astic. If anything like so much responsibility had been urged upon her at first, she would have been frightened away from the work entirely. (Smith 1892, p. 54)

The literature emphasized that the agent's administrative, educational, and supportive responsibilities were most effectively implemented in the context of a positive relationship. In 1901, Smith said:

> In order to make friendly visiting succeed . . . the agents must care to really help the visitor—not merely to give what the visitor asks, but, with tact and patience what he needs and to go at it simply and informally. The agent . . . must learn patiently to know and understand the new visitor. . . . Thought must be given to his problems and both direct and indirect means used to help him help himself in working them out wit'1 the poor family. (1901a, pp. 159–60)

Earlier she had noted that "the agent should be one able to guide and inspire others, ready to step in and help when necessary in what is properly visitor's work but sufficiently patient with the imperfections and delays of volunteers not to usurp the visitor's place" (1884, p. 69).

It was noted that education of visitors should emphasize the principles for worker action: "The meetings of visitors rightly managed are a great power of education. In these meetings, and in talking or writing to visitors, details should not be allowed to hide principles on which the work rests. The principles should be discussed and the reasons for them given again and again as new visitors come to the meetings or new knowledge invites a change of policy" (Smith 1887, p. 160).

While group meetings of visitors were frequently the context for such instructions, individual supervision, using the visitor's case record as the text for training, was employed more and more frequently.

Not only were the present functions and approaches of supervision foreshadowed in this earlier development of the process but so was the present hierarchical position of the supervisor. While the "paid agent" acted as supervisor to the volunteer visitor, the paid agent "supervisor" was himself supervised by the district committee which had ultimate authority for case decisions. Early charity organization records speak of members of the central executive committee coming to "consult and advise with Agent concerning the work"

(Becker 1963, p. 256). The paid agent supervisor was then in a middle management position, as is true of supervisors today—supervising the direct service worker but being themselves under the authority of the agency administrators.

The amplifying effect of supervision in extending the influence of a limited number of trained and experienced workers was recognized early. "The agent's knowledge and experience was extended over a far wider field than he could have covered alone. The inexperienced worker was trained by actual service without the risk of injuring the beneficiaries in the process, and the family visited had the advantage of both the agent's professional knowledge and the visitor's more intimate and personal friendliness" (Conyngton 1909, pp. 22–23).

By the turn of the century there was a gradual change in the composition of agency staffs, which affected supervision. Difficulty in depending on a staff of volunteer visitors who needed to be constantly "obtained, trained and retrained" became more evident as demands on agencies expanded. With the growth of industrialization and urbanization in late-nineteenth-century America and the large increases in immigration, the need for paid staff increased. As a consequence there was a gradual decrease in the ratio of volunteer friendly visitors to paid staff. Although such staff still initially required training by more experienced agent-supervisors, a cadre of trained workers who remained on the job for some time was being built up and the demands for supervisory education and support became somewhat less onerous. At the same time the burden of educating workers in the supervisory context was partly relieved by other resources.

From the very beginning of the Charity Organization movement, discussion groups of visitors and agents had been encouraged. Evening reading groups met to discuss current literature and to share experiences. The 1892 annual report of the Charity Organization Society of Baltimore notes that short papers, followed by discussion, were presented at meetings of visitors on the following topics: "How to Help Out-of-Work Cases," "The Treatment of Drunkards' Families," "Sanitation in the Homes of the Poor," "The Cost of Subsistence," "Deserted Wives," "Cooking and Marketing." The Boston South End District visitors and agents heard lectures on "Housing the Poor," "The Sweating System of Boston," "Trade Unions," "The

Social Situation at the South End," and one, by Professor John R. Commons of the University of Wisconsin, on "Training of the Friendly Visitor."

The better-established Charity Organization societies gradually began to conduct more formal training programs which involved systematic education of those selected to be paid agents. For instance, the Boston Charities Organization initiated in-service training programs for new agents in 1891. The new agents were "apprenticed" to more experienced workers, participated in group teaching sessions conducted by the general secretary of the organization, and were assigned readings from the well-developed agency library. The supervising, experienced agents met periodically with the general secretary to discuss problems of educational supervision. By 1896 the Boston Organization stated in its annual report:

> We have a higher standard for our agents. When the society started, there were no experts at this work; the agents and committees had to work together to acquire their training as best they could; while now, we have a well-organized system for training agents by having them work under direction, both in the Conferences and in the Central Office, before they are placed in positions of responsibility; so that there is always an agent qualified for the place should a vacancy occur. . . . We have undertaken to prepare our [agents] for their work by a system of preliminary training which we hope will make them more positively efficient and guard them from errors unavoidable among the untrained. . . . We have had hopes of being able carefully to train new volunteer visitors. . . . We have thought, thus, to develop wisely the good intentions of those who join us with the generous, if sometimes indefinite, purpose to do good.

State and national conferences offered an opportunity for the exchange of information and ideas among people working in welfare organizations and institutions. They were, in effect, a source of training. The first National Conference of Charities and Correction was held in Chicago in 1879. In 1882 Wisconsin organized the first State Conference of Charities and Correction. The published proceedings of such conferences provided material for education and training. These were supplemented by a growing body of periodical literature that spoke to the concerns of people working in the field. Texts and tracts devoted to the work of charities' agency personnel were also published. In addition to the texts referred to above, Mary

Richmond, then General Secretary of the Charity Organization Society of Baltimore, published *Friendly Visiting Among the Poor: A
Handbook for Charity Workers* in 1899, and Edward Devine, General Secretary of the Charity Organization Society of New York City,
published *The Practice of Charity* in 1901.

The 1887 annual report of the Brooklyn Bureau of Charities states
that "the nucleus of a library has been formed at the Central Office
and now includes some 2,500 books, pamphlets and papers relating
to the principles and methods of charitable work and cognate sub-
jects. The collection is already worth the attention of those interested."

Gradually a body of practice wisdom was being developed, codified, and made explicit for communication through published
channels. A group of practitioners interested in a particular phenomenon that ultimately became known as social work was gradually being identified and was developing a sense of conscious self-
identification. The development of a knowledge base was accompanied by growing recognition that sympathy and interest alone
were not sufficient to make a good worker. The 22d annual report of
the Charity Organization of Baltimore (1903) comments that the
"day is long passed when the only necessary qualifications for social
service are good inclinations. To minister successfully to a family
whose own resources have broken down requires intelligence and
skill of a high order." The prerequisites associated with the emer-
gence of a profession gradually began to become clear.

The development of a knowledge base made it possible to offer
courses on social work content in colleges and universities—the
beginnings of professional education—by departments of sociology
and economics. These disciplines were closely allied with "social
work" at that time and saw it as applied sociology. Frequently the
academic courses used the Charity Organizations as social laboratories for student education. In 1894 it was reported that 21 of 146
colleges and universities contacted in a survey were giving courses
in charities and correction (cited by Brackett 1904, p. 158). For
instance, the University of Wisconsin offered courses in practical
philanthropy in the early 1890s. Professor Richard T. Ely, who was
responsible for the development of that program, arranged for a
course of lectures on charities by Dr. Amos G. Warner. "Expanded
and published as 'American Charities' in the Library of Economics

and Politics edited by Dr. Ely, these lectures became the first standard book on the subject" (Brackett 1904, p. 162).

These various approaches to training personnel for the emerging profession culminated in the movement for development of a formal comprehensive program of specialized education. Anna L. Dawes is generally credited with making the initial suggestion for "training schools for a new profession." In a paper presented at the International Congress of Charities in Chicago in 1893, she argued that "it ought to be possible for those who take up this work to find some place for studying it as a profession." Students in such a training school could be taught "what is now the alphabet of charitable science—some knowledge of its underlying ideas, its tried and trusted methods and some acquaintance with the various devices employed for the upbuilding of the needy so that no philanthropic undertaking, from a model tenement house to a kindergarten or a sand heap, will be altogether strange." The motion was seconded by Mary Richmond, who argued for the need for a training school in applied philanthropy at the 24th National Conference of Charities in 1897. Richmond (1897a) reported that while it was true that each Charity Organization Society took some responsibility for training its visitors and its workers through the district-committee conferences and the activities of the paid agent-supervisors, such education was apt to be agency centered and parochial: "This training specializes too soon and our leaders have but the need for a more intimate and sympathetic acquaintance on the part of our agents with almshouse work, reformatory work, care of defectives and all the other branches of work represented at this [National] Conference. . . . The school that is to be most helpful to our charity organization agents, therefore, must be established on a broad basis" (p. 184).

In June 1898 a six-week summer training program was offered to 27 students by the New York Charity Organization Society. This program is regarded as the beginning of professional education in social work. The summer course was repeated for a number of years and then expanded to become the New York School of Philanthropy, the first full-time school of social work. It is now the Columbia University School of Social Work. A school for social workers was established by Simmons College and Harvard University in 1904, and in 1907 the Chicago School of Civics and Philanthropy (now the

University of Chicago School of Social Service Administration) was established.

By 1910 five schools of social work had been established in the United States. Primary responsibility for training a cadre of social work professionals was vested in such schools. Agency supervision was seen as a supplementary educational resource. But since the number of schools was so limited, the greatest bulk of paid agents (later called charity workers and ultimately social workers) still reviewed their training through apprenticeship programs in social agencies under the tutorship of more experienced agent-supervisors.

Although charged with this responsibility for educational supervision, almost none of the supervisors had any formal training in supervision since none was available. A short course in supervision was offered for the first time in 1911 under the aegis of the Charity Organization Department of the Russell Sage Foundation. The department was headed by Mary Richmond at that time.

Thus, starting with the development of the Charity Organization movement in the 1880s, supervision gradually emerged as a necessary aspect of Charity Organization work. The agent-supervisor organized, directed, and coordinated the work of visitors and paid agents and held them accountable for their performance; he advised, educated, and trained visitors and paid agents in performance of their work and supported and inspired them in their discouragements and disappointments. The three major components of current supervision were thus identifiable among the tasks assumed by the early agent-supervisor. The case record had been identified as the principal vehicle for supervision, and the individual conference as the principal context.

By the turn of the century the educational apparatus of a profession was being organized and was assuming the main responsibility for training. Supervision continued to perform an educational function but now more as a supplement to such formal training institutions. Over time, supervision achieved more visibility in the agency administrative structure, and the process itself gradually became more formalized. Time, place, content, procedures, and expectations of supervisory conferences received clearer definition. As social work became more diversified, supervision took root not only in family service agencies where it had had its origins but also in corrections, psychiatric social work agencies, medical social work agencies, and schools.

As supervision became a more identifiable process, it was subjected to explicit analysis. Between 1920 and 1945 *Family* and then *Social Casework* published some 35 articles specifically devoted to supervision.

The Milford Conference Report (1929) concluded that "supervision of the staff should be conceived as having two functions, first to keep the work of the agency up to the standard it has set for itself; and second to promote the professional development of staff" (p. 55). The conclusion makes explicit the administrative and educational functions of supervision during this earlier period.

A number of books were written that were devoted exclusively, or primarily, to social work supervision. Virginia Robinson published a pioneer work in 1936, *Supervision in Social Case Work*, followed by *The Dynamics of Supervision under Functional Controls* (1949). In 1942 Bertha Reynolds wrote *Learning and Teaching in the Practice of Social Work*, which is devoted in large measure to educational supervision. In 1945 Charlotte Towle included an extended section on social work supervision in her widely distributed pamphlet *Common Human Needs*, published by the Federal Security Agency and later reprinted by the National Association of Social Workers. Towle enlarged on that work in *The Learner in Education for the Professions*, published in 1954.

A review of the published material tends to indicate that the direction and concerns of social work supervision have mirrored, over time, some of the changes in orientation of social work generally and casework in particular. Early in the history of social work it was thought that the worker, or friendly visitor, knew what was best for the client. Knowing this, the worker offered the client clear advice as to what should be done and she arranged, independently of the client, to make resources available on the client's behalf. This was sometimes called an "executive treatment" approach (Lee 1923). Analogously the supervisor, knowing what was best, told the worker what needed to be done.

As social work developed a greater appreciation of the need to actively involve clients' participation in, and planning of, their own solutions to problems, there was a complementary change in the approach in supervision. Supervision moved from telling the supervisees what to do to a greater encouragement of supervisee participation in planning and an increased mutuality in the supervisor-supervisee relationship (Glendenning 1923).

Although the impact of psychoanalytic psychology on the actual service offered the client in the 1920s may have been exaggerated (Alexander 1972), many of its ideas do seem to have influenced the orientation of supervision during that period. Supervision was seen as a kind of relationship therapy analogous to casework for the client. In order to be effective with clients, workers needed to be aware of, and have the help of the supervisor in resolving, their own intrapsychic conflicts (Glendenning 1923). Marcus (1927) suggested that

> the supervisor consider herself a caseworker whose case work must embrace not only the student's cases but the student herself. This demands, of course, that the supervisor investigate and treat the personal problem of the student as the latter investigates and treats those of the client. . . . If casework is an art and a philosophy and not merely a trade practiced on the handicapped and helpless, it was to be just as thoroughly a part of the caseworker's attitude toward herself. (p. 386)

In the midst of the "psychiatric deluge," however, Paige (a supervisor) writes of supervision in terms which emphasize accountability. She talks about the supervisor's holding the worker "to the meticulous adherence to the enforcement of social legislation in which minimum social standards have been crystallized" (1927, p. 307).

During the same period, Dawson (1926) explicitly stated the functions of supervision in traditional terms, as administrative (the promotion and maintenance of good standards of work, coordination of practice with policies of administration, the assurance of an efficient and smooth-working office); educational ("the educational development of each individual worker on the staff in a manner calculated to evoke her fully to realize her possibilities of usefulness"); and supportive (the maintenance of harmonious working relationships, the cultivation of esprit de corps) (p. 293).

At different points of time, the preferred model for the supervisor-supervisee relationship reflected the preferred model of the worker-client case work relationship rather than any of the models of group-worker or community-worker interaction. This is, of course,

not surprising since the supervisor-supervisee relationship, like the worker-client relationship, is dyadic. Whatever the profession at any one time thinks makes for an effective dyadic relationship will be reflected in the models applicable to both the worker-client and the supervisor-supervisee relationship.

The component of supervision that overall has received the greatest emphasis in the literature is educational supervision. Theoreticians of social work supervision have attempted to apply a more general theory of growth and change to the educational process in supervision. Robinson, in the first book written on case work supervision (1936) and in her subsequent work (1949), attempted to apply the Rankian-functional approach to behavioral change to the supervisor-supervisee relationship. Towle (1954), on the other hand, attempted to analyze the relationship between supervisor and supervisee in terms of Freudian ego psychology. Supervision was seen as a change-oriented process, the dynamics of which were made explicable by application of ego psychology theory.

Some explanation for the heavy emphasis in social work supervision on the educational component stems from the strong influence of psychiatry on social work. Supervision in psychiatry is implemented almost exclusively in the context of the professional preparation obtained in the psychiatric residency program. The emphasis is on training and growth of a clinician and the supervision is clinically oriented. As Langs (1979) says in discussing psychiatric training, "The goal of supervision" is the "education of the therapist" (p. 83)—echoing another influential psychiatric supervision text by Ekstein and Wallerstein (1972).

The balance between the administrative, educational, and supportive components of supervision has varied widely over the course of the last eighty years. While educational supervision, teetering toward therapy, was in ascendancy during the 1920s and 1930s, more recently the administrative aspects of supervision have moved toward center stage—especially with the continuing development and diversification of large-scale public welfare programs during the 1950s and 1960s.

During the period of intensified concern with social action on the part of social workers in the 1960s and early 1970s there was a reaction against supervision generally. Sensitivity to the rights of all oppressed subordinate groups carried over to the supervisee as an oppressed group. Freedom from supervisory control, a greater emphasis on participatory democracy, and mutuality in the supervisory relationship were given greater emphasis (Mandell 1973).

Growing concern with accountability in the 1970s intensified an emphasis on the administrative aspect of supervision, which is further accented by current agency needs to accommodate to budgetary shortages. At the same times the "discovery" and growing interest in burn-out has put greater emphasis on the supportive components of supervision.

Since roughly 1975 there has been a marked increase in the number of books devoted to social work supervision. In addition to the first edition of this book published in 1976 there have been books by Westheimer (1977), Abels (1977), Pettes (1979), Powell (1980), Austin (1981), Shulman (1982), and Munson (1983). Collections of articles on supervision were edited by Kaslow and associates (1972; 1977) and by Munson (1979c). Books on field instruction in social work containing general material on supervision were published by Wilson (1981) and Shaefor and Jenkins (1982). Increased interest in supervision is also demonstrated by the new journal *The Clinical Supervisor*, which began publication in the spring of 1983.

A general characteristic of the recent publications is the heterogeneity of their approaches to supervision and the differing kinds of emphasis they employ. Each text tends to select one or another of the components of supervision as the focus of its concern. For example, Munson (1983), Shulman (1982), and Pettes (1979) are primarily concerned with clinical-educational supervision; Austin (1981) is primarily concerned with administrative supervision.

Almost all of the literature cited above derives from work in casework agencies and is casework oriented.

As Kutzik (1977) notes, consultation rather than supervision "was the rule among settlement staff" (p. 37). The egalitarian nature of settlement house movement ideology was less receptive to the hierarchical implications of supervision and, according to Kennedy and Ferra (1935), implementation of supervisory functions in settlement houses was limited through the 1920s.

With the development of group service agencies, supervision was enriched by contributions from this segment of social work. Williamson's book *Supervision* (1959, revised 1961), while general in nature, was oriented toward the YMCA worker. Two additional texts on supervision were similarily directed toward group service agencies (Lindenberg 1939; Dimock and Trecker 1949).

Supervision nonetheless continued to be strongly influenced by its origins in casework. Miller (1960), in one of the few articles written by a group worker on supervision, deplores the tendency of group work to pattern its supervisory procedures in accordance with those developed by casework. Supervision is less clearly formalized in group work agencies. Spellman (1946) noted the "odd assortment of practices which had grown up" in response to the need to perform supervisory functions but without explicit consideration of the process:

> We've had the "trouble shooter method"; "let me know if anything goes wrong and you need me for any emergency—and I'll be right there." Then there is the "hit-and-run method"; "I'll see you in the hall a couple of minutes after the meeting is over and we'll check on what happened and what you want for next week." Others had worked out the "crutch philosophy"; "I'll help you get started until you can stand on your own two feet." (p. 125)

A 1972 study of Chicago group work agencies showed that "most executives confer with staff members individually when necessary without planned supervisory conferences" (Switzer 1973, p. 587). Another study of group work supervision finds some additional distinctive elements. Olyan (1972), studying group work supervision as compared with casework supervision, found that group work supervisors were more likely to feel that social workers were not ready to assume responsibility and needed close supervision. They gave administrative supervision greater emphasis than did casework supervisors and used observation procedures more frequently.

Supervision in community organization is even less explicitly formulated. Community organizers often work in agencies with limited staff or are members of a small specialized unit in large agencies. In either case there is no elaborate hierarchical structure which includes supervisory personnel. The nature of the work of the community organizer often tends to be diffuse and the goals amorphous. This requires a great measure of on-the-job autonomy in dealing with the demands of the nonstandardized situation.

The functional requirements of supervision in community organization—assignment of work, review and assessment of work done—may be performed by the agency administrator. These functions have to be performed, however infrequently or casually, but often no one is clearly designated as supervisor and there is no explicit recognition that supervisory tasks are being discharged. The failure to recognize supervision is intensified by the particularly negative connotations the term has for community organizers. Of all the specialized subgroups in social work, community organization feels most strongly the need for worker autonomy. Supervision suggests a subservience that runs counter to this strong value. "This generally activist philosophy of many community workers does not regard with enthusiasm such organizational concepts as bureaucracy, authority and accountability" (Pettes 1979, p. 23).

A book devoted to the practice and training of community workers in England clearly reflects the community worker's uneasy attitude toward supervision while it indicates the value of supervision to the community worker (Briscoe and Thomas 1977). Community workers see their primary loyalty and commitment to the community in which they are working and to the people in that community. They are hesitant about being identified with an agency and its bureaucracy which often represent what the community is struggling against. The community workers suspect that the purpose of supervision is to exact conformity with the goals and norms of the agency with which they are affiliated—an affiliation they would rather not acknowledge. They feel that supervision

> may also be perceived as a way of controlling community work activities that may be politically embarrassing to the department or local authority. Community workers generally see themselves as agents of social change and they are suspicious of those in organizations, like supervisors, who seem to represent the status quo and who provide a method of control over field workers. (Harris 1977, p. 33)

Rejection of supervision is an effort to "avoid being contaminated" in the context of the community worker's conflicting loyalties and identification with the community and the agency. As part of their struggle to maintain their integrity in a situation of conflicting loyalties and commitments "supervisors are kept at a safe distance" (Thomas and Warburton 1978, p. 29).

Supervision is not only associated with the agency and its bureaucracy, it is also associated with professionalism. This too is resisted, since developing expertise and theorizing about community work increase the social distance between the worker and members of the community. Community workers "may feel morally or politically compromised in taking up skill development opportunities" (p. 28) within the agency. Consequently the educational as well as the administrative component of supervision is rejected. There is a tendency, then, to reject the idea that any supervision is appropriately associated with community organization and there is an almost total lack of literature on this subject.

In some respects, however, the need for supervision is even more urgent in community organization than in other areas of social work. The community organizer inevitably represents the agency. Working in a highly politicized arena, the worker is subject to a variety of pressures and power plays. In dealing with community groups he may commit the agency to activity or to policies that the agency finds difficult to defend or support. Consequently there is a great need for the agency to know what might have been promised, what deals are being contemplated, what action the worker plans to take. This requirement for accountability to agency administration is a task of supervision.

Despite the desirability of supervision, the nature of the community organizer's work may sometimes make it difficult to apply supervisory procedures. "Community workers function frequently in less well defined situations than workers in other methods. In part this is due to the experimental nature of much of the practice" (Pettes 1979, p. 24). Brager and Specht (1973) note that

> whereas casework interviews can be scheduled and group workers conduct meetings on some regular basis, the activities of community workers defy regulation and scheduling. Work time is absorbed with informal telephone conversation, attending meetings in which they may have no formal role, talking with other professionals, and other difficult to specify activities.

This argues for very loose supervision since the worker has to be provided with maximum discretion.

Confirmation of the disproportionately greater concern with supervision in casework as contrasted with community organization and group work is indicated by the responses to the NASW 1982 Data Bank Survey of membership. Of the respondents who identified their primary job title as supervisor, 99.3 percent were from casework settings, .006 percent were from the community organization settings, and .002 percent were from group services settings.

Toward a Definition

The word supervision derives from the Latin *super* "over" and *videre* "to watch, to see." Hence a supervisor is defined as an overseer, one who watches over the work of another with responsibility for its quality. Such a definition of supervision leads to the derisive phrase "snooper vision." The orthodox definition stresses the administrative aspect of supervision, the concern with seeing that a job is performed at a quantitatively and qualitatively acceptable level.

In developing a definition of supervision for our purposes, it is helpful to discuss in turn each of the different considerations which, in aggregate, contribute to a comprehensive definition. These include: (1) the functions of supervision; (2) the objectives of supervision; (3) the hierarchical position of supervision; (4) supervision as an indirect service; (5) the interactional process of supervision.

The Functions of Supervision

A review of the social work literature shows that supervision has been defined primarily in terms of the administrative and educational function, the emphasis varying with the author. Robinson, in the first social work text on this subject, *Supervision in Social Casework* (1936), defined supervision as "an educational process in which a person with a certain equipment of knowledge and skill takes responsibility for training a person with less equipment" (p. 53). The first edition of the *Encyclopedia of Social Work* (1965) defines supervision as an educational process. It is the "traditional method of transmitting knowledge of social work skills in practice from the trained to the untrained, from the experienced to the inexperienced student and worker."

The second (1971) and third (1977) editions of the *Encyclopedia* emphasize the administrative function. It defines supervision as "an administrative function, a process for getting the work done and maintaining organizational control and accountability" (p. 1544).

On occasion both functions are included in the definition. Towle (1945) defines social work supervision as "an administrative process with an educational purpose" (p. 95; similarly Burns 1958, p. 6). A standard group work text states that "the supervisor's responsibilities are both administrative and educative in nature. . . The ultimate objective of supervision is that through more effective effort on the part of its workers, an agency's services are improved in quality and its central purposes come nearer to fulfillment" (Wilson and Ryland 1949, p. 587).

Each of the definitions presented is only partially correct. It is true that supervision is both an administrative and an educational process. The social work supervisor has responsibility for implementing both functions in contact with supervisees. There is, however, an additional and distinctively different responsibility that needs to be included in the definition. This is the expressive-supportive-leadership function of supervision. The supervisor has the responsibility of sustaining worker morale, helping with job-related discouragements and discontents, giving supervisees a sense of worth as professionals, a sense of belonging in the agency, and a sense of security in their performance.

These three major functions of supervision are complementary. All are necessary if the ultimate objective of supervision is to be achieved.

Admittedly there is an overlap between the administrative, educational, and supportive functions of supervision. However, each function is different from the others in terms of problems and goals. The primary problem in administrative supervision is concerned with the correct, effective, and appropriate implementation of agency policies and procedures; the primary goal is to insure adherence to policy and procedure. The primary problem in educational supervision is worker ignorance and/or ineptitude regarding the knowledge, attitude, and skills required to do the job; the primary goal is to dispel ignorance and upgrade skill. The primary problem in supportive supervision is worker morale and job satisfaction; the primary goal is to improve morale and job satisfaction. The above presents a functional definition of social work supervision.

The Objectives of Supervision

The objectives of social work supervision are both short- and long-range. The short-range objective of educational supervision is to improve the worker's capacity to do his job more effectively. It is to help the worker grow and develop professionally, to maximize his clinical knowledge and skills to the point where he can perform autonomously and independently of supervision. The short-range objective of administrative supervision is to provide the worker with a work context that permits him to do his job effectively. The short-range objective of supportive supervision is to help the worker feel good about doing his job.

However, these short-range objectives are not ends in themselves, but are the means for achieving the long-range objective of supervision. This objective is to effectively and efficiently provide clients with the particular service the particular agency is mandated to offer. The ultimate objective is, then, efficient and effective social work services to clients. It is toward this objective that the supervisor administratively integrates and coordinates the supervisees' work with others in the agency, educates the workers to a more skillful performance in their tasks, and supports and sustains the workers in motivated performance of these tasks.

The Hierarchical Position of Supervisors

The position of the supervisor in the hierarchy of the agency further helps to define supervision. It is clearly a middle-management position. The supervisor is responsible for the performance of the direct service workers and is accountable to administrative directors.

The supervisor is sometimes described as an "in-between" functionary. The position of the supervisor is aptly described by Austin (1981), who notes that the supervisor has "one foot in the work force and one foot in the management module, not being clearly associated with either" (p. 32). They are "leaders of their subordinates" but subordinate to agency administrators. The supervisor is sometimes referred to as the "highest level employee and the lowest level manager," a "sub-administrator and a supra-practitioner" (Towle 1962). A member of both management and the work group, he acts as a bridge between them.

While agency executive administrators are primarily responsible for program planning, policy formulation, agency funding, and community relations, primary supervisory managerial responsibilities center on program management and program implementation. Supervision has a more pronounced internal operations focus as contrasted with the more external orientation of top agency administrators. It is said that administration controls the domain of agency policy and planning; supervisors control the domain of management; workers control the domain of service.

Supervision as an Indirect Service

The supervisor's position in the agency organizational structure further defines supervision as an indirect service. The supervisor is in indirect contact with the client through the worker. The supervisor helps the direct service worker to help the client.

Supervision as an Interactional Process

Supervision is defined as a process. In implementing the functions of supervision, the supervisor engages in sequential series of deliberately and consciously selected activities. There is an ordered beginning, middle, and end to the process of supervision and the activities engaged in at each point in the process are somewhat different from activities engaged in at other points in the process.

The process of supervision is implemented in the context of a relationship. Being a supervisor requires having a supervisee much as being a parent requires having a child. A supervisor without a supervisee makes as much sense as saying my brother was an only child. Since at least two people are involved, their interaction is a significant aspect of supervision. Supervisor and supervisee(s) establish a small interlocking social system that at its best is cooperative, democratic, participatory, mutual, respectful, and open.

Definition of Supervision

A comprehensive definition of social work supervision attempts to combine all the elements noted in the five sections above. As the term will be used in this book, then, a social work supervisor is an agency administrative staff member to whom authority is delegated to direct, coordinate, enhance, and evaluate the on-the-job perform-ance of the supervisees for whose work he is held accountable. In implementing this responsibility the supervisor performs admin-istrative, educational, and supportive functions in interaction with the supervisee in the context of a positive relationship. The super-visor's ultimate objective is to deliver to agency clients the best possible service, both quantitatively and qualitatively, in accor-dance with agency policies and procedures. Supervisors do not di-rectly offer service to the client, but they do indirectly affect the level of service offered through their impact on the direct service supervisees.

Empirical Validation of Definition

The definition is derived from a general analysis of social work supervision. To what extent do empirical studies of supervision sup-port the validity of the definition—to what extent does it reflect the reality of social work supervision? We have only limited empirical data on this. In 1977, the Wisconsin Department of Health and Social Services (1978) sponsored a study of the tasks performed by those holding the position of social work supervisor I. A task book of 574 possible supervisor tasks was developed and the supervisors were asked to identify which of these tasks they actually performed. Usable responses were received from 38 supervisors. The fact that only 20 percent of the 574 tasks were selected by 50 percent or more of the respondents indicates that there was considerable variation in the actual job tasks performed by those holding the similarly designated Supervisor I position.

The largest number of tasks performed by the largest number of supervisors were those that are essentially administrative in nature. This group of tasks constituted some 60 percent of all tasks per-formed. These included assigning, directing, reviewing, coordinating, and evaluating work; making personnel decisions regarding hiring, promoting, termination, program planning, and budget development; intra- and interagency communication of policy; and handling complaints.

Tasks related to educational supervision—staff development and training—constituted 10 percent of tasks performed. These included activities such as assessing training needs of workers; facilitating training; suggesting, teaching, and demonstrating; orienting and inducting new workers into their job; and providing needed information.

Tasks related to supportive supervision were rarely explicitly identified although some of the task items selected indicated the supervisor's responsibility for maintaining productive levels of morale.

Patti (1977) asked 90 "social welfare managers" to delineate the activities they engaged in during a typical work week. The respondents included administrators and department heads as well as supervisors. Differences in activities were related to differences in levels of management. While executive management level administrators were more concerned with "representing the agency in the community," "negotiating with groups and organizations," "setting agency goals and objectives," "designing program structures," and "budgeting," respondents at the supervisory management level "spent a major portion of their work week in 'directing', 'advising,' and 'reviewing' the work of their subordinates" (Patti, 1983, p. 45). Supervisors were seen as having day-to-day contact with front line staff, maintaining work flow, delegating and assigning work, seeing that services were provided in a manner consistent with policies and procedures, consulting with front line workers on case level decisions, providing advice and instruction on technical aspects of work, providing opportunities for upgrading areas of knowledge and skills, pointing out deficiencies, and evaluating individual performance (p. 44). Administrative and educational functions and activities of supervisors are clearly identified in the findings.

A detailed study between 1975 and 1977 of social work team practice in England, Scotland, and Northern Ireland involved repeated interviews with some 300 social workers and participant observation of their practice. Some 700 interviews were tape recorded and transcribed. Asked about how they perceived the functions of supervision which they experienced, the practitioners identified administrative, educational, and supportive aspects, although here support was given more explicit mention.

> In the social worker's eyes, the most important purpose was to provide them with the support which came from talking things over, sharing worries, and seeking practical and procedural advice. Reflection on interaction with clients was considered almost as important as immediate support. Social workers generally considered that another purpose of supervision and an appropriate one was checking on their work and, linked with this, ensuring that they were not making serious mistakes. Supervision, some mentioned, imposed a necessary discipline upon them. (Parsloe and Stevenson 1978, p. 201)

Shulman (1982) reports on a study in which 109 supervisors were asked to "indicate the percentage of time they allocated to various tasks." Responses indicating that about 20 percent of the time was spent on "management," 18 percent on "coordinating," and some 11 percent on "personnel"—all of which can be regarded as administrative considerations—leads to the conclusion that about 49 percent of the supervisors' time was spent in administrative supervision. About 40 percent of the time was devoted to "supervision-consultation," which can be interpreted to mean educational supervision (p. 22).

Poertner and Rapp (1983) did a task analysis of supervision in a large public child welfare agency. Having identified, through interviews with selected supervisors, the tasks that they performed, a refined listing of 35 explicit tasks of supervision was sent to 120 supervisors and 227 direct service workers. The supervisors were asked to state whether or not they performed the tasks listed and the workers were asked to identify the tasks they perceived the supervisors performing. Responses indicated that supervisors performed administrative-management tasks primarily. Some 80 percent of the tasks performed were concerned with (1) caseload management ("evaluate case plans for compliance with department policy," "projects case placements and service needs," "examines case plans with case workers"); (2) worker control ("assign new cases," "reviews forms for accuracy and completion," "monitors team goal attainment"); (3) organizational maintenance ("responds to instruction or requests from central office," "determines records keeping procedures," "checks and approves forms"); (4) interacting with community ("meets with community agencies to discuss service plans," "participates with community groups to identify and define new service priorities," "meets with community groups to elicit cooperation to meet department goals"). The remaining 20 percent of tasks performed were divided between supportive and educational supervision. In implementing supportive supervision, supervisors said they "encouraged, listened to, and responded to staff concerning cases." In implementing educational supervision, supervisors said they "educated caseworkers on the role of the juvenile court"; "taught caseworkers court procedures."

Here once again an empirical study of supervisor's tasks confirms the fact that administrative, educational, and supportive components are responsibilities of the position. In ranking the allocation of emphasis, administrative supervision once again has clear priority.

A Theory of Social Work Supervision?

No single comprehensive theory of supervision is available, nor is one likely to be formulated. No such theory or model is proposed in the text. The justification for the contention that no comprehensive theory or model of supervision is likely to be formulated lies in the fact that supervision consists of many separate, if related, functions.

A theory regarding administrative supervision would need to draw on theories available in the literature of organizational sociology and social psychology regardng organizational structure, organizational functions, organizational communication, organizational development and change, etc.

A theory regarding educational supervision would have to draw on an entirely different and equally massive body of literature and research, namely theories regarding teaching and learning in the individual and group contexts.

A theory regarding supportive supervision would relate to still another body of theory and research. This is the voluminous literature relating to therapy, counseling theory, and research regarding the conditions which facilitate attitudinal and emotional change.

Each of these principle functions of supervision relates to different clusters of theory, research, and knowledge, dealing with distinctively different phenomena.

Not only is it likely that a theory applicable to supportive or educational supervision would have little relevance to administrative supervision, but furthermore a theory of supervision applicable to the dyadic supervisory context is not likely to be applicable to the group supervisory context.

At the highest level of generality, it may be true that one can formulate a general theory of supervision. This is what Shulman attempts in his book, *Skills of Supervision and Staff Management* (1982). What emerges, however, is a theory regarding interpersonal, interactional behavior which, at that level of generality, is equally applicable to any situation in which two people interact: the relationship between supervisor and supervisee, worker and client, parent and child, husband and wife, friend and friend. To deserve the title, a "Theory of Social Work Supervision" would have to be more specifically aimed at the unique nature of the supervisory context.

Given the different but related functions of supervision, such a theory is not likely to be formulated. What is more likely, and feasible, are separate theories applicable to administrative, educational, and supportive supervision.

Social Work Supervisors—A Demography

The 1982 National Association of Social Workers Data Bank Survey of over 60,000 respondents found that 7.1 percent of the membership indicated that their primary position title was that of supervisor. Extrapolating to the total NASW membership the estimate is that some 6,400 NASW members are supervisors. Some 20 percent of respondents identified themselves as holding a "management/administrative" title. It might be supposed that some percentage of this group of respondents had some supervisory responsibilities even though their primary job title was something other than supervisor.

The supervisors responding to the survey were mostly employed in child and youth service, in mental health, and in medical care. Most frequently they were employed in social service agencies or organizations.

While the 1982 NASW Data Bank Survey is the best and most recent information available, it presents a somewhat skewed picture of the social work supervisor. A very high percentage of the supervisors responding were graduate social workers since most members of the NASW have an MSW, but this leaves uncounted a number of supervisors who do not have graduate social work training. Social workers employed in voluntary agencies are disproportionately represented among NASW members. Consequently the data does not adequately reflect additional numbers of supervisors employed in county, municipal, state, and federal agencies, many of whom are, in fact, not NASW members.

Shyne's (1980) report of a national study of services to children and families found that in the public agencies studied "only about one third of direct-line supervisors had professional social work education" (p. 31). Given these considerations, it might be safe to estimate that there are some 10,000–15,000 social workers whose primary job responsibility is that of supervision.

Patti and Rauch (1978) studied the hiring preferences of 138 Public Welfare Administrators for the position of supervisor. Administrators gave high priority to an applicant who had familiarity with the program they were to supervise and direct practice experience. Having an MSW and formal education in social work administration were less critical in determining a decision to hire.

Patti and Maynard (1978) reviewed the job specifications for supervisory positions in Public Welfare Agencies in 42 states. Most frequently the positions required an MSW with an additional two years of direct service practice. While social work training was "clearly considered the most desirable type of advanced education for supervisory positions in the State Social Service Programs and Mental Health Programs," it was not considered as desirable in Corrections. Study of the specifications also suggested that while MSWs with practice experience had the best possibility for qualifying for supervisory positions, there was growing competition from people holding other masters degrees who had agency experience. This reflects the situation as of 1977 when the last available study was done. Bringing the study findings up to date might require emphasis on the author's warning that "social workers will increasingly be competing for these positions with people from a variety of educational backgrounds and experiences."

A detailed design of a social service system for children and families sponsored by the Child Welfare League of America advises that to fulfill the roles of supervisor "effectively it is recommended that a supervisor be assigned a maximum of five social workers, two case aides, and one or two clerk typists" (U.S. Dept. of H.E.W. 1978).

In 1983 supervisors in child welfare agencies earned a median salary of $23,000 (Jones and Moore 1983).

The Importance of Supervision in Social Work

We have noted that, historically, supervision has always been an important element in social work. Supervision is not, of course, unique to social work, but the function and process of supervision have achieved special importance in social work as contrasted with most other professions. This prominence might be explained by some distinctive aspects of the profession, the nature of its service delivery pattern, the problems with which it is concerned, the clientele to whom service is offered, and the characteristics of social workers.

1. Social work, as contrasted with other, more entrepreneurially oriented professions, offers service to the client group through an agency. An agency is a complex organization and therefore needs to develop some bureaucratic structure if it is to operate effectively. The work of different people, each performing some specialized task, has to be coordinated and integrated. The social agency thus requires a chain of command, a hierarchy of administrators. Since the greatest percentage of social workers perform their professional functions within an agency, they find themselves in a bureaucratic structure in contact with the supervision which a bureaucracy requires.

A very small number of social workers operate autonomously as private practitioners outside an agency. To the extent that the profession moves toward implementation of its function outside an agency setting, a concern with supervision may be de-emphasized. However, the current situation, in which social work is practiced primarily in an agency setting, is likely to prevail for some time.

Other professions that find the bulk of their practitioners working in agency settings have been concerned with supervision for similar reasons. This is true particularly for teachers and nurses. As the more traditionally entrepreneurially oriented professions become bureaucratized (as is happening currently with medicine and law), they find themselves building a bureaucratic apparatus that includes supervisory personnel and supervisory controls.

Social work, however, from its inception has been organizationally based. It knows no other tradition. Having a longer history in an organizational context, it has had a more prolonged concern with supervision. Considerable educational and training effort is expended in helping social work recruits understand and identify with organizational models and values. Social workers are evaluated in terms of their identification with, acceptance of, and adherence to agency policies and procedures.

The whole orientation of the profession gives centrality to the agency. While other professions socialize recruits in terms of a professional image that is largely modeled after the independent entrepreneur, social work has always heavily emphasized the organization-agency context as the locus of the worker's activity. Consequently, as Scott (1969) notes, "social workers, unlike members of other professions, expect to enter an organization where their work will be subject to routine hierarchical supervision" (p. 92). As a result of tradition and training, the "social worker is a sophisticated and accomplished 'organization man'" (Vinter 1959, p. 242; see also Epstein 1970; Rothman 1974, p. 96).

2. A significant component of social agency activity is concerned with the distribution of services and supplies which the agency does not own. Very substantial amounts of agency resources, supplied from community appropriations, are allocated through decisions made by workers. Assigning a child foster care can involve the commitment of thousands of dollars over a five- to ten-year period. The decision to assign a homemaker to a family or provide day care at community expense, or institutionalize a brain-damaged child or a senile aged person, involves a substantial increase in community expenditures. The community feels entitled to know that such decisions are made with some oversight and procedural safeguards, not solely on the basis of the worker's autonomous discretion. As Levy notes, "Organization funds, materials, and all other resources placed at the disposal of staff members are not personal assets. They are assets held in trust for the community" (1982, p. 51). Howe

(1980) suggests that professions such as social work, which "involve economic externalities" that are provided by the community and whose use affects the community, cannot expect to be fully autonomous (p. 179). There is justification for community control of such organizations.

Accountability to the community is also required by the fact that the community provides the agency with its clientele. Policies established by the community, regarding eligibility requirements for certain programs and definitions of needs, channel people to the agencies. As a result, the social work situation brings great pressure from the community for explicit accountability procedures regarding agency activity. This, once again, leads directly to a need for a supervisory apparatus.

One might argue that traditional accountability procedures in other professions require the professional to be self-disciplined and self-accountable, subject where necessary to peer review. However, even in the oldest and most solidly established professions there is a demand for more formal procedures of accountability once public funds are involved, procedures which are supervisory in nature.

In 1972 Congress passed legislation which provided for Professional Standards Review Organizations (PSRO) "to monitor the quality of every doctor's professional work whether it be performing open heart surgery or making a house call, if the services are being paid for by Federal [Medicaid and Medicare] programs" (*New York Times*, December 3, 1973). Neither Congress nor the American Medical Association (which ultimately approved the legislation) felt that the individual physician's self-accountability was sufficient. Given the large amount of public funds being expended for medical programs, supervision here, too, is regarded as necessary.

3. Not only the finances and resources which the agency employs to help its clients, but very frequently also the policies which the agency implements originate elsewhere. Policy for public social-welfare agencies is often created by political bodies such as public welfare boards and commissions. The agencies are then answerable to these political entities for correct implementation of policy. This circumstance, too, creates an organizational pressure for some system of accountability for workers' activity within the agency.

Scott (1965) terms professional organizations that are controlled, in some measure, by external agencies "heteronomous organizations" and includes social agencies, schools, and libraries under such a rubric. His study of their administration confirms their greater concern with supervision and supervisory procedures.

The outside dictation of agency policy is justified not only by the fact that public funds are being used in offering the service but also by the fact that social agencies are concerned with problem situations which present a great danger to the community, situations in which the community has a strong vested interest. Crime, dependency, discrimination, and family breakdown are particularly costly financial and ideological threats to society. Response to these problems involves the embodiment of society's values, its ideological commitments in sensitive areas—family structure, legal conformity, sexual mores, the work ethic, racial conflict. The community feels impelled to indicate how such situations should be handled through its articulation of social policy. The fact that social work agencies are concerned with problems which pose not only a financial but also an ideological danger to the community again leads to external control of agency policy and internal agency control of worker autonomy. The public is anxious about the kinds of decisions made by the agency which can affect public policy on controversial questions.

4. The autonomy granted any member of a profession reflects the degree of autonomy granted the profession as a whole. If the community is hesitant about granting full autonomy to a profession, there will be pressure toward supervision of the individual professional. The degree of autonomy granted is a function of the extent to which there is general consensus about the profession's objectives. Where powerful segments of the community disagree about the ultimate aims of a profession's activity, there will be greater reluctance to grant autonomy to the profession since this will permit the profession to decide on its own objectives. Autonomy enables a few professionals to decide for the many in the community. There is less general consensus as to the objectives of social work than there is regarding, for instance, the objectives of the health services. Hence, there is greater community reluctance to grant social work a full measure of autonomy.

Community confidence in the competence of a professional group to effectively implement society's mandate is a necessary prerequisite for the grant of full autonomy. Whether the opinion is justified or not, it seems clear that the community has doubts about social work competence. Since society's grant of autonomy to the profession is limited as a result of these considerations, there is less protection of autonomy of any individual professional.

5. Research suggests that when a profession, such as social work, performs nonuniform tasks in an uncertain and unpredictable context, toward the achievement of diffuse and ambiguous objectives with heterogeneous populations, there is more decentralization of decision making and a greater need for worker autonomy (Dornbusch and Scott 1975, pp. 76–87; Rothman 1974, 152–57). These findings logically argue for less bureaucratic structure since they suggest difficulty in codification of procedures, formulation of standardized rules of action, and routinization of performance. They would also seemingly argue for a less elaborate supervisory apparatus. One can, however, deduce the opposite need from the same considerations. Where objectives are unclear, where there is great uncertainty as to how to proceed, where the effects of interventions are unpredictable and the risk of failure is high, workers may need, and want, the availability of an administrative representative with whom they can share responsibility for decision making, from whom they can receive direction, and to whom they can look for support. Consequently, the conditions under which the work of the profession is performed argue for the desirability of a supervisory cadre.

Because of this nonroutine, nonstandardized, unpredictable, highly individualized nature of social agency activities, it is difficult to design a comprehensive formal management information system. Even the best forms fail to collect a good deal of significant information about the worker's activity. Consequently the nature of the social worker's function and activities requires that the administration gather information through other channels. The conference between supervisor and supervisee is such a channel. The need for such personalized, intensive, and flexible channels for gathering this information further highlights the need for social work supervision.

6. Social workers perform their functions under conditions that do not permit direct observation. The ethos of the profession encourages such protection from direct scrutiny, and practice principles further support it. We hold interviews in private and discourage

observation as an intrusion on the privacy of the encounter. We contend that direct observation of our practice would create hazards for effective worker-client interaction. We thus create an unusual situation of role performance invisibility and interdicted observability. This being the nature of our practice procedures, the client would be left without effective protection from practice which might be damaging if there were no system for supervisory review of what the worker was doing. Many other professionals perform their services publicly and their work is thus open to more general evaluation. The lawyer can be observed in the courtroom, the musician on the concert platform, the professor in the lecture hall. These situations make less imperative the need for supervisory review of performance as a protection to clients. The fact that group workers to some extent and community organizers to an even greater extent perform "in public," mitigates some of the pressure for supervision in these areas of social work.

7. Certain other professionals such as doctors and dentists do perform their functions privately, but the outcome of professional activity is more objective and observable than in the case of social work. The doctor may perform his functions in private without benefit of supervisory review, but consistently inadequate professional performance means sick or dead patients. The cause-and-effect relationship between social work activity and changes in the client's situation is much more subtle, and difficult to define. Since the damaging effects of poor practice are not so self-evident and observable, protection of the client requires a procedure for explicit periodic review of worker activity.

8. Two additional aspects of the social work delivery system create a need for supervision: the agency provides the workers with their clientele and clients are often "captives" of the agency.

A captive clientele reduces the need for self-discipline and critical self-evaluation. The professional entrepreneur, the lawyer or doctor, pays a price for ineptitude, inefficiency, and out moded professional skills, in a reduction in income owing to loss of clients. The social worker, operating in an agency that provides the clients, does not face the same kind of penalties which alert him to the need for examining and correcting his practice. The setting again dictates a greater need for controls since the practice does not automatically provide such controls.

Furthermore, the client's use of agency service is often involuntary, dictated by organs of social control such as schools and courts. Even without such formal directives, situational imperatives may deny the client the freedom of choice. The need for food, shelter or medical care may determine the client's need for agency service, a service for which the agency is granted a monopoly.

The fact that the client's use of the agency is often compulsory means that greater provision needs to be made to protect the client than would be the case in situations where the client could choose to withdraw if dissatisified with the service.

9. Despite the fact that social workers use resources provided by the community, are required to implement policies formulated by groups outside the agency, peform their tasks in private on clients who often have no alternative options, and are concerned with outcomes which are difficult to discern and evaluate objectively, is there a real need for supervisory review and control in regard to accountability and client protection? One might counter that the supposition that such conditions argue for the necessity of supervision is demeaning and insulting to the worker. All of these conditions might accurately characterize the social work situation yet not require supervision if we granted the social worker her professional prerogative. One would expect that the direct service professional in contact with the client would herself be concerned about protecting the client and implementing agency policy in a clearly responsible manner. Operating autonomously, she would provide, for herself, the controls of supervision. But it is here, once again, that we encounter a situation characteristic of social work which creates a need for the development and elaboration of a supervisory apparatus.

Kaufman (1960) identifies the significant conditions which ensure that the autonomously operating worker will be self-supervised so that agency policy will be adhered to and the needs of the client protected. These conditions include extensive professional education, a strong interest in the tasks to be performed, a commitment to the ends to which these tasks are directed, and periodic agency indoctrination reinforcing the saliency and legitimacy of these goals. The result of these conditions is to socialize the worker so that she does, as a matter of personal preference and professional conscience, those things that are professionally required. The composition of social work agency staff, now and in the past, raises questions about the degree to which these conditions are met. In the absence of these conditions there is greater pressure to develop a supervisory control system to insure that work performance is in accordance with professionally desirable norms.

The process of professional recruitment, selection, and education has implications for the kind of supervisory system a profession establishes. If the process of occupational selection is deliberate, and if the program of training is prolonged, the need for elaborate supervisory procedures is lessened.

A candidate who deliberately makes a choice of some profession after careful evaluation of alternatives is apt to feel a sense of commitment to the profession. The very process of applying for, and being selected by, a graduate professional school acts as a screen which ensures recruitment of those applicants who, in some way, share the values, assumptions, and predispositions characteristic of those performing the work. This is reinforced by the professional training experience.

The objective of professional training is not only to teach the knowledge, skills, and attitudes that would enable the recruit to do a competent job but also to socialize the student to the ways of the profession, to develop a professional conscience. It is the elaborate process of professional socialization, during a prolonged program of intensive training, which permits workers in all professions to operate autonomously, free of external direction and control but subject to internal direction and control on the basis of competence and values incorporated during training. The supervisor is, in effect, internalized during the transformation of the lay person into a professional, and supervision does not then need to be externally imposed. Discipline becomes self-discipline; accountability is accountability to one's professionalized self. Such constraints are further maintained and collectively sustained by strong professional organizations to which the professional feels an affiliation, even if he is not formally a member, and by periodic in-service training courses, conferences, meetings, and professional journals.

All of this is quite different from the situation which characterizes job entrance for the largest percentage of social workers— currently and throughout the history of the profession. For most social workers who have ever occupied the position, entrance to the job has not been the result of a serious commitment to social work as a lifetime career but rather a decision of limited commitment, frequently made because other, more attractive, alternatives were not available. Workers often come to the job with no previous knowledge of social work, no firm identification with the profession, its objectives, standards, and values—an identification which might have been developed during a prolonged period of professional training—and with no resolute commitment to the profession.

In 1983 there were approximately 380,000 people in the United States occupying positions as "social workers." Reviewing statistics on the demographics of American psychotherapists and basing his conclusions on data from NASW and data from states reporting their numbers of licensed MSWs, Beitman (1983) concludes that there were 100,000 practicing MSWs in the U.S. in 1983 (p. 42). It might be estimated then that some 27 percent of all social workers in 1983 were professionally trained to do the job prior to accepting the position. Including BSW graduates, this figure might be raised to 30 percent. A 1978 national study of social services to children and their families notes that "about 80 percent of the children were assigned to caseworkers whose highest degree was a bachelor's degree with about one in five of these degrees in social work. Five percent were served by workers with less than a four year college degree while 9 percent had workers with graduate degrees in social work and 6 percent were assigned to graduate degrees in other fields" (Shyne and Schroeder 1978, p. 25). The largest majority (75 percent) of the workers in public child welfare, a major field of social work practice, apparently came to the position without any prior social work training, suggesting the clear need for supervision.

The low ratio of professionally trained to the total work force reflects a situation which has been typical throughout the history of the profession. In fact, the situation in 1983 was more favorable than in the past. A 1926 study showed that only 7 percent of the workers had full professional training (Walker 1928, p. 108). In 1940, of the 69,000 social workers listed by the 1940 census only 11,000 (16 percent) were members of the American Association of Social Workers, which enrolled most of the professionally trained social workers at that time (Hathway 1943). By 1960, some 25 percent of the 116,000 people holding social welfare positions had graduate social work degrees (National Social Welfare Assembly 1961, p. 1).

Lacking control of job access and job entry, the profession can dictate to only a limited extent the personal and professional qualifications of personnel. This situation has implications not only for education and training that recruits bring to the position but also for their attitudes toward, and commitment to, the work they are called on to perform. Chatterjee (1972) found that public welfare workers manifested limited commitment to their job. Miller and Podell (1970) concluded that only about 10 percent of the caseworkers in the New York City Department of Social Services were "socialized professionals with a commitment to social work combined with a positive disposition to the department" (p. 12).

It is difficult to know how significantly the situation has changed since these studies were done. A tightened labor market during 1980 has reduced turnover and increased the number of workers who are experienced and committed. Declassification of social work civil service positions may have increased the percentage of workers without prior training.

Court decisions on discrimination suits filed under the Civil Rights Act of 1964 challenged the use of hiring requirements that could not be validly proven to be related to the job. As a consequence of the resulting declassification of civil service positions previously reserved for applicants who offered professional educational credentials, more people were hired who had no prior training in social work. Training by supervisors of such recruits was required to compensate for lack of pre-employment educational preparation. Nationwide declassification of social worker positions increased the importance of educational supervision.

There are, in effect, two different kinds of staff to which supervision is directed. One (often found in highly professionalized, generally voluntary agencies) is composed of people who have made a career choice of social work after considerable exploration and deliberation, who have invested effort and money in a prolonged program of professional education, and who have thereby developed some beginning competence in performing social work tasks, and some identification with and commitment to the social work profession.

At the same time there is an even larger number of workers (more often concentrated in large public welfare agencies), holding the job title of social worker and performing social work tasks, who often have come to the job fortuitously, because an opening was available. They often have had no prior exposure to social work, have not considered it seriously as a career, have had little if any education or training for the job and have little if any identification with and commitment to social work. This second group is, of course, highly diversified.

Thus, there always has been and continues to be a need for agencies to induct, train, and socialize new recruits. And because of tenuous commitment, or lack of prior opportunity to socialize toward a firm commitment to the mission of social work on the part of many recruits, social work has had to assign supervisory personnel to perform the functions of educational and administrative supervision.

10. The need for organizational controls in supervision on the part of the agency is made more imperative by the absence of effective organizational controls on the part of the profession itself. The professional associations in medicine and law, controlling entry into and expulsion from the profession, can effectively be delegated the responsibility of policing their members to limit abuses of professinal autonomy and guarantee professionally responsible behavior. Until very recently the National Association of Social Workers did not even accept for membership the non–MSW social workers who filled the majority of social work positions. While technically eligible, few such workers are affiliated with the professional organizations. The ability of professional social work organizations to guarantee the conduct and competence of the social worker's performance is seriously limited. This absence of effective professional control groups in social work, as compared with more traditionally established professions, argues for an alternative control system such as agency supervision.

11. Bureaucratization, of which supervision is a component, results not only from the limited training of a large number of people carrying the title of social worker but also from the limited knowledge base and technology available even to fully trained workers. Where the level of development of a profession's knowledge and techniques is such that the professional often finds himself encountering situations in which he cannot operate with full confidence that he knows what to do and how to do it, as is true in social work, there is a greater tendency to share decisional responsibility with a supervisor and less readiness to resist supervisory "sugges-

tions" and rules that dictate action. A person needs to be very confident of his ability to make use of autonomy if he is going to claim it aggressively and defend it tenaciously. "Control over the work of semi-professionals is possible because they lack the weapon—knowledge—with which professionals resist control. . . . The motives which drive professionals to seek autonomy are strong intrinsic commitment to specialize knowledge and skills together with confidence in their ability to exercise such skills" (Simpson and Simpson 1969, pp. 198–99).

12. The distinctive nature of the problems encountered and the tasks performed by social workers makes desirable, perhaps even necessary, the availability of supportive supervision. Social workers are in constant contact with highly charged affective situations that make heavy demands on emotional energy in behalf of the client. The problems encountered—parent-child conflict, marital conflict, illness, death, dependency, deviance—are those that a social worker struggles with in one way or another in her own life situation. The principal instrumentality for helping the client is the worker herself, so that failure to help may be sensed as a personal failure. The responsibilities are great; the solutions available are ambiguous; the possibilities for happy solutions are limited. The risks of guilt, anxiety, discouragement, and frustration are numerous. There are few professions that come close to social work in developing in the worker the need for support, encouragement, reassurance, and restoration of morale—a need met by supportive supervision.

The nature of social work not only argues for the need for supervision for new recruits, but also for the more experienced worker.

> The nature of social work . . . is work with people through relationships where the personality of the worker is one of the tools for the work. It can be argued that no one, however skilled or experienced, can ever be entirely objective about the way they use themselves in relation to another person. A third person is essential to help the social worker stand back from the relationship and then return to it in ways which are helpful to the client. If one accepts such arguments then, in the words of one social worker, "supervision is essential for every social worker." (Parsloe and Stevenson 1978, P. 205)

13. Supervision in social work may have developed prominence and significance because it performs necessary and important

functions in response to the distinctive characteristics of the profession. At the same time it may have been assisted toward prominence by a lack of active opposition to development of a supervisory apparatus. The personality characteristics of people attracted to social work and the large proportion of women in the field may further help explain the prominence of supervision.

The tendency toward bureaucracy and toward administrative controls (including supervision) is characteristic of all professions that have complex organizations. It is particularly characteristic, however, in those professions with a complex organization and a predominantly female labor force. Approximately two-thirds of all social workers are women.

A sociologist, writing about the social work profession, declares that

> the way in which the female role is defined in general may still mean that women will be more submissive in an organizational context than men and therefore more likely to allow their work to be controlled by administrators. It is difficult to know whether organizations such as social work have taken this form because of the high percentage of female employees or whether they recruit females to fit that kind of context. (Heraud 1970, p. 256)

Socialization to the professional identity through a prolonged period of training is only one of the factors associated with levels of commitment (Geer 1966). Intensity of commitment is also related to the priority given the professional role as against possible alternatives, such as motherhood, which compete with the professional role for the allegiance of many workers (Chafetz 1972; Reid 1967; Tropman 1968). As a result, some percentage of social workers may offer the professional role a commitment of limited intensity and limited duration.

A 1982 study of career plans of 181 students in a graduate school of social work indicated that "significantly more women (76 percent) than men reported that they planned to leave the field of social work for at least six months and then return. Time out for child care was a major aspect of women's career planning and appeared to be irrelevant to men's" (Kravetz and Jones 1982, pp. 81–82).

Less unreservedly committed to the occupational role, more discontinuous in work history, less interested in long-range career goals, often responsive to the cultural norms regarding assertiveness on the part of the female, the women who constitute a high proportion of social agency staffs "submit more willingly to bureaucratic subordination than men and strive less for autonomy as professionals" (Simpson and Simpson 1969, p. 244). This pattern reinforces the tendency toward bureaucratization in social work agencies and the acceptability of supervision.

These last paragraphs might be regarded as sexist, but they reflect the results of empirical studies on the sociology of professions rather than a personal point of view. Given the women's liberation movement, the changing status of women, and the devaluation of the "sacredness" of motherhood as *the* principal female role, these contentions may be less true in the future. But while such considerations may move in the direction of progressive attenuation, they currently retain some measure of explanatory potential regarding the limited opposition to the *development* of supervision in social work. In a world that is undergoing rapid change in community perception of what women can and should be doing, such statements are open to question.

For institutions as well as for individuals the past is structured in the present and traditional, if changing, patterns help us to understand how things came to be what they are. Furthermore the limited opposition to the development of supervision in social work is not gender specific. In this respect social workers in general seem to be androgynous in their orientation.

Different occupations attract and produce different occupational personalities. The conjecture is that people with particular kinds of personalities are attracted to different professions; that the process of professional socialization then tends to reinforce those aspects of personality which are congruent with, and conducive to, smooth adjustment to the professional subculture.

Some of the selective personality characteristics of social workers may have relevance to the supervisor-supervisee relationship. Gockel's nationwide study of undergraduate students who major in social work indicates that they are "significantly less likely to express a desire for freedom from supervision than are those who remain out of the field. . . . They bring their acceptance of supervision (whatever its genesis) to the career decision when they decide to shift into social work" (1967, pp. 95–96). Gockel notes that this is true for both male and female social-work recruits. Morris Rosenberg (1957), in a study of occupational values, found that the highest concentrations of compliant, acceptance-seeking students were among those selecting social work and teaching as preferred careers. These students showed a willingness to be dominated, a reluctance to dominate others, and a general concern with "approval, acceptance, warmth, support" (p. 42). Strauss (1964) finds that social workers as compared with clinical psychologists function more willingly and effectively in a subordinate role vis-à-vis psychiatrists (p. 83).

A questionnaire study of job orientations of social workers indicated a "primary interest in job security and personal comfort. Less concern was expressed for jobs that provided opportunity for risk-taking, high competition, and possibilities for creative and autonomous practice " (Cohen and Rhodes 1977, p. 287).

Interestingly, McCune found that community organization students rated highest in independent job orientation and medical social workers rated lowest (1966, p. 123; also see Brager and Michael 1969). Supervision is least highly developed in community organization and perhaps most highly developed in medical social work.

Cournoyer's (1983) report of the assertiveness of more recent groups of social work students is as an indication of changing values and behavior. Some 142 MSW students completed *The College Self–Expression Scale*, which measures levels of assertiveness. Social work student scores indicated that they were more assertive than a normative population of West Virginia University students with which the scale had been used.

To conclude, the distinctive personality characteristics of social work recruits as well as the fact that it is a predominantly female profession may help account for the lack of a history of active opposition to the *development* of supervision in social work.

. No single factor cited in this section can account for the significance and prominence of the process of supervision within social work. In aggregate, however, they form an impressive explanatory array.

Summary

Following a brief historical review of supervision, I noted the variety of definitions of social work supervision. For the purposes of this book, the supervisor was defined as a member of the administrative staff offering an indirect service which included administrative, educational, and supportive functions.

In explaining the prominence of supervision in social work, I noted that organizationally based workers offer resources provided by the community in implementation of community-formulated policies. Working with clients who often have no alternative options, workers who are often untrained and need frequent support offer service under conditions of privacy, with ambiguous outcomes. The predominantly female composition of the work force and some selective personality characteristics of people attracted to the profession tend to reduce opposition to the development of supervision in social work.

CHAPTER TWO
Administrative Supervision

SUPERVISION is a special aspect of organizational administration. When a number of people are brought together and are then provided with the necessary equipment and facilities to get a particular job done, there needs to be systematic coordination of effort if the objectives of the group are to be efficiently accomplished. The systematic, cooperative, coordinated effort of a group of people in getting a desired job efficiently accomplished, if sustained for any period of time, leads inevitably to the development of some kind of formal organization of the work. Schein (1970) defines organization as "the rational coordination of the activities of a number of people for the achievement of some common explicit purpose or goal through division of labor and function and through a hierarchy of authority and responsibility" (p. 9). More tersely, Blau and Scott (1962) define an organization as "a social unit that has been established for the explicit purpose of achieving certain goals" (p. 1). Organizations are thus "consciously planned and deliberately structured" so as to increase the probability of achieving organizational goals and objectives.

A bureaucracy is a specialized kind of organization. The term "bureaucracy" is used here not pejoratively but descriptively and neutrally, to designate a particular organizational form. A bureaucracy is, theoretically, the most rational, efficient, effective organizational format for coordinating the cooperative efforts of a sizable group of people, each of whom is engaged in a different task necessary for the achievement of common organizational objectives. A bureaucracy may be characterized as follows:

1. There is a specialization of function and task, a division of labor, among units of the organization and among different employees within each unit.
2. There is a hierarchical authority structure, different people being assigned positions of greater or lesser responsibility and power.

3. People in the hierarchy exercise authority on the basis of the position they hold.
4. People are recruited, selected, and assigned to positions in the organization on the basis of objective, impersonal, technical qualifications rather than on the basis of who they are or whom they know.
5 There is a system of rules and procedures, universally and impersonally applied, which determine the rights and duties of people occupying each of the positions in the agency.
6. All organizational activities are deliberately and rationally planned to contribute to the attainment of organizational objectives. Bureaucracy is sometimes described as the "rational organization of collective activities."

These are the essential characteristics of the bureaucratic organizational structure in its ideal form; actual bureaucracies achieve the ideal in varying degrees. Consequently any bureaucratic organization can be more or less bureaucratic.

Most social work organizations have employees who engage in specialized tasks, and have an administrative hierarchy, a set of clearly formulated rules and procedures, clearly defined roles and statuses, all designed to achieve specific objectives. In short, not only are social agencies organizational in nature, they conform to the definition of a particular kind of organization—a bureaucracy.

Any organization, and particularly a bureaucratic organization, needs administration. Administration is a process which implements organizational objectives. Stein (1965) describes it as a "process of defining and attaining the objectives of an organization through a system of coordinated and cooperative effort" (p. 58).

In organizations with highly differentiated hierarchical structures, there are first line supervisors, supervisors directly responsible for and in contact with the direct service workers, and an additional layer of second line supervisors, supervisors who supervise the first line supervisors. Our concern here is primarily with the front line supervisors, those who supervise direct service workers.

The supervisor is a link in the chain of administration—the administrator who is in direct contact with the worker. As an administrator, the supervisor has responsibility for agency management, and specific, clearly defined, administrative-managerial functions are assigned to her. These functions are the essence of administrative supervision.

Tasks

What specifically are the tasks the supervisor is called upon to perform in discharging the responsibilities of administrative supervision? They include the following:

1. Staff recruitment and selection
2. Inducting and placing the worker
3. Work planning
4. Work assignments
5. Work delegation
6. Monitoring, reviewing, evaluating work
7. Coordinating work
8. The communication function
9. The supervisor as administrative buffer
10. The supervisor as change agent

1. Staff Recruitment and Selection

The effective achievement of organizational objectives requires making a collectivity out of a group of individuals. There has to be some consensus as to how individuals will work together, how they will perform their assigned tasks, and how they will coordinate their activities with others in the collective. Harnessing a group of people to cooperatively and collaboratively work toward a common objective necessitates limiting the effects of human variability.

One step in limiting variability lies in the process of selection for membership in the organization. The supervisors charged with hiring people as agency social workers seek to select candidates who are likely to "fit in." The task requires selecting those applicants who have the personal characteristics, attitudes, and maturity that will allow them to feel comfortable and accepting in implementing agency objectives.

The process of prolonged education in other professions is a sorting mechanism which selects out those recruits who are not likely to be a good fit for the job. However, many people apply for social work jobs without having encountered the educational sorting process. Furthermore, the nature of the job is so ambiguously defined in the mind of the general public that many applicants cannot clearly determine whether they want to do it. As a consequence, the administrative gatekeeper has an important function in social work selection.

Since personnel recruitment and selection involve fitting people to a particular job, the nature of the job that needs to be done requires specification. The supervisor is in the best position to know the details of the job that needs to be done and the attitudes, skills, and knowledge required to do it. Consequently, supervisors make a significant contribution to the process of staff recruitment and selection.

Since supervisors know the work that needs to be done they participate in establishing criteria for hiring staff and in implementing these criteria in interviewing job applicants. Having interviewed applicants, they provide input into decisions about hiring. Even if they do not always make the final determination, the supervisors' recommendations are invariably given careful consideration.

The supervisors, who are in immediate contact with the direct service workers, are in the best position to know if additional staff needs to be recruited. They are the first to know about anticipated resignations and staff turnover. Once again their position in the agency calls attention to their administrative responsibilities in regard to recruitment and hiring.

2. Inducting and Placing the Worker

Once an applicant has been recruited and hired, the supervisor to whom the new applicant is assigned has the function of placement and induction. Workers need to find their place in the organizational framework. Knowing clearly to whom they report, and who reports to them, enables workers to find their "particular location in the invisible geography" of the agency's human-relations network. Through the supervisor, their immediate administrative link, workers are tied into the total organizational apparatus.

The process of such placement and identification has its beginning in the worker's induction into the agency, a function for which the supervisor is administratively responsible. The supervisor prepares to induct the worker by reviewing the worker's personnel folder, informing other workers in the unit that a new worker has been hired, finding an office and a desk, selecting some reading material about the agency and its functions, and selecting a limited number of tasks to discuss with the worker for possible assignment.

On meeting the newly hired worker, the supervisor discusses the function of the unit to which the worker has been assigned, how it fits into the total agency operation, the relationship of the supervisor to the worker, and his relationship with other workers in the unit. Hopefully, questions about job specifics have been discussed as part of the formal job offer, but they may need further clarification.

Such specifics include details around salary, pay periods, work hours, health insurance, pension, vacations, holidays, absences, overtime, sick leave, reimbursement for travel, national meeting and workshop attendance support policy, receiving and making local and long distance telephone calls. Induction includes sharing helpful information about parking, local eating facilities, and location of bathrooms. The supervisor makes arrangements for a door and/or desk nameplate and for a mailbox.

The supervisor tells the worker how to obtain forms and office supplies, how and under what conditions to use the xerox. One supervisor says:

> All of this is nitty-gritty stuff but I have found that it is essential to outline these things for my supervisees so that they could provide themselves without having to ask me something or other every five minutes, but more important so that they could develop a sense of belonging to the agency. Knowledge of office operations allowed for a feeling of confidence, competence, and comfort and a sense of being one of the group.

If the worker is new to the city as well as the agency there may also need to be at least an offer of help in finding housing, day care, a doctor, a dentist.

The supervisor personally introduces the worker to peers, office personnel with whom he will be working, and administrative officers. She is aware that the man or woman on a new job, in a new organization, is likely to be lonely. The supervisor might ask one of the more experienced employees in the unit to act as sponsor for the new worker, answering routine questions and being available to help the new worker during the first week or so. If the new worker is not isolated at lunch time the first week, but is included in some group, it is a great comfort to the new staff member.

New workers may have little if any idea of the purpose and nature of supervision, so there is a need for some kind of preparation for the role of supervisee. Just as it has been found useful to prepare clients for psychotherapy through the use of a preinduction preparation interview, it would be helpful to provide such help to beginning supervisees. This will give the supervisee some idea of what to expect and will ensure the more active participation of the supervisee, who might otherwise see himself as "receiving" supervision. Also, the orientation should be gradual so that the supervisee doesn't become overwhelmed with too much too early.

Some of the hazards of induction, and the supervisor's handling of them, are detailed in a social worker's recollection of her first day as a psychiatric social worker in a mental hospital:

> From the start, the supervisor seemed to be sensitively aware of possible anxiety on my part. She had made considerable plans in advance as to what I would do my first few weeks at the hospital. The first day she arrived fifteen minutes early and met me at the door. We went to her office, she took my coat and offered me a cup of coffee. She then took me with her to get it so that I would know where the pot was for future use.
>
> We had to go through two locked doors and as we did so, Ms. B. explained that she would see that I got a set of keys for my own by the end of the day. (She did this and I was to find that she was equally prompt with other matters as well. If I asked a question she would either answer it or be on the phone immediately to find out from someone who knew.) These two gestures served to make me feel like one of the staff and, as such, accepted and very comfortable.
>
> As we sat drinking our coffee, Ms. B. explained her plans for me for the day. First off, she would show me around the immediate area and introduce me to the people with whom I would be in frequent contact. She noted that she would not confuse me by giving a tour of the whole grounds. She confided that this is what was done when she first came to the hospital and she ended up not remembering where anything was nor who any of the people were.
>
> As we toured the second floor, Ms. B. introduced me as a new worker. This made me extremely uncomfortable, as such a label is

generally a hindrance in working with a client. I wished that, as some of the literature suggested, a name such as "assistant caseworker" or "intern" or "trainee" had been used. I brought this up later and Ms. B. agreed that the label of "new worker" might present problems and that henceforth she would just refer to me as a social worker around patients unless asked. Unfortunately, she did not inform other staff members of this and so half of them still referred to me as the "new worker."

Ms. B. gave me some pamphlets on the functions of the hospital and the specific expectations of social workers.

Unfortunately, she then handed me great volumes of material to read, the content of which had little meaning at the time as it dealt with specifics such as addresses and special policies of agencies with which the hospital might have contact. Glancing at the indexes would have been just as useful since even the regular social workers at the hospital did not know these infrequently used specifics without referring back to the manuals. I was considerably chagrined at the assignment of this task as I knew from past experience how fruitless it would prove to be and had hoped that my supervisor would also have remembered from her past. Before I got around to reading very much of this, Ms. B. suggested that I attend a staffing by a psychiatrist other than the one on whose service I would be working. This proved to be very worthwhile as I was able to be more fully appreciative of the great variation in psychiatrists and the way in which they staffed patients.

3. Work Planning

Once the direct service worker has been recruited, hired, inducted, and placed, the supervisor has to plan what the agency needs him to do.

Administration sets general policies and objectives. These then need to be broken down into specific duties and, ultimately, into specific tasks—a certain unit of work to be completed within a given period of time. This is a process of progressively greater refinement of general policy objectives at each descending administrative level so that they can be parceled out in small, manageable units. It is at the first-line supervisory level that agency policies and objectives get their ultimate translation into tasks to be performed by direct service workers.

The supervisor is directly in charge of a group of employees responsible for maintaining a productive flow of work, which "flows from points of decision to points of action." In less elegant terms, this key administrative responsibility of supervision is called "getting the work out," "putting the job description to work."

Providing service to the group of clients for which any unit has responsibility requires planning and the delegation of tasks. A unit may be allocated responsibility for 300 clients with a variety of social problems. Each supervisor, allocated 5 to 7 workers, has the responsibility of delegating to each worker some component of the entire unit caseload so that in aggregate the 300 cases are covered.

Planning the distribution of cases is not, however, an automatic mathematical process. Good planning requires familiarity with the supervisees and with the cases requiring action. It also requires familiarity with the tasks the unit is responsible for, so that all tasks will be concluded within a given time frame without unduly overloading the workers or requiring overtime work. The supervisor has to have the competence to plan for judicious deployment of her work force. Planning them involves deciding what needs to be done and how it's going to get done through selective assignment and delegation of tasks to staff. Planning involves decisions regarding scheduling and prioritizing work, not only who will do it, but when it has to get done. Thus, work planning, of necessity, precedes work assignment.

The unit supervisor has some responsibility for long-range planning as well as for immediate planning. Long-range planning involves preparation of a unit budget as a component of the total agency budget. This is based on some assessment of the future work load of the unit and the fiscal, technical, and human resources that might be required to complete it.

4. Work Assignment

Having planned the overall work of the unit the supervisor selects tasks for individual workers in line with the total unit work plan. In making task assignments the supervisor needs to take a variety of factors into consideration.

CRITERIA FOR ASSIGNMENT

1. In social agencies, case or group assignment generally is made in terms of the specific strengths and weaknesses of individual

workers. Consequently, in discharging this responsibility the supervisor needs to know the individual worker's capacities intimately. Implied here is not only a knowledge of the areas that are likely to be problematic for a certain worker, but also the level of complexity of casework demands that the worker can handle with some likelihood of success.

2. Selection for assignment may depend on job pressures carried by the different workers for whom the supervisor has responsibility. Good administration requires an attempt to equalize the demands made upon workers at the same title and salary level. The supervisor needs to consider the current total caseload carried by each worker, in terms of number of cases and also in terms of the activity likely to be demanded of the worker. The supervisor then assigns new cases so as to ensure some equitable distribution of work load. Otherwise, for instance, a worker might be stigmatized by her peers as one who is not really carrying her load in the group.

3. Another criterion in assignment of tasks should be variety. Too great a concentration on one particular kind of task, one kind of case, or one kind of problem situation denies the worker the satisfactions and competence derived from variety in job assignments. This criterion needs to be balanced against assignment in terms of workers' strengths and weaknesses. Some workers do better, and derive greater satisfaction, from highly concentrated job assignments. Others resent this practice and find it stultifying.

4. The worker needs the stimulation of challenge as well as variety if motivation is to be sustained and professional growth increased. Assigning tasks clearly below the level of the worker's capacity is likely to be less desirable than the opposite.

5. Some consideration might need to be given to the question of matching worker and client in terms of age, sex, race, or ethnicity.

WORK ASSIGNMENT AND CASELOAD MANAGEMENT

Work assignment involves scheduling. Assignments need to be made and tasks allocated with some understanding of the time span in which the work needs to be completed, so that deadlines can be met. The supervisor is responsible for scheduling that ensures the workers' ability to perform their jobs without undue stress. The scheduling of meetings, supervisory conferences, dictation time, and report due dates must be made with some appreciation of the total load imposed on the workers and the time available to do the work.

Wherever possible, workers should have an opportunity to express preference for certain kinds of case situations in which they may have a particular interest. Joint discussions of case assignment might further elicit the workers' subjective reactions to work loads. While having the same number of cases as peers, a worker may nevertheless feel overloaded. Sharing her sense of resentment with the supervisor can be helpful. In addition, the supervisor has the opportunity to discuss techniques of caseload management with the worker. The total caseload might be reviewed and some decision made as to those cases on which minimum effort might be expended because the situation is stable and not subject to much change. Other cases might be selected for more intensive consideration. The client in such cases may be more vulnerable, or the client and the social situation may be open to positive change in response to active intervention by the worker. At the same time the supervisor can make clear to the worker where the agency's preferred priorities lie, which cases should receive service if time and energy are limited, and which need not be done until time is available.

WORK ASSIGNMENT PROCEDURE

A study of case assignment procedures in voluntary and public welfare agencies shows that the most frequent system, by far, is for the supervisor or other administrator to assign cases "based on knowledge of case characteristics, worker ability and experience, etc." (Haring 1974, p. 5). In only about 5 percent of the agencies did the procedure entail "division of labor by staff members among themselves either at periodic meetings or by rotating responsibility for intake" (p. 4). A high percentage of the workers reacted favorably to the assignment of work by the supervisor.

A supervisee writes about her reaction to case assignments by her supervisor:

> I, personally, felt that a random distribution of cases and task assignments provided me with a far greater array of experiences than would

have been available had I selected cases and assignments more in accord with my own preference. Under these circumstances, I was often forced into situations that, had I been operating of my own volition, I might have tried to avoid. I think that this produced an environment for substantial personal growth. Allowing an individual to select cases or work assignments which he feels are suited to his personal preferences may lead to stagnation, rather than the development of a flexible individual who can work with a diversity of problems and people. Too often personal preference can be used as an avoidance mechanism or a "cop-out." This does not mean that individual preferences should be categorically ignored or denied, but that the supervisor should evaluate the request for certain assignments or cases critically before giving his assent, to insure that such action would primarily be in the best interests of the client and/or the agency and not just the worker.

An innovative alternative to assignment of cases by the supervisor alone is assignment by unit members in a group meeting. The cases to be assigned are introduced and summarized, and supervisor and supervisees decide on assigning the case together. While this ostensibly is a more democratic procedure, a study of this procedure among social work teams showed that group pressure replaced supervisor authority. One worker said, "The allocation meetings allegedly allow a democratic choice. In reality it works out that the less strong-minded get lumbered. . . . However in practice it was apparent that the social workers felt under an obligation to take a fair share of the referrals and not to leave all the work to their colleagues" (Parsloe and Stevenson 1978, p. 73).

Group allocation did involve a considerable expenditure of worker time and worked best if the supervisor was willing enough and strong enough to exert authority to shield some workers from weakness or excessive self-demands. However, workers were stimulated by the discussion, got a better overview of the total referral caseload, and welcomed the status that came with involvement.

PROBLEMS IN WORK ASSIGNMENT

In assigning cases the supervisor faces a number of contradictory pressures that are difficult to resolve. While willing to accede to a worker's preference, the supervisor still must assign every case for service. Even if no supervisee has expressed preference for some particular kind of client, or worse, even if all supervisees have expressed dislike for that kind of client, the supervisor must nonetheless assign the client for service.

> Ms. P., a medical social worker, has been assigned cases on the Pediatrics Ward. The large number of handicapped and defective children, especially children requiring institutional placement, has been disturbing to her. After three months at the hospital a case is assigned of a three-year-old spastic boy to discuss institutional possibilities with the parents who are felt to be receptive to placement. Rather reluctantly, Ms. P. tells her supervisor that she would rather not be assigned this case and mentions that a child of a friend was placed in a colony for the mentally defective a year ago. Ms. P. visited with her friend, and the institution seemed depressing.
>
> Rather than acceding to or rejecting the request or resorting to her positional authority to back up her assignment of the case, the supervisor engaged Ms. P. in elaborating on and examining her feelings about the assignment. The supervisor did this with the acceptance of the fact that every worker has limits to tolerance and there are some cases that should not be assigned because the worker has strong negative feelings about the assignment. At the same time, there was a recognition that workers have to be helped in extending their limits of tolerance. To permit Ms. P. to reject every assignment with which she might feel uncomfortable would do an injustice to her capacity for growth. In addition to discussing with Ms. P. her own feelings about the situation, the supervisor reviewed the knowledge available regarding the advantages and disadvantages of institutionalization for such children. She helped Ms. P. apply this knowledge to the particular situation of the family of this particular spastic child.

There are further conflicts—between the supervisor's desire to assign every case to the most competent and experienced worker and the need for equitable distribution of caseload, and between the desire to give each client the best worker and the need for new, inexperienced workers to learn the job.

A more global problem of case assignment for the supervisor is determining whether or not a case assigned by administration to the unit is appropriate. This is a gatekeeping function that guards against the unit being saddled with cases that are more appropriate to the functions and expertise of other units.

In assigning tasks the supervisor has the additional problem of deciding on the amount of direction given in assigning the task and the level of discretion permitted the worker. But this is a problem which relates more directly to another major function of supervision—work delegation.

5. Work Delegation

In assigning work the supervisor not only has to deal with the problem of task selection, using the criteria discussed above, but also has to decide the explicitness with which she instructs the worker about action that needs to be taken in implementing the assignment. Task assignment indicates what work needs to be accomplished. Task delegation indicates how it is to be accomplished. Where work is assigned under conditions of maximum worker autonomy and discretion, the objectives of task assignment are clearly stated and the worker is permitted to initiate any action, at any time, which he feels will result in accomplishment of the objectives. Under conditions of more limited autonomy, the worker may be delegated authority to act only after obtaining prior approval or he may be told in advance what to do.

There are a variety of procedures that can be used to delegate tasks in a way that can modulate the extent of autonomy granted. One can provide a series of explicit and detailed directives as to how the task should be carried out; one can provide a very general series of directives, giving the worker considerable flexibility on detail; one can plan cooperatively in discussions with the worker how the task should be carried out; or one can merely leave the worker free to implement the task with no particular restrictions other than general objectives and a time limit.

Most frequently the more adequately trained and experienced workers are given the freedom of deciding the details in implementing an assignment. The supervisor assumes little responsibility for specifying how the assignment is to be implemented. In supervising the less adequately trained and inexperienced worker, the supervisor may have to take more administrative responsibility for the specifics.

Intrinsic job satisfaction and heightened motivation tend to be associated with greater autonomy in implementation of job assignments. The more discretion he is given, the greater the likelihood that the supervisee will feel he is trusted and worthy of trust. Con-

sequently, on a continuum of directivity, the supervisor should permit the workers as much discretion as they can safely and
productively handle. Whenever possible, the supervisor indicates
what results need to be achieved without specifying the procedures
to be employed. However, the supervisor should be ready, when
necessary, to be more directive, not only assigning the task but
clearly specifying how it should be done.

Often even the more experienced worker may want some directive assistance in task implementation. This function—"analysis
and planning of client contact with supervisees"—is rated by supervisors as one that occupies a very high percentage of their time
(Kadushin 1974). In effect, such planning is like a briefing session.
The assignment is explained, the objectives are clarified, the
method of implementation is discussed.

Even maximum worker autonomy, however, is exercised within
constraints that derive from the objectives of the agency, the requirements of agency survival, the tenets of the profession. Autonomy in task implementation is "an exercise of discretion toward
prescribed ends, within prescribed limits."

Delegation goes beyond the assignment of a task. It involves the
supervisor sharing some measure of her authority with the supervisee, who is then empowered to make decisions and to take action
in the performance of the assigned task. But while responsibility for
the task and the authority to take action can be delegated it cannot
be relinquished by the supervisor.

Delegating in social work is risky, unlike some other supervisory
situations, because there are more limited subsequent controls
available permitting a check on the work. A work force whose activities are visible and subject to supervisory observation permits
ongoing application of controls if the decision to delegate proves to
be an error. No such ready controls are available in social work to
reverse an error in delegation.

Task delegation is a complex function dependent on a number of
interacting variables. These include supervisor attributes, supervisee attributes, the nature of the task delegated, and the organizational climate, all of which will be discussed in some detail below.

The amount of discretion that the worker is granted to operate
autonomously is a function of the supervisor's ability and willingness to delegate responsibility, which in turn are affected by a vari-

ety of factors. Supervisors differ in the anxiety they feel about delegating tasks. Some are less willing than others to accept the risk of mistakes and failure in their supervisees, for which they might be held accountable. This unwillingness may stem from a supervisor's lack of confidence in himself or from an anxious relationship with his own supervisor. Some are less ready to encourage the development of independence on the part of their supervisees and are gratified by the continuing dependency exemplified by controlling the work decisions of supervisees. Some obtain satisfaction by vicarious involvement in direct practice. More active direction of the work of their supervisees gives them a sense of being involved in the worker-client relationship. The more authoritarian, controlling supervisor will be less ready to delegate than will the democratic-egalitarian supervisor. The supervisor who is oriented toward upward mobility and anxious to please administration is less likely to delegate responsibility than is the supervisor who is free of such internal pressures. In summary, "The ability of a supervisor to delegate effectively depends on the way he relates to his job, his subordinates, his superior and himself" (Bishop 1969, p. 112).

Other factors that determine delegation relate to the worker rather than the supervisor. A supervisor may be reluctant to delegate because he perceives the worker as incapable, at this point, of operating independently. The worker may be ambivalent about accepting responsibility because this implies accepting blame for failure as well as commendation for success.

The supervisor may be deterred from delegating because the worker communicates a reluctance and discomfort in accepting independent responsibility for the task, but worker readiness to accept responsibility reciprocally affects the supervisor's readiness to grant responsibility.

Supervisees who feel uncertain about their competence to do the job will press for greater direction and more precise delegation from supervisors than will their more confident peers. Supervisees who feel a strong need for independence, who are ready to risk mistakes and who need less structure, will encourage the supervisor to delegate tasks in a less specific way. Workers have different levels of readiness to tolerate ambiguity in a situation that is not clearly defined or structured for them.

Other factors that determine readiness to delegate relate to the task situation itself. If the nature of the situation is one which is likely to have high visibility, relates to a sensitive public policy question, or effects personnel and/or organizations that have considerable power, there will be increased hesitancy to delegate since the embarrassing consequences of any error are more likely to be intensified.

Where clients are more vulnerable, as in the case of children who might be subject to abuse and/or neglect, where decisions might involve commitment of scarce resources such as large amounts of public money or large amounts of worker time, or where errors in worker judgment might have serious consequences for the client, the situation may dictate a reduction in delegated discretion.

The complexity of the task and the pressure of time available for completion also affect the nature of delegation. More complex tasks may require more precise specification in delegating. The pressure of time allows for fewer errors and less experimentation with possible false starts and consequently a greater measure of supervisor control.

Still other factors that determine the supervisor's willingness and readiness to delegate lie with administration. Supervisors are more apt to delegate responsibility if they have the assurance that administration will support rather than berate them if the worker commits an error.

Where there is pressure for precise accountability of agency activity from groups to which the agency is responsible, supervisors will feel a greater pressure to delegate tasks with exactness and limit worker discretion.

Operating in a host setting alongside professionals of other disciplines increases the hesitancy to delegate. In schools, hospitals, and psychiatric clinics, supervisors are sensitive to the fact that their supervisees are being closely observed by others. Supervisors further have to negotiate with other professionals for the position and prerogatives of social work within the host setting. This situation is more tenuous than one in a setting controlled by social workers.

In summary, the decision around task assignment and the degree of autonomy granted the worker in implementing a task are determined by such factors as: the complexity of the task, level of worker skill and interest, worker caseload in terms of nature and number of cases, vulnerability of and risk to the client, sensitive nature of the problem and likely visibility of error, readiness of supervisor and supervisee to incur risk, and administrative penalties for supervisory failure.

Ultimately, the supervisor retains administrative responsibility for the work assigned, and supervisors accept the fact that they are responsible for the work done by their supervisees. Seventy percent of the supervisors studied by Olyan (1972) agreed with the statement, "The supervisor is responsible for the work done by each of his supervisees" (p. 162).

Supervisors tend to direct delegated tasks in terms of suggestions or advice. "It might be helpful if. . . ." "It might be advisable to. . . ." But advice, suggestion, or persuasion may not always be sufficient to direct or redirect the worker. In such cases the supervisor has responsibility for being expicitly directive. As one supervisor said,

> There are times, let's be frank about it, when I have to be an arbitrator, when it is so obvious that the [worker] is heading for trouble and the client is going to become adrift as a result. I don't mind if from time to time I can afford the luxury of the social worker making a mistake and learning from it but in this work we can't afford to make a mistake if it's going to backfire on the client.

The difficulty is determining the point where "advice stops and direction begins," where "professional responsibility ends and managerial responsibility begins" (Parsloe and Stevenson, p. 222).

6. Monitoring, Reviewing, Evaluating Work

At this point the process leads to another distinctive function of administrative supervision. Having delegated the assigned task with the appropriate level of discretion, the supervisor has the further responsibility of monitoring the task assignment to see that it gets done in the allotted time and in a way which is in line with agency procedures.

An interview study of 20 supervisors in a state public welfare department found that 55 percent of the supervisors saw their primary role as monitoring worker performance (Weatherley et al. 1980). Monitoring involves obtaining verbal reports from workers, reading records, reviewing statistical reports. At the minimum the objective of performance monitoring and review is to see that no harm is done. But in addition it may involve sharing favorable feedback and verbal approval. Work review is necessary to determine if the work is being accomplished as planned. Work review also involves the general responsibility of seeing that supervisees are available to cover the work load. This function, then, involves monitoring both the worker and the worker's work.

The principal resource the supervisor has available to ensure that the work of the agency gets done is the time and skill of the supervisees. In accepting the role of employee of an agency the supervisee implicitly agrees to place his time and skill at the disposal of the agency for some specific period during the day and week. Consequently, the supervisor has the responsibility of knowing when and if the supervisees are available for work during the agreed-upon period. The supervisor needs to be concerned with tardiness, absences, requests for time off, sick leave, vacation schedules, and projected and emergency overtime personnel needs to ensure adequate coverage of work assignments. If the supervisor does not have final authority with regard to these questions, as she should, she often has the power of decisive recommendation.

Tardiness and absenteeism reduce the human resources available to the supervisor for getting the work done. Both are such routine occurrences that they need to be accepted by the supervisor as a fact of life. In time, supervisors get to know the tardiness and absentee patterns of their supervisees. They make decisions as to whether they are avoidable or unavoidable, controllable or accidental. Allowing for a certain amount of sanctioned tardiness and absenteeism, supervisors try to follow a policy that is clearly and explicitly communicated to supervisees and one that is reasonable, fair, and equitable.

In implementing the work-assignment and work-delegating responsibilities of administrative supervision, the supervisor is concerned with assuring continuity of service. The worker represents the agency to the community. The supervisor represents the agency as well, though once removed. If a worker leaves the agency, the supervisor is there to step in and ensure that the agency is still responsible for offering service, so that there is no break in the continuity of contact, but merely an interruption and possible delay. If the worker is absent or sick, the supervisor again ensures continuity of contact and work coverage.

The supervisor or administrator not only has to review the assignment to be assured that it is actually being accomplished, and accomplished in accordance with agency policies and procedures, but further has to make some judgment as to whether it is being accomplished at a minimally acceptable level. The supervisor then has responsibility for evaluation. Formal evaluation of the workers' performance is an administrative act. If the agency is to operate efficiently, then someone has to share clearly with the workers an objective appraisal of the things they are doing right, the things they are doing wrong, to point out the behaviors that require changing. Agency procedures regarding raises, promotions, and changes in job assignment require periodic formal evaluation if such decisions are to be implemented in a rational manner. Since evaluation is a very important function of administrative supervision and is the source of much confusion and difficulty, we have reserved a more detailed discussion for chapter 6.

Monitoring, review, and evaluation are the inspectional aspects of administrative supervision. Inspectional supervision deserves the onerous reputation it has achieved only if done autocratically and to excess. These are not inherently undesirable procedures. They are functions that are administratively necessary if the client is to receive satisfactory service. The administrative supervisory function of monitoring, reviewing and evaluating work implies further the supervisor's responsibility to take disciplinary action if the work is clearly unsatisfactory.

7. Coordinating Work

The overall agency objectives have to be subdivided into manageable and differentiated tasks that are assigned to different units and then are once again subdivided and assigned to individual workers. If organizational objectives are to be effectively implemented all of this breaking down has to be coordinated and integrated.

Through coordination the supervisor brings workers into relationship with other workers involved in activities that are reciprocal, supportive, or supplementary to their own work. Coordination unifies different workers' efforts toward achievement of agency objectives. Cooperation among workers and work units is maximized, conflict minimized, and greater complementarity assured.

The supervisor also coordinates and integrates her own unit with other units of the agency and with other agencies in the community's social welfare network. The supervisor thus not only occupies a position in the vertical hierarchy but relates horizontally to other administrative units on the same hierarchical level. The supervisor in the family service unit of a multiservice neighborhood center, for example, might help coordinate the activities of her supervisees with the homemaker unit, the employment unit, the day-care unit, the protective services unit.

The supervisor activates support staff resources to facilitate the work of the direct service line workers. Through coordination the supervisor makes available to the worker human, fiscal, and physical resources required to do the job. She might help coordinate the supervisees' activity with that of the clerical unit, seeing that typing time is available, a dictaphone provided. She might help make available psychiatric consultation and psychological test resources to the supervisees. She functions here to ensure the availability and smooth scheduling of a variety of different agency and community resources for the supervisees.

The supervisor organizes and orchestrates the activities of a number of different workers so that their joint efforts are cooperatively directed toward accomplishing some significant aspects of the mission of the agency. Coordination involves ensuring that the different workers understand the goals and objectives of the agency in the same way and accept them—or at least behave as though they accepted them—so each worker can operate in the confident expectation that others in the group are working together rather than at cross purposes.

Coordination requires that the supervisor adjudicate conflicts between workers in his unit and between his unit and other units of the agency. Two workers may be competing for the same assignments, or may disagree about who should be doing what with regard to a complex problem for which they have joint responsibility. The unmarried mothers' unit may be dissatisfied about the availability of adoptive homes for which the adoptive unit is responsible; the family care worker may be getting little cooperation from the agency's employment unit or housing unit. The supervisor has the responsibility of seeing that such conflicts are satisfactorily resolved. Put positively, the supervisor maintains harmonious working relationships within the unit and between his units and other units in the agency.

Spergel (1966) gives an interesting example of such coordination in his analysis of the outreach program working with street gangs.

> Service to fighting and highly delinquent groups requires a high degree of cooperation among street workers along with representatives of other agencies, especially the police. . . . One example of a device for coordinating and controlling the area-oriented worker is the central communications system. When a critical situation arises, the worker is expected to relay information to the supervisor as soon as possible via a central control switchboard. The supervisor can then deploy other workers and involve the police, if necessary. This kind of communication system assists the supervisor to know where workers are in the field, and permits him to inform, advise, or direct them as to the most appropriate way of handling the emergent situation. (pp. 243–44)

The supervisor has the responsibility of facilitating the supervisees' work. However skillful the individual workers, their effectiveness is reduced if they operate in a defectively organized unit. The supervisor is responsible for providing the supporting organizational setting that would maximize the workers' contribution. The supervisor relates effective people to effective programs through effective organization of the work context. This means making sure that workers are provided with adequate facilities, supplies, staff help, and information.

Supervisors need the authority to require that facilities be made available. Strong chief unit clerks often contend with weak supervisors about the allocation of facilities and the work time of typists and file clerks. Despite the fact that the agency table of organization gives the supervisor greater authority, inability to effectively exercise this power may put the supervisor's workers at a disadvantage regarding access to the resources they need to do their work effectively.

The supervisor performs the additional function of acting for agency administration in authorizing and legitimizing supervisees' decisions and recommendations. This gives official agency support to the workers' actions. In doing this the supervisor acts to coordinate the claims of the worker on behalf of his client with the services the agency is ready and willing to offer.

8. The Communication Function

The supervisor acts as an integral link in the chain of administrative communication. In the vertical line of authority, she faces two ways—toward the administrators above her in the hierarchy and toward the workers below her. The supervisor's position is, then, one of the administrative control centers for gathering, processing, and disseminating information coming from above and below in the chain of command.

A small group cooperatively performing certain tasks can rely on face-to-face communication among all members of the group. A complex organization, in which administrators rarely have direct contact with workers, requires other approaches if messages are to reach their proper destinations and be understood and accepted. Formal channels of communication need to be provided, and the nature of the work to be done and the conditions under which it is to be completed need to be precisely stated and clearly defined.

Communication permits more effective coordination of the work of the agency through linkages provided by the flow of information and feedback. The volume of communication varies with the degree of diversity of a social agency. There is a greater necessity for coordination in more complex organizations. Communication as a vehicle for coordination is particularly necessary in organizations such as social agencies, where tasks are ambiguously defined and where it is difficult to explicitly codify procedures for task implementation. Rather than being able to rely on written manuals and handbooks, administrators need to make frequent efforts to clarify and check to see if messages have been understood.

"In a sense the formal structure [of an organization] acts as a highway system guiding both the direction of information flow (up, down, sideways) and the distribution pattern and its terminal points" (Steiner 1977, p. 1980). The supervisor is one of the principal gatekeepers in the communications highway system, gathering, interpreting, distilling and evaluating information received *from* others in the hierarchy and transmitting this information *to* others in the hierarchy.

What administrators have to say to the workers in interpreting agency objectives, policies, procedures, and structure, and what they have to share about proposed agency changes, they channel through the supervisor, who is administration's spokesperson to the workers. Messages from workers to administration also have to be channelled through the supervisor. The administrator needs to depend on the supervisor to find out how agency policies and procedures are being implemented, the successes and problems in implementation, and the workers' feelings about agency objectives, policies, and procedures. This is the kind of information which only the direct service worker possesses, and the kind of information the administrator needs to know about if the agency is to be successfully run.

The supervisor has the responsibility of encouraging relevant communication from supervisees, establishing a climate of receptivity and a readiness to listen. Conversely, the supervisor has to demonstrate a readiness to share relevant information with supervisees, keeping them informed, indicating a willingness to answer questions fully and to correct misconceptions. The supervisor should avoid assumptions. "Don't assume that the supervisees know; tell them. Don't assume that you know how they feel; find out. Don't assume that they understand; clarify" (U.S. Civil Service Commission 1955, p. 22).

A large-scale study found adequate and effective communication within the agency to be a very important determinant of worker satisfaction. The study of 1,600 workers in 31 agencies found that "the biggest problem is that higher levels in an organization usually assume communication is adequate but lower level personnel do not agree. The great majority of personnel feel they do not have all the information they need to do their jobs effectively" (Olmstead and Christensen 1973, p. 13).

Almost every aspect of the supervisor's work involves skill in communication. Clear unambiguous communication is required in inducting the worker, assigning and delegating work, reviewing, evaluating work, giving feedback, and coordinating work. If communication between supervisor and supervisee is to be effective, it needs to be relevant, distortion free, sufficiently detailed, and prompt.

In acting as a channel of communication from administration to the direct service staff the supervisor has a responsibility beyond mechanical transmission of information. The additional responsibilities are to see that the message is understood and accepted and to motivate the worker to act in accordance with the information transmitted. It is especially important to communicate information about changes in policies and procedure to the individual worker directly affected by them.

Concern with effective communication requires some decision as to how the message from administration to supervisees and supervisor to administrator might best be transmitted. The supervisor has a variety of channels through which to communicate information: personal face-to-face communication, phone communication, writing a memo or a report. The personal face-to-face choice provides instant feedback, which enables the supervisor to tailor the communication to fit the individual recipient. The message is apt to be more potent since it is transmitted personally. Phone messages are apt to be shorter or more abbreviated, and there is less feedback, both verbal and nonverbal.

However, both face-to-face and phone communication may get sidetracked and be dominated by other concerns, and since there is no record of the communication it is not repeatedly visible as a reminder. Also, face-to-face and phone communication require additional time since the message has to be repeated to every recipient. Furthermore, oral messages can be distorted in transmission.

In using the written channel of communication, the supervisor can be more precise. There is greater possibility for control of the content of the message. There is a record of the communication which can be reread by the recipient at her own convenience as a reminder. There is time saved in simultaneous distribution of the message to a number of recipients. However, written messages are less flexible, and there is no possibility of interpretation and elaboration to the individual recipient.

The supervisor may choose to employ multiple channels for repeated transmission of the same information. Redundancy in communication has the effect of reducing the possibilities of message distortion.

To be effective, the supervisor has to do more than act as a messenger. Lacking direct contact with administration, supervisees look to the supervisor to represent their interests and actively press for the implementation of necessary changes. Effective administrative supervision requires active representation of supervisees' interests and viewpoints as an intermediary with administration. Blau and Scott (1962) found that those supervisors in a public welfare agency who related to administrators in an independent manner and who regularly backed their subordinates commanded high loyalty from their supervisees (p. 155). A psychiatric social worker in a state hospital says that in one case she

> judged it necessary to call in an outside consultant-advocate in an incident involving the civil rights of a patient. My supervisor supported this decision verbally and by attending the meeting which was held to discuss the patient's situation. She did this even though the hospital administration disapproved of my action. It was gratifying to see that my supervisor was open to the facts and exercised judgment based on client need rather than on official administration policy.

The act of communication is abortive unless it is accompanied by some confidence in the possibility that the message will have an effect. Supervisee satisfaction with supervision appears to be related to the level of influence the supervisor has with administration (Pelz 1952). There was dissatisfaction with the supervisor who promised much but was able to deliver little. There was high satisfaction with the supervisor who communicated worker requests and was able to get action. The lesson for administrators is that they should make a sincere effort to respond to communications from supervisees via supervisors. The lesson for supervisors is that they must honestly share with the supervisees the limits of their power, to forestall unrealistic expectations about the effects of upward communication.

Some studies have shown that workers are not confident that supervisors will take responsibility for decisions when these are questioned by higher-ups (Greenleigh Associates 1960, p. 133). The most frequent complaint about supervisors listed by supervisees in a questionnaire study of N.A.S.W. members is that the supervisor was "hesitant about confronting agency administration with the needs of his or her supervisees" (Kadushin 1974).

> Mr. E., a school social worker, was indignant at the judgmental attitude of the Board of Education's policy regarding admission of unmarried mothers to special school programs. The supervisee informed his supervisor that it had been his experience that school officials were discouraging unmarried mothers from attending school by erecting unnecessary procedures for admission to school. Mr. E. had hoped

that the supervisor would either join him in talking with Board of Education officials or support him in doing so. Instead the supervisor chose to focus on Mr. E.'s "indignation" and "hostility" toward the Board of Education and was insensitive to the need for change in school policy.

PROBLEMS IN ORGANIZATIONAL COMMUNICATION

The above account suggests one of the principal barriers to the free flow of communication up and down administrative channels. The supervisor may be reluctant to communicate negative information to people to whom he is administratively responsible because he fears incurring hostility or displeasure. Similarly, the supervisee is reluctant to communicate negative information to the supervisor because he fears rejection, a negative evaluation, a censuring reaction. Consequently, rather than a sharing of dissatisfactions and problems in offering service, communication is carefully restricted to telling others only what they want to hear or what will reflect favorably on one's own performance. The safest procedure is to act the part of a not-too-obvious "yes man" and "play it close to the chest." Freedom to speak is felt only as freedom to agree. This pattern operates more intensely for supervisees who are motivated to obtain the approval of supervisors and who are seeking a good evaluation.

Barriers to organizational communication result from conflicting group loyalties as well as from a need for self-protection. The supervisee is reluctant to share information that may discredit peers or groups of clients with whom he might feel identified. Supervisors may be reluctant to share with administration their critical, but accurate, assessment of some subsection of the agency with which they must continue to work.

Information is power. It is not true that what people don't know won't hurt them. They can very well be harmed because they have not been informed about things they need to know in order to perform effectively. This suggests an additional barrier to the free flow of communication. The supervisor may withhold information from supervisees because this increases their dependency on him.

If these barriers to the free flow of communication do not result in withholding information which should be shared, they more often result in "selective emphasis" and "selective omission" in transmission. Communication takes place but is tailored to the needs of the communicator.

One might realistically anticipate that every agency faces impediments to the free flow of communication. Even in the best of circumstances one might expect supervisees to be pragmatically self-protective in the information they choose to share. But if one cannot hope to achieve the best communication, one might perhaps attain better communication. And here the supervisor is a key figure. Olmstead (1973) claims that

> The climate created by an individual's immediate supervisor is probably the most important influence affecting his communication. Every encounter with the supervisor teaches him something. When the supervisor gives an order, reprimands, praises, evaluates performance, deals with a mistake, holds a staff meeting or contacts [supervisees] in any other way (or fails to contact them), the [supervisees] learn something. They learn about the kinds of information that will be rewarded or punished and the means of communication which the [supervisor] views favorably or unfavorably. (p. 47)

Credibility is important for effective communication. Supervisees need to have an attitude of confidence and trust in the motives and sincerity of the supervisor. This attitude develops when supervisors are truthful in their communications and when words and action go together. Supervisees are constantly engaged in "search behavior" in an effort to distinguish the reality from the rhetoric.

In general it might be said that communication in the agency flows down more easily than it flows up. Communication in the organizational hierarchy has often been described as a system where information flows up through a series of filters and comes down through a series of loudspeakers.

Even in a communication system free from inhibiting influences, the supervisor still has a problem of deciding what information needs to be shared and can be shared. Not all of the information that comes from administration should automatically be communicated to supervisees, and not everything shared by supervisees needs to be transmitted to administration. Applying some general principle of selectivity, such as that one should transmit only information which helps supervisees do their job more effectively, implies that the supervisor needs to have an intimate, detailed knowledge of the worker's job. Only on the basis of such knowledge and understanding can the supervisor assess the value of information for the supervisee.

Making human relationships work is supposedly the stock in trade of social work, and it applies as well to making for effective communications between supervisor and supervisee. A respectful, empathic, understanding orientation, a willingness to listen, an accepting nonpunitive attitude, establish the context for good communication.

Because the orientation of the direct service workers to task-related information is different from that of the supervisor, the supervisor needs to be sensitive to the fact that the same communication may be differently perceived by them. A message from the administrator to the supervisor may consist of asking that the agency be more accountable to the community. This is translated by the supervisor to mean that he will need to assign tasks so that they are more objectively measurable and this message is communicated to the workers. The workers translate the supervisor's message to mean that they will have to fill out more forms with greater care than previously. The responses to essentially the same message are apt to be different at the different levels of communication because at different levels the message has different implications for action.

LATERAL COMMUNICATION

We have noted that the supervisor is a channel of communication in the vertical hierarchy. The supervisor also communicates horizontally—within the agency and with other agencies, between her unit and other units through peers at the supervisory level. Lateral communication from supervisors in one unit to supervisors in related units is concerned with problems of conflict and overlap, changes which might make for more effective coordination of efforts, information about impending changes which may affect coordination of activities. Such communication may be for the purpose of reducing duplication of services, soliciting resources, increasing utilization of services, making referrals, reducing inappropriate referrals, or integrating services.

The supervisor needs to be aware that in addition to the formal organizational communication network described here, there is a parallel communications network operating through the agency's informal structure. While this network transmits much in the way of gossip and rumors it also acts to amend, interpret, and elaborate on the supervisor's communications up and down the hierarchical ladder. The informal channel is particularly active when the situation is ambiguous or unpredictable, or when the formal channel has not provided sufficient information.

The grapevine exists side by side with the official formal channels of communication, and often the supervisor is not included in it. Such informal channels tend to be more active in those situations where the formal channels do not encourage a free flow of information.

9. The Supervisor as Administrative Buffer

The supervisor serves as a buffer in relation to agency clients, and administration looks, in general, to the first-line supervisory staff to handle problems relating to service. Consequently, the supervisor performs the function of dealing with clients who want to discuss a complaint with someone other than the worker. A child welfare worker writes:

> When an irate and emotionally disturbed parent wished to visit her child in foster placement and I had denied her request, she contacted my supervisor when I was out of the office. My supervisor listened supportively, gathered the facts, upheld me in my decision but suggested that the client come to the office to discuss the situation with both my supervisor and me.
> The parent came in a day or so later . . . and we had a very productive meeting. Client was able to express some of her hostility and anger at the child's removal from her home—which anger had been focused on me—however, my supervisor completely supported my position which then freed me from becoming defensive and allowed me to support the client also. The result was a better relationship with the client and more cooperation from her, which ultimately worked to her advantage in the later return of her children to her.
> Having reviewed the case material my supervisor had decided to support my decision. However, she also gave client respect and courtesy which eased the tensions of the interview and allowed us all to gain by it. The client did not feel we were in league against her as she

could have if my supervisor had not been skillful in encouraging her feelings and right to them; nor did the client manage to manipulate my supervisor and me into opposite corners.

The supervisor should be ready to accept appeals from clients who are dissatisfied with a worker's decision and want to speak to a higher authority. In doing so they protect the worker from having to deal with clients' strong feelings about a negative decision, and from a possible arbitrary or incorrect decision. They provide a channel for managing client advocacy efforts. Without such a channel direct service workers may become overloaded with the extra time and effort required to deal with vigorous client dissent.

While serving as a buffer between client complaints and the agency, the supervisor also functions as a buffer between the worker and the agency. The supervisor protects the worker from imposition by administrators of unreasonable workload standards, for example.

The supervisor also has the responsibility of protecting the supervisee from any kind of sexual harrassment within the work unit for which the supervisor is accountable. The American Psychological Association definition of sexual harrassment may be relevant here. It is defined as "deliberate or repeated comments, gestures, or physical contact of a sexual nature that are unwanted by the recipient."

The supervisor as a buffering person helping in negotiating organization complexities is described by a supervisee.

> She radiated a lot of caring, which was very important. I feel it's important. She was an intricate part of the system and really familiar with it; and I wasn't. And I think a knowledge of the hierarchy—of the system, the relationships that exist in it—is very important, and an ability to deal with those. If I had trouble with someone within the agency, she always dealt with it. She didn't do it for me but she helped me to deal with it. (Diane 1977, p. 128)

In addition, the supervisor is expected to protect the organization from potentially embarrassing deviance and heresy. Deviance involves behavioral contravention or subversion of agency regulations; heresy involves ideological opposition to the presuppositions on which the rules were formulated. The worker in a Catholic child welfare agency who helps an unmarried pregnant girl solve her problem by obtaining an abortion is deviant in that context. If she champions the point of view that there is really nothing wrong with an out-of-wedlock pregnancy and questions the legitimacy of agency efforts to help women conform to society's traditional sexual mores, she would be heretical.

An agency operates in, and is tied to, an external environment whose components include clients, funding sources, regulatory agencies, and the general public as well as other agencies with which it competes for income and resources. The agency needs to maintain the good will and support of the external environment. Activities that undermine the legitimacy of the agency with its donor constituency threaten its existence. The elimination of many agencies during the past decade testifies to the fact that the threat is real.

Agency self-preservation is a legitimate objective. More than a question of opportunistic defense of selfish vested interests is involved. If agency workers have a sincere belief in the value of the agency's mission, their concern for agency preservation is ultimately a concern with providing a needed service. The failure to obtain continued funding results in denial of this service to a client group.

The supervisor acts as a guardian of the organization's belief system. For workers to reject significant aspects of agency policy and procedure is regarded as an act of hostility and a challenge to organizational authority. It threatens agency operation because "it suspends the rules that produce loyalty and cohesion" (Peters and Branch 1972, p. 290), without which the agency finds it difficult to operate.

The conflict between worker and organization is manifested first at the level of contact between worker and supervisor. Consequently, "in many organizations it seems systematically to become part of whomever is formally designated as first in command of each particular work unit to occupy the buffer zone which contains heretical confrontations between the individual and the social organizations" (Harshbarger 1973, p. 264). The function is one of "crisis absorbency" and prevention of a threat to the agency's relationship with its supporting constituency.

This administrative function of supervision is implemented by offering workers the opportunity to discuss with the supervisor their questions and doubts about the agency's philosophy, rules, and procedures. Patient, open discussion of the workers' views in an accepting atmosphere is designed to help them understand the rationale of the agency's approach. If the workers remain unconvinced, the supervisory conference still offers a safe channel for the open expression of opposition. The cathartic effect of such an opportunity results, as Goffman (1952) says, "in cooling the mark out"—a reduction in the intensity of feeling of indignation, an increased readiness to conform to organizational demands. Another frequent procedure in the management of heresy is cooption, an attempt to retranslate the worker's opposition so that it can be channeled into kinds of changes that the agency can accept.

In a study of authority relationships in a public welfare department (Peabody 1964), 83 percent of the welfare department employees said that at one time or another they had received instructions from above which seemed to conflict with their own standards, often with regard to regulations for processing welfare grants. The most frequent reactions to such a conflict situation, in descending order, were "discusses with immediate supervisor and works for change but still complies"; "consciously questions but accepts as binding"; "informs immediate supervisor of views but complies or seeks to be converted" (p. 107). (Interestingly, welfare workers were more inclined than police officers and elementary school teachers included in the study to discuss situations of conflict with their supervisors and to work for change.)

The responsibility of acting in defense of agency policy can be a source of considerable dissatisfaction for supervisors. Frequently they find themselves in disagreement with some particular agency policy, rule, or procedure. Nevertheless their role requires communication of the policy and attempts to obtain compliance with it. Forced by their position to perform such functions, supervisors feel uncomfortably hypocritical. In a survey of dissatisfactions felt by supervisors, the "need to get workers' adherence to agency policy and procedure with which I strongly disagree" was among the dissatisfactions most frequently checked (Kadushin 1974).

10. The Supervisor as Change Agent and Community Liaison

Buffering client complaints and worker deviance and heresy suggests the exploitation of the supervisor in the service of preserving the agency status quo. Preserving organizational stability is, in fact, a function of administrative supervision. But the supervisor also has an equally significant parallel administrative responsibility as an organizational change agent. Buffering contributes to the preservation of the agency, but rigidity and unresponsiveness to change threaten the preservation of the agency.

There is a danger that too rigid "management" of deviance and heresy, the "absorption of protest and domestication of dissent," may be counterproductive for the agency. An unperceptive supervisor would then be performing a disservice. The agency must balance contradictory needs—accepting change while maintaining stability. It would be impossible to run an efficient organization and maintain effective working relationships with other agencies if the agency were not essentially stable and predictable. However, too much stability can foster rigidity which becomes ossification. And this can result in the agency failing to respond to the needs of a changing situation. Consequently, while defending the agency against deviance and heresy, the supervisor has to be open to suggestions for useful innovation. As Reich (1970) says, agency administration "is always neutral in favor of the Establishment" (p. 100). The bias needs to be explicitly recognized, but lightly held.

The supervisor can be an active participant in the formulation, or reformulation, of agency policy. Having learned from the direct-service workers about client and community needs, having learned about the deficiencies and shortcomings of agency policy when workers have attempted to implement it, the supervisor should do more than act as an inert channel for upward communication of such information. The supervisor has the responsibility of using her knowledge of the situation to formulate suggested changes in agency policy and procedure. The supervisor is in a strategic position to act as agency change agent. Standing between administration and the workers, she can actively influence administration to make changes and influence workers to accept them.

Supervisors may, however, hesitate to advocate change because of apathy, lack of conviction in the change being requested, competing pressures from routine work which demands all of their time and energy, or an unwillingness to take the risk of punitive reprisals if they challenge administration. In general, the administrator prefers a passive conforming supervisor; the supervisees want an aggressive advocacy-oriented supervisor.

In the service of agency preservation supervisors have to be sensitive and receptive to pressures from direct service workers for changes in policies and procedures which they perceive as archaic, unworkable, ineffective, unproductive, inequitable, or oppressive.

If the supervisor sees a need for changes, then she should actually encourage and collaborate with supervisees in seeking those changes, rather than being a mere mediator. She must collect and organize supporting information, help staff clearly identify what it is they want changed, and help staff articulate as clearly and as honestly as possible why they want change. Unless the desired change can benefit the agency and client group, and will receive the support of the staff, the chance for change is diminished. The supervisor has to mobilize allies in the agency that would support the change, maximize receptivity to the message, and minimize opposition and defensiveness on the part of the administration.

If unconvinced about the necessity for change the supervisor may act as a mediator between direct service staff and administration around changes that supervisees see as necessary. The supervisor may arrange to have the administrator meet with the supervisee group to explain and, if necessary, defend policy in response to staff challenges.

The responsibility of the supervisor in mediating between the agency administrator(s) and the staff "is to open up areas of difference so that both parties in the conflict can deal with them honestly—to search out and implement the common ground . . . by challenging obstacles that make it difficult for both staff and administration to see their mutual interests . . . by acting as a third force in relations between the staff group and the administration" (Shulman 1982, pp. 264–66).

It is at this juncture that conflict between the worker and the organization often become most clearly manifest. The whole philosophical debate regarding the obligation of civil disobedience to unjust laws is applicable to the problem faced by social workers in meeting agency requirements for conformity to policies and procedures which they are convinced are oppressive. Workers are encouraged to seek redress and change within the agency. There is a rich literature available on tactics that workers can employ in attempting to effect changes in agency policies and procedures in the face of resistant or inaccessible administrators (Weissman 1973; Resnick and Patti 1980). Going outside the agency, outside of channels which include the supervisor as the first point of contact, is enjoined—although there are more frequent examples of such "whistle blowing" recently (Peters and Branch 1972; Nader, Petkas, and Blackwell 1974).

While the problem which generates the most indignation is agency temporization, or outright rejection, of workers' suggestions for changes, there is often a problem in the other direction. Progressive, innovative administrators often have difficulty getting supervisees to accept changes in policies and procedures (Preger and Specht 1968). A whole host of factors understandably stand in the way of acceptance of change. Additional energy needs to be expended in overcoming habitual patterns of dealing with work problems, in unlearning old ways and in learning new ways of working; there is anxiety about whether one can adequately meet the demands of new programs and new procedures; there is reluctance to accept an increased measure of dependency while learning new patterns; there is a struggle involved in developing a conviction in the value of the change; there is anxiety about rearranged interpersonal connections in the agency as work procedures change.

Change is best accomplished if supervisees participate from the start in planning the change, if they are informed early of the nature of the planned change, if the change is introduced slowly, preferably with some initial trial effort, if expectations are made clear and understandable, if the change is in line with perceived agency norms and objectives, if there is some assurance that the change will have the effect predicted, if the administration, including supervisors, communicate strong belief in the desirability of the change, if there is some appreciation of, and empathy with, the difficulties that change generates for the staff, and if provision is made to reduce the costs of change to the staff. Putting herself in the supervisees' place, the supervisor has to make an effort to understand the possible costs and benefits the change implies for them.

Not only is the supervisor responsible for changes within the organization, but she must be sensitive to needs for changes in the network of agencies whose operations affect the work of her supervisees. In reviewing, coordinating, and planning work supervisors may become aware of a lack in the community social service system of some needed service. The supervisor contributes to facilitating the increased effectiveness of the work of her supervisees by advocating in the community for support of the needed service. By doing so the supervisor enriches the resource network for both clients and supervisees.

Summary

The following principal administrative functions of supervision were identified and discussed: (1) staff recruitment and selection; (2) inducting and placing the worker; (3) unit work planning; (4) work assignment; (5) work delegating; (6) monitoring, reviewing, and evaluating work; (7) coordinating work; (8) acting as a channel of communication; (9) administrative buffering; (10) acting as a change agent and community liaison.

In implementing her administrative responsibilities and functions, the supervisor organizes the work place, agency facilities, and human resources to achieve agency administration objectives in a way which, quantitatively and qualitatively, is in accordance with agency policies and procedures.

CHAPTER THREE
Administrative Supervision— Problems in Implementation

HAVING OUTLINED the functions, tasks, and responsibilities of administrative supervision in the preceding chapter, we are concerned in this chapter with some of the principal problems encountered by social work supervisors in implementing administrative supervision.

The Problem of Vicarious Liability

It was noted in the preceding chapter that the supervisor is ultimately responsible for the work that is assigned and delegated. Malpractice complaints and legal decisions have clearly confirmed the principle of the supervisor's responsibility for decisions and actions of supervisees. This is supported by doctrines variously termed "vicarious liability," "imputed negligence," and "respondeat superiore." The doctrine states that the "superior" is responsible for the acts of his agents within the scope of their employment. The supervisee is legally regarded as an "extension" of the supervisor, and the two are considered a "single persona."

When action is taken, the supervisor is perceived to have reviewed and sanctioned it. If the acion was performed incompetently, the supervisor is responsible for having entrusted the implementation of the decision to a worker who she should have known was not competent to perform it. "It is assumed that the supervisor . . . knows or should know what is going on and that the supervisor has an impact on the quality of work done" (Slovenko 1980, p. 60).

A worker's incompetence is an indictment of the supervisor. In a malpractice suit against the worker, the supervisor can be implicated as an accessory. This is in response to the legal principle of *respondeat superiore*—"let the master answer."

The *N.A.S.W. News* (June 1982) reported that "employees of the El Paso, Texas, Department of Human Resources, including the Director of the Child Welfare Division . . . were indicted by a county grand jury for criminal negligence in a child abuse case in which a 14-month-old girl under child welfare supervision died. . . . The *supervisor* of the social worker handling the case was also indicted" (p. 10).

Following the death of an abused 5-year-old boy under guardianship of the Illinois Department of Children and Family Services, a state legislator "demanded that the family services division caseworker and *supervisor* be suspended without pay pending an investigation" (*Capital Times*, Madison, January 14, 1981).

In another case a child who had been returned home by the agency after a short stay in foster care was fatally abused by the biological parents.

> An investigation by top state child welfare administrators into the events surrounding the decision to return the child to her home led to the highly publicized and controversial dismissal by DPW officials of social workers and two *supervisors* for professional negligence in the case . . . the *supervisors* and administrators were found to be negligent because they failed adequately to review the clinical judgments of the workers under their supervision. (Aber 1982, p. 217)

Slovenko (1980) reports the case of a client referred by the court to a mental health clinic for evaluation. "A social worker did the interviewing, found that he was without mental disorder, and the supervising psychiatrist signed the report without interviewing him. A few days later [the client] killed his wife and children. The *supervisor* was sued in a malpractice action" (p. 469).

"The State of California, acting through its placement office in the Youth Authority, placed a sixteen-year-old child in the home of foster parents. . . . Subsequently the foster mother was physically beaten by the foster child" (Cohen 1979, p. 124). The foster mother sued the agency for damages on the basis of the fact that they failed to warn the foster parents of the possibility of violent behavior on the part of the foster child. The child had a background of violent behavior about which the agency had a record.

A probation officer made a discretionary decision, in violation of department rules, not to take a probationer into custody upon complaint by the probationer's girlfriend that he had physically and sexually assaulted her. Six weeks later the probationer sexually assaulted and killed a 10-year-old child. The probation officer "was suspended for three days without pay and his *supervisor* was suspended for five days without pay (*Capital Times*, May 11, 1982).

A psychotherapy clinic supervisor assigned a client to a counselor who, allegedly, engaged in sexual intercourse with the client. Under the doctrine of vicarious liability, the client initiated a lawsuit against the *supervisor*, who was named as the defendant rather than the counselor (Cohen 1979).

The doctrine of vicarious liability places the supervisor in a very vulnerable position. Schutz (1982) advises that "basically, any major decision that the [supervisee] makes ought to have been reviewed—and modified if necessary—by the supervisor" (p. 49). The NASW Professional Liability Insurance Agency warns that as a social worker you are "Liable to be Liable." To reduce liability risk it suggests: "If you are responsible for the actions of other employees, be sure proper practices are fully understood and followed" (*NASW News*, February 1983, p. 14).

Discussing the concept of "respondeat superiore" and vicarious liability, Cormier and Bernard (1982) note that it has far-reaching implications for supervisors. "The supervisor needs to ensure that supervision does occur. . . . In order to prevent negligent supervision, the supervisor has to be familiar with each case of every supervisee" (p. 488). The supervisor has to be clear about the level of competence of each supervisee to be able to guarantee that a case assigned can be competently handled. Referrals and case terminations need to be made in a way that protects the supervisor from any charge of negligence.

> Given the fact that the worker is accountable through the supervisor to the agency administrator and through the agency administrator to the legislature and ultimately to the public means that the supervisor not only has the managerial right but also the managerial duty to direct, instruct, review, appraise, and if necessary, discipline the worker. The worker is subject to these normal management rights. (Rowbottom, Hay, and Billis 1976, p. 130)

The Problem of Authority and Power

Rationale for Authority and Power

If one agrees that the functions of administrative supervision reviewed in chapter 2 must be performed if the agency is to operate efficiently and effectively, if it is further agreed that the supervisor is ultimately responsible for seeing that these functions are efficiently and effectively implemented, it follows that the supervisor needs to be granted the authority and power which would enable her to satisfactorily enact these tasks. As Studt (1959) says, authority is delegated and sanctioned when "in order to get the job done properly a person in one position in an organization is authorized to direct the role activities of a person in another position" (p. 18). Assigning supervisors the responsibility for implementing the essential functions of administrative supervision without at the same time granting them the necessary authority is the organizational equivalent of asking them to make bricks without straw. The organizational axiom is that delegation of authority is a necessary concomitant of administrative responsibility.

The need for administrative authority in an agency derives from organizational complexity and task specialization. If groups of individuals are to work together to accomplish desired ends, their efforts must be integrated. Some administrative officer, in this case the supervisor, has to be given authority to direct and coordinate individual activities toward the achievement of a common purpose, to review and evaluate work, and to hold workers accountable. Formal channels of authority must be established since it must be clear who has the authority to assign, direct, and evaluate work and who is being directed and evaluated.

Since compliance with directives toward the achievement of joint efforts cannot be left to chance, individual desires, or whim, some kind of authority-control system is an organizational imperative. It is designed to "minimize discretion based on subjective considerations" (Stein 1961, p. 15). Vinter says, "All organizations create means for ensuring that cooperative action is oriented toward desired objectives. To avoid a state of anarchy among participating personnel, an explicit structure of authority and responsibility is defined in every social agency. . . . This structure seeks to ensure predictable behavior of workers in conformity to policy" (1959, pp. 199–200).

Tannenbaum (1968), in his study of organizational controls, notes that

> organization implies control. A social organization has an ordered arrangement of individual human interactions. Control processes help circumscribe idiosyncratic behaviors and keep them conformant with the rational plan of the organization. Organizations require a certain amount of conformity as well as the integration of diverse activities. It is the function of control to bring about conformance to organizational requirements and achievement of the ultimate purposes of the organization. The coordination and order created out of the diverse interests and potentially diffuse behaviors of members is largely a function of control. (p. 3)

In a study of the social work profession Toren (1972) states: "Supervision is the institutionalized built-in mechanism through which the attitudes and performance of social workers are controlled" (p. 65). The rationale for any supervisory control review system is to assure that the workers will act in ways that will lead to the achievement of organizational objectives.

The danger of indifference to procedures for controlling and/or influencing the behavior of workers is the possibility that the workers will make decisions and act in ways that reflect their own desires and preferences, whether or not they are congruent with organizational objectives. Furthermore, unless there is some predictability in the decisions and behavior of one worker, a predictability that reflects adherence to agency objectives and procedures, it is difficult to coordinate and integrate that worker's performance with that of other workers.

The authority delegated to the supervisor ultimately derives from the community. In public agencies the collective intent is embodied in the statutes that established the agency and in accordance with which the agency operates. In private agencies, the collective intent is manifested in the support the agency obtains for its existence and continuation through voluntary Community Chest contributions. Agency objectives reflect what the community wants done, and use of supervisory authority to ensure achievement of these objectives can be seen as an act in furtherance of the collective will.

Legal authority derives its legitimacy from the fact that it, supposedly, represents the common good. The objectives of the agency similarly are supposed to represent the common good. Authority employed to achieve the common good is regarded as legitimate authority.

The legitimacy of this ultimate authority may be questioned by workers, who thereby also question the legitimacy of the supervisor's authority. They may feel that neither the statutes which establish the public agency nor the community welfare council which sponsors the voluntary agency do, in fact, represent the will of the community.

The agency depends on the supervisee's acceptance of the legitimacy of organizational authority to achieve agency goals. When the agency and the supervisees are committed to the same objectives, the supervisee will more freely grant the right to be controlled if this contributes to the achievement of the accepted task. The common goal becomes the common good which justifies acceptance of authority.

Supervisory Authority and Sources of Power

Authority needs to be distinguished from power. Authority is a right which legitimizes the use of power; it is the sanctioned use of power, the accepted and validated possession of power. Authority is the right to issue directives, exercise control, require compliance. It is the right to determine the behavior of others, to make decisions which guide the action of others. In the most uncompromising sense, "authority is the right to demand obedience; those subject to authority have the duty to obey."

This right of authority is distributed to the supervisor through the agency administrative structure. The supervisory relationship is established through authority delegated the supervisor by the agency and through the supervisee's reciprocal acceptance of the supervisor's legtimate entitlement to authority.

Power is the ability to implement the rights of authortiy. The word "power" derives frm the Latin *potere*, "to be able." If authority is the *right* to direct, command, and punish, then power is the *ability* to do so. The distinction is clearly seen in situations in which a person may have authority but no power to act, and vice versa. Extreme examples are the hijacker of a plane, who has power but no authority, and the prison warden held hostage by prisoners, who has authority but no power.

The distinction between authority and power is aptly illustrated by this discussion between a judge and a priest: the priest claimed that his position was the more important one because he could condemn sinners to hell; the judge countered by saying that his position was more important because when he condemned people to be hung, they actually were hung. The priest had the authority to condemn people to hell, but there was considerable question about his power to enforce the verdict. The same distinction is illustrated in Canute's Law—"Even a king cannot control the tides." Authority is the right to supervise; power is the ability to effectively exercise that right.

The source of the supervisor's authority is the agency administration, which in turn represents communiy will. What are the sources of power which energize authority and make possible the implementation of the right to command? Recognizing the legitimacy of the authority invested in the supervisor, what prompts the supervisee to actually comply with the supervisor's directives?

There are a variety of descriptive systems that categorize sources of power (Etzioni 1961; Presthus 1962; Weber 1946). Among the most frequently used is the classification developed by French and Raven (1960), who have identified five distinctive bases of social power: reward power, coercive power, positional power, referent power, and expert power. We will attempt to apply these categories to the social work supervisory situation.

REWARD POWER

The supervisor has the ability to control tangible rewards for the supervisees, such as promotions, raises, more desirable work assignments, extra secretarial help, a better office, recommendations for training stipends, agency-supported attendance at conferences and workshops, a good reference on leaving the agency. Rewards can be psychic as well—approval, commendations, supervisory expressions of appreciation.

Rewards such as pay increases and promotions are zero-sum. There is just so much to go around and distributing these goodies to some means denying them to others. But there are many unlimited non-zero-sum rewards. Praise, recognition of achievement, providing a feeling of satisfaction in work done, can be freely given to one without denying them to others.

If reward power is to be effective, it needs to be individualized and clearly related to differentials in performance. If rewards become routinized, as in the case of across-the-board raises, they lose their power to stimulate improvements in worker performance. The supervisor therefore has to be knowledgeable about the quality of the performance of different workers if he is to make a fair determination of allocation of rewards. Furthermore, the supervisee needs some confidence that the supervisor does, in fact, control access to rewards, that administration has granted him the authority to make crucial decisions relating to dispensation of available rewards.

As contrasted with certain other employers, social agencies have limited reward power because they control only a limited range and variety of rewards. Production incentives, stock options, and so on are not available as possible rewards. Uniform pay scales dictated by civil service and/or union regulations make it difficult to reward meritorious performance. Similar constraints make it difficult to fire a worker, or take any disciplinary action.

COERCIVE POWER

The supervisor has the ability to control punishments for supervisees. These include demotion, dismissal, a poor "efficiency rating," a less satisfying work assignment, a negative reference on leaving the agency. There are psychic punishments as well—expressions of disapproval and criticism, snubs, and avoidance. Reward power and coercive power are overlapping, since the withholding of rewards is in effect a punishment.

Whereas in the case of reward power the supervisees are induced to comply with supervisory directives in order to achieve a reward, here compliance results from the effort to avoid punishment. The strength of coercive power depends on the extent of belief in the likelihood of disciplinary action. If the supervisees have reason to believe that little serious effort will be made to apply punishments, this is not an effective source of supervisory power. However, "while most competent supervisors are reluctant to exercise coercive power, except in extremely serious conditions, the important point is that most subordinates behave in accordance with the belief that such power could be exerted at any time" (Austin 1981, p. 21).

LEGITIMATE OR POSITIONAL POWER

By virtue of being invested with the title, the supervisor can claim the authority that goes with the position. We accept the authority of the office and in doing so accept as legitimate the authority of the person occupying it. The supervisee in taking a job with the agency has implicitly contracted to accept direction from those invested with agency authority. There is a sense of moral obligation and social duty related to the acceptance of positional authority. Consequently the supervisee feels that the supervisor has a legitimate right, considering her position, to expect that her suggestions and directions will be followed.

Positional power derives its force not only from prior reinforcing experiences in which obedience to those in positions of authority was rewarded by acceptance and approval, but also from its effect in making one's job easier. Barnard (1938) notes that the initial presumption of the acceptability of organizational authority enables workers to avoid making issues of supervisory directives without incurring a sense of personal subserviency or a loss of status with their peers.

REFERENT POWER

The supervisor has power which derives from the supervisees' identification with her, a desire to be liked by the supervisor and to be like the supervisor. Referent power has its source in the positive relationship between supervisor and supervisee, in the attraction the supervisee feels toward the supervisor. It is relationship power. In effect, the supervisee says, "I want to be like the supervisor and be liked by her. Consequently, I want to believe and behave as she does" or "I am like the supervisor, so I will behave and believe like her." The supervisor is perceived as a model of the kind of social worker the supervisee would like to be.

The relationship, once established, provides the supervisor with a power base for influence. The stronger the relationship, the stronger is the power of the supervisor to influence the behavior and attitudes of the supervisee. As a consequence of the relationship, the supervisee is strongly motivated to seek the approval of the supervisor. The supervisor becomes a person of meaning and significance whom the supervisee would like to please and to whom she feels a sense of personal loyalty.

As a consequence of a strong interpersonal relationship, the supervisee is receptive to influence efforts on the part of the supervisor. As a result of identification, the supervisor's expectations become internalized. Supervisees then act as their own "supervisor," behaving as they expect the supervisor would want them to.

Reward power reinforces referent power because the dispenser of rewards becomes a more attractive and liked figure as a consequence of this. Studies of modeling behavior indicate that the more power and authority the model has over the recipient of modeling efforts, the more likely it is that behavior of the model will be imitated.

EXPERT POWER

Expert power derives from the special knowledge and skills which the supervisor has available and the supervisees need. This is the power of professional competence. The supervisee who attributes expertise to the supervisor must have trust in her decisions and judgments. The supervisor who has an MSW, who has passed the Academy of Certified Social Workers' written examination, is initially perceived as having more expertise than a supervisor who does not possess such credentials. But ultimately the supervisor has to prove in practice that she can live up to the promise of her credentials.

The supervisor is able to influence the kinds of behavior that supervisees will manifest because she has the knowledge which indicates the way in which it is desirable or necessary for them to behave if they are to deal satisfactorily with work problems.

Referent power has a potentially broader influence than expert power. The influence of expert power is confined to the content areas defined by the expertise. Expert power is difficult to achieve since the evidence of expertise needs to be validated continually. It can dissolve as the supervisee comes progressively closer to the supervisor in level of expertise. A supervisor's continued absence of contact with direct services can result in technical obsolescence and a consequent reduction in expert power.

Interrelationships Between Types of Supervisory Power

The five sources of power have frequently been subdivided into two groups, functional and formal power. Functional power, which includes expertise and referent power, depends on what the supervisor knows, is, and can do. Functional power resides in the person of the supervisor. Formal power is related more directly to the title the supervisor holds and the authority with which the title is invested. Formal power includes positional power and the power of rewards and punishments. The two groups of powers are complementary and support each other. The most desirable situation for effective exercise of power is one where the formal power and functional power are congruent. This is the situation when the person accorded positional authority and the power of the office to reward and punish is, by virtue of his human-relations skill and knowledge of the job, also capable of demonstrating the power of expertise and of developing referent power. Functional authority tends to legitimize and make acceptable formal authority. Difficulty arises when the person with formal authority knows less or has less work experience than the supervisee or does not gain the respect of the supervisee. The supervisee is therefore less willing to grant the person's entitlement to the power of his position and this tends to attenuate and undermine his formal authority.

Since formal power is related to the office of the supervisor and functional power is related to the person of the supervisor, the latter is apt to be more variable. There is little difference between one supervisor and another in the same agency in their positional, reward, and punishment power. There may be considerable difference, however, in their total ability to implement their authority because of differences in their expertise and relationship skills.

The supervisees' readiness to accept the supervisor as an expert and as an object of identification and emulation is subject to change. If they find, as they grow in knowledge and experience, that they are less dependent on the supervisor for help in solving their work problems, if in testing the supervisor's advice and suggestions in practice they conclude that she is not the expert she claims to be, or the expert they previously perceived her to be, expert power tends to be eroded.

Formal authority is received automatically by ascription when a person is assigned to the position of supervisor. Functional authority has to be achieved by the supervisor and continuously validated. If the supervisees do not perceive the supervisor as an expert, the supervisor has no expert power; if supervisees feel no attraction to the supervisor and do not care whether or not the supervisor likes them, the supervisor has no referent power.

The different sources of power available to the supervisor to induce behavioral change in supervisees, and to control their actions, have different kinds of applicability and costs associated with their use. Both reward power and coercive power relate to specific kinds of supervisee behavior that are either encouraged or discouraged. The effect of using such power is apt to be rather limited in scope. Both require the opportunity and constancy of surveillance. Only if the supervisor knows what the supervisee is doing or not doing can these sources of power be applied. Supervisees feel a pressure to engage in the required behavior only if there is some chance that the supervisor will know about it. The use of reward and coercion as sources of power only achieves compliance.

Expert power and referent power, by contrast, are more diffuse in their effects. Once these sources of power have been established, then whatever the supervisor says, whatever the supervisor requests, is likely to be considered seriously by supervisees. The effect of such power is internalization of the supervisor's authority, which then exerts pressure toward conformity whether or not the supervisor can witness the behavior. While reward and punishment power can achieve compliance and a change in behavior, the exertion of expert and referent power in achieving internalization of influence can achieve changes in feelings and attitudes as well.

Referent and expert power give the supervisory relationship a leadership orientation. As a consequence of the supervisee's liking the supervisor and admiring and respecting her expertise the authority of the supervisor is freely accepted rather than felt to be imposed. The supervisee is voluntarily motivated to conform to the requests, suggestions, and tasks assigned by the supervisor. The supervisor obtains supervisee compliance with a minimum of resistance. The supervisee is open to and accepting of the efforts of the supervisor to guide and influence and the supervisee feels led rather than bossed.

Warren (1968) has analyzed the various sources of power as related to conformity to agency norms under conditions of the low-visibility performance characteristic of social work. Under these conditions, expert power and referent power are most effective in ensuring both attitudinal conformity (implying internalization of norms) and overt behavioral conformity.

Because the force of positional power as felt by supervisees is the result of earlier socialization, this source of power is vulnerable to problems concerning a supervisee's relationship to authority figures. The supervisee who has had developmental experiences which result in opposition to, and hostility toward, parents and parent surrogates is more likely to resist the power of position.

Studies of worker satisfaction in a variety of contexts as related to supervisory sources of power show expert power and referent power to be positively related to supervisee satisfaction, coercive power least frequently related to satisfaction (Burke and Wilcox 1971).

Studying the relationship between supervisees' satisfaction with supervision and the perceived source of the supervisor's authority, Munson (1983) found that satisfaction with supervision was clearly related to competence and experience as the source of power. By contrast supervisors whose power was perceived as deriving from hierarchical sanction of their position were seen as less friendly, less open, less understanding.

Coercive power frequently leads to a downward cycle—punishment resulting in resentment which incites behavior which elicits punishment. If performance is not visible, coercive power can encourage deception, false reporting, and cover-ups to avoid punishment.

Coercive and positional power may be sufficient to induce supervisees to work at a level which meets the minimal requirements of the job. This is what they have technically contracted for in accepting the job. Referent and expert power, however, can induce supervisees to exert themselves beyond this level. They want to do better to please the supervisor, whose referent power makes him a person of significance for the supervisee. They get satisfaction doing a better job as they are helped to solve job problems through the supervisor's use of expert power. Reward power can also have this effect if the range of rewards available is sufficiently attractive to the supervisees and if they feel assurance that better work will, in fact, be rewarded.

The various sources of power are interrelated. Reward power increases the likelihood of developing a positive relationship. A positive relationship, once established, increases the potency of psychic rewards (praise, approval) offered by the supervisor. The use of coercive power tends to increase the difficulties of establishing a positive relationship and hence impedes development of referent power as a possible source of influence.

The exercise of power, when accepted by the supervisee, results in some change in her behavior. She acts, and refrains from acting, so that her behavior conforms to the needs of the organization in achieving its objectives. Power is used to attain some deliberate, intended effects. Where power is successfully applied, we can talk of control.

What sources of supervisory power are perceived by social workers as influencing their behavior? In a study of non-MSW supervisees supervised by non-MSW supervisors in a public welfare agency, positional power was most frequently mentioned, followed by expert power (Peabody 1964). Referent power was seen as a less significant source of influence. In a second study involving MSW supervisors and supervisees, both groups saw expert power, professional competence, as the main source of the supervisor's influence (Kadushin 1974). The supervisors saw this as almost the exclusive source of their power. A sizable percentage of supervisees, however, saw positional power as a significant source of supervisory influence. Apparently supervisees were readier to grant supervisors the power of their position in the administrative hierarchy than supervisors were ready to accept this as a source of power. It is interesting that in neither study was referent power, relationship power, seen as a significant source of supervisory influence. As was expected, neither reward power nor coercive power was seen as a preferred source of power.

A study of some 1,600 employees in 31 social welfare and rehabilitation agencies shows the same relative ranking of the sources of supervisory power. "Expert power" was listed as the principal reason which induced supervisees to "do things my immediate supervisor suggests or wants me to do," followed by positional power as the second source of supervisory influence. Referent power was given middle-range ranking. Reward power and coercive power were perceived as the least potent sources of influence (Olmstead and Christensen 1973).

Although it is clear that expert power is the kind of power most readily acknowledged and most comfortably employed between social work supervisor and supervisee, the question might be raised whether this is a viable and potent power base for the social work supervisor.

The base of reward, coercive, and positional power is the community through the agency. The base of referent power is the person of the supervisor. The base of expert power, however, is the profession. The profession provides the knowledge which makes the supervisor an expert. Consequently the potency of expert power depends on the "state of the art" of the profession. If a profession has well-developed, highly sophisticated techniques and the supervisor is well educated in what the profession has available, the gap in expertise between the supervisor and the supervisee recruit is very wide. If, however, there is little specialized knowledge available, if the techniques which the supervisor possesses are limited, the gap is narrow and can be eliminated within a short period.

There is a question as to the real extent of this gap between supervisors and supervisees in social agencies. The limited empirical material available does not substantiate a gap. Supervisors' scores on the Academy of Certified Social Workers' qualifying examinations were not generally higher than those of supervisees. Research projects that required both supervisors and supervisees to perform a practice task did not demonstrate higher skill on the part of the supervisory group (Brieland 1959; Brown 1970). Rapid changes in the field with reference to what is accepted theory, techniques, and interventions tend to erode the supervisor's authority of expertise. Socialized in terms of an earlier view of social work, skilled in approaches generally used in the immediate past but somewhat outmoded in the present, the supervisor may know less than the supervisee about what is *au courant*.

Difficult as it is for the supervisor to maintain authority on the basis of expert power when there is, objectively, little real expertise, the task becomes even more difficult in an ideological climate in which possible differences in expertise are explicitly rejected. Where the ideological emphasis is toward a declaration of equality between client and worker, teacher and student, supervisor and supervisee, where differences in roles are denied and all become peers and colleagues, authority based on expert power is further eroded.

It must be noted, however, that the preceding paragraphs refer to the extent of the gap in expertise relating to general professional knowledge and skills. Expert power may be validated on the basis of other kinds of information. If the supervisor has more experience in the agency than the supervisee, as is usually the case, her greater expertise may relate to her knowledge of agency policy, procedures, and operations. The supervisor, in this instance, has the knowledge and skill which enable her to help the supervisee "work" the agency system, find her way in the agency system so as to get the work done. She is party to much-needed organizational intelligence.

This base of expert power is supplemented by the supervisor's strategic position in the agency communications network. Not only does she know more about agency operations because she has had more intra- and inter-agency experience, but she also possesses much-needed knowledge about agency policies and procedures because she has initial access to such information from administration.

Legitimation of Authority

Supervisory authority, once accepted, is reinforced for the individual supervisee by the pressure of the peer group of co-workers.

Authority requires legitimation. And while authority can be exercised in pair relations, it can originate only in a group because only a group can provide legitimation of the control exercised. What social process legitimates the control exercised by a supervisor? The supervisor's ability to help subordinates solve complex problems commands their respect, and his willingness to furnish help and do favors for them commands their allegiance. As the members of the work group share their respect for and loyalty to the supervisor, there develops a consensus among them that they should comply with his wishes and suggestions. Once established, these norms of allegiance and respect are enforced by the group because all might suffer if some members failed to repay their obligations to the supervisor. In this fashion, compliance within certain bounds becomes a group norm . . . internalized by group members and enforced by group sanctions. These values legitimate the extension of the supervisor's authority beyond the legally prescribed limits. (Blau and Scott 1962, p. 143)

Despite our distaste for the words and our resistance to the activities implied, authority and power are built into the supervisory relationship. Miller (1960) suggests that "it would help a great deal to give up the sentimental sham that the worker-supervisor relationship exists between equals or between professional colleagues who happen to have different functions and responsibilities. This kind of well-meaning distortion obscures the power and authority inherent in the supervisory function" (p. 76).

In an analysis of social welfare administration Patti (1983) says "We acknowledge that authority is inherent to the administrative and management process. The manager does indeed direct and control and there is nothing to be gained by clouding the reality" (p. 26).

> Authority is intrinsic to the [supervisor's] role. Its constructive use is indispensible to the manager's performance and that of the organizational unit for which he or she is responsible. (Patti 1983, p. 218)

> The manager who consistently shrinks from using the authority of the office when there is disagreement with subordinates ultimately loses the ability to coordinate activities toward the achievement of organizational objectives. (p. 217)

The supervisor must accept, without defensiveness or apology, the authority and related power inherent in his position. Use of authority may sometimes be unavoidable. The supervisor can increase its effectiveness if he feels, and can communicate, a conviction in his behavior. If he acts with confidence and with an expectation that his authority will be respected, his directives are more likely to be accepted.

Nonauthoritarian Authority

If, in order to perform functions that are necessary for achievement of organizational objectives, the supervisor must be granted, and must exercise, some measure of authority, how can this authority be most effectively manifested? The likelihood of the supervisees' accepting the supervisor's authority is increased if certain caveats are observed. They are designed to help the supervisor exercise authority without being officious or authoritarian.

In general, the most desirable use of supervisory authority is "exerting power with minimal side effects and conflicts," and seeking approaches "for the limiting of the exercise of power to the least amount which will satisfy the functional requirements of the organization and for maximizing role performance without the exercise of power" (Kahn 1964, p. 7).

There is apt to be greater voluntary compliance with supervisory authority if its sources are perceived as legitimate, the methods employed in its exercise are acceptable, the objectives of its use are understandable and approved, and it is exercised within the limits of legitimate jurisdiction.

The attitude, the spirit with which authority is employed, is significant. If it is used only when the situation demands it, when it is required to achieve objectives to which both supervisor and supervisee are jointly committed, it is more likely to be accepted. If it is exercised in a spirit of vindictiveness, in response to a desire for self-aggrandizement, a pleasure in dominance, a delight in self-gratification, it is less likely to be accepted. The best use of authority comes out of an expression of care and concern for the worker.

Supervisees can more easily understand and accept the exercise of authority if it is clear that authority is being used for the achievement of organizational goals rather than because its use is intrinsically pleasurable to the supervisor. If supervisees are committed to the achievement of the organizational goal, acceptance of authority is then congruent with their own needs and wishes.

If authority is employed in a manner which indicates that the supervisor is flexible and open to suggestions for changes in "commands" on the basis of relevant feedback from supervisees, it is less likely to be viewed as capricious and arbitrary. If, in exercising authority, the supervisor shares with his supervisees the reasons which prompt the directive, if he gives an opportunity for questions and discussion of the directive, the supervisees' feeling that this is a rational procedure over which they have some control is further enhanced. Through such participation the supervisees share control.

If authority is exercised in a predictable manner, the supervisees again feel they have some control over the situation. They can clearly foresee the consequences of certain actions on their part. Arbitrary exercise of authority is unpredictable and inexplicable.

Authority needs to be used with a recognition that supervisees, as adults, tend to resent the dependence, submissiveness, and contravention of individual autonomy implied in accepting authority. And authority is best exercised if it is depersonalized. Even in the best of circumstances, we are predisposed to resent and resist authority. It is, in its essence, antiegalitarian. It suggests that one person is better than another. Depersonalizing the use of authority is designed to mitigate such feeling. The attitude suggests that the supervisor is acting as an agent of the organization rather than out of any sense of personal superiority. The supervisee is not asked to acknowledge the superiority of the supervisor as a person but merely her assignment to a particular function in the agency hierarchy.

If it is not to be resented, authority has to be impartially exercised. Impartial does not necessarily mean equal. It means that in similar situations people are treated similarly. If there is an acceptable reason for unequal, preferential treatment, this is not resented. One worker can be assigned a much smaller caseload than another. If, however, the smaller caseload includes difficult, complex cases, the assignment will not be regarded as an unfair exercise of supervisory authority.

The supervisor needs a sensitive awareness that her authority is limited and job-related. The administrative grant of authority relates to a specific set of duties and tasks. The legitimacy of the supervisor's authority is open to question if she seeks to extend it beyond recognized boundaries. For example, attempting to prescribe a dress code for supervisees or to prescribe off-the-job behavior causes difficulty because the supervisor is exceeding the limits of her legitimate authority.

The supervisor has to be careful to refrain from using authority unless some essential conditions can be met. Barnard (1938) points out that supervisory directives will tend to be resisted unless the supervisee can and does understand what needs to be done; believes that the directive is consistent with his perception of the purpose of the organization; believes it is compatible with his personal interests and beliefs; and is able to comply with it. Similarly, Kaufman (1973) notes that supervisee noncompliance results from the fact that the supervisee does not know clearly what needs to be done, cannot do it, or does not want to do it (p. 2).

The most effective use of authority is minimal use. Persistent use of authority increases the social distance between participants in supervisory relationships and results in a greater formality in such relationships. It intensifies a sense of status difference between supervisor and supervisee and tends to inhibit free communication. The supervisor therefore should make authority explicit as infrequently as possible and only when necessary.

Using other means of influence, as alternatives to the use of power, is desirable. The desirable procedure is for the supervisor to use the least amount of authority and power to achieve the aims of supervision. If one can, by providing certain information, or by modeling, or by expressions of empathic understanding and acceptance, induce the supervisee to behave in the desirable manner, this should be the most preferred intervention. As Sennett (1981) notes, "Naked power draws attention to itself. Influence does not." The "veiling of power" (p. 174) humanizes it.

Supervisory authority can be more effectively implemented if agency administration observes some essential considerations. Most basically, only those who are qualified as supervisors should be appointed to the office, and appointment should be a result of fair and acceptable procedures. Only then will supervisees be likely to grant the supervisor's legitimate right to the title and to the authority associated with it.

Administration needs to delegate enough authority to enable the supervisor to perform the functions required of him, and to delegate it in a way that conforms to the principle of unity of command. This principle suggests that a supervisee be supervised by, and answerable to, one supervisor. The exercise of authority is difficult if more than one administrative person directs the supervisee with regard to the same set of activities. There is difficulty, too, if no one has responsibility for some significant set of duties that the supervisee has to perform. Both gaps and overlaps in administrative responsibility create problems.

When agency administration, as the immediate source of the supervisor's authority, consistently supports the authority of the supervisor, this tends to stabilize his power. And, of course, inconsistent, unpredictable support from the administration of a supervisor's authority tends to erode his power.

The administration needs to make clear to both supervisors and supervisees the nature of the authority delegated to the supervisors, the limits of that authority, and the conditions under which the authority can be legitimately exercised. A supervisee writes:

> A reporter of a local paper asked the supervisor for permission to attend a group session of AFDC mothers who had been meeting with me for some time. The supervisor referred the question to me. I indicated that I would like a chance to discuss it with the group. However, when the supervisor pressed for an immediate answer since a decision needed to be made without delay I said no, I didn't think the reporter should attend the meeting. The next day the supervisor decided that agency policy dictated that the reporter should be permitted to attend because of the public relations opportunity for the agency. If I [the supervisee] had no real authority to make the final decision, the supervisor should not have asked me. It should have been clear in the beginning who had the right and responsibility for a decision of this kind.

Problems in the Implementation of Supervisory Authority

While theoretically social work supervisors have an impressive array of potential sources of authority and power, the available descriptive and empirical data tends to indicate that (1) social work supervisors are reluctant to use the authority and power they have available; (2) they are particularly reluctant to use their power and authority toward implementing the administrative-instrumental productivity objectives of supervision (i.e., "getting the work out"); and (3) even if social work supervisors were more motivated to use their authority and power toward the administrative objectives of supervision, the likelihood of their success in achieving this objective can often be effectively blunted by the countervailing power possessed by supervisees.

Avoidance and Abrogation of Authority and Power by Supervisors

Administrative exercise of authority and power is perceived as being ideologically antithetical to some of the fundamental values of social work—values which emphasize egalitarian, democratic, non-coercive, nonhierarchical relationships. These practice precepts reinforce supervisors' ideological uneasiness about the exercise of administrative authority and power.

Vinter (1959), speaking to this problem, says that a "strain . . . arises from juxtaposition of the nonauthoritarian ideology of social work and the exercise of authority and control within the administrative context. Valuation of autonomy and self-determination for the client has pervaded the administrative structure of social welfare" (pp. 262–63). Indeed, as Levinson and Klerman (1972) say, "The predominant view of power . . . in mental health professions is much like the Victorian view of sex. It is seen as vulgar, as a sign of character defect, as something an upstanding professional would not be interested in, stoop to engage in" (p. 66).

Unfortunately, but inevitably, it is difficult to respond to authority, power, and control in functional terms alone. While authority, power, and control are functionally necessary for achieving organizational objectives, they get all mixed up with feelings of prestige, self-esteem, superiority and inferiority, dominance, and submission. It may be significant to note that the words "power" and "potent" derive from the same roots. Strong currents of feeling are evoked by power relationships in any context because they reactivate memories of our first encounter with authority and control in the parent-child relationship.

Organizational studies of social agencies show that very few human service organizations have "management control systems that are in any way comparable in quality to those in the private sector" (Herzlinger 1981, p. 207). Complex measures of quality control and recipient satisfaction are hardly ever found (p. 208). "Even if such data were present it is unclear that they would be used for control" because they are managed by professionals "whose norms are antithetical to the hierarchical corporate version of the control process" (p. 209).

The question of power and authority in the supervisory relationship is just a special instance of the problem of authority in social work generally, a difficulty which has received special attention in the professional literature (Foren and Bailey 1968; Orchard 1965; Studt 1954, 1959; Yelaja 1971).

The reluctance of supervisors to express their authority is noted by Satyamurti (1981) in a participant-observation study of a British agency. In this excerpt supervisors are designated as "seniors."

> In terms of the formal hierarchy, seniors had a supervisory role which implied the exercise of authority. It was apparent that this was distasteful to many seniors, particularly those with a traditionally professional orientation. Their model of the relationship between them and their team was far more along the lines of consultant to co-professionals, despite their awareness of wide differences among fieldworkers in respect of experience and skills. Even the more managerially oriented seniors were reluctant to insist on a social worker accepting their judgment if they were unable to persuade them to do so voluntarily. Thus one said that if he disagreed with a social worker over a financial payment, and was unable to convince him/her that it should not be made, then he would allow the payment to go ahead, and provide the required signature. Seniors' reluctance to exercise authority, and to emphasize the difference in organizational status between them and fieldworkers, made them open to pressure. (p. 57)

In an interview study, over 300 British direct service social workers identified "checking on their work" as an appropriate purpose of supervision. On the other hand, supervisors were more reluctant to acknowledge the "checking process." They "seemed to fight shy of what they regarded as authoritarian aspects of their role and concentrated on the supportive rather than the controlling aspects of supervision" (Parsloe and Stevenson 1978, p. 202). Supervisors "were obviously skilled, some would suggest too skilled, at denying or disguising checking aspects of their role which fundamentally concern their use of authority" (p. 221).

Using standardized research instruments inventorying managerial styles and managerial philosophy, a number of different research reports concerning the approaches of social work supervisors lead to similar conclusions. At best they show social work supervisors having limited concern for monitoring task performance and worker productivity and greater concern for the human relations aspects of supervision. At worst they show social work supervisors demonstrating indifference to both task requirements and human relations aspects of supervision, connoting a general abrogation of supervisory responsibilities.

Using a standardized Leadership Opinion Questionnaire, Olyan (1972) obtained responses from 228 supervisors in three different settings. One scale included in the questionnaire concerns structure and is designed to reflect

> the extent to which an individual is likely to define and structure his own role and those of his subordinates toward goal attainment. A high score on this dimension characterizes individuals who play a very active role in directing group activities through planning, communicating information, scheduling, criticizing, trying out new ideas and so forth. A low score characterizes individuals who are likely to be relatively inactive in group direction in these ways. (p. 172)

Low scores on the structure scale suggest a reluctance to exercise control and authority.

A second scale included in the questionnaire is the consideration scale, designed to measure

> the extent to which an individual is likely to have job relationships with his subordinates characterized by mutual trust, respect for their ideas, consideration for their feelings, and a certain warmth between himself and them. A high score is indicative of a climate of good rapport and two-way communication. A low score indicates the individual is likely to be more impersonal in his relations with group members. (p. 172)

While the social work supervisors scored relatively high on the consideration scale as compared with 35 other occupational groups for which scores are available, they ranked lowest of all 36 occupations on the structural scale. Olyan concludes that the data "suggests that supervisors in this study group are not oriented toward goal attainment techniques such as planning, communicating information, scheduling, criticizing" (p. 178). These are the activities central to implementation of the responsibilities of administrative supervision and related to the exercise of authority.

According to the studies which have used the Leadership Opinion Questionnaires in management research, the most desirable combination is that of a supervisor who scores high both on consideration and structure. The pattern of the social work supervisors with high scores on consideration, very low scores on structure, suggests a situation in which supervisees would not take the supervisor seriously. This pattern is conducive to a relationship in which the supervisee finds it easy to ignore the supervisor. Proficiency and goal attainment, key objectives of administrative supervision, are likely to suffer as a result.

Granvold (1978) found along with Olyan (1972) that the 108 social work supervisors he tested using the Leadership Opinion Questionnaire were high on consideration but low on the structure dimension which was "considered" to measure the supervisor attitudes that reflect a commitment to satisfying organizational objectives. Results indicated that "the study group ranked rather high on the consideration subscale and extremely low on the structure subscale" (p. 42).

A major implication of this study is that social work supervisors "had the appropriate attitude set to effect worker objective satisfaction." However, with regard to organizational objectives, the findings suggested that respondents not only failed to manifest supervisor behavior in support of these objectives but that their attitudes toward such responsibilities were weak (p. 44; see also Cohen and Rhodes 1977).

Using a series of standardized instruments and obtaining responses from 44 supervisors and 510 supervisees, Russell, Lankford, and Grinnell (1984) studied styles of supervision in a large state public welfare agency. Styles of supervision were elicited through the use of a *Styles of Management Inventory* based on the Managerial Grid concept of Blake and Mouton (1961). The grid balances concern for production and concern for people. It consists of five explicit dimensions, the extremes of which are maximum concern for production and minimum concern for people; and maximum concern for people and minimum concern for production. The most desirable combination is one which integrates task requirements and human requirements. The least desirable combination is one which reflects minimal concern for both dimensions—on the grid the 1.1 dimension.

The unexpected finding of the study was that supervisors described, and supervisees perceived supervisors using, the least desirable style of supervision—the 1.1 style, with minimal consideration given to both dimensions. The style is a very atypical supervisory approach. As compared with the mean based on data obtained from business, industry, government, and service organizations representing 4,819 supervisors with whom the forms have been used, the unusually high proportion of public welfare supervisors identified as using a 1.1 style of supervision ranked the agency in the "one percentile of organizations that have such a high proportion of 1.1 supervisors."

The 1.1 style of supervision suggests a detachment from the responsibilities of supervision. Supervisors avoid any contact or involvement with supervisees except when it is absolutely necessary. It is "management by exception" which provides minimal direction, review, and support of the worker's work. There is considerable reliance on the agency manual and forms in implementing supervision. It reflects a feeling that effective production is unobtainable, that satisfactory relationships are difficult to establish, and it reflects a lack of certainty about entitlement to vigorously exercise the authority of supervision.

Such research repeatedly shows social work supervisors failing to use their authority and power in implementing the responsibilities of administrative supervision.

Organizational Factors Attenuating
Supervisory Power and Authority

Reluctance and avoidance in the exercise of administrative authority by supervisors may be only partially the consequence of the fact that vigorous exercise of power and authority is antithetical to social work values and practice precepts. It may also derive from, and be reinforced by, a recognition that the supervisor's actual power and authority is more apparent than real.

Some of the attenuation of supervisory power results from factors which are inherent in a human service agency's organization and structure and the nature of the social worker's tasks.

Effective exercise of supervisory authority and power requires that certain prerequisite conditions be operative. Administrative control requires clarity in goals and objectives so that both the worker and the supervisor know the activities the workers should undertake. It also requires the supervisor to know clearly what the worker is doing and to judge whether or not what the worker is doing is being done correctly. None of these conditions, however, are generally characteristic of the social work supervisory situation.

Human services very often have multiple, sometimes even conflicting, goals expressing the ambivalence of the community regarding the problem the agency addresses and the clients they serve. Which goal has agency priority in regard to the unmarried mother—adequate support for her and her child, control of her sexual behavior, or punishment for immoral conduct? Which goal has priority for the AFDC program—giving the recipient the option of self-determination of child rearing alternatives, or making certain the program resources are conserved and that every able-bodied mother be self-supporting through employment? In the conflict between the needs of aged parents and the needs of their adult children, whose preferences are given priority by the agency?

> The social programs that public service bureaucrats are charged with administering are almost invariably complex and controversial. As a result the goals of these agencies are multiple, contradictory and vague, reflecting as they do the political and social forces and compromises that formed them. (Prottas 1978, p. 295)

Handler (1979) points to the fact that the enabling legislation establishing most social service programs are replete with vague, ill-defined, ambiguously-stated objectives and criteria. "Vague language in the statutes—creates a 'downward flow' of discretion—until the lowest level field officer interprets rules and guidelines for specific cases" (p. 9). The direct service worker is thus invested with a considerable amount of discretion in selecting objectives in individual cases.

In addition to the fact that agency objectives are often multiple, vaguely stated, and open to a variety of possible interpretations, the need to individualize the application of agency service also constrains supervisors' administrative authority. Lipsky (1980) notes that the characteristics of the direct service social workers' jobs "make it difficult if not impossible to severely reduce discretion. They involve complex tasks for which elaboration of rules, guidelines, or instructions cannot circumscribe the alternatives." The situations encountered are too complicated, too unpredictable, too individualized, and too idiosyncratic to "reduce to programmatic formats." Workers need discretion "because the accepted definition of their tasks calls for sensitive observation and judgments which are not reducable" to specific rules, regulations, procedures. They are granted, or take discretion, because the community "to a degree seeks not only impartiality from its public agencies but also compassion for special circumstances and flexibility in dealing with them" (p. 15). To the extent that every client is like all other clients the agency can standardize practice and direct the workers' behavior. But since each client is in many respects like no other clients, this requires that discretion be given the worker in responding to the unique aspects of the situation.

Direct service workers "enjoy considerable discretion in part because society does not want computerized public service and rigid application of standards at the expense of the individual situation" (p. 23) and only the worker can know the details of the individual situation. Personalizing social services requires giving the worker considerable discretion.

The nature of the social worker's job makes it difficult to control since each situation encountered is nonstandardized, diffuse, uncertain, unpredictable, and highly individualized. These are the characteristics of a work situation that demands allocation of a large measure of discretion to the person in actual contact with the client—the supervisee. The relevant research shows that the less specific the task, the less standardized the job, the less likely it can be controlled (Litwak 1964).

Complex, ambiguous, and uncertain situations can best be responded to incrementally, each step determining the next step. Only the worker in direct contact with the client and aware of the details regarding each step is in a position to implement such a strategy.

Not only are the situations the worker needs to address nonstandardized, but so are the intervention techniques that the worker needs to apply. The services provided by most social agencies

> rely heavily on the application of technologies that are nonroutine, complex, and indeterminate. The variability of client needs and requests and the difficulties involved in understanding the problems they present when combined with the relatively unspecific nature of the techniques employed and the still considerable uncertainty about their effects, make it unfeasible for the organization to prescribe uniform technical processes. (Patti 1983, p. 137)

Social work activity is characterized by what has been variously termed "role performance invisibility" and "low compliance observability." This factor, inherent in the work situation, further attenuates the supervisor's administrative power. The possibilities of direct control and observation of workers' behavior are very limited. Consequently, while the supervisor can "order" that certain things be done, and that they be done in a prescribed manner, there often is no way she can be certain that the directives will be carried out. Ultimately, she is dependent on the worker's report to her that work has been done in the way it should be done. As Gummer (1979) notes:

> In social agencies supervision is based on the workers' reports of what they are doing rather than a supervisor's direct observation of the work. Organizations with this structure have significant control and accountability problems since the line workers are able to operate with a high degree of autonomy and can screen their behavior from the direct surveillance of administrators. These structural conditions promote discretionary behavior of workers, who in the privacy of the interviewing room are free to interpret and apply agency policy and procedure as they see fit. While confidentiality is designed to protect the client, it protects the worker as well. (p. 220)

Arguing that workers currently have too much autonomy, Handler (1979) notes that

> it is extremely difficult to monitor social service activity (i.e., to obtain reliable information on decision making so that performance can be evaluated); and if activity is not readily susceptible to monitoring then supervisory offices lack the necessary information to assert control. A system that limits the amount of information available to supervisors and controller increases the discretionary power of field-level personnel. (p. 18)

The less information the supervisor has about the worker's activity, the less amenable is the "worker to supervisory control and discipline" (p. 108).

The general organizational demand imposed on supervisors makes it difficult to effectively implement the authority to monitor, review, and assess the worker's activity. Gambrill and Wiltse (1974), in their study of California foster care, found workers had considerable decisional discretion. But the supervisor's failure to adequately monitor the worker activity, they note, is inherent in a situation in which a typical unit caseload for which the supervisor is responsible consists of 245 children. "Even if the supervisor was extremely conscientious there would have to be a well-developed monitoring system to enable him/her to keep up with what is happeneing to 245 different children. . . . The problem of too great a discretionary component is heightened by the impossibility of adequate supervision under the current system" (p. 18).

Noting some of these characteristics of the human service organization's delivery system, Hasenfeld (1983) concludes that "These characteristics . . . accord line staff [the direct service worker] considerable discretion . . . line staff function quite autonomously from the rest of the organization; task interdependence is low between work units and there are significant barriers to effective supervision" (p. 157).

To sum up briefly, authority and power are difficult to exercise effectively in the face of ambiguous objectives, uncertain procedures, and indeterminate interventions about which the supervisor has only speculative knowledge.

The problem of control is intensified in the context of increasing caseload pressure. In an empirical study of the effects of higher caseloads on worker autonomy and discretion, Brintnall (1981) found that "Caseload pressures tend to make effective supervision of staff by upper level officials unusually difficult increasing the lattitude afforded lower level staff to act independently" (p. 296).

Supervisee Countervailing Power

The supervisor's authority and power are limited not only by ideology, reluctance, and organizational considerations, but also by the countervailing power of the supervisees. The traditional social work literature has underestimated the power of the worker and overestimated the power that the supervisor is actually able to exert in implementing the functions of administrative supervision. Although control in the relationship is asymmetrical, it is not unidirectional. While the supervisor has, clearly and admittedly, more authority and power than the supervisees, the supervisees also have some power in the relationship even though they may lack formal authority (Mechanic 1964; Janeway 1980).

The concept that power is ultimately based on dependency might be usefully applied in analyzing the countervailing power of the supervisees (Emerson 1962). The supervisees depend on the supervisor for rewards, for solutions to work problems, for necessary information, for approval and support. However, the supervisor is also dependent on the supervisees. The supervisor may have the formal power to assign, direct, and review work, but she is dependent on the supervisees' willingness and readiness to actually do the work. If supervisees fail to do the required work because of opposition or resistance, the supervisor is in trouble with the administration, which holds her responsible for getting the work done. Supervisees thus have the power of making life difficult for the supervisor. In discussing her present assignment a supervisee said she could

> drive her supervisor frantic if she wanted to—and she sometimes did. She was responsible for processing foster home applications. If she wanted to gum up the works she just took longer to do them—always for legitimate reasons—it was difficult to schedule an interview with the father or the last time she scheduled an interview with the family they had to cancel it when she got out there because of some emergency, or there were special problems which required more detailed exploration, etc.

A supervisee writes that a supervisor newly appointed to the unit

> had the tendency to "command" his supervisees to carry out specific tasks and responsibilities, refusing to discuss the reasons behind them and replying coldly, "Because I said so," when asked. Our group of supervisees resented this approach to the extent that they "boycotted" the supervisor, flatly refusing to do anything more than minimum work required and giving him the "silent treatment." Once this reaction became apparent to the supervisor, he began to be more communicative and understanding and less strictly authoritative than he had been previously.

The willingness to obey is sometimes given key consideration in defining authority. In this view, authority is not delegated from above in the hierarchy but granted from below; it is based on the consent of the governed. If this is the case, then the legitimacy of the supervisor's authority is, in fact, controlled by the supervisees and can be withdrawn by them (Barnard 1938, pp. 161–65). Although agency administration legitimates the authority of the supervisor, such authority must be endorsed by supervisees before it can be fully implemented. Both official legitimation and worker endorsement of authority are necessary (Dornbusch and Scott 1975, pp. 37–42).

In the last analysis the supervisees have the ultimate veto power. They can refuse consent to be governed by resigning from the organization. "You can't fire me, I quit." Realistically, however, the labor market situation may act as a constraint on the worker's "veto power."

The potency of the supervisor's authority is related to the worker's commitment to the job. If the worker does not care whether the agency retains him or not, if he has little concern about whether the client receives or does not receive adequate service, the supervisor has little power to influence the worker's behavior.

Workers not only have the power of not cooperating, they have the power of overcompliance or rigid compliance. Good Soldier Schweick was able to bring the army to its knees by compulsive, meticulous compliance with every order in the rule book. Supervisees can effectively sabotage the work of an agency by the literal application of all policies, rules, and procedures. This is sometimes termed "malicious obedience."

The worker is the only one who has the knowledge of the intimate details of the client's situation. The worker comes into possession of this knowledge on the basis of a contact which the supervisor cannot observe. The worker then is in the possession of considerable knowledge about the case situations for which the supervisor has ultimate responsibility. Such information, which only the worker possesses, can be shared freely, shared partially and selectively, distorted, or withheld in communications with the supervisor. This means that while the worker has no formal grant of authority in relation to the supervisor, the worker has considerable actual power in this relationship.

As a consequence, the supervisor is dependent on the worker for the information which is basic to the exercise of authority. Such information is provided by the workers in verbal reports and/or written records, the substance of which is determined by the worker. Outright falsification in records or verbal reports is infrequent and atypical. But there are no independent sources of information by which to check the reports made by the worker whose work is being supervised. The written and spoken records either support the worker's decisions or do not include information that might arouse doubts about the decision. Since the record is written by the worker, "it is not unreasonable to suppose that information would not be included that contradicts [the direct service worker's] judgments or that reports his unsanctioned behaviour" (Prottas 1979, p. 153).

Workers can manipulate the supervisor by manipulating the information they feed to her about the client and the client group. A worker might exaggerate the difficulties which some procedure occasioned for his client and exaggerate client opposition to the procedure.

The power of the individual supervisee in controlling the work flow (how much work or what kind is done within a given period of time) and his control of information fed to the supervisor may be augmented in coalition with other supervisees. Supervisees acting as a group can develop considerable power in controlling their supervisor.

The supervisor is also dependent on the supervisees for some kinds of psychic rewards. Approbation from supervisees, expressions of commendation and appreciation from supervisees, is a source of intrinsic job satisfaction for the supervisor. It hurts the supervisor never to be told by a supervisee that she has been helpful to her, that she is a good supervisor. Supervisees can manipulate supervisors' dependence on such gratification by studied deference and apple-polishing. Blau and Scott (1962) found that one significant source of emotional support for the supervisor was the loyalty of his supervisees (p. 162). The threat of withdrawal of loyalty acts as a constraint on the supervisor's exercise of his authority and power.

Workers have power by virtue of the problems and losses involved in replacing them. Dismissal is a weapon that is used, workers realize, with considerable hesitancy. If a worker is dismissed, the agency has to spend considerable time and energy finding a replacement and then more time and energy training the replacement.

While the supervisor uses her authority to control, she is at the same time controlled by that authority. The nature of the delegated authority sets clear limits to her jurisdiction and clearly prescribes boundaries to her authority. She is not authorized to employ certain sanctions, offer certain kinds of rewards, intrude on certain aspects of the workers' behavior. Authority is the domestication of unregulated power. It explicates the prerogatives and limitations in the exercise of power (Dornbusch and Scott 1975).

These factors mitigating the potency of administrative supervision which are inherent in the work context are further reinforced by characteristics of the supervisor-supervisee relationship that can neutralize the supervisor's authority.

The power of the supervisee also derives from the supervisor's need to be considered a "good" supervisor as described in the literature—a self-image which the supervisor seeks to establish and maintain. Manifesting attitudes of acceptance and respect, adhering to the principles of participatory democracy and mutuality, communicating approachability and openness, the supervisor is perceived as responsive to pressure from a strongly motivated and assertive supervisee. Supervisees who want the supervisor to meet their requests try to generate guilt in the supervisor by suggesting that in refusing they are being authoritarian, unprofessional, more concerned about the agency and its rules than the workers and their clients. In the face of escalating assertiveness on the part of the supervisee, the supervisor

> who follows good practice remains courteous, understanding and calm—the more a [supervisor] follows good practice the less a subordinate will fear retaliation when he places pressure on the [supervisor]. The more a supervisor follows good practice, the more a subordinate will exert social pressure on him to reverse a disapproval. A "no" need not be taken as a final answer if the administrator has already demonstrated that he is open to the ideas of his colleagues. (Zander 1977, pp. 96–97)

The supervisee can control the use of power by the supervisor by appealing to the norms of fairness, of colleagueship, of professional behavior. This is not the way one should treat another human, another colleague, another professional. To the extent that such norms are accepted by the supervisor, they act as constraints on his behavior.

A knowledge of agency rules can be used effectively by the supervisee in exerting influence on the supervisor. The supervisor is as much constrained by agency rules as is the supervisee. Quoting a relevant rule to the supervisor is among the more effective techniques used by supervisees in studies of upward influence procedures (Schilit and Locke 1982, p. 310). Comprehensive knowledge of agency rules and procedures helps the supervisee equalize power with supervisors.

The fact that the direct service worker has considerable power despite the fact that there is no formal grant of authority is aptly illustrated in the following vignette written by a supervisor in a day care agency whose supervisee, Joan, was a child care worker.

> There were times that I thought Joan was taking advantage of my understanding nature. For example, I felt it was important for her to be on time so she could greet all the children when they arrived. This would establish for the children a mood for the day, a feeling of continuity, a trust that all is going to be well again. Often Joan would be late or would arrive early only to leave in order to buy coffee across the street. She had a million excuses—buses not being on time, dying of hunger, and alarms not going off. I had a feeling that Joan's most creative part of the day was in the morning thinking up excuses to give me for not being in the room when the children arrived. There was a point where I should have said something like, "All right, Joan, either you're here in the classroom at 8:40 or I will start taking money out of your paycheck." Why didn't I take action? There were several reasons, the most unattractive being that I didn't want Joan to see me as unfriendly, insensitive, and unempathetic. This was a mistake on my part.
>
> There was another reason for not confronting Joan on the issue of lateness that is a litle more complex than just wanting to be liked. Joan could have been made to be in her room welcoming children as they arrived from 8:40 on. But what concerned me as much as her attendance was the quality of her welcome. Joan was used to arriving around 9:00 and apparently saw little importance in warmly greeting each child in some special way. For Joan to be forced to change what she perceived to be her schedule without proper preparation would, in my opinion, be detrimental to the children. There would be a great danger that Joan would feel imposed upon and unjustly abused, and direct her anger towards the children. What I believed I needed to handle this situation was time set aside in the day for me to schedule regular meetings in order to discuss with Joan such matters as the importance of greeting children on arrival. (Miller, Mailick and Miller 1973, p. 88)

The countervailing power of the supervisee vis-à-vis the supervisor is central to the question of worker autonomy and the demands of the organization mediated by the supervisor. The strain between these often conflicting pressures is a persistent theme in organizational literature. This will be discussed once again in chapter 9 in dealing with the question of worker independence from supervision.

The Problem of Rules, Noncompliance, and Disciplinary Action

While the considerations cited above indicate the problems involved in implementing authority and power in monitoring and controlling supervisees' decisions and actions, it does not absolve the supervisor of the responsibility for performing those functions. The supervisor still has to implement administrative supervision in accordance with agency procedures and rules.

The Functional Value of Rules

The supervisor, in monitoring conformance to agency rules and procedures, permits the agency to get its work done effectively. In prescribing and proscribing, in monitoring what should be done and what cannot be done, the supervisor is ensuring predictability and reliability of performance. Workers doing different things, whose work needs to be coordinated, can be assured that the work their partners are doing will be in accordance with some uniform expectations. The worker in the unit of the agency offering service to the unmarried mother interested in placing her child for adoption can discuss the characteristics of an approved adoptive home without having herself seen one. She can do this because she knows the requirements and procedures which regulate the work of her colleagues in the adoptive home-finding unit. Workers have to have confidence in the reliability with which these fellow workers will follow prescribed procedures, as a prerequisite for performing their own tasks.

The supervisor, as protector of agency rules and procedures, has the responsibility of seeing that policy is uniformly interpreted. If each worker were permitted to establish his own policies, or to idiosyncratically interpret centrally established policies, this would ultimately set client against client, and worker against worker. A liberal interpretation of policy by one client's worker is an act of discrimination against the client of a second worker. It would encourage competition among workers in an effort to tap agency resources to meet the needs of their own clients, with whom they are, understandably enough, primarily concerned.

The general emphasis in social work on autonomy, self-determination, and individualization tends to encourage a negative attitude toward rules. Rules suggest that people are interchangeable rather than unique and different. The negative attitude toward formalization of prescribed behavior in rules and procedures has, of course, support in the real negative consequences which can result from their application. They do limit the autonomy of the worker, they discourage initiative, they tend to make the agency muscle-bound, less flexible and adaptable, "set in its ways." They predispose toward a routinization of worker activity. Rules can become ends in themselves rather than means for achieving organizational objectives; they restrict the freedom to individualize agency response in meeting particular needs of particular clients and encourage deception and duplicity as workers feel a need to "get around" the rules.

Social workers are generally well aware of, and sensitive to, the negative consequences of rules. It might be helpful to the supervisor who inevitably faces the responsibility of communicating and enforcing rules and uniform procedures if some conviction could be developed regarding the positive aspects of standardization.

While each rule and prescribed procedure, if taken seriously, limits worker autonomy by deciding in advance what action should be taken in a particular situation, the rules permit more efficient agency operation. When the recurrent situation to which a rule is applied is encountered, it need not be subject to an exhaustive process of review and decision making. The supervisee does not need to discuss the situation with the supervisor and can act with the assurance that the decision, congruent with the procedure, has agency sanction. This relieves anxiety and frees the supervisee's energies to deal with those unique aspects of the client's situation that cannot be codified in some formal policy statement. If everything in every case had to be decided afresh, the worker could easily be overwhelmed and immobilized. Here, as elsewhere, there is no real freedom without clearly defined laws. They provide a structure within which workers can operate with comfort, assurance, and support. Rules provide a clear codification of expectations. They communicate to the worker how he is expected to respond in a variety of recurrently encountered situations. This understanding is particularly important in social work where the various groups the social worker faces communicate contradictory, and often conflicting, expectations. The community may expect him to respond in one way to client problems, the client a second way, the profession in still another way. The rules offer a worker the serenity of unambiguous guidelines as to how the agency expects him to respond in defining clearly the "minimum set of behaviors which are prescribed and proscribed." The rules mitigate conflicts to which workers might otherwise be exposed.

While rules and regulations have the negative effect of decreasing worker discretion and autonomy, they have the positive effect of decreasing role ambiguity and increasing role clarity. As a result of a set of formalized rules and procedures and a detailed job description, the worker knows more clearly and with greater certainty what she should be doing and how she should be doing it. Having guidelines increases the ability of people to work together in the agency and tells workers what behavior they can expect from each other (Organ and Greene 1981). Rules also can increase organizational stability in a potentially hostile environment (Kurzman 1977).

If the agency wisely formulates its rules and procedures with active worker participation and if it further provides for a periodic critical review of them, the agency, of necessity, must make a systematic analysis of professional practice. The best rules are, after all, merely a clear codification of practice wisdom, what most workers have found is the best thing to do in certain situations. The call for rules and procedures is, consequently, a call for a hard analysis of practice.

Ultimately rules protect the client, since the procedures to which all workers adhere in a uniform manner assure him of equitable service. He is assured that another client will not be given preferential treatment because his worker likes him better and that he will not be treated worse because he has antagonized the worker by his militancy. If a client meets the qualification as codified in agency procedures, the worker is under some constraint to approve his application for adoption, to authorize his request for a special assistance grant or whatever. Rules and regulations are definite; the worker may be capricious.

Rules reduce the possibility of friction between supervisors and supervisees. They set impersonal limits to exceptions that the supervisee might press for. They are also a source of support and sanction to the supervisor in making decisions that threaten the relationship. Rules depersonalize decisions which might be resented as a personal affront by the supervisee: "I wish I could go along with your request, but agency regulations prevent this." More positively, the procedural norms substantiate the desirability of the decision the supervisor is making: "In these kinds of problems we have found such an approach is not particularly helpful. In fact, based on our experience, we have developed a procedure which requires that the worker not take such action."

Rules protect the worker from arbitrary, personalized decisions by the supervisor, from favoritism, and from discriminating acts based on irrelevant criteria. While rules constrain those "to whom they are applied," they constrain the "behavior of the rule applier as well." In fact, a sophisticated worker armed with a detailed knowledge of the rules can use them to control the authority and discretion of the supervisor (Mechanic 1964).

Rules reduce the possibility of supervisor-supervisee friction because they operate as remote-control devices. Supervision can occur through adherence to a universally applied rule rather than through the direct, personal intercession of the supervisor suggesting that this or that be done in this or that way. Control takes place at a distance in the absence of the supervisor. A rule is a "definition of expectation." The explicitness of a rule makes clear when a required action was not taken or when a prohibited action did take place. A rule therefore provides the supervisor with a guideline to nonperformance and objectively legitimates the application of sanctions.

Gouldner (1954) has pointed out that rules can be used as devices to create social obligations. Supervisors, by deliberately refraining on occasion from enforcing rules, can create a sense of obligation on the part of supervisees. Because the supervisor has been lenient about enforcing certain requirements, she can more freely ask the supervisee to extend himself to do some things which need to be done. Blau and Scott (1962) found that supervisors in a county welfare department actually did differentially enforce rules to attain the effect of developing loyalty and social obligation. The supervisor

employing such an approach, however, needs to have a sophisticated knowledge of the work situation so that she can "judge which
operating rules can be ignored without impairing efficiency" (Blau
and Scott 1962, p. 143).

The relaxed supervisor can adopt a flexible attitude toward
agency rules. She accepts the fact that some degree of noncompliance is, in all likelihood, inevitable. She recognizes that not
all procedures are of equal importance and that some can be ignored or subverted without much risk to agency or client.

Helping the staff to understand clearly the nature and purpose of
the agency's rules lessens the dangers of ritualism and overconfor-
mity. Rules, regulations, and procedures often become ends in
themselves rather than a means of more effectively serving the
client. If workers are encouraged to participate in the formulation of
rules and procedures, if they are helped to understand and critically
evaluate the situations which required formulation of the rules,
they will have less of a tendency to apply them in a rigid, routine
way. Supervisees will be able to apply the rules more flexibly, more
appropriately, and with greater conviction. Furthermore, understanding clearly the rationale for the particular rule, the worker will
be in a better position to suggest modification in those situations
where the procedure seems inappropriate or self-defeating. To
encourage and reward such initiative the supervisor needs to be receptive to such suggestions for change communicated by the
supervisees.

In the context of adherence to rules and procedures, we again
encounter the problem of conflict between the organization and the
worker, between the need for stability, predictability, and standardization of behavior and the need for change, innovation, and the
freedom to develop imaginative behavioral responses to novel situations.

Steggert (1970) raises this question when he asks, "How then
does the [supervisor] in a bureaucratic structure resolve the conflict
between the organization's legitimate need for predictability (and
thus for a variety of formal controls and coordination procedures)
and the human unpredictability resulting from allowing subordinates to function more autonomously (and thus engaging in more
needs-satisfying behavior); how does he simultaneously maintain
that part of the organizational system for which he is responsible

while satisfying . . . the human side of the enterprise?" (p. 47). As Green (1966) notes,

> The problem . . . is essentially one of reconciling the professional worker's need for autonomy and the organization's need for employees to be integrated within the complex of its activities. For the social worker autonomy means maintaining professional standards, developing a creative and resourceful approach to practice and finding opportunity for professional development and research activity. For the organization integration involves maintaining administrative standards and rational coordination of activities together with development of responsibility and loyalty in the employees. (pp. 82–83)

One characteristic of bureaucratic organizations is that the prescribed behavior for any role in the agency is formulated objectively and impersonally without reference to the individual who might become the role incumbent. Consequently there is always the likelihood of differences between the job requirements and the need dispositions of the series of individuals who are at different times hired to fill the job. The individual worker's definition of the specifics of the role behavior is the result of his attempt to reconcile the demands of the job with his own particular need dispositions. The supervisor's responsibility is to help supervisees reduce the gap between organizational demands and personal idiosyncracies. Her task is to "integrate the demands of the [agency] and the demands of the staff members in such a way that [the job] is, at once, organizationally productive and individually fulfilling" (Getzels and Guba 1957, p. 428).

The sensitive supervisor needs to be selective in efforts to achieve greater congruence between the individual's way of performing his role and the agency's definition of role performance. The supervisor will select for discussion, and possible change, only those differences which do negatively affect efficient and effective service to the client. The supervisor gives priority to behaviors which are "required" and those which are "prohibited." The rationale for designating the behaviors as either required or prohibited is, we assume, that they have greatest potency for helping or hurting the client. Consequently, they have to be most carefully monitored. But between "required" and "prohibited" there are many behaviors which are less crucial and critical for the effective implementation of tasks the worker performs in offering service to clients. Consequently, the supervisor can view such modifications of prescribed role behavior with greater permissiveness and equanimity, formulating a zone of indifference.

Another problem faced by supervisors is to decide on the relative balance between standardization and uniformity in procedure and supervisee autonomy and flexibility. Formally codified rules and procedures to which all workers have to uniformly adhere restrict the workers' autonomy in flexibly responding to the needs of the individual case situation. On the other hand, if all workers were permitted to formulate rules and procedures differently for each case situation, the result would be organizational anarchy. As Stewart (1972) says, "No organization can set order as its overriding aim nor can any put flexibility as its prime concern. All organizations need elements of both and the problem is to decide what is the appropriate balance between them" (p. 151). The general principle might be to grant supervisees as much freedom as is compatible with efficient, effective, and equitable implementation of the agency's goal. This of course is a nice, rounded statement which, admittedly, is often difficult to apply in specific situations.

Understanding Noncompliance

The supervisor should make an effort to understand and, if possible, help the supervisee understand noncompliant behavior. Here, as always, the assumption is that behavior is purposive. It may be that the supervisee does not know clearly what is expected of him and does not clearly understand what it is he is supposed to be doing. Noncompliance might then yield to a clarification of what is called for by agency policy. The worker may understand what is required, may be in agreement with what is required, but be unable to meet the demands of the rule or procedure. He does not know enough or is not capable enough to comply. Education and training are required, rather than criticism, to obtain compliance.

Although it had been agreed that Mr. F. would arrange for group meetings of the patients on his ward, he had consistently and adroitly avoided scheduling such meetings. Despite repeated discussion of the need for this and tentative plans, no meetings were held. Finally, in response to the supervisor's growing insistence and impatience, Mr. F.

shared the fact that he knew very little about how to conduct a group meeting, despite all his early verbalized knowledge, and was very anxious about getting started with a group.

The rules and regulations of large, complex social agencies are often voluminous and sometimes contradictory, and are frequently undergoing revision and modification. Noncompliance may result from failure to know which rule to apply or how to apply it. Such actions might more properly be classified as practice errors rather than noncompliance. They are mistakes that are not due to any willful deviance or negligence.

Ability to fulfill task responsibilities may also relate to the client and the client's situation rather than to any inadequacies on the part of the worker. The client may be so resistive to help, or the resources available to change the situation so limited, that the worker avoids contact with the family.

Children in foster care had been ordered by the court to be returned to the physical custody of the mother against agency recommendations. The worker, prior to this order, had been working with one of the teenage children, Sally, around school adjustment, adolescent conflicts, etc. Following the return of Sally to the mother, the worker failed to keep a scheduled appointment with Sally and did not schedule another appointment. When this was discussed in a supervisory conference, the worker indicated that with Sally's return to her own mother she felt no confidence that she could be of any help. The situation in the house was such that she did not feel that anything she could do would enable Sally to change.

Noncompliance may result from a disagreement with policy or procedure. The worker may regard compliance as contrary to his definition of the agency's objective. This might require some discussion of the purpose of the policy in an effort to reconcile it with the worker's view of agency objectives. The worker may in fact be correct in claiming that agency objectives would best be served by ignoring the rules in this instance and amending or revising them. For instance, during the 1960s, social workers in west coast public welfare departments were fired after they refused to conduct "midnight raids" to check on the continued eligibility of AFDC clients. They strongly felt that such procedures were a violation of clients' rights and their own professional standards.

Noncompliance may result from some incompatibility between agency policy and procedures and the worker's personal values or the values of his reference group.

> Mrs. R's caseload included a black family with four children. Part of the difficulty resulted from inadequate housing and Mrs. R. was helping them to find a larger apartment. However, she avoided exploring the possibilities which might be available in a large neighborhood housing project. In discussions with the supervisor, she indicated that she felt it inadvisable for black and white families to be living together and was reluctant to help her clients move into the housing project. This was in contradiction to the nondiscriminatory policies of the agency.

> A point of persistent difficulty in Mrs. L's handling of her caseload is her consistent failure to inform clients of the different kinds of services and financial help to which they might be entitled despite the fact that the procedure calls for sharing this information. She has a strong feeling that many of the clients are getting as much, or more, than they need and sharing this information is just inviting a raid on the county treasury.

Noncompliance may result from a work conflict. The worker makes a discretionary decision to do one thing and not another because she cannot do both. Thus the worker may have failed to get an important report in on time because she had to arrange an emergency placement for a child.

The worker's noncompliance may be in response to a conflict between the needs of any one client and the need for efficient, expeditious task performance in order to provide service to the client group. Unless the worker can rapidly meet the administrative demands for obtaining the information necessary to make valid decisions regarding foster care or adoptive applications, for instance, the system may become overwhelmed as new applications wait to be processed. This means that only that content which would help answer the questions required for administrative decision would be explored in interviews. Other considerations, however significant they may be to the applicant and the agency, are likely to be discouraged as extraneous to the immediate task of completing the home study. The fault then lies with excessively heavy demands on the agency rather than with the unwillingness of the worker to explore aspects of the situation which the agency wants reviewed.

Noncompliance may result from disagreement about interpretation of policy. A supervisor writes:

> A worker refused to follow policy. She asked for a clearance from the supervisor in the state office. A written interpretation was provided which was in accord with my interpretation of policy. The worker insisted on acting her own way. Because of the "semantics" of wording in the agency manual, the worker contended that she had the prerogative.

Sometimes policies, rules, and procedures are contradictory, and adherence to one requires noncompliance with another. Protecting the suicidal patient from himself, for example, may require breaking the rules of confidentiality.

Noncompliance may result from a conflict between bureaucratic demands and casework goals as perceived by the supervisee.

> Ms. B had accepted a gift from a client. Her supervisor called attention to the fact that acceptance of gifts from clients was not in accordance with agency policy. Ms. B. said, in response, that she was aware of this but felt that if she had not accepted the gift the client would feel that she was rejecting her. She had accepted because this helped strengthen the relationship.

In general terms this is the classic conflict between the bureaucratic orientation and the service orientation, identified in social work by Billingsley (1964a) and Piven and Papenfort (1960), among others. Workers may decide that there are some actions which need to be taken in behalf of service to the client even though the actions conflict with agency policy. In this sense, noncompliance comes close to innovation, permitting individualization of agency policy and enabling the agency to serve the client more effectively. It illustrates the fact that noncompliance may be functional.

Such noncompliance was noted by a participant observation researcher in a British social agency:

> Sometimes social workers found themselves in a situation of conflicting loyalties, particularly when a client was in conflict, or potential conflict, with authority—usually doing something that was illegal or which involved deception of some kind. Examples of this were dealing in stolen goods, taking drugs, "fiddling" with the gas meter, or with-

holding information about earnings from DHSS. Social workers, as part of "the authorities" themselves, felt that they were, at least in principle, expected to be on the side of respectability and observance of the law. But they also felt that their relationship to the client necessitated loyalty to him or her. In this situation there was a range of strategies that social workers could adopt. They could, first of all, avoid knowing about the client's deviant behaviour. Sometimes social workers confided in their colleagues that they suspected that Mrs. X was on drugs, or Mrs. Y had a cohabitee, but would not discuss this with the client concerned. Often clients played along with this, and withheld information from the social worker about some of their activities. Thus Mrs. J only told her social worker that she was on drugs when the police had raided her flat and she was about to appear in court.

Second, the social worker might know what was going on, but maintain a neutral attitude in relation to the client, neither encouraging the deviant behaviour nor informing the relevant authorities.

Social workers might, on the other hand, side with the client secretly, so long as the conflict did not come out into the open. They might, for instance, encourage the client to earn extra money and not notify the DHSS. For some social workers, being "in on" the deviant act was to them a token of being trusted, which they valued for its own sake. (Satyamurti 1981, p. 160)

A clear majority of the 65 social workers Pearson (1975) interviewed in a study of "industrial deviance" in a social agency admitted complicity in such acts of client violation of rules and procedures of the agency. Pawlak (1976) reports a similar kind of "tinkering" with the system on the part of the worker.

On many occasions workers will clearly signal clients whom they wish to help that they do not wish to be told about minor occasional income. Aside from any other considerations such income greatly complicates grant application completion (Prottas 1979, p. 34).

A survey study of 1,300 workers in a state department of public welfare found that "more than two-thirds of the workers reported they bent, ignored, conveniently forgot or otherwise subverted departmental rules" (O'Conner and Spence 1976, p. 178; see also Weatherly et al. 1980).

Such noncompliance may be a necessary and useful expedient in dealing with conflicting and irreconcilable demands. The worker, subjected to the pressure of client needs in the context of bureaucratic rules and procedures which make difficult the satisfaction of such needs, bends or breaks the rules. In such instances supervisors often tolerate or ignore nonconformity (Jacobs 1969).

Green (1966) points out that the pull toward overidentification of social workers with the client is likely to be greatest in large, highly bureaucratic organizations. The client is often a "victim" of the same bureaucracy. "Thus the social work victim unconsciously identifies with the client victim" (Green 1966, p. 75). This leads to the temptation to make an alliance with the client against agency regulations and procedures, resulting in noncompliance with agency policy.

Noncompliance may result from the fact that the supervisee is subject to a variety of pressures from the client and is dependent on the client for psychic gratification. In this sense the client has power over the supervisee which may force him to act in contravention to agency policy. Supervisees are subject to rewards from clients such as expressions of gratification, praise, affection, and friendship. They are subject to punishments from clients such as expressions of aggression, hostility, deprecation. Supervisees would like to be told that they have been helpful to the family, that they are loved for it, and that they are wonderful people; supervisees tend to avoid taking action which might result in the client's telling them that they are "stupid bastards who never did know what it was all about and have never been of much help to anybody." Noncompliance may then follow from supervisees' being pressured by the client to do what the client wants them to do, not what the agency or their professional conscience dictates to be necessary and desirable. A supervisee in protective service writes:

> The agency is reasonably clear as to the circumstances which require initiating a petition for removal of the child. Of course, only the worker knows the specifics of a particular case so a lot depends on the worker's discretion. But in this instance of a black 4-year-old boy in the home of a single-parent AFDC family, I really knew the kid was being abused. Yet whenever I even hinted at starting procedures to remove the child, which is what I should have done according to agency policy, the mother began to get hostile and abusive, accusing me of being a "meddling white racist." She knew how to manipulate me, making me feel anxious, guilty, and uncertain. I could, of course, have discussed this with my supervisor but I was afraid that it would end on a firm decision to remove the child and, given the control this

mother had, I did not want to have to fight with her in implementing such a decision.

Supervisee noncompliance may be prompted by a desire to make the job easier, less boring, more satisfying. Noncompliance is, in such instances, a response to the worker's effort to "increase his own power and status and freedom and security while shedding uncongenial work and unwelcome responsibilities" (Jay 1967, p. 89). These are the pragmatic rewards of noncompliance. As Levy (1970) notes in discussing the activities of some workers in a county welfare department,

> employees begin to identify with and work within the logic of the "system." This entails the playing of a highly elaborate game in which the general idea is to make one's job as easy as possible through meeting enough statistical requirements to keep administrators and supervisors off one's back, doing just enough for clients so [one] won't be bothered by them and keeping [one's] caseload as low as possible by "transferring out" as many cases as possible and accepting as few as [one] can. (p. 172)

Noncompliance may result from the effort to cope with the requirements and stress of the work. It may be an expedient adaptation in managing the work so as to get it done with the least possible harm to the client and reduced discomfort and increased satisfaction to the worker. The nature of the work they do and the stringent constraints which limit their ability to be of help pressures direct service workers to adopt such expedients in implementing their job. Noncompliance or modified compliance may then be seen to be the direct service worker's response to the problems the job poses for her. A supervisee writes:

> After a time you get to be self-protective. You learn how to "manage" the clients so that they impose less of a burden. I remember one case of a middle-aged woman in marital counseling. She was very dependent, talked incessantly and called me continually. Even though I recognized it was part of the service, I always "arranged" to be going out if she caught me in. She gradually got the message, "Don't call us, we'll call you."

A supervisee in corrections writes:

> There are a number of different circumstances which require revocation of parole. But that's a lot of extra work and a lot of harder work

because it means a big hassle with the parolee. Okay, if something is very serious you play it according to the regulations. But if it is something ambiguous and you figure that even if something happens you can justify not having revoked parole, you figure, "To hell with the regulations, why bust your ass?"

Noncompliance may be due to psychological considerations, as in the case of the worker who fails to turn in a sufficiently detailed record because of anxiety regarding self-exposure. Similarly, noncompliance may relate to developmental experiences. A supervisor writes:

I had a 25-year-old worker who seemed unable to follow rules. When she first came to the unit, she seemed bright, eager and intelligent. I was aware her father was a judge in a small town in another state. I did not realize how this was affecting her until several months passed. She never let me know, through "out" slips, where she might be in case of emergency. One day she was needed for an emergency, had not left an "out" slip or any word of where she might be located. I kept going to her office and asking other workers if they had seen her. Finally, she came bursting into my office where my secretary and another worker were and started blasting me. I stated, "Just a minute, young lady." The two people in my office quickly left. I pointed out to her that certain rules and regulations are necessary for running our unit efficiently and why I had been requesting "out" slips from her. What I had failed to realize was that her actions were those of an adolescent, that she still was rebellious and was projecting some of her own rebellion toward her father (an authoritarian figure in two ways—father and judge) on me and the department (the "System").

The supervisor, of course, is making a speculative inference that needs confirmation in discussions with the supervisee. If confirmed, the incident illustrated noncompliance based on personal developmental problems.

Noncompliance may also be an act of hostility toward the supervisor or the agency he represents, as when the worker deliberately fails to implement agency policies or procedures as an act of defiance. There is personal satisfaction in such covert manifestations of hostility.

Noncompliance may be a deliberate act of defiance in a conscious effort to call attention to policies which need to be changed. In such cases the worker is pointing to the need for change by challenging the system (Merton 1957, p. 360).

Noncompliance may be a response to real dangers encountered on the job. The worker, often a young, white female, is obliged, in many instances, to go into apartment buildings in areas characterized by high rates of crime. Social workers have, in fact, been mugged, assaulted, and molested during the course of their work. As a result there is considerable anxiety, and visits to clients may be resisted and not scheduled (Mayer and Rosenblatt 1973a).

Understanding the worker's behavior is not the same as excusing it. Even though there may be understandable reasons for noncompliant behavior, clients are still harmed as a result and the agency's objectives are not implemented. Being "therapeutic" to workers in permitting them to continue to operate contrary to agency policy may be antitherapeutic to the clients.

From an ethical perspective supervisors are in a defensible position in requiring workers to do what the agency asks of them and in enforcing agency policy, rules, and procedures. The Milford Conference Report (1929) early emphasized the professional obligation of the worker to adhere "to the policies and regulations of the organization . . . policies once adopted by an agency are binding upon its entire personnel." The Code of Ethics of the National Association of Social Workers states that the social worker should adhere to commitments made to the employing agency. Levy (1982) notes that "the very acceptance of employment in a social organization constitutes, in itself, a promise of loyalty to the organization and devotion to its purpose and function (p. 48) . . . whatever procedures have been defined for accomplishing the work of the social organization nonadministrative staff are obliged to follow" (p. 50).

Compton and Galaway (1975) strongly support this obligation. They clearly state that they do not believe that a "worker who accepts a position as a member of an agency—and who utilizes agency resources—can act as though he were a private practitioner—as a staff member, the worker is bound by the policies of the agency" (p. 481). Of course, "loyalty and devotion to the employing organization is neither absolute nor infinite" (Levy 1982, p. 48). Opposition to, and deviance from, agency policy may be ethically required where clients are harmed by policy and the policy itself is unethical. Deviation is then justified on the grounds of superseding values.

The profession of social work and the community has looked to the supervisor as the first line of defense in behalf of the client, the agency, and the community, in responding to worker behavior that might represent a danger to the client, agency, or community. This charge is embodied in the monitoring, review, and evaluative functions of administrative supervision. When the supervisor has failed, either because of ideological hesitancy, incompetence, or indifference in implementing the functions of administrative supervision, the community has imposed external review-control procedures on the agency.

The child welfare services system reflects the consequences of such failure. Widespread criticism was directed against foster care throughout the 1960s and 1970s. It was said that children were unjustifiably placed and replaced, that children were lost in a system insufficiently and carelessly monitored, that damage was done to children who lived for long periods of time in limbo because of failure to review their situation. In the drive to achieve "permanence for children" as early as possible, procedures were developed outside the agency—in court review of placements and in citizen review boards.

In many states Juvenile and Domestic Relations Courts are authorized to review child welfare cases to determine whether the worker's decision is in the child's best interest—this in effect is judiciary supervision of the agency's work. Citizen Review Boards are authorized to monitor and review the worker's activities to determine among other things "what efforts have been made to carry out permanent placement" plans for a child and "make recommendations" about actions that might be taken (Conte et al. 1981).

By 1980 there was, in most states, monitoring and review by some external agency of the decisions and the work of the direct service child welfare social worker. The ultimate explanation of and justification for such procedures was the perceived failure of the internal agency monitoring and review system—a failure of agency supervision.

The fact that Citizen Review Boards, generally consisting of volunteers, have been legally authorized and established in a number of states to assess the performance of direct service workers and recommend changes in service intervention is a testimonial to the perceived failure of supervisors, who initially had this review responsibility (Conte et al. 1981). It is clear that if first-line supervisors inadequately review and monitor the work of their supervisees, others outside the profession will take over a measure of this responsibility, as has already happened in foster care in response to similar problems.

In response to this concern and the possibility of imposition of external controls, a national study of social work in England sponsored by the National Institute for Social Work recommended a "formal system to enable senior management to monitor what goes on and by which they can ensure that clients with similar needs are treated with reasonable consistency, that resources are fairly allocated, and that staff overstep neither the boundaries of law nor generally agreed standards of conduct" (Barclay Report 1982, p. 129).

A more committed adherence to the implementation of the essential functions of administrative supervision may help to modify the stereotypical perceptions of "policy makers, governmental executives, and top level agency managers" as well as the public "that somehow social work is antithetical to good management. The training and personal predispositions of social workers, in this view, make them ill-suited for managerial positions that require, among other things, rational analysis, a willingness to ferret out inefficient practices and force compliance with policies and procedures" (Patti 1984, p. 25).

Taking Disciplinary Action

It needs to be noted that most workers, on most occasions, do conscientiously comply with agency policies, rules, and procedures. Noncompliance is the exception. However, the limited number of exceptions give the supervisor a maximum amount of difficulty. A disproportionate amount of time and psychic energy needs to be devoted to the few workers who frequently are noncompliant.

The supervisor in his role as protector of agency policies, rules, and procedures may have to get supervisees to do some things in some particular way or have them stop from doing some things in some particular way. The supervisor may find himself in a position where he has to employ sanctions in requiring compliance with agency policy, rules, and procedures, where he has to take corrective action. Supervisors face situations in which workers consistently fail to get work done on time, are consistently late or absent, fail to turn in reports, or complete forms carelessly, conspicuously loaf on the job, disrupt work of others by excessive gossiping, are careless with agency cars or equipment, are inconsiderate, insulting, or disrespectful to clients, or fail to keep appointments with personnel of cooperating agencies and services.

Such situations should not be permitted to develop unchecked. There generally are prior indications of resistance or opposition to compliance. If earlier manifestations have been ignored, if the supervisor "looks the other way," it becomes progressively more difficult to take action when action can no longer be avoided. The supervisee can rightly claim that the supervisor has been remiss in never having earlier discussed the behavior he now wants stopped. The supervisor's effectiveness in dealing with the situation is reduced by feelings of guilt and defensiveness. A supervisor writes:

> In our last conference of the year, I hesitantly raised the question of B's persistent lateness to meetings and conferences. I had been aware of this failure on her part, but for a variety of reasons, had overlooked to deal with this directly. At this time, my opening this issue resulted in [B's] unburdening herself of a number of severe personal and family problems. I dealt with these as appropriately as possible, but referred back to the lateness, etc. B acknowledged her discomfort with her behavior, but felt she had not been sure about my expectations because I had not previously made an issue of this. I agreed . . . and we ended with some appreciation for not having completely overlooked an important part of her development. The timing was unfortunate, in that this problem should have been dealt with much earlier in the year for it seemed to be symptomatically tied to important personal blockings that were interfering with [B's] development. Perhaps my "better late than never" behavior was similar to what she had been doing all year!

The supervisor should discuss in private the problem that calls for a reprimand. To criticize a worker in front of his peers makes it more difficult to help him change his behavior. A supervisee writes that she was late in submitting a monthly statistical report:

> The supervisor meeting me in the hall loudly reprimanded me in the presence of other workers and threatened to put my report-lateness in his evaluation. The supervisor returned to his office without giving me a chance to reply. The supervisor had a chance to release his anger but

he was unsuccessful in getting my report in any sooner. I was sore. He publicly called attention to what I had done. It was nobody else's business. He never gave me a chance to explain—or even asked for an explanation.

A reprimand is also best delivered at a time when the supervisor is not upset about the incident, as well as in private. These two suggestions, which require delay, contradict a third suggestion, that a discussion of the incident should take place as soon as possible after it occurs. However, they can be reconciled by noting that while a delay is desirable for cooling off and for provision of privacy, the delay should be as short as possible.

In what follows a supervisor takes peremptory but necessary action in dealing with noncompliance. The context is a probation and parole office.

I happened to be passing by Helen's door as a client was leaving and overheard her say that he shouldn't worry about completing auto operation and permission forms (an agency requirement) because "they weren't that important." I felt upset that she was cooperating with a client to decrease compliance with important agency regulations. I asked that she meet with me and asked if her client had secured a car, if she had seen proof of a driver's license, insurance, and really thought about giving him permission to drive? I was being accusatory and Helen stated that it was stupid that a grown man should have to have our permission to own and operate his own car. I suggested that perhaps she wasn't aware that without completing the procedures with the required proof, if he committed another offense in which the vehicle was used, the agency would be accountable—that if he were stopped without a permission form he would be taken to jail. It became more a rebuking lecture than I meant it bo be. She said that she wasn't aware of all of this (another failure on my part) and thought that it was just a repressive measure to keep the clients under control. I left her office with the comment that the forms must be completed (an order), that they protected the agency, the client, the community, her, and myself.

The best approach is one which communicates concern for the supervisee, a willingness to listen to his explanation of what happened, a desire to understand how he sees the situation and a readiness to help him change. The emphasis is on a change of behavior so as to increase the agency's effectiveness of service rather than on the apprehension and punishment of noncompliance. If the supervisor perceives noncompliance as a threat or an act of hostility, any discussion of the incident is apt to be emotionally charged. Regarding it as a learning opportunity for the worker or as an opportunity for improving the supervisor-supervisee relationship generates a different, more positive, attitude.

The objective of such supervisory intervention is preventative and corrective rather than punitive. In reprimanding, the supervisor must be impersonal, specific as to the facts, and consistent in his approach. The supervisor needs to be aware that in disciplining one she is disciplining all. Supervisor behavior manifested in dealing with one supervisee in a disciplinary action will affect the reactions of all supervisees.

The supervisor should make some record of the incident so that if there is a recurrence, and more severe sanctions need to be employed, they can be justified by the record. There is a series of actions the supervisor might take, graded in terms of increasing severity. The first is a joint review of the situation by supervisor and supervisee. The supervisor can offer the worker a warning, followed, if the behavior continues, with a verbal reprimand. This might be followed by a written reprimand which is placed in the record, a lower than average evaluation rating, suspension for a limited period, demotion, and ultimately dismissal.

Serious disciplinary action such as suspension without pay for a period of time, demotion, or firing requires documentation. Such action will in all probability require a defense in response to a grievance procedure currently operative in most agencies, particularly those under civil service or union contracts.

If individual noncompliance is not effectively dealt with at the supervisory level, the administration may make it a matter for agency policy decision making. Such matters, when made agency policy, reduce flexibility at the direct service level. All the workers then suffer from some reduction in autonomy as a result of the dereliction in compliance by a few workers. Because of the possibility of such an eventuality, workers tend to support supervisors in their efforts to obtain compliance.

A supervisor details the positive use of sanctions in the following example:

> A woman in her mid-50s with a college education but no work experience was hired by a public welfare agency as a caseworker. Serious

problems began to manifest themselves and the worker appeared over-whelmed by the poverty she observed visiting the homes of welfare clients. She became emotionally involved with clients' problems and attempted to personally meet their needs, supplying money from her own funds, clothing from her family, even cooking and delivering meals to the sick. At the same time she showed little sensitivity to the feelings of the clients and no conception of the meaning of confiden-tiality. Other problems that interfered with effective social work were chronic tardiness, conducting personal business and going to the beauty shop on agency time, habitual reckless driving which resulted in a series of minor accidents, a poor relationship with other staff members and aggressive resistance to supervision.

The supervisor in this situation recognized the problems and the emotional needs of the worker and planned for more intensive super-visory help than usually given an average new worker. When no im-provement was noted and the problems even became worse, the supervisor arranged for the worker to be transferred to another unit with a different supervisor. When this did not result in improvement in any of the problem areas, the decision was made to terminate em-ployment before the end of the probationary period. At each step the supervisor had attempted to discuss the problems frankly with the worker although she seemed to have no insight into her role in them and advised her to seek employment in another type of work. The worker appealed her dismissal but the supervisor's decision was up-held. Shortly afterwards the woman took a job as a bookkeeper and held it for over ten years to the apparent satisfaction of herself and her employer.

The supervisor's early recognition of the problem, implementation of vigorous and planned efforts to deal with it, recognition of the futility of these efforts, and prompt, appropriate and firm action bene-fited both the employee and the agency.

Summary

This chapter reviewed some of the significant problems in imple-menting administrative supervision. The supervisor is responsible for the actions of her supervisees in accordance with the principles of vicarious liability and respondeat superiore. The supervisor is granted a measure of authority and power by agency administration in support of this ultimate responsibility. Authority was defined as the legitimation of the use of power. Power was defined as the ability to implement the right authority. Five sources of power were dis-cussed: reward, coercive, positional, referent, expertise.

A further distinction was made between functional power (relating to the personal attributes of the supervisor), and formal power (inherent in the position of supervisor).

The supervisor needs to come to terms with the delegation of authority and power. Power and authority should be used only when necessary to help achieve the objectives of the organization, in a flexible, impartial manner and with a sensitive regard for worker response.

Despite the grant of authority, supervisors are reluctant to actively employ their power. Power and authority are further eroded by the nature of social work tasks and by the countervailing power of supervisees. As a consequence of the reluctant and difficult utilization of supervisory power, external sources of control have been developed, particularly in child welfare.

In implementing the functions of administrative supervision the supervisor needs some appreciation of the utility of rules and an understanding of the factors relating to noncompliance. The process of disciplining workers for noncompliant behavior was reviewed.

CHAPTER FOUR
Educational Supervision

EDUCATIONAL SUPERVISION is the second principal responsibility of the supervisor. Educational supervision is concerned
with teaching the worker what he needs to know in order to do his
job and helping him to learn it. Every job description of the supervisor's position includes a listing of this function: "instruct workers
in acceptable social work techniques"; "develop staff competence
through individual and group conferences"; "train and instruct staff
in job performance."

Studies of functions which supervisors identified as those which
they performed included such educational activities as "teaching,"
"facilitating learning," "training," "sharing experience and knowledge," "informing," "clarifying," "guiding," "helping workers find
solutions," "enhancing professional growth," "advising," "suggesting," "helping workers solve problems."

Educational supervision is sometimes termed clinical supervision. It is concerned with teaching the knowledge, skills, and attitudes necessary for the performance of clinical social work tasks
through the detailed analysis of the worker's interaction with the
client.

I noted earlier that one of the singular aspects of social work is
that a very sizable percentage of agency staff come to the job without prior training. There is also considerable turnover and lateral
job movement from agency to agency. Consequently there is a constant need to train people to do the job of the social worker and to do
the job in a particular agency. The responsibility for such training is
assigned to staff-development personnel, which include first-line
supervisors when they are engaged in educational supervision.

Some distinction needs to be made between staff development,
in-service training, and educational supervision. Staff development
refers to all of the procedures an agency might employ to enhance
the job-related knowledge, skills, and attitudes of its total staff, and
includes in-service training and educational supervision. Training

140   EDUCATIONAL SUPERVISION

sessions, lectures, workshops, institutes, information pamphlets, and discussion groups for caseworkers, administrators, clerical staff, and supervisors are staff-development activities.

In-service training is a more specific form of staff development. The term refers to planned, formal training provided to a delimited group of agency personnel who have the same job classification or the same job responsibilities. In-service training programs are planned on an a priori basis in terms of the general educational needs of a group of workers. The generic teaching content is applicable to all members of the group but is specifically relevant to none. Educational supervision supplements in-service training by individualizing general learning in application to the specific performance of the individual worker.

Educational supervision is a still more specific kind of staff development. Here training is directed to the needs of a particular worker carrying a particular case load, encountering particular problems and needing some individualized program of education.

The supervisor in discharging the responsibilities of educational supervision helps the worker implement and apply the more general learning provided through the in-service training program. He teaches "the worker what he needs to know to give specific service to specific clients" (Bell, n.d., p. 15) and helps the worker make the transition from knowing to doing. In-service training and educational supervision complement each other. The supervisor will reinforce, individualize, and demonstrate the applicability of the more general content taught in planned, formal in-service training sessions (Meyer 1966).

Educational supervision is a line, rather than a staff, function. The supervisor has administrative responsibility for the supervisees to whom she is offering training. Other staff-development activities may be the responsibility of specialized personnel whose sole concern is education of staff and who have no administrative responsibility for the staff they are training.

Educational supervision is a very significant dimension of the supervisor's activities and responsibilities. Two of the three strongest sources of satisfaction for supervisors are "satisfaction in helping the supervisee grow and develop as a professional" and "satisfaction in sharing social work knowledge and skills with supervisees." Two of the three main sources of supervisee satisfaction with supervision are related to educational supervision: "my supervisor helps me in dealing with problems in my work with clients" and "my supervisor helps me in my development as a professional social worker." In addition both supervisors and supervisees agreed that "ensuring the professional developments of the supervisee" was one of the two most important objectives of supervision (Kadushin 1974).

Conversely, when supervision fails, the failures are most keenly felt in the area of educational supervision. Two major sources of dissatisfaction expressed by supervisees relate to this function: "my supervisor is not sufficiently critical of my work so that I don't know what I am doing wrong or what needs changing" and "my supervisor does not provide much real help in dealing with problems I face with my clients" (Kadushin 1974).

Shulman (1982) studied the reports from both supervisees and supervisors regarding the actual functions the supervisors were perceived to perform and preferred functions. Both groups indicated that a considerable amount of the supervisor's time was spent in teaching-consulting. Furthermore the "largest increase of preferred to actual time spent" indicated by both supervisiors and supervisees involved increased time in "teaching practice skills" (pp. 22–23). An interview study of 20 supervisors in a state public welfare department found that 60 percent of the supervisors rated assisting workers as the most satisfying part of their job. (Weatherley et al. 1980).

Relationship of Educational Supervision to Administrative Supervision

Administrative supervision and educational supervision share the same ultimate objective, to provide the best possible service to the clients. Administrative supervision provides the structure directed toward this goal; educational supervision provides the training which enables workers to achieve it.

Administrative supervision is concerned with structuring the work environment and providing the resources which enable the workers to perform their job effectively. Educational supervision provides the knowledge and instrumental skills which are the workers' necessary equipment for effective practice.

Educational and administrative supervision also reinforce each other. Educational supervision is designed to increase the effectiveness of administrative supervision. As a consequence of educational supervision the tasks of administrative supervision are alternatively implemented. "Training and guided experience [take] the place of detailed and close supervision as a means of accomplishing the same control functions" (Olmstead 1973, p. 90). With more education, workers can act more autonomously and independently, reducing the burden of administrative supervision.

Attitudes of commitment and loyalty to agency values, aims, and procedures are developed through educational supervision. If the agency can, through education, indoctrinate workers with a personal interest in doing what the agency wants done, in the way the agency wants it done, toward objectives the agency wants to achieve, the agency will be less hesitant to delegate authority for autonomous performance. Educational supervision provides administrative controls through a process of helping the worker internalize such controls.

We are using the term "indoctrinate" here in its least pejorative sense, to mean a form of consciousness raising. As Olmstead says, "Indoctrination is the process by which personnel internalize sets of principles and values that will, in part, govern their behavior. Much of professional education is, in effect, indoctrination" (1973, p. 87).

Educational supervision involves the communication of a belief system which has, as one of its tenets, the legitimation of the agency's authority structure. Such socialization has, as one of its aims, the "engineering of consent" so that ultimately the supervisee voluntarily endorses the legitimacy of the supervisor's positional authority.

Simon (1957) cogently summarizes the relationship between the functions of educational and administrative supervision:

> Training influences decisions "from the inside out." That is, training prepares the organization member to reach satisfactory decisions himself without the need for the constant exercise of authority or advice. In this sense training procedures are alternatives to the exercise of authority or advice as means of control over the subordinate's decision. . . . It may be possible to minimize or even dispense with certain review processes by giving the subordinates training that enables them to perform their work with less supervision. Training may supply

the trainee with the facts necessary in dealing with these decisions, it may provide him with a frame of reference for his thinking; it may teach him "approved" decisions; or it may indoctrinate him with the values in terms of which his decisions are to be made. (pp. 15–16)

Recruited from a wide variety of backgrounds having different sets of experiences, having learned the language and mind set of different academic disciplines, recruits to social work positions need to be educated to a common frame of reference, a common view of agency objectives and a uniform commitment to common goals. Unless differences can be reduced there is little possibility of having a staff operating in some consistent manner. One of the educational tasks of supervision is to help the worker accept the frame of reference, point of view, and objectives to which other workers in the agency subscribe and which guides their actions and behavior.

While the organization's control apparatus, manifested in administrative supervision, exerts an external pressure encouraging workers to conform to agency policies and procedures, educational supervision ultimately results in an internalization of such influence efforts. Both administrative and educational supervision are directed toward changing worker behavior in the direction necessary for effective performance as an agency worker. The achievement of this objective in moving from administrative supervision to educational supervision is the movement from direction by the supervisor to self-direction by the supervisee.

Professional socialization involves the reduction of idiosyncrasy. Lay attitudes and approaches to problems are diverse; professional approaches tend to be more homogeneous. Professional socialization involves taking on a professional identity and a special outlook regarding one's work which is shared with colleagues. Educational supervision is the context for role transition from lay person to professional, providing the supervisee with this sense of occupational identity.

Because administrative supervision and educational supervision provide alternative procedures for control of workers' performance, more of one requires less of the other. Hall (1968) concluded from a study of the relationship of bureaucracy and professionalism in a number of different professions, including social work, that "an equilibrium may exist between the levels of professionalization and bureaucratization in the sense that a particular level of professionalization may require a certain level of bureaucratization to maintain social control" (p. 104). Higher levels of professionalization were associated with lower levels of bureaucratization. Similarly, Hage and Aiken (1967), in a study of 16 social welfare and health agencies, found that "close supervision is less likely when members of an organization are professionally active . . . and when they have been professionally trained" (p. 90).

Development of knowledge and skills, as a consequence of educational supervision, permits relaxation of administrative controls. Not only will the worker feel a personal obligation to do a good job, he will have the necessary competence and capability to do so.

Educational supervision permits smoother administrative coordination and more effective communication. Having learned how the agency operates, and what the functions of other people are in the agency, the worker can coordinate his own work with others. Having learned the specialized language of the agency and the profession, the worker can communicate with colleagues with fewer risks of misunderstanding. The shared "universe of discourse" aids communication. Making decisions on the basis of mutually shared values, presuppositions, and knowledge increases the predictability of the workers' actions. Thinking in a way which is similar to the thinking of their fellow professionals, they are likely to come to the same conclusions independently. And homogeneity of thinking among fellow agency workers makes it easier to coordinate the work of different groups in the agency.

Studying changing interpersonal perceptions of social work supervisors and supervisees over a period of a year, MacGuffie, Janzen, and McPhee (1970) found a growing congruence in perception. Supervisor-supervisee interactions toward the end of the year were based on developed communalities in perception which tended "to minimize the chance of distorted communications and to clarify both cognitions and feelings of co-communicators" (p. 268). Education of the supervisee to the consensus of values, uniformity of perspectives, and standardization of language shared by other workers in the agency reduces the likelihood of intra-agency conflict while increasing the level of intra-agency cooperation.

As a result of educational supervision the worker is in a better position to evaluate his own performance. He learns the difference between good and poor practice and has some criteria by which he can be self-critical. Thus the administrative supervisory functions of control, coordination, communications, cooperation, and evaluation are all made easier as a consequence of educational supervision.

Conditions for Effective Teaching and Learning

The supervisor's principal responsibility in educational supervision is to teach the worker how to do the job. Our task here is to delineate what promotes effective teaching and learning. The teacher can organize content, provide a suitable atmosphere for learning, and make learning available but cannot ensure its acceptance and certainly not its use. This only the learner can do. Teaching is essentially the "art of assisting another to learn." As Robinson says, "Teaching provides the subject matter, the stimulus, the materials, sets the tasks and defines the conditions. But learning is the process of utilizing opportunity and limits in one's own way for one's own ends" (1936, p. 128). Learning is a creative personal experience.

The supervisor, in implementing educational supervision, has the responsibility of knowing the content that needs to be learned, of knowing how to teach it effectively and for creating, sustaining, and managing a social and emotional environment which facilitates learning.

Our interest, therefore, is in how learners learn. The supervisor needs to be aware of some of the factors that facilitate learning and know something about techniques that maximize it. In this section I outline some general principles of learning and some techniques derived from these principles that are applicable to the supervisory conference. In the absence of a comprehensive, generally accepted "integrating theory in pedagogy," there is "principally a body of maxims" (Bruner 1971, p. 31) which may, nonetheless, be highly useful.

Principle

We learn best if we are highly motivated to learn. In applying this principle the supervisor can use the following techniques.

Techniques

1. Explain the usefulness of the content to be taught. We owe the worker some explanation as to why it might be important for him to know this material if he is to discharge his professional responsibilities effectively. Motivation increases as usefulness of the content becomes clear. The new worker may not appreciate the importance, for instance, of learning effective referral procedures. If we can show, by citing the relevant research, the sizable percentage of people who need referral service and the effects of different referral procedures on subsequent client experience, the worker may better understand the significance of this unit of learning. The adult learner is concerned with current problems that require learning for solution. In teaching-learning situations involving adults we can take advantage of this orientation by stressing the utility and applicability of what is learned.

2. Make learning meaningful in terms of the individual worker's motives and needs. However useful or significant the material is generally, the worker is not likely to be motivated unless one can show its usefulness and importance for a problem or situation that is meaningful to her. Showing how the supervisee could have improved on her last interview if she had had a surer grasp of the dynamics of behavior will do more to increase motivation than lectures on the general importance of such knowledge.

The closer the training is to the job of the worker, the more specific it is to the worker's problems, the more directly it is perceived by the worker as meeting his needs and satisfying her concerns. This has been found repeatedly in a national study of in-service training in child welfare (Vinokur 1983).

3. Tie areas of low motivation to areas of high motivation. The worker may be highly motivated to help the client but indifferent to the content which the supervisor is attempting to teach—for instance, recording. If the supervisor can demonstrate that recording

permits the worker to be more helpful to the client, he may then be motivated to learn it.

One needs to be aware of the variety of the possible motives for learning. Motivation is "an internal process initiated by a need which leads to goal seeking." Intrinsic motives are tied to the content itself. People want to study the content because they are interested in the material itself, because there is satisfaction in meeting the challenge of the content and mastering it, because there is pleasure in solving professional problems and in acquiring knowledge.

Motives may be largely extrinsic, however. Learning the content is only a way of reaching other goals. There may be psychic rewards from the approbation of peers, the supervisor, parents, one's own professional superego. Other psychic rewards are derived from competitively learning better than sibling-peers in the agency. Learning the content may be motivated by a desire for autonomy and independence, so that one does not have to turn to the supervisor for help. There may be administrative rewards such as pay raises and promotions.

Motives for learning may result from a developing commitment to the agency, its staff, and its objectives. Having a strong conviction in the agency's objectives, the worker wants to see them achieved as effectively as possible. Motivation is strengthened by identification with the agency and colleagues. Feeling identified with the agency, the worker wants the agency to be favorably perceived by the community; feeling loyal and close to his colleagues, he wants their good opinion. As a consequence of these considerations, the worker is motivated to learn so as to be as competent as possible.

Research on the nature of job satisfaction helps clarify the incentives that are likely to motivate on-the-job learning. The main studies on job satisfaction have been done by Herzberg and his group in a wide variety of contexts (Herzberg 1968; Herzberg, Mausner, and Snyderman 1959). Five factors were identified as the principal sources of job satisfaction for most people. Arranged in order of frequency, these are: achievement (feeling pleased with something done in which one would take pride); recognition (good work was commented on and complimented); the work itself (the work was interesting, challenging, varied); responsibility (freedom to do the work independently and autonomously); and advancement (the possibility of moving up to more responsible positions). These factors can be used to motivate learning. For instance, there is greater possibility of meeting the need for achievement if the worker learns how to do the job more effectively; learning to do the job increases the probability that the worker will be granted more responsibility, more opportunity to work independently; and learning to do the job enhances the possibility of advancement.

We would do well to utilize any and all motives to optimize learning. If the worker wants a promotion or raise, or a student wants a high grade, we can tie these motives to the need to learn the content as a requirement for achieving their goals.

Motivation increases receptivity to learning and makes energy available for learning. It thus sets the stage for learning and provides the teachable moment. But it does not in itself make for learning. The supervisor has to take advantage of the teachable situation to teach something of significance. Motivation needs to be provided with a learning opportunity and direction. The supervisor provides guidance to the learning that motivation seeks.

4. Since motivation is of such crucial significance, the supervisor needs to safeguard and stimulate motivation where it exists, and instill motivation where it does not. Motivation indicates a readiness for learning. A worker who lacks motivation to learn certain content may have no felt need for it. He is satisfied with what he is doing, in the way he is doing it. He has no problem that requires additional learning for its solution. The worker may be right, in which case the supervisor has nothing to teach him.

If the supervisor, however, is convinced that the worker's perception of his performance is wrong and that there is much he needs to learn, she would first have to stimulate dissatisfaction with his performance. The supervisor may want to confront the worker with the gap between what he is doing and what he can do, what he is doing and what needs to be done, what he is doing and what he wants to be able to do. Dissatisfaction with his current performance is a necessary prerequisite before the worker is ready to learn new and better ways of working with the client.

Consequently, the supervisor makes a deliberate but compassionate effort to create some desire for, or curiosity about, the learning she has to offer. Rather than being passive in the face of lack of motivation, the supervisor acts as a catalyst for change, creating tension that needs to be resolved. The worker's equilibrium needs to be disturbed if receptivity to learning is to be stimulated.

At times the "supervisor must awaken anxiety by penetrating the rationalization and defenses that bind it. If the supervisor avoids conflict for purposes of keeping the supervisory relationship untroubled and outwardly smooth he will have abdicated his responsibility to the supervisee and will have compromised his trustworthiness" (Mueller and Kell 1972, pp. 30-31).

Motivation for learning follows the general principle that all behavior is purposive. We learn only when we want to learn, when we feel a need to learn. While this justifies stimulation of a need, such a procedure may be unnecessary. The first assumption about an apparently unmotivated supervisee might well be that we are not sensitive enough to discern the motives that he does have. It would initially be better to attempt to understand and use those motives which the learner himself brings to the situation. We might need to recognize that in some cases the problem is not that the worker is unmotivated but that he is differently motivated. The problem is not lack of motivation but difference in motivation. Discovering the nature of these different motivations we might be able to exploit them in the service of motivating learning.

Principle

We learn best when we can devote most of our energies in the learning situation to learning. Energy needed to defend against rejection, anxiety, guilt, shame, fear of failure, attacks on autonomy, or uncertain expectations, is energy deflected from learning. We can maximize the amount of energy available to learning in the following ways.

Techniques

1. Clearly establish the rules of the game regarding time, place, roles, limits, expectations, obligations, and objectives. If the worker is anxious because he is uncertain of what is expected from him in the role of supervisee, he is not fully free to devote full attention to

learning. The nature of the supervisory relationship should be clear. The frequency of supervisory meetings, the length of such conferences, the respective responsibilities, expectations, and obligations of supervisee and supervisor in preparation for, and in the conduct of, such conferences should be clearly established, mutually understood, and mutually accepted. Such details provide the comfort of an unambiguous structure.

Clarity relates to learning objectives as well. The supervisor needs to know, and to share with the supervisee, some idea of where he hopes the learner is going, what she will know and be able to do after she has learned what the supervisor hopes to teach. Objectives give meaning to each discrete learning unit and permit us to measure progress. As Seneca said, "No wind is favorable if you do not know your destination."

2. Respect the worker's rights, within limits, to determine his or her own solutions. The structure, while supportive in its clarity, should not be so rigid that it becomes restrictive. Some flexibility needs to be permitted the supervisee so as to prevent psychic energy from being diverted from learning to deal with rising hostility and resentment at infantilization. This is particularly true in adult education since the learner operates with considerable freedom and autonomy in other significant areas of his life. Here, however, he is partially dependent, as is every learner who needs to turn to others to teach him what he does not yet know. As a generally independent adult, he is more apt to resent this necessary dependency. The supervisor should then permit the greatest amount of independence that the learner can profitably use without danger to the client. Respect for the worker's autonomy and initiative ensures that psychic energy necessary for learning will not be dissipated in defense of autonomy.

3. Establish an atmosphere of accepting, psychological safety, a framework of security. Learning implies a risk of mistakes and a risk of failure. It implies, too, a confession of ignorance. A worker who fears censure and rejection for admitting failure or ignorance will devote psychic energy to defense against such anticipated attacks. The supervisor should be the supervisee's mentor rather than tormentor. An atmosphere of acceptance permits a freer involvement in risk-taking and a greater psychic concentration on learning rather than on self-defense.

The effects of the supervisor's attitude of acceptance on the worker's performance is described by a worker.

> I didn't feel that I was getting criticized for what I was doing. So a lot of my feelings of anxiety and discomfort began to dissipate as I was not getting criticism from him; therefore, I wasn't criticizing myself— as harshly anyway. And I was feeling more comfortable. As I began to feel more comfortable—the more comfortable I felt, it's like the more ready I was to take that more critical look at what I had done. The more sure I felt that I wasn't a complete asshole, that I wasn't blowing it right and left, that I was O.K. in the room—I wasn't going to perma- nently damage anybody or any of that—and that the person I was presenting was really myself and not something that I was trying to do for my absent supervisor, the more ready I became to ask questions of myself and what I was doing in technique and all that. It wasn't laden with all the feelings and all the anxiety and all that. (Diane 1977, p. 136)

The impact on the supervisee of a supervisor who communicates nonacceptance is described by a supervisee.

> I would just get angrier and angrier inside and I would get tighter and tighter and more closed, and whatever it was that we were supposed to be talking about around my client no longer became important be- cause the dynamics that were going on between the two of us were so heavy that I couldn't even think about whatever it was that I was supposed to be thinking about. (Diane 1977, p. 95)

Learning does not merely result in adding knowledge and skills to those already available to the learner. Learning involves the risk of change in attitudes, values, and behavior as the new learning modi- fies the perception of the world and of people. The risk of change is anxiety-provoking. We often fear what the consequences of change might be for us. If the supervisor is empathic in regard to the anx- iety created by change resulting from learning and is supportive, there is less of a need to devote psychic energy to defend against change and to bind associated anxiety.

But acceptance involves expectations. Psychological safety does not mean a permissiveness that ignores the demand for adequate performance on the part of the worker. We must make firm de- mands on the worker for learning what she needs to learn. But our demands are made in a friendly way, out of a desire to help rather than to hurt. They do create tension. However, such tension is necessary to motivate the supervisee to learn.

The supervisor has to be consistently helpful to the supervisee rather than consistently popular. This means challenging error, calling attention to ignorance, pointing to mistakes and deficiencies in performance. The supervisor has to offer a judicious balance between stimulus and support. The supervisor is responsible for maintaining the balance between a degree of tension which motivates and challenges, and a degree of tension which immobilizes. We utilize the tension which derives not from the fear of failure but from the discrepancy between what the worker knows and what he wants to know. It involves making demands with the utmost possible respect, compassion, and understanding. It would be foolish to pretend that balancing these contradictory and vaguely defined variables is anything but the most difficult of tasks.

4. Acknowledge and use what the worker already knows and can do. This technique decreases anxiety since it indicates to the worker that he can draw on what he already knows to meet the demands of supervision. Affirmation and use of the already rich learning the worker brings to the teaching-learning situation is an advantageous aspect of adult education.

5. Move from the familiar to the unfamiliar. The unfamiliar provokes anxiety. If the supervisor can relate new material to familiar material, the new learning seems less strange, and less difficult to learn.

6. Demonstrate confidence, if warranted, in the worker's ability to learn. He himself may have doubts about his ability, doubts against which he needs to defend himself at some expenditure of psychic energy robbed from learning. Communication of a feeling of confidence in the worker's ability, where warranted, helps to allay feelings which detract from learning. Confidence in the learner's ability to learn is contagious. Communication of confidence increases motivation for, and interest in, learning.

At the same time the supervisor has to accept, and make allowances for, the fact that learning is a growth process and takes time. One must expect nonproductive plateaus where little progress is being made. There needs to be time for reflection, absorption, consolidation of learning. There is likely to be some regression in learning, much zigging and zagging. Like all growth processes, it is uneven and variable, and different kinds of content are learned at different rates of speed.

7. Know your content; be ready and willing to teach it. The supervisor not only needs the wish but also the ability to be helpful. The worker does not know what he needs to know and this makes him anxious. His anxiety is tempered, however, by the fact that if he does not know, at least the supervisor knows the answer to some of his questions. Not only does she know but she is willing to share this knowledge with him, if necessary. If the supervisor does not know, or seems unwilling to share her knowledge, this increases tension since it suggests to the supervisee that he faces the prospect of dealing with situations for which he has no adequate assistance available. Inevitably on some occasions, the supervisor might have to say, "I don't know." But then she needs to add, "We will try to find out." Lack of knowledge in a situation which requires responsible action is anxiety provoking. Knowing that someone knows and is ready to provide the helpful knowledge diminishes anxiety. It might be noted that supervisor competence rather than omniscience is all that the supervisee does, and can, expect. But the greater professional competence of the supervisor can help to meet the supervisees' legitimate dependency needs. And the supervisor has to be capable and ready to meet these needs.

The negative effect on the supervisee when perceived legitimate dependency needs are thwarted is described by a supervisee.

> And sometimes her tone would get condescending: "Now, B., you're bright. You can think of that." For instance, if I was having difficulty with something and asked for some suggestions, that would be the sort of response she would give me. It was like, unless I did everything on my own, I wasn't putting forth enough effort. I could've used at times more help from her—very direct help—rather than, "What do you think?" There were a couple times when we went back and forth—it's amazing—where she'd say, "Well, what do you think?" after I asked for help; and I'd say, "I don't know, what do you think?" And she would—very straight-faced—comes back with, "Well, what do you think?" And I'd say, "Look, H., I really thought about it very hard; and I can't come up with anything else. That's why I'm asking you." (Diane 1977, pp. 154–55)

Principle

We learn best when learning is attended by positive satisfactions—when it is successful and rewarding. We seek to repeat what has been satisfying and avoid repeating what is painful.

Techniques

1. Set conditions of learning so as to ensure high probability of success. A successful experience in one's practice rewards and reinforces the behavior associated with the successful experience.

It would be inadvisable to present the worker with a learning demand that is clearly beyond his capacity to meet it. If there is little chance of success, there is little motivation to try. The learner needs some assurance that he can succeed if he is going to risk himself in trying. On the other hand, the task needs to be sufficiently challenging to engage the worker's interest and prompt him to extend himself. If a task is too easy, one is not likely to experience a feeling of success in achieving it. Selecting a learning task that is challenging but not overwhelming is a neat trick. It is, admittedly, much easier to describe than to do, particularly without any gauge by which to measure how much challenge a worker can hope to meet successfully.

2. We increase positive satisfactions in learning if we praise, where warranted, success in professional accomplishment. Praise is a psychic reward that reinforces the behavior that prompted the commendation. Indiscriminate praise is counterproductive, however. The supervisee is an adult capable of independent critical assessment of his own performance. If we praise performance which he recognizes as substandard, we lose credibility in his eyes and our subsequent assessments are discounted. The worker might feel he cannot trust our judgment. It is, therefore, important to commend only what can be defended as objectively praiseworthy. The supervisor should be specific about the behavior which has elicited approval. Not the general statement, "You really indicated your understanding of Mr. P.'s behavior," but the specific statement, "You really indicated your understanding of Mr. P.'s behavior when you said . . . in response to his comment about. . . ." Such specif-

icity not only ensures that such learning is attended by positive satisfactions because it is being rewarded but also makes conscious and explicit the behavior which the supervisor hopes to reinforce.

Pleasure and pain, reward and punishment overlap with the question of motivation in learning. We are motivated to learn so that we can avoid the pain that comes from inability to deal successfully with problems in job performance. We are motivated to learn so as to feel the pleasure of doing a job competently and effectively. We are motivated to learn so that we can avoid the punishment of being dependent and can obtain the reward of acting autonomously. We are motivated to learn so that we can avoid the pain of criticism and guilt and be rewarded with praise and approbation from ourselves and from "significant others," including the supervisor. We are motivated to learn to avoid the dissatisfaction which comes from the uncertainty of not clearly knowing what we are supposed to be doing or how to do it. We are motivated to learn in order to feel the satisfaction in the security which comes from knowing, with assurance, what it's all about.

3. Praise through positive feedback. Such reinforcement is most effective if offered while the learning situation to which it applies is still fresh and vivid. This fact emphasizes the importance of regularly scheduled conferences at reasonably frequent intervals (once a week perhaps) so that the supervisor can offer his critical reaction to recently encountered experiences in which learning has been applied by the supervisees. Assessment of results is necessary if the learner is to experience a feeling of success which is a reward.

4. Periodic stock-taking provided in a formal evaluation conference at less frequent intervals (every six months perhaps) further ensures learning attended by positive satisfaction because it permits a perspective on long-range progress. The supervisee can get some sense of progress in learning over time, which is rewarding.

5. We ensure the greater probability of success if we partialize learning. "A man can eat whole steer—one steak at a time." We offer learning in digestible dosages. The agenda for a particular conference should cover a limited, defined unit of learning, which is clear, acceptable, and attainable.

6. Success and positive satisfactions in learning are more likely if the material is presented in a graded sequence, from the simple to the complex, from the obvious to the obscure. It is easier for a

worker to understand concrete situational needs such as a home for a totally dependent, abandoned infant than it is to undertstand the psychological dependency needs of a middle-aged neurotic. It is easier to understand that feelings are facts than to grasp the idea of ambivalence. Grading the complexity of content is more difficult in social work than in mathematics or chemistry. Seemingly simple situations have a tendency to present unanticipated complexities. However, to the extent that we can discern the measure of comparative difficulty of material to be taught, we should attempt to teach the simpler content first.

There are some general criteria for differentiating between simpler and more difficult social-work learning situations. The client who is motivated to use the service, has good ego strength, is not unduly defensive, and with whom the worker can in some way identify presents less difficulty. A situation in which cause-and-effect relationships are clear, for which remedial resources and services are available, and in which the problem is well focused, presents less difficulty. These characteristics represent treatable clients in treatable situations, ensuring greater probability of the successful application of learning.

7. We ensure the greater probability of positive satisfaction in learning if we prepare the worker for failure. It may be necessary to expose the worker to situations of a complexity and difficulty for which he is as yet not fully prepared. The demands of case coverage may not always permit the assignment of cases that are within the worker's competence. In such instances it would be helpful to explicitly recognize with the worker the possibility of failure in the encounter. He is then less likely to be overwhelmed by personal guilt or shame and be more open to learning from the experience.

Principle

We learn best if we are actively involved in the learning process.

Techniques

1. The supervisee should be encouraged to participate in planning the agenda for the supervisory sessions. This technique

ensures the supervisee's active involvement in the learning situation. In addition it increases the probability that content of primary interest and concern to the supervisee will be discussed.

Active participation in selecting the content for learning tends to heighten commitment to the task of learning. This is the content the learner herself suggested she was motivated to learn. The objectives of the learning-teaching encounter are therefore probably acceptable to her. But while we might need to start where the worker is, we have an obligation to educate toward where the agency wants him to be. There are objective performance standards that need to be met. We cannot, in a gesture of mutual egalitarianism, give priority to the worker's educational choices. We are constrained to teach what he needs to learn, not what he wants to learn. But the two are often reconcilable, and knowing what the individual learner is interested in learning may enable the supervisor to bring "wants" and "needs" closer to each other.

2. We ensure the greater active involvement of the supervisee in learning if we encourage and provide opportunity for him to question, discuss, object, express doubt. The supervisor should supplement, rather than substitute for, a supervisee's thinking. Thinking is trial acting. The worker will use what is being taught in active encounters with clients. He can, however, also be encouraged to engage with the content to be learned through discussion. This is a cognitive rather than behavioral engagement with the learning but one which nevertheless requires active participation in learning. Such involvement of the supervisee is only possible in an atmosphere of psychological safety in which the supervisee feels comfortable about questioning the supervisor and presenting his own, perhaps opposing, point of view.

3. Provide the explicit opportunity to utilize and apply the knowledge we seek to teach. If we are teaching the worker some of the principles of client advocacy, we would need to provide an assignment which involves the worker in client advocacy. The worker then, of necessity, is actively engaged in testing the learning through use. We learn by doing. Learning determines action, but successful action reinforces learning.

The worker may, however, engage in incompetent practice. Consequently, providing practice experience has to be followed by a critical review of what was done. Such feedback enables the worker to know specifically what might need correction and change. This review should again be followed by the opportunity to practice the corrected learning.

Principle

We learn best if the content is meaningfully presented.

Techniques

1. As much as possible, select for teaching the content that is of interest and concern to the supervisee. Readiness for learning is often related to some specific situation. The worker needs to know what will help her deal with a problem she is having with a particular client. This is the teachable moment for the presentation of the relevant content. At this point the content has meaning for the supervisee and can be most effectively taught.

2. Content is meaningfully presented if it fits into some general theoretical framework. Different supervisors adhere to different theoretical systems—psychoanalytic psychology, behaviorism, existential psychology, etc. The choice of system is not as important as the fact that there is belief in some comprehensive, internally consistent configuration which satisfactorily explains the mysteries of human behavior (at least for its adherents). Our subject matter is people. We need some cognitive map, some cosmology, which makes sense of why people do what they do in the way they do it.

It is difficult to learn discrete, unrelated details of behavior. If, however, the supervisor is knowledgeable about some well-articulated scheme, she can relate details to principles which act as an organizing focus for details. Whatever one's opinion is regarding id-ego-superego, or drive-stimulus-response, one needs to recognize that these ideas suggest large-scale, coherent, explanatory frameworks of human behavior which meaningfully organize details regarding the human condition. The supervisor needs to have available some reasonably comprehensive explanatory framework which meaningfully organizes the content she is attempting to teach. Such ideational scaffolding provides the "unity behind the plurality of experiences" and gives a sense of connectedness to discrete learnings.

Bruner (1963) notes that "perhaps the most basic thing that can be said about human memory after a century of intensive research is that unless detail is placed into a structured pattern it is rapidly forgotten" (p. 24). "Organizing facts in terms of principle and idea from which they may be inferred is the only known way of reducing the quick rate of loss of human memory" (p. 31). Bruner further comments that "the principal problem of human memory is not storage but retrieval" and that "the key to retrieval is organization."

3. Meaningful teaching is selective teaching. Some things are more important than others, some content requires more attention, emphasis, repetition than other content. The supervisor needs to have priorities that guide the choice of content to be taught.

4. Imaginative repetition makes learning more meaningful. If we select a number of experiences that teach the same idea in different ways, it is easier to grasp and accept. Through comparison and contrast, illustration of similarities and differences, the same content is more meaningfully presented.

Practice of skills is, after all, the opportunity to repeat in different situations the exercise of such skills. But repetition is not haphazard. It is carefully selected in terms of organizing principles. As Tyler (1971) states, "in order for educational experiences to produce a cumulative effect they must be organized so as to reinforce each other" (p. 83). The best repetition involves not sheer drill of old learning but some variation that includes new elements to capture the learner's interest. We learn best if the material is presented in a way which is novel, varied, and challenging. Such presentations tend to keep the learner stimulated and interested.

5. Teaching that is planned in terms of continuity (reiteration of important content—deepening learning), sequence (successively building toward greater complexity—broadening learning) and integration (relating different kinds of content to each other) is apt to be teaching presented in a more meaningful context. Content has to be planfully organized and systematically presented if it is to be taught effectively.

6. Some of the techniques mentioned in relation to previously cited principles of learning are applicable here as well. The content is more meaningful if the supervisor can relate new learning to

previously acquired learning, moving from the unfamiliar to the familiar, and if the content can be presented in logical progressions, moving from simple to complex.

7. Learning is more meaningful if it can be made conscious and explicit. We are not always aware of what we have learned. To the extent that we can consciously articulate and label what we have learned, the learning is apt to be more meaningful and transferable. This fact calls attention to the need for periodic recapitulation and summarization of units of completed learning.

Principle

We learn best if the supervisor takes into consideration the supervisee's uniqueness as a learner.

Techniques

1. Individualize the learner through educational diagnosis. We study the learner so that we can understand how she learns. Educational diagnosis of a supervisee includes a statement regarding what she already knows well, what she needs to learn, what she wants to learn, and how she wants to learn it. To individualize teaching we need to know not only where the worker is but where she wants to go. With such an educational diagnosis we are in a better position to fit the learning situation to the learner rather than the learner to the learning situation. The advantage of tutorial teaching in the supervisory context is precisely that the supervisor can tailor his choice of approach and content to the learning needs of the individual supervisee.

In making an educational diagnosis of supervisees, one needs to consider the special attributes of the adult learner. Adult learners have a long attention span, can sustain learning activity and postpone gratification for long periods. A good deal of adult learning might more properly be termed relearning rather than primary learning, and the learning process therefore involves some necessary unlearning. There is more resistance to accepting the temporary dependency that learning often requires. Adult learners are, of course, often able to articulate what they want to learn and why they want to learn it. Maximum participation of the learner in the teacher-learner interaction is not only desirable but eminently feasible. The adult learner has a fund of learning and life experience that might be adapted to the current learning situation.

The educational diagnosis of the individual adult learner is developed in ongoing contact with him. The supervisor observes the supervisee's use of supervision, the level of motivation manifested, the balance of rigidity and flexibility in learning, the level of preparation for and participation in conferences, and the general attitude toward the content to be learned and toward the learning situation. The supervisor attempts to discern the procedures which elicit the supervisee's best response. Some people learn best in a highly structured situation, some people learn best in a loosely structured situation; some learn through listening, others through reading; some learn only through action in a practice situation, some cannot begin to act until they have learned; some learn best in an individual tutorial situation, others learn best through group interaction; some learn best through ready acceptance of teaching, some learn best through active opposition to content presented; some are ready to learn but are less ready to be taught.

Is resistance to learning manifested in submissiveness, detachment, arrogance, aggression, self-deprecation, dependence, ingratiation? What failures in performance are due to ignorance or inexperience, amenable to change through education and experience, and what problems are the result of personality difficulties? What character defects impede learning and tie up psychic energy that might otherwise be available for learning? Is content learned for self-protection or for mastery of problem situations? Is learning collected as a possession or acquired for the aggrandizement of status? Does the supervisee think his way through a problem or feel his way through it? Is he responsive to a deductive pattern of instruction, moving from the general idea to the particular situation, or does he learn more readily inductively, requiring an experience with a series of similar situations before he can truly grasp the relevant generalization? Is he a fast learner, always ready and anxious for new material, or a learner who needs to take more time in integrating learning? Does the supervisee acknowledge his learning deficiencies and demonstrate a readiness to learn or is his response characterized by denial and defensiveness? To what extent is the supervisee ready, willing and able to take responsibility for his own learning needs? To what extent is the learner comfortable with uncertainty and ambiguity in the knowledge base available? To what extent does he need the certainty of unequivocal answers?

How can the worker be described in terms of the variety of motives that energize people's interest and behavior? In McClelland's terms, is the worker motivated by a need for interpersonal affiliation, for task achievement, or for power to influence others? In terms of Maslow's hierarchy of needs, is the worker motivated by a strong need for belonging, love, and social interaction, by a need for esteem and status or by a need for self-actualization? In Herzberg's terms, is the worker motivated by maintenance needs, job security, salary, and working conditions, or by needs for growth and development, increased responsibility, and recognition of accomplishment? And what is the degree of cognitive complexity with which the worker approaches a situation—the extent to which she can perceive the multidimensional aspects of a problem?

A comprehensive educational diagnosis which individualizes the supervisee also includes some attention to learning problems associated with more personal aspects of the supervisee's functioning in interaction with the clients. These include learning problems relating to the reactivation of the worker's personal developmental problems in the interaction with the client and problems of selective identification with one aspect of the case situation. As a result of transference, the worker's perception of the client is distorted by seeing the client not as he is but as representing in some measure significant others from the worker's past. As a result of reactivation of developmental problems the worker may distort the client's situation by avoidance of significant content which it would be important to recognize. As a result of selective identification, the worker may distort perception of the client's situation by "taking sides" with the child in a parent-child problem or with the wife in a marital problem.

An educational diagnosis requires some attention to these sources of distortion which adversely affect the worker's ability to offer effective service. In the effort to identify such difficulty, the supervisor needs to be aware of some relevant symptomatic manifestations. The consistent failure on the part of the worker to discuss content that might logically be presumed to be important is a diagnostic one. The total absence of any mention of the husband-father in the case of a child with a behavior problem, or the lack of any information regarding sexual adjustment in the case of a marital problem might be suggestive.

An atypically sharp, disproportionate feeling reaction to some aspect of the client's situation might be another cue. The worker's response, if exaggerated, might suggest that the source of the reaction is only partially the client's situation, and more due to the worker's own problems. Persistent stereotyping of the client based on limited evidence might suggest distortions in perception stemming from the worker.

Individualization implies some understanding of what the learner risks in learning this content, and there are both internal risks and external risks. The internal risks relate to the meaning this learning has for his self-image and his current belief and attitudinal system. The external risks concern his relationship with his reference group. Those who believe that the Bible is literal truth, for instance, cannot afford to learn the proof in support of the theory of evolution, and the right-wing conservative might feel out of place with his friends if he accepted liberal ideas about social welfare.

In an analysis of learning patterns of social workers as compared with other professional groups, Kolb (1981) identified the social worker's learning orientation as "concrete-active." The pattern suggests a preference for learning through active involvement rather than detached, reflective, analytic observation of phenomena, learning through immersion in experience, a tendency to solve problems in an intuitive trial-and-error manner. "The dominant philosophy is pragmatism and truth as defined by workability. Inquiry centers around the question of how actions shape events. The case study is the common method of inquiry and analysis" (p. 244).

2. The educational diagnosis should be used. The supervisor, in preparation for a conference, would need to review what the supervisee most needs to learn at this particular time, how best to approach teaching the content to this particular supervisee, how the supervisee is likely to react in response to the efforts to teach him this content, and so on.

Individualization implies that each of us has his own unique, best way of learning. However, while it is recognized that the supervisor may not always be capable of modulating her approach to be neatly congruent with the needs of the learner, she should at least be understandingly aware of the nature of the learner's educational diagnosis.

3. It is desirable to engage the supervisee actively in an assessment of what he already knows and what he wants to learn. This, once again, individualizes the learning needs of the particular supervisee, spares him the boredom of redundant learning, and spares the supervisor the effort of teaching what does not need to be taught. In addition, the learner's employment record and his record of experience at the agency give relevant information about his educational and experiential background.

Adult learners have at their command a variety of previously learned skills which may be retranslated for use in a social work context. In implementing educational supervision the supervisor might try to help the supervisee identify these skills and help the supervisee to use them appropriately.

4. We individualize teaching according to differences in the pace of learning. It takes time to integrate newly learned material, to assimilate it with previous learning and make an accommodation to a new equilibrium in thinking and feeling which the incorporation of learned material requires. Being asked to absorb too much too quickly threatens internal coherence and stability.

While it is true that people learn more effectively when they learn at their own pace, there needs to be some recognition that both the agency and clients pay a heavy price for the slow pace of the slow learner. Neither can tolerate for long an excessively slow learner.

The Significance of the Supervisor-Supervisee Relationship for Educational Supervision

Throughout this section we have made allusions to the supervisor-supervisee relationship as having crucial significance for learning in supervision. The teacher-learner relationship is of prime importance because teaching is mainly a problem in human relationships. The term "relationship" as used here means the nature of emotional interaction. In general, learning can take place best when the nature of such interaction is positive, when teacher and learner accept each other and are comfortably relaxed with each other. The level of participation is higher and anxiety is lower in the context of a positive relationship, facilitating learning. There are a number of additional factors which suggest the importance of a good relationship for educational supervision.

Not only must the learner be motivated to accept the content of what needs to be learned, but he must be motivated and ready to accept it from the teacher. A worker resists accepting content offered by a supervisor he does not like and respect. The relationship, if positive, is the bridge over which the material passes from teacher to learner. If the relationship is negative, communication is blocked.

A positive relationship intensifies the impact of the supervisor's educational efforts. There is considerable empirical support for the contention that the nature of the relationship is a powerful variable in determining the supervisee's openness and receptivity to the supervisor's efforts to educate toward change (Goldstein, Heller, and Sechrest 1966, pp. 73–91).

Identification with the supervisor heightens the worker's motivation to learn. As a consequence of identification, the worker wishes to be like the supervisor, to have her competence, and to learn in order to emulate her. Only if the relationship is positive will the worker identify with the supervisor.

In the following quotation the supervisee describes how she uses her supervisor, Morrie, as a source of identification. "I find myself in situations thinking 'Well now, what would Morrie do?' And I'm kind of generalizing from what he does with me. I've never seen him with a client. You know, thinking if I was feeling a certain way, how would he react? I kind of use that" (Amacher 1971, p. 36).

The supervisor as model for identification is also aptly described in the following, written by a supervisee:

I guess his personal way of being was very strong in supervision. It was very warm, very relaxed, very comfortable—he smiled, laughed, sat back in his chair, and gazed off and smoked a cigar—and was just very interested but wasn't like sitting on the edge of his chair waiting for the next thing I would say so that he could respond to that. And I perceived that as indirectly giving me a model 'cause I figured that must be in some ways what he's like in therapy; and that's more what I would be like in therapy if I were myself. And it would also kinda make the client a lot more comfortable since it made me comfortable in supervision. "Aha!" I figured, "I should try to do that." It's very relaxing, and he uses strokes—makes supportive, reinforcing comments, but not overbearingly so—just does enough of that that I can believe it when he does it. And he never makes harsh, critical statements and his suggestions are usually specific, and he explains what he means by them and gives an example of it but somehow manages to do that without making me feel like a jerk for not having known to do that in the first place. (Diane 1977, pp. 139–40).

In learning through identification, the supervisor needs to give the supervisee the freedom to accept what he can use and reject or discard what does not seem appropriate for him. Such freedom leads to selective identification and selective learning rather than an indiscriminate mimicry of the supervisor. In the beginning, identification may involve a sizable component of imitation, but as Steinbeck says, "Only through imitation do we develop toward originality" (*Travels with Charley*).

Establishing and maintaining a positive relationship with the supervisee teaches essential social work skills, because in developing such a relationship, the supervisor is modeling the way in which the supervisee might effectively relate to the client. Having experienced a helping process in educational supervision, the worker is then in a better position to understand what is involved in seeking and using help. As Robinson states, "Since supervision in social casework teaches a helping process, it must itself be a helping process so that the [worker] experiences in his relationship with the supervisor a process similar to the one he must learn to use with his client" (1949, p. 30).

It needs to be noted, however, that the superordinate-subordinate role relationship still holds, even in the educational component of supervision. The supervisor is sanctioned by the agency to engage in educational activity. Secondly, the supervisee, while participating in determining what should be taught and learned, faces constraints determined by what the agency requires that he learn to do. Consequently the supervisor has considerable responsibility for what is included in the educational program. Thirdly, the supervisor is responsible for evaluating whether or not the supervisee has in fact learned what it is that he has to know and what she is mandated to teach. These considerations make it clear once again that super-

visor and supervisee are not acting as equals in educational supervision.

Content in Educational Supervision

Any delineation of the content of supervisory teaching has, of
necessity, to be general. An overview of supervision, such as this
book, is directed toward workers in many different kinds of agencies
who must learn different kinds of content to do their jobs well.
However, since all social work agencies have elements in common,
there are certain uniformities in what needs to be taught. The following discussion of the basic content of educational supervision is
derived from material developed by Helen Harris Perlman. Perlman
(1947) points out that what evey social worker needs to know is
concerned with people, problems, place, and process—the four P's.
To this might be added a fifth P—personnel, the person of the
worker offering the service.

The nuclear situation for all of social work is that of a client
(individual, family, group, or community—*people*) coming, or referred, to a social agency (*place*) for help (*process*) by a social
worker (*personnel*). The client comes with a *problem* in social functioning.

Supervisors in every social agency will be teaching something
about each of these five content areas. However diverse the specifics of *people, place, process, problems,* and *personnel,* these will be
matters for the agenda of educational supervision. Despite differences in specifics, in each instance there is a particular group of
people, either an individual or collectivity, presenting a particular
kind of social problem, seeking help from a social worker who is
affiliated with a particular social agency and offers some particular
approach to helping. And the worker, in order to perform his job
effectively, would need to know about the process by which he
hopes to help, about the agency through which he is offering such
help, about the people with whom he will be working, about the
problems which they present, and about himself as the principal
instrumentality for helping.

For each of these content areas—people, problem, place, process,
and personnel—there are objectives in terms of knowledge, atti-

tudes, and skills. For instance, in learning to help senior citizens adjust to the problems of institutional living, the worker needs to have some knowledge of the biopsychosocial aspects of aging and to have interpersonal skills in reláting to senior citizens. But teaching-learning also involves value-related attitudinal changes toward the aged. It involves the dissolution of some stereotypes so that a more realistic, more optimistic attitude is developed; a change from disdain, dread and repulsion, despair, and negativism to the perception that the aged have strength and a sense of self-worth, can respond to interests, are likable, friendly, and capable of change (Cohen 1972).

However diverse the agency, the supervisor has to teach something about how the agency is organized and administered, how it relates to other agencies and fits into the total network of community social services, what the agency's objectives are, what kind of services it offers and under what conditions, how agency policy is formulated and can be changed, and what is the nature of the agency's statutory authority.

However diverse the social problems with which different agencies are concerned, the supervisor will have to teach something about the "causes" of social problems, community response to particular social problems, the psychosocial nature of these problems, the impact of social problems on different groups in the community, the effect of a particular problem on people's lives, the relationship of agency services to the social problems that are of primary concern to the agency's mandate.

However diverse the clientele served, the supervisor will have to teach something of human behavior in response to the stress of social problems. While the casework supervisor might be primarily concerned with teaching how individuals and families respond to social problems and adjust to them, the group work supervisor and community organization supervisor might be more concerned with teaching how people in collectivities such as groups and communities behave in responding to social problems. In order for the supervisee to understand problematic individual and collective responses to social stress, the supervisor needs to teach something of "normal" individual and collective development and behavior.

Whatever the processes employed in helping the client to a restoration of a more effective level of social functioning or ameliorating or preventing social disfunctioning, the supervisor will have to teach something of the technology of helping. This, in the end, is where everything gets put together. Knowledge about people, problem, and place is taught because ultimately it enables the worker to help more effectively. The supervisor has to teach what the worker is to do, how he is to act if he is to help individuals, groups, or communities deal effectively with their social problems. And he has to teach something of the theory that explains why the particular helping technology the agency espouses, whatever it is, is likely to effect change.

In any agency, whatever the methodology for helping, the supervisor teaches something of the sequential nature of the helping process. It is described in a variety of ways: social study, diagnosis, treatment; data gathering, data processing, intervention; obtaining information, processing information, exerting social influence. All of these descriptions, however diverse, imply a process of remedial action based on understanding derived from the facts.

The supervisor further has to teach the supervisee something about himself in developing a greater sense of self-awareness. Nathanson (1962) defines self-awareness as "the capacity of an individual to perceive his responses to other persons and situations realistically and to understand how others view him" (p. 32). Grossbard (1954) notes that "broadly speaking, self-awareness is a person's ability to recognize with a reasonable degree of accuracy how he reacts to the outside world and how the outside world reacts to him" (p. 381; see also Purvis 1972).

People are, of course, not helped by a social agency in dealing with problems of social functioning but by social workers representing the agency. Furthermore, the principal instrumentality for helping is generally the social worker herself. There are, of course, social utilities administered by social workers which are essential resources for helping, such as homemaker service, foster care, institutions, day care, and grants of income. Most frequently, however, the principal resource the agency makes available in the process of helping people is the skill and competence of the worker herself. It is the social worker who leads the group, organizes the community, acts as advocate, supports, sustains, clarifies, offers herself as a model for identification, rewards and shapes behavior, and so on.

In work environments where instruments, machines, or mechanical devices of one sort or another are used, they determine how the work is to be done and limit the effects of personality differences among workers. In social work, where the worker is the main instrumentality, the person of the worker determines what is done and how it is done.

Since the worker's personality and behavior are significant determinants of what happens in the worker-client interaction, the supervisee herself, her attitudes, feelings, and behavior become a necessary and inevitable subject of educational supervision. The aim is to develop a greater measure of self-awareness in the worker so that she can act in a deliberate, disciplined, consciously directed manner in the worker-client interaction so as to be optimally helpful to the client. The capacity to perceive one's behavior as objectively as possible, to have free access to one's own feelings without guilt, embarrassment, or discomfort, is a necessary, if not sufficient, prerequisite for the controlled subjectivity the helping process demands. The freedom to use feelings imaginatively and creatively for helping also requires considerable self-awareness.

Developing a high level of worker self-awareness is further necessary because the social problems that are the professional concerns of the worker also affect him personally. Here, unlike the situation in many other professions, there is considerable interpenetration between life and work. The worker may be involved, to some extent, in many of the kinds of problems encountered by the client—parent-child conflict, aging, marital conflict, deviance, illness, financial problems, death. "Living on a job that is so closely allied to life itself makes separation of work from other areas of life exceptionally difficult. Since, in social work, the work task and living are often simultaneously experienced, anxiety is greater than in many other fields of endeavor" (Babcock 1951, p. 417). A supervisor in medical social work writes:

> We got to that part in the record where one relative began talking about problems with unexpected bowel movements with the patient at home. The relative asked R a question to which she didn't know the answer. R offered to invite a doctor to the next group meeting. She read on, but I stopped her and said: "I feel that you have missed the relative's concerns. Let's go back into the experience. What were your feelings at that moment?" She began to laugh uncomfortably and

spoke about the whole bowel movement business making her uncomfortable. I asked her: "What did you feel at that moment?" After a pause, she responded that at that moment she didn't really want to listen, to get too closely involved with the relatives re giving patients digitalis. I responded that I could understand and suggested that she might have felt hopeless. "Like what good is talking about these things going to do?" She agreed, describing her anxiety and a sense of being trapped by it. After having her assume the role of the relative and obtain a "feel" for the specific underlying concerns, we role-played different ways in which she might have reached for the member's concerns. She particularly liked her idea of reflecting the member's concern to the group, asking whether anyone else had similar concerns or experiences. I found myself being caught in her excitement as we both threw ourselves into the role-playing. R searched the record for other places where she disconnected and suggested a doctor to "explain" the reasons behind problems, e.g., bowel movements, catheter, sex. She exclaimed, "Wow, I see how I ran away—that was really scary, but I do sense how I will do it differently next time." (Gitterman 1972, p. 37, reprinted with permission of Jossey-Bass)

Education toward a greater development of self-awareness permits the worker to think objectively about these matters. It provides a greater assurance that the worker's own reactions to these professional problems will not adversely contaminate the helping relationship.

In the following brief excerpt the worker is talking to the supervisor about a 12-year-old girl named Thelma. The youngster is described by the worker as provocative, snide, impudent, and upsetting. She teases adults, including the supervisee.

As the student talked about Thelma's behavior and described it in some detail in response to my questioning, she suddenly looked as though a thought had struck her and said, "You know, I was very much like her when I was her age." The student went on to describe how she had taunted a Junior High School teacher with certain remarks, daring the teacher to punish her. I felt that the worker was really working on something and confined myself to listening and encouraging her to speak, with an occasional comment. (Gladstone 1967, p.11)

Awareness of similar life experiences permits the worker to understand the client's behavior.

A somewhat different group of problems relating to educational supervision also calls for developing self-awareness. Any systematic educational program is in essence a program of planned change, the teacher being the change agent, the learner being the target for change. But the pressure to change, resulting from learning, generates ambivalence and resistance.

The particular content that needs to be learned, the attitudes that need to undergo change, sometimes result in blocks to learning, to problems in learning. We learn only what we can emotionally afford to learn. If the content learned is a threat to our self-esteem, strongly discordant with attitudes and beliefs that are essential to the maintenance of emotional equilibrium, we refuse to learn this content. The repertoire of maneuvers that permit us to shield ourselves from content include all the mechanisms of defense. Educating toward self-awareness may help the supervisee resolve some of these resistances to learning. Persistent blocks to learning are the exception rather than the rule. However, such problems are encountered in a less intense and less pervasive form by all learners. For the reasonably mature learner the work of the ego in the service of adaptation is sufficient to counter the work of the ego in the service of defense. Learning takes place despite resistance because of the learner's need and desire to meet the demands of the job.

In a supervisory context which supports freedom and safety to do this, the healthy supervisee is open to introspective self-analysis. Introspectively examining his responses, the worker is in a double position, both the subject and the object of self-examination. Aware that he is reacting resentfully or punitively, or warmly or sympathetically, to some clients, feeling intimidated or threatened or repulsed by other clients and introspectively examining the basis for such responses helps the worker develop self-awareness. The supervisee, in applying knowledge of human behavior to himself and his own interactions, understands this material in a more meaningful affective way. Education in self-awareness has as one of its objectives this kind of heightened affective sensitivity.

This discussion of the justifications for concern with development of self-awareness reflects the fact that it is an important content area of educational supervision. The supervisor has the responsibility of teaching the worker about himself as well as teaching the worker about people, problems, place, and process. In fact, social workers tend to perceive the education toward self-awareness as one of the unique aspects of social work supervision. In a study that asked about factors which differentiated social work supervision, "the commonest theme expressed" by the 100 social work respondents was the following: "Because the skill to be developed is the disciplined use of self in professional relationships, supervision in casework affects personality more closely than supervision in other fields which are more dependent on objective skills" (Cruser 1958, p. 23).

The requirement of a didactic psychoanalysis for certification as an analyst is an institutionalized testimonial to the importance of self-awareness in the people-helping professions. The desirability of this objective of educational supervision receives support from at least one empirical study of social workers which suggests a relationship between level of self-awareness and practice competence (Bruck 1963).

The content around place, problem, people, process has often been previously encountered by the supervisee in undergraduate or graduate courses in psychology, social psychology, sociology, political science, anthropology, social work, counseling, etc. The supervisor can often build on previous learning in teaching this content. Teaching supervisees content relevant to personal self-awareness may not be able to build on previous learning.

What content do supervisors themselves assign priority? Data gathered from structured interviews with fifty public welfare supervisors concluded that they gave high ratings to content involving interpersonal skills—"know how to relate well, communicate, listen, interview and understand the client" (Brennen, Arkava, Cummins, and Wicks 1976, p. 20). Lowest priority was given to content "concerning the role of the social worker in relating to the community and in bringing about change in the agency" (p. 21).

More details regarding knowledge and skills to be taught are embodied in the more detailed evaluation statements (see pp. 359–73). The listing of content areas to be evaluated indicates what the worker needs to know, to believe, and to do.

Educational Supervision versus Therapy

The task of developing self-awareness as a responsibility of educational supervision presents social work with a persistent and

often-discussed dilemma. Development of self-awareness is analogous to the insight objectives of psychotherapy. The supervisory
context is in many essential characteristics similar to the therapeutic context. Both situations involve a continuing, intimate, highly
cathected, dyadic relationship in which an effort at exerting interpersonal influence to effect change is made by one member of the
dyad toward the other.

How then does the supervisor develop self-awareness in the supervisee without being accused of "caseworking the caseworker"? A
distinction needs to be made between educational supervision and
therapy.

Differences Between Supervision and Therapy

Differences between educational supervision, concerned with developing self-awareness, and therapy relate to (1) purpose and
focus, (2) roles, and (3) process.

1. PURPOSE AND FOCUS

The supervisor recognizes and respects the limits and restrictions
of her purpose. Her responsibility is to help the supervisee become a
better worker, not necessarily a better person. Her legitimate concern is with the professional activities of the supervisee, but she has
no sanction to intrude into the personal life of the supervisee. The
concern is with changes in professional identity rather than
changes in personal identity. The supervisor asks, "How can I help
you do your work?" rather than "How can I help you?" Ekstein and
Wallerstein (1972) note that "in supervision we aim at a change in
skill, a change in the use of the professional self while in psychotherapy we aim at changes which embrace the total adaptive functioning of the individual" (p. 92).

The valid focus of attention is the supervisee's work, rather than
the supervisee herself. Only as the supervisee's behavior, feelings,
and attitudes create some difficulty in the performance of professional tasks, then and only then, do they become a legitimate matter
for supervisory concern. The supervisor is not entitled to intervene
with regard to behavior, feelings, and attitudes which, however

problematic or deviant, are not clearly manifested in some job-related interaction.

In educational supervision we are not primarily dealing with the total person as in therapy. We are dealing with only one of the many roles that make up the worker's total identity—the specific, particular role of agency employee. The supervisor, unlike the therapist, is not concerned with the causes of personal pathology, but only with the consequences of such problems for the worker's performance on the job.

What is of exclusive concern is the supervisee's work rather than her worth. This is not to deny that professional growth does have consequences related to personal growth. The professional self is, after all, a significant aspect of the total personal-self configuration. But if the personal self undergoes growth and change, as is likely, this happens as an incidental, serendipitous, unplanned, unintended byproduct of the focus on professional growth.

Although the following comments by Ekstein and Wallerstein (1972) relate to supervision of the psychiatric resident, they are pertinent to this discussion. The authors comment that

> both supervision and psychotherapy are interpersonal helping processes working with the same affective components, with the essential difference between them created by the difference in purpose. Though both are helping processes, the purpose of the helping experience is different. Whatever practical problems the patient may bring to his psychotherapist, they are always viewed in the light of the main task: the resolution of inner conflict. Whatever personal problems the student may bring to his supervisor, they are likewise always seen in terms of the main task: leading him toward greater skill in his work with his patients. While it is true that the patient may occasionally benefit in practical matters, or perhaps even from direct practical advice, and while it is equally true that the student will frequently benefit in a personal sense, they have made these gains in the course of following the main purpose of their relationship with the helper. If the main purpose of a relationship is maintained throughout, the difference is clearly apparent between the type of relationship called psychotherapy and the one called supervision. . . . In psychotherapy the patient essentially sets his own goals, with . . . the proviso always that these goals may change as the therapeutic process itself develops and makes for change. The therapist has no vested interest in any particular degree or direction of change. In supervision, on the other hand, the clinical setting, whose representative is the supervisor, sets

both its requirements and its goals in terms of standards of professional performance and clinical service currently rendered and to be attained. The institution thus furnishes the external yardstick to which both supervisor and student must measure up. (pp. 254–55, reprinted with permission of International Universities Press)

The therapist is free to work toward any goal that the client selects. The supervisor is responsible for the behavior of the supervisee and is not free to work toward any goal the supervisee selects. The agency requirement is that he help the worker become an effective agency employee. The therapist helps the client achieve an individualized, personally satisfactory solution to his problem. The supervisor helps the worker achieve a resolution to his problem that is satisfactory to the organization. The objective of the supervision is improved technical performance in contrast with the therapist's objective of personality reconstruction or remediation. The objectives of educational supervision and therapy are different. Learning to become a social worker does not necessarily result in the resolution of personal pathology; undergoing psychotherapy does not make a person a social worker. Supervision is oriented to the needs of the client; therapy is oriented to the needs of the worker.

If the supervisee becomes a client of the supervisor in a shift from educational supervision to psychotherapy, the focus of supervisory attention must shift from the agency client to the worker. The needs of the supervisee as client then take precedence over the needs of the agency client. This is a subversion of the primary responsibility and obligation of the agency toward its client. Instead of the focus of attention being on service, the client is used to advance the therapy of the worker. This is an inequitable manipulation of the client, without the client's permission and in contravention to the client's objectives in coming to the agency. The client becomes an involuntary coparticipant in the worker's therapy.

To accept the supervisee for psychotherapy requires a modification of work standards. The criteria for a decision regarding enforcement of agency standards become the therapeutic needs of the supervisee-client rather than the needs of agency clients. This too is contrary to the primary obligation of the agency. Exercise of administrative sanctions required in maintaining adequate standards may be antitherapeutic for the supervisee-client. The supervisor cannot at the same time be a psychotherapist to the supervisee and a guardian of agency standards.

In implementing the focus on supervision as against therapy, the supervisor keeps the discussion centered on the client's situation and experience rather than the worker's situation and experience. The discussion is work-centered, not worker-centered. Further, the focus is on *what* the worker did or failed to do rather than *why* he did it. If there is any discussion of the reasons that may help explain the worker's behavior, it is centered on the current work situation rather than in any psychodynamic exploration of developmental antecedents. In indicating what should not be done, Feldman, Sponitz, and Nagelberg say:

> Supervisors, in discussing their workers' performance, put undue emphasis on discovering the inhibitions of their supervisees, looking for psychological causes. They look for the remote cause of an earlier relationship of the worker to his mother, even going so far as to think of possible frustrations in early feeding. Though any of these factors may still apply, a supervisor should examine carefully whether a worker's negative reactions are not based on the worker's present relationship with his symbolic parent, the supervisor, who should be supplying needed technical knowledge. (1953, p. 158)

Current reality as an explanation of workers' problems should always be examined first. Personal problems should be discussed through their derivative manifestations in the work assigned. A worker may

> reveal marked anxiety in trying to help a client who rejects her child. . . . [The supervisor] does not explore the [worker's] early experience in his relationship with his own mother. She focuses instead on eliciting and on understanding the [worker's] feelings about *this* mother. She directs him to consider how this woman came to feel and act as she does and she holds the worker accountable to try to understand and meet the woman's need for help. (Towle 1954, p. 123)

2. DIFFERENCE IN ROLE RELATIONSHIPS

Shifting from educational supervision to psychotherapy involves an unwarranted and inappropriate shift in roles. As Stiles (1963) says, "A supervisory relationship contains an implicit contract: the worker is responsible for attempting to maximize his performance and continuing his professional development; the supervisor is responsible for helping him achieve these goals" (p. 24). The parameters of the contract, as noted, are the worker's "performance" and "professional development." Concern with personal development is an unwarranted and unanticipated extension of the explicit contract. Having consented to an administrative-educational process, the worker cannot legitimately have a psychotherapy process imposed on him. "Therapizing" the relationship suggests that the supervisor is entering areas of the worker's life concerning which he has no organizational sanction or authority.

Unlike the client in psychotherapy, the supervisee is not free to terminate his relationship with the supervisor. Thus, attempted transformation of educational supervision into psychotherapy is even more likely to be resented by the captive worker. Supervisees understandably resent any invitation to engage in a psychic striptease: "I had gotten into this conversation with my supervisor where he managed to dig into a whole lot of personal stuff and I bite pretty quick; if someone encourages me, out it comes. And I walked out of the office really angry with myself for having done it" (Amacher 1971, p. 225).

In educational supervision, the worker contracts for knowledge and guidance, not the alleviation of symptoms. There is no treatment contract that would sanction the supervisor to subject the supervisee to some of the psychic pain that may be necessary for effective therapy, no contract that would make the supervisee aware that he might have to accept some of the inevitable discomforts of therapy.

In accepting the role of patient to therapist, certain prerogatives of privacy are waived. In a supervisory relationship which is redirected to a therapeutic relationship, there is no clear agreement on the part of the supervisee that he has agreed to the suspension of such entitlements.

3. PROCESS DIFFERENCES

Subverting educational supervision so that it becomes psychotherapy in disguise not only contravenes the agreed nature of reciprocal supervisor-supervisee role relations, it also violates the conditions for effective therapy. Effective therapy is not likely to be possible unless a complete detailed history has been taken, a clear diagnosis of the problem formulated. Effective therapy would require considerably more detailed exploration of developmental data and current functioning than is possible, or acceptable, in the supervisory relationship.

Effective therapy requires a psychosocial diagnosis of the client and a therapeutic alliance between therapist and client. Effective educational supervision requires an educational diagnosis and a teacher-learner alliance between supervisor and supervisee.

In educational supervision, the supervisor universalizes the content she is teaching rather than personalizing the teaching, which would be more appropriate to therapy.

In therapy unconscious feelings are explored for their genesis and worked through for their resolution. In supervision, unconscious feelings may be identified but are neither explored nor resolved. While listening with the understanding of a therapist the supervisor responds, not as a therapist, but as an educator.

The supervisor seeks to promote identification, but not transference. If therapy depends for some of its effectiveness on transference elements, then converting the supervisory situation into a therapeutic relationship increases the probability that therapy will fail. In the usual therapy situation, the contact between patient and therapist is confined to their interaction during the therapy sessions. Supervisor and supervisee, on the contrary, have contact with each other in many different contexts in the agency. This tends to dilute the potency of transference for effective therapy.

The evaluative component inherent in supervision makes it difficult to effectively engage in therapy. In addition to the risk of loss of self-esteem, of possible rejection and blame in sharing intra- and interpersonal problems, is the added risk that this content might be used in evaluating the supervisee's potentialities for professional performance and advancement. There is increased tendency to share selectively rather than fully and openly. The responsibilities of supervision compromise the requirements for effective therapeutic interaction.

In therapizing the supervisor-supervisee relationship, the supervisor risks doing the supervisee an injustice. It reduces the supervisee's incentive to get outside help clearly designed to provide therapy and thus denies the supervisee the full benefit of a relationship exclusively devoted to his therapy.

Research studies indicate that supervisors tend to behave differently in supervision than in therapy. Lambert and Beier (1974) compared the interaction of five therapists with their own clients and with their supervisees. The focus of the tape-recorded comparison was the level of facilitative conditions (empathy, respect and genuineness, specificity) offered in each of these interactional contexts. The levels of empathy and specificity were significantly lower in the supervisory context. A global rating showed that the interactional orientation in supervision was significantly less therapeutic than that offered in counseling. The results suggest that there is a recognition of the difference in objectives between therapy and supervision which requires the supervisor to behave differently in the two contexts.

The fact that psychiatric residents undergo a personal analysis while in supervised training is a recognition of the fact that there is, or should be, a clear distinction between therapy and supervision.

To summarize, confusion results from the fact that educational supervision toward developing job-related self-awareness and psychotherapy are similar in some essential respects. Both encourage self-examination in the context of a meaningful relationship, both are directed toward personal growth and change, both provoke anxiety. The psychodynamics of both processes and the techniques employed are the same. The distinction lies primarily in purpose, focus, role expectations, and process employed.

Acceptance of Distinction Between Supervision and Therapy: Empirical Data

The available data suggest that most supervisors and supervisees understand, and accept, the limited definition of the supervisor's responsibility as outlined here. Most of the 853 respondents to a questionnaire made a clear distinction between professional development and personal development. The *professional* development of the supervisee was selected by both supervisors and supervisees as one major objective of supervision. Conversely, both groups selected "ensuring the more complete development of the supervisee as a mature *person*" as among the three least important objectives. Satisfaction "in helping the supervisee grow and develop in *professional* competence" was the main satisfaction in supervision for the largest percentage of supervisors (88 percent). Less than 1 percent of them, however, checked "helping supervisees with their *personal* problems" as a source of satisfaction. Similarly, the statement of dissatisfaction in supervision least frequently checked by supervisees was "My supervisor tends to become too involved in my personal problems," indicating that transformation of supervision into psychotherapy was not currently a problem for most of the respondents (Kadushin 1974).

Supervisors responding to admonitions that they have no right to "casework the caseworker" adhere to the dichotomy of professional versus personal development even more rigorously than do supervisees. If anything, supervisees indicate a greater willingness to accept the therapeutic intrusion of the supervisor than supervisors appear willing to offer it. In response to the incomplete sentence, "If personal problems came up in my work with clients I would prefer that my supervisor. . . ," 48 percent of the supervisees said that they wanted the supervisor to "identify the problems and help me resolve them" whereas only 30 percent of the supervisors prefer this response. Conversely, 44 percent of the supervisors would "identify the problem and help supervisees get outside help" but only 11 percent of the supervisees preferred this response. Supervisors, more often than supervisees, saw the legitimate source of help for job-related personal problems as lying outside the supervisory relationship (Kadushin 1974).

The hesitancy by social work supervisors to therapize the relationship reflects a similar tendency in psychotherapeutic trainers of psychiatrists. Goin and Kline (1976) videotaped conferences between 24 supervisors of second-year psychiatric residents for the purpose of examining how the supervisors dealt with the residents' countertransference reactions to their patients. Countertransference was defined as the "therapist's conscious as well as unconscious reactions toward and feelings about their patients" (p. 41). Surprisingly "for a discipline that often stresses the need for open communication" (p. 42), only 12 of the 24 supervisors discussed countertransference at all, despite the fact that it was evident in each case. Of the 12 supervisors who did, only 4 discussed it at any length. The supervisors tended to avoid such discussion because of hesitancy about converting the educational situation to therapy, and because of hesitancy in creating anxiety in the supervisee.

When countertransference was discussed effectively the supervisors, in a frank, no-nonsense way, called attention to the therapist's feelings about the patient which were affecting his work. There was no attempt to "explore personal motivations, conscious or unconscious, for residents acting or feeling as they did. It was merely an attempt to acknowledge the feelings that were there" (p. 43). The objective in raising these feelings for discussion was to make the resident aware of them so as to give him "a greater chance for rational control over his interactions with the patient" (p. 42). The objective was not to "probe deeper into the roots of these feelings" for the purpose of therapeutic resolution (see also Hunt 1981). As Haley (1977) notes "A person's personal life is too important to be tampered with by teachers," including supervisors (p. 187). (See also Mayer; Rosenblatt 1975.)

Problems in Implementing the Distinction

These problems "leave the supervisor in the dilemma of having to be more than a teacher, but less than a therapist. Inevitably this demands sensitive and difficult decisions on the part of the supervisor, who must always be aware of when his professional concern becomes personal intrusiveness and yet deal directly and realistically with countertransference phenomena which interfere with the ongoing therapeutic work" (Gizynski 1978, p. 203). Furthermore, "It is a matter of extreme delicacy to maintain a warm and interested human relationship on the one hand and on the other not to respond to the therapeutic needs that the [supervisee] may reveal either directly by the development of symptoms or indirectly in the handling of case material" (Zetzel 1953).

Consequently, establishing guidelines for what is appropriate in a supervisory conference is easier than applying them. The following excerpt is a supervisor's introspective review of the difficulty in making a decision in such a situation. The problem lies in deciding when a worker's difficulty is purely personal and when it is task-related.

Vera [the worker] brought up the fact that she was experiencing some confusion herself about the prospect of marrying her present boyfriend and that the two of them were involved in premarital counseling. She expressed doubt as to her ability to help someone else deal with a problem similar to the one she herself was experiencing.

I was caught a little off guard and likewise experienced a certain element of confusion—a few quick thoughts ran through my mind, and I responded by doing "nothing." My quick thoughts leading to this response went something like this: avoid taking on the role of therapist; personal problems of the supervisee are not relevant here unless they interfere with job or learning performance and there is not yet sufficient evidence to this effect; the fact that Vera is both aware of and getting outside help for her problem is good; I want to convey to her that having some problems does not necessarily prevent a person from providing effective professional help; perhaps the best way to operationalize all of the above thoughts is to simply shrug off Vera's remarks and keep the discussion focused on how to help the client. Vera had no trouble picking up the fact that I preferred not to get into a discussion of her personal problems. She did not pursue the matter any further and appeared able to continue concentrating on her client's situation. With the exception of a brief comment or two, she has not brought the matter up in subsequent sessions, nor have I.

On hindsight, I am neither totally dissatisfied nor completely overjoyed with the way I handled this matter. The basic issue is if, when, and how a supervisor should get involved in dealing with the personal problems of a supervisee. In the literature I have looked at, the issue is frequently raised and always answered in essentially the same way—that is, the supervisor should be aware of and deal with the emotional aspects of learning (fears, resistances, etc.) but should not focus on the personal needs and problems of the supervisee unless these difficulties are such as to significantly interfere with work performance—and then the supervisor should not "treat" the supervisee but encourage him to seek outside help.

I am satisfied that my response and the rationale behind it were in accord with the literature on this issue. However, I now question one of the basic assumptions upon which this response was based, i.e., the lack of interference with work-learning performance. In starting the process of evaluating Vera's work, I have become aware of a tendency on her part to shy away from offering help to clients in the area of marital conflict, although not hesitating to offer and provide it in other problem areas (housing, child-parent relationships, etc.). Also, it now occurs to me that Vera may not have been asking for any help with her personal problems (she was already involved in outside counseling), but only for help in resolving her concern about being able to help someone else with a problem she saw was similar to her own. If this was the case, I would consider her concern to represent the kind of emotional aspect of learning which is the responsibility of the supervisor to deal with. In retrospect, viewing the pattern of Vera's work performance I think the problem was more job related than I had originally thought.

The problem is noted by another supervisor in the following:

> A recurrent problem was Dick's hesitancy about helping a family arrange for a nursing home placement for an aged client, even when this seemed clearly necessary. At some point, I felt that it was important to explore Dick's feelings towards nursing homes to be sure that he wasn't allowing a personal bias to interfere *against* nursing home placement. I attempted to deal exclusively with job-related awareness, but when Dick admitted that much of his feeling came from the experience of his own father being placed in a nursing home, the session began to focus more and more on the supervisee rather than on the work-related issue. We became caught up in dealing with the psychology of Dick's relationship with his father, but eventually I was able to redirect our attention and move back with some difficulty to the issue of nursing homes for his clients.

The problem is a difficult one because the worker is likely to react negatively to both indifference and excessive interest. If the supervisor ignores the supervisee's comment about what is apparently a purely personal problem, he is likely to feel rejected. If the supervisor shows excessive interest in the problem, it can be interpreted as an unwarranted intrusion. Recognition of the worker's statement without pursuing it might be the difficult response of choice. A frank, explicit statement by the supervisor of what he is doing might help: "I appreciate that this must be a difficult problem for you but I really don't think it is appropriate for us to discuss it at length here." However, it needs to be recognized that a "rigid boundary between the personal and professional lives of (supervisees) seems simplistic and artificial" (Gurka and Wicas 1979, p. 404).

The Individual Conference

Structure and Scheduling

The most frequent context for supervision is the individual conference. It is often supplemented and sometimes replaced by alternatives such as the group conference (see chapter 6). Nevertheless the individual conference is still the principal locus of supervision; 86 percent of supervisors and supervisees indicated, in response to a questionnaire, that this was true in their experience (Kadushin 1974).

The individual conference is essentially a dyadic interview to fulfill the administrative, educational, and supportive functions of supervision. It is, for educational purposes, an individual tutorial. Like all interviews, the individual conference requires certain formalities, structure, and differential role assignment. It should be a regularly scheduled meeting at some mutually convenient time. It should be conducted in a place that ensures privacy and protection from interruption, is physically comfortable, and conducive to good, audible communication.

The effects of failure to guard against interruptions and of differences in supervisor-supervisee orientation to conferences are illustrated in the following comment by a supervisee.

> We only have one hour, which is really poor because when I do see him there are constant interruptions. And I make a list before I go in there. First of all because I know I have to go boom, boom, boom. And John doesn't go boom, boom, boom. He's much slower than me in his pace of communicating, much more thorough. I would take a quick answer and go on to the next thing. . . . Today he couldn't see me at the regular time but could see me for half an hour after the staff conference. Well the conference was late and then there were interruptions. So it's gotten so that I reduce my discussions to the most specific, concrete kinds of things. (Amacher 1971, p. 71)

Although formal scheduling is desirable, there may be occasions when informal, on-the-spot conferences are necessary. Social work is full of stressful emergencies that often cannot wait for the regular conference. At the point of crisis the worker's motivation for learning is apt to be most intense. Consequently it is good to seize the teachable moment.

However, the unscheduled, off-the-cuff, "may-I-see-you-for-a-quick-minute" conference has its own disadvantages. Because it does come up suddenly, there is no time for preparation. Judgments are made without sufficient opportunity to carefully consider alternatives. Because such conferences snatch time from other scheduled activities, they are apt to be hurried and harried. The worker may feel guilty and apologetic about intruding on time the supervisor had scheduled for other activities. In contrast, the worker can comfortably use the scheduled conference time with a guilt-free sense of entitlement. A separate time, a separate place, a planned encounter symbolically affirm the importance of supervisory conferences. Persistent requests for conferences on the run tend to depreciate their significance.

An attempt to understand the individual worker's pattern of using supervision may be helpful. Some workers may deliberately, if not entirely consciously, force the supervisor into frequent informal conferences as a way of avoiding formal conferences. This pattern may express the worker's undue dependence on, or hostility toward, the supervisor. The supervisor must decide when an emergency is truly a crisis and when it is more an expression of a supervisee's rather than a client's need.

Preparation

A scheduled conference begins before it actually starts, and this is one of its prime advantages. It begins in the preparation for the conference by both supervisee and supervisor. The supervisee submits some record of his work—written recording, tape recording, log forms, work schedules, reports completed, a work plan. The supervisee's formal preparation of this material requires some explicit self-review of his work.

The supervisor reviews whatever examples of the supervisee's current activity have been made available. Reviewing the material with the responsibilities of educational supervision in mind, the supervisor develops the teaching syllabus for the next conference or series of conferences. A conscious effort is made to select some cluster of information or concepts for teaching. The supervisor, in preparation for teaching, might review his own notes and the relevant literature on the material he plans to teach. Preparation for a tutorial requires the same care as teaching a seminar in a school of social work.

Practice knowledge and competence are indispensible for effective first-line supervision generally, and for educational supervision in particular. The power of expertise, which is a principal source of the supervisor's administrative authority, requires this. The responsibilities of educational supervision further require a solid grasp of the subject matter relevant to agency practice. The supervisor as a source of identification, as an admired practitioner, and as a model of effective practice, needs to project the image and the reality of competence.

Scott (1969) found that professionally oriented workers preferred a supervisor "to know the theoretical fundamentals of their discipline—be skilled in teaching casework methods and capable of offering professionally competent assistance" (pp. 94–95). The supervisee looks to the supervisor to have available a fund of previously developed solutions to practice problems. Studies of student evaluation of teaching show that a thorough knowledge of subject matter content is a necessary, if not sufficient, requirement for good teaching.

The worker's activity, as evidenced in the material submitted, is the "textbook" for the "course." It provides the basic relevant material for teaching, and the teaching objectives selected should be tied in with the worker's on-the-job activity; therefore the supervisor not only needs to know the content to be taught, but also to be thoroughly familiar, through preparatory review, with the worker's activity.

In administrative supervision, case records, worker's reports, and other forms are reviewed for evidence of services rendered in compliance with agency procedure; in educational supervision the same records are reviewed for evidence of deficiencies in performance which require training.

In addition to the content and context of the material to be taught, the supervisor also has to review his knowledge of the learner. Given the special learning needs and unique learning patterns of this particular supervisee, how can the selected teaching objectives be best presented? What teaching techniques and approaches might work best with this supervisee? To answer these questions the supervisor should review the educational diagnosis of the supervisee and where he is now in his learning. In preparation the supervisor reviews both the material presented by the supervisee and the supervisee who is presenting it.

Preparation involves ensuring the availability of instructional materials that might be needed in conference teaching. If the use of certain agency forms is to be taught, copies should be at hand. If policies are to be discussed, the agency manual should be accessible. If references are to be cited to support teaching and to stimulate out-of-conference reading by the supervisee, the books and articles should be obtained in advance and made available.

The advance planning and preparation provide the supervisor with a focus and a structure which she holds lightly and flexibly, ready to discard or change in response to a supervisee's learning needs as they are actually manifested in the conference. Selectivity in choosing what to teach is a significant aspect of preparation. To attempt to teach everything, all at once, is to guarantee failure to teach anything. The supervisor has to select some limited focus for teaching.

Conferences concerned with the supervisee's clinical work generally have two interrelated objectives. One focus is on case management—enhancing an understanding of the client in her situation, planning strategies for intervention, etc. The second focus is on developing the knowledge and skills of the worker.

Process

Once the conference is under way, how does the supervisor teach? We have noted that the starting point for educational supervision is the report of the worker's activity on the job, shared with the supervisor in advance or verbally during the conference. "Supervision is 'post-facto' teaching, a retrospective scrutiny of interactions and their reciprocal effects" (Fleming and Benedek 1966, p. 238). The supervisor engages the worker in a systematic, explicit, critical analysis of the work he did and the work he is planning to do, with an individual client, a family, a group, or a community. The endeavor is to provide the worker "with a structured learning situation which facilitates maximum growth through a process which frees potentialities" (Ekstein and Wallerstein 1972, p. 10). The conference is an opportunity for guided self-observation, for systematic introspective-retrospective review of work that has been done, for thinking about the work as "recollected in tranquility." Experience is fragmented and seemingly chaotic. The supervisor helps the su-

pervisee impose some order and meaning on experience, and identify the principles that can guide him in understanding what he
needs to do.

The supervisor does this by asking questions, requesting clarification, freeing, supporting, stimulating, affirming, directing, challenging, and supplementing the worker's thinking. The supervisor
calls attention to errors in the worker's performance, missed opportunities, apparent misunderstandings, gaps and inconsistencies.
The supervisor introduces new ideas, shares relevant knowledge
and experience, explains and illustrates similarities and differences
between this and other situations, enlarging the worker's perspective. The supervisor poses relevant alternatives for consideration. A
study of tape-recorded conferences indicated that the supervisor's
questions very seldomly came across with the message of

> "I am testing you to see if you know this," but more often as "What do
> you think, because we have to decide this together?" or "What do you
> know about this, because I want to help fill in what you don't know so
> you can help the client more effectively?" That is, [supervisors]
> seemed interested in knowing what the [worker] thought, to put their
> ideas together or to help the [worker] become more knowledgeable,
> not to evaluate in the judgmental sense the worker's amount of knowl-
> edge. (Nelsen 1973, p. 190)

The supervisor can offer a small lecture, engage the supervisee in
a Socratic dialogue or a give-and-take discussion, offer a demonstration, role play, listen to and analyze with the supervisee a tape-
recorded playback, and offer material for reading.

Most supervisors apparently use a mix of expository, didactic
teaching and dialectical-hypothetical indirect teaching procedures.
Didactic teaching amounts to "telling"; dialectical-hypothetical
teaching involves questions and comments which help the supervisee think things out for himself and attempt to find his own answers. It comes close to the guided discussion method.

Some things the worker can learn himself from an analytical
examination of his own experience with the client. For such kinds
of learning the best approach by the supervisor is to be like a mid-
wife, helping the worker give birth to his learning, assisting by
active listening, guiding questioning, clarifying, paraphrasing, encouraging elaboration. "Tell me more of what you felt at that point";

"Could you explain that?"; "What prompted you to say that then?"; "What were you thinking when the client told you that?" This kind of learning depends on supervisee self-discovery, but the supervisor engages in actions that increase the probability that self-discovery will take place. The approach is in line with the recommendations of the classical educator Comenius, who noted that the principal objective of the educator is "to find a method of instruction by which teachers teach less but learners may learn more." Comenius is seconded in this by Rousseau, who noted that "our urge to instruct leads us to teach that which the student could better learn on his own."

Some things cannot be learned by even the most astute, insightful examination of the worker's interactional experience with the client. Some things have to be taught didactically—the agency's eligibility requirement for the variety of services it offers, the research findings regarding factors associated with success in adoption, community resources available to help with problems of single parenthood.

Most of the teaching for which the supervisor is responsible in implementing educational supervision results from a process of reciprocal interaction between the teacher and learner, both actively participating in the process, both contributing to the process. It is a combination of didactic teaching and dialectical-hypothetical self-discovery learning.

Some have proposed a more explicit learning theory approach to supervision, advocating the use of behavior modification approaches (Levine and Rose 1970; Tilker 1974; Mead and Crane 1978; Morton and Kurtz 1980). The emphasis is on changing the supervisee's behavior through clearly specifying behavioral learning outcomes, particularizing and sequencing teaching objectives, and explicitly rewarding and reinforcing desirable responses.

Other approaches to educational supervision have been suggested for helping the supervisee achieve the necessary changes in thinking and feeling. Moffat (1977) has outlined a task-oriented approach and Schmidt (1979) has presented a cognitive restructuring approach. According to Schmidt, learning problems in supervision are the result of feelings triggered by thoughts or self-statements. The corrective is to change these thoughts so that they do not impede learning. Thoughts such as "I must show the supervisor how perfect I am"; "I must make the right decision or something terrible will happen"; "I should like all my clients and I should never feel angry" are counterproductive. If changed, the supervisor would be freer to learn.

Given the fact that supervision is conducted in the context of an interpersonal dyadic relationship, with the objective of effecting change, it is not surprising that the approach that supervisors adopt in supervision reflects the approach they employ in case work (Frances and Clarkin 1981). Lacking training in teaching but possessing clinical skills, the temptation for the clinician turned supervisor is to utilize a clinical approach to teaching.

The behavior modification caseworker is a behavior modification supervisor. The Rogerian caseworker is a Rogerian supervisor; the ego-psychology-oriented caseworker is an ego-psychology-oriented supervisor. Even the family therapist is likely to transform supervision into a replica of family therapy. Supervision is most often conducted in a group as group supervision, family metaphors and family sculptures are used in discussing group interaction; supervisees may discuss their own genogram and family experiences.

Some significant content cannot be taught either didactically, through discussion, or through some form of behavior modification. Such content can only be taught through modeling.

A good deal of what is most effective in social work is based on a special human attitude and approach to the client. As Grotjohn (1949) asks, how can this be taught? "How do you teach patience and devotion, tact and timing, decency and tolerance, empathy and intuition, modesty and honesty and frankness . . . the dangers of abusing a position of confidence and trust?" Such things are learned more effectively through a cathected identification with a supervisor who models such attitudes rather than through didactic teaching or discussion.

Imaginative modeling involves more than watching the supervisor as implied in the term "role modeling." Modeling involves "observing" desirable worker behavior available from a wide variety of sources—reading typescripts of interviews, listening to audiotapes, watching movies and videotapes, watching interviewing through a one-way screen, or sitting in on an interview. All these procedures provide the supervisee with a model of how a worker should behave in contact with a client.

It should be noted that incidental learning goes on side-by-side with intentional teaching. Much is caught that is not explicitly taught. Consequently the supervisor has to be careful that her interpersonal behavior is congruent with her teaching about such interpersonal behavior. The supervisor who behaves nonacceptingly toward workers is not likely to teach the concept of acceptance successfully. In this instance the supervisor does not exemplify in her own behavior the attitudinal approach she is professing to teach.

The supervisor who says, "I am telling you that what you are supposed to do is to let the client make his own decision about what he wants to do," is not teaching what he intended to teach, namely self-determination.

Good supervision is good social work practice once removed. Much of what is desirable behavior in the worker-client interaction is analogous to desirable behavior in the supervisor-supervisee interaction. Good supervision is then a model for what the supervisee needs to learn and an instrumentality for facilitating such learning. Educational supervision is both a model and a method.

But the choice of approach depends not only on the nature of the content to be taught, but also on the nature of the learning preferences of the learner. Even content that lends itself to learner self-discovery through Socratic questioning by the supervisor may be preferred to be learned didactically by some particular learners. A supervisee says:

> I am aware, or at least I hope, the supervisor knows some of the answers. Maybe it's better to do things for yourself. You may learn better by trying to reach for the answers by yourself. But I know myself and I learn what I need to learn pretty effectively if I am just told what answers others have formulated. I can use their experience and know-how.

The choice of approach is based on the goodness-of-fit between the content to be taught and the learning preferences of the supervisee.

The supervisor selects her approach not only so that it is congenial with the learning patterns of the supervisee but also so that it is appropriate to the content to be taught. Agency forms and procedure can be taught didactically and by providing relevant reading material. Interviewing techniques cannot be effectively taught in that manner; role playing is the more appropriate teaching approach for this kind of content.

A supervisor says, "The worker expressed his anxiety about medical terms and his limited understanding of them, and I recommended a book which contained useful information about them," illustrating an appropriate approach for the content to be taught. In a different situation, however, another supervisor says that "her supervisee faced a difficult decision whether to recommend foster care for these children or placing a homemaker in the home. I engaged [her] in a discussion [in which we thought] of the advantages and disadvantages of each of the alternatives." In each of these conferences the teaching methods were appropriate for the different content that needed to be taught.

The methods employed have to be appropriate to the ultimate objective of educational supervision, which is knowledge for use. Rapoport's (1954) definition of supervision as a "disciplined tutorial process wherein principles are transformed into practice skills" calls explicit attention to this focus. The classroom teacher can be satisfied with intellectual acquisition of content by the learner. Educational supervision has to aim at emotional assimilation of the content so that behavioral changes result from teaching. The progression is from information into knowledge, knowledge into understanding, understanding into changed behavior in interaction with the client. New behavior is then tested in interaction with the client to see whether the change is effective. Feedback from the client and the supervisor permits the worker to correct his learning, modify his behavior, test it again, and examine the second feedback.

To promote transfer of learning so that the same problems do not have to be rediscussed as they are encountered in different cases, the teacher directs learning toward a clarification of general principles that can be validly applied from case to case. She moves from the specific to the general, relating the case situation to the principle and the principle to the case.

Situational learning of the technical requirements for dealing with the particular case situation, which is the subject of the conference, is supplemented by an effort to conceptualize and generalize what is taught. Conceptual teaching generalizes the particular experience; practice teaching particularizes the generalization. The supervisor's approach in moving from the specific to the general, in helping the supervisee conceptualize practice, is illustrated in the following comment.

> Oh, one other thing that I think has to do with his teaching style is that when we're talking about a specific client, he will often now—he didn't at first—but now he will say, "Well, what do you think about this general issue of—?" and then he'll take what we're talking about—say it's a very verbal client or a very nonverbal client, or it's a client who has terminated early—he'll say, "What do you think about this style in general?" not just related to this client, but with others. Or a client who terminates: "If you had it to do over again with this client, what might you have done differently now that you have hindsight?" I guess it's typical of him to say, "Now that we're operating on the basis of hindsight, what might we do differently?" which does not mean to me, "Well, schmuck, what could you have done better with this case?" But "Now that we have all the data in, thinking back on it, do you have any thoughts?" So he pushes me to think in a more general way about the processes of therapy with particular kinds of people or particular kinds of techniques or whatever, and how I would do that again in the future—how I would use that. I guess sort of asking me to conceptualize things on a broader level, to think about things on a broader level than just one client. (Diane 1977, p. 143)

Teaching techniques have, of course, different effects depending on the attitude, skill, conviction, and appropriateness with which they are used. "What do you think?" and "How do you feel about it?" can sound like tired clichés. They can also be said, however, in a spirit which suggests that the supervisor warmly welcomes a more active participation of the supervisee in the learning process. The aim is to develop an interactional pattern of mutuality. Despite the elements of mutuality in the relationship there is, or should be, an imbalance in the knowledge and skills which the participants bring to the encounter. The supervisor has to accept the responsibility for having more experience, being more knowledgeable and skillful and having available what the profession provides in practice wisdom and problem solutions. Supervisor and supervisee are not peers. As Robinson says, "to start with an assumption of equality is to deny the student her right to any learning process" (1949, p. 42). The supervisor has the ultimate responsibility for what takes place in the teaching-learning situation.

In the following passage a supervisor describes how she found her own congenial approach to educational supervision in offering leadership in the context of mutuality.

Perhaps one of the most difficult aspects of the role of supervisor, for me, was making criticisms and suggestions. As nice as my supervisory theory sounded, when I attempted to put it into practice, I had trouble.

I found myself saying to Ruth, as she reported her meetings to me, "Did you find out about . . .?" "Did you turn this in yet?" "Well, did you think of trying this . . .?" Ruth's reaction to all of these "did you's" was, naturally, very defensive. Her answer was, most often, something like "Well, I didn't have time" in a very cold, flat voice, or "It seemed more important to. . . ." I was sounding more like a policeman-mother than a helpful supervisor.

I began to experiment with different ways of saying the same things, or getting the same point across, without such an authoritarian ring. My first idea was to hedge a little, to not come on so strong. I began saying "Well, you know, you might be interested in trying something like this. . ." or "Maybe one thing you could do, too, is to attempt to. . . ." When I hedged and hawed in this manner, Ruth wasn't nearly as defensive, but I still wasn't getting the desired result. Now she wasn't taking me seriously. I seemed to have no authority at all now, rather than too much. Her answer very often was "Maybe I'll try it" or "I'll think about it," very lethargically. When I realized that this approach was failing also, I put my head to work, and came up with another idea. I was trying to learn from Ruth and she from me. I needed to respect her and encourage her; I needed to give her the chance to express herself in an open and nonjudgmental atmosphere.

What I was attempting to teach her was my own techniques, my way of doing things and of thinking, of handling groups, of being a social worker. Therefore, when I suggested something to Ruth, I was giving her my ideas, what I thought, what I needed to know, what I would do. Individual supervision is a very personal experience. Therefore, I felt I could say these things to Ruth in just that way. At our next meeting together I said to Ruth, "I think what I would like to know from this girl is. . . ," "I think the first thing I might try, would be to. . . ," "For me to do this. . . ."

At first I was afraid of what Ruth's reaction would be to my great emphasis on "I," but my fears were quickly dispelled. It worked beautifully. Ruth's reactions were something like "Oh yeah? I didn't think of that" or "Wait a minute, why would you do that?" When I gave her my thoughts, as a person in a supervisory capacity, she was able to relate herself to me as a person in the student role.

I realize this type of approach wouldn't work well for everyone, although it did work for me in this one case. One snag, however, that came hand in hand with this new way of doing things, was that it evoked questions such as "Why would you do that?" I was pleased she wanted to know my thoughts and that she wanted to discuss it further. Nevertheless, I didn't feel comfortable just telling her my reasons, without her having to think about it. Yet I dislike it when someone tries to "play teacher" with me, and tuns my questions back around on me. I didn't want to answer, "Because X, Y and Z," nor did I want to reply, "Well, why do you think?"

My solution again stemmed from the philosophy I tried to adopt; that I was there to learn from her as well as she from me. The next time she asked me my reasons why, I told her of this dilemma; that I didn't want to give her all the answers, but I didn't want to be the quiz master either; and then we struck a compromise. If she would tell me some reasons she could find for doing it that way, I might learn some new things. Then I would tell her my reasons for taking that approach, and she might learn some new things from me.

As funny as it all sounds right now, and was at that time too, it really worked well. Whenever Ruth started to ask why, she would stop herself and say "Is that because. . . ?" To which I would always reply politely, "Yes, and not only that. . . ." It became a kind of a game I suppose, but the game, and the very ritualized aspect of it provided some very necessary elements to our interviews. It helped us both to realize our roles more fully, through spelling them out so clearly in this one aspect of the supervisory relationship. It added humor to our sessions. It helped us deal with our embarrassment, by laughing a little and thereby relieving the tension. And perhaps most importantly, it brought us closer to each other; we began to like each other and to work much better together.

Orientations to the Process of Educational Supervision

Several distinctly different orientations toward supervision have been identified which tend to result in different approaches to educational supervision. An experiential-existential supervisee-centered orientation sees supervision as concerned with the development of supervisees' self-understanding, self-awareness, and emotional growth. The emphasis is on the worker's feelings. The supervisee has major responsibility for what he wants to learn, and the focus of supervision is on the *way* the worker does his work and the nature of his relationship to the client.

A didactic–task-centered orientation sees supervision as primarily concerned with the development of the supervisees' professional skills. The emphasis is on the workers' thinking. The supervisor has the primary responsibility for what is taught, and the focus of discussion is on the content of *what* the worker is doing, his activities with, and in behalf of, his clients.

An experiential-existential orientation to educational supervision involves establishing a relationship with the supervisee and engaging in interaction which is analagous to the worker-client relationship. The focus of interaction is the supervisee and the content for discussion is the supervisee's feelings about the case problem, his reaction to and feelings about the client, the client's response to the supervisee as the supervisee perceives this, the supervisee's feelings about the client's response, etc. The supervisor concentrates on this focus by reflecting, clarifying, probing, and interpreting the feelings of the supervisee. Suggestions, advice, evaluative comments which might reinforce or discourage certain supervisee behaviors are held to a minimum. The goal of educational supervision here is to help the supervisee to find his own orientation through an exploration of his own experience.

A scale listing these two orientations (didactic vs. experimental) as opposite poles was offered to supervisors and supervisees (Kadushin 1974). They were asked to indicate the point on the scale which denoted the orientation that they thought worked most effectively for them. The tendency for both supervisors and supervisees was to check the midpoint, indicating that the most desirable orientation was a rather even mixture of the two approaches. Despite the general overall agreement, however, supervisors leaned toward the didactic–task-oriented–professional growth approach somewhat more decidedly than did supervisees.

An Israeli study of 29 workers and 26 supervisees found that workers preferred an "advisory" approach to a "learning" approach in dealing with practice problems (Yodefet, Yaakovson, and Pinto 1978). An "advisory" approach, as defined in the study, provides "advice on specific cases in order to solve specific problems that the worker encounters" (p. 81). "Learning" involves "searching for answers" and was the preferred orientation of supervisors.

Goin and Kline (1974) videotaped those supervisors of psychiatric residents who were consistently evaluated as most competent by students. They then analyzed the videotapes of these and other supervisors in an effort to determine the distinctive behaviors manifested by such supervisors in individual conferences. "Good supervisors were shown to be those who made supervision a didactic experience with the focus of attention on the patients" (p. 213). This research finding supports the value of more didactically oriented educational supervision. Other studies of learning in supervision tend to indicate that even in teaching such interpersonal skills as empathy, a didactically oriented approach is effective (Payne, Winter, and Bell 1972). In summarizing a review of the research comparing the effectiveness of experiential and didactic supervision Boyd (1978) says "very little research supports a claim for the effectiveness of experiential supervision or for the hypothesis that experiencing facilitative conditions within supervision will enable the supervisee to offer these same therapeutic ingredients to others" (p. 73).

In summarizing the analyses of supervision of field training among a number of human service professions, Kurpius and Baker (1977) note that

> The dominant approach to applied training across all of the professions is a didactic one. Direct instruction by an expert to one or a small cluster of students is the dominant and traditional mode of training. The didactic process is the matrix in which more specific techniques are embedded. . . . Experiential events in field training tend to be incorporated into the didactic approach to further instructional aims. (p. 235)

Counselor Education and Supervision has published three reviews of research in supervision on counselor trainees—a review by Hansen and Warner (1971) of 25 research studies published between 1960 and 1970, a five-year review (1970–74) by Hansen, Pound, and Petro (1976) of 29 research articles, and a third review by Hansen, Robins, and Grimes (1982) of 19 articles published between 1975 and 1980. The review of the research in 1976 reported that the use of modeling in supervision was an effective educational procedure but that didactic approaches were more effective than experiential approaches in training (p. 113).

In the third review of research reports on supervision in counseling education covering the period 1975–80, Hansen, Robins, and Grimes (1982) conclude that while "modeling is an effective approach to teaching facilitative communication, the findings are inconclusive as to whether didactic or experiential methods are most effective" (p. 201).

The cumulative summary of the three research reviews tends to support the overall conclusion that, on balance, the didactic-behavioral approach to achieving the objectives of educational supervision yields somewhat better results. But it should be noted that each approach receives some empirical support.

The research seems to point in the direction of integrating both approaches, to an approach of technical eclecticism. Each approach seems more effective with different kinds of content and perhaps with different groups of learners. The question that has been posed more and more insistently for social work outcome research generally seems equally applicable here: what kinds of approaches to educational supervision work best with what kinds of supervisees under what kinds of circumstances?

Process-Feedback

The supervisor teaches and the supervisee learns through feedback. It would be impossible to learn to play golf if we never saw where the ball went after we hit it. We need to know how we are doing, what we are doing right, what needs to be changed. Feedback reinforces learning that "works" and helps correct faulty learning. We learn from our mistakes only if we can find out what they are and have the opportunity of analyzing them.

Whereas supervisors tend to hesitate about being critical of a supervisee's work, supervisees welcome appropriate and constructive criticism. One survey found that among the main sources of supervisee dissatisfaction was that supervisors "were not sufficiently critical so that the worker did not know what he was doing wrong or what needed changing" (Kadushin 1974). Workers seem both to anticipate and to welcome instruction, direction, and structure from the supervisor. They do, apparently, look to her to learn what they need to know in order to do their job effectively. Supervisees deserve and appreciate explicit, definite feedback. Goldhammer (1969), discussing supervision of schoolteachers, makes this point:

Perhaps the most rapid and efficient way to alienate one's supervisees is by hedging and by pussyfooting. Teacher: So you think I was really sarcastic with them? Supervisor: Uh, no, I didn't really say that. You are generally sympathetic and friendly with the youngsters, but some of your remarks today, were, uh, less kindly than I've known them to be in the past. Teacher: Some of my behavior today was unkindly? Supervisor: Well, uh, no, not really, but, uh. . . . (p. 344)

To engage in the following kind of dialogue is not very helpful either: "You're doing fine! Keep it up." "Keep what up?" "Just what you're doing" (Ekstein and Wallerstein 1972, p. 145).

Heppner and Handley (1981) researched the behaviors of supervisors that correlated with counselor trainees' perceptions of their supervisor's trustworthiness. The results "seem to indicate the importance of providing honest evaluative information on teaching with a supportive relationship. Perhaps when supervisors only provide positive feedback and do not confront trainees with nonfacilitative behaviors, trainees quesion what is not being said and subsequently the trustworthiness of the supervisors" (p. 244).

Block and Brown reported that when "given the opportunity to rate the clinical supervision they had received, a group of [communicative disorder trainees] emphasized that the supervisors should provide specific feedback to the trainee and that it should be offered in such a way that it would be 'supportive of students' and 'would help them to feel confident' " (quoted in Culatta and Helmick 1981, p. 23).

We can expect the workers, as reasonably healthy people, to be able to take valid criticism without falling apart. It is, therefore, not necessary to balance every criticism with a compliment. Not only does this often put the supervisor in a false position, it is also demeaning to the worker. One supervisee said, "I knew something bad was coming up because she started to give me all that sweet-talking praise." A supervisor expresses her own response to the dilemma:

Should I always temper a criticism with a compliment? Should I make up compliments, or pick out small, good points, if I can't find enough to go around? Should I just offer each compliment as it occurs to me? I'm sure it sounds silly now, but at the time, it was really a problem. The solution I arrived at was simply to play it by ear. I couldn't bring myself to make up phony compliments, or pick out petty points to compliment her on, or to temper each criticism with a compliment.

My main focus here was to be open, honest and realistic. If something could have been done better, I felt it was important to let Carol know. If something was done well, this was also important information.

The supervisee needs feedback to help him overcome his performance deficiencies so that he can do better work. Feedback helps make learning explicit and conscious. The supervisor has the perspective, the objectivity, and the knowledge of what good performance is supposed to look like.

Aside from the client the supervisor is the only other person who has detailed knowledge of the supervisee's performance. Furthermore, the supervisor is sanctioned to give feedback and is explicitly charged with this responsibility. Given these considerations, the supervisor is most often the primary source of feedback for the supervisee and supervisees are eager for this.

Receptivity to feedback is a function of the source of the message and the nature of the message. If the source of the feedback has credibility for the receiver, if the source has power over the receiver, if the source is regarded as an expert, the feedback is more likely to be regarded seriously.

Feedback is more effective if certain guidelines are observed by the supervisor in offering feedback.

1. Feedback should be given as soon as possible after the performance. This increases motivation and interest in learning what might have been improved. Rewarding commendable performance by praise as soon as possible after the event increases the potency of reinforcement.
2. Feedback should be specific. One should be able to point to a specific intervention, act, or comment that needs praise or correction. A specific illustration of poor question formulation or a ragged, ambiguous transition is better than general feedback, which suggests a need to improve interviewing skills.
3. Feedback should be objectifiable. One should be able to point to the concrete behavior which illustrates a deficiency in performance. Vague, general, global statements have less credibility.
4. Feedback should be descriptive rather than judgmental. "I notice that your response to Mrs. P. resulted in her becoming silent and changing her focus," rather than "Your response to Mrs. P. was not very good."

5. Feedback should be focused on the behavior of the supervisee rather than on the supervisee as a person. "After he told you he was gay, your next series of comments had a punitive phrasing," rather than "From your comment, it seems that you don't like gays or are uncomfortable with them."
6. Feedback should be offered tentatively for consideration and discussion rather than authoritatively for agreement and acceptance.
7. Try to tie feedback as explicitly as possible to what you want the supervisee to learn, what you think he needs to learn.
8. Good feedback involves sharing ideas rather than giving advice, exploring alternatives rather than giving answers. It is focused on behavior which can be modified and is accompanied by specific suggestions for change.
9. Feedback needs to be selective in terms of the amount that a person can absorb. The principle is to keep the amount to what the supervisee can use, not all of the feedback you have available to give.

Feedback is important for the supervisor as well as the supervisee. Monitoring verbal and nonverbal responses, specifically requesting reaction where only limited or ambiguous reactions are communicated, the supervisor needs to be constantly alert to whether teaching is resulting in learning. What has been well taught is not necessarily well learned.

Growth Process in Educational Supervision

A number of different attempts have been made to formulate the process of educational supervision in terms of stages of development (Hogan 1964; Littrell et al. 1979; Ralph 1980; Stoltenberg 1981; Hart 1982; Miars 1983; Reising 1983; Friedlander 1983; Cross and Brown 1983; Heppner and Roehlke 1984).

A developmental approach to supervision presupposes that there is growth in supervision and that each stage of such growth requires modification in the supervisor's approach to the supervisee. The modifications are required in response to changing needs of supervisees at different levels of the growth process.

The central idea in these formulations is that the supervisee moves through a series of identifiable, characteristic stages in learning to be a professional social worker, counselor, or clinical psychologist and in developing an identity as a professional.

According to the available research, at the beginning stages in the growth process supervisees need high levels of instruction, structure, and support. They are method and technique oriented with a considerable concern for skill development. The focus in instruction is on the worker-client relationship and the instructional-expert role of the supervisor is given emphasis. The supervisee has a variable sense of professional identity. A coherent theoretical conception of practice is in the process of formulation. Expectations need modification toward a greater acceptance of realistic limitations. The supervisor is directive in a support-security context.

At a later stage in the growth process, the relationship between supervisor and supervisee is less formal and less structured. The supervisor-supervisee relationship is given greater focus and attention. Personal-professional growth concerns, rather than technical-skills concerns, have higher priority. The supervisor as counselor rather than expert is the preferred image. The supervisee has developed some confidence in his technical skills, is less anxious about the possibility of making mistakes, is more autonomous in performance. A clear sense of professional identity has been achieved. The supervisee has come to terms with unrealistic expectations.

The supervisee has established some coherent frame of reference regarding practice. Given an assured base of professional identity and an established conceptual framework, the supervisee is more flexible in his practice, can afford to be more speculative and critical about practice. The supervisee welcomes critical feedback in response to desires to refine a self-assured practice. Beginning supervisees want to develop skills, intermediate level supervisees are more concerned with conceptualization of their practice and advanced supervisees are interested in developing self awareness through examining personal issues affecting their practice. The movement is from skills acquisition to increasing focus on the person of the supervisee.

The progression for the supervisor is from a didactic-instructional-structured relationship with heavy emphasis on technical skills, expertise, and support to a less structured, more informal relationship with a greater emphasis on critical expectations and personal-professional development of the supervisee.

Earlier in the process of professional growth, workers may be motivated by rewards and punishments. At a later stage in the process, workers are more likely to respond to motives relating to satisfaction in the supervisor-supervisee relationship. At each of the different stages a different teaching approach may be more appropriate.

The Parallel Process Component in Educational Supervision

The parallel process, sometimes called the reflection process, has been identified as a phenomenon in supervisory interaction which has considerable significance for educational supervision (Searles 1955; Marohn 1969; Mattinson 1975; Doehrman 1976; Sachs and Shapiro 1976; Kahn 1979; Calligor 1981; Bromberg 1982; Gasiorowicz 1982).

The parallel process is an exemplification of isomorphism—the tendency for patterns to repeat at all levels of the system. We can view the supervisor-supervisee-client interaction as one large system which includes two subsystems, the worker-client subsystem and the supervisor-supervisee subsystem. Isomorphism would suggest that as the worker deals with the client in the worker-client subsystem this would tend to get reflected in the supervisor-supervisee subsystem as a parallel process.

The parallel-reflection process suggests that the supervisee re-enacts in the supervisory conference the behavior which the client manifested in the casework interview. The supervisor then has available in the here and now of the supervisory conference this additional experiential dimension for understanding the worker's performance. Without being consciously aware of this the supervisee, in attempting to understand the client's behavior, identifies with it and mimics it for presentation in the supervisory conference so as to obtain help in dealing with it.

The reflection process involves a recognition that the worker-client relationship involves reciprocal interaction, in which the worker is influenced by the client as well as influencing the client. A client who evokes a sense of disorganization, confusion, and puzzlement in the worker is paralleled by the supervisee's evocation of confusion and puzzlement in the supervisor when the supervisee presents the case for discussion. Experiencing a client who is evasive and resistant, the worker, in discussing the case, displays an analogous kind of evasiveness and resistance in interaction with the supervisor. And just as the client generated a feeling of helplessness, frustration, and anger in the worker, the worker evokes feelings of helplessness, frustration, and anger in the supervisor. If the supervisor is aware of the source of his feelings in the parallel process she can more effectively help the supervisee in working with the client.

Manifestations of parallel process supposedly enable the supervisor to perceive what is occurring in the situation between worker and client as it is replicated in the supervisory interaction. Parallel process thus permits secondhand "observation" of the worker performance with the client through its reflection in supervision.

The parallel process may work in reverse. If the supervisor does not actively extend himself to help the supervisee, the supervisee may repeat this by being indifferent to the client. If the supervisor dominates the supervisee, the supervisee may dominate the client.

The supervisee is the constant element in the two dyadic subsystems. Both involve interaction; both are concerned with the process of helping. Similar psychodynamics operate in both sets of relationships. It might be expected then that the feelings evoked in one context by and in the supervisee might be similar to the feelings evoked in the other context in and by the supervisor. This provides the basis for a parallel process. From the vantage point of the parallel process the two dyadic systems, worker-client and supervisor-supervisee, become one triadic system.

If the worker acts so as to obtain the approbation of the supervisor this is parallel to the behavior of the client in attempting to solicit the approbation of the worker. In both situations, however, the "parallel" behavior is a very natural response to a person having positional power with reference to significant aspects of one's life. Structural and dynamic similarities between therapy and supervision foster parallelisms. Analogous situations evoke analogous behavior (Gediman and Wolkenfeld 1980).

Despite the intriguing nature of the hypothesis, the "reflection process," in its more restricted sense, is as yet difficult to identify. Mattinson (1975) notes that "There is no one 'thing' always easily recognized which is called the reflection process. It can be manifested in a variety of ways, sometimes blatantly, sometimes very subtly. Its recognition and the practice of using it can, in some instances, be very difficult" (p. 22). Furthermore, she says that the "reflection process is only a small part of a supervision," likely to "concern the most difficult and disturbing cases" (p. 48).

Termination of Educational Supervision Conference

A supervisory conference, like an interview, is hard work. Consequently, after an hour and a half, it is likely to be progressively less productive. The end of the conference should be planned at the beginning so that the agenda selected for the conference can be completed within the allotted period of time.

Toward the end of the scheduled time, the supervisor should be looking for a convenient point of termination. It should be at a point where closure has been obtained on a unit of work. The emotional level of the interaction should not be intense. The worker should have been given some prior opportunity to ask those questions and discuss those issues that were of most concern to her. To say to the supervisee, "We have two minutes left for the conference. Was there something you wanted to bring up?" is very frustrating.

Termination involves a summarization of the conference, a recapitulation of points covered and content taught. A supervisor says, "The sessions seemed more worthwhile when I reiterated at the end what we had talked about because it made it seem like we covered a lot. The ending seemed much more together and planned out when I summarized. We both saw these conclusions as a pronouncement of the end of the session. We consequently then proceeded to relax."

Since the conference terminates before it actually ends in the minds of the participants, it might be good to finish with some explicit questions for the worker to think about, some specific reading suggestions relevant to what has been discussed and in line with his interests. The questions might serve as a transition to the next conference. Thinking about the questions raised, both the supervisor and supervisee would be preparing for their next meeting.

In general, it might be said that a good conference in educational supervision has the following characteristics:

1. It involves planning and preparation by both supervisor and supervisee.
2. It has a shared, consensually agreed upon objective.
3. Its focus is the clinical work of the supervisee.
4. It gives priority to critical self-analysis by the worker of his performance, assisted by the guidance of the supervisor and supplemented by her contributions as a resource person.
5. It provides the worker with clear, unambiguous, relevant feedback designed to help improve performance.
6. It takes place in the context of a facilitative learning atmosphere.
7. It follows desirable principles of learning-teaching.
8. It provides follow-through and a tie to the next conference.

It might be noted that while the supervisor has the principal responsibility and sanction for formal education of the supervisee, the supervisor needs to remember that there is considerable informal, unsanctioned education of the supervisee going on at the same time. Workers turn to their peers in learning how to do the job. The client is actively engaged in teaching by her responses to what the worker does. When interventions work, the client is helped and the worker is rewarded. The worker learns that this is a good way to go. As Langs (1979) notes, the "ultimate supervisor for the therapist is the patient" (p. 205). Supervisors need not feel competitive about these auxiliary teachers but welcome their assistance.

Process Studies

There is only one social work study available that attempts a systematic and detailed examination of what actually goes on in individual conferences. Nelsen (1973, 1974) studied tapes of 68 supervisory conferences conducted in a variety of casework agencies. Although these conferences were between students in a school of social work and their field-instructors (supervisors), the findings are applicable to supervisory conferences generally. In response to the question, What do participants really talk about in supervisory conferences? Nelsen finds that

by the fourth taped conference, the following discussion pattern was fairly common. First, field instructor and student would together go

208 EDUCATIONAL SUPERVISION

case by case through the student's submitted written material, with
field instructor asking questions for clarification or student volunteer-
ing extra details, with interrelated discussion of dynamics and handling, with occasional brief exposition by the field instructor of
relevant theoretical or skills information which the student had apparently not known, and with eventual agreement on what was going on
with the client and what to do next. Second, there might be brief
discussions of cases on which there had been new developments but
not dictation, e.g., a broken appointment requiring further action from
the student. Third, there might be some, usually brief, discussions of
learning content such as whether a student was recording properly, or
agency-field content such as monthly statistics or the need to find a
resource for a client. (1973, p. 189)

Both field instructors and students usually participated actively [in
the discussion]. The field instructors freely gave didactic material although not often lengthy exposition. (1974, p. 149)

Supervisors also engaged in supportive activity (to be discussed in
chapter 4) and gave directives "requiring particular behavior" by
the supervisee, i.e., "fill in social service cards in each case"; "to
find a nursing home, call the homes, find out whether they have a
bed, if not find out when they will, find out the cost." Directives
tended to be associated with agency administrative procedures and
concrete services. The context in which the directives were given
indicated a sort of summing up of mutual discussion rather than
the issuing of an order. The reciprocal interaction between supervisor and supervisee is suggested by the fact that supervisors gave
more directives to supervisees who often requested direction than
to those who did not.

Studies of supervisory conferences in closely related fields are
instructive. Culatta and Seltzer (1976; 1977) developed an instrument for scoring categories of interactional events in supervisory
conferences of communicative disorder clinicians. Six categories
were related to the interventions of the supervisor and six to analogous contributions by the supervisee.

The supervisory conference event categories included positive or
negative evaluation statements (supervisor evaluates observed behavior or verbal report of supervisee and gives verbal or nonverbal
approval or disapproval); strategy interventions (statement by supervisor given to clinician for future therapeutic intervention);

questions (any interrogative statement made by the supervisor relevant to the client being discussed); and observation or information statements by supervisor.

Five-minute segments of the tape-recorded supervision conferences were scored by six supervisors who were instructed in the use of the instrument. Two different studies yielded very similar findings. The principal activity in the supervisory interaction tended to be concerned with provision by the clinician-supervisee of "information about therapeutic sessions while supervisors essentially used this information to suggest strategy for future sessions—the picture that evolves is one of the clinicians feeding raw material to the supervisors who used it to plan overall therapy strategy for the clients." This was in marked contrast to the supervisor's perception of "themselves as sounding boards to be used by the supervisee as resource people" (1976, p. 12)—a perception similar to the one generally held by social work supervisors of their activity.

In analyzing differences in talk-time by supervisors and supervisees in the conference, supervisors almost invariably talked more than supervisees.

Questioned about their style of supervision, supervisors were sorted into 3 distinct groups—"Those who felt they were directive in style by providing specific suggestions and comments about methodology and client performance; those who believed they were nondirective, using a nonprescriptive method relying on the clinician to explain the methodology employed; and a group who said they favored a combination of approaches." However, analysis of the content and sequence of the conference revealed that all supervisors seemed to function in similar patterns regardless of their own evaluation of their supervisory styles (1976, p. 12).

A surprising finding was the very limited number of evaluation statements made by supervisors. This generally left the supervisee with little explicit guidance as to what he was doing correctly and/or well and what was done incorrectly and/or poorly.

Schubert and Nelson (1976) corroborated the Culatta and Seltzer findings using a somewhat different instrument for explicitly analyzing supervisors in the conferences. They found that supervisors were most frequently engaged in providing opinions or suggestions. The second most frequent behavior was providing information. In this study also, supervisors talked more than supervisees.

Problems in Offering Educational Supervision

Supervisors may exploit educational supervision to meet their own needs without being fully aware of it. The situation provides the opportunity for developing protégés, for making workers over into the supervisor's own professional image. The supervisor becomes, in such instances, more an object of direct imitation than an object of identification. The worker's success is the supervisor's success; the worker's failures are perceived as the supervisor's failures. The supervisee is less an independent entity than an extension of the supervisor.

The supervisor who, in response to the triadic situation of client-worker-supervisor, is still more a worker than a supervisor, will focus too heavily on the client. Such a supervisor is still primarily interested in practice, albeit vicariously through the supervisee. He has not yet made the psychological transition from worker to supervisor. The consequence for educational supervision is that the supervisor denies the supervisee his freedom to learn. Giving exclusive priority to client needs, the supervisor is so fearful of mistakes by the supervisee that he tends to be overdirective and overcontrolling. The supervisor acts more like a guard than a guide.

A supervisor may be hesitant in sharing his knowledge and expertise with the supervisee out of anxiety about competition from a "sibling." If the supervisor derives gratification from the supervisee's dependency, he will perennially tend to perceive her as "not yet ready" for next steps in education. In both these situations the supervisor tends to teach the content of educational supervision grudgingly, in small doses, at an inappropriately slow tempo. Evidence of workers' growing independence and competence is viewed with anxiety rather than pleasure. An imperious "need to be needed" on the part of the supervisor will further conflict with the responsibility to grant the supervisee as much autonomy as she can responsibly handle.

Overidentification with the worker may make the supervisor overly protective, shielding the worker from possible mistakes, anxious that the worker may not be able to accept normal failures: "She was afraid to take the risks necessary for learning and I was afraid to let her."

A supervisor who is anxious about his own relationship with the

administrator may overcontrol the worker to prevent embarrassment at worker errors for which the supervisor is held responsible.
Conversely, supervisors may act out their own rebellious impulses
toward the agency through their supervisees, from the safety of
their middle-management position.

The supervisor who has considerable therapeutic skills but limited pedagogic skills, or feels more comfortable with the role of
caseworker than with that of teacher, may convert educational supervision into psychotherapy. There is greater gratification in cast-
ing the supervisee in the role of client than that of learner.
Questions brought into the supervisory conference by the supervisee tend to become personalized and interpreted as problems of
personal pathology with which the supervisee might need help.

A supervisor may be sufficiently uncertain about her own knowledge that she cannot permit the supervisee the freedom to experiment and to learn. A supervisor writes:

> Because of my discomfort with the supervisory relationship,I found it
> easier to simply introduce final decisions matter-of-factly, rather than
> risk challenge of my own choice of alternatives in a give and take
> process. I was perfectly happy with this "dictator" method but feared
> an open exercise of authority which might be called for in joint demo-
> cratic decision-making if the worker didn't accept my reasons as valid
> and challenged my choices.

Such a supervisor may tend to be defensive and find it difficult to
acknowledge ignorance.

Educational supervision provides the opportunity for a narcissistic display of knowledge and skills. Whether or not this is educa-
tionally helpful to the supervisee becomes a secondary consideration. The supervisor who made the following comment caught
himself indulging in such behavior.

> In discussing the client with the worker during that session, I made
> another mistake: that of "lecturing" the worker on the psychological,
> social, cultural and economic factors affecting clients' behavioral pat-
> terns without any reference to the particular situation at hand. And
> when I did talk about the client, I started to discourse on the effects of
> emotional and cultural deprivation on the lives of children, and the
> psychoanalytical implications of Henry's father having run away from
> the home. . . . I finally caught myself in the middle of the oedipal
> complex bit. "B.S. !" I said to myself and changed the subject immedi-

ately, hoping that the worker had not realized the pompousness of it all, and if she did that she would forgive me for it. I then realized how easy it is to get carried away when one has a captive audience. The "teaching" aspect of supervision is an art not easily mastered. I must remember to do more teaching and less preaching.

Some egalitarian-oriented supervisors may, on the other hand, be afraid of showing what they know. Revealing that they are actually more knowledgeable than the supervisee destroys a pretense of equality in the relationship. Teaching freely requires the ready acceptance by the supervisor that she does, in fact, know more than the supervisee and is entitled to teach it.

Some supervisors, vicariously reliving their own difficult experience in supervision, may want to give the supervisee as hard a time as they had—"Why should he have it so easy when it was so hard for me?" The supervisee becomes a target of displaced hostility over whom the supervisor has sanctioned control. Other supervisors may hesitate to be appropriately critical, fearing hostility or rejection by the worker.

Every supervisor has her own likes and dislikes regarding supervisee learning patterns. If she is not aware of such predilections, there is less probability that she can control differences in her response to different supervisees. Some supervisors like rapid, avid learners who absorb teaching quickly and voraciously; some like the slow, plodding learners who are less challenging and for whom considerable repetition of content is required. Some supervisors like the supervisee who presses the supervisor-supervisee educational relationship in the direction of peer consultation and colleagueship; others find gratification in the supervisee who accepts a parent-child relationship. Some like the exuberant, extroverted learner; some like the shy, introverted learner. Some are more comfortable with learners who do best in the individual-tutorial situation; some are more comfortable with group-oriented learners.

These are some of the considerations which a supervisor of supervisors needs to be aware of in making an educational diagnosis of supervisors.

Case Illustrations

The following vignettes illustrate the supervisor implementing the responsibilities of educational supervision in individual conferences. They have been submitted by supervisees as examples of good supervision.

> The case involved my counseling a husband and wife. The wife was to come to hospital for tubal ligation and wanted an operation. She stated her husband wanted her to have the operation, but was being un-cooperative in helping her arrange day care for the 3 children. She also complained bitterly about desperate financial conditions and how her husband would not follow through on his responsibilities. She stated that her husband would be willing to talk to me but would not be able to come to my office at the hospital. A home visit was arranged. After visiting the home, conditions that the wife had commented upon seemed verified; the husband was civil, but not very communicative. We discussed the reason for the wife's impending hospitalization, home conditions, his ability to budget. We left with agreement that they would come to my office next week. After the interview I felt I had gone to the home and unconsciously sided with the wife. I had moved too quickly in establishing a relationship with the husband and almost ended up telling him how to be more responsible. My super-visor discussed the case with me and (1) gave me positive support regarding my concern for the family and my attempted outreach; (2) supported and verified the fact that perhaps I had been "too pushy"; (3) suggested reasons why I might have acted this way (since this was not my usual style); (4) suggested how I might salvage the relation-ship with the family on next visit. We did a role play to help me feel more comfortable.

> Supervisor noticed that the supervisee appeared to be in a state of frustrated agitation. Supervisor learned that the supervisee was im-mobilized because she had to be at an important meeting in the office within an hour and she had a client who needed her to do "something right now" and she had already spent over an hour talking with the client and making calls trying to find the client a place to live. The client, a 16-year-old unmarried girl with her baby, had come to the agency asking for help in finding a new place to live as her mother had kicked her and the baby out of the house the night before. The super-visor did not stand on ceremony but took initiative to help supervisee immediately. She asked the supervisee to her office to discuss the situation so that perhaps together they could figure out a solution. She assured supervisee that time is still relative, most emergencies not always what they seemed and the supervisee did have access to super-visor which could help spread the responsibility. Supervisor focused in on the problems of the "dependent child mother" who is living with her own mother. She assessed supervisee's knowledge of family as a unit and enabled supervisee to see, and talk about, over-identification

which usually occurs without sufficient facts about a problem. This enabled the supervisee to call client's mother which resulted in a solution to immediate problem and demonstrated to supervisee that she did not have to face problems alone.

The problem was more clearly defined after the worker called the mother of the client only to learn that "she had not put her daughter out, but had lost her temper and her daughter had grabbed the baby and left. It had been late, they were both tired and they had quarreled over the baby's diapers!" The mother was sick with worry and came to agency. When the mother and daughter were tearfully reconciled, the worker was invited to come to their home on the next day to talk about some "real things."

———

During one of our conferences, I was discussing a "social study" I had completed on a client seeking individual counseling. I was relating my impressions of the client, using diagnostic labels and social work "jargon" rather freely. My supervisor listened carefully, but without commenting. When I had concluded, she smiled warmly and queried, "What's this woman like?" I was somewhat taken aback, but began to describe her, again using diagnostic terminology. My supervisor interrupted me, saying, "Well you've already said that and I agree with you completely. But what is she like?"

I feel the interaction my supervisor engaged me in was extremely important, as it forced me to take a serious look at the pitfalls of using diagnostic labels too freely. I realized more clearly than before that labels should serve mainly as a helpful means of classifying behaviors and character disorders—that even though you may attach the "right" label, this does not automatically mean you understand the client. My supervisor asked me to describe a typical interaction between the client and her primary family as I would envision it having happened in her childhood. After struggling with this, she then asked me to again relate my diagnostic impressions, this time without using labels and jargon. I was successfully able to accomplish this, and feel that the steps my supervisor took were important in that they forced me to individualize my client. As a result, I was able to relate in a more personal and individual manner with my client in treatment, thus providing a more effective service.

The following is a more detailed analysis of part of an individual conference with Jim F., a worker in a state child-welfare district office.

Jim began by saying that he wanted to talk about Frank. He brought out that it was important to preserve Frank's placement—he did not think the problem would be solved by replacing him and I agreed. He thought he had made some impression on the boy, and that Frank realized he wanted to help him. I said this was good, and suggested that worker was really on the spot with foster mother ready to put Frank out if his behavior did not change. He agreed to this and said he had made it clear to Frank that he must get a job and stay away from the old crowd, since they are undesirable. I said from his recording I could see he had tried very hard with Frank—did he think it had worked?

The worker here selects the content for the teaching agenda ("he wanted to talk about Frank"). This is in accordance with the principle that learning takes place when the supervisee actively participates in the learning process. It also ensures a higher level of motivation to learn, since the worker, given the opportunity, will select for discussion that content which presents a problem for him.

The supervisor helps to clarify and define the nature of the problem situation that confronts the supervisee. The problem is not Frank's replacement but how to preserve his current placement for him.

The supervisor rewards by explicitly commending ("I said this was good"), in accordance with the principle that we learn best when we receive rewards for learning.

The supervisor communicates empathic understanding and acceptance of the worker's situation ("he was really on the spot"). This probably will be regarded as emotionally supportive by the worker, and helps to establish a good atmosphere for learning. Recognition that the supervisor is empathic and accepting makes the supervisee more receptive to content. The supervisor, however, might be concerned with teaching in saying that the worker is "on the spot." The supervisor is redefining this matter as a problem for him in his responsibility as the social worker assigned to the case. The supervisor is not concerned with Frank's behavior. That is Jim's responsibility. The supervisor is, however, concerned with Jim's behavior and case planning. The worker, rather than the client, is the immediate responsibility of the supervisor.

After Jim has shared with the supervisor what he has done on the case, the supervisor confronts Jim with a challenging question, "Did he think it had worked?" Because the question is challenging and apt to induce defensiveness, it is preceded by an introduction that makes it emotionally easier to accept: "I said . . . I could see he had tried very hard with Frank." The question, "Did he think it had worked?" solicits an objective, self-critical analysis. In inviting reflection, the supervisor is increasing the worker's involvement, intensifying his level of participation in learning.

Didactically stating that the approach was mistaken or, more gently, that it left something to be desired, might have engendered a need for Jim to defend his behavior, since this might be perceived as an attack. People learn less effectively when psychic energy is devoted to self-defense. Encouraging self-examination may result in the worker's explicit recognition of some of the shortcomings of his approach. He may then be more ready to consider alternatives.

It might be noted, too, that the supervisor has actually read the record and is using his knowledge derived from it in this conference. This in itself is encouraging to the supervisee because it indicates that the supervisor is serious about these encounters, is interested in preparing for the supervisory sessions, is keeping to their mutual agreement. Since the justification for recording lies partly in its utility in supervision, use of the recording in the supervisory session rewards the worker for having done the work. It further helps develop a positive supervisor-supervisee relationship. Emotional interaction between the two is more apt to be positive if the supervisor shows respect for the supervisee by respecting his product—the recording.

As yet the supervisor has not taught much, at least not explicitly, although he has taught something about good human relations. He has taught too, by implication, that it is helpful to define a problem clearly and to partialize it if possible. He has encouraged an attitude toward one's work—a reflective self-critical approach—which is a necessary prerequisite for the development of self-awareness. Principally, however, the supervisor is not so much concerned with teaching at this point as he is with developing an atmosphere which is conducive to learning.

> Jim shook his head, indicating he was very doubtful, then burst out with "Frank makes me mad, he's just lazy like Mrs. D says. He doesn't ever try to get work." He went on to tell how at Frank's age he had been earning his own spending money for several years by doing odd jobs that he found himself. I agreed that it would be hard for him to understand why Frank could not do this too—could he see any differ-

ence in Frank's situation and his own. He thought for a moment and then pointed out that he had his family and Frank was in a foster home. I wondered what difference that would make? He could not see that it would make any. After all Frank was only two when he went to a foster home and does not even remember his own family—it was probably the best thing that could have happened because his mother did not take care of him.

Here the atmosphere of psychological safety established by the supervisor permits the supervisee to express his negative feelings about the client. It frees the supervisee to express disagreement with some of the things for which social work supposedly stands. In effect he says the client is lazy, he's no good; if he's in trouble, it's his own fault; he makes me mad; each man is the architect of his own fate, and if Frank just tried harder he would be able to resolve his problems.

The supervisor is understanding enough to accept this outburst, and, rather than express disappointment or chagrin that a social worker should react to his client in a manner which suggests rejection, expresses empathy with the supervisee's difficulty in understanding Frank. Responding in this way the supervisor is teaching, by example, the concept of acceptance—that judging the client and his behavior in moral terms may be satisfying, but it is not very helpful; that in problem-solving it is more helpful to try to understand than to judge. She then asks a question which shifts the focus from an evaluation of Frank's behavior to an attempt to understand the behavior: what helps to explain Frank's actions, what prompts him to act differently from the supervisee?

The supervisee, whose thinking has been channeled by the question, comes up with a descriptive statement of difference. The supervisor further questions him because this, as yet, does not explain why people should behave differently when confronted with similar situations. A less perceptive supervisor might be satisfied with the answer and develop a short lecture on the implications of differences in developmental history. This supervisor prefers to elicit the supervisee's perceptions of the implications that differences in developmental history have for behavior. This, once again, maximizes supervisee participation in learning. Implicit in the supervisor's questions are some behavioral concepts, e.g., the past is structured in the present, behavior is purposive, all generalizations need to be individualized, feelings are facts and determine behavior. These ideas, however, are not taught explicitly.

The worker continues to voice doubts about the point the supervisor is making; he questions whether this difference in background explains the difference in behavior between himself and Frank.

> I suggested we think back to when all this happened. I asked how he thought Frank felt when he had to leave his parents and go to a strange place, or did it seem that he was too young for it to make any difference. Worker looked dubious and remarked that after all, a kid of two could hardly talk. We discussed this for a while, and he was thoughtful at my suggestion that it might even be harder for a little child like Frank who could feel, but was too young to understand what was happening, than for an older child. I said here we were talking about what had happened to Frank and about his feelings when he was two years old, perhaps this did not seem to have much connection with the present. He said, thoughtfully, that he could see it might, adding that Frank never hears from his family and that must be "rough on the kid"; I said he was telling me that out of Frank's life experiences and his own they would bring something different in terms of feeling to the present. With an expression of surprise, Jim commented that he felt sorry, not angry at Frank anymore, how come? Did he think it was because we were trying to understand Frank? He decided this was it, and wondered why he had not thought about all that before.

The supervisor does not directly counter the worker's doubts about her implied "explanation." She invites the worker to examine his thinking further, but this time by attempting to empathize with Frank (how did he think Frank felt? etc.). She goes on to suggest a line of thought which the supervisee grasps ("or did it seem that [Frank] was too young for it to make any difference"). Such an approach can be helpful if the supervisor senses that this is the nature of the worker's thinking but that he is either not ready or not clear enough to articulate it. The supervisor, in making it explicit, exposes it so that it can be discussed. Unless the message from a worker is clear, however, there is danger that this kind of interpretation will project onto the worker the supervisor's own conception of the situation, which the supervisee then employs for his own ends.

In any event, the supervisor is trying to make a teaching point: that a two-year-old can "know" and his "knowing" does affect later behavior—an idea with which the supervisee disagrees. At this juncture the supervisor, if she thinks the point important enough to warrant concern with its acceptance, should be prepared with didactic research material to reinforce it. What studies, if any, support the contention that a child of two can remember and that such memories affect later behavior? What clinical material supports the contention? The student has a right to know and the supervisor has an obligation to make this information available. Otherwise, the supervisor is exploiting the authority of her position to solicit acceptance of what may well be a presumption with little supporting evidence.

The past is of concern, however, not for itself but only as it affects the present. The supervisor shifts the discussion back to this area of greater importance. She does so by a question that suggests another principle in learning—that we learn best when the material being presented is meaningfully related to problems that concern us. The supervisor is trying to relate the questions she raised about Frank's past to the problems that the worker faces in dealing with Frank. The supervisee makes this connection and makes a deduction in line with what the supervisor is attempting to teach about the effects of the past.

The supervisor then summarizes and makes explicit the meaning of the interaction ("I said he was telling me," etc.). In summarizing, the supervisor uses another principle in learning—namely, we learn best and retain best if we are clear about what we have learned, if we can put it into words and look at it.

What needs to be taught is not only a change in thinking, not only the injection of new ideas for the worker's consideration (some of which may affect his thinking, some of which may not), but a change in feeling as well. The supervisor's approach, which focuses on understanding rather than judging, leads to a change in feeling. The worker begins to feel sorry for Frank, rather than angry at him. This is an advance toward greater helpfulness but still not as helpful as an understanding of Frank, which the supervisor is aiming to teach. The approach toward developing understanding is only partly in the questions the supervisor raises ("could he see any difference between Frank's situation and his own"; "I wondered what difference that would make"; "I asked how he thought Frank felt"). It is also in the supervisor's approach to the worker. She is not judging the supervisee and his responses but rather attempting to understand why he answers in the way he does. She presents a pattern for identification which the worker might emulate in thinking about Frank.

> Jim then reminded me of the foster mother's complaints and of how he had tried to handle this with Frank by telling him he should find a job and give up his "bad" associates. I said he seemed to be questioning this himself, did he think people always did what they were told to do? In the Army they did. This was always true? What about the men who went A.W.O.L.? He pointed out that they took the consequences and I agreed that we all have to do that. He reminisced about the difference in officers, how some were not liked and had a lot of trouble because the men would not obey them. In other words, I said, it made a difference how the men felt about their superiors. Of course, if they trusted them it was O.K. I said I was sure this was true, and suggested we get back to Frank. "You mean with Frank it's different, I'm not still in the Army." I thought it must be hard getting away from giving orders or carrying them out. "Yes, I see what you mean, I don't think mine are going to work with Frank."

Earlier in the conference the worker has allied himself with the foster mother against Frank ("he's just lazy like Mrs. D. says"). Here the supervisee is separating himself from the foster mother and this change follows from his change of feeling about Frank.

The supervisor uses comparison and contrast to teach a sensitivity to the unique, individualized aspects of this situation. She helps Jim factor out the essential differences between this and an apparently comparable situation, his army experience. The supervisor employs a context which is meaningful for the supervisee and which also follows the principle of moving from the familiar to the unfamiliiar. The supervisor keeps to a relevant focus, however, by relating this situation to the problem which is of concern to them, how best to help Frank. To the good teacher, nothing introduced by the worker is irrelevant. It is the responsibility of the supervisor to take what has been presented and relate it to the tasks of the supervisory conference.

> I asked Jim how, then, he thought he could help Frank, and he replied ruefully that he was not sure—it had seemed simple before, he would just tell him what he should do. Now he realizes Mrs. D. has been doing this right along and it hasn't worked. I asked if he thought he

could help the foster mother understand Frank better. He thought he could try and added that he guessed she felt annoyed at Frank like he did. "How do you think Frank feels?" He said he had just been thinking about that and thought he might well be feeling all alone, like nobody cared, and that must be awful. I agreed and said, "I can see you do care what happens to Frank and I think if you got that over to him, maybe in time Frank can learn to trust you."

Having helped Jim come to the conclusion that the approach he had been using with Frank was not likely to work and having helped him learn why it was not likely to work, the supervisor returns to the basic question that is the focus of the conference—how to help Frank. Now the question can be discussed with greater clarity and with greater motivation on the part of Jim to consider new approaches. The preceding discussion has made possible a teachable moment. The supervisor optimizes the supervisee's involvement by asking how he now thinks he can be helpful to Frank.

The supervisor recognizes and accepts the supervisee's dependence on her for suggesting possible new approaches at this point. In response to this need she suggests an approach ("I asked if he thought he could help the foster mother understand Frank better").

Jim is not only achieving a greater understanding of Frank but, in applying a general approach focused on understanding rather than judging, he is achieving greater empathy with the foster mother as well ("he guessed she felt annoyed at Frank like he did"). The supervisor teaches here, as she did somewhat earlier ("it made a difference how the men felt about their supervisors"), the importance of feelings in relationships—the fact that people behave toward one another in terms of how they feel about one another ("You do care what happens to Frank and . . . maybe in time Frank can learn to trust you"). The supervisor goes on to teach that the worker is part of this complex interaction; that his feelings toward the client are a determinant of the interaction in the relationship (feeling frustrated, he might feel angry toward Frank); that the worker's feelings which intrude in the relationship, once identified, can be controlled.

Jim said he too could see how it would take time whereas he had thought he could do it all in one interview. I said it was hard to realize that change comes slowly in people. I thought he had made a good beginning and realized that he had noticed Frank seemed more cheerful and spoke more easily at the end of the interview. He hoped so but felt he needed to do a lot more thinking before he saw Frank again.

He guessed it wasn't the way he thought, that you can learn all about casework in ten easy lessons. I laughed and said it was good that he was realizing this, but I knew it was hard too when he wanted so much to know all the answers. When we didn't, we could feel frustrated, and perhaps that was some of the reason he had felt angry at Frank. Jim was very thoughtful and said this helped him to understand something that had happened in another interview and we went on to discuss that.

Utilizing the experience Jim has just gone through, the supervisor teaches about expectations for change. Inferentially the supervisor reassures and supports Jim by indicating that she does not expect him to change Frank overnight—nor should Jim expect this for himself. The supervisor supports and excuses his frustration at not being able to learn all about casework in a few lessons.

The supervisor's general approach is consistent with that communicated throughout the conference. Her accepting, understanding, supportive attitude, her readiness to praise the worker where commendation is warranted, her willingness to grant the worker autonomy and to move at his pace have created a nonthreatening climate favorable to learning.

The approach is not so permissive, however, as to be totally without anxiety. There is clear indication that although the supervisor accepts Jim's current professional deficiencies, she does expect him to learn to do better. This is the best kind of anxiety for learning—anxiety based not on fear but on the discrepancy between what the worker needs to know and perhaps wants to know and what he does, in fact, know.

This section of the conference concludes before the conference itself is ended. The next section is introduced by the supervisee once again, this time on the basis of association with related problems—a natural and desirable procedure for transition, indicating the supervisee's ability to generalize his learning.

Some readers might regard the supervisor's approach as too passive or too Socratic. She might have been more active in stimulating Jim to think about certain significant aspects of the case which were largely ignored. It might have been helpful to clarify the target of change efforts—Frank, the foster mother, or both. While suggesting that Jim help the foster mother to understand Frank better, she made no effort to develop how this might be accomplished. There was little exploration of how the foster mother felt and the basis for her reaction in the situation. Rather than agreeing readily with Jim that replacement was undesirable, the supervisor might have helped him clarify his thinking about the advantages and disadvantages of replacement in this particular situation. While indicating the importance of developing Frank's sense of trust in Jim, the supervisor offers little in the way of specifics as to how this might be accomplished. The worker needs help in more clearly identifying the kinds of approaches and interventions on his part that will enhance trust. Little effort was made to explain the nature of the general social situation relating to Frank's employment and job-training opportunities. The fact that some things are not covered may reflect the principle of partialization. Only so much can be included on the teaching agenda of any one conference, and the supervisor always has to be somewhat selective.

We might further note that the supervisor was aided in her efforts by an apt, willing, and capable supervisee; that the conference might have gone less smoothly if Jim had been less cooperative and more resistive. This observation illustrates that teaching and learning require the cooperative efforts of all the participants in the interaction. The best supervisor will fail with some highly sensitive supervisees with limited capacity for learning, and the worst supervisor will succeed with some highly cooperative and capable supervisees.

Summary

Educational supervision is concerned with helping the worker learn what he needs to know in order to do his job effectively. Educational and administrative supervision have the same objectives, and educational supervision supplements administrative supervision by furthering the internalization of administrative controls, developing a professional orientation and a sense of loyalty among colleagues.

The following conditions make for an effective learning situation in the context of a positive relationship. We learn best if:

1. We are highly motivated to learn.
2. We can devote most of our energies to learning.
3. Learning is attended by positive satisfactions.
4. We are actively involved in the learning process.
5. The content to be learned is meaningfully presented.
6. The uniqueness of the learner is considered.

The supervisor has the responsibility of teaching the worker content regarding people, problems, process, and place and developing the self-awareness of personnel with regard to aspects of functioning that are clearly job related.

The regularly scheduled individual conference is the main locus of educational supervision. The teaching content is the supervisee's performance, and the teaching approach is based on an educational diagnosis of the supervisee. Preplanning and preparation are necessary, and during the conference the supervisor engages the supervisee in a systematic, critical analysis of the work he did and is planning to do.

CHAPTER FIVE
Supportive Supervision

THIS CHAPTER is concerned with the third major component of supervision—support. Supervisees and supervisors face a variety of job-related stresses. Unless some resource is available to help them deal with these stresses, their work may be seriously impaired, to the detriment of agency effectiveness. The supervisor is responsible for helping the supervisees adjust to job-related stress. Higher administrators are usually responsible for support to first-line supervisors. The ultimate objective of this component of supervision is the same as the objective of administrative and educational supervision—to enable the workers, and the agency through the workers, to offer the client the most effective and efficient service.

The *NASW Standards for Social Work Practice in Client Protection* make this responsibility of the supervisor explicit. As one of the supervisor's tasks, the *Standards* lists "management of work-related stress and assistance to staff—in coping with their work-related stress."

If one were to categorize the research findings on characteristics associated with effective supervision and leadership, two kinds of factors turn up repeatedly. One cluster of factors relates to getting the job done, seeing that the people who do the job are provided with the facilities, services, information, and skills they need to do the job. These are the task-centered, instrumental considerations of supervision. The second cluster of factors is associated with seeing that the people who do the job are comfortable, satisfied, happy in their work, and have a sense of psychological well-being. These are people-centered, expressive considerations of supervision. Expressive tasks meet the needs of system maintenance. They are the equivalents of oiling the parts and cooling the works of a mechanical system to reduce abrasion and the possibility of overheating. Such expressive system-maintenance functions permit the achievement of instrumental goals.

Blake and Mouton (1961) employ these two variables in the development of their managerial grid—concern for production (the instrumental consideration) and concern for people (the expressive consideration). The best managerial style, both psychologically satisfying and economically productive, is an optimum combination of the two concerns. The Ohio State Leadership Studies (Stodgill and Coons 1957) identified "initiating structure" and "consideration" as the two basic dimensions of leadership. A leader who rates high on initiating structure is task oriented, organizes the work to be done, and clearly defines work objectives, group member roles and expectations. This is a concern with the instrumental aspects of the job. The leader who rates high on consideration communicates trust, warmth, friendliness, and support—a concern with expressive considerations. The Ohio studies found that the most effective leaders were those who rated high on both dimensions. The Michigan Studies on Management (Likert 1967) came to the same general conclusions. The supervisor who communicates both support and high performance-goal expectations is likely to have the most effective work group.

Fiedler's (1967) research on leadership suggested that the optimum mix of these two major dimensions was largely a function of the situation. Some jobs and some settings require a greater component of instrumental, task-oriented, production-centered concern; other situations require a greater emphasis on the expressive, worker-oriented, human-relations aspects. The mix also depends on idiosyncratic needs and characteristics of the supervisees, some requiring more structure and direction, others requiring a more decidedly expressive orientation.

In studies of job satisfaction and dissatisfaction, these two aspects of supervision are, once again, clearly distinguishable. Herzberg, Mausner, and Snyderman (1959) found that worker dissatisfaction might be related to either "technical supervision" or "interpersonal supervision." Dissatisfaction with technical supervision resulted from the fact that the supervisors lacked competence in the technical skills they were assigned to supervise, the instrumental component of supervision. Dissatisfaction with interpersonal supervision resulted from failures in the human-relations responsibilities of the supervisor, the expressive component of supervision.

If these considerations operate even in the organizations that depend most strongly on machines as the means of production, they are substantially more important for social work organizations in which the medium of service offered is the worker herself. Machines do not have to feel a conviction in the work they are doing in order to do it well; they never suffer from depression, guilt, a sense of inadequacy. They are not jealous or envious of the achievements of other machines and do not feel competitive. They do not need to be inspired in order to work at an optimum level. But these kinds of feelings—and more—determine the effectiveness of the social agency worker. Consequently the social work supervisor must be concerned with the feeling reactions of supervisees to their job and their job situation. Where the technology is centered mainly in human resources, the protection and development of human capacities will be a dominant supervisory concern.

In terms of the categorization of the major components of supervision as used in this book, both administrative and educational supervision are primarily, although not exclusively, directed toward instrumental considerations. The supportive component of supervision is primarily concerned with expressive considerations.

Administrative supervision provides the organizational structure and access to agency resources that facilitate the workers' job; educational supervision provides the knowledge and skills required for doing the job; supportive supervision provides the psychological and interpersonal resources that enable the worker to mobilize the emotional energy needed for effective job performance. Administrative supervision is concerned with organizational barriers to effective services; educational supervision is concerned with ignorance barriers to effective service; supportive supervision is concerned with emotional barriers to effective service.

Further, administrative supervision is responsible for relating effective workers to effective organizations, increasing the effectiveness of the organizational structure and the resources available to the worker. Educational supervision is primarily concerned with increasing the effectiveness of the worker through upgrading knowledge and skills. Supportive supervision is primarily concerned with increasing effectiveness of the worker through decreasing stress which interferes with performance, and increasing morale which enhances performance.

Performance is a function of ability and motivation. Effective ad-

ministrative and educational supervision may increase the supervisee's ability to do an effective job. The worker, however able, may
still perform inadequately because he is not sufficiently motivated.
Motivation determines how vigorously, conscientiously, and persistently abilities will be mobilized to do an effective job. Supportive
supervision is concerned with increasing motivation.

If administrative supervision provides supervisory authority with
the power of position, reward, and coercion, and educational supervision provides the power of expertise, supportive supervision provides supervisory authority with referent power. The worker complies with agency policies and procedures so that he can obtain the
ego support the supervisor can make available.

The different components of supervision provide the workers
with distinct but complementary models of the social worker for
emulation. Administrative supervision provides a model of an efficient worker; educational supervision provides a model of a competent worker; supportive supervision provides a model of a compassionate, understanding worker.

And once again it might be noted that administrative, educational, and supportive components of supervision are interrelated
rather than categorically distinct. For instance, effective educational supervision, by helping the worker become more skilled, results not only in increased competence but also in greater job
satisfaction and reduced anxiety about ability to meet job demands.

Definition and Use

In chapter 3 we were concerned in part with some of the therapeutic aspects of educational supervision. Our concern, however,
was with particular kinds of therapeutic consequences of a good
supervisory relationship. These pertained to developing greater
self-awareness and self-understanding with reference to job-related
behavior. In effect we were focusing on the insight-clarification
outcomes of educational supervision.

Supportive supervision is concerned with another kind of therapeutic responsibility of supervision, related to different kinds of
needs and directed toward different kinds of outcomes. The two
therapeutic objectives, insight and support, while differentiated

here for clarity, are often interrelated. As Towle (1954) notes, the supervisee oftens "gains insight as anxieties are lowered and defenses relax" in reponse to support (p. 145).

Supportive supervision includes those interventions that reinforce ego defenses and strengthen the capacity of the ego to deal ˘ with job stresses and tensions: such procedures as reassurance, encouragement and recognition of achievement, realistically based expressions of confidence, approval and commendation, catharsis-ventilation, desensitization and universalization, and attentive listening which communicates interest and concern. In implementing the responsibilities of supportive supervision, the supervisor attempts to help the workers feel more at ease with themselves in their work. As Bloom and Herman (1958) state, "one of the major functions of the supervisor is to provide certain emotional supports for the worker. She must encourage, strengthen, stimulate and even comfort and pacify him" (p. 403). The supervisor seeks to allay anxiety, reduce guilt, increase certainty and conviction, relieve dissatisfaction, fortify flagging faith, affirm and reinforce the worker's assets, replenish depleted self-esteem, nourish and enhance ego capacity for adaptation, alleviate psychological pain, restore emotional equilibrium, comfort and bolster and refresh. Supportive supervision is concerned with tension management on the job.

These supportive "therapeutic" aspects of supervision do not make supervisors uneasy nor are they the subject of controversy. This is unlike the uneasiness relating to the "therapeutic" aspects of developing supervisee self-awareness.

As Goin and Kline (1976) note, "Relieving anxiety, providing support, and establishing a positive relationship are all synonomous with therapy but they are not avoided. No supervisor is purposely harsh to avoid the therapeutic effect of kindness and empathy" (p. 43). Here we are concerned with being "therapeutic" with a small "t," as distinguished from doing Therapy in Supervision. This concern was discussed above (pp. 174–80).

If social workers are to do their job effectively, they need to feel good about themselves and about the job they are doing. The reality is, however, that they often, for a variety of reasons to be explicated below, feel discouraged, disaffected, powerless, frustrated, devalued, inadequate, confused, anxious, guilty, apathetic, alienated, and burdened with a sense of futility. A worker expresses disillusionment:

The supervisee is a male caseworker in a public welfare setting. He had had graduate training and this is his first job. He has been with the agency for nine months. While a number of clients have marital and parent-child problems, he feels that because of the size of his case load he cannot offer the service he would like. He feels discouraged and says that "the things I am doing, any intelligent clerk could do, they are hardly professional."

A supervisee expresses dismay:

> I don't really know what the things are that are making me draw back. I think it's not really wanting to get involved in the world of Mrs. Garcia because it's such a horrible world. She has seven children and no husband and lives in a project and now she's very sick. You know that's not the nicest world and I'm not sure I want to be there. (Amacher 1971, p. 164)

Another worker expresses discouragement:

> First, the girl ran away from home, fine. She took an overdose, fine. Then her mother's boyfriend is living in the house; her father's an alcoholic; her boyfriend just gave her VD and then she found out she is pregnant. Bang, bang, bang, right down the line. (Amacher 1971, p. 159)

Inevitably it is more difficult to do an effective job when oppressed by such feelings. If these feelings are frequent in an agency, the low level of morale results in high turnover, repeated absenteeism and tardiness, loafing and inattention to work, noncompliance, frequent grievance reports, and interpersonal friction. Not a happy way to run an effective agency. Furthermore, only as the workers feel confident can they communicate confidence and hope to the client. A feeling of hope is an important variable in determining the success of worker-client interaction.

Thus far the general responsibilities of supportive supervision have been stated in a negative sense. A similarly restricted definition of physical would be the absence of disease. We might broaden the definition of physical health so that it suggests a complete sense of physical health well-being rather than merely the absence of disease. In the same way we might define psychological well-being, the goal of supportive supervision, as a state of complete emotional health, the maximum a person is capable of achieving.

In this sense the supervisor, in implementing the responsibilities of supportive supervision, not only relieves, restores, comforts, and replenishes, but more positively, inspires, animates, and exhilarates. The supervisior "motivates toward excellence," helping the worker develop those feelings and attitudes which are conducive to their best efforts, rather than "merely protecting against incompetence." Such supervision makes the difference between joyless submission and eager participation, between playing notes and making music. A supervisee writes,

> I am not sure what the supervisor did or how she did it, but the spirit she inspired in the group was unmistakable. Somehow we felt hopeful, light, cheerful, and optimistic. We felt confident that we could accomplish much that was good and worthwhile. It's a good feeling and it's hard to sustain but while it lasts it's a wonderful high, a really good trip.

The need for supportive supervision has long been recognized in social work supervision. One of the earliest studies of worker turnover, in 1927–28, noted "unhappiness in work," a question of worker morale, as the second largest category of reasons for leaving the job. It included such reasons as "dissatisfaction with social work," "depressing work," "clients hopeless," and "caseload too heavy" (Pretzer 1929, p. 168). These problems would have been the concerns of supportive supervision at that time.

Supportive functions currently are seen as an important responsibility of supervision. A study of supervision in 31 social welfare and rehabilitation agencies, based on questionnaires to 1,600 employees and detailed interviews with a sample of direct service workers, showed "support" to be one of the key functions of supervision. It was defined as "provision of emotional support to subordinates and enhancement of subordinates' feelings of importance and self-worth." "Overall, personnel report that supervisors provide a great amount of support. . . . In fact, in comparison with scores on other scales, providing support is what supervisors do best" (Olmstead and Christensen 1973, p. 189). An earlier study found that "support and encouragement" and "appreciation of efforts" ranked second and third in a 12-item listing of helpful aspects of supervision (Cruser 1958, p. 20).

Nelsen (1973, 1974) studied tape recordings of a series of 68 supervision conferences. She found that 69 percent of the taped units "contained three or more supportive comments" (1973, p. 336), indicating the high frequency of such kinds of interventions. Relating the level of supervisor support to strain in the supervisor-supervisee relationship, Nelsen concluded that "the use of support was one of the most important skills for the [supervisor] to master if the relationship strain was to be avoided" (1973, p. 340). She notes that the "technique of . . . offering support was used both more extensively and more flexibly than might have been expected" (1974, p. 153).

Burn-out: Definition and Symptoms

Work stresses adversely affecting human services personnel have received explicit, almost explosive, attention with the identification of the burn-out syndrome. First named in the literature in 1974 by Fraudenberger, burn-out has been the subject of a small library of books and articles, and a national conference on burn-out was held in 1981 in Philadelphia (Brodsky and Edelwich 1980; Cherniss 1980; Fraudenberger 1980; Pines, Aronson, and Kafry 1981; Maslach 1982; Paine 1982). Burn-out is clearly a hot topic. A major component of these studies is devoted to defining burn-out and identifying the attitudes, feelings, and behavior associated with burn-out. In order for the supervisor to help a worker with problems of burn-out the supervisor needs to be able to recognize its manifestation.

"Burn-out can be defined as a syndrome of physical and emotional exhaustation" resulting from occupational stress "involving the development of negative self-concepts, negative job attitudes, and a loss of concern and feeling for clients" (Pines and Maslach 1978, p. 233). Burn-out has been defined as an "exhaustion reaction, the result of constant or repeated emotional pressure associated with the intense involvement with people over a long period of time" (Pines, Aronson, and Kafrey 1981, p. 15). This reflects the dictionary definition of burn-out "as debilitated or excessively worn by excessive consumption of energy or physical resource." Burn-out is not the same as job dissatisfaction; it more closely resembles battle fatigue.

In characterizing a worker as burned out, we are not pointing to the transient, temporary feelings which every worker experiences when a case has blown-up. The term is validly applicable only to a persistent, chronic condition which results from a culmulative, prolonged, undissipated build-up of stress.

Mechanical devices have a fuse which shuts the machine down on over-stress, computers flash "overload" when demand exceeds their capacity, and a pinball machine registers "tilt." Humans have no built-in protective devices which flash lights on in an overload.

An awareness of the symptom of burn-out enables the supervisor to more easily recognize its onset. The symptoms are physical, emotional, and behavioral. Workers experiencing burn-out manifest weariness and chronic fatigue. Feeling physically drained, they are more susceptible to colds, tension headaches, digestive difficulties, and sleep disorders.

Emotionally burned-out workers feel a sense of disenchantment with the work and alienation from the work. Discouraged, hopeless, and pessimistic about the work they are doing, they feel depressed and emotionally depleted. Workers experiencing burn-out tend to feel angry and resentful as a consequence of a sense of work failure and futility.

There is a loss of enthusiasm, excitement, sense of mission, a gradual erosion of commitment and interest in the job. Instead of being interesting and satisfying, the job becomes something to be "tolerated and survived."

Behaviorally, workers suffering from burn-out, or impending burn-out, manifest a resistance to going to work, and increased tardiness and absenteeism. When at work they tend to watch the clock, postpone or cancel client appointments, take more frequent and longer coffee breaks. Where workers may have previously felt concern when a client failed to show up, they now feel relieved. They resist taking phone calls from clients and postpone calling back. They display a more cynical, detached, indifferent, apathetic approach to a client in a effort to distance themselves emotionally from the client. There is an increased tendency to treat the client in a mechanical, rigid, petty, bureaucratic manner, making less of an effort to help. In discussing clients, they are more likely to stereotype and disparage them, show a loss of caring and concern, and talk about them as "cases" rather than as individuals.

When interacting with clients, burned out workers are more

likely to avoid eye contact, increase their physical distance from the client, subtly discourage the client from sharing emotional material, and keep the interview as short as possible. Feeling physically tired and emotionally depleted, burned out workers tend to be more impatient with clients, and more easily irritated by them. Burned out workers do only those things which enable them to get by. They are going through the motions, merely putting in their time.

A worker describes some of her behavior which she identifies as associated with burn-out.

> Sometimes I would be late for home appointments. I would make stops on my way to home visits and do my errands just to have time that had nothing to do with my work. I sometimes spaced out during interviews with clients and I started referring people to other agencies or counselors. I would have a negative attitude before I even went in; I would be very curt, with no warmth at all. In retrospect I think that I was fighting to create this distance so the clients wouldn't like me. I thought that if I wasn't helpful and I wasn't sympathetic, when I asked if they wanted another appointment, they would say no. (Pines, Aronson, Kafry 1981, p. 47)

Overall the worker's behavior suggests emotional withdrawal from the job and emotional distancing and detachment from clients.

Empathic, accepting, and authentic responses are difficult to communicate when one is psychologicaly detached from the client. In the novel, *The Caseworker,* George Konrad describes the introspective, cynical, uncaring comments of a burned-out social worker.

> Go on, I say to my client. I say it routinely, out of habit because I can guess what he is going to say and doubt his truthfulness. He complains some more, justifies himself, puts the blame on others. From time to time, he bursts into tears. Half of what he says is besides the point; he reels off platitudes, he unburdens himself. He thinks his situation is desperate; it seems perfectly normal to me. He swears his cross is too heavy to bear; it seems quite bearable to me. He hints at suicide; I let it pass. He thinks I can help him; I can't tell him how wrong he is. (p. 3)

Burn-out results in a dehumanization of the client. Empathy, understanding, and individualization require a psychological effort which the worker can no longer emotionally afford. A worker in a community mental health agency expresses the sense of frustration and futility that characterizes burn-out.

> The situations started looking so much alike to me. I could never see changes. It was always the same people, in the same situations. I would get angry when I'd go in. After a while, I stopped listening, I stopped being empathetic. I had to lose my compassion in order to survive emotionally. It wasn't a job where you got many thanks from the clients. It was a vicious circle; because the more angry I became,the less I felt like putting out in the counseling sessions, so of course less happened with the clients. (Pines, Aronson, Kafry 1981, p. 46)

A worker details the changes she experienced in the development of burn-out:

> When I started, I was deeply involved in every aspect of the sixty families I had. I really cared and was supportive of everything that went on. But if you continue at this level of involvement you get to be crazy very soon. So I started to withdraw a bit and see things as the client's problem. I went from total involvement to a kind of standing back. In the end I developed a callousness towards the people I was working with. I was so emotionally detached that I might as well not have been there. I was earning money, but I didn't feel the work was part of my life. (Pines, Aronson, Kafry 1981, p. 58)

The feelings which contribute to the development of burn-out are circular. Feeling disenchanted, hopeless, and cynical, sensing a growing hostility toward and resentment of clients and their unending problems, the conscientious human service worker responds with guilt, shame, and discomfort. The additional stressful emotional burden associated with such feelings further contributes to the development of burn-out. Dealing with feelings of guilt, shame, and a sense of failing to respond positively to the client requires an expenditure of psychic energy.

The supervisor needs to be aware that there is an element of contagion in the loss of morale in the development of burn-out. One worker's depressed, disenchanted feelings tends to contaminate other workers and reduce their own level of enthusiasm for the job.

Sources of Job-Related Tension for the Supervisee

Having learned to recognize burn-out and the stresses and symptoms associated with its gradual development, the supervisor has to understand its etiology and the nature of the specific, recurrent sources of tension encountered by supervisees.

Administrative Supervision as a Souce of Tension

The previously discussed components of supervision are in themselves sources of tension for the worker. As discussed in chapters 3 and 7, administrative pressures toward compliance with agency policies and procedures and the requirement for work assessment and evaluation are sources of tension for the worker. Workers face the stress related to the conflict between the bureaucratic and service orientations. At the same time, good administrative supervision is, in and of itself, supportive in that it offers supervisees a well-defined structure in which to operate, a clear definition of realistic and appropriate objectives, a chance to participate in agency decision-making. It also keeps them informed through full and free communications.

Educational Supervision as a Source of Tension

Similarly, educational supervision is a source of both tension and support. Education implies change, and the target of change efforts is the worker. Change involves, of necessity, a temporary disequilibrium, an "unfreezing" of the old equilibrium. Educational efforts, then, inevitably induce some anxiety.

New situations are encountered for which the supervisee does not have a readily available solution. Ideas that were thought correct are explicitly examined and questioned; some are found to be incompatible with new ideas to which the supervisee is introduced. The transition period is characterized by anxiety and a temporary loss of confidence. The old procedures are being rejected, but the new procedures are not yet fully accepted. Besides, the supervisee is ambivalent about taking the next step. He is "not sure that he is willing to change what it took him so long to learn" (Rothman 1973).

All learning presents the learner with a need to adjust to these emotional concomitants, but their intensity varies, depending on the nature of the subject matter. Where the subject matter is largely external and unrelated to the personal self (for example, in mathematics or chemistry), the demands of the learning situation do not pose a significant emotional problem. Where the subject matter intimately affects the perception of self and the nature of the learner's interpersonal relationships, the effects are likely to present greater difficulties. The subject matter of social work is likely to develop the kinds of intrapersonal reverberations which make the changes resulting from learning more problematic. What Lazerson (1972) says about psychiatry is also true for social work: "It is important to emphasize that the very nature of what is to be learned . . . adds greatly to the stress already inherent in the learning situation and adds its own special challenge to the learning alliance" (p. 89).

Social work content is emotionally charged and ego-involved. It is content which reflects the way a person views himself and the world around him. In learning about human behavior, we are learning about ourselves, about our defenses, our motives, our unflattering impulses. In dispassionately examining the sources of our most cherished attitudes and illusions, we are throwing open to question the way in which we order our lives. Whereas the usual educational situation asks that the student critically examine and hence possibly change his ideas, social work supervision is often directed toward a change in behavior and perhaps personality.

The threat of change is greater for the adult student because learning requires dissolution of long-standing patterns of thinking and believing. It also requires disloyalty to previous identification models. The ideas and behavior that might need changing represent, in a measure, the introjection of previously encountered significant others—parents, teachers, highly valued peers—and the acceptance of other models implies some rejection of these people. The act of infidelity creates anxiety.

Much of social work education is concerned with secondary socialization. As a consequence of primary socialization, strong attitudes have developed toward minority groups, welfare recipients, divorce, discrimination, racism, sexual deviance, crime, juvenile delinquency, violent confrontation, the class struggle, etc. The learner has become accustomed to particular patterns of behavior in relating to other people. Socialization in educational supervision requires changing those attitudes and behavioral patterns that impede competent job performance.

The supervisory tutorial is a threat to the student's independence. Readiness to learn involves giving up some measure of autonomy in accepting direction from others, in submitting to the authority of the supervisor-teacher. Supervisees also face a threat to their sense of adequacy. The learning situation demands an admission of ignorance, however limited. In admitting ignorance, supervisees expose their vulnerability. They risk the possibility of criticism, of shame, and perhaps of rejection because of an admitted inadequacy.

Supervisees have the choice of being anxious because they do not know how to do their work or being anxious about confessing ignorance and obtaining help. The recognition and acceptance of ignorance is a necessary prerequisite to learning. Towle (1954) presents the most detailed and perceptive analysis of the problem of tension associated with educational supervision.

While educational supervision produces these kinds of anxieties, it also contributes to reducing tensions. The knowledge and skills, the problem solutions, which educational supervision makes available give the worker a feeling of confidence and a sense of assurance in job performance. Until the worker learns what he needs to know, he is "realistically helpless, confused and fearful out of the lack of know-what, know-how, and know-why" (Towle 1954, p. 33). The supervisor, in meeting workers' "realistic dependency fully and truly" (Towle 1954, p. 149), is being supportive. In learning what he needs to know, the worker can adapt more successfully to the demands of the work situation. This, in itself, is gratifying and supportively ego-enhancing.

The Supervisor-Supervisee Relationship as a Source of Tension

The relationship between supervisor and supervisee is another main source of both tension and support. Mayer and Rosenblatt (1973b), who obtained some 233 protocols of stress situations encountered by social work practitioners, state that "the worker's anxieties appeared to be basically a function of the two main relationships in which he was involved, his relations with his supervisor and those with his clients" (p. 3). Furthermore, the two sources of anxiety are interrelated. "If the worker felt secure with his supervisor this was apt to make him less anxious with clients. On the other hand, if he felt insecure with his supervisor this was apt to make him more anxious with clients" (p. 3).

In her treatment of social workers, Babcock (a psychiatrist) maintained that they felt "less inadequate with clients than with the supervisor to whom they fear to reveal their inadequacies. . . . These patient-workers in discussing their work experience accept intellectually that they need the supervisor, yet . . . they often admit to unreasonable anxiety" (1951, p. 418).

Why should the relationship be a source of tension? The supervisory relationship is an intense, intimate, personalized situation that has considerable emotional charge. As is true for any highly cathected, meaningful interpersonal relationship, it becomes infused with transference elements, with ambivalence and resistance, with residuals of earlier developmental conflicts.

The supervisor-supervisee relationship evokes the parent-child relationship and, as such, may reactivate anxiety associated with this earlier relationship. If the supervisor is a potential parent surrogate, fellow supervisees are potential siblings competing for the affectional responses of the parent. The situation therefore also threatens to reactivate residual difficulties in the sibling-sibling relationship. It is a particularly fertile context for the development of transference.

A rich literature tends to support the contention that the supervisory relationship does, in fact, mobilize these kinds of tensions (Ekstein and Wallerstein 1972; Fleming and Benedek 1966; Schuster, Sandt, and Thaler 1972; Langs 1979). The worker often reenacts his problem with the client as a problem in supervision.

Doerhrman (1972) studied this reciprocal interaction by analyzing eight sets of concurrent supervisor-supervisee-client relationships over a period of 20 weeks. She studied two supervisors and four supervisees offering service to eight clients. Both the supervisors and the supervisees were interviewed each week with regard to what had happened in the supervisory sessions. She was struck by the intensity of the supervisees' reactions to their supervisors.

Rather ordinary action on the supervisor's part seemed, at times, to have a profound effect not only upon the therapist's feelings about himself as a therapist but also upon the way he conducted his therapy.

Following a disagreement with her supervisor, a worker said: "Just how much the supervision gets into mother images was really brought home to me. It was very clear that the degree of upset was not reasonable. . . . All it was was that my supervisor was angry with me. Well you should be able to tolerate people being angry with you. I was thrown into a massive depression. . . . I know I over-reacted" (Doehrman 1972, p. 116).

The major findings of the study were that there is a "meshing of transference and resistance patterns of the therapist and supervisor and that the therapist acts out with his patients the effects of the conflicts engendered in him by his supervisor. . . . It is therefore concluded the supervisors should be extremely sensitive to unknown and intense effects that they will have upon their supervisees, as well as effects their supervisees may have on them, and not assume that their relationship to the [supervisee] is a simple didactic one" (Doehrman 1972, pp. 205–6). "The results indicate that tension in the supervisory relationship is inevitable" (p. 211).

Supervisees face a problem in determining what content is "on-stage," or admissible for discussion in conference, and what content is "off-stage." Material which they have confidentially shared with the supervisor in social situations on the assumption that it was "off-stage" is sometimes used in interpreting on-the-job difficulties. This is regarded as an unwarranted use of personal information. Because of the ambiguity regarding what information can legitimately be used by the supervisor in conferences, supervisees are under some tension in selecting content to communicate to the supervisor.

Tension also is generated around the interpretation of content. There may be a conflict between the supervisor's and the supervisee's definition of the situation. The worker seeks to "negotiate" the validity of his definition with the supervisor. Here he is at a decided disadvantage. Since the "correctness" of either interpretation often cannot be objectively determined, where there is a conflict the supervisor's interpretation of the situation is apt to prevail. As Scott (1969) points out,

The use of methods by which a caseworker's motives are scrutinized and questioned raises problems because such tactics are subject to abuse: from worth as a method of helping the worker to attain insight, such procedures can degenerate into devices for the manipulation of the worker. The danger inherent in the possibility that at any moment the worker can be reduced from a participant in the discussion to its subject may act to curb the working out of honest differences of opinion between worker and supervisor. The worker who disagrees with his superior may be met with the response that he is "unable to accept supervision," or that he is exhibiting "resistance," or "immaturity." At worst, the supervisor becomes omnipotent: a worker is not even entitled to his own opinion in an honest diagreement with his supervisor because the latter can devalue his arguments by questioning his motives. (p. 109)

There may be further tension which results from unwarranted attempts to make the worker into a client. A supervisee discusses her relationship with her supervisor:

Feeling that "honesty" was the hallmark of the good caseworker, I included in my process recordings all of the doubts, fears and anxieties that I experienced in my interviews. At first the supervisor was delighted with my openness. However, in time she began to question what lay behind all my uncomfortable feelings. At one point, we were spending more time in discussing me than in discussing my patients. We explored my pathology in all its gory details. I would come out of the supervisory conference shaking with self-doubt and feeling vulnerable and picked apart. (Mayer and Rosenblatt 1975, p. 186)

Some conflict between worker and supervisor results inevitably from differences in perspective. The worker faces the client directly. The client is in a position to punish the worker with hostility, contempt, rejection, and apathy or reward the worker by change in behavior, by praise and appreciation. The worker is concerned with client needs for these reasons as well as in response to a desire to be helpful. The supervisor is not exposed to client reaction but is directly exposed to administrative reaction, from which the worker is buffered. The supervisor's concern is to see that agency administration is pleased with his work. Given their different positions in the agency hierarchy, the worker and supervisor have different perceptions of their world. The worker tends to see the case, the supervisor to see the caseload.

The supervisor, having already resolved many of the problems faced by supervisees, may underestimate the disturbance such problems create for them. It is easy to minimize the difficulty of these problems and to take them for granted. The supervisor may develop the unwarranted expectation that the supervisee should be as efficient as she is in dealing with these problems. The supervisor, in empathizing with the supervisee, needs to recall her own first encounter with an abused child, a client with terminal cancer, a slum tenement reeking with booze, feces, and exposed garbage, her first efforts of placing a child.

The worker often becomes explicitly aware of many of the different kinds of tensions encountered in doing the work in discussions with the supervisor. Supervision might be perceived, by the worker, as the source of such tensions. The worker then finds "some relief in being able to blame some of his problems on the supervisor who tends to become, at this point, more or less the 'villain' " (De la Torre 1974, p. 303). Supervisee dissatisfactions with supervision point to additional sources of stress relating to the supervisor. Table 5.1 ranks some of them as obtained from supervisees in a questionnaire study.

The Client as a Source of Tension

Relationships with clients are an additional source of stress for the worker. Workers deal with people who are living under considerable stress. They encounter the clients at a time of crisis, when their emotional reactions are overt and strong. It is very enervating to deal with a great deal of raw emotion—anxiety, anger, depression, grief—and with the constant exposure to highly charged emotional situations while under the necessity of controlling one's own emotional responses. "The worker, face to face with the client in the interview, is exposed continually to an onslaught of unrepressed primitive feelings. The avalanche of feeling with which the . . . social worker is confronted is an unusual stress situation peculiar to the task of extending psychological help. It is, in a sense, an occupational hazard" (Feldman, Sponitz, and Nagelberg 1953, p. 153).

The effect of exposure to clients' feelings is intensified by the fact that social work training is designed to increase sensitivity and response to such feelings. If training were aimed at shielding us

Table 5.1   Sources of Supervisee Dissatisfaction in Supervision

	Percentage of supervisees checking item as a strong source of dissatisfaction (N = 384)
1. My supervisor is hesitant about confronting agency administration with the needs of his (her) supervisees.	35
2. My supervisor is not sufficiently critical about my work, so that I don't know what I am doing wrong and what needs changing.	26
3. My supervisor does not provide much real help in dealing with problems I face with my clients.	25
4. My supervisor tends to be capricious and arbitrary in the use of his (her) authority.	23
5. My supervisor does not provide enough regularly scheduled, uninterrupted conference time.	21
6. My supervisor is too controlling and dominant, so that he (she) restricts my autonomy and initiative as a professional.	20
7. My supervisor shows little real appreciation of the work I am doing.	15
8. My supervisor tends to encourage unnecessary dependency.	14
9. My supervisor is hesitant about making decisions and/or taking responsibility for decisions, so that the total burden of case decisions rests with me.	12
10. Other (miscellaneous).	22

Source: Kadushin (1973).

from displays of emotionality, of learning tactics and procedures to distance ourselves from feelings, the impact would be mitigated, attenuated. Social work training moves in the opposite direction—to dismantle the barriers which protect us from being affected by the feelings of others and learn to receptively open ourselves to such feelings.

The need to be empathetic implies the need to feel with the client. If the worker is truly empathetic, he must feel some of the pain, the anguish, the despair, the hurt which many of the clients feel. A supervisee says:

When you're working with people then you're under pressure straight away. You can't just treat a person like a piece of paper and file it away to be forgotten until another day. If that person came into you with

what to them is a very pressing problem, you have to do your damned-
est to help them and therefore you put yourself under pressure, this is
part and parcel of the work. (Parsloe and Stevenson 1978, p. 300)

And during the course of the day's work, the emotional expenditures in each interview are cumulative, leaving the worker emotionally depleted and exhausted. A worker says:

> A really black day. I had a series of four interviews, one right after
> another with several depressed women. The atmosphere in my office
> became progressively more funereal as the day went on. Gloom and
> doom, dejection and despair. And the very worst was the last interview
> of the day with Ruth, who, having been told by her lover that he was
> breaking off with her, wanted me to convince her that she has some
> reason for living. I had been contaminated by the mood of the other
> clients and feeling dejected, had a hard time screwing myself up to
> sound positive about life.

Workers encounter "clients" who have neither asked for nor want
agency service and who are hostile and resistant to their efforts to
help. And the caseload includes groups of clients whose behavior is
offensive to many workers—child molesters, wife beaters, rapists,
child abusers.

Despite such hostility and the workers' own very human reaction
of antipathy to some clients, professional practice principles require
that they act acceptingly. In the following excerpt a worker describes her feelings before an interview with a hostile client. The
worker was scheduled to visit a mother whose children had been
removed and who wanted them back.

> I was very frightened of the upcoming visit. I have a difficult time
> dealing with hostility and I expected Mrs. P. to be quite hostile. . . . My
> anxiety mounted steadily the morning of the visit. I lingered at the
> office as long as I could, wanting to remain in the presence of other
> workers. Finally I left to drive to Mrs. P's house. I arrived at her
> neighborhood only too soon. I trudged up the steep hill with dragging
> feet, wishing with all my strength that I was going in the other direc-
> tion. . . . I remember hoping that Mrs. P. would have forgotten the
> appointment and wouldn't be at home. But there she was, opening the
> door for me. I felt somehow like a condemned man at his own execu-
> tion. (Mayer and Rosenblatt 1973a, p. 8)

Social service agencies are often the agencies of last resort. Some
percentage of our clients come to us after every major institution in

society has failed in their efforts to help them toward achieving adequate adjustment, self-sufficiency, independence. The family has failed, the school has failed, the church has failed, in some cased the legal system has failed. We often inherit the failures of other human service systems.

With limited capacity to effectively use the kind of help we can make available, often indifferent or resistant, if not openly hostile, the best the worker can hope for is a limited tenuous adjustment, despite the best efforts. The problems are often relatively intractable. The client's interpersonal environment is often unsupportive and deprived, if not actually noxious. Such clients make very heavy and stressful demands on the worker's time and emotional energy and offer limited professional satisfaction in return. Dependent and emotionally taxing clients drain the worker's store of emotional energy, leaving them feeling emotionally depleted and exhausted, powerless and impotent.

There is often no sense of closure—a feeling that the work is finished, objectives accomplished. Experience has taught the worker that contact frequently is recurrent and episodic, rates of recidivism high. A community mental health clinic worker says:

> This woman had a boyfriend who moved in and out. While he was living with her, he gave her a lot of support with her children. Whenever they quarreled and he walked out, she'd call me in despair. At first I would go out and spend two hours saying whatever was needed to lift her out of her misery. This happened pretty regularly every few months, and after a year or so I became less responsive to her. Instead of going to see her, I'd talk to her on the phone. "So he left again," I'd tell her. "He's left before." If she remained upset, I'd tell her I'd be out to see her within a few days. Sometimes I never did go. I was beginning to put things off. (Brodsky, p. 186).

In a study of the satisfactions and stresses of psychiatrists, psychologists, and social workers Farber and Heifetz (1981) found that "doubts regarding the efficacy of therapy was one of the principal sources of stress" (p. 626). They were stressed by "giving so much, receiving so little, and through it all remaining vulnerable to doubts that one's efforts are effective" (p. 674). "Most therapists cited lack of therapeutic success as the single most stressful aspect of therapeutic work" (Barber and Heifetz 1982, p. 5).

There is stress associated with physical dangers encountered on the job. The fear of possible physical harm from clients is not entirely imaginary. "A study directed by Dr. Roger M. Whitman, Chairman of the University of Cincinnati School of Medicine, found that 24 of 100 psychiatrists and psychologists they surveyed had been assaulted in the preceding year by at least one patient" (*New York Times*, June 14, 1983; see also *Star* 1984).

While it may be objectively true that the actual danger from physical abuse is not very great, there is a constant underlying anxiety about such a possibility. While actual physical abuse may be relatively infrequent, the worker is more often subjected to verbal abuse. Clients under considerable stress are not always in full control, so that angry feelings are openly expressed in verbal attacks on workers. There is the stress associated with being on the receiving end of bitter complaints about the worker's supposed inadequacies and failures, of insults and verbal derogation. A foster care worker says:

> The interview left me shaken. When I told Mrs. N. that given her situation, we could not return Johnny home, she said "Could not? You mean *you* don't want to." Her voice rising and her face getting flushed, she lost her cool and she, "You lousy bitch. You shit. I knew all along you didn't like me, but I didn't think you would go so far to hurt me, you little bastard." Its hard to get talked to like that without feeling upset.

The recipient of a worker's service is a fellow human being. The worker's decisions often have considerable implications for the client's living situation. A child is placed for adoption, a parolee can be released from prison because a job has been found, funds are obtained for a day-care center. This is an awesome responsibility, and awareness of the possible consequences of such decisions is a source of occupational stress. Often the worker has to make these crucial decisions in the face of unnerving uncertainty, ambiguity, and limited information and with a recognition that full understanding of the prodigious complexities of unpredictable human situations is beyond the wisest person's true comprehension.

Working in what is, in effect, an emotional hot house, the worker is required to act decisively in the face of considerable uncertainty. And because we know such recommendations and/or suggestions are not all that unequivocally correct, the worker is stressed by the burden of guilt and anxiety in the direction she gives to people's lives. A community mental health clinic worker says:

> In this field you have to make life and death decisions, consequential decisions that have very serious effects on the life of your clients. Is there any amount of training or wisdom that can prepare you to make decisions that would baffle even Solomon? There is always an element of uncertainty that you have to deal with—an uncertainty that nags at you.

Offering help inevitably involves the helper in another person's life and problem. Having accepted the responsibilities of helping, one must accept the burdens and risks associated with it—of rejection, worry, concern, failure.

Many situations encountered by child welfare workers have all the essential elements of Greek tragedies. They involve conflicting but legitimate and justifiable interests and needs. There may be a conflict between the rights and privileges of a foster parent and the rights and privileges of a natural parent. The conflict may be between the right of grown children to live autonomously and the rights of aged parents for protection and support.

There are also problems of deciding between competing needs of different clients. Devoting a considerable amount of time to one client means neglecting another. As one worker put it,

> The conflict that I felt was not only between the regulations and the clients but between client and client. If you want to help clients get schooling or job training or discuss personal problems with people who may be very eager to talk to you about them, you do so with the knowledge that you are not using this time to help get basic material things to people who just as desperately need them. (Miller and Podell 1970, p. 24)

Some stress results from the workers' uncertainty about the outcome of their intervention. Certain changes are obvious—a neglected child is placed in a comfortable foster home where he is well cared for. However, many changes which social workers attempt to bring about are not so visible. Changes in parental attitudes toward children, in adjustment of a child to a foster home, in an adoptive parent's sense of security in his role, may not be overtly manifested. There may be dissatisfaction for workers in the lack of observable changes which reward their conscientiousness and competence.

The Nature and Context of the Task as a Source of Tension

Stress can result from the nature of social work tasks and the conditions under which the work is done. We noted earlier that the task in which the worker is engaged interpenetrates with his own life. Encountering separation experiences, the worker is made anxious as he remembers his own separation fears at the hospitalization or death of a parent, the threat of divorce, and so on.

Babcock (1953) says, "Living on a job that is so closely allied to life itself makes separation of work from other areas of life exceptionally difficult. Since the work task and living are often simultaneously experienced, anxiety is greater than in many other fields" (p. 417). A worker says,

> Sue was pregnant out of wedlock again. She went on and on about how easy it seemed for her to become pregnant—said it with pride as well as with some regret. And as she went on and on about this, my insides knotted with envy. Why so easy for her and so hard for me? We had been trying for a year and with increasing desperation, to have a child. I, who wanted a child so much, could not get pregnant; Sue, who did not want a child, got pregnant effortlessly. It was hard to keep listening to Sue discuss her problem since listening increased the hurt I felt so deeply.

The work setting often produces stress. Wasserman (1970) describes a typical public child-welfare agency:

> The new professional social worker's home base is usually a district office. His desk is one of many on an open floor. There is a little or no privacy. He is surrounded by other workers, welfare assistants, clerks, and supervisors, all crowded together with one desk adjoining another. Telephones are constantly ringing, and there is a steady hum of conversation, typewriting, and people moving from place to place. The office is not an environment in which a worker can think clearly and and calmly about the complex and painful situations he faces and the fateful decisions he must sometimes make. There is no quiet place where one can go to think for a few moments or consult with colleagues. Interviewing clients, which occasionally takes place at the agency, is carried out in a small, open cubicle. There is no privacy. In sum, the setting is not one usually conceived of as "professional"; in fact, the environmental image is more industrial than professional. (p. 95)

Other stresses result from the fact that the workers' responsibilities exceed their power and resources. Society supports social work agencies because they are part of the necessary apparatus for social control. They mitigate the effects of situations that might lead to social conflict, and alleviate the most extreme effects of social dysfunction. The limited support given to agencies allows them to perform this secondary function. The support necessary to carry out their primary functions—to provide adequate measures for prevention and rehabilitation—society is not yet willing to grant. The workers therefore have to implement a policy that reflects society's ambivalence toward the groups whom they are asked to help. Very often what they are asked to do is in conflict with society's willingness to provide the resources which will enable them to do it.

Furthermore, neither the worker nor the profession has the power to change those significant social pathologies—discrimination, unemployment, housing shortages, etc.—which directly limit what the worker can do. These crucial externalities, beyond the workers' power to remedy or change, affect their practice and determine the outcome of their efforts.

The results of the workers' best efforts to help the client in the face of overwhelming odds, under conditions which are beyond their control, lead to a sense of impotence, frustration, and failure. A clear sense of achievement is hard to come by. In addition, "the pain the staff experiences in their awareness of client sufferings is heightened by resentment that their efforts are depreciated and that they are blamed for inadequacies over which they have no control" (Arndt 1973, p. 50).

One study of MSW recruits' reactions to a public child-welfare agency during their first years of employment found them

> disheartened and overburdened by the large numbers of biological parents, foster parents, and children with whom they had to work and overwhelmed by the large number of emergencies they had to face on an almost daily basis. . . . The worker is often overwhelmed by the cumulative impact, perhaps the cumulative terror, of a large number of cases—by the human suffering, deprivation, disorder, ignorance, hostility, and casualty he must face as part of his everyday work situation. . . . The two principal feelings expressed by the twelve new professional social workers during the two-year period were frustration and fatigue. (Wasserman 1970, p. 90)

A worker writes about her reaction to trying to help in the face of overwhelming odds:

> I'm tired of hearing about rats and roaches, and politely ignoring the latter as they crawl over walls and floors. I'm tired of broken boilers, toilets, and refrigerators, plumbers who never come, junkies in the halls and junkies who break into apartments and steal clocks, irons, sheets, children's clothes, food—anything they can lay their trembling hands on. I'm tired of hearing abut asthma, high blood pressure, anemia, arthritis, toothaches, headaches, and "nerves" . . . I don't want to hear the same things: "He just left . . . not enough for . . . I don't know where he . . . like to work but . . . think he's you know, slow . . . not sending up heat . . . some mornings it's so bad . . . went to the clinic but they . . . do you give money for . . . need . . . teacher sent him home because he . . . only got to the eighth. . . ." Poverty jams into a mold which permits few variations. (Walton 1967)

There is stress in working in the context of ambiguous objectives. Society often gives the agencies a poorly defined charge. The community sometimes does not make clear what response it expects from agencies in the face of social problems. Workers ultimately have the task of making decisions in the face of poorly defined or even conflicting objectives. Should the AFDC mother be encouraged to work or stay home with her children? Should prisons serve the purpose of punishment or rehabilitation? Should the community share with the parents the burden of care for the severely retarded child? Should homosexuals be accepted as foster parents? In these situations, and others, workers frequently face the stress of making decisions and taking action about moral and ethical questions on which both they and the community are still undecided. In a survey of over 1,300 workers in a state Department of Public Welfare, "60 percent said it was difficult to know what was expected of them on the job" (O'Connor and Spence 1976, p. 178).

Some of the occupational stress to which workers are subject stems not only from uncertainty about what they should be doing but also how they should be doing it. Techniques and approaches for helping the client are not so well established as to provide clear-cut guidelines for the workers' behavior. For many situations there is no validated professional consensus on the most effective approach. In addition to incomplete or imperfect mastery of available knowledge, workers have to accept the limitations of professional knowledge itself.

The worker is faced with the stress of balancing antithetical demands and expectations. He is required to be objective and maintain some emotional distance from the client. But at the same time, he is required to be empathetic, feeling what the client feels, putting himself figuratively in the client's situation. These are contradictory demands.

The worker is required to individualize the client, seeing her in all of her special uniqueness. At the same time, the worker is often required to label the client for diagnostic reimbursement and administrative purposes. Labeling inevitably involves some deindividualizing stereotyping. There is a need to nonjudgmentally accept clients as they are. At the same time the worker is expected to make assessments about the client's behavior, the client's treatability, the client's motivations, the client's manipulations. The worker is asked to accept and respect the client as a person, but reject his dysfunctional behavior, to reject the sin but not the sinner. This is a difficult separation to make since the behavior is a significant component of a person's identity. The worker is asked to accept the client as he is and is expected to help him to change because what he is is not acceptable. The worker thus has to balance antithetical attitudes of acceptance and expectations of change.

We are asked to be authentic and genuine and at the same time consciously controlled in our interview behavior. The requirement for "spontaneously controlled" behavior once again involves contradictory demands.

There is stress associated with the antithetical pressures of being a professional in a worker-client relationship, on the one hand, and our humanistic tradition on the other. The professional relationship implies inequality in knowledge and power in our favor; the humanistic tradition strives for equality and colleagueship in the relationship. As professionals we are "better," in the specific sense of our expertise, than the clients. The therapy relationship is inherently a relationship of unequals. We are the helper, they are the ones needing help. But this inequality offends us and we feel a sense of stress from the dissonance between the reality of difference and our egalitarian orientation (Klienman 1981).

The factor which tends to provide satisfaction and hence counter negative feelings in most jobs is the recognition by oneself, confirmed by others, that the work has been well done and that there is a desirable outcome. The work social workers do does not confirm itself. There are no observable, objective, tangible indications of whether our interventions have been successful. We do not see the car we helped build roll off the line, a defective heart corrected by a coronary bypass, a jury verdict in favor of our client. Social workers are not often rewarded by the unmistakable indications that their interventions have made a difference.

Since the work is done in private, workers do not get the confirmation of their competence from other professionals who, having witnessed the performance, might commend the worker. The doctor in the operating room, the lawyer in the courtroom might be congratulated by peers who have observed the competent professional in action.

The performance of actors, athletes, musicians are applauded by their clients, the audience. Applause is an overt, instant expression of approval. In leaving a tip for the waiter or waitress, we signify applause of their work. In contrast, workers rarely get direct confirmation of their competence by applause from their clients. Most clients are too absorbed in their own troubles to concern themselves with efforts to express commendation or gratitude for the worker's efforts.

Working in private toward objectives the worker can only guess have been achieved, and only rarely receiving spontaneous and voluntary gratitude by the client, the worker is under stress from doubts about his competence and about the significance of his work.

The worker is the principal instrumentality for helping the client. Failure in social work is more directly felt as a reflection on the adequacy and competence of the worker as a person than in many other kinds of work. A facilitative relationship is the necessary, if not the prime, ingredient for success in much of our work. Developing such a relationship depends to a considerable extent on what we as people contribute to the interaction. Consequently when things go wrong we tend, in an exercise of self-awareness, to focus on ourselves to identify how our needs and feelings might have intruded in the interaction. More so than in most other jobs, the social worker *is* her work. Failure then is more easily personalized.

The occupational title, Social Work Professional, arouses expectations in others which result in stress. Just as people who hold the title of minister, priest, or rabbi are expected to be more perfect morally than the population at large, the title, Social Work Professional, leads to expectations that the person so identified would be better adjusted, be more successful in interpersonal relationships, be better parents, and have better marriages than others. Workers may feel a stressful pressure to live up to the expectations communicated by the title. When they encounter difficulties in relationships with their children and spouses, as is inevitable in any complex human relationship, workers may feel more keenly than others a sense of disappointment and failure.

The Organization as a Source of Tension

The burn-out literature repeatedly points to organizational considerations as a source of tension and stress for workers. Organizational turbulence, frequent reorganization, and rule changes are stressful. An organization with a high degree of centralization of decision making, a highly formalized hierarchical system, and elaborately structured rules and procedures is associated with a greater likelihood of burn-out. As a result of such an organizational configuration, workers find it hard to achieve the "motivation" that Herzberg (1959) defines as associated with job satisfaction. These include opportunities for growth and development on the job, meaningfulness of work, opportunities to participate in organizational decision making. While job dissatisfaction and burn-out are different concepts, job dissatisfaction contributes to the development of burn-out.

Workers in many large public agencies face the stress of adapting to constantly changing directives.

> Frequent interruption of routine income maintenance and service activities further overburden caseworkers. The perpetual changes in welfare law keep administrators and caseworkers off balance, requiring them to constantly learn and relearn. When asked how often rules

are changed, a Detroit caseworker answered, "Every time you put your pencil down. As soon as you make a change, a change has been made on what you just changed." An Atlanta caseworker agreed: "We get so many manual transmittals with so many changes that it's impossible to stay on top of everything." Changes are so frequent that agencies cannot keep manuals up to date. (Galm 1972, p. 30)

Because the client's welfare is not necessarily equivalent to the agency's welfare, professional and bureaucratic orientations provide competing claims upon loyalty. Billingsley (1964a), who has studied this conflict in child welfare agencies, finds that

> in spite of the social worker's intellectual and emotional commitment to meeting the needs of his client it is apparent that these needs must be met within the framework of structured approaches imposed by the agency and the profession, even over the worker's own estimation of the needs of the client. This is consistent with findings in studies of other professions. (p. 403)

The conflict between the two orientations leads to a strain between the agency demand that a given number of units of work be performed and the desire of the professional to do the best possible job. Billingsley identifies this as the conflict between quantitative output and qualitative performance.

There is stress associated with salaries paid many workers. Admittedly, income may not have been a strong source of motivation in the choice of social work. Other kinds of satisfaction had greater priority. But if adequate income is not of first importance it is, as someone said, "wonderfully soothing to the nerves." We cannot ignore the fact that salary is often perceived as an objective measure of one's worth to society. Since lower income levels signify that we are considered of lesser importance this makes it difficult to maintain a respectable level of self-esteem. Pay levels become particularly important as an objective measure of society's estimate of our worth in those instances where there is an absence of other objective measures of our work as noted above.

The actual salary is not as important as the relative salary in comparison with other members of our reference group. The important comparison for the worker is her salary compared with her peers—people with similar education, achievements, background. The worker with an MSW compares her salary and associated possible life-style with people in other professions who have also invested six years in professional preparation. The comparison often puts the social worker at a disadvantage.

There is the further stress, not previously encountered in the history of social work, associated with the possibility of losing one's job and not being able to find a comparable position. Budget cuts, reduction in staff, program discontinuance, rising social work unemployment, are now matters of common concern exciting anxiety and stress.

Workers in some special settings face particular stresses. All organizations interact, of course, with the environment in which they are embedded. However, not all professionals are required to interact on intimate terms with other professionals. The social worker in a host setting (the medical social worker in a hospital, the school social worker in a public school, the psychiatric social worker in a mental institution) is placed in this position. They have to justify and define their decisions to a critical audience of other professionals. They have to learn a pattern of deference in interacting with higher-status professionals. Research indicates that such "boundary positions" are apt to produce tension (Kahn 1964). Even though doctors, for instance, are supposedly colleagues and peers of the social worker in a hospital or mental health facility, the reality is that the doctor is "primus inter pares," first among equals. A psychiatric social worker on an inpatient hospital psychiatric ward says,

> My feelings of anxiety and stress have been mainly a result of working in a host setting. Initially, I was extremely anxious about working with residents and psychology fellows. I felt inadequate even though I thought I had much better training and had better skills in working with people. I tended to be concerned with status, prestige, etc. They were psychiatrists—they had medical degrees or else they had Ph.D.'s. I was really intimidated by their status.
>
> When I began to work with residents, I tended to defer to them. I was sure that they knew what was best and that I shouldn't question them. Besides, if I did question them, I would have to be damned sure I could justify my position.
>
> My one-down position became problematic and stressful for me. And the fact that I am a woman and almost all of the residents and psychology fellows are men didn't help either.

The hazards of sexism and the resentments associated with heirarchical elements in interprofessional relationships interact with each other. Hierarchy and gender segregation overlap. The higher-status psychiatrists and clinical psychologists are more apt to be male. Social workers are likely to be female.

There is stress that derives from the necessity of working cooperatively with other institutions in society which are based on values that are somewhat at variance with the values to which the social worker owes allegiance. The worker often has to work with the legal system, with the educational system, and the health system, which see the problems of her clients from different vantage points. The worker faces the stress of communicating in different universes of discourse and accommodating to different points of view regarding the same problematic situation.

Community Attitudes Toward Social Work as a Source of Tension

The worker is affected by the general community attitude toward social work and the function it performs. While the community has always been ambivalent about the profession, more recently there has been an intensification of the negative components of the ambivalence.

Earlier in our history, the effectiveness of social work interventions was not critically questioned. It was presumed and generally accepted that our interventions had positive results.

The thrust during the recent past has been to question this presumption. Demands for accountability became more insistent. The imputation of competence and expertise now had to be demonstated and validated through research. A series of research efforts were mounted to objectively, critically, and dispassionately examine the consequences of our activity. The results were somewhat disappointing. We were doing some good, but not nearly as much as was assumed. As a consequence, some of our confidence has been shaken and stress is felt not only because of the skeptical imputation of others, but also because of doubts about the work felt by the worker herself.

Not only was social work previously granted unquestioned presumptions about its expertise and effectiveness, it was also granted a presumption about the benign nature of its intentions. There was a consensus that what the social worker did was done altruistically and unselfishly for the benefit of the client. The community attitude toward social work was generally respectful and approving.

Even conceding that our interventions are not as effective as either we or the community had hoped, we had previously been given high marks and prestige for our moral integrity, our altruism, our disinterested benevolence. But now all this has been called into question. Lawyers, historians, and radical therapists have argued that our apparent benevolence is a mask of social control for intrusion into client lives, for a violation of client's rights, and for coercive domination. In effect, they claim, our work is an exercise of power and paternalism in disguise. Rather than acting in a benevolent manner for the client's own good, we represent in reality an oppressive society and the results of our interventions are often far from benign. These groups have introduced a vocabulary of client's rights as against the social work's emphasis on client's needs. (Donzolet 1979; Gaylin, Glasser, Marcus, Rothman 1978; Lasch 1977).

Rather than being universally perceived as benevolent and benign, social workers are more frequently now perceived as intrusive and controlling. While we intend to liberate, some claim that we more often succeed in dominating.

Over the years public attitudes toward social work have moved from approval, trust, and confidence through questioning ambivalence, to a greater measure of critical mistrust and cynicism. Certainly the early sets of public attitudes were less stressful for workers than the more current, more negative ones.

Even more recently, with the support of the Reagan administration, more of the public has gone beyond the stage of questioning the effectiveness and benevolence of what social workers do. A more fundamental question, a more basic philosophical question, has been raised as to whether we should be doing it at all with the support of public funds. It is a question regarding the responsibilities of government toward its citizens. The welfare state orientation which led to the development and support of social welfare programs is based on the idea that the community, the collectivity, has some responsibility for helping people with their social problems. Anti-welfare-state ideology says that this is not an appropriate function of government and support for such programs is not an appropriate expenditure of public funds.

In response to the philosophy of more limited government, social work has faced the stress of cuts in funding and diminished support for our programs. In being forced to do more with less, we are asked to manage organizational change to lower levels of service. This is a situation in sharp contrast to the political philosophy prevailing between 1930 and 1970. The change in political philosophy and the implementation of the changed philosophy is felt as an additional stress by workers. "When the profession has dubious status, the worker must not only prove his worth as a professional person but his profession's worth as a profession" (Towle 1954, p. 16).

With this growing public disenchantment with the benevolence and competence of professionals, progressively greater encroachments were made on the autonomy of workers' decision-making power by community groups representing clients. Organizations of one kind or another representing welfare recipients, foster parents, adoptees, the mentally ill, etc. were empowered or empowered themselves to contest workers' decisions. Workers face the stress of explaining and defending their decisions in response to critical questions from such groups.

With the growth of political activism during the 1960s and 1970s, clinical social workers began to feel a sense of guilt and betrayal about a clinical approach to the problems of their clients. Some still suffer from the residual effects of this. Focusing on the intrapsychic and interpersonal problems of the individual client and their families suggests that they are "blaming the victims" of social pathology and social disorders and that they are placing the burden for change on the individual client. Clinicians were being told that their work was futile and perhaps even destructive because they were ignoring the larger issues of racism and sexism and failures in the economic system. This makes clinicians defensive, ambivalent, and uneasy about their work.

In summary, it is noted that the supervisor providing supportive supervision has to understand the stresses and tensions workers encounter on the job. Such understanding is a prerequisite to offering interventions that are likely to be helpful. The source of stresses and tensions include such factors as administrative and educational supervision, the client, the nature of the work itself, the social agency organizational structure, and the attitude of the general community toward social work and social workers. The worker encounters problems of role ambiguity, role conflict, role overload, and role strain.

Worker Personality as a Factor in Burn-out

In effectively implementing supportive supervision, not only does the supervisor have to be aware of the various stresses cited above which are encountered by the worker, but he must understand the worker's reaction to stress.

Subject to the same stressful stimuli, some workers burn out and others do not, and different workers manifest different degrees of burn-out. The attitudes which people bring to the job is a factor. The worker who is relaxed and doesn't take his work too seriously, who has a high self-esteem which is not threatened by occasional failures on the job, who is not too self-demanding and self-punitive, is less frequently a candidate for burn-out. Such attitudes help immunize the worker against burn-out (Caron et al. 1983).

The worker who consistently tends to blame himself for failure rather than realistically assigning some component of failure to the client and the social situation is more likely to respond negatively to job stress.

The paradox is that the more conscientious, concerned workers are the ones that are most likely to be susceptible to burn-out. It is said that "one has to be on fire in order to burn out." The commitment and dedication which characterize "determined idealists" may result in a greater discrepancy between great effort expended, intensified expectations, and limited outcome. The sense of disappointment in their work is apt to be greater for such workers. The worker becomes a prisoner of his own sensitivity.

The self-image that is characteristic of many people who select social work as a career—the image of an accepting, tolerant, understanding, helpful person—increases vulnerability to burn-out. Encountering difficult problems, many workers find that they are, after all, not angelic, but only human. When angry, unkindly or critical feelings about clients begin to surface, a considerable amount of psychic energy is expended in defending against such feelings in an attempt to preserve the more acceptable self-image. This reaction is often intensified when the client is of a different race or sex and the worker feels self-accused of sexism or racism.

There are differences among workers in the significance which the job has for them in regard to their total life configuration. For some workers, the job is the most important thing in their lives, having clear priority over other interests. For other workers, the job is a more peripheral aspect of their lives. The worker who builds his life around the job is more likely to risk burn-out. Investing more of himself in the job, he is more likely to be disappointed and depressed if things go wrong on the job.

Stress is cumulative and incremental. Consequently, the worker whose off-job life is generally unstressful can withstand considerable stress on the job without risking burn-out. However, if the worker's social, marital, or parental situation is stressful, even limited additional stresses on the job may make him vulnerable. Stress from the home front spills over, adding to stress on the job.

Just as the supervisor is guided by a diagnostic assessment of the learning needs and learning style of the supervisee in educational supervision, a diagnostic assessment of the needs for emotional support is useful in supportive supervision.

Workers who have limited personal investment in their work, who are not strongly oriented toward seeking emotional fulfillment from their client contacts, who tend to make situational rather than personal attributions of failure in their work, who are bureaucratically oriented toward acceptance of rules, regulations, and procedures are likely to have less need for supportive supervision. The nature of their orientation defends them from emotionally disturbing aspects of their work. They are the indifferent, conformist workers somewhat immune to job frustrations.

A worker who is concerned about but not emotionally involved in the job, who is satisfied with meeting minimal standards and who is primarily concerned with extrinsic rewards—pay, job advancement, desirable office space—is likely to be in the greatest need of supportive supervision when some situation is encountered which threatens job security.

Workers who are idealistic, independent, individualistic, nonconforming are likely to need more supportive supervision. They are strongly affected by the conflict and the discrepancy between what they think service to the client should be like and what they actually experience it to be. They are sensitive to ethical conflicts in their work, and affected by the frustrated impulse to effect change. They chafe at requirements to conform to organizational needs. Such workers need supportive supervision in reconciling their conflicts, their discontents, their disappointments. Where reconciliation is not possible, supportive supervision would at least provide the opportunity of openly discussing their disagreements with a receptive representative of the organizational hierarchy.

The more dedicated the worker, the greater the likelihood of the need for supervisory support. Workers who feel a strong sense of "calling," who are imbued with a dedicatory ethic toward their work, who have a strong professional superego are more strongly affected by inevitable failure. Such workers, who bring the best of what is needed to social work, are more likely to require the guilt-dissolving absolution of a supervisor, someone in a position of authority who gives permission to moderate the demanding rigidity of a strong, punitive superego. Supportive supervision provides the antidote to the tyranny of the ideal—the unrealistic expectations that such highly committed workers impose on themselves. Supportive supervision is designed to help such workers take themselves less seriously.

The worker who is upwardly mobile and achievement-oriented may need the frequent reassurance from supportive supervision that she is doing well. Any imputation of work failure is threatening and anxiety-provoking to such workers, and calls for supportive supervision.

In maintaining supervisor awareness of the negative effects of job stress and in raising supervisee consciousness of this, the periodic scheduled evaluation conferences might include a burn-out check review. This would keep both supervisor and supervisee alert to the development of dangerously high levels of chronic tension.

Implementing Supportive Supervision

Having learned to identify burn-out and understand the factors which help explain its development, the supervisor has the responsibility of responding to the problem in a way which might prevent the development of, and mitigate the effects of, stress and tension.

Supportive supervision is often implemented not as a separate, explicitly identifiable activity, but rather as part of the work of edu-

cational and administrational supervision. Assigning work, reviewing work, or training for the work can be done in a manner that is
supportive. The functions of educational and administrative supervision can be performed in a way that communicates respect for,
interest in, and acceptance of the supervisee. As we discussed earlier, the consequences of good administrative supervision and good
educational supervision can be supportive in the structure and the
skills they offer the supervisees.

Increasing job performance and improving competence through
educational supervision provides a sense of accomplishment,
makes the job more meaningful, and leads to greater job satisfaction. In a study of how human service professionals cope with burn-
out and the suggestions they have for coping with burn-out,
"building competence" is the most frequently cited response (Shinn
and Morch 1982, p. 231).

Beiser (1966) notes that it is very difficult to separate the precisely educational from the purely supportive components of supervision. In discussing her own supervisory practice with child-
psychiatry residents, she says that

> although I gave a great deal of didactic information both as to theory
> and specific skills, sometimes this was to alleviate anxiety, sometimes
> to encourage identification or to demonstrate a model of flexibility.
> When I tell of my own errors I use them not only to illustrate a particu-
> lar point but to encourage a less experienced therapist or to interfere
> with hopes of omnipotence through identification with me. (p. 138)

The supervisor's availability, in and of itself, is reassuring and
supportive. A questionnaire study of worker reaction to supervision
indicated that supervisors' availability and regularity of contact
were positively correlated with satisfaction with supervision and the
level of perceived helpfulness of the relationship (Shulman 1982,
p. 27–28).

The negative effect of harassed supervision and lack of availability in response to a worker's need for support is illustrated in the
following:

> I had just completed my home visit with an extremely angry, hostile
> mother. She was angry with me because I had had to remove her child

some time ago and still did not feel she was ready to assume her maternal responsibilities. I had endured her curses and hysterics; now, as I left her home I was trembling and angry. But, I was also filled with self-doubt. Was I doing the right thing? Maybe there was something I should have done differently or might do now so that mother and child could be reunited? I returned to the office absorbed with the incessant dialogue taking place in my mind and proceeded to my supervisor's office. As she looked up, I blurted, "I am so angry with Mrs. S." Before I could finish my story we had several interruptions and then the phone rang. After the phone conversation, she said, "What is it you were saying?" "Nothing," and sulking I stalked out of her office. I was frustrated all afternoon.

The supervisor's response to the development of stress and tension on the part of the worker and the ultimate danger of burn-out involves a series of specific interventions. The supervisor can act to (1) prevent stress and tension from developing; (2) remove the worker from the source of stress; (3) reduce the impact of stressors; (4) help the worker adjust to stress.

Prevention of Stress

At the very beginning, the probability of burn-out might be reduced by the supervisor's effective performance of the administrative supervisory function of hiring and inducting. This permits the selection of personnel so that there is a "best fit" between applicant and the work that needs to be performed.

Providing accurate information about the job permits the applicant to make a more objective decision as to whether it is the kind of job that fits his needs and expectations. As a consequence of clearly learning what the work realistically entails, some applicants who might have had difficulty on the job select themselves out.

But accurate objective information about the job is also helpful to those who decide to accept the position. As a result of having been clearly told what they might expect, there is less likely to be disillusionment and disappointment when they encounter the realities of the job. Such anticipatory guidance and realistic preview is a psychological innoculation associated with increased survival rate on the job (Wanous 1975).

Reducing and Ameliorating Stress

The supervisor can supportively help to reduce stress impinging on the worker or remove the worker temporarily from a stressful situation. These procedures are analogous to environmental modification procedures in working with the client. The supervisor can arrange for a temporary reduction in caseload, or a temporary shift to less problematic clients. The supervisor might also arrange for a temporary increase in clerical help available to the worker.

Conferences, institutes, and workshops not only provide learning and stimulating personal contacts but also enable the worker to get away from the office and the caseload. They are, in effect, supportive "rest and recreation" devices removing the worker from stress.

The supervisor might sanction time-outs as a tension-reducing measure. A day off in the middle of the week or an afternoon off after a difficult morning might be permitted, the time to be made up when the worker feels more in control.

Imaginative, flexible work scheduling, and arranging for job sharing of high-stress tasks, are stress-reducing procedures. Helping the worker organize his work load, sanctioning the prioritization of tasks so that some responsibilities are temporarily neglected, and allowing for deadlines to be delayed with the supervisor's authorization help reduce the development of stress.

The supervisor can remove the worker from stress by job enrichment, job diversification, job rotation. As Davis and Barrett (1981) note: "Rotation of workers to alternate services within the agency can be used to provide a change of pace with relief from stressors" (p. 59).

Job enrichment attempts to help the worker find more meaning in tasks assigned while job diversification involves increasing the variety of job-related tasks. Caseworkers might be assigned to work with a group, teach homemakers or foster parents, engage in work-related research, or write a work-related report for administration.

A temporary change of assignment from the field to the office with temporarily diminished responsibility for contact with clients helps the worker to catch his psychic breath and recharge emotional batteries.

Careful assignment of a reasonable caseload balanced between cases with a high risk of failure and cases that might provide an experience of success prevents tensions arising from quantitative or qualitative role overload.

In an attempt more specifically related to helping the worker cope with developing tension, supervisors in some agencies have arranged for stress management workshops. This might include instruction on biofeedback, meditation, or relaxation techiques.

The supervisor can be supportive by frankly sharing some of his own difficulties with the supervisee. This confirms the fact that examined failure is acceptable and that the supervisee need not feel so guilty and inadequate.

> Gretchen then commented that it was so hard to know when she should say something to someone and when she should keep quiet. I asked her what she meant. She said, . . . "if the girls want to talk about sex, I let them talk about sex even if I know that maybe I am going further than they want to go." I agreed that this was a rough struggle, one that I was going through too. I elaborated by saying that many times I was torn when Gretchen asked me something as to whether or not to tell her or to let her do the work. This struggle, I said, I could feel with her since it was a struggle that I had too. Gretchen looked at me and said, "Do you really?" I said that I did. She looked very comfortable and at ease with this. (I cannot describe the look but at that moment I felt that there was a strong feeling of closeness between Gretchen and me.) (Gladstone 1967, p. 9)

The worker may be upset about a problem he is facing with the client. Discussing it with a supervisor who is calm about the situation is supportive. Some of the supervisor's calmness is contagiously communicated to the worker. A supportive orientation encourages expression of feelings, which is in itself supportive. Nelsen (1973) found that supervisees "volunteered feelings after they had been encouraged *and* supported in expressing feelings on a conference by conference basis" (p. 209, emphasis in original).

It is presumed that anxiety is reduced by externalization, by open expression of anxious feelings.

Perception by supervisees of the level of a supervisor's helpfulness was positively associated with the supervisor's encouraging such ventilation. Positive responses to the statement "when I am upset about something my supervisor says or does, he/she encourages me to talk about it" were highly correlated with supervisory helpfulness in Shulman's study (1982, p. 157).

The supervisor who suspects that the supervisee feels anxious about his next visit to a family, his next group meeting, or his next community-action planning conference, might supportively ask, "How do you feel about this meeting?" Or she might hazard an inference coupled with an invitation: "You seem somewhat upset about this upcoming meeting. Would you like to talk about it?"

Considerable stress is encountered in exercising control and communicating acceptance in response to a client's hostility and rejection. To react with anger, defensiveness, or withdrawal (eminently human and socially acceptable reactions) would be regarded as a violation of professional norms. Such a response would then evoke guilt and a feeling of professional failure. Even the thought of such reactions creates discomfort. "The client aroused some negative feelings in me—like anger, impatience, and frustration. And I became angry at myself for having these feelings" (Mayer and Rosenblatt 1973a, p. 8).

While holding to the norms of professional conduct, the supervisor can supportively sanction such feelings. Paraphrasing Freud, the supervisor might say that the professional superego is like a good hotelkeeper who doesn't care what goes on in the privacy of the individual rooms as long as it doesn't disturb other guests. All thinking and feeling is acceptable as long as it is not manifested in unacceptable behavior. A worker says,

> I think that one of the important functions of suportive supervision is to help the worker deal with negative feelings about the client. Social work attitudes tend to reinforce general societal constraints about thinking negative thoughts about other people. So this is quite a job for supervision. In my case I was asked to physically describe a client. I proceeded along the line of height, weight, etc., when my supervisor asked me if the person was attractive. I was really caught off guard and felt hesitant about expressing my thoughts that, no, the person wasn't attractive at all. With the supervisor's support I have become more at ease with expressing negative thoughts and feelings and have come to accept these as part of any relationship.

The supervisor supports workers in carrying out tasks that must be done but that cause anxiety. Workers are often initially reluctant to reverse the usual pattern of amenities and ask intimate details about the life of a relative stranger, the client. Such behavior is seen as an unwarranted intrusion on client privacy, a manifestation of unacceptable "aggressive voyeurism." The supervisor supports the workers by reassuring them about their entitlement to such information if they are to do the job of helping the client.

Reinforcement, or confirmation, of the workers' decisions is supportive because it assures them that the supervisor shares the responsibility for what they are doing or planning to do. It is reassuring for workers to know that their decisions are in line with more expert opinion.

The supervisor mitigates stress by supportively sharing the responsibility for difficult decisions with the worker. A social worker in an AFDC program said,

> In talking with Mrs. H. about how she disciplined the children, she told me that yesterday she had caught her 4-year-old playing with matches—lighting them and tossing them in the air. Frightened and anxious, she grabbed the kid, slapped his hand repeatedly, then lit a match and burned the kid's hand slightly. Mrs. H. thought that feeling the pain would teach the kid to keep away from matches. She sure handed me a tough one. According to the law, I was really supposed to report Mrs. H. for child abuse. But if I reported her I would blow the chances of continuing a relationship with Mrs. H. and possibly being of help to the children. What to do? After discussing this with my supervisor, I held off reporting Mrs. H. for abuse. That shares the guilt for the decision.

Discussing this stressful aspect of the social worker's job, Brearley (1982) makes explicit the relationship between work stress and supportive supervision:

> Social workers are subject to many pressures which create stress. Working in a situation of uncertainty, having to deal with a lack of knowledge and often with uncontrollable factors in an environment which militates against change inevitably creates stress. Social work has therefore developed techniques to manage stress, particularly the supervision process. . . . Supervision is a way of sharing the burden of uncertainty, of gaining support in a practice context in which decisions are almost invariably made with incomplete information and knowledge. Through supervision, the worker is helped to manage his own response to being unsure and also helped to clarify decisions and share responsibility for decision making. (pp. 136, 139; see also Shapiro 1982)

Mayer and Rosenblatt (1973a,b) found, in their study of stress among social workers, that new workers had an unrealistically high expectation of what social work could accomplish. When this overly optimistic picture met with inevitable failure, the workers tended to blame themselves. The supervisor can offer the exculpation of a practiced professional who reduces guilt by excusing failure. The supervisor helps workers move from an unrealistic sense of idealistic omnipotence to an acceptance of a realistic limitation of themselves, social work technology, and the clients. The shift is supportive and results in less anxiety and guilt. The supervisor legitimizes limits of expectations. The supervisor depersonalizes responsibility for some failures and relieves the worker of the burden of unearned guilt.

One significant aspect of supportive supervision is concerned with what Stelling and Bucher (1973) have identified as "vocabularies of realism." "Acquiring a language for coping with failure and human fallibility can be seen as part of the process of acquiring a professional orientation and frame of reference toward the work of the profession" (p. 673).

"Vocabularies of realism" help the worker cope with stress by a cognitive restructuring of his approach to the work. It helps to reduce the pressure of work demands, providing sanction for detached concern and psychological distancing from the client. It revises expectations so that they are less idealistic and more realistic, and depersonalizes failure when it occurs.

The need for vocabularies of realism is greater in those professions where risk of failure is high and the consequences of failure are significant. "A profession which rests on a body of knowledge characterized by uncertainties and gaps runs a relatively high risk of error and failure" (p. 673). These factors are operative in social work. As a consequence, collective responses to recurrent probabilities of failure have tended to develop, and the supervisor passes these on in supportive supervision. Stelling and Bucher, studying these procedures in medicine and psychiatry, identify basic exculpatory themes that are similar to those employed in social work. One theme is "doing-one's-best"; a second is "recognition-of-limitations." In the following example we see the doing-one's-best theme communicated supportively by a supervisor to a psychiatric resident.

Another very important time came when one of my supervisors said to me, in dealing with this very manipulative patient, "Look, you know, she may commit suicide, we may lose her—we could try, but there is a very good chance that she will kill herself sooner or later, no matter what you do," and I think once I had accepted that idea that patients do kill themselves and that . . . there are some things I can do to prevent this, but there are also some things that I can't, I think I had kind of an "aha" experience. (Stelling and Bucher 1973, p. 667)

The second theme supportively communicated in supervision is a recognition of limitations, expressed by the following psychiatric resident:

One thing one learns in this residency program is not to have therapeutic ambitions in anywhere near the quantities that you have when you first come here. Patients thwart that right, left, and center, and you learn that it is therapeutically unhelpful to have a large therapeutic ambition for patients. . . . I can now say that there are large numbers of people who suffer symptomatically, but who are untreatable. . . . I had many sorts of rescue fantasies about patients when I came into the residency, and it's taken me a long time to shift focus and learn that I didn't have to rescue everybody, that, one, it wasn't necessary, and two, it wasn't possible. (Stelling and Bucher 1973, p. 669)

The supervisor reduces tension by helping the worker resolve the problem of conflicting role obligations. If the worker is torn between finishing a report and helping a client facing an emergency, the supervisor can sanction delaying the report so that the worker can devote full attention to client needs. Where two performance objectives conflict, for instance detailed intensive interviews with clients at intake and the need to expeditiously complete intake interviews so as to process more applicants, the supervisor can reduce anxiety by officially assigning clear priority to one of the objectives.

The supervisor provides the support of perspective. The view that both the client and the relationship are fragile often inhibits workers from doing what may be helpful. The supervisor can validly reassure the worker that both the client and the relationship can survive a mistaken intervention, a poor interview, or a temporary lapse in professional conduct. Unlike the experienced worker, the new worker "does not have a backlog of successful cases to which he can refer in reverie when things don't go well with the client who is sitting across from him. When things go awry in relationship to a particular client nothing can shore up a therapist's defenses faster

270 SUPPORTIVE SUPERVISION

than his recall of the many successful cases he has terminated" (Mueller and Kell 1972, p. 104). Borrowing the perspective of the more experienced supervisor can be supportive.

A beginning worker might express doubts about his ability to be helpful to the client. The supervisor can supportively universalize by sharing the fact that most new workers feel this way, that she has been able to assist others to be helpful, that she has confidence in the worker's ability to learn, and that she would be available to discuss with the worker the problems he meets in trying to be helpful. This single intervention contains a number of different kinds of statements, all of which have a supportive intent.

Supervisors provide support for workers in helping them formulate a clearer conception of agency policies, their own work goals, and their role within the agency. Unless supervisees have a reasonably clear idea of what they are supposed to be doing, why they are doing it, toward what objectives, they are likely to be burdened with unnerving doubt and confusion. Uncertainty is generally related to increased tension. A worker whose supervisor clearly communicates performance objectives, performance standards, and performance expectations, feels a sense of support in such clarity.

If role ambiguity is a potential source of tension, clarity in definition of work objectives, expectations, and reciprocal responsibilities prevents the development of such tension. In the following, a supervisee writes of the nonsupportive effects of lack of clarity regarding objectives:

> I was given the task of being an indirect leader in a new setting. I continually reported back to the supervisor what I was doing and what problems existed. The supervisor briefly commented that what I am doing is good. When I asked direct questions such as what goal does the agency have as a priority now, or what are new developments from conferences, the supervisor answered that there are no goals, no new developments, you do your own thing. I feel that a task like the above is extremely difficult and threatening, demanding support and a certain amount of direction from the supervisor, which serves the purpose of giving the supervisee a sense of direction and support in the work setting itself. The supervisor's lack of direction made my task more difficult.

The supervisor, in discharging the responsibilities of supportive supervision, attempts to provide workers with the opportunity to experience success and achievement in performance of professional tasks and provides increasing opportunities for independent functioning. Herzberg, Mausner, and Snyderman (1959) found that feelings of achievement and responsibility were two of the most potent sources of job satisfaction. Both help people feel good about the job they are doing.

The supervisor supports by praising and commending good performance and communicates agency appreciation for the workers' efforts. Compliments from the supervisor are particularly gratifying and ego-enhancing because they come from someone who is identified as capable of making valid evaluations. In sharing their victories with an appreciative supervisor, workers know that they are talking to someone who understands the difficulty of the task they have successfully achieved. To perform this support function effectively a

> person must fulfill two important criteria: he or she must be an expert in our field and someone whose honesty and integrity we trust. In other words this person must understand the complexities of the job we do and must be courageous enough to provide honest feedback. If these requirements are met we can accept support as genuine. Mothers, spouses, or nonexpert friends can provide general encouragement but that is probably not as meaningful as support from someone who can appreciate the technical intricacies of our job. (Pines 1983, p. 158)

Partial praise should be offered where warranted: "It was good you realized something was going on here, but I am not sure this was the best way to respond to it. Let's talk about how to handle clients' anxiety." The worker is commended for knowing that something needed to be done, even though what she did was not especially helpful. One supervisor writes, in detailing her supportive intervention,

> On the days I didn't find a lot of glory to give her, I gave her encouragement and pointed out that at least she was aware of what she did wrong and how it could have been improved. When she had a miserable meeting with the girls and was angry with herself, I tried to interject some realistic reassurance. When she had a good meeting, I tried to help her feel justified in her high spirits. I'm sure that getting along together as people had a great deal to do with it as well.

Unwarranted praise, however, is antisupportive. It may reflect the supervisor's rather than the supervisee's anxieties, which then tend to decrease the supervisee's self-confidence. "He seems much too worried about me, like I am about to fall apart or something"; "I get the feeling that he is afraid to criticize me, afraid that I can't take it"; "I don't think I am so fragile, but he is so supportive about not hurting my feelings that I begin to wonder if he thinks I am fragile"; "I appreciate the gentleness of her approach to me but it suggests a kind of condescension that I tend to resent."

As was true for educational supervision, the act and its intent may be at variance with the effect. Just as teaching is not learning, supportive activity on the part of the supervisor may not be perceived as supportive by the supervisee. The supervisor must be sensitive to any feedback that gives information as to the actual effect of her behavior. Reassurance may not reassure; catharsis may lead to an increase in anxiety.

The following are two examples of situations that were regarded by workers as good examples of supportive supervision:

One conference dealt with the relationship of the supervisee in working with a group of severely mentally handicapped children. The worker mentioned the fact that such children "make me physically ill," "they are repulsive to me." I pointed out how I could understand her feelings and how I myself had at one time shared somewhat the same feelings. I went on to talk about my growth in this as a result of experiences I had had in working in a school for retarded children, the warmth of relationships that had developed.

I do not know if she has changed her bias, but I know that she did a good deal of thinking about it, and told me how I had helped her manage her feelings so that she could work more effectively in that program. What helped the supervisee was some understanding and sympathy toward her feelings coupled with warmth and empathy and a positive stand on what this type of work could entail, how it could be meaningful, etc.

A worker in a surgical ward of an acute-care hospital expressed to her supervisor her resistance to visiting a patient, long known to her, who was in terminal stage of cancer. Supervisor helped worker to express her fear, and then to look at why she was afraid. Worker finally concluded that she was afraid patient might die while she [worker] was visiting her. Further exploration revealed that the worker had many warm, close and positive feelings about the patient and the worker was afraid she would break down and cry. The supervisor's response to this was, in effect, "so what!" Discussion followed regarding the reality of such fears and emotions, the need for the worker to remain an individual whose real feelings are not to be confused with concepts of "professionality," and that expression of honest feelings can only serve to strengthen relationships between people. Subsequently, the worker reported freedom to share feelings with the dying patient. The supervisor had effectively provided support to the worker, had accepted her fears and emotions, enabled her to express them, and freed her to overcome fears.

Recapitulation—and Some Caveats

In general the supervisor, in implementing the responsibilities of supportive supervision, engages in the same kinds of intervention that characterize supportive psychotherapy. The supervisor acts to prevent stress, reduce stress, or temporarily remove the worker from stress. The supervisor praises the workers' efforts where warranted, reassures and encourages, communicates confidence, depersonalizes and universalizes the workers' problems, affirms workers' strengths, shares responsibility with workers for difficult decisions and/or lends his sanctions to the workers' decisions, listens attentively and sympathetically, providing an opportunity for cathartic release. All of this takes place in the context of a positive relationship characterized by respect, empathic understanding, acceptance, sympathetic interest in and concern for the worker as a person. The fact that such interventions are employed in the context of a meaningful positive relationship increases the saliency of the supervisor's communications. Praise, reassurance, encouragement, any supportive comment expressed by the supervisor, have greater significance for, and effect on, the supervisee because they come from somebody whose responses he values highly.

The aim of supportive supervision is to reduce anxiety, allay guilt, increase self-esteem, enhance the workers' capacity for adaptation to the demands of the work situation, and free psychic energy for more adequate job performance. By increasing the supervisees' feeling of emotional well-being, the supervisor increases their emotional fitness to offer more effective service.

It needs to be recognized, however, that even the best supervisory relationship is not potent enough to resolve some dissatisfactions and job-related conflicts which derive from the nature of the work itself and the conditions under which it frequently has to be performed. Some potential dissatisfactions are inherent in agency structure, the social work task, the state of available professional technology, the position of the social work profession in modern society.

It would be asking far more of supervision than it is capable of achieving if a good supervisory relationship is expected to eliminate work dissatisfaction, worker disenchantment, and worker turnover. This is part of the vocabulary of realism for supervisors.

Because of the selective emphasis on stresses and tensions associated with the social worker's job there is a decidedly negative bias in the material presented above. Because of my conviction in the importance of the positive contribution which social work makes to peoples' lives, a parenthetical note seems necessary here. The fact is that, while the stresses and tensions noted above are real, most social workers do not burn out, and most social workers find considerable satisfaction in their work.

A comparison of mean values for tedium and burn-out for a variety of human service professions shows social workers having a high mean value, but on a lower level than education or nursing (Pines, Aronson, Kafry, Table A.3, p. 208). A study of 108 family service agency direct service social workers found that "Burn-out scores generally fell on the lower end of the scale, indicating that the majority of workers experienced little or no burn-out" (Streepy 1981, p. 60). A national study of some 400 MSWs in a variety of agencies indicated a high level of satisfaction with their jobs. Over 80 percent of the workers stated that they were "very satisfied" or "somewhat satisfied" with their jobs (Jayaratne and Chess 1982, p. 6).

This does not mitigate the need for supervisors to be aware of stresses encountered by workers in doing their job. Worker and supervisor recognition of the significance of job stress is confirmed by the results of a 1980 national study of training needs of 1,500 child welfare supervisors and direct service workers. In selecting priorities for training from a list of 44 content items, both workers and supervisors listed "identifying and lessening workers stress" as among the very highest priorities (Vinokur 1983, pp. 78, 86).

The Value of Supportive Supervision—Research Findings

Studies are available which demonstrate the positive effects of supportive supervision. One study experimentally tested the effects of supportive and nonsupportive orientations to supervision (Blane 1968). Counseling students who experienced supportive supervision showed a significant difference in empathic understanding after such supervision as compared with scores before supervision. Students who experienced nonsupportive supervision did not show this change.

Another study testing the differential consequences of the two approaches showed that nonsupportive supervision tends to shift the worker's focus of concern away from the client and toward himself (Davidson and Emmer 1966). Blau (1960) found that reductions in the lèvel of workers' anxiety as a result of supportive supervision were related to a less rigid use of agency procedures and encouraged better service to clients.

The available research also supports the supposition that good supervision reduces the development and negative effects of burnout. Berkeley Planning Associates (1977), a research organization, studied worker performance in eleven protective service demonstration projects across the country. Comparing differences in the level of burn-out between workers in the different agencies, they concluded that the nature of supervision offered the workers was a crucial determinant of the level of burn-out. "It was found that those demonstration projects in which workers report inadequate supervision had the highest incidence of burn-out. Good supervision is crucial to workers' performance and satisfaction" (p. 57). Where workers experienced inadequate supervision, inadequate leadership, and inadequate communication, burn-out was more frequent. Adequate supervisory structure and support, provision of timely, appropriate, and adequate information were associated with lower levels of burn-out (Armstrong 1979).

In a study of stress encountered by 183 workers and supervisors in a public welfare agency, Munson (1983) found that "regular supportive supervision was the most effective aid in combatting burnout" (p. 217). Contrawise poor supervision is associated with increased risk of burn-out. In a survey of 183 protective service workers, Gillespie and Cohen (1984) found that burn-out was related to failure of supervisors to provide support and technical assistance to workers.

A research study of case management systems at four settings providing service to the chronically mentally handicapped found that "sites in which the content of supervision included supportive enabling and problem-solving activities were also sites in which case managers exhibited no antagonism toward management, low levels of absenteeism, no stereotyping of client groups, and less of the other symptoms associated with burn-out" (Caragonne 1979, p. 24).

Supervisors were perceived as being one of the key figures in their social support network, along with coworkers and friends, as reported by human service workers in a number of related studies (Pines, 1982, p. 157). The availability of such support was significantly and negatively correlated with burn-out; that is, the better the support network the less burn-out occurred. The support network was defined as including people with whom one had "enduring interpersonal ties" and "who could be relied upon to provide emotional sustenance, assistance, and resources in time of need and who provide feedback and with whom we share values and standards" (p. 156).

Correlational data from 541 MSWs clearly support the existence of a negative relationship between emotional support from supervisors and co-workers and stress and strain. For example, "emotional exhaustion was negatively correlated with supervisor support" (Jayaratne, Tripod, Chess 1983, p. 23).

A detailed interview study of psychotherapists, including social workers, in private practice indicated that "most therapists found the role of support systems essential" in dealing with stress encountered in their work. "All who could, utilized supervisory relationships to help them through difficult moments" (Farber and Heifetz 1982, p. 6).

In a study of organizational responses to burn-out, White (1978) concludes that "The provision of effective *clinical case supervision* [emphasis in original] is the most consistent mechanism needed to provide staff with emotional rewards that may be only minimally provided by their clients with whom they work—the positive stroking of staff in the supervisory process may do more to enhance the treatment of clients than the actual supervision of details of the treatment process" (p. 15).

The stimulation and challenge the work offers was clearly related to social workers' job satisfaction and to the reporting of burn-out in one national study of social workers (Jayaratne and Chess 1982). It was noted that through job assignment and case selection, the supervisor is in a key position to control the level of job challenge offered the worker and prevent boredom and stagnation.

The crucial significance of supervision for worker satisfaction is highlighted in a study of the effects of role conflict and role ambiguity among protective service workers. Harrison (1980) assessed the degree of role conflict ("incompatible demands made on worker") and role ambiguity ("lack of clarity as to what is expected, appropriate or effective role behaviors") among 112 such workers and found evidence that mean levels for both factors was higher than for other occupational groups studied.

> The most problematic outcome of such heightened role conflict is likely to involve the social worker's attitude about the supervisor. It is realistic to speculate that the supervisor in child protective services is an especially important source of role information. Thus the supervisor who is perceived as sending either contradictory role prescription or role information which contradicts that from other role information sources . . . may be viewed as a source of dissatisfaction. Perhaps the worker looks to the supervisor as one who should help sort out inevitable role conflict issues and when this supervisory function is not fulfilled to the worker's expectation, dissatisfaction results. It appears, at any rate, that the supervisor is in a particularly important position with reference to role conflict phenomenon.

Additional Sources of Support for Supervisees

1. The Client

The supervisor is not the only source of support for supervisees in dealing with stresses encountered on the job. Clients can be a source of support as well as stress. In their responses to workers, and to the service offered by workers, they confirm the workers' competence and sense of self-worth. Appreciative comments regarding the workers' efforts are supportive. Client movement and change provide workers with a gratifying feeling of achievement.

2. The Peer Group

The informal agency structure provides the worker with an additional source of support. Some interpersonal relationships in the organization are required by agency structure—the supervisor has no choice but to establish a relationship with the supervisee, and vice versa. Informal relationships are voluntarily selected; they are the primary, close relationships one establishes in the organization in response to personal interests and preferences without reference to any formal work requirements.

The agency is, after all, a small social system composed of a network of human relationships that follow idiosyncratic desires rather than the organizational chart. The formal structure reflects the needs of the organization. The informal structure reflects the needs of the individuals.

Resorting to the informal structure, workers turn to others with whom they feel comfortable to talk about their dissatisfactions, discouragements, doubt about the job, to express feelings of anxiety about inadequate performance and feelings of guilt about mistakes made. The peer group on the job, the work clique, is very often the primary resource to which workers turn to talk about such concerns. These are people who most likely have experienced similar problems. They are knowledgeable about the job situation and can discuss these matters with some sophistication. The worker who feels the need to talk about these feelings and the peer group to whom he turns share experiences and a common frame of reference, increasing the likelihood of empathic understanding. In addition, they have no administrative power to evaluate the worker. Consequently the worker may feel freer in sharing his doubts and dissatisfactions with fellow workers than with his supervisor. The peer group has the additional advantage of being not only psychologically accessible, since social distance between peer and peer is minimal, but also physically available. You do not have to make an "appointment" with co-workers.

When workers were questioned about who would be the first person they would turn to if they were feeling frustrated or upset with some aspect of work in the agency, 53 percent said a work associate, 24 percent said a supervisor, and 15 percent said an administrator (Austin et al. 1977).

Co-workers provide mutual support, assistance, and protection. They use each other as models for identification and teach each other much that is important about the job. "A social worker may use the [peer] group as a sounding board for a particularly difficult case problem or ways to get around a trying regulation may be devised" (Peabody 1964, p. 72). Parallel to the formal system of administrative, educational, and supportive supervision there exist the administrative, teaching, and supportive functions as performed by the peer group. The person holding the position of supervisor is formally invested with the title but should recognize that the supervisee has, in fact, other "supervisors" without title or official position.

The idea that the peer group and the supervisor are alternative sources for meeting similar needs is supported by Marcus's (1961) research. He found that those workers who were supervised by unpopular supervisors interacted more with each other and sought each other out more often. Blau and Scott (1962) have detailed the supportive activities of the peer group:

> Discussions among colleagues served to relieve the tensions engendered by conflicts with clients. Informal observation over a period of several months and interviews with the staff revealed that there were three topics of conversation prevalent among staff officials during working hours. The most frequent topic involved complaints about clients. An interviewer would, in effect, say to a colleague, "Look what this client did to me!" The discussions served as an escape valve for releasing aggressive feelings against clients in a harmless form. But this could not have been their sole function, for they often occurred after an official had penalized a client, perhaps by sending a notification that might disqualify him from further unemployment benefits. In these cases, the practice did not serve to relieve pent-up aggression, which had already been expressed directly by penalizing the client, but to obtain social support for one's decision and thereby mitigate feelings of guilt. The sympathetic listener, who laughed at the client's stupidity or expressed indignation at his impertinence, im-

plicitly justified the speaker's punitive or inconsiderate action by con-
demning the client's behavior, and this social approval relieved
impending feelings of guilt.

A second type of discussion took the form of joking about clients.
Ridicule is a form of aggression, but it also relieves guilt. The laughter
elicited by a story about a client constituted social evidence that his
behavior was ludicrous or incongruous, thus placing the blame for the
client's troubles on his own shoulders and relieving the official from
having failed to mitigate these difficulties; it conveyed the message,
"Nobody could have helped such an impossible person!" Joking about
clients not only relieved tensions created by work situations but also
strengthened group cohesiveness by uniting its members in laughing
together. . . . Finally, some interviewers did not joke or complain
about clients but often told colleagues about outstanding clients they
had encountered. This third topic of conversation was characteristic
of the interviewers who were most considerate in their treatment of
clients. Their sympathetic attitudes toward clients constituted over-
conformity with the service ideals in violation of group norms, according to which concern with helping clients must be tempered by
willingness to "put them in their place" when necessary. By selecting
for their conversations with colleagues accounts of exceptional clients
who clearly deserved special consideration, interviewers with overly
favorable attitudes toward clients sought to escape the onus of being
defined as deviant by soliciting social approval of their treatment of
clients. In these cases, the listeners were invited to agree, the extremely considerate treatment was surely justified. Thus, [workers]
felt compelled to seek the social approval of colleagues for both inconsiderate and overly considerate treatment of clients, because the former violated their service philosophy and the latter their unofficial
norms. These discussions about clients furnished social support and
reduced tensions. (pp. 84–85)

In a study by a sociologist of the interaction among colleagues in
a social agency, it was noted that according to the peer culture
"nearly everyone clearly recognized an obligation to listen if colleagues wished to express anxiety, anger, or frustration, or to re-
count their experiences in the knowledge that they too could claim
colleagues' attention in similar circumstances" (Satyamurti 1981,
p. 59). Peer-group gripe sessions are effective cathartic devices permitting discharge of tension and providing release and relief.

In providing supportive supervision, the supervisor can actively
mobilize the assistance of the peer group resource. The supervisor
can stimulate supportive peer-peer interaction and encourage coop-

erative mutual aid among staff in reinforcing the supportive activities of the supervisor.

Supervisors might facilitate the development of the peer-peer interactional system by arranging for group supervision and frequent unit meetings.

The supervisor might encourage supportive peer-peer interaction by helping to organize peer supervision and consultation.

3. Supervisees' Adaptations

Supportive supervision is further supplemented by the workers' own adjustive capacities.

Supervisees respond to the stress of supervision by actively "psyching out" the supervisor. Their purpose is to determine the kinds of behavior that will obtain acceptance and those that will elicit disapproval. Supervisees then manage a presentation of self that will net maximum approval and minimum disapproval. What Goldhammer (1969) says of teachers in supervision can be applied equally well to social workers. They have learned, in adapting to stress in the supervisory relationship, "how to second guess the supervisor, how to anticipate what will please him, how to stage appropriate performances for him to observe and how to jolly him up for their own protection" (p. 64).

Humor helps reduce worker tension by making the impermissible permissible. The friendly sarcastic remark permits an excusable expression of hostility toward clients and supervisors. It suggests that the worker does not really mean what he is saying and expects to be excused. If the supervisor reacts punitively, it is an indication that he cannot take a joke. "The supervisor said she was stumped, she really did not know what to suggest. A smile slowly spread over the worker's face as she said in a gentle voice, 'My, that really surprises me—I thought you were all-knowing, all-loving and all-forgiving.'"

Supervisees have developed a series of well-established, identifiable games that are, in effect, defensive adjustments to the threats and anxieties which the supervisory situation poses for them. In the description that follows, these games are grouped in terms of similar tactics. It may be important to note that some supervisees almost

never play games. However, even the least anxious supervisees resort to such adjustive games occasionally. Supervisors also play
games for similar reasons. These are discussed following the description of supervisees' games.

Supervisees' Games*

1. Manipulating Demands Levels

One series of games is designed to manipulate the level of demands made on the supervisee. One such game might be titled
"Two Against the Agency" or "Seducing for Subversion." The game
is generally played by intelligent, intuitively gifted supervisees who
are impatient with routine agency procedures. Forms, reports,
punctuality, and recording excite their contempt. The more sophisticated supervisee introduces the game by noting the conflict between the bureaucratic and professional orientation to the work of
the agency. The bureaucratic orientation is one that is centered on
what is needed to ensure efficient operation of the agency; the
professional orientation is focused on meeting the needs of the client. The supervisee points out that meeting client needs is more
important, that time spent in recording, filling out forms, and writing reports is robbed from direct work with the client, and further
that when he comes to work and goes home is not important as long
as no client suffers as a consequence. Would it not therefore be
possible to permit him, a highly intuitive and gifted worker, to
schedule and allocate his time to maximum client advantage and
should not the supervisor be less concerned about his filling out
forms, doing recording, completing reports, and so on?

It takes two to play games. The supervisor is induced to play this
game because he identifies with the supervisee's concern for meeting client needs; he himself has frequently resented bureaucratic
demands and so is, initially, sympathetic to the supervisee's complaints; and he is hesitant to assert his authority in demanding
firmly that these requirements be met. If the supervisor chooses to

---

* Much of the material in this section originally appeared in my article entitled
"Games People Play in Supervision," *Social Work* 13 (1968): 23–32. It is quoted with
permission of the National Association of Social Workers.

play the game, he has enlisted in an alliance with the supervisee to subvert agency administrative procedures.

Another game designed to control the level of demands made on the supervisee might be called "Be Nice to Me Because I Am Nice to You." The principal ploy is flattery. "You're the best supervisor I ever had," "you're so perceptive that after I've talked to you I almost know what the client will say next," "you're so consistently helpful," "I look forward in the future to being as good a social worker as you are," and so on. It is a game of emotional blackmail in which, having been paid in this kind of coin, the supervisor finds himself unable to hold the worker firmly to legitimate demands.

The supervisor finds it difficult to resist engaging in the game because it is gratifying to be regarded as an omniscient source of wisdom; there is satisfaction in being perceived as helpful and in being selected as a pattern for identification and emulation. An invitation to play a game that tends to enhance a positive self-concept and feed one's narcissistic needs is likely to be accepted.

In general, the supervisor is vulnerable to an invitation to play this game. The supervisor needs the supervisee as much as the supervisee needs her. One of the principal sources of gratification for a worker is contact with the client. The supervisor is denied this source of gratification, at least directly. For the supervisor the analogous satisfaction is helping the supervisee to grow and change. But this means that she has to look to the supervisee to validate her effectiveness. Objective criteria of such effectiveness are, at best, obscure and equivocal. To have the supervisee say openly and directly, "I have learned a lot from you," "You have been helpful," is the kind of reassurance needed and often subtly solicited by the supervisor. The perceptive supervisee understands and exploits the supervisor's needs in initiating this game.

2. Redefining the Relationship

A second series of games is designed to lessen the demands made on the supervisee by redefining the supervisory relationship. These games depend on ambiguity in the definition of the supervisory relationship; it is open to a variety of interpretations and resembles, in some crucial respects, analogous relationships.

One kind of redefinition suggests a shift from the relationship of teacher and learner in an administrative hierarchy to worker and client in the context of therapy. The game might be called "Protect the Sick and the Infirm" or "Treat Me, Don't Beat Me." The supervisee would rather expose himself than his work, and so he asks the supervisor for help in solving his personal problems. The sophisticated player relates these problems to difficulties on the job. If the translation to worker and client is made, the nature of demands shifts as well. The kinds of demands one can legitimately impose on a client are clearly less onerous than those imposed on a worker. The supervisee has achieved a payoff in a softening of demands, and since so much time is spent discussing his personal problems there is less time left for discussing his work.

The supervisor is induced to play because the game appeals to the social worker in him (since he was a social worker before he became a supervisor and is still interested in helping those who have personal problems); it appeals to the voyeur in him (many supervisors are fascinated by the opportunity to share in the intimate lives of others); it is flattering to be selected as a therapist; and he is not clearly certain that such a redefinition of the situation is impermissible. All the discussions about the equivocal boundaries between supervision and therapy feed into this uncertainty.

Another game of redefinition might be called "Evaluation Is Not for Friends." Here the supervisory relationship is redefined as a social relationship. The supervisee makes an effort to take coffee breaks with the supervisor, invite her to lunch, walk to and from the bus or the parking lot with her, and discuss common interests during conferences. The social component tends to vitiate the professional component in the relationship. It requires increased determination and resolution on the part of any supervisor to hold the "friend" to the required level of performance.

A more contemporary redefinition of the supervisor-supervisee relationship is less obvious than the two kinds just discussed, which have long been standard. The game of "Maximum Feasible Participation" involves a shift in roles from supervisor and supervisee to peer and peer. The supervisee suggests that the relationship will be most effective if it is established on the basis of democratic participation. Since he knows best what he needs and wants to learn, he should be granted equal responsibility for determining the agendas of conferences. So far so good. However, in the hands of a determined supervisee, joint control of agenda can easily become total supervisee control. Expectations may be lowered and threatening content areas avoided.

The supervisor finds himself in a predicament in trying to decline the game. There is truth in the contention that people learn best in a context that encourages democratic participation in the learning process. Furthermore, the current trend in working with social agency clients is to encourage maximum feasible participation, with as yet ambiguously defined limits. To decline the game is to suggest that one is old-fashioned, undemocratic, and against the rights of those on lower levels in the administrative hierarchy—not an enviable picture to project of oneself. The supervisor is forced to play but needs to be constantly alert in order to maintain some semblance of administrative authority and prevent all the shots being called by the supervisee-peer.

3. Reducing Power Disparity

A third series of games is designed to reduce anxiety by reducing the power disparity between supervisor and worker. One source of the supervisor's power is, of course, his position in the administrative hierarchy vis-à-vis the supervisee. Another source of power lies in his expertise and superior skill. This second source of power is vulnerable in this series of games. If the supervisee can establish the fact that the supervisor is not so smart after all, some of the power differential is lessened and with it some of the need to feel anxious.

One such game, frequently played, might be called "If You Knew Dostoyevsky like I Know Dostoyevsky." During the course of a conference, the supervisee alludes casually to the fact that the client's behavior reminds him of Raskolnikov's in *Crime and Punishment,* which is, after all, somewhat different in etiology from the pathology that plagued Prince Myshkin in *The Idiot.* An effective ploy, used to score additional points, involves asking the supervisor rhetorically, "You remember, don't you?" It is equally clear to both supervisee and supervisor that the latter does not remember—if, indeed, he ever knew. At this point the supervisee proceeds to instruct the supervisor. The roles of teacher and learner are reversed; power disparity and supervisee anxiety are simultaneously reduced.

The supervisor acquiesces to the game because refusal requires a confession of ignorance on his part. The supervisee who plays the game well cooperates in a conspiracy with the supervisor not to expose his ignorance openly. The discussion proceeds under the protection of the mutually accepted fiction that both know what they are talking about.

The content for the essential gambit in this game changes with each generation of supervisees. My impression is that currently the allusion is likely to be to the work of systems theoreticians or family therapists—Minuchin, Framo, Byng-Hall—rather than to literary figures. The effect on the supervisor, however, is the same: a feeling of depression and general malaise at having been found ignorant when his position requires that he know more than the supervisee. And it has the same payoff in reducing supervisee anxiety.

Another game in this genre exploits situational advantages to reduce power disparity and permit the supervisee the feeling that he, rather than the supervisor, is in control. This game is "So What Do *You* Know About It?" The supervisee with a long record of experience in public welfare refers to "those of us on the front lines who have struggled with the multiproblem client," exciting humility in the supervisor who has to try hard to remember when he last saw a live client. A married supervisee with children will allude to her marital experience and what it "really is like to be a mother" in discussing family therapy with an unmarried female supervisor. The older supervisee will talk about "life" from the vantage point of a veteran to the supervisor fresh out of graduate school. The younger supervisee will hint at his greater understanding of the adolescent client since he has, after all, smoked some marijuana and has seriously considered LSD. The supervisor, trying to tune in, finds his older psyche is not with it. The supervisor younger than the older supervisee, older than the younger supervisee, never having raised a child or met a payroll, finds himself being instructed by those he is charged with instructing; roles are reversed and the payoff to the supervisee lies in the fact that the supervisor becomes a less threatening figure.

Another, more recently developed, procedure for "putting the supervisor down" is through the judicious use in the conference of strong four-letter words. This is "Telling It Like It Is," and the supervisor who responds with discomfort and loss of composure has forfeited some amount of control to the supervisee, who has exposed a measure of the supervisor's bourgeois nature and residual puritanism.

Putting the supervisor down may revolve around a question of social work goals rather than content. The social action oriented supervisee is concerned with fundamental changes in social relationships. She knows that obtaining a slight increase in the budget for one client, finding a job for another client, or helping a neglectful mother relate more positively to her child are of little use since they leave the basic pathology of society unchanged. She is impatient with the case-oriented supervisor who is interested in helping a specific family live a little less troubled, a little less unhappily in a fundamentally disordered society. The game is "All or Nothing at All." It is designed to make the supervisor feel he has sold out, been co-opted by the Establishment, lost or abandoned his broader vision of the "good" society, become endlessly concerned with symptoms rather than with causes. It is effective because the supervisor recognizes that there is an element of truth in the accusation for all who occupy positions of responsibility in the Establishment.

4. Controlling the Situation

The games mentioned have, as part of their effect, a shift of control of the situation from supervisor to supervisee. Another series of games is designed to place control of the supervisory situation more explicitly and directly in the hands of the supervisee. Control of the situation by the supervisor is potentially threatening since he can then take the initiative of introducing for discussion those weaknesses and inadequacies in the supervisee's work that need fullest review. If the supervisee can control the conference, much that is unflattering to discuss may be adroitly avoided.

One game designed to control the discussion's content is called "I Have a Little List." The supervisee comes in with a series of questions about his work that he would very much like to discuss. The better player formulates the questions so they relate to problems in which the supervisor has greatest professional interest and about which he has done considerable reading. The supervisee is under no obligation to listen to the answers to his questions. When question 1 has been asked, the supervisor is off on a short lecture, during which time the supervisee is free to plan mentally the next weekend or review the last weekend, taking care merely to listen for signs that the supervisor is running down. When this happens, the supervisee introduces question 2 with an appropriate transitional comment, and the cycle is repeated. As the supervisee increases the supervisor's level of participation he is, by the same token, decreasing his own level of participation, since only one person can be talking at once. Thus the supervisee controls both the content and the direction of conference interaction. The supervisor is induced to play this game because there is narcissistic gratification in displaying one's knowledge and in meeting the supervisee's dependency needs, and because, in accordance with good social work practice, the supervisee's questions should be accepted, respected, and, if possible, answered.

Control of the initiative is also seized by the supervisee in the game of "Heading Them Off at the Pass." Here the supervisee knows that her poor work is likely to be analyzed critically. She therefore opens the conference by freely admitting her mistakes— she knows it was an inadequate interview, she knows that she should have, by now, learned to do better. There is no failing on the supervisor's agenda for discussion to which she does not freely confess in advance, flagellating herself to excess. The supervisor, faced with this overwhelming self-derogation, has little option but to reassure the supervisee sympathetically. The tactic not only makes it difficult for a supervisor to conduct an extended discussion of mistakes in the work but also elicits praise for whatever limited strengths the supervisee has manifested. The supervisor, once again, acts out of concern for troubled people, out of his predisposition to comfort the discomforted, out of pleasure in acting the good, forgiving parent.

Another variation is "Pleading Fragility." The supervisee communicates "that he is extremely brittle, is easily hurt or may even go over the brink if pushed too hard. This communication effectively prevents the supervisor from exploring any painful or threatening issues with the supervisee" (Bauman 1972, p. 253).

Control can also be exerted through fluttering dependency, a case of strength through weakness. It is the game of "Little Old Me" or "Casework à Trois." The supervisee, in his ignorance and incompetence, looks to the knowledgeable, competent supervisor for a detailed prescription of how to proceed: "What would *you* do next?" "Then what would *you* say?" The supervisee unloads responsibility for the case onto the supervisor and the supervisor shares the caseload with the worker. The supervisor plays the game because, in fact, she does share responsibility for case management with the supervisee and has responsibility for seeing that the client is not harmed. Further, the supervisor often wants the gratification of carrying a caseload, however vicariously, so that she is somewhat predisposed to take the case out of the supervisee's hands. There are, in addition, the pleasures derived from acting the capable parent to the dependent child and from the domination of others.

A variant of this game in the hands of a more hostile supervisee is "I Did Like You Told Me." Here the supervisee maneuvers the supervisor into offering specific prescriptions on case management and then applies them in spiteful obedience and undisguised mimicry. The supervisee acts as though the supervisor were responsible for the case, he himself merely being the executor of supervisory directives. Invariably and inevitably, whatever has been suggested by the supervisor fails to accomplish what it was supposed to accomplish. "I Did Like You Told Me" is designed to make even a strong supervisor defensive.

"It's All So Confusing" attempts to reduce the authority of the supervisor by appeals to other authorities—a former supervisor, another supervisor in the same agency, or a faculty member at a local school of social work with whom the supervisee just happened to discuss the case. The supervisee casually indicates that in similar situations his former supervisor tended to take a certain approach, which is at variance with the approach the current supervisor regards as desirable. And "it's all so confusing" when different "authorities" suggest such different approaches to the same situation. The supervisor is faced with defending his approach against some unnamed, unknown competitor. This is difficult, especially because few situations in social work permit an unequivocal answer in which the supervisor can have complete confidence. Since the supervisor was somewhat shaky in his approach in the first place, he feels vulnerable to alternative suggestions from other "authorities," and his sense of authority in relation to the supervisee is eroded.

A supervisee can control the degree of threat in the supervisory situation by distancing techniques. The game is "What You Don't Know Won't Hurt Me." The supervisor knows the work of the supervisee only indirectly, through what is available in the recording and shared verbally in the conference. The supervisee can elect to share in a manner that is thin, inconsequential, without depth of affect. He can share selectively and can distort (consciously or unconsciously) in order to present a more favorable picture of his work. The supervisee can be passive and reticent or overwhelm the supervisor with endless trivia. In whatever manner it is done, the supervisee increases distance between the work he actually does and the supervisor who is responsible for critically analyzing it with him. This not only reduces the threat to him of possible criticism of his work but also, as Fleming and Benedek (1966) point out, prevents the supervisor from intruding into the privacy of his relationship with the client.

A supervisee can manipulate the level of the supervisor's response to worker performance deficiencies by games such as "Who Me? No Me" and "Mea Culpa, But Just This Once."

In playing "Who Me?" the supervisee tries to shift the burden of responsibility for his own shortcomings in task performance onto other things. Pointing to failures by others—the client, clerical staff, workers in other agencies, "the system"—acts to shift responsibility from the supervisee himself. Pleading extenuating circumstances—traffic problems, the weather, temporary indisposition—mitigates responsibility.

"Mea Culpa, But Just This Once" is an apology coupled with a show of repentance which reduces the supervisor's inclination to reprimand the supervisee for task failures. The apology is an acknowledgment of error, a confirmation of the supervisor's right to point out the error. Repentence is both an act of self-punishment and a promise not to repeat the error. In the face of all of this, supervisors find themselves disarmed.

Supervisors go along with these games because of their reluctance to reprimand workers. They, along with the workers, are looking for excuses which might make it possible to avoid confronting the worker's performance deficiencies.

Countering Games

Although such defensive games help the supervisee cope with anxiety-provoking stress, they may be dysfunctional and subvert the purposes of the supervisory encounter. Consequently the supervisor may be required to break up the games.

The simplest and most direct way of dealing with games introduced by the supervisee is to refuse to play. Yet a key difficulty in this approach has been implied by discussion of the gains for the supervisor in playing along. The supervisee can successfully enlist the supervisor in a game only if the supervisor wants to play for her own reasons. Collusion is not forced but is freely granted. Refusing to play requires that the supervisor be ready and able to forfeit self-advantages. For instance, in declining to go along with the supervisee's request that he be permitted to ignore agency administrative requirements in playing "Two against the Agency," the supervisor has to be comfortable in exercising her administrative authority, willing to risk and deal with supervisee hostility and rejection, willing to accept the accusation that she is bureaucratically, rather than professionally, oriented. In declining other games the supervisor denies herself the sweet fruits of flattery, the joys of omniscience, the pleasures of acting as therapist, and the gratification of being well liked. She incurs the penalties of an open admission of ignorance and uncertainty and the loss of infallibility. Declining to play the games demands a supervisor who is aware of and comfortable in what she is doing and who accepts herself in all her "glorious strengths and human weaknesses." The less vulnerable the supervisor, the more impervious she is to gamesmanship—not an easy prescription to fill.

A second response lies in open confrontation. Goffman (1959) points out that in the usual social encounter each person accepts the line put out by the other person. There is a process of mutual face-saving in which what is said is accepted at its face value and "each participant is allowed to carry the role he has chosen for himself," unchallenged (p. 11). This is done out of self-protection since, in not challenging another, one is also ensuring that the other will not, in turn, challenge one's own fiction. Confrontation implies a refusal to accept the game being proposed; instead, the supervisor seeks to expose and make explicit what the supervisee is doing. The supervisory situation, like the therapeutic situation, deliberately rejects the usual rules of social interaction in attempting to help the supervisee.

Confrontation needs to be used, of course, with due regard for the supervisee's ability to handle the embarrassment and self-threat it involves. The supervisor needs to be aware of the defensive significance of the game to the supervisee. Naming the interactions that have been described as "games" does not imply that they are frivolous and without consequence. Unmasking games risks much that is of serious personal significance for the supervisee. Interpretation and confrontation here, as always, require compassonate caution, a sense of timing, and an understanding of dosage.

Never openly confronting each other with what is happening protects the symbiotic nature of the relationship. A supervisee who was aware that she engaged in game playing, and who was aware that the supervisor was aware that she was playing games says, "In a sense, we collaborated to provide each other with what we wanted: I needed a good job reference; she needed to feel that she was a competent administrator and supervisor."

Another approach is to share honestly with the supervisee one's awareness of what he is attempting to do in adjusting to work-related stress but to focus the discussion neither on the dynamics of his behavior nor on one's reaction to it, but on the disadvantages for him in playing games. These games have decided drawbacks for the supervisee. They deny him the possibility of effectively fulfilling one of the essential purposes of supervision—helping him to grow professionally. The games frustrate the achievement of this outcome. In playing games the supervisee loses by winning.

Kolevson (1979) attempted an investigation of the extent to which games are actually played in supervision by information solicited from social work student supervisees. The results indicated that "gamesmanship was relatively infrequent," but that "students who were more critical of their supervisory relationship" were more likely to engage in games (p. 243). The research goes on to note that the gamesmanship "in the supervisory relationship may be . . . difficult . . . to measure since exposing one's games may be a threatening venture" (p. 244).

Comparative Enactment of the Principal Components of Supervision

This chapter and the previous chapters have discussed the three principal components of social work supervision—administrative supervision, educational supervision, and supportive supervision. The three components effectively cover both the instrumental and expressive responsibilities of supervision—ensuring that the work is done, and done by people who know how to do it and who feel good about themselves and their job while doing it.

Supervisors tend to view the administrative component of supervision as less important than other components. "Ensuring that the client gets full entitlement to service" and "ensuring the professional development of the supervisee" are ranked as the two more important functions of supervision. "Ensuring compliance with agency policy and procedure" and "ensuring accountability for the use of public funds" are ranked among the least important functions of supervision (Kadushin 1974).

In general the evidence available seems to show that the responsibilities of supportive supervision are more effectively implemented than the responsibilities of either administrative or educational supervision. A study of the reactions of 211 beginning social workers (caseworkers, group workers, and community organizers) to their job indicated that a major source of dissatisfaction was the technical competence of the supervisors. At the same time, the workers were very much satisfied with the interpersonal relationships they enjoyed with their supervisors. Expressive needs were satisfied, instrumental needs were not (Miller 1970).

A study of the differences between the social work students' ideal picture of supervision and actual supervision encountered shows the greatest discrepancy with regard to the "cognitive-structuring behaviors" of their supervisors. These included such instrumental problem-solving aspects of supervision as the following: "As I need them, he suggests specific intervention techniques"; "He helps me to apply theoretical concepts in the analysis of my practice"; "He assists me in systematically structuring my own thinking in the problem areas where I am not clear" (Rose, Lowenstein, and Fellin 1969).

Similarly, Kadushin (1974) asked supervisors to describe their conception of an ideal supervisor by reacting to a series of 39 statements about different kinds of supervisory behavior. Supervisees were given the same statements and asked to describe their current supervisor. The 39 statements offered were designed to cluster into six different dimensions. (1) supervisor interest in supervisee ("ready and willing to meet the supervisee and shows real interest in discussing the supervisee's work"); (2) empathic understanding of the supervisee ("when the supervisee is discouraged or anxious, supervisor seems to recognize this"); (3) acceptance of supervisee ("creates the kind of emotional atmosphere so that supervisees feel free to discuss their mistakes and failures as well as their successes"); (4) willingness to grant autonomy ("can permit the supervisee to make his own mistakes"); (5) openness ("is ready to acknowledge occasional inability to help supervisee"); (6) competence ("has a detailed accurate grasp of agency policies and procedures"). Discrepancies between the ideal picture of supervision and the actual picture of supervision were frequently greater with regard to the instrumental (technical competence) components rather than with the expressive (relationship skill) components.

The nationwide study of social agency supervision by Olmstead and Christensen (1973) shows that supervisors were ranked lowest on "work facilitation" scales involving such activities as "showing personnel how to improve performance and providing help in solving job-related problems" (p. 195). Supervisors were ranked considerably higher, however, on scales concerned with supportive activities in supervision.

The apparently greater success in implementing the supportive responsibilities of supervision may merely reflect the fact that, in implementing this function, the supervisor is closer to the job for which she was trained and which she knows best. Supportive supervision is more like the professional social work direct-service function than is either administrative or educational supervision.

Summary

Supportive supervision is concerned with helping the supervisee deal with job-related stress and developing attutudes and feelings conducive to the best job performance. Whereas administrative and educational supervision are concerned with instrumental needs, supportive supervision is concerned with expressive needs.

The main sources of job-related stress for the supervisee are the performance and compliance demands of administrative supervision, the learning demands of educational supervision, the clients, the nature and organizational context of social work tasks, and the relationship with the supervisor.

In implementing the objectives of supportive supervision the supervisor seeks to prevent the development of potentially stressful situations, removes the worker from stress, reduces stress impinging on the worker and helps her adjust to stress. The supervisor is available and approachable, communicates confidence in the worker, provides perspective, excuses failure when appropriate, sanctions and shares responsibility for different decisions, provides opportunity for independent functioning and for probable success in tasks achievement.

The client, the peer group, and the worker's own adjustive capacities are additional sources of support for the supervisee.

Supervisees engage in a variety of procedures and games which can help deal with job-related tensions.

CHAPTER SIX
Stresses in Becoming and Being a Supervisor

THE PREVIOUS CHAPTER detailed some of the strains and stresses encountered by direct service workers which require a supportive response on the part of the supervisor. In this chapter we are concerned with the stresses and strains encountered by supervisors themselves. In chapter 7, however, there will be a fuller discussion of one of the most pervasive sources of stress and tension for supervisors, namely the function of worker evaluation.

Transition—Worker to Supervisor

The supervisee is not alone in encountering job-related tensions that call for adjustive responses and supportive help. The supervisor also struggles with problems that create tension for him in becoming, and being, a supervisor. Promotion to supervisor involves a drastic change for the worker. The newly appointed supervisor "is essentially entering a new occupation, not simply a new position. This occupation will have its own set of job specifications . . . precedents . . . expectations. In the performance of his duties he finds himself in a new set of role relations with his former peers, with his new administrative colleagues and with his new superiors" (Moore 1970, p. 213).

The transition from worker to supervisor is in some measure analogous to developmental transitions "such as adolescence, marriage, or retirement. As with other transitions, it may involve a period of disruption, of depression or defensive hyperactivity, of personal and professional growth. . . . Changes in external aspects of the career are likely to be accompanied by inner changes in personality" (Levinson and Klerman 1967, p. 13–14). Conceptions of personal identity change so as to be congruent with changes in professional identity.

The motive which prompts the transition suggests different problems for different workers. Some have had strong attraction to moving into a managerial position and this move is in line with their true intentions. Others move into supervision by reason of default of more preferred alternatives. Advancement up the career ladder in the direct service position is limited. Few agencies have super-advancd senior case work positions. Career advancement in pay, status and prestige, and continuing professional growth and challenge almost require acceptance of the supervision option.

A sizable percentage of social worker administrators would have preferred to remain as clinicians if salaries and status at the clinicial level were the equivalent of those available with promotion to administration (Scurfield 1981).

For such workers, moving into supervision means deprivation of the satisfaction of direct practice. Movement into supervision comes almost automatically to "survivors," as a reward for the faithful who have considerable seniority on the job. There is often neither a great incentive nor a great opposition to the change. Both Patti et al. (1979) and Scurfield (1981) in their studies of workers' motives for transition to managerial positions found a variety of motives, "interest in administration" being the principal motive of only a limited number of respondents.

The transition involves a temporary disequilibrium in identity. The new supervisor had previously developed a firm sense of who he was and what he could do in his identity as a direct service worker. This identity had been repeatedly confirmed by responses from peers, supervisor, and clients, who accorded him the recognition that comes with this role identity. Moving into the position of supervisor required dissolving the old identity as direct service worker and slowly building a new sense of identity as supervisor. This new, and at the beginning alien, identity needs confirmation from supervisees, fellow supervisors, and administrators, whose behavior toward the new supervisor attests to the fact that they recognize and accept him as a supervisor. Initially the supervisor has to work to obtain this confirmation from others of the new position and title, which involves proving one's competence to others.

Becoming a supervisor may involve moving to a new agency and all that this implies in the way of adjustment. But even if the worker stays in the same agency after becoming a supervisor, the shift requires some of the adjustments involved in accepting a new job. As one beginning supervisor said, "Rather than being at the top of the ladder as a caseworker, I was starting all over at the bottom again in my new trade—supervision" (H.C.D. 1949, p. 161). The shift has been compared with that of a person who has often ridden as a passenger in a car and who now has the responsibility for driving the car, watching traffic, getting the group safely to its destination.

The new supervisor may have some anxiety about his ability to meet the demands of the new job. While all supervisors have experienced some anticipatory socialization to the position as a result of their experience as supervisees, there is an uneasy recognition that this is inadquate preparation. Being a supervisee does not make one a supervisor just as being a student doesn't make one a teacher.

Some of the stress related to becoming a supervisor was detailed in a study of the reaction of 40 supervisors to the experience of transition (Woodcock 1967). Becoming a supervisor was regarded as a career crisis, "the first and most striking finding being the degree of alarm that the prospect of supervision proved to arouse" (p. 68). Since few supervisors had had formal training in supervision prior to the appointment, they felt considerable anxiety about whether they could do the job. This fear related particularly to the demand of educational supervision. Did they know enough to teach others to do the work? New supervisors reported "increased reading, thinking, consulting, attending lectures, seminars, meetings, anything which would illuminate the road ahead. . . . One supervisor said, 'I bought a pile of social work books, only one of which I read.' Another 'made notes on the principles of casework and determined to exemplify all these in all cases'" (p. 69).

Becoming a supervisor forces one to explicitly examine one's practice in order to conceptualize it for teaching. "Supervising forced me to put my ideas, knowledge and experience together. I was placed in the position of having to communicate or try to communicate what I knew." As Ewalt (1980) says, "Moving from doing to teaching requires what may be thought of as a conscious disintegrating process in which the supervisor purposefully recalls and conceptualizes elements in the decision-making process" (p. 5).

The shift from diagnosis of clients' social problems to diagnosis of supervisees' educational problems, from helping in the personal

development of the client to helping in the professional development of the worker, involves a shift from therapeutic techniques
previously acquired to pedagogic techniques that need to be
learned. Accepting the title of supervisor involves a shift in self-
perception from a treatment person to an administrator-teacher.

In moving into supervision, the worker assumes the stress of
greater responsibilities. She has responsibility to the supervisees for
administration, education, and support, and ultimate responsibility
for service to the client. She assumes greater responsibility for policy formulation in the agency and community-agency relationships.
Whereas previously the worker was responsible only for her own
work, she now has the larger responsibility for the work of a number
of others. Instead of being responsible for a caseload, the supervisor
is now responsible for a number of caseloads.

Because of a frequently distorted perception of the supervisor's
position, new supervisors experience "reality shock" as they encounter the actualities of supervision. As one new supervisor said,

> When I was a caseworker, I thought the supervisors had it all worked
> out and knew what they were doing. It all looked so easy. Now I see
> how great the responsibilities are and that everything isn't so neat at
> the supervisory level. There are power struggles, games, and turf bat-
> tles among the supervisors. When I first became a supervisor, I felt
> very confused and depressed, and there was no one to help. (Abra-
> mczyk 1980, p. 83)

In becoming a supervisor, the worker gives up the satisfaction of
direct practice and contact with clients. She has to learn to offer
service through others. One supervisor said, "As a caseworker I was
very 'social work' oriented. I enjoyed working with clients and helping them if possible. As a supervisor I no longer feel the stimulation
I did as a worker" (Miller and Podell 1970, p. 36). Some supervisors
ask for a small direct-practice caseload as a way of meeting the need
for these satisfactions.

Some stress derives from the defensiveness that a supervisor
might feel in comparing administrative work with direct service
work. According higher status to direct service activity as the only
work worth doing in an agency, the supervisor may be somewhat
apologetic about a desk job without client contact (Berliner 1971).

As discussed earlier, some of the administrative requirements of the supervisor's job run counter to the ethos of social work. The need to exercise authority, the need to judge the worker, the need to deindividualize the client in formulating and implementing policy require some adjustments in attitude. Patti et al. (1979), studying the problems of worker transition from the direct service position to the management position, found that "the use of authority, particularly as it implied directing, supervising, and changing subordinates, was the most difficult area of adjustment for respondents when they assumed their first administrative job" (pp. 146–47).

A study of 285 social work administrators, most of whom had been clinicians, indicated once again that adaptation to authority was a problem in making the transition from direct service to adminstration. The move was from indirect leadership to more direct leadership, from permissiveness to assertive direction, from covert use of power to more overt use of power. In reporting the research, Scurfield (1981) says, "It is clear that the exercise of authority in relationships with subordinates in contrast with the exercise of authority in relationships with clients is a major area of change reported by some former clinicians in their transition to administration" (p. 497).

In direct service work, the workers may advise, suggest, and influence, but never direct the client to engage in certain actions. The ultimate decision and responsibility for action rests with the client and the consequences of the client's decision is borne only by the client. The authority of supervision extends beyond advice, suggestion, and influence to the imperative of directing the worker to act in some particular way. And the consequences of the worker's decision to accept, respect, or modify the supervisor's directive is borne not only by the worker but by the supervisor and the agency as well. Since the supervisor is given the power to actually require certain actions by the supervisee, it is appropriate that supervisors accept responsibility for the worker's failure to act. The limits of authority and responsibility are broader and more pervasive in supervision as contrasted with direct service.

Worker adherence to the clients' right to self-determination permits the client, with worker acquiesence, to reject worker suggestions. The principal of self-determination is not applicable, however, to the supervisor-supervisee relationship. "When a subordinate fails to accept the suggestion of the [supervisors] the latter must be prepared to press for compliance even in the face of appearing to be arbitrary. Certainly there are times when it is appropriate to defer to subordinates or engage in collaborative decision making, but inevitably there are occasions in which the manager must take courses of action that may not be agreed to or supported by staff" (Patti 1983, p. 217).

The beginning supervisor also has to make other adjustments in perspective. He moves from a process orientation as worker to a more focused concern with product as a supervisor. He has to become more organizationally oriented.

The movement from worker to supervisor is accompanied by a stronger identification with the agency, increased support, loyalty, and commitment to the organization and its policies. Agency policy and actions now seem more justifiable, acceptable, morally correct and fair. The new supervisor's attitudes become more like those supervisors whose ranks he is joining and different from the attitudes of direct-service workers from whom he is disengaging.

Lieberman (1956) tested the hypothesis that a person's attitudes will be influenced by the role he occupies in a social system. "Johnny is a changed boy since he was made a monitor in school"; "She is a different woman since she got married"; "You would never recognize him since he became a foreman" (p. 385). He studied the attitudes of men in industrial concerns before and after they became supervisors. He found that, since the supervisory role entails being a representative of management, workers who were made supervisors did tend to become more favorable to management.

The change from worker to supervisor involves a change in reference group affiliation, which leads to changes in attitudes and therefore behavior. The change in functions performed also requires changes in behavior. Attitudes are revised so that they are consistent with changed behavior required by changed functions. One supervisor expressed her change in orientation as follows:

My orientation definitely changed as I moved from the role of supervisee to the role of supervisor. In the first place, I took agency policy much more seriously. I also felt a marked increase in responsibilities and in the importance of realizing the full responsibilities of this position. I also saw problems in a wider scope and found it easier to analyze them when the details and the client were not as close to me

The change in position and the responsibilities that go along with becoming a supervisor in and of itself force a change in the worker's perception of agency rules, policies, and procedures. But this change is reinforced by information about agency operation from a broader perspective than had been available earlier. Such change is also reinforced as a consequence of "experiencing" as supervisor the political effects of agency policy which the worker only "knows" about.

As he moves from worker to supervisor, the new supervisor becomes more sensitive to the effects—on policy, agency survival, and agency image—of actions taken with, or in behalf of, individual clients. He adopts an administrative perspective with regard to service decisions (Piven and Pappenfort 1960).

A change in perspective implies further a change in perception of the effects of agency policy. As a former worker, the supervisor measured the effects of agency policy on the client with whom she had direct contact. As supervisor, she is in a better position to see the effects of agency policy in a wider perspective. A policy which may have impacted negatively on her own former clients may be seen as meeting more effectively the needs of a wider group of clients as a collectivity.

The transition involves a change of orientation from individual justice in which the unique needs of the individual client is given priority to the idea of proportional justice which requires fairness and equity in prioritizing the competing claims of many clients.

The new supervisor has to reassess the balance in a conflict between an orientation which gave priority to resources and an orientation which gave priority to people. The conflict is often expressed by business managers who complain that "social workers don't care what they do with the money" and social workers who complain that managers "don't care what they do to people." In making the transition the supervisor as a member of the management team has to give greater recognition to the fact that resources are scarce, that painful choices have to be made, and that priority of client needs is not absolute.

As a worker, the newly appointed supervisor may have thought of management as concerned primarily with survival, with little real commitment to the needs of the client. Now as Matorin (1979) says, the practitioner as supervisor "has become a member of the 'establishment' and is propelled into what may have previously been the enemy camp. They are now responsible for all of the deficiencies of the system, yet expected to defend and identify with it" (p. 15).

Some problems arise from the fact that the supervisor, in a position immediately adjacent to the caseworker, has the same professional background and experience as the supervisee. Identified and empathic with the problems and orientation of the direct service worker, the supervisor nevertheless represents management. "This creates both a role conflict and a personal dilemma for the supervisor. Professional norms stressing autonomous integrity for practitioners still make a claim on him which he considers legitimate but so does the organization's need for control" (Abrahamson 1967, p. 83).

Becoming a supervisor requires changes in the worker's relationships with others in the agency. The supervisor is no longer a member of the peer group of direct service workers. She has become one of "them." Not only is the new supervisor deprived of what may have been a satisfying source of pleasure and support, but she is further penalized by feelings of rivalry and jealousy from former colleagues. There may be "a certain feeling of distance that I had arrived and they hadn't" or "that I was doing better than them" (Woodcock 1967, p. 69). A new supervisor says,

> One's colleagues like to see a person get ahead all right—but not too far ahead, and not too fast. If fortune seems to be smiling too often and too broadly on one person, his friends begin to sharpen their knives to even up the score a bit. I was philosophical about this, as by this time I realized that an occasional knife in the ribs goes with supervision just as June bugs go with June and must be accepted as stoically. I marked my promotion by buying a bigger brief case, enrolling in an advanced seminar in supervision, and having a drink with a few sympathetic friends—also supervisors. (H.C.D. 1949, p. 162)

Social distance is increased between the worker-turned-supervisor and his former peers. There is more formality, less spontaneity in their interaction, a greater guardedness and hesitancy in communication. The talk slows down and alters as he sits down to drink coffee with them. What was formerly identified as interesting ingroup gossip is now perceived as squealing when shared with a former peer who is now a supervisor.

Charles Lamb noted this change in his essay "The Superannuated Man":

> To dissipate this awkward feeling, I have been fain to go among them once or twice since; to visit my old desk fellows—my co-brethren of the quill—that I had left below in the state militant. Not all the kindness with which they received me could quite restore to me that pleasant familiarity which I had heretofore enjoyed among them. We cracked some of our old jokes, but methought they went off but faintly.

Former peers wonder about the new supervisor. Will he act with favoritism toward best friends; will he pay off grudges against old enemies; will he grow into the job or just swell? "He must neither commit the sin of officiousness nor the folly of fraternity."

The ghosts of one's predecesors can be a source of tension. The new supervisor wonders if she can be as good as the former supervisor; if, in changing some of the patterns of work established by the former supervisor, she will insult the old loyalties of the supervisees and incur their hostility.

Having lost her old peer group, the new supervisor has to obtain acceptance in a new peer group, that of the other supervisors. Maintenance of some marginality, some social distance, from both groups to which the supervisor is hierarchically related, the supervisees who are his subordinates and the administrators who are his superiors, is functionally useful. Blau and Scott (1962) found that "detachment from subordinates was associated with high productivity and independence from superiors with greater solidarity in the work group and [that] both kinds of social distance, although the two were hardly related to one another, were associated with commanding the loyalty of subordinates" (p. 238).

The limits of the supervisor's responsibility are less definite than the worker's. Consequently, some beginning supervisors find themselves working harder than ever before. "I soon found that I was doing about twice as much work as I had done formerly. When I brought this to my executive's attention she was very nice about it. She patiently explained that this was one of the privileges of my new position" (H.C.D. 1949, p. 161).

New supervisors found that their prior casework training and experience was of considerable help to them in effectively dealing with the very significant interpersonal relationship aspects of supervision. In addition, their previous clinical experience was considered "to be a major source of credibility with their subordinates" (Patti et al. 1979, p. 148). "The transition to management involved adapting knowledge and skills previously acquired, rather than comprehensive and fundamental retraining" (Patti et al. p. 151).

However, while most of the managers continued to feel that a clinical background was a necessary ingredient in preparation for human services administration, it was clear that there are some differences in the demands made of the direct service workers as contrasted with those made of the supervisor. The transition requires the mobilization of skills that are not so directly required in direct service practice. While direct services practice requires maximization of potentials for expressive behavior—caring, concern, empathy, compassion—transition to supervisor requires maximization of potential for instrumental behavior—integrating, organizing, coordinating, manipulating. Bamford (1978) notes that

> The very qualities which make a good social worker are often the antithesis of those required in management. Talking things through patiently and determinedly is an admirable quality applied to work with clients. Applied indiscriminantly to management decisions great and small, it is a recipe for administrative paralysis. (p. 11)

There is stress associated with the fact that many supervisors have limited preparation for assuming the position and little educational support available following assigment to the position.

Some training in supervision is of course absorbed as a consequence of being a supervisee. In one study, supervisors indicated that the most important source of learning their job was the role model of supervisors with whom they had had contact as supervisees (Olyan 1972, p. 213). Being supervised not only helps a person learn how to become a social worker; it also helps in learning how to become a social work supervisor.

But many supervisors do not feel adequately prepared for the job. The average response of 109 supervisors who were asked by Shulman (1982) to respond to the statement, "I received adequate preparation for the tasks and problems I faced as beginning supervisor" was between "uncertain" and "disagree." Deficiencies in training for social work supervision were further identified in a national survey of the needs in child welfare training. Respondents, all of whom had expertise in child welfare, cited training in "Supervision in Child Welfare" as having second highest priority among training needs listed (Vinokur and Gray 1981).

Summary—Stress Associated with Becoming a Supervisor

In accepting the transition, the new supervisors face the complex processes of developing a clear conception of what the new position entails behaviorally and attitudinally; they have to divest themselves of old behaviors and attitudes appropriate to the direct service worker's position and learn and commit themselves to behavior and attitudes appropriate to the new position; they have to emotionally accept a changed image of themselves and a changed relationship with former peers and newly acquired colleagues.

Overall, however, clinicians moving to supervision see the transition as not being particularly problematic. Researching the actual experience of such a transition, Scurfield (1981) notes, in reporting responses from administrators who made this transition, that he "expected that former clinicians would report that their transition to administration had been difficult. The findings show, however, that former clinicians tended to minimize differences between clinical and administrative practice. This suggests that little difficulty may be experienced in the transition period" (p. 498).

On the basis of their research of the actual transition experiences from clinician to administrator, Patti et al. (1979) second Scurfield's findings but are somewhat more sanguine. They note that "despite the obvious difficulties in making the transition to management, the data also suggests that in many respects the respondent's past clinical education and experience was perceived by them as an aid in the process. As a consequence the role discontinuity and identity problems encountered, although quite apparent, appear to have been much less intense than we had assumed" (p. 151).

Ongoing Supervisor Stress: Being a Supervisor

In addition to the stresses encountered in becoming supervisors, there are ongoing job-related stresses involved in being a supervisor. Supervisors, like supervisees, face heavy work pressures.

Wasserman (1971) questions whether "the supervisor, responsible for five workers with a total of 175–200 cases or more, can make reasoned and balanced judgements about any problematic human situations, particularly when he must base his judgements on what the workers say about clients" (p. 91). A study of supervisors' work load in a public welfare agency concluded that "casework supervisors did not have time to supervise" (Galm 1972, p. 34). Faced with such pressures, supervisors feel anxious about the kind of job they can do. A supervisor writes:

> My greatest dissatisfaction came with the realization that supervision takes an incredibly large amount of time. I now understand why I have received so little of it in my former placements. To do the job correctly, one needs to devote great time and energy to supervising each [worker]. It resembles teaching anything. To maximize effectiveness, the teacher must prepare several hours for each hour spent actually instructing. I would have liked to have been able to analyze each recording of the worker, for instance, in depth, prior to our discussion of it, but instead I found myself listening to it for the first time in conference and responding spontaneously.

Supervisors are aware of, and feel concerned about, the limits of the help they can give supervisees. A supervisor says: "A big part of my anxiousness is that I won't know the answers for them and that I won't satisfy them with the answers that I have to give. I think even our profession doesn't know that much and that's a hard thing. They walk out feeling they didn't get what they wanted" (Amacher 1971, p. 262). Workers can stand the uncertainty and doubt better than the supervisor can because they feel that if they do not know the answers they need, the supervisor can make them available. The worker has the sanctioned luxury of acceptable dependence on the supervisor. The supervisor is granted the dubious prerogative of independence. She becomes the question-answerer rather than the question-asker. Furthermore, she has little opportunity to turn to others in the hierarchy who might be able to answer her own questions. The worker's status gives absolution from some mistakes; the supervisor's status reduces the grant of immunity. In meeting the needs of the worker, the supervisor requires a confidence in her convictions and in decision-making that is hard to come by. The pressure to act with certainty, when inwardly one feels very uncertain, is stressful.

There is also stress which results from the lack of clear definition of the supervisor's tasks, responsibilities, and authority. In one interview study of 20 supervisors, half said they were unclear about their role in the agency (Weatherley et al. 1980). And there is stress as a consequence of current attacks on the legitimacy of the position of supervisor. The discussion in the literature, which suggests that supervision is an archaic, unnecessary drag on the profession, tends to erode the confidence of supervisors that they are engaged in a meaningful and appreciated task.

Supervisors worry that they may be growing away from the job they have to supervise. In some measure the supervisor's image of practice is not as it is but as it once was; practice in the supervisee's experience is as it is today. Such anxiety is exacerbated by the rapidity of change. "Given the rapid changes in knowledge and state of the arts, the administrative professional is in danger of losing 'professional authentication'" (Moore 1970, p. 211). Changes involve new orientations and new techniques. Supervisors may often lack mastery of some of the new techniques and knowledge about some of the new programs. Hanlan (1972) cites an example of this:

> The merger of a number of small, independent, sectarian agencies in Philadelphia under one administrative organization is one illustration of how the change in functions has broad ramifications throughout all levels of the organization. In this particular case, the tension was particularly noticeable at the level of the first-line supervisor. The situation became critical when supervisors who formerly performed casework teaching functions were now required to train their staff and themselves in a wide range of community-organizing functions. (p. 43)

A supervisee notes another kind of difficulty:

> I had a systems-family perspective developed in family therapy training. My supervisor was psychoanalytically oriented. I had difficulty in relating what I was doing with my clients. Since we had adopted different perspectives so too we had adopted different vocabularies to describe the dynamics of the problems and the proposed interventions. When I would indicate that a mystification process was operating or that an individual's matrix of identity was unbalanced or that a battle for bilaterality existed within the therapeutic relationship, my supervisor did not understand me. I found myself in an uncomfortable

position of trying to explain these concepts and their applicability. My supervisor did not have any answers consistent with my perspective. It became difficult to rely on her for guidance on questions concerning my analysis of a problem, my methods of intervention, or my goals for a client.

The supervisor has to deal with the stress of competitiveness between supervisees while diplomatically maintaining a cooperative spirit in the group. "Several workers with the same supervisor are like a big family, each demanding the . . . attention of a busy mother who has her own housework to do. The supervisor has to learn to give each what he needs without seeming to give anyone more than the others" (H.C.D. 1949, p. 163). Here, too, the supervisor walks a tightrope.

Formal supervisory conferences with supervisees are a source of stress for the supervisor. It is in this interaction that the supervisor has to prove her competence, her value to the supervisee. The conference is the context in which the administrative, educational, and supportive abilities of the supervisor are subject to test; the worker, in providing materials for the conference agenda, has exposed his work for critical analysis. The supervisor, in responding to the supervisee's work, questions, and problems, is subject to critical analysis by the supervisee.

The supervisor is apt to be pulled between conflicting expectations from above and below. Placed at the boundary between the direct service worker and agency administration, the supervisor is simultaneously a member of both the working unit and the organizational unit. As is true for all who operate in boundary areas, the supervisor is in a difficult position. He has only marginal membership in each unit and is faced with pressure from both as he attempts to act as a buffer and mediator between them. Sometimes the directives from administration and the demands from the workers are contradictory. In responding to one group, he risks incurring the hostility of the other group and compromising his power to influence.

I noted earlier that the supervisor is dependent on the worker to some extent. In terms of instrumental needs the supervisor gets compliance, communication, and information from the worker; in response to expressive needs, the supervisor gets appreciation, respect, and loyalty from the worker. Failure or refusal of the worker to meet the instrumental and expressive needs of the supervisor creates stress for the supervisor. The worker can be uncooperative, resistive, make the work of the supervisor more difficult, threaten the supervisor's good conception of herself and her competence. The supervisor is identified with her supervisees in the agency and in the community, and any complaints about their work reflects negatively on her.

Supervisors also face the problem of implementing seemingly antithetical demands—permitting the greatest degres of worker autonomy while adequately protecting the rights of the client; helping preserve agency stability while promoting agency change; being supportive to the worker while communicating challenging expectations; acting as an agent of the bureaucracy while being loyal to the profession; balancing the individual needs of the worker and the needs of the organization. Also, workers want an aggressive supervisor; administrators generally prefer a passive supervisor. The supervisor has to balance these antithetical expectations. Thus, the supervisor has to learn to live with the tensions generated by all sorts of conflicting demands and expectations.

The supervisor can effectively implement her responsibilities only if the agency provides her with enough resources to do the job. This means that the supervisor has to have enough workers assigned to her unit and enough workers with a particular level and variety of skills. Many supervisors face problems resulting from being in short supply of workers available to cover the caseload or from assignment of workers with deficiencies in knowledge and skills that limit the productivity of the unit.

The supervisor, like the worker, faces the frustration of limits to autonomy and discretion. The sources of constraints may be different but the experience of constriction is the same. The supervisor is constrained by administrative policy, union regulations, client advocacy organizations, the reporting requirement of legislative sources of agency funding, accrediting standards, and licensing standards.

Certain situations present special problems for the supervisor. In some instances the official hierarchical relationship is contrary to the usual pattern of social arrangements. The younger person is generally expected to defer to older people; people with less experience on the job are expected to defer to those with more experience.

Consequently, when the supervisor is younger than the supervisee or has less experience on the job, the situation presents additional problems. The supervisor in such instances may feel less secure, more defensive, less certain of her entitlement to the position. Positional authority is called into question because it runs counter to social expectations.

If there is a substantial age difference between supervisor and supervisee, there is a problem of "generation gap" or "cultural lag" between the older, experienced supervisors and the younger, recently trained supervisees. However, the young supervisor with the young supervisee faces other kinds of problems. A young supervisor with limited practice experience writes:

> I feel that my age and amount of experience in social work are both my greatest strengths and my greatest weaknesses. They are strengths because it has only been a few months since I was in the same position as my supervisee, with strong feelings of inadequacy and nervousness. They are weaknesses because I don't feel that I know enough about social work yet to supervise and teach someone else.

Race as a Factor in Supervision

Where the supervisor and supervisee are of different races, some of the problems of race relations in society at large are apt to intrude in the relationship. Despite this, a review of five leading social work journals between 1950 and 1982 revealed no social work article on supervision dealing directly with racism (Swanson and Brown 1982, p. 59).

White Supervisor—Black Supervisee

The more frequent pattern is of a white supervisor and a black supervisee. A white supervisor says:

> The black worker felt that I was not meeting her needs, probably because of our racial differences. The worker was angry and I felt threatened (maybe I am a racist). We spent a great deal of time discussing these feelings. We got a lot of talk going but no real change in attitude. Finally I said, "Look, we've talked about it long enough. Let's

get on to the business of the agency. If a specific example comes up that seems related to our differences in race we can then discuss it." The situation improved after this. It seemed to me in retrospect that the worker was suffering from insecurity about how she was doing the job. I got hooked onto looking at racism (with some valid concern) when actually the worker needed more help to feel she could do the job.

White supervisors of black supervisees will have to work harder to elicit their trust and confidence and provide evidence of their ability to understand the black experience. The white supervisor may feel uneasy and awkward in a close black-white relationship.

Studies tend to show that we are more confident in making judgements about people who are similar to ourselves. Having limited experience with minority group supervisees the white supervisor may feel uneasy in making judgements about performance without a minority-group-related base line. This implies that there may be a tendency to evaluate performance differently based on the worker's race. The most desirable approach to evaluation suggests, of course, that all workers should be evaluated in the same way in response to the same criteria. The actuality is that some supervisors out of sympathy, guilt, fear, or negative prejudice may evaluate minority group workers differently and less confidently than white workers. Fear of being labeled racist or the desire to openly proclaim that they are not racist may lead to a hesitancy to criticize black supervisees for deficiencies in their work.

The effects of race are the result of a complex relationship between the race of the supervisee, the supervisor, and the clients being discussed. Black supervisees offering service to a black client may not share all of the client's pathology with the white supervisor because it reflects negatively on the black community. A white supervisor and a black supervisee offering service to a black client presents a challenge to the supervisor's expertise. "A minority worker claiming the expertise of life experience can challenge the [white] supervisor's knowledge and ability to deal with racial/ethnic problems and issues" (Swanson and Brown 1952, p. 65).

A white supervisor in contact with a white supervisee offering service to black clients may not be able to be of help because of lack of knowledge of the black experience, black lifestyle, black problems, and adaptations. A prejudiced white supervisor may actually be harmful by communicating racist attitudes to the supervisee.

The white supervisor has some responsibility for self-education around the minority group experience, and for developing an awareness regarding her own attitudes toward race. It is part of the responsibility of acting as a nonracist role model to both white and black supervisees. The factor of race should not be ignored nor should it be overemphasized. A sensible, relaxed sensitivity to race seems to be the most desirable approach.

A white supervisor in contact with a black supervisee who ignores the factor of race may be perceived negatively. Saying in effect "you are like me; I don't think of you as black" may be seen by blacks "as a negation of their black identity and a subliminal message that they would be acceptable if they were not black—that is if they would repudiate parts of themselves." If on the other hand the black supervisee "is asked to comment on every black patient or issue relevant to blacks he or she cannot help but wonder whether there is stereotypical thinking behind the question such as all blacks think alike" (Bradshaw 1982, p. 205).

Black Supervisor—White Supervisee

Where a black supervisor supervises a white worker positional authority is again in contradiction to the usual social arrangement pattern. Few whites have experienced a situation of subordination to a black person. A black woman supervising a white woman writes about the learning advantages of such an arrangement: "This was an opportunity for the worker to get information on black life-styles, feelings, etc., that she may otherwise not have had a chance to learn. It also gave me a chance to teach some therapeutic techniques to use in dealing with black clients that aren't usually printed in the literature." Royster, a black social worker, notes that "the black supervisor must decide whether or not to assign white workers to black clients, given the prevailing belief in much of the community that black workers are more effective with black clients and given the knowledge of racism within each white person" (1972, p. 81).

Feeling that they might be less acceptable to white supervisees, black supervisors may have a tendency to be less directive and less assertive with such supervisees. They might be hesitant to exercise close supervision even when it is necessary.

Based on the supposition that blacks in supervising whites might attempt to minimize a status situation that might be perceived as incongruent, it is suggested that the black supervisor might exercise general rather than close supervision and might encourage supervisees to initiate activity. This will tend to reduce the conspicuousness of their superior supervisory status.

Black Supervisor—Black Supervisees

Royster feels that the black supervisor may have even more difficulty with black workers. The black supervisor, representing management in agencies that often have racist policies, may be in conflict with those black workers who are more wholeheartedly oriented to the views of the black community (p. 80).

Black supervisees may resent black supervisors, who may be perceived as identified with oppressive management and also as having betrayed their group in "acting white." The process of acculturation to membership in the management team may, it is felt, tend to attenuate minority subcultural differences.

Minority supervisees of minority supervisors may seek to exploit their joint membership in the minority group to obtain preferential treatment in work assignment and evaluation.

A more positive view is that the black supervisees feel more comfortable with a black supervisor and "they may see the black supervisor as a role model with whom they can unambivalently identify" (Bradshaw 1982, p. 217).

Blacks appointed to managerial positions are apt to feel that they are under constant scrutiny to prove they can do the job adequately. There may be some feeling of doubt not only on the part of their white colleagues but on the part of their subordinate minority supervisees as well (Bush 1977, p. 19).

Minority supervisors are often called on to act as either "showcase" personnel or "fire-fighters." They might be "displayed" as evidence of the progresive thinking and affirmative action orientation of agency administration. They might also be called upon to deal directly with minority group clients who might have some beef against the agency and are interested in making a complaint (Bush 1977).

The black supervisor may feel a special pressure to act as a representative of the agency's black service workers with special advocacy responsibility, and to help interpret the needs of black staff members to agency administration (Vargus 1980).

Gender as a Factor in Supervision

Differences in gender between supervisor and supervisee can present some problems. Caplow (1954), in an earlier study of sociology of work, pointed to the fact that men find it contrary to the norm to be directly subordinate to women in the work situation and that they are resistive to accepting women supervisors. Subsequent research in a number of different occupations tended to confirm this as a prevalent attitude among males.

While there might be a continuing discomfort felt by traditionally oriented male workers generally in being supervised by women, this does not seem to be true of male social workers. Male social workers tend to be more androgynous than men in general in their orientation toward sex role behavior and consequently are apt to be less disturbed or threatened by women in supervisory positions (Dailey 1983, p. 22). The more accepting attitude toward supervision by women manifested by male social workers as contrasted with men in general is confirmed by their positive responses to their actual experiences as supervisees of female supervisors. In an interview study of the experience of 65 supervisees with their supervision, Munson (1979a) found that male social workers supervised by females reported high levels of satisfaction with their experience. The level of satisfaction of these male supervisees was even higher than the level expressed by males supervised by fellow males.

On the other hand Behling, Curtis, and Foster (1982) obtained responses from 276 graduate social work students about their experiences in supervision with field instructor supervisors, and, focusing on the effects of sex matching between instructors, supervisors, and student supervisees, they found the female-student versus male-instructor combinations to be clearly the most stressful and problematic combination. "The stresses in the combination primarily were attributed to traditional sexist attitudes held by male instructors."

Working with a female supervisor, for some men, is "the first time in their adult life, except in their relationship with parents, that they are presented with a woman in a position of authority. This experience exposes the beginning therapist to his own system of unrecognized values, attitudes, and thus potential countertransference problems" (Nadelson and Notman 1971).

The female supervisor can provide the male supervisee with a consciousness-raising learning situation regarding women's experience. This can provide an antidote to the "countertransference deafness" of some males toward their women clients' needs and aspirations, increasing their capacity for empathic understanding (Alonson and Rutan 1978; see also Scher 1981).

A female supervisee supervised by a female supervisor has a positive role model with whom she can identify for moving up the administrative ladder.

Participants in cross-gender supervisory relationships may be hesitant to freely discuss the sexual problems of clients because of a fear of eroticizing the supervisory relationship (Brodsky 1980, p. 516).

Male supervisors need to be sensitive to avoid talk and behavior that might suggest sex bias or sex role stereotyping or derogatory labeling.

Much as it would be unwise and inexpedient to ignore factors of racial difference between supervisor and supervisee, it would also be a mistake to regard gender differences between the two as a matter of no potential significance. For most supervisory dyads, gender differences may be of neutral significance, the supervisor and supervisee relating to each other as one professional to another. However, some female supervisees may exploit gender differences in seductive ploys, making their relationship with the male supervisor more advantageous. Some male supervisors may employ their positional power covertly to solicit sexual favors. In less extreme interactional encounters, gender difference may result in flirtatious displays of femininity and male narcissism that interferes with good supervision. Male supervisors in response to stereotypic male roles may have difficulty with a manipulatively dependent female supervisee and female supervisors may enact the nurturing earth mother role to male supervisees who need firm expectations.

Male supervisors may act in a traditionally courtly, protective manner toward female supervisees, being careful to avoid "hurting" them by being critical, even when this is appropriate. Or a female supervisor with a male supervisee may be reluctant to display the same level of assertive leadership behavior that she might comfortably manifest in contact with a female supervisee (Megargee 1969).

Sexual harassment is a possible danger in cross-gender supervision because the power differential is so clearly in the supervisor's favor. As a consequence, the supervisee is vulnerable and the supervisor might use the position to obtain sexual advantages. Where there is a difference in power, there is no true, voluntary, informed consent.

The relationship is one which provides the supervisor with the possibility of exerting "undue influence." "Undue influence" situations are defined as those situations where there is inequality in the relationship, where one member of the pair is dependent for some reason on the other, where one member of the pair is induced to have confidence in the other. In the context of a relationship of undue influence the potential impact of the supervisor's power is intensified.

The fact that the supervisor does possess real power with regard to the worker's career and that such power is exercised in response to evaluations which have considerable elements of subjectivity makes the supervisee vulnerable to advances from the supervisor. Such vulnerability requires protection from sexual harassment.

Furthermore it needs to be recognized that the supervisor-supervisee relationship has many of the elements of an intimate relationship. People meet with some regularity in private to discuss matters which often are of an emotional, personal nature. The affective intensity of the relationship is deliberately fostered because it provides the necessary context for effective supervision.

Because the advantage of power lies with the supervisor, in this close relationship he/she must take greater responsibility for aborting any action which risks converting a professional relationship to a social-sexual relationship. The supervisor has to be held to a higher standard of conduct than the supervisee. This does not absolve the supervisee from the responsibility of refraining from any action, suggestion, or innuendo which implies directly or indirectly interest in such a change in the relationship.

The American Psychological Association's definition of sexual harassment accurately describes the activity as "deliberate or repeated comments, gestures, or physical contacts of a sexual nature that are unwanted by the recipient." Sexual harassment is typically much more of a problem in dyads composed of a male supervisor and a female supervisee.

While we have no information available regarding sexual contact between social work supervisors and supervisees a nationwide survey of the American Psychological Association's Psychotherapy Division is instructive. Of the 126 females who received their degree between 1973 and 1979, 25 percent reported sexual contact with their educators, about half of whom had been their clinical supervisors (p. 689).

The NASW Code of Ethics in the section on ethical responsibility to clients unequivocally states that "social workers should under no circumstances engage in sexual activities with clients" (II-5), however, there is no specific mention of a prohibition of such activity between supervisor and supervisee in the section on ethical responsibility to colleagues.

The possibility of sexual harassment seems most likely in the vertical hierarchical relationship (worker-supervisor; worker-administrator) where there is considerable power differential. However, the supervisor needs to be aware that co-worker relationships and worker-client relationships are also the possible context for sexual harassment.

A questionnaire returned by 319 NASW members in a Midwest state in 1982 indicated that 36 percent of the female respondents and 14 percent of the male respondents had experienced sexual harassment on the job. The most frequent kind of harassment experienced was verbal—jokes, propositions, demeaning flattery. Unwanted touching was less frequent. The person doing the harassing was equally often a client, co-worker, or supervisor/administrator (Maypole 1983).

It is disconcerting to note that workers who experienced sexual harassment from co-workers and/or clients rarely sought the protection of their supervisor or reported it to them (Maypole and

Skaine 1982, p. 690). It was felt that the report might be treated lightly if not ridiculed and there was little conviction that any effective action would be taken.

The current sensitivity to the possibilities of sexual harassment in supervision is justifiable and necessary. However, it may present a problem for both male and female supervisors. Maccoby (1976) notes that male supervisors, anxious about imputations of sexual harassment, often withhold needed encouragement from female supervisees; contrawise, female supervisors may feel hesitant about assuming a warm, nurturing, supportive approach with male supervisees. Vigorous supportive supervision may be regarded as an invitation to intimacy.

A case which most graphically illustrates this complication involves, paradoxically, a charge by a male supervisee against a female supervisor. The worker alleged that his female supervisor made sexual advances, and when he failed to respond he was denied recommendation for promotion. A jury awarded the male supervisee $196,500 in compensatory and punitive damages. In commenting on the verdict, the Wisconsin Assistant Attorney General who defended the supervisor noted that "supervisors, especially those who are women, will have to step carefully through management techniques that call for being supportive to subordinate personnel. Otherwise it would be difficult to avoid the allegation of sexual harassment" (Madison, *Capital Times,* July 17, 1982). The accused supervisor said that as a result of the verdict, she was changing her approach to supervision, giving fewer compliments and being more direct in criticism (Madison, *Capital Times,* July 24, 1982).

The supervisor faces the stress of making sure that significant decisions around hiring, evaluations, promotions, discipline, and discharge are defensibly free of any imputation of racial, sexual, or age discrimination. In marginal instances, where the supervisor has some doubts about the possibilities of such a change being made, she might need to consult agency legal council about how to proceed in implementing such decisions.

The relationship between supervisor and supervisee established over time may be more significant than the factors of gender and race. Prejudice, misunderstanding, residuals of sexism and racism may decline or be resolved for the particular supervisee dyad as a consequence of continuing contact and development of a positive relationship. The supervisor's competence in performing her administrative, educational, and supportive functions vis-à-vis the supervisee may take precedence over considerations of race or gender.

Summary of Stresses Encountered by Supervisors

We have noted the stresses supervisors face in making a transition to the position and the stresses they encounter in implementing their responsibilities as supervisors. These relate to the demands of the position, the conflicting needs of administration, workers, and clients, and problems relating to age, gender and race.

Table 6.1 recapitulates some of the dissatisfactions with the supervisory role, as noted by supervisors, which reflect the different kinds of stress encountered on the job.

Coping with Stress—Supervisors' Adaptations

In general, supervisors have fewer supportive resources available to help them cope with work-related stresses than do supervisees. Griping as a form of cathartic release is not as readily available to the supervisor.

> Caseworkers could freely complain about agency policies and even, on occasion, defy them, but such options were hardly open to supervisors. Supervisors did critically discuss some aspects of agency functioning in supervisory staff meetings, and such discussions sometimes resulted in policy changes, but many regulations were outside their control, having been set by legislative bodies and the lay board. Regardless of their own feelings, supervisors were expected to enforce all current agency policies. These circumstances created problems for all supervisors, although professionally oriented supervisors were placed in a particularly difficult position. It was their task to help workers to accommodate to the agency's program—to reconcile bureaucratic requirements with professional principles. (Scott 1969, p. 133)

There appear to be fewer provisions made for the formal induction of supervisors into their new role and fewer formal, regularized

Table 6.1 Supervisor Dissatisfaction in Supervision

	Percentage of supervisors checking item as strong source of dissatisfaction (N = 469)
1. Dissatisfaction with administrative "housekeeping"—red tape, details in caseload audits, time sheets, statistical reports, etc.	71
2. Dissatisfaction because other heavy responsibilities of the job not related to work with supervisees prevent me from giving as much time as I would like to supervisees.	53
3. Loss of the direct worker-client contact and relationship.	46
4. Dissatisfaction related to need to get workers' adherence to agency policy and procedure with which I disagree.	41
5. Dissatisfaction with having to work with supervisees who are resistive or hostile or dependent or slow learners, etc.	39
6. Dissatisfaction from being tied to the desk and to the office.	27
7. Anxiety at the responsibility of making decisions for which there is no clear-cut agency policy or procedure.	27
8. Dissatisfaction associated with the conflict between administrative, evaluative aspects of the relationship with supervisees and the educational aspects.	26
9. Anxiety from not feeling certain that I know enough to be an adequate supervisor.	22
10. The need to exercise administrative authority in relation to supervisee performance and to evaluate the work of the supervisee.	21
11. Dissatisfaction at the socially and professionally isolated position of the supervisor in my agency.	21
12. Dissatisfaction with the physical aspects of my job—office, equipment, parking, etc.	18
13. Dissatisfaction at finding myself becoming part of the Establishment.	15
14. Anxiety from being responsible for somebody else's work and being looked to for leadership.	12
15. Anxiety at having to supervise workers who are older and/or more experienced than myself.	2
16. Other (miscellaneous).	2

Source: Kadushin (1973).

channels provided to assure support for new supervisors during the transitional period.

Whereas the supervisee has a formal channel of feedback in the supervisor that provides opportunities for commendation, the supervisor has no such formally assigned sources of feedback. Many supervisors live with the stress of not knowing how well they are doing and what, if anything, they should be doing differently. Perhaps the assumption is that if the person is experienced enough to be selected for the position, he or she should be able to operate independently without the need for such support. A supervisor wryly expresses some resentment about this:

> My first supervisee was a rather dependent person, who, as we expressed it professionally in her evaluation, "worked best with considerable reassurance and support." In practical terms, this meant that I propped her up while she propped the clients up, and in the end the whole weight fell on me. This left me in need of "considerable reassurance and support" too, but no one thought of that. I was the supervisor and I was paid to have shoulders that were broad. I soon became accustomed to this, however, and eventually I was able to prop several workers up—something like the bottom man in a human acrobatic act—and hardly feel it at all. (H.C.D. 1949, p. 162)

The supervisory peer group is less often a resource for emotional support than is the direct-worker peer group. There are not as many supervisors, so there are fewer possibilities for choice of those with whom one might feel comfortable and congenial. Competition for promotion becomes keener as one moves up the administrative ladder because there are progressively fewer positions available. Consequently there is less tendency for the supervisors to act as a group and a greater tendency to act as individuals in seeking administrative favor.

It is far more difficult for supervisors than for direct service workers to develop a colleague support group. There are few, if any, functions or activities that require that supervisors work together. There is no formal arrangement analogous to unit meetings which would enable supervisors to get to know each other and develop a relationship. The work of the supervisors, even more than that of the workers, tends to isolate them psychologically and geographically.

Studies of social interaction and peer consultation among direct service workers and supervisors showed a considerably greater amount of interchange among direct service workers as compared with supervisors (Blau and Scott 1962).

Supervisors are also subject to burn-out. High expectations that they can significantly influence supervisee professional growth or that they can effect consequential changes in the agency are often frustrated. Balancing the needs of the organizations against the needs of supervisees and/or clients, facing the necessity of obtaining compliance with policies and procedures with which they disagree, trying to carry out their responsibilities with increasingly limited resources of personnel and funds, emotionally depleted by the need to support and nurture and sustain a unit of supervisees lacking a support group, supervisors experience burn-out (Harvey and Raider 1984).

Supervisors, in adjusting, make deliberate efforts to buffer themselves from supervisees. Too much social contact, too little distance, exposes the supervisor to constant pressure from the demands and needs, explicit or implicit, of the supervisees. But since the supervisor needs the cooperation of the supervisees, and a positive relationship with them, too great a social distance is undesirable. In a somewhat formalized, controlled contact the supervisor seeks an optimum balance between too great a familiarity, which risks constant pressure, and too little, which encourages supervisee resistance and alienation.

Supervisors adjust to their situation by developing their own vocabularies of realism. They learn to accept the limitations of their power and authority by discovering that, despite their restricted knowledge and control, most often the terrible things they fear just don't happen. They learn to turn a blind eye and a deaf ear to relatively inconsequential examples of deviance and noncompliance. They learn to recognize the limits of their influence, that while they can teach the worker to be responsible for his learning, while they can facilitate interest, motivation, and commitment in the work, only the worker can feel that interest, motivation, and commitment.

Some supervisors may adjust to the stresses of the position by becoming indifferent and doing the minimum to satisfy the requirements. Such a supervisor rewards supervisees who handle their assignments without bothering him, who do not bring up any problems, who do not generate any complaints from clients or other agencies, who do not allow emergencies to develop and, when they do develop, handle them by themselves. The supervisor's actions are motivated not by a concern with helping the supervisees develop autonomy but rather by a desire to be trouble free. He settles for the absence of negatives in the performance of his supervisees rather than encouraging the presence of positives. He is not concerned with noncompliance as long as the supervisees take the risk and are not too blatant about it.

There are numerous compensating gratifications that offset, and make acceptable, the increased stresses occasioned by the appointment to supervisor. Table 6.2 ranks satisfactions in supervision as described by supervisors. The list points to the kinds of social and emotional returns from their jobs which sustain supervisors in dealing with job-related tensions.

Supervisors' Games

It would be doing both supervisor and supervisee an injustice to neglect a description of games initiated by supervisors. Supervisors play games for the same reasons that supervisees play. The games are methods of adjusting to stresses encountered in performing their role. Supervisors play games out of felt threats to their position in the hierarchy, uncertainty about their authority, reluctance to use their authority, a desire to be liked, a need for the supervisees' approval—and out of some hostility to supervisees that is inevitable in such a complex, close relationship.

One of the classic supervisory games can be called "I Wonder Why You Really Said That." This is the game of redefining honest disagreement so that it appears to be psychological resistance. Honest disagreement requires that the supervisor defend her point of view and be sufficiently acquainted with the literature to present the research evidence in support of her contention. If honest disagreement is redefined as resistance, the burden is shifted to the supervisee. He has to examine the needs and motives that prompt him to question what the supervisor has said. The supervisor is thus relieved of the burden of validating what she has said, and the onus for defense now rests with the supervisee.

Table 6.2   Supervisor Satisfaction in Supervision

	Percentage of supervisors checking item as strong source of satisfaction (N = 469)
1. Satisfaction in helping the supervisee grow and develop in professional competence.	88
2. Satisfaction in ensuring more efficient and effective service to more clients through my supervisory activity.	75
3. Satisfaction in sharing my social work knowledge and skills with supervisees.	63
4. Satisfaction in the greater opportunity and leverage to affect changes in agency policy and procedures.	45
5. Satisfaction in the stimulation provided by curious, idealistic and enthusiastic supervisees.	44
6. Satisfaction in helping the supervisee grow and develop as a person.	37
7. Satisfaction in a more diversified job.	31
8. Satisfaction in having others look to me for leadership, advice, direction.	24
9. Satisfaction in being able to provide emotional support to supervisees when needed.	23
10. Satisfaction in increased salary that goes with job.	23
11. Satisfaction in contacts with professionally qualified and interesting fellow supervisors.	18
12. Satisfaction in the status and authority the position gives me.	9
13. Satisfaction in being free from contact with difficult clients and a heavy caseload.	5
14. Satisfaction in helping supervisees with their personal problems.	1
15. Satisfaction with the physical aspects of the supervisor's job—better office, parking, privileges, etc.	1
16. Other (miscellaneous).	2

Source: Kadushin (1973).

Another classic supervisory game is "One Good Question Deserves Another." A supervisor writes:

I learned that another part of a supervisor's skills, as far as the workers are concerned, is to know all the answers. I was able to get out of this very easily. I discovered that when a worker asks a question, the best thing to do is to immediately ask for what she thinks. While the worker is figuring out the answer to her own question (this is known as growth and development), the supervisor quickly tries to figure it out also. She may arrive at the answer the same time as the worker, but the worker somehow assumes that she knew it all along. This is very comfortable for the supervisor. In the event that neither the worker nor the supervisor succeeds in coming up with a useful thought on the question the worker has raised, the supervisor can look wise and suggest that they think about it and discuss it further next time. This gives the supervisor plenty of time to look up the subject and leaves the worker with the feeling that the supervisor is giving great weight to her question. In the event that the supervisor does not want to go to all the trouble, she can just tell the worker that she does not know the answer (this is known as helping the worker accept the limitations of the supervision) and tell her to look it up herself. (H.C.D. 1949, p. 162)

Some games are designed to validate the supervisor's authority on the basis of ascription. Subtly appealing to experience or credentials, the supervisor solicits endorsement of authority and seeks to deflect any challenge to such authority. Playing "Parents Know Best," the supervisor asserts her unquestioned authority on the basis of her MSW or years on the job (Hawthorne 1975). A soft form of the game is to openly recognize the supervisee's difference of opinion but not accept it. "I know you don't agree with me, but later when you get more experience you will find that I am right."

Some supervisors' games are concerned with protection from the burdens of supervision. The supervisor can avoid the inconvenience of individual conferences by finding justifiable reasons to postpone or cancel conferences or significantly shorten those which are unavoidable. The game might be termed "I Can Hardly Catch My Breath." The supervisor indicates that because he has suddenly received an administrative request for a special report or some special statistics, he is very sorry but the scheduled conference will have to be postponed (Hawthorne 1975).

A judicious arrangement of the supervisory conference agenda may provide protection from the need to confess inability to help. The more difficult questions are relegated to the last ten minutes of the conference. Then, regretfully noting that "I wish we had more time to discuss this," the supervisor gives these questions a cursory and hurried review, leaving no time for possibly embarrassing questions.

Protecting themselves from the necessity of exerting authority, supervisors play pseudodemocratic games trying to hide the fact that they are supervisors. The emphasis is on reducing any heirarchical differences and drawing the worker closer to them by drawing closer to the worker. The game is "I Am Just Like You."

Appealing to the limits of the supervision power protects the supervisors from some difficult decisions. In playing "I Would If I Could But I Can't," the supervisor indicates that she would be willing to go along with some request that the supervisee is making except for the fact that the administration will not permit it.

The worker has considerable administrative discretion in how liberally or rigidly she might interpret agency policy in contact with the client. The supervisor has similar maneuverability in applying administrative requirements in supervision. The supervisor creates an obligation by leniency in enforcing agency procedures. "After All I Did for You" is a supervisor's game which seeks to cash in on such obligations. It calls for explicit attention to the obligations which the supervisee has incurred and asks that restitution be made. "After all I did for you" can be communicated almost as effectively nonverbally as verbally. The pained expression, the sigh of resignation at impending disappointment bring the supervisee up short.

The supervisor is selective in her demands for adherence to agency rules and procedures or modulates the vigorousness with which she requires such adherence. The extent to which the supervisor feels free to do this depends on the security she feels in her own relationship with administrators to whom she is responsible and the number of "reciprocity credits" that she has earned with them.

The obverse of reciprocity credits is of course "obligation deficits." Supervisees seek to obligate the supervisor for extra work they have done in meeting the request for a report on short notice, in agreeing to cover an uncovered client, and so on. Being "obligated" to the workers, the supervisor has to reciprocate by softening, for a time at least, her demands on the workers in order to maintain their loyalty.

Supervisors, in avoiding a response to a supervisee's request for a decision, information, or guidance, may engage in double-talk. From the supervisee's point of view this might be termed "Waddid She Say?"—sometimes called the "old song and dance" approach. The game involves using as many esoteric, preferably psychoanalytic, terms as possible, giving the appearance of knowing what you're talking about. It requires considerable self-assurance on the supervisor's part and the ability to phrase a response with considerable ambiguity. The effectiveness of this game derives from the fact that it is difficult for the supervisee to challenge the supervisor and request clarification and from the fact that the confusion generated by the statement makes it impossible to formulate a sensible question. Having made the statement, the supervisor prudently disappears in the smokescreen.

Summary

Supervisors are also subjected to a variety of job-related stresses. The transition to supervisor is a difficult change involving a reorientation of relationships with colleagues, and alterations in self-perception and in attitudes toward agency goals and procedures. The additional responsibility, along with the lack of preparation, ongoing support, and clarity in role differentiation, combined with conflicting demands, all contribute to supervisors' feelings of tension. The problems of race and gender in supervisory interaction are other sources of stress. Satisfactions, however, balance some of the dissatisfactions for supervisors. Games played by supervisors can help supervisors in their efforts to cope.

CHAPTER SEVEN
Evaluation

EVALUATION in supervision is defined as the objective appraisal of the worker's total functioning on the job over a specified period of time (Schmidt and Perry 1940). It is a process of applying systematic procedures to determine with reliability and validity the extent to which the worker is achieving the requirements of his position in the agency. An evaluation should be a judgment based on clearly specified, realistic, and achievable criteria reflecting agency standards. It is job related and time limited. It is concerned with both the "quality of performance and the quantity of accomplishment." Evaluation is an administrative procedure that should, and can, contribute to professional growth. It is therefore a component of both administrative and educational supervision. It is further a component of supportive supervision. Explicit feedback helps the worker get a sense of meaningful achievement, reduces the tension associated with role ambiguity, and provides the positive reinforcement for good work well done.

Written, signed evaluations have legal implications as well as supportive, educational, and administrative implications. Due process requires that a worker be periodically informed of the acceptabilty of his performance to the agency. If a decision is made to dismiss the employee, failure to have provided the worker with such periodic assessments can legally be regarded as a violation of due process as well as being in contravention to many union contracts.

Equal opportunity regulations require that any administrative personnel action requires validation by specific objective evaluation procedures. Without such substantiating documentation, decisions affecting women and/or minorities are open to challenge.

Evaluations are as ubiquitous and necessary as they are inevitable. There is no way of not communicating an evaluation message. Refraining from evaluating is, in itself, an evaluation. An anxious worker to whom no evaluation is communicated may read the message as "I am so bad he can't even tell me about it"; the cocksure, conceited worker may read the same message as "my work is so exemplary that there is nothing to discuss."

Every time the supervisor nods in agreement, says "yes," "okay," "you're right about that" in response to something the supervisee has said, an evaluation is being made. Every time a pained expression crosses the supervisor's face, every time he gestures impatiently, every time he says gently, "come now, I am not so sure about that," or more forthrightly, "I disagree with you about that," an evaluation has been made.

We cannot abstain from informal assessment, and workers are aware of this. Each supervisor has some idea of how she ranks a particular worker as compared with others in terms of a level of performance she regards as adequate. Evaluations require us to formalize such assessments, to make them explicit, to communicate them to the workers, and to defend them if necessary.

The formal evaluation conference differs from the ongoing assessments which are, or should be, part of each supervisory conference. In the individual conferences the focus of concern is the current case situation. The formal evaluation conference is concerned with an overview of the entire caseload. It is a period of stock-taking and review. As Pettes (1967) says, it is "a chance to see how the whole orchard is growing rather than concentrating on individual trees" (p. 114). Given the uncluttered opportunity to take a more general view of the worker's activity, the worker and supervisor make a conscious effort to discuss general patterns of performance.

At this point, greater precision in terminology might be helpful. One might reserve the use of the term "evaluation" for the formal, periodic event concerned with reviewing the worker's total performance. The term "assessment" might be an appropriate term for the ongoing, informal review of the limited segment of the worker's performance which is the concern of each particular conference. The formative "assessment" during each conference ultimately leads to the summative "evaluation." Our concern in this chapter is with "evaluation" rather than "assessment."

Values of Evaluation

Evaluation has value to the client, the agency, the supervisor and, most importantly, to the supervisee.

Value to the Worker

Evaluation relieves supervisees' anxiety since it helps them know where they stand. The only thing more anxiety provoking than evaluation is no evaluation. Supervisees are then in doubt about how adequately they are meeting agency expectations and how they compare with other workers of similar education and experience.

A period set aside for formal evaluation gives supervisees a perspective on change and achievement. Assuming that a worker has improved during the period of time covered by the evaluation, the process tends to encourage him and to enhance a sense of accomplishment. For the worker the evaluation is an opportunity to obtain explicit approval of his work from somebody who is thought to have the information, ability, and experience to make such a judgment. It provides the worker with a presumably objective, authoritative perspective on his abilities and deficiencies. Recapitulating the real progress in professional development made by the worker while acknowledging the existence of deficiencies, the supervisor helps the supervisee to view his work more realistically and optimistically. This mitigates the counterproductive tendency, particularly on the part of young, conscientious workers, to deprecate their achievements.

Evaluations help motivate, direct, and integrate learning. The supervisee is stimulated to learn and change in order to achieve a good evaluation. A systematic review of what one has learned helps to consolidate it. Having identified explicitly what he has learned to do, the supervisee can recognize the learned behavior and more easily repeat it.

Evaluations help direct learning. The standards by which he is evaluated help to clarify for the supervisee the specific kinds of activities on which he has to focus. Selection of a task for inclusion in an evaluation-assessment instrument increases the visibility and significance of that task. The workers are likely to expend more energy in learning such tasks and pay more attention to the performance of such tasks.

Evaluation helps make learning conscious, because it requires an explicit assessment of performance. It points to how much the worker has learned, how far he has come. At the same time it helps to clearly identify the nature of performance weakness and what needs to be learned more adequately. It makes possible further goal-directed teaching. An evaluation is concerned with an assessment in the present of work during the immediate past period, for the purpose of determining future teaching and learning activity.

Evaluations help set the pattern for self-evaluation by the supervisee. Before standards of service can be internalized for self-regulation, they need to be clearly identified for the worker. Having become acquainted with performance standards and criteria as a result of evaluation conferences, the supervisee is in a better position to critique his own work. Evaluation "increases self-awareness to further self-improvement."

Every worker has the responsibility for self-evaluation and self-regulation. The worker's continuous, critical assessment of his own performance is the best guarantee of effective and efficient service. But to do this analysis requires not only the will to engage in critical self-evaluation but a knowledge of the standards and criteria that distinguish good practice from poor practice, learned as a consequence of evaluation conferences.

Evaluations assist the worker in career planning. Many workers need reasoned feedback in helping them determine whether or not they have the necessary aptitude for success in social work. Marginal employees may be helped to consider alternatives as an outcome of evaluation. Others may find they have aptitudes for supervision and/or administration and can be helped by the evaluation conference to consider preparing themselves for these responsibilities.

Value to the Agency

Discharging the responsibility toward public accountability by evaluating the extent to which the agency is achieving its goals and objectives starts with an evaluation of the degree to which the individual worker's performance is meeting agency standards. Just as the agency is accountable to the community, so the individual worker is accountable to the agency. Evaluation by the supervisor of the work of the supervisee is one link in the chain of accountability to the community for which the entire agency is responsible.

Periodic, systematic evaluation of worker performance may point to needed changes in agency administration. Careful review may show that the workers are not failing the agency but that instead the agency is failing them. Evaluation leads to communication from supervisors to administrators regarding administrative procedures that are adversely affecting worker performance.

A review of a series of evaluations of a number of different workers can help in planning in-service training programs and staff-development procedures. Such analysis may disclose consistent weak spots in staff performance to which agency administration needs to give attention. Evaluation helps define for the staff generally, and for the individual worker in particular, those aspects of professional performance that require further special attention and effort, and it points to the kinds of learning experiences that need to be provided. Evaluation further helps the agency to identify special skills manifested by individual staff members who might then be assigned special tasks.

Evaluations are procedures for controlling and standardizing the behavior of the worker. The evaluation criteria make explicit and visible the kind of behavior expected, the kind of behavior that is approved, the kind of behavior which will be rewarded. As Dornbush and Scott (1975) note, evaluation is an exercise "in the authorized use of power to control task performance by the distribution of organizational sanctions" (p. 157). Evaluations thus serve the agency purpose of administrative supervision.

If promotions, dismissals, reassignments, and merit pay increases are necessary and acceptable responsibilities of administrative supervision, then we must accept as legitimate and necessary the procedures that permit such decisions to be made on a reasonable and defensible basis. Evaluation also helps validate agency policy regarding worker selection. Through evaluation the agency can determine if its selection requirements do, in fact, tend to result in the recruitment of personnel capable of doing an effective job.

Evaluation of performance for administrative decision becomes more important in the context of diminishing agency budgets and downsizing agency programs. If staff has to be cut, retaining the best workers depends on the accuracy and objectivity of performance evaluation.

Value to the Client

Social work, like other professions, claims the freedom to operate without control by outsiders. One justification frequently advanced to support the demand for autonomy is that professionals will regulate each other to prevent abuse and ensure efficient practice. The professional association code of ethics exemplifies such self-regulation by members of a profession. But the sanctions available in the professional codes of ethics are rarely applied, and then only for the most egregious violations. The community, in granting a profession freedom from outside regulation, control, and interference, has a right to expect some more immediate, more routinely applied measures of control. The principal benefit of evaluation for the client is that as a consequence he is more likely to be assured of effective service and protected from continuation of inadequate service.

Value to the Supervisor

As a consequence of a systematic evaluation of the worker's performance, the supervisor knows what has been learned and what still needs to be taught. Evaluation provides the agenda for future educational supervision.

Explicitly evaluating the strengths and weaknesses of the individual workers in her unit, the supervisor is in a better position to efficiently deploy the human resources available. Assignments can be made more efficiently as a consequence of evaluation. The supervisor can make a better match between tasks that need to be completed and interests and aptitudes of individual workers.

Formal, explicit evaluation protects supervisors from their own biases in rewarding or sanctioning the worker. The evaluation criteria and the need to justify her judgments helps to discipline the supervisor's thinking in assessing the worker's performance.

The evaluation report and associated documentation of the worker's performance provides protection for the supervisor in cases where personnel decisions are contested. The requirements of the Equal Employment Commission, union contracts, and civil service regulations make supervisors vulnerable to such complaints.

The standards and criteria explicated in a good evaluation form are, in effect, a translation of the objectives of the agency at the Administrator's level to specific tasks at the performance level. As such it not only acts as an instrument of worker behavior control as noted above, it also helps reduce role ambiguity and role conflict. Consequently the evaluation form and process assist the supervisors in implementing the administrative functions of supervision.

Having noted the values of evaluation, we may now ask who might best be delegated the task of making evaluations. The logical response is that the person in the agency who is most directly and intimately acquainted with the details of the worker's day-to-day activity would be in the best position to make a reasoned and defensible assessment of peformance, i.e., the worker's immediate supervisor. Consequently it is not surprising that when any organization requires a formal, periodic evaluation of worker performance, almost invariably the immediate supervisor is given this responsibility.

Objectives of Evaluation

Having indicated the value of evaluations for the different constituencies which are directly or indirectly concerned with the process, the specific objectives of evaluation need to be noted. Evaluation has two principal objectives. One is an administratively focused objective. Evaluation provides a systematic product, a report, which administration uses in making informed administrative decisions— retention, merit pay increases, promotion, suspension, etc. A second principal objective is focused on the worker's professional growth and development. Evaluation is a teaching-learning process which identifies strengths and weaknesses in the worker's job performance so as to enable the worker to improve his performance. As a product for administrative purposes, evaluation focuses primarily on past performance. As a teaching-learning process, evaluation focuses on past performance for the purpose of improving future performance. As a product, the evaluation report is used by "others" to make decisions about the worker; as a process, evaluation is used by the worker himself for changing his way of working. Evaluations have the objectives of motivating the supervisee as well as recognizing good work.

Based on information obtained from 196 voluntary social service agencies, Wiehe (1980) determined that "performance improvement" was regarded as the primary purpose of evaluation by 49 percent of the agencies. Other purposes such as "salary raises" (26 percent), "promotion from probationary period" (15 percent), training (7 percent), discharge (2 percent) and promotion (1 percent) lagged behind (p. 5).

Dislike of Evaluations

Despite the value and necessity of evaluations, they trouble most supervisors and tend to be avoided, if not actively resisted. There are a number of reasons which explain supervisors' dislike of evaluations.

Evaluation is among the supervisory procedures that most explicitly call attention to the difference in status between supervisor and supervisee. As such, it tends to increase the social distance between them. It is difficult to maintain the fiction that supervisor and supervisee are colleagues in a peer relationship when the supervisor has the responsibility and authority to evaluate the work of the supervisee. The possible reward-punishment consequences of evaluation clearly express the power of the supervisor, which on other occasions may be muted and obscured. Some supervisors feel uncomfortable with the authority inherent in their position. In many other kinds of supervisor-supervisee interactions their authority need not be explicitly employed and so can be conveniently ignored; in evaluation it is openly exercised.

Any evaluation of the worker is in effect an indirect evaluation of the supervisor. If the worker is performing inadequately, the evaluation might reveal that the supervisor has not taught the worker what he needs to know, has not given the worker the help he had the right to expect. A supervisor reports:

> I felt a pressure to give her a good evaluation, and I wonder now if my desire to do this was because I felt it was therapeutic for her. It was also a kind of reward for myself for being a good therapist in helping Ms. G. become a better worker. Both of these reasons are inappropriate but it was a kind of validation that I was a good supervisor.

Evaluation can evoke strong negative feelings. Supervisors may be anxious that evaluation will precipitate a hostile reaction from the supervisee; there is guilt at the possible consequences of a negative evaluation, consequences that have considerable significance for the job status and professional career of the worker. A supervisor says:

> If I told Mr. R. what I really think—that he's a lousy worker—he'd blow his top and I'd have psychic debris all over the office. Besides, he would challenge me on every word, and I am not so sure I could cross the *t* and dot the *i* on my judgments. So who needs all that grief? I kind of tone the evaluation down.

While supervisors may feel uncomfortable and apologetic about making evaluations, supervisees are apt to be anxious and defensive. Comparative evaluation more often than not becomes a subject of agency gossip. Consequently not only is self-esteem involved but reputational standing in the peer group is affected by such assessments. In addition there are clear career-related penalties associated with a poor evaluation.

The supervisor is keenly aware of the possible career consequences of evaluations for the supervisee. Many of the benefits that are possibly available as a result of very good evaluation are nondivisible—there are only so many promotion slots. Not knowing the rigorousness with which other supervisors are evaluating their supervisees, the supervisor is made hesitant by the realization that she might be placing her supervisee at a competitive disadvantage.

There is a reluctance to be appropriately critical because the criticism might be discouraging to the worker. The supervisor may hesitate to inflict pain and discomfort or may fear that the supervisee will like her less as a result. The supervisor's task is to be uniformly helpful, not invariably popular, to be consistently useful and responsible rather than consistently loved. Aware of this ambivalence, a supervisor notes:

> I was flattered by his evident liking and respect for me. It gave me pleasure. I was not so ready to risk this by arousing his hostility if I pressed him about some of the things he was doing poorly, which needed improvement. If I did what I thought I had to do I would be giving up, or at least risking, some of the satisfactions for me in the relationship.

To be comfortable with the threats implied in evaluating, the supervisor must accept the legitimacy of the evaluation process and feel entitled to make an evaluation. The supervisor has to feel confident that she is capable of making a valid judgment, that she has enough accurate information on which to base a valid judgment, and that the standards on which the judgment is based are clearly defined and defensible. However, many supervisors question the legitimacy of evaluation and lack a sense of entitlement. They do not think they should or can judge the work of another. Further, they are oppressed by conflicting, ambiguous evidence of performance and by imprecise, vague standards available for judging performance. Consequently they neither feel qualified to make such a judgment nor confident that they can make a true evaluation. Such doubts may make supervisors hesitant about being critical—not being without sin, they are reluctant to cast the first stone. As one supervisor said,

> I know the agency wants us to recommend dismissal for workers who don't meet minimum requirements. But I am not so sure what these requirements are or how to measure them and how much emphasis to place on achievement versus individual progress. It's hard for me to be confident recommending dismissal for even my poorest supervisees so I give them a passing evaluation.

A positive evaluation is an endorsement, a certification of proficiency. Hence it involves a considerable responsibility to the general community, to the specific community of clients, to the agency, and to professional peers. Being invested with, and having to carry out, such a responsibility is apt to be somewhat unnerving.

The requirement for evaluation seems to contradict the ethos of social work. The professional value orientation puts great emphasis on being nonjudgmental. Evaluations, of necessity, involve a judgment of performance. The admonition to be responsibly critical, frank, and direct in rigorous evaluation clashes with the professionally inculcated disposition to be accepting and compassionate, supportive and reassuring. The felt conflict causes discomfort.

Most supervisors are aware of the possible loss of staff as a result of a negative evaluation. This realization suggests an additional motive for resisting evaluations. A study of worker attrition in the New York City Department of Public Welfare showed that "workers with one or more positive evaluations were about half as likely to leave the Department within nine months of their appointments as those with none; workers with a plural number of negative evaluations showed a significantly greater tendency to leave the Department than those with one or none" (Podell 1967, p. 22).

Every time a supervisee with some experience is fired or quits in response to a negative evaluation, a new, inexperienced worker has to be hired in his place. During the period of transition, extra burdens are placed on the supervisor. The uncovered caseload has to be temporarily assigned. Prospective candidates for the position have to be interviewed and a selection made. Once a person has been hired, the supervisor again faces the tasks of worker introduction and orientation. The supervisor can avoid all this additional work by placating the supervisee with a laudatory, if not entirely accurate, evaluation.

On a cost benefit analysis balance, the supervisors have much to risk and little to gain by extending themselves to conscientiously undertake detailed formal examinations. There is little overt reward. It is part of the job so that there are no special compliments or fringe benefits which result. On the other hand, it is a difficult, time-consuming job requiring a lot of painful soul-searching. It involves a risk of evoking hostility, resentment, or rejection in the worker. It is understandable then why so often evaluations are delayed and, when done, are done perfunctorily.

So evaluations generally tend to be avoided, but negative evaluations tend to be avoided most of all. Yet such evasion only compounds the supervisor's problem. Refraining from critical evaluation does the worker an injustice and promises future difficulty. Performance failures that are ignored do not disappear. The worker continues to practice his mistakes and becomes more proficient in making them. With time the errors become more serious and, having been ignored, are more difficult to deal with. The easy avoidance of critical evaluation today comes back to haunt the supervisor tomorrow.

Hesitancy to deal openly with deficiencies in performance becomes in itself an incentive to continued concealments. The supervisor is aware that if she raises the problem for discussion after some delay, the worker can justifiably accuse her of early dishonesty and deception.

Failure to be appropriately critical substitutes a problem of group morale for a problem of individual morale. The worker who is appraised too leniently may be happier, but his fellow workers will be less happy. Peers are perceptive in their evaluation of each other's competence. If a worker whom they know to be inefficient and ineffective is given a raise along with better workers because the supervisor has not been appropriately critical, they feel resentful and cynical. They become suspicious about the validity of the supervisor's evaluation of their own work. They are robbed of some of the motivation to improve their own performance, since the system appears to reward good and bad work equally.

It may reassure supervisors to note that most social work supervisees recognize and accept the fact that the agency, as their employer, has a right to evaluate the work they are doing. They face this challenge along with millions of other employed workers. In fact, one study found that supervisees expressed strong dissatisfaction with the fact that supervisors were not sufficiently and specifically critical of their work. Anxious to do a better job, supervisees looked to their supervisor for help in identifying deficiencies in their work which needed correcting. They were disappointed when they failed to receive such critical analysis (Kadushin 1974). When supervisees raise objections to evaluation, the reason is not the legitimacy of agency entitlement to evaluate their work but rather the fact that evaluations are often inequitable, arbitrary, and unhelpful.

Desirable Evaluation Procedures

Despite the clearly identifiable reasons which feed supervisory antipathy toward evaluation, it is both necessary and inevitable. What approaches are most likely to contribute to a productive evaluation?

1. Evaluation should be a continuous process rather than an occasional event. The formal evaluation conference may be a summation of the small assessments that take place as part of each conference. Regularly devoting some part of each conference to assessment, however brief, helps desensitize the worker's anxiety regarding it. This practice also helps prepare her for what is likely to be shared at the formal conference so that it does not come as an unexpected, disconcerting surprise. As one worker complained, "The supervisor never mentioned my overidentification with Jane [a

girl on probation] until the evaluation conference. If I had been aware of it sooner I certainly could have made some effort to control overidentification in my contacts." The formal, periodic evaluation is a summary recapitulation of familiar, previously encountered assessments rather than an unexpected, unanticipated critique for which the worker is unprepared.

2. The supervisor should discuss the evaluation procedure in advance with the supervisee. Supervisees may be less anxious if they know in advance when evaluations are to be scheduled, what information and standards are to be used as a basis for evaluation, what they might be expected to contribute to the evaluation, with whom the evaluation will be shared, what use will be made of the evaluation. But, of even greater importance, supervisees will be in a better position to prepare for the evaluation over a period of time and to participate more productively in the process. This approach implies that the evaluation outline should be shared with workers in advance and that they be given the opportunity of asking questions about the outline for clarification.

3. The evaluation should be communicated in the context of a positive relationship. The positive relationship acts as an anodyne to the pain of criticism (however warranted) and makes the worker more receptive to, and accepting of, the criticism as a basis for constructive change. If the supervisor and supervisee dislike each other, the supervisee is predisposed to reject the criticism as invalid and unfair.

All criticism of performance should be offered out of a sincere desire to help, not out of pleasure and satisfaction in criticizing. The supervisor needs to be sensitive to the worker's reaction, to manifestations of anxiety and resistance. These feelings can then be discussed openly, and appropriate reassurance and support can be offered. The most important aspect of evaluation is the attitude with which the process is conducted.

A formal evaluation generates anxiety because it is a threat to narcissism and self-esteem. There is a fear of failure and rejection. It raises such questions as, Will I be able to measure up to expectations? Will I be able to maintain the good opinion of me held by people I like and respect? How do I compare with my peers? What effect will this have on my professional future? Evaluations become part of our official records. There is much at stake. A good supervisory relationship helps support the worker through this anxiety-inducing procedure.

4. The evaluation procedure should be a mutual, shared process. The supervisor should attempt to maximize the worker's participation in, and contribution to, the evaluation. The worker could be asked to write a self-evaluation or to write a critique of the supervisor's evaluation. The worker's reaction to the evaluation should be solicited. Mutuality implies not only encouraging the worker's participation but also active use of those contributions that are valid and applicable in the final evaluation write-up. Evaluation is done "with" the worker, not "to" the worker. Mutual participation in the evaluation process increases the probability of a more valid evaluation and of its acceptance and use by the supervisee.

Participation lessens anxiety. Having been invited to participate, the worker retrieves a measure of control of the proceedings. Sharing in control and being able in some measure to determine content, direction, and emphasis in the evaluation conference, the supervisee tends to feel less anxiously helpless. Participation also tends to reduce the discomforting imbalance in power between supervisor and supervisee. Power is manifested in the ability to control. In encouraging the supervisee's active participation in the evaluation process, the supervisor is sharing his control.

5. Evaluations should be made with some recognition and consideration of reality factors that might be determinants of the worker's performance. The supervisor needs to assess whether or not the worker's caseload was atypically heavy or included more than the usual number of specially difficult cases. Was this a period when the turnover in personnel was greater than normal, when things at the agency were unusually hectic? Allowances need to be made for situational aspects of the job—lack of office space, lack of secretarial help, the unavailability of essential support services, periods of low agency morale which adversely affect workers' performance. The worker who has a routine caseload of minimum complexity, imposing few unusual decision-making responsibilities, is in a different position from the worker with a caseload of clients who frequently present unique and complex problems.

6. The principal, if not the exclusive, focus of evaluation should be the work performance of the supervisee rather than any evaluation of the worker as a person. The only social role of concern to

evaluation is that of the supervisee as an employee of a social agency and, specifically, as the person assigned to do a particular job in this agency. None of the other aspects of the worker's life are legitimate areas for review. This concept is stressed by the Family Service Association of America in defining evaluation as "an accurate appraisal of the performance of the incumbent [of the position] in relation to specific duties assigned" (1957, p. 53).

7. The evaluation should review both strengths and weaknesses, growth and stagnation, and should be fair and balanced. Isolated, atypical examples of the worker's performance should not be used to make a general case for failure. Rather, recurrent patterns of behavior in job performance are the legitimate bases for evaluation statements. Nor should the supervisor's personal standards be substituted for agency standards as a basis for evaluation.

Fair evaluation focuses on behavior because "behavior provides structure and articulation for objectives and judgments that might otherwise be vague and excessively open to interpretation" (Goldhammer 1969, p. 326). The total configuration of the worker's performance needs to be considered. Recent incidents may over-influence the evaluation because of their very recency, and dramatic incidents because of their vividness. Furthermore, if behavior patterns are cited as factors in the evaluation, there should be some reason to believe that the worker's behavior had some significant positive or adverse effect on the client.

Admittedly, fairness is difficult to achieve. It has been said that what makes life so complicated in supervision is that the supervisee can almost always find some technical defense for his actions while his supervisor can almost always find some basis on which to criticize them (Goldhammer 1969, p. 172).

The evaluation should not be used by the supervisor to support some predetermined decision.

8. A good evaluation is not like a final game score but rather a review of how the game was played. It should be more than a listing of good and bad performance, being instead an analysis of why certain behaviors and procedures are desirable and effective and why other behaviors and procedures are not. As one worker said in complaining of her evaluation conference, "The supervisor said my work was satisfactory but what was satisfactory about it or why it was satisfactory she didn't say, so I don't know."

9. The evaluation should suggest tentativeness rather than finality and should focus on modifiable aspects of the worker's performance: this is the way the worker performs at this particular time; the expectation is that she will develop and improve. The good worker can become a better worker, and the poor worker a good worker. The spirit of the evaluation should communicate the idea that "success is not final; failure is not fatal." The evaluation is, after all, not an unchangeable verdict but an incentive for change.

In achieving comprehensiveness an evaluation should look to the future as well as the past. The worker's performance speaks to what he has already done. Focusing on capacities and potentialities says something about what he might be able to do in the future.

10. Evaluations should be formulated with some consistency. Both intra- and inter-supervisor consistency is desirable. The supervisor needs to apply the same standards in the same way to all of her supervisees who have approximately the same education and experience. Likewise, different supervisors responsible for different units of workers with similar backgrounds need to act similarly in evaluating their respective supervisees. It is difficult to think of any other factor so corrosive of morale as differences in evaluation procedures applied to a homogenous group of supervisees.

11. It is desirable for the supervisor to indicate a willingness to accept evaluation of his own performance from the supervisee. If the process of evaluation is helpful in the development of the supervisee, it can likewise contribute to the supervisor's professional development.

The supervisee will be more accepting of evaluation, and less likely to see it as a manifestation of capricious authority, if she has the opportunity, in turn, to evaluate the supervisor. Certainly, as a recipient of supervision, as the consumer of the product, she is in a position to assess the supervisor's performance. Teaching faculty currently are more and more frequently open to student evaluation; it is difficult to defend supervisor immunity from supervisee evaluation. Two-way evaluations exemplify agency orientation toward evaluation. Evaluation of the worker's performance should be only one manifestation of the overall evaluation of personnel at all levels as part of a periodic review of the agency's total program.

12. Involvement of staff in establishing evaluation criteria is likely to ensure the selection of more relevant criteria, to intensify

commitment to the evaluation process, and to clarify expectations with regard to evaluation. Workers who have helped develop standards to which they will ultimately be held accountable will feel a greater obligation and responsibility to see that the evaluation process achieves its objectives. Research indicates that ability to have significant input in determining evaluation criteria and procedures is clearly related to satisfaction with evaluation (Dornbusch and Scott 1975, pp. 186–87).

13. Since the worker does his work in an organizational context which might impede as well as facilitate satisfactory performance, some effort should be made explicitly to identify organizational difficulties over the evaluation period. One should ask whether there has been a change in administration; a reorganization of the agency; a temporary shortage of staff due to high turnover rates; new legislation directly effecting agency operations, etc. Due allowance should be given these destabilizing considerations in making the evaluation.

Evaluation Conference—Process

1. Scheduling the Conference

The worker should be informed at least a week in advance about the specific date and time of the evaluation conference. In some agencies, evaluations are scheduled at regular intervals—every half-year or every year. In other agencies, evaluations are tied to transition points in the supervisee's professional career, for example, at the end of the probationary period, when the worker's assignment is changed, when there is a change of supervisors, when the worker is leaving the agency, when a merit increase is due.

2. Supervisor's Conference Preparation

The supervisor prepares by reading a sampling of the worker's recording, reports, special project write-ups, by reviewing the statistical material, time sheets, and supervisor's notes or logs covering the period of performance to be evaluated, as well as by reviewing previous evaluations.

In a more general fashion the supervisor's preparation should be a continuous process. Utilizing all sources of information, the supervisor should make notes of ongoing activity that illustrates the worker's typical performance. She should be constantly alert for critical incidents that relate performance to agency standards. A thorough knowledge of the details of the worker's performance is one of the most effective antidotes to supervisory anxiety about making evaluations. Criticism can be shared with less anxiety if there is a feeling of certainty that it is warranted and if the criticism can be adequately documented.

Since the total caseload cannot be reviewed in equal detail, preparation involves selecting typical representative examples of the worker's performance for illustrative reference during the conference. This includes selection of good work showing specific skills; examples of poor performance illustrating the need for skills requiring additional work; and case examples indicating the worker's professional growth.

The supervisor further prepares by introspectively examining his attitudes toward, and feelings about, the supervisee which might contaminate an objective appraisal of performance. The supervisor needs to be aware of such feelings as hostility toward the supervisee, which might make him punitive in evaluation; a desire to control, which might make him manipulative; or a tendency to identify with and defend the supervisee, which might make him overprotective. The supervisor has an investment in the professional progress of his supervisees; eager for their success, which is the supervisor's success once removed, he may be reluctant to perceive the workers' failings.

The supervisor should also prepare for the conference by reviewing some of the classic and persistent pitfalls in evaluating, in order to avoid them. These include the "error of central tendency"—the tendency, when in doubt, to rate specific aspects of the worker's performance as "fair" or "average"; the "halo effect"—the tendency to make a global judgment about the worker's performance and then to perceive all aspects of the worker's performance as consistent with that general judgment; the "contrast error"—the tendency to evaluate using oneself as a standard, the very conscientious supervisor seeing most workers as less conscientious, the highly organized supervisor tending to see others as less well organized; "leniency bias"—a reluctance to evaluate negatively and critically. Such errors will be discussed in greater detail below (pp. 354–57).

3. Worker's Conference Preparation

The worker should also prepare for the conference by reviewing the agency evaluation outline or evaluation rating form which has been shared with her. She might follow the outline in thinking about and making notes for a self-evaluation. In addition, she might be asked to consider the way her performance six months or a year ago compares with her performance now, what she thinks she has accomplished during the period to be covered by the evaluation, where she thinks she needs more help, and the kinds of professional experiences she missed and would like to have.

Despite the desirability of familiarizing the supervisee with the criteria of evaluation, a large percentage of supervisees responding to a national study reported that they were not given a formal statement which informed them of these criteria. Only about one in four supervisees was asked to formulate her own evaluation statement in preparation for the evaluation conference. Less than half indicated that they were given a written evaluation that was supplemented by an oral discussion. Almost half of the supervisees (46 percent) reported that no formal, individual evaluation conference was scheduled with them. When such conferences were scheduled, they usually occurred at one-year intervals (Kadushin 1974).

4. Evaluation Conference Interaction

If both supervisor and supervisee thoughtfully prepare for the evaluation, there may be much agreement to begin with. The following are an excerpt from a self-evaluation review by a supervisee and an excerpt, related to the same problem, from her supervisor's preliminary evaluation note.

Supervisee self-evaluation:
With both Jane [an unmarried mother] and the Allens [a foster family] I continued to demonstrate what appears to me to be excess zeal. Jane was more capable of handlng her problems than I gave her credit for

and did not need as much help as I was ready and anxious to offer her. She was capable of applying for AFDC without my intervention. The Allens too had enough skill and practice as parents to do an adequate job of making Paul [the foster child] comfortable with the transition to their home without all my hovering over them. In these, and in several other instances, I tend to be the all-loving, overprotective, anxious mother figure.

Supervisor's preliminary evaluation:
Miss M [the supervisee] frequently manifests a need to be helpful, to encourage the dependency of clients, to solicit client approbation and appreciation by doing for them what they can, perhaps, do as well for themselves. The general attitude of concerned helpfulness which Miss M manifests is a desirable attitude for which the worker should be commended. However, Miss M's current indiscriminate, helpful behavior needs to be exercised with more self-control and self-discipline. Miss M needs to learn to offer her help more discriminatingly in situations where it is appropriately required. In such situations and under such circumstances her help is likely to be more truly helpful. Perhaps we can, in future supervisory conferences, center on the criteria which will enable Miss M to distinguish when a client is truly objectively dependent on her for her intervention and when the client can do for himself.

The mutual awareness of the same general problem may be a tribute to the supervisor's continuous efforts at assessment during the regularly scheduled ongoing supervisory conferences. Sharp differences in how the supervisee and supervisor assess the performance would suggest some difficulty in the relationship, some failure in communication.

At the beginning of the evaluation interview, it may be useful to deal explicitly with worker anxiety, to review the procedure, and to briefly recapitulate what will be covered. If made at all, these comments should be very brief; the worker is primarily concerned about the evaluation itself. Another tactic in opening the evaluation conference is suggested by a supervisor who said, "I asked the supervisee to check her case load with me for the period to be sure nothing had been omitted. I find this is a good comfortable way for both supervisor and supervisee to get into the evaluation conference, and it sets the tone for the supervisee as an active participant."

It is suggested that the interview start with positives, move to problems and deficiencies, and end with reviews of positive performance. This has been termed the sandwich approach—a slice of negatives between two positives.

Since the supervisee is probably anxious to hear what the supervisor has to say, this is one conference in which the supervisor should take the initiative. The supervisor should open the main body of the conference-interview by presenting clearly, simply, and unambiguously a general evaluation of the worker's performance as she sees it. Evaluation provides explicit formal feedback. Its effectiveness is intensified if it is specific, if it can be communicated so that it is appropriate to the needs of the worker, if it is clear and accurate.

The supervisor, in his anxiety, can be so careful that he drains the assessment of all meaning and significance. Euphemisms and qualifications are often added to elaborate circumlocution so as to soften the message to the point where it fails to be communicated.

> I said that, on occasion, I had some feeling that in particularly difficult situations, with overly demanding clients, when she herself was hurried and harassed, her behavior tended to reflect aspects of an attitude which suggested some elements of disrespect—even though I recognized that generally this might not be typical of her approach. I wondered if she herself thought this was the case—did she think there was some truth in this or perhaps not.

The formal evaluation is the opportune time for plain, direct statements adequately supported by specific citations from job performance. Workers may feel puzzled by ambiguous evaluation statements. "I guess I am doing all right because she didn't say I wasn't." "She talked a lot about my mature approach to people but I don't know exactly what she meant." Supervisees are interested in an honest evaluation of their performance. In expressing dissatisfaction with evaluations that failed to provide specific feedback in a supportive manner, a supervisee says:

> My evaluations were short, not in depth, and limited to general, positive feedback. Little criticism of my work was included. Overall my evaluations were positive but dissatisfying to me because they felt empty as I really wanted to spend some time on areas on which I needed improvement.

Since a principal responsibility of the supervisor in this conference is to provide explicit, honest feedback in a supportive manner, the principles of effective feedback are applicable here. These have been discussed previously (pp. 199–202) and need not be repeated here.

The main body of the conference is a discussion of the worker's performance using criteria such as those described in a later section of this chapter. The conference concludes, as does any good interview, with a summary of the principal points covered. The implications of the conclusions for immediate future conferences are explicated and outlined. There is a clear statement of "where we go from here." Attention is paid to the supervisee's emotional responses to the evaluation at the end of the conference, and an effort is made to resolve, or at least mitigate, the most disturbing feelings.

Having explicitly identified some aspect of the worker's performance needing improvement, the supervisor and supervisee might give some consideration, in terminating the conference, to a plan of action for change. Both participants should agree on a specific period of time during which the objective for change will be accomplished. Some evaluation forms even have an entry labeled "Development Plan: List specific plans for improvements, objectives to be achieved, schedules for development to be undertaken."

The evaluation conference is not finished when the participants leave the room. Both supervisor and supervisee continue to mull it over. Hopefully, this reflection on what was discussed will lead the supervisor to a better understanding and appreciation of the supervisee's work, and the supervisee to a better awareness of his strengths and weaknesses as a social worker.

But even when the conference has finished, the evaluation process continues. Each evaluation is directed toward the ultimate achievement of the termination of evaluations, when the worker is truly self-directed and capable of valid self-evaluation. At that point in his professional development, an objective, critical, outside review of his work can still be helpful, but the agency has sufficient confidence in the worker so that formal evaluations are no longer administratively required. It is then that evaluation is terminated.

Communication and Use of Evaluations

The supervisee is not in a position to accept or reject the evaluation, as would be true if the relationship were consultative. The agency cannot grant the supervisee this option if it is to responsibly meet its obligation to the community and the clients. Assuming the evaluation is valid, the supervisee is given the option of modifying his behavior so that it meets the standards of performance required by the agency.

The supervisor, in preparing an evaluation, needs to have confidence that recommendations for administrative action, which follow from the evaluation, will be supported by the administration. However, the ultimate responsibility for implementing the consequences of the evaluation rests with administration. This practice protects the supervisee from possible arbitrary evaluations and accompanying negative recommendations. Thus, if the supervisor needs the confidence that administration will generally accept his evaluatory recommendations, he also needs to be aware that good administration will make a considered rather than an automatic decision to support such recommendations.

Once the evaluation has been formulated, it should be written out and the worker should have an opportunity to read it and to keep a copy. NASW Standards for Social Work Personnel Practices, as revised in 1971, require a written statement by the agency "of standards of performance" as the basis for evaluation. Furthermore, "the evaluation shall be in writing . . . and the employee shall be given the opportunity to read it, to sign it (signifying he had read it) and to file a statement covering any points with which he disagrees. A copy of the evaluation shall be furnished the employee." The statement notes that "the authority of the evaluator must be recognized on both sides and final authority belongs to him" (National Association of Social Workers 1971, p. 19).

In a written evaluation, the supervisor can be deliberate and precise. She can review it carefully and reconsider it at leisure for possible changes in content, emphasis, and balance. None of this is possible in the heat and stress of an oral evaluation, when a word uttered is beyond recall or change. Because they are a matter of record, written reports have the advantage of being available for use by those who might supervise this worker in the future.

Several arguments can be made in support of having the worker read the evaluation. Oral evaluation is open to misinterpretation and is the source of considerable fantasy about what the supervisor actually said. A written evaluation is definite and available for re-

reading and rechecking. While still open to some misinterpretation, it is not as readily distorted as an oral evaluation. It is easy for the worker to fail to hear what he does not want to hear or to suppress what he has heard but is reluctant to remember. It is possible, but more difficult, to engage in such defensive maneuvers with a written document. The evaluation conference is often a stressful experience during which the supervisee finds it difficult to absorb what is being said. The opportunity to read the material improves the chances for distortion-free communication.

Being permitted to read the evaluation reduces any anxiety the worker may feel about whether the evaluation that is shared verbally is the same as the written evaluation actually filed with administration. The privately written evaluation is often more critical than the evaluation verbally communicated, and supervisees are aware of this. The fact that the evaluation will be read acts as a constraint on the supervisor. It is likely to intensify the care with which the statement is prepared and increases the probability that the evaluation will be more objective and accurate.

The context provided for reading the evaluation is important. The worker should have the opportunity to read the evaluation in the presence of the supervisor. If he has questions or objections regarding content, or desires clarification of ambiguously phrased material, this can be handled immediately. If the evaluation is negative, the presence of the supervisor provides an immediate target for hostility or an immediately available source of reassurance and support.

If objections are raised which the supervisor accepts as valid, the evaluation statement is amended accordingly. If objections are raised which are not agreed to by the supervisor, the supervisee should have the right to ask that a statement of her reservations be included in her file in her own name. Evaluation forms often include provision for supervisor signature, supervisee signature, and signature of agency administrator. Alongside the supervisee's signature the forms might include a proviso such as the following: "The contents of this evaluation have been shared with me. My signature does not necessarily mean agreement."

Some supervisors claim, with a certain amount of justification, that a careful safeguarding of the supervisee's right to read the evaluation will result in less useful and perhaps less valid evaluations. Torn between doing justice to agency administration and agency clients and protecting themselves from enervating argumentation, supervisors may choose to write bland, noncommittal, generally favorable evaluations, saying little to give offense but, at the same time, saying little that is significant. Hunches, intuitions, sharp guesses which supervisors feel are true but which they cannot actually substantiate by citing the specific supporting evidence, will tend to be excluded.

Some supervisors also feel that such procedures suggest that the supervisor is not trustworthy, that supervisory evaluations are likely to be unfair, unjust, and untruthful. They reject and resent such implications. These supervisors assert that where the supervisory relationship is positive, the professional self-discipline of the supervisor is a sufficient guarantee that the evaluation will be fair and honest—without the requirement that the supervisee have a right to check it.

The agency should make available procedures for appealing an evaluation that the supervisee thinks is unfair. The supervisor needs to support access to such procedures without any suggestion of retaliation. It is not the use of such procedures that is important to most workers but the knowledge that the option is freely available and accessible.

In summary, both supervisor and supervisee should prepare for the conference by reviewing their notes and tentatively formulating an evaluation. After they have discussed their respective perceptions of the worker's performance in the evaluation conference, the supervisor writes a formal evaluation statement. This is given to the worker for reaction and comment.

The above presentation indicates desirable social work evaluation procedures. We know little of how such evaluation conferences are actually conducted. Nichols and Cheers (1980) analyzed the recordings of 23 evaluation conferences. While these were between supervisors and social work students, they may be instructive for what they can tell us about the conduct of practice evaluation conferences. In 30 percent of the cases no evaluative comments were made. With regard to about a third of the evaluative comments made, "little or no evidence was presented to support the evaluative comment. When evidence was produced, it was primarily a descriptive statement rather than a specific example" (pp. 63–64). In 87 percent of the cases, the supervisor introduced the topics that were discussed.

A study of evaluation of workers in protective services concluded that

> where assessment skills of workers' performance has been rigorously examined, it appears that supervisors tend to make global assessments of workers' performance and fail to make discriminating ratings of different performance criteria. It was further noted that personal characteristics of the supervisors influenced their ratings. Supervisors, in general, were not prepared to carry out accurate and detailed performance assessment of supervisees' work. (Thomas and LaCavera 1979, p. 4)

Errors in Evaluation

On page 346 above we listed some of the recurrent classical errors that are persistently committed in making evaluations. Such errors require more explicit discussion.

1. *The Halo Effect* derives from the perception of one aspect of the worker's performance which is outstanding. The very favorable impression resulting from this one aspect then radiates to all other aspects of the worker's performance. Judgment in all aspects of performance is biased by the impression generated by one aspect of performance.

A dubious supposition of performance consistency supports the halo effect. The supposition is that the worker's performance is all of one piece. If he is good in this aspect, he is likely, if he is consistent, to be good in all aspects.

Halo effects operate in a negative as well as in a positive direction. Perception of a worker's total performance may be biased by deficiency in one aspect of his work.

The term halo effect is also used when the judgment of specific aspects of performance is biased by a global judgment of performance—the tendency is to make a global judgment and rate specific aspects of performance in a way that is consistent with the global judgment.

The halo effect is a major hazard to objective evaluations. The relevant research shows that "those individuals who behave in such a way as to satisfy the personal needs of the supervisor will generally be rated higher; those subordinates who interfere with the satisfaction of the personal needs of the supervisor will generally be rated lower. The specific ratings by supervisors are likely to be determined by the more global, conscious or unconscious, reaction to subordinates" (Kallejian, Brown, and Wechsler 1954, p. 168). A good evaluation may reflect the ability to please the supervisor rather than objectively superior performance in contact with the client.

Green (1972) notes that research on supervisory evaluations tends to indicate that an evaluation "begins with a field instructor's assessment of a student's *overall* performance which then determines whether he or she will not find any specific qualities which are being sought" (p. 53). This is the halo effect in operation.

2. *Leniency Bias* reflects a hesitancy to evaluate negative performance fairly and honestly. The evaluation is more positive than warranted by the actual performance. The result is that all ratings are skewed toward the positive end. There is little differentiation in the evaluation and the utility of the evaluation for administration is reduced.

Leniency bias does the supervisee a disservice. It is falsely reassuring, encourages unrealistic confidence and avoids coming to grips with performance deficiencies which require attention.

A leniency bias damages the morale of the best workers. If everybody gets a very good evaluation, questions are raised about the validity and fairness of the evaluation process. Objectively better workers wonder if extending themselves is really worth the effort since superior performance is not differentially rewarded.

Leniency bias is endemic in social work. We do not like to say anything that might be hurtful. Given the paucity of data available and the ambiguity of the definitions of good and bad work, we are not secure enough in our judgments. Negative evaluations risk a bad scene.

The Educational Testing Service used to have the contract for administering and scoring the reference vouchers and tests used for certification to The Academy of Certified Social Workers (ACSW). The Service's review of the judgments of supervisors and peers on the reference voucher rating forms indicates "a strong 'leniency effect' in the ratings which is evidenced by uniformally high average ratings, low variabilities and a total reluctance by the rater to employ the low or unfavorable categories" (Educational Testing Service 1973, p.3).

Brandon and Davies (1979) note, in studying the process of evaluating marginal graduate social work students, that workers are evaluated as acceptable "if there is no evidence of incompetence." This is different from an orientation which requires "that there be positive evidence of good practice" (p. 315). Leniency bias is reflected in the general conclusion of the study— that, in the program of professional education for social work, "People pass who do not fail."

Brandon and Davies' comments are supported by Brennan's (1982) findings that of a "combined total of 463 grades awarded first and second year graduate students in field instruction courses in a school of social work during the 1976–77 academic year, less than 1 percent of such grades were C or below" (p. 77).

3. *Central Tendency Error* refers to the tendency when in doubt to rate all work as "average" or "fair." As a consequence all evaluations are bunched together at the center of the distribution. An average rating may, in fact, reflect true performance. Central tendency error is only an error if it is made because an evaluation has to be given and the supervisor does not know enough about the worker's performance to make a defensible judgment. Average ratings are easy to justify, are rarely controversial, and meet the demands of the evaluation procedure. All in all, it is an easy way out and follows the line of least resistance.

4. *Recency Errors* and *Errors of Overweighting*. Evaluations cover some definite time period and the supervisor needs to make the evaluation in terms of performance over that time period. Otherwise there is the tendency to be unduly influenced by recent performance. This is similar to the error of being unduly influenced by dramatic events which tend to have disproportionate visibility. Both recency and drama distort perspective on total performance over the period to which the evaluation speaks. Evaluation should be based on patterned, typical performance.

5. *Contrast errors* are of two kinds. One is related to the field, the context, in which the evaluation is embedded. If most of the supervisees in a unit are relatively poor performers, an average performer looks much better by virtue of the contrast. Rather than being eval-

uated in terms of his performance based on some objective standard the evaluation is based on the supervisee's performance as it compares with a poorly performing group.

The other contrast error is the result of comparing the supervisee's performance with that of the supervisor's assessment of how she/he might have performed in similar circumstances. Here the supervisor uses herself as the standard against which the supervisee is contrasted. This is then an idiosyncratic standard against which the worker is evaluated.

Evaluation Outlines and Rating Forms

Many of the suggestions to make the evaluation process more positive and productive depend for their effective implementation on the availability of an evaluation guide or outline. An evaluation outline ensures more precise definition and specification of the criteria for evaluation; it suggests the explicit kinds of information that need to be obtained for evaluation; it assures a greater likelihood that uniform standards will be followed by different supervisors and by the same supervisor with different supervisees; it tends to depersonalize the evaluation for the supervisee since the outline is an all-agency guide, and reduces a supervisor's guilt and anxiety as she employs agency-sponsored standards and is protected from her own subjectivity; it increases the certainty of covering the same points in successive evaluations; it simplifies sharing with the supervisee, in advance, the areas of performance to be covered by an evaluation.

The availability of an evaluation outline related specifically to the job responsibilities of a classified group of workers in a particular agency ensures that the process of assessment will be directed to the worker's performance on the job, a job for which the duties have been clearly defined. The evaluation outline further serves as a convenient interview guide for evaluation conference discussion.

Evaluation outlines in any social work agency reflect basic social work skills, methods, and general objectives—the enhancement, support, or restoration of psychosocial functioning. Hence it is to be expected that evaluation outlines have some general similarities. However, since each agency has a particular responsibility, a particular problem area, and operates in a particular community, with staff of some particular composition, each agency has to adapt and modify a generally applicable outline to make it optimally appropriate to its own situation. One agency may be concerned with use of community resources, another with the development of those resources; workers in one agency may be involved in considerable collaborative effort with other professional workers; in another agency they may have minimal working contact with other professionals. These factors alter the kinds of competencies that need to be evaluated.

Any evaluation, of necessity, starts with a statement of objectives and a description of the job the worker is being asked to perform. It is axiomatic that we cannot tell how well we are doing unless we know what we are trying to do. The process of evaluation involves the explication of worker tasks; the clear, concise, and meaningful definition of criteria by which we can measure the extent to which the tasks have been achieved; and the actual measurement of worker performance in terms of the criteria which reflect the task objectives. A criterion is a standard against which a comparison can be made.

Criteria are the specific aspects of the worker's performance which are given consideration in forming a judgment. Criteria should represent important, significant aspects of the worker's performance. Criteria, in aggregate, should cover the total job description. They need to be well defined and formulated so that they are measurable in objective terms.

One of the difficult problems faced by the social work profession, and shared with other human-service professions, is establishing standards of productivity in the absence of a standard product. The ultimate aim of social work intervention is the more effective psychosocial functioning of the client—individual, family, group, or community. The most immediate criterion, then, in evaluating the productivity of the worker is the number of clients who have been helped, as a consequence of the worker's activity, to achieve more effective psychosocial functioning over a given period of time. Any review of the literature concerned with evaluating the outcome of social work service will testify to the problems of definition, measurement, and data procurement which would be encountered in applying such a criterion in evaluating the worker's performance. In recognition of the difficulties of evaluating worker performance in terms of outcome, the content of evaluation in virtually all agencies has been generally concerned with second-order criteria, which are easier to apply. The use of such criteria is based on the supposition that if the worker possesses relevant knowledge, displays professionally approved behavior, manifests the proper attitudes, and follows professionally prescribed procedures, clients will be helped. Consequently, the evaluation is focused on relevant knowledge, approved behavior, proper attitudes, and prescribed procedures rather than on the frequency, consistency, and quality of client change, as such, attributable to worker intervention.

Evaluation on the basis of process and procedure rather than outcome is defensible because so many factors that determine outcome are beyond the control of the worker. One might often legitimately claim that "the operation was a success although the patient died."

Despite the necessary emphasis on process, outcome data when available should be included as a consideration in evaluation. Such material helps increase the reliability of evaluative judgments (Kagle 1979). With the recent use of behavior modification approaches and the specification of identifiable, measurable objectives to be achieved through the worker's intervention, evaluation on the basis of outcome variables has become more frequent. The worker's performance is evaluated in terms of the degree to which specific, measurable objectives have been achieved.

It is suggested that some of the instruments employed in studying the therapeutic relationship might be adapted to the evaluation process. Scales developed to determine levels of empathy, non-possessive warmth, and self-congruence might be so employed (Lechnyr 1975).

Evaluation Content Areas

An overview of the principal content areas usually included in reasonably comprehensive evaluation outlines follows:

I. Ability to establish and maintain meaningful, effective, appropriately professional relationships with client system.
   A. Attitudes as manifested in appropriate worker behavior to-

ward client: interest and desire to be helpful; respect; empathic understanding; nonjudgmental acceptance; nonstereotyped individualization; assent to client self-determination; warmth and concern.

B. Objective, disciplined use of self in relationship in behalf of client: empathy and sympathy without overidentification.

C. Adherence to professionally accepted values in client contact: confidentiality.

II. Social work process—knowledge and skills.

A. Social study (data-gathering) skills: discriminating ability to discern psycho-social-cultural factors of significance to service situation that needs to be explored; ability to gather relevant information from client, collaterals, records, tests; observation and exploration of relevant items of social study are accurate and appropriately detailed.

B. Diagnosis (data assessment) skills: demonstrates understanding of interrelationship of intrapsychic, interpersonal, and environmental factors; effectively applies knowledge of human behavior and social systems so as to derive meanings from social study data; shows appreciation and understanding of client's perceptual, cognitive, and emotional frame of reference; capable of formulating a descriptive, dynamic diagnostic or data-assessment statement.

C. Treatment (intervention) skills: capacity to plan and implement a program of remedial action based on understanding (diagnosis), derived from the facts (social study); ability to use, as appropriate to the client's situation, specific treatment interventions, e.g., environmental modification, psychological support, clarification, insight, advocacy, brokerage, social action; interventions are appropriately timed and relevant.

D. Interviewing skills: ability to establish, with client, clear interview purpose; ability to maintain interview focus in order to achieve interview purpose; maintains a good balance between flexibly and responsibly following client lead and offering appropriate direction and control; ability to tactfully and nonthreateningly help client communicate feelings as well as facts.

E. Recording skills: recording demonstrates capacity for organization and communication of worker's thinking and feelings; recording is discriminating, selective, accurate, succinct.

III. Orientation to agency administration—objectives, policies, procedures.

Knowledge of, commitment to, and identification with agency objectives, policies, and procedures; ability to work within limits of agency policies and procedures; imaginative use of agency policies and procedures in helping client; takes responsibility for working toward orderly change in policies and procedures which require improvement.

IV. Relationship to, and use of, supervision.

A. Administrative aspects: prepares adequately for conference, is prompt and regular in attending scheduled conferences, provides supervisor with necessary, appropriate material for conference.

B. Interpersonal aspects: freedom in seeking and using supervisor's help without undue dependency; acceptance of supervision and instruction without subservience; positive orientation to supervisory authority; active and appropriate participation in supervisory conferences; ability to recognize when consultation is needed and how it might appropriately be used.

V. Staff and community relationships.

Contributes to harmonious and effective relationship with agency staff at all levels; develops positive relationship with, and makes appropriate use of, colleagues from allied disciplines; constructively represents the agency to other professionals and to the general community; has good knowledge of relevant community resources.

VI. Management of work requirements and work load.

Covers work load with regularity and adequacy; shows ability to plan and organize work schedule within time allotted; shows capacity to set selective, valid priorities and to schedule work accordingly; is prompt in submitting recording, statistical reports, time sheets, service reports, etc.; absences and lateness infrequent and justified; productivity is at the expected level for workers of similar responsibility and experience.

VII. Professionally related attributes and attitudes.

Realistic critical assessment of own limitations without undue anxiety; adequate level of self-awareness and capacity for self-evaluation; flexible and cooperative on the job; enthusiasm for, and conviction in, the work he is doing.

Generally behaves on the job in accordance with the values and ethics of the profession; shows identification with the profession; takes responsibility for continued professional development by reading, informal discussion, participation in relevant, available training programs.

Evaluation outlines like the preceding one result in a narrative statement of performance. There is a growing dissatisfaction with detailed narrative statements and increasing use of standardized check forms as guides to evaluation. The use of such a form imposes less of a burden on the supervisor, it results in a more precise product for comparative evaluation of one worker with another or the same worker with himself at different points in time, and it encourages greater standardization in evaluation. It is an expeditious way of summarizing evaluative statements.

From experimental study, Schubert (1960) concludes that "application of a schedule to student process records has been found an effective and relatively economical means of making objective evaluations of performance and discriminating between several levels of performance" (p. 298).

Table 7.1 shows a humorous, but clear, example of an objective format for performance evaluation.

The following examples illustrate different kinds of formats used in social work evaluation forms. The material comes from evaluation forms obtained from a number of schools of social work and a wide variety of agencies. The items have been modified and edited to suit our present purpose. I have included only a limited number of items in each form but have varied the content so that, in aggregate, the items employed illustrate the kinds of content areas included in a comprehensive evaluation outline.

The following example illustrates the use of a step scale. Each step in the scale identifies the level of performance which relates to a particular area of performance.

What are the worker's attitudes toward clients as shown in supervisory and/or group conferences?
1. Acceptance without sentimentality, without overidentification, without denial of unlikable qualities in client.

Table 7.1. Example of a Performance Evaluation Format

Performance factor	Performance level				
	Far exceeds job requirements	*Exceeds job requirements*	*Meets job requirements*	*Needs some improvement*	*Does not meet minimal requirements*
Quality of response	Leaps tall buildings with a single bound	Must take running start to leap over buildings	Can only leap over short building or medium with no spires	Crashes into building when attempting to jump over	Cannot recognize buildings much less jump over them
	1._____	2._____	3._____	4._____	5._____
Tempo of performance	Is faster than a speeding bullet	Is as fast as a speeding bullet	Not quite as fast as a speeding bullet	Would you believe a slow bullet?	Wounds self with bullet when attempting to shoot gun
	1._____	2._____	3._____	4._____	5._____
Communications skill	Talks with God	Talks with the agents	Talks to himself	Argues with himself	Loses the argument
	1._____	2._____	3._____	4._____	5._____

2. Acceptance tinged with overidentification, but not so much so as to impede learning.
3. Acceptance varies in different cases; predominantly positive attitude toward clients.
4. Some negative attitudes toward clients, but these are not so excessive as to impede learning.
5. Strong overidentification impedes learning.
6. Hostile, withholding attitudes impede learning.
7. Neutral and guarded attitudes.

To what extent does the worker perceive his own part in the worker-client relationship?
1. Sees that his own feelings affect work with the client, and tries to handle his own feelings for the client's benefit.
2. Acknowledges feelings but does nothing about them.
3. Protests or denies feelings.
4. Guarded in acknowledging feelings; maintains a bland surface, so there is nothing to take hold of in teaching.

What is the quality of the worker's diagnostic perception as revealed in verbal and written evidence?
1. Very high quality both in recording and in verbal material. Expresses diagnostic thinking freely. Sees the total problem and implications. Sees the meaning of behavior both in the client's life situation and in the worker-client interaction. Explores supervisory suggestions rationally. Weighs evidence.
2. High quality, but less consistently or pervasively so than in 1.
3. Mixed quality: variations in different cases, or sees major problem but not its implications.
4. Mixed quality: does fairly well verbally but does not organize ideas on paper very well.
5. Limited quality: diagnostic thinking is in general rather thin or something distorted, but enough is going on that there is something to take hold of in teaching.
6. Poor quality: distortions in thinking do not yield to discussion, or observation is so superficial that clues are not available for supervisory discussion.

What attitudes does the worker characteristically show in the conference with the supervisor?
1. Thoughtful, spontaneous, generally positive.
2. Somewhat scattered, spontaneous, positive.

3. Challenging and somewhat hostile; but hostility not so great as to impede learning.
4. Guarded; apparently some fearfulness of the supervisor's intent; bland.
5. Passively hostile; negative attitude that impedes learning.
6. Actively hostile; negative attitude that impedes learning.
7. Other

What is the level of the worker's attempts to engage client participation?
1. Very high: imaginative, individualized, relevant, with full recognition of obvious factors and some recognition of the less obvious. Flexibly related to case situation. Well-timed.
2. High: individualized and relevant, with recognition of obvious factors; fairly flexibly related to case situation; fairly well-timed.
3. Moderate: incomplete or inadequate or superficial, but not predominantly irrelevant, inappropriate, inflexible, or poorly timed. May be somewhat inconsistent.
4. Low: predominantly somewhat irrelevant or inappropriate, and/or mildly distorted or rigid; not very well-timed.
5. Very low: predominantly irrelevant or inappropriate, and/or grossly distorted or rigid; poorly timed.

Table 7.2 shows a five-step scale with a further gradation of two different points within each step.

The evaluation instrument might be a check form with evaluation items stated, giving the supervisor four or five possible choices of responses. The performance response levels might be stated in several ways.

1 = clearly above expected level	1 = excellent	1 = outstanding
2 = above expected level	2 = above average	2 = very good
3 = at expected level	3 = average	3 = good
4 = below expected level	4 = below average	4 = poor
5 = clearly below expected level	5 = poor	5 = unsatisfactory

A zero is often provided to be checked when the supervisor does not have sufficient information or when the item is not relevant to the worker's job assignment. Any one of these three scales might be employed with the following evalution-item listing.

Table 7.2. A Step Scale
For each factor to be rated select the behavior description along the 10-point scale which *most nearly describes the worker.* Decide which of the two numbers above the behavior description represents the more accurate, most consistent description of the worker and circle this number. Rate each factor without reference to any other. If you have had no opportunity to observe the worker in the relevant activity, circle 0. (National Association of Social Workers n.d.)

	0	1 2	3 4	5 6	7 8	9 10
1. Ability to develop and maintain working relationships with clients.	No opportunity to observe.	Difficulty in forming relationships even in relatively uncomplicated situations.	Able to form productive relationships but this may be inconsistent and the range may be limited.	Generally forms productive relationships, but has some difficulty in unfamiliar situations.	Consistently forms productive relationships in familiar situations and often in unfamiliar and challenging situations.	Unusual and consistent ability to form relationships with wide range of persons in complex situations.
	0	1 2	3 4	5 6	7 8	9 10
2. Ability to take professional action on behalf of client.	No opportunity to observe.	Usually expresses little concern for the rights of clients.	Recognizes the rights of clients but generally does not stand up for the client.	Sensitive in general to the rights of clients and takes a stand for the client in usual situations.	Greater than usual sensitivity to rights of clients and leadership in advocating for those rights.	Has in-depth awareness of the rights of clients in complex situations and consistently takes a stand for clients.

	0	1 2	3 4	5 6	7 8	9 10
3. Diligence and dependability in performing assigned work.	No opportunity to observe.	Frequently does not work hard or long enough or has "forgotten" to carry out assignments.	Some supervisory prodding necessary to get work done.	Works fairly steadily at assigned tasks.	Can be depended on to stick to a job until it is finished.	Puts every possible effort into his work.
4. Commitment to continuing professional development.	No opportunity to observe.	No apparent interest in professional development. Not self-critical, apathetic about increasing skill and knowledge, very limited view of professional responsibility. Does not respond to stimulus. Not committed to continuing professional development.	Inconsistently responds to outside stimulus to increase knowledge and skill, rarely takes initiative. Commitment somewhat questionable.	Usually responds to outside stimulus but does not initiate many efforts toward increasing knowledge and skill. Interest somewhat restricted but there is some positive evidence of commitment.	Definite evidence of commitment to continuing professional development, though this may be spasmodic or limited to particular areas. Some initiative in self-evaluation. Demonstrates some sense of professional responsibility beyond immediate tasks.	Consistently seeks to extend knowledge and improve skill, evaluates own practice, formulates ideas and shares them, clear sense of professional responsibility beyond the immediate job, systematically prepares self for new responsibilities.

Evaluation items	*Performance level*
a. Is aware of own feelings in relationship and controls them so as not to impede help to client.	1 2 3 4 5 0
b. Establishes a relationship characterized by rapport, ease, psychological safety.	1 2 3 4 5 0
c. Able to communicate acceptance of wide variety of different kind of behavior while not condoning unacceptable behavior.	1 2 3 4 5 0
d. Able to obtain clear and accurate picture of problem situation with which client wants help.	1 2 3 4 5 0
e. Able to organize and synthesize social study data in understanding client in his situation.	1 2 3 4 5 0
f. Confirms, refines, modifies diagnostic formulation as appropriate.	1 2 3 4 5 0
g. Able to mobilize community resources in client's behalf.	1 2 3 4 5 0
h. Able to accept limited treatment goals without feeling immobilizing frustration.	1 2 3 4 5 0
i. Facilitates client communication in interview.	1 2 3 4 5 0
j. Understands and responds to nonverbal as well as verbal communication in interview.	1 2 3 4 5 0
k. Recording reflects nature of worker-client interaction and worker's diagnostic thinking.	1 2 3 4 5 0
l. Is constructively and appropriately critical of agency policies and procedures which impede service.	1 2 3 4 5 0
m. Able to contribute constructive disagreement in supervisory conference.	1 2 3 4 5 0
n. Takes responsibility for establishing own learning needs in supervision.	1 2 3 4 5 0

The following three items illustrate the use of a seven-point scale anchored by descriptive statements at the high and low ends, clearly defining the behavior being evaluated.

1. *Relationship with client* (individual or group): *level of rapport, warmth, acceptance*
   HIGH Has regard, respect, and concern for person regardless of behavior which worker may reject; established warm, nonthreatening, nonpunishing, easy, relaxed, psychologically safe atmosphere; compassionate, gentle, sympathetic; client given freedom to be himself, to express himself freely, in all his unlovely as well as lovely aspects; client feels at ease and is encouraged to communicate since he trusts worker and has confidence in him.
   _1. Extremely good.
   _2. Very much better than average.
   _3. Somewhat better than average.
   _4. Average.
   _5. Somewhat poorer than average.
   _6. Very much poorer than average.
   _7. Extremely poor.
   _8. Not enough information available to make confident judgment.
   LOW Moralistic and judgmental; cold, distant, aloof, derogatory, disapproving, critical; establishes an atmosphere which is psychologically threatening and potentially punitive; client not permitted freedom to be himself; client feels uneasy, unrelaxed, hesitant to communicate since he mistrusts worker and has little confidence in him.

2. *Diagnostic skills* (individual or group)
   HIGH Recognizes, identifies, demonstrates understanding of and appropriate use of psychosocial, individual and group dynamics; tends to individualize diagnosis using pertinent social-study material; capable of conceptualizing and verbalizing psychodynamics of client situation and psychodynamics of the worker-client (individual or group) interaction; uses theoretical constructs regarding individuals and groups to make relevant, valid inferences from appropriate case data; technical language precisely and/or appropriately used.
   _1. Extremely good.
   _2. Very much better than average.
   _3. Somewhat better than average.
   _4. Average.
   _5. Somewhat poorer than average.

___6. Very much poorer than average.

___7. Extremely poor.

___8. Not enough information available to make confident judgment.

LOW Misses most significant psychosocial, dynamic cues; understanding of client's situation and dynamics of worker-client interaction superficial and/or distorted; tends to stereotype client and apply theoretical constructs inappropriately; technical language imprecise and/or inappropriately used.

3. *Management of work load*

HIGH Management of work load is smooth, efficient, inconspicuous, requiring little or no prodding or checking; worker output and efficiency high; meets deadlines, fulfills assignments.

___1. Extremely good.

___2. Very much better than average.

___3. Somewhat better than average.

___4. Average.

___5. Somewhat poorer than average.

___6. Very much poorer than average.

___7. Extremely poor.

___8. Not enough information available to make confident judgment.

LOW Management is poor, seems unable to manage work load without considerable reminding, prodding, checking; work output and efficiency low; frequently fails to meet deadlines or fulfill assignments.

More precise distinctions can be made on a scale such as the following. The supervisor is requested to check the scale at the point which appropriately reflects level of performance.

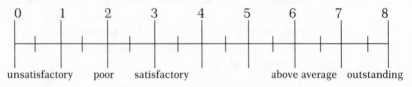

The scale is repeated for each of the items, such as the following:

a. Recognizes and disciplines own biases, prejudices, negative reactions to client.

b. Accepts limitations in clients' capacity and motivation and works with clients at their own tempo.

c. Uses good judgment in determining what information needs to be obtained in a particular situation.

d. Makes relevant inferences from social study data through appropriate application of social work theory.

e. Able to use the relationship as a medium for help.

f. Achieves good balance in treatment between stimulating the client to act on his own behalf and, when necessary, acting in behalf of the client.

g. Can identify and utilize appropriate strategies of intervention relevant to client system need.

h. Understands client's latent as well as manifest communication in interview.

i. Effectively handles pauses, silence, transitions in interview.

j. Recording is well organized and reflects essentials of case situation.

k. Understands his position in agency structure and the appropriate channels for intra-agency communication.

l. Shows little need to defend himself against learning in supervision.

m. Shows evidence of use of supervisory learning in subsequent client contacts.

n. Able to function as a productive, contributing member of a team of colleagues.

Evaluation outlines might include a series of graded statements, the supervisor checking the one that most clearly approximates the worker's performance. The following are illustrations of this.

Supervisee's Relationships with Clients
__1. Shows an exceptional ability to relate.
__2. Demonstrates a high degree of relating.
__3. Relates adequately with most clients.
__4. Has difficulty relating to clients.
__5. Often relates in a manner which turns clients off.

Supervisee's Treatment Planning
__1. Has ability to formulate, develop, and implement sound treatment plans which prove effective for the client.
__2. Develops sound treatment plans but finds implementation difficult.

_3. Develops treatment plans which are sometimes question-
able.

_4. Formulates treatment plans which prove ineffective for the
client.

With recognition of the difficulty of making precise distinctions
in levels of performance, some evaluation forms provide only for
very broad categorizations, i.e., acceptable, needs improvement,
unacceptable.

An evaluation form can include negative as well as positive and
neutral statements. The following examples are taken from such a
form.

Instructions: Below are listed some statements which relate to
evaluation of worker task performance. Using your knowledge of
the worker's activity, please mark each statement according to how
strongly you agree or disagree that this is characteristic of the work.
Mark the statement $+3$, $+2$, $+1$ or -1, -2, -3 to represent the
following:

$+3$ I strongly agree	-1 I disagree slightly
$+2$ I agree	-2 I disagree
$+1$ I agree slightly	-3 I strongly disagree

_a. Demonstrates an interest in client's problems.

_b. Tends to be cool and aloof in contact with client.

_c. Tends to respond punitively to the hostile, resistive client.

_d. Shows empathic understanding of most client behavior.

_e. Participates actively and willingly in supervisory sessions.

_f. Accepts and acts on constructive criticism.

_g. Lacks sensitivity to dynamics of self in supervisory relation-
ships.

The content of the evaluation outline and the content items included in the above illustrative standardized forms are designed to
be generic and applicable, with some adaptation, to all social work
methodologies. In addition to the core generic items illustrated, it
may be helpful to list some performance items that are more specific to group work and community organization.

Group work:

1. Skill in the use of group process to effect individual change.

2. Skill in helping individuals establish positive, productive group relationships.
3. Skill in the use of program activities to effect group change.
4. Skill in participating effectively in group interaction.
5. Knowledge of, and ability to use, a variety of group roles in effecting group movements.
6. Skill in discriminating and appropriate use of program media.
7. Skill in effecting change in intragroup interaction.
8. Skill in relating to group members as individuals.
9. Knowledge of various types of groups and their differentiated structure and function.
10. Skill in group leadership.

Community organization:
1. Skill in assisting community group to articulate needs and problems.
2. Skill in helping community residents develop organizational capacity necessary for effective social action.
3. Skill in establishing positive and productive relationships with leadership people at a variety of levels.
4. Skill in employing a range of educational and/or promotional techniques to enhance community understanding and support of social welfare programs.
5. Knowledge and understanding of community dynamics and power structure.
6. Skill in bringing together disparate citizen groups, professional groups, and social agencies in a working relationship addressed to the solution of community problems.
7. Skill in translating expressed community concerns into a feasible course of remedial action.
8. Skill in increasing motivation and participation of community residents in problem-solving activities in their own behalf.
9. Skill in negotiating with citizens' groups and community agencies.
10. Skill in effecting change in intergroup relationships.

In applying rating scales, supervisors make use of the knowledge which comes from experience in evaluating the performance of different workers. A lack of such experience makes it difficult to use some rating scales, as one supervisor notes:

It was difficult to evaluate using ratings such as above average, average, below average. Having no substantial supervisory experience other than this year's, it was difficult to determine what average behavior would be. This must be a dilemma faced by other beginning supervisors, who have little other than their own behavior by which to compare.

Even the most detailed rating form may fail to include a performance item that is of particular significance in the case of an individual supervisee. Furthermore, a valid evaluation is a complex configuration of many discrete items. The standardized form tends to fractionate performance since it is generally a listing of separate items. It is clear that something more is required, which involves putting the items together in some general, inclusive statement that relates the different items to each other. Using the same itemized information, one can get quite different evaluations depending on how one interpretively puts the items together. Failure to understand the interrelationship of discrete performance items is illustrated by the efficiency expert who evaluated the work of members of a symphony orchestra. He noted that for

> considerable periods the oboe players had nothing to do. The number should be reduced and their work spread out more evenly over the whole of the concert, thus eliminating peaks of activity. It is noted that all twelve first violins were playing identical notes; this seems unnecessary duplication. There is too much repetition of some musical passages. No useful purpose is served by repeating on horns and woodwinds a passage which has been already adequately handled by the strings.

In an evaluation, as in an orchestra, the whole is greater than the sum of individual parts.

In view of the need for a summary statement that integrates the itemized listing, most standardized forms leave space for this at the end. The instruction to the supervisor might be to "consider and assess the staff member's total performance as a social worker during the period covered by the evaluation, taking into account those factors covered by the form and any others you might believe to be important." More succinctly, the form might end by asking for the supervisor's general overall impression of the worker. All items in the outline or on the standardized scale appear to have equal value, but some are more mechanical, more peripheral, and require less skill than others. The overall summation is an opportunity to give differential weighting to the more significant aspects of the worker's performance which require more skill and competence.

The rating forms generally provide for fact-sheet information which includes the name of the worker, classification of the worker, education, the name of the supervisor, the identifying department or unit, the date of the evaluation, the reason for it, the period it covers.

Once a standardized rating scale has been formulated, it might be helpful to schedule meetings of supervisors alone, supervisees alone, and of the two groups together in order to discuss the use of the form. Such training in the use of the scale will ensure more uniform and efficient use of the instrument.

The evaluation outline or rating form is uniformly applicable to all the workers in the same job classification, that is, those positions having similar duties and responsibilities and requiring similar levels of knowledge and skill. Because the workers have the same classification, they have the same status in the agency and receive similar pay.

The standard for a job activity is defined as the quality of performance and the quantity of accomplishment which the agency feels it is legitimate to ask from all the workers assigned this job activity who have similar levels of education and experience. Evaluations for the same job classification differ in terms of experience on the job. The evaluation outline for the Caseworker I employee with five years of service is necessarily somewhat different from that for the newly hired Caseworker I. The performance items are similar in many instances. The difference lies in the greater consistency, adequacy, appropriateness, and autonomy of performance by the experienced worker. It calls for a performance executed with greater self-assurance as applied to a caseload of greater complexity. For example, the evaluation outline in table 7.3 makes distinctions in expectations varying with experience.

In addition to narrative evaluation reports, rating scales, and checklists, a "results oriented" approach is sometimes employed by social agencies. Unlike the narrative form outline, rating scales, or checklists, the "results oriented" evaluation content cannot be standardized in advance. The central point of a "results oriented" ap-

Table 7.3. Distinctions in Expectations, Based on Experience

Performance criteria	Experience level		
	1st year	3rd year	5th year
Understanding of the relationship of this agency to other agencies	beginning understanding	good understanding	full grasp
Commitment to agency program	awareness and a feeling of responsibility	growing facility	full commitment
Anxiety level	still a good deal of unfocused anxiety	no pervasive anxiety except in particular cases—expect some regression	anxiety minimal; worker should handle it herself except in serious cases
Degree of enthusiasm for work	high degree	still some unbridled enthusiasm	seasoned with compromise
Capacity to take criticism and deal with it constructively	accept with some objectivity; needs help in dealing with it	take and use with a minimum of help	take and use without defensiveness
Capacity for effective functioning as team member	growing awareness of need to fit self in; still needs much help	accomplished fact	accomplished fact plus helping others to do it
Use of supervision	willingness to expose but still quite dependent; produces material but not too clear on what needs to be learned	takes initiative; use of time for specific needs; knows what he wants	consultation

proach is that the subject matter for evaluation will be determined collaboratively by supervisor and supervisee in advance and the contract established forms the content for the performance appraisal. Based on a specific review of job function and a specific review of the supervisee's performance level, goals are established for achievement within a specific time frame. The statement of specific goals jointly arrived at is translated into behaviors. The goals and associated behaviors then form the basis for the evaluation at the end of the time-frame period. Management-by-Objectives and Goal Achievement Scaling Procedures lend themselves to results oriented evaluation.

"Competency based" approaches to social work curricula design and evaluation have increased interest in greater precision in evaluating educational growth and change. Such approaches argue for defining learning objectives in performance terms and learning outcomes in behavioral terms.

The above discussion reviews some of the approaches in formalizing an evaluation so that it results in a report. We might now ask what approaches agencies actually employ in making evaluations.

Wiehe (1980) obtained information from 196 voluntary social service agencies regarding their procedures for staff evaluation. The largest number of agencies (45 percent) used an essay form. This involved "Statements often in response to open-ended questions regarding the employees' good and bad points." Such descriptions of performance generally included statements of strengths and weaknesses and might include guidelines for improved performance. The second most widely used procedure was a rating scale (30 percent of the agencies). Twenty-three percent of the agencies used a "results oriented appraisal method as the primary evaluative technique."

In discussing the results of his study, the author comments that the limited use of a "results oriented approach" by social agencies is "rather surprising in the light of the emphasis in recent years on program evaluation which assumes the identification of measurable goals" (p. 6).

In studying evaluation procedures employed in field education programs in social work graduate programs, Kettner (1979) also found that a narrative format was used much more frequently than objective check lists. Only 27 percent of 35 schools studied "specified the use of learning contracts as a basic document . . . for evaluation purposes" (p. 55).

Sources of Information for Evaluation

In addition to knowing what to look for, which is spelled out in the criteria of the evaluation outlines, we have to know where to look in sampling worker performance. The supervisor needs to be able to obtain sufficient valid and reliable information representing the typical performance of the worker if she is to apply the criteria in making an assessment. The possible sources of information available to the supervisor regarding the worker's performance might include:

1. Supervisee's written records.
2. Supervisee's verbal reports of activity.
3. Tape recordings of supervisee-client (individual, group, or community) contacts.
4. Video tapes of supervisee-client contacts.
5. Observation of supervisee's performance via one-way screen.
6. Observation of supervisee in joint interviews.
7. Observation of supervisee's activity in group supervisory meetings.
8. Observation of supervisee's activity in staff meetings and/or joint professional conferences.
9. Client evaluations of supervisee's performance.
10. Supervisee's correspondence, reports, statistical forms, weekly schedule, daily action logs, monthly performance records, etc.

A study of the actual sources of information utilized by supervisors in formulating evaluations indicates high dependence on a very limited group of sources, principally the supervisee's written record material and the supervisee's verbal reports of activity.

Recorded material includes data regarding the worker's program efforts. Quantifiable productivity outputs such as the following are reviewed for evaluation: number of interviews conducted, children placed, applications processed, discharge plans completed, home visits made, contracts written, institutions licensed, foster home evaluated, group meeting held, number of collatorals contacted, etc.

Less frequently utilized, but of some importance, are correspondence, reports, and statistical forms, and worker activity in staff meetings and group supervisory meetings. Audio and video tape recordings, direct observation of the worker, and client evaluations are almost never utilized (Kadushin 1974).

The use of audio and video tapes and one-way-screen observation is discussed in detail in chapter 9, which is concerned with innovations in supervision. I might note here, however, that other human-service professions use such devices in supervision much more frequently, and there is beginning to be an acceptance of their use in social work as well.

In all of the above the worker himself, either alone or in interaction with the supervisor, generates the data which is utilized for evaluation. It must be conceded that supervisors "see" a worker's performance from just one vantage point. Others in different hierarchical relationships with the worker may see her differently because different aspects of the person's performance are manifested in the different relationships. Peers and clients may evoke different aspects of the worker's repertoire of behavorial responses. This argues for the fact that a more comprehensive appraisal of the worker's total performance would need to include the perceptions not only of the supervisors but of peers and clients as well.

While the clients' experience with the workers makes clients an important source of information about a worker's performance, it needs to be recognized that the client is not in a good position to evaluate the worker. The client is not knowledgable about agency job requirements, lacks a perspective on social work performance in general, and may find it difficult to be objective because of an intense personal relationship with the worker.

In one study, supervisor and supervisee evaluation ratings were significantly correlated with each other but both were at considerable variance with client ratings of the supervisee. Client ratings of performance were much more favorable (Bishop 1971). Nevertheless, there is growing acceptance of clients' reactions as a source of information regarding workers' performance. Client reaction has frequently been a productive source of information in program-evaluation research. Clients may provide equally valid information regarding their contacts with individual workers.

The research tends to indicate that peers make very accurate assessments of each other's performance. However, efforts by the supervisor to solicit information from peers for purposes of evaluation presents problems. Peers are in competition with each other and this may determine the nature of information selected for sharing. Peers "telling" on each other is apt to create morale problems within the peer group and there is a question of violation of each other's confidentiality.

Evaluation of Supervisors

While the supervisee is accountable to the supervisor, the supervisor in most agencies is not formally evaluated by anybody. There is frequently no evaluation of the supervisor's performance by agency administrators. While supervisors may be conscientious about self-evaluation and attempt to make efforts to modify performance accordingly, this may not be a sufficient incentive to effect change. Calutta and Seltzer (1977) instructed clinical speech therapist supervisors in the use of charting systems for their audiotaped supervisory conferences. Faced with a self-generated critique of their performance as a result of a charted analysis of their interaction, the supervisors became explicitly aware of some undesirable aspects of their supervision. Despite this, analysis of continuing supervisory sessions indicated that self-knowledge "per se of how a supervisory session is being conducted may not exert enough force to motivate change in supervisory behavior" (p. 526). Apparently additional incentive through external feedback and evaluation may be necessary. However Hegarty (1974) did find that supervisors did change as a result of feedback from supervisees about their supervisory performance.

Evaluation of supervisors presents more of a problem than evaluation of supervisees because supervisors produce fewer "products." There are no case records and fewer reports of one kind or another. The supervisee has the most intimate, detailed knowledge of the supervisor's performance. Consequently some efforts have been made to obtain evaluations of supervisors from their supervisees.

Some of the items included in such evaluations concern the relationship with the supervisee. The relationship measure might be in a semantic differential form:

Describe the response you think is characteristic of your supervisor's relationship to you.

Accepting	1_ 2_ 3_ 4_ 5_	Rejecting
Warm	1_ 2_ 3_ 4_ 5_	Cold
Cooperative	1_ 2_ 3_ 4_ 5_	Uncooperative

Sometimes it is in the nature of a scale soliciting different levels of agreement.

1. My supervisor recognizes and respects my autonomy.
   Strongly Agree__; Agree__; Undecided__; Disagree__; Strongly Disagree __.
2. My supervisor offers a supportive, open relationship which facilitates my learning needs.
   Strongly Agree__; Agree__; Undecided__; Disagree__; Strongly Disagree __.

Evaluations of supervisors by supervisees may be in the nature of a series of related statements. The supervisee is asked to choose the statement that best describes the supervisor's behavior.

__1. When conflict arises my supervisor tries to cut it off and win his(her) position.
__2. When conflict arises, my supervisor tries to identify reasons for it and to resolve underlying causes.
__3. When conflict arises, my supervisor tries to be fair but firm and to get an equitable solution.
__4. When conflict arises my supervisor tries to remain neutral or stay out of it.
__5. My supervisor tries to avoid generating conflict but when it does appear he(she) tries to soothe feelings and to keep people together.

It may be in the nature of a series of graded statements, the supervisee selecting the one most characteristic of the supervisor's performance.

My supervisor's attitude toward supervision is:
1. Enthusiastic—enjoys supervising
2. Very interested

   3. Somewhat interested
   4. Only routine interest displayed
   5. Uninterested

My supervisor's apparent knowledge of social work is:
   1. Very well informed
   2. Well informed
   3. Could be better informed
   4. Not well informed
   5. Gives misinformation

Sometimes evaluation items are in the nature of a scale indicating the level of consistency of behavior emitted by the supervisor. The scale uses terms like "Almost always," "Often," "Sometimes," "Rarely." Items include statements such as the following:

   1. My supervisor helps me gain a sense of achievement in my work.
   2. My supervisor gives me an opportunity to do challenging work.
   3. My supervisor is accessible when needed.
   4. My supervisor provides opportunities for me to suggest changes in agency policy.
   5. My supervisor treats me as though I could be easily replaced.
   6. My supervisor helps me conceptualize my client's situation.
   7. My supervisor confronts me with ineffective practice when this is appropriate.
   8. My supervisor helps me to assess my strengths and weaknesses.
   9. My supervisor encourages me to find my own style in helping clients.
   10. My supervisor provides direct suggestions and advice when this is appropriate.

The content areas of supervisor performance evaluations follow from the supervisor's functions. The supervisees are asked to evaluate the supervisor's adequacy with regard to:

   1. The clarity of communication
   2. Planning and assigning work
   3. Delegating authority and responsibility

4. Guiding and reviewing work
5. Coordinating and integrating work
6. Resolving technical problems
7. Ability to motivate workers
8. Inducting and integrating worker into agency
9. Instructional skills
10. Supportive interventions
11. Objectivity and comprehensiveness of evaluation

Some content areas are concerned with the supervisor's attitudes and behavior regarding the responsibilities of supervision. Supervisees are asked to rate the supervisor's availability when needed, his level of commitment to supervision, his willingness to extend himself to help supervisees, the consistency with which he implements promises to the supervisee.

Supervisees might be asked to indicate (1) the extent to which they regard the supervisor as a desirable professional role model and (2) whether they would choose this supervisor for themselves if they had the option of making a selection.

It might be of assistance to supervisors in examining their performance if supervisees were asked such questions as "What do you think are your supervisor's principal strengths?" "Principal weakness?" "What do you think your supervisor needs to work on?"

An evaluation of supervisors by agency administrators might ask such questions as (1) changes in the level of productivity of unit; (2) the unit's error rate; (3) number of complaints received from clients; (4) rate of unit staff turnover; (5) absentee and tardiness record of the unit; (6) relationships with other agencies; (7) interpretation of agency functions to the community; (8) ability to represent needs of her workers to administration; (9) capacity to communicate service effects of agency policies and procedures to administration.

Controversial Questions

There is some controversy about whether evaluation should be concerned with assessing the worker against objective, uniform standards or against the worker's own development. A profession accountable to the community and concerned with effective service to the client cannot, it seems to me, accept as legitimate an orientation toward evaluation which employs the worker's own development as the standard. Some minimal external requirements need to be met. Even if the worker is ten times more proficient today than yesterday, if he still does not meet minimum standards of acceptability we do the clients an injustice in retaining the worker on the job. We are concerned about individual development, but as measured against some general, established standard.

Earlier I mentioned the controversy around separating administrative and educational supervision. Some proponents for separation suggest that the administrative responsibility of evaluation be given to the supervisee's peers. Studies have shown that when peers are provided with the necessary information about a worker's performance their assessment of performance correlates very highly with evaluations of the same work made by the supervisor (Friesen and Dunning 1973). Under usual conditions, however, workers do not know enough about the work activity of their peers to make a reasoned judgment. Social work generally involves face-to-face activity between worker and client in privacy rather than any public performance open to observation by others. Studies of doctors in a clinic performing under analogous conditions indicated that they did not have enough knowledge of their peers' activity to judge their performance validly and reliably (Freidson and Rhea 1965).

Evaluation by peers would require sharing with each other all of the recordings, case reports, and statistical forms ordinarily used as a basis for evaluation. Even if such materials were shared with peers openly and willingly, the peers would still be denied the rich information that supervisors obtain from the conference-to-conference discussion of work activity. The limited availability of basic information needed for valid evaluation, and the time expenditure such a procedure would impose, make peer evaluation for educational purposes open to criticism. Peer evaluation as a basis for administrative decision would be open to even more serious question. Where peers are in competition for scarce resources (a merit raise, a promotion, a more desirable caseload), the burden of trying to be fair, honest, and objective in evaluating one's competitors is very great. Some additional difficulties of the relationship of peers to the evaluation process have been discussed above (p. 380).

The same problems regarding adequate knowledge of the worker's total performance would militate against assigning the responsibility for ongoing educational supervision to one person in the agency and responsibility for evaluation to another. Other aspects of this controversy are discussed in chapter 9.

Another problem relates to the antithetical functions of education and evaluation. We noted that the two principal objectives of a good evaluation are educational and administrative; evaluation is designed to further professional growth but also provides a basis for administrative decisions. Attempting to achieve both of these objectives in a single conference is likely to fail because the defensiveness generated by judgments operates against the openness required for learning. The suggestion is that these two objectives be separated. One evaluation conference would focus on professional development. Another evaluation conference, held at a different time, would focus on producing an evaluation report for administrative use (Meyer, Kay, and French 1965).

In essence, evaluation for admininistrative purposes is uncoupled from evaluation for developmental purposes.

There is a question about the reliability and validity of supervisors' judgements in evaluation. The supervisor is faced with a very difficult, albeit inescapable, task in evaluating. Unable to observe worker performance directly, denied access to a clearly defined finished product, employing imprecise criteria applied to activities which are difficult to measure, the supervisor is asked to formulate an evaluation that accurately reflects the reality of the worker's performance.

There is general agreement that standards for evaluation in social work have been vague, "pragmatic, observational and intuitive rather than precise, standardized and scientific" (Kagan 1963, p. 18). But they have not been totally unsophisticated, casual and without merit.

Some confirmation of the validity of a supervisor's assessments can be derived from the fact that such assessment shows significant correlation with scores achieved by workers on written tests developed from job analysis (Kleinman and Launsbury 1978; Cope 1982).

In an experiment conducted in 1955 under the sponsorship of the Council on Social Work Education (Lutz 1956), records of four casework interviews were sent to casework faculty of schools of social work throughout the country for independent assessments. Records of four group-work meetings were sent to group-work faculty. Faculty members were asked to evaluate the performance of the caseworker or group worker as reflected in the record on a seven-point scale from "definitely inadequate" to "definitely superior." A total of 143 responses were received. In three of the four casework records the consistency in judgments made was at a level of statistical significance ($p = .01$). This indicates that there was a considerable consensus regarding judgments. However, there were some supervisors who rated the same record "definitely inadequate" while others rated it "definitely superior." Consistency in rating all of the group-work records was stastically significant, and there was less variability in the ratings. There is therefore reason to believe that supervisors can achieve close agreement about the level of performance of a particular worker based on some generally accepted criteria.

Kagle (1979) asked 435 registered clinical social workers to evaluate the social worker's performance in two case analogues sent to them. One was a case of child neglect, the second of marital conflict. The Case Evaluation Form which the respondents were asked to use included criteria generally employed in evaluating social work practice. Findings indicated that "there was much disagreement among evaluators on case one. Overall less than 75 percent of the respondents agreed on thirty-nine of the fifty-four evaluation criteria . . . . Respondents failed to agree in twenty-nine of the fifty-four criteria" on case two (p. 294). The researcher concluded that "a case record is clearly insufficient information on which to base a valid judgement" of the worker's performance (p. 295).

Even if more adequate data were available to supervisors, some of the essential problems of evaluation would still persist. This is the conclusion of a study conducted by Liston, Yager, and Strauss (1981). They obtained videotapes of six psychiatric residents interacting with patients at midphase of psychodynamically oriented therapy. Using a previously validated schedule, the Psychotherapy Assessment Schedule, they asked thirteen Board certified psychiatrists, all experienced supervisors and clinicians, to evaluate the resident's performance based on the videotape. Interrater agreement was statistically better than chance. For practical purposes, however, it is noted that "the strength of interrater agreement was low on every case" (p. 1071). "Interrater agreement tends to be worse among ratings for those conditions or behaviors which are especially important to assess accurately. . . . The most difficult performance category for the raters to agree about was that of dealing with the specific skills of therapy" (p. 1072).

Chevron and Rounsaville (1983) arranged to have the work of nine psychotherapists evaluated by five different procedures:

1. Didactic examination
2. A composite global rating by faculty in the training program attended by the subject therapists
3. Therapists' self-ratings
4. Independent evaluators' ratings of videotaped psychotherapy sessions
5. Supervisor's traditional method of evaluation on the basis of the therapists' retrospective reports of therapy sessions

Results showed little agreement among assessments of the therapists' skills based on the different data sources. The most disconcerting finding was the lack of agreement between ratings based on review of videotaped sessions and those based on the supervisor's discussion of process material with the therapist.

Optimistically, however, only the supervisor's ratings were correlated with client outcomes, indicating that the supervisor's ratings had validity in terms of positive client change.

In explaining these confounding findings, the researchers note that supervisees typically reported on client behavior, client themes, and client progress in discussions with supervisors. Thus the most salient information focus in supervisory sessions may be associated with client variables. In contrast, in evaluating videotaping of therapy sessions, the focus of attention tends to be on the therapist's behavior and interventions. The tie between what is discussed with supervisors in conferences is closer to client outcome than is the link between the videotape focus of evaluation and outcome.

Evaluations require some consensual agreement on the part of the profession about what constitutes good practice. Explicit criteria might have been formulated and standards established. Supervisors may be willing and able to evaluate and yet there may be problems in providing the worker with a fair evaluation. Since there are many schools of thought about what is good practice, the supervision might hold one theoretical position regarding this and the supervisee an equally acceptable but quite different position. Because the supervisor is charged with making the evaluation his theoretical bias may determine the judgements made.

> Until data firmly establishes the superiority of a well defined set of procedures or interpretation for a given clinical problem, the very same behavior of a clinician may be rated appropriate or inappropriate depending on the point of view of the observer. . . . the behavior assessable only through the individual "filters" of a clinical supervisor. (Shriberg et al. 1975, p. 159)

The fact that supervisors employ their own theoretical biases in evaluating the work of supervisees is neatly illustrated in the responses of three different supervisors to the same segment of work by a counselor.

> This particular interview involved a beginning counselor and an exceedingly fluent and verbal high school senior who proceeded to monopolize the counseling hour so completely that the counselor actually said only two sentences, namely, "Would you tell me your reasons for coming to counseling," and "Our time is about up; would you like to make another appointment?" The three supervisors of varying theoretical positions proceeded to examine what should have been done in this particular interview, which perhaps in actuality was what *they* would have done under the circumstances. One of the supervisors, of a Freudian bent, asserted that he would have done exactly what the counselor in question had done; that is, permitted him to free associate as much as he pleased during this first interview without any direction or interruption. This supervisor felt the counselor had done a marvelous job. The second supervisor, of a more directive-clinical orientation, expresssed the opinion that, as he saw it, the counselor had done an atrocious job and indeed posed the question, "Who was doing the counseling?" He felt that the counselor should definitely have curtailed the client's excessive flow of verbiage and probed, analyzed, hypothesized, and clarified to a greater degree. The third supervisor took a somewhat middle-of-the-road position and felt that there were several opportune times for the councelor to reflect, clarify, and recapitulate, but praised the counselor's permissiveness and patience. (Demos 1964, p. 705)

The general difficulties in evaluation are compounded currently by rapid changes in social work responsibilities, procedures, and acceptable methodological approaches. For example, the psychoanalytically oriented supervisor has great difficulty in evaluating the work of the behavorially oriented supervisee. Accepting that "different" does not necessarily imply "better" or "worse," the super-visor is not in a position to evaluate work based on a much different basic orientation to the clients.

Recognizing and accepting the necessity for evaluation and the difficulties that reduce the likelihood of achieving a wholly satisfac-tory, reliable and valid evaluation, what can one say to supervisors faced with this responsibility? The task and concomitant authority are inherent in the position. To accept the position of supervisor involves acceptance of the task. In accepting the task one must also, unavoidably, accept the burden of guilt and anxiety associated with it. But this is a truth to which the supervisor is no stranger. The social worker offering service to the client accepts the burden of guilt and anxiety associated with implementing decisions that are frequently made on the basis of tenuous evidence and haz-ardous inference. Every decision of consequence to which one is a responsible party excites a keen and discomforting awareness of personal fallibility.

One might further say to supervisors that they should recognize and accept their humanity, that *all* evaluations have, inevitably, elements of subjectivity, that all are, in a measure, in error. But the supervisor, in immediate contact with the day-to-day work of the supervisee, is best informed about the work and best able to evalu-ate it. The measure of probable error in the supervisor's evaluation is less than the supervisee would be subjected to if evaluated by anyone else. And the systematic, conscientious effort at assess-ments by the supervisor, despite subjectivity and error, is "far kinder (and more accurate) than the commonly employed gossip by which professional judgements are circulated in the absence of a structure" (Ekstein and Wallerstein 1972, p. 291). If "true," com-pletely accurate, evaluations are not attainable, adequate and use-ful approximations are achieveable.

It must be recognized and accepted that, however fallible it may be, the best instrument currently available to make complex judg-ments, such as performance evaluations, is the trained, perceptive, informed mind of the supervisor.

"Subjective judgements are imprecise and run to danger of being distorted by biases and preferences. But they are broader, richer, more complex and, in the end, perhaps truer to reality than highly specific, narrowly defined, objective criteria" (Hayward 1979). More precise instruments are desirable but not yet devised. Currently, "the making of such assessments is as much an art to be cultivated as it is a science to be applied" (Green 1972, p. 54). Neither the community, the agency, the clients, nor the supervisee can legitamately ask for infallibility in evaluation. What they can ask for and expect is a "reasonable approximation to an estimate" (Reynolds 1942, p. 280). This most supervisors are capable of offering, while striving for infallibility.

Summary

An objective appraisal of the worker's total functioning on the job over a given period of time, in terms of clearly defined criteria reflecting agency standards, has value for the supervisee, supervisor, agency, and client. It is a responsibility of administrative supervision.

Supervisors dislike evaluating because they are reluctant to accentuate status differences, feel dubious about their entitlement and ability to evaluate, perceive evaluation as an indirect assessment of supervision, regard it as contradictory to the ethos of social work, and fear the strong negative affect which might be evoked.

Evaluation should be a continuous process that encourages active supervisee participation and input. It is based on defensible related criteria that are openly shared with the supervisee. It takes situational factors into consideration, is tentative and concerned with both strengths and weaknesses. It is enacted in the context of a positive relationship, and the supervisor is ready to accept an evaluation of his own performance.

Both supervisor and supervisee prepare for the evaluation conference by reviewing the work done during the evaluation period. The conference is concerned with a mutual sharing of the outcomes of the reviews, using the evaluation outline as the basis for discussion. The final evaluation is written and given to the worker.

A variety of performance evaluation outlines were presented. The worker's written and verbal reports of her work are the principal data used in assessing performance. Evaluations are most frequently used in motivating professional growth and making personnel decisions.

CHAPTER EIGHT
The Group Conference in Supervision

ALTHOUGH the individual conference is the most frequent context for supervision, it is not the only one. In a few agencies the group conference is the principal form of supervision. In many more agencies the group conference is used in addition to the individual conference.

A 1973 questionnaire study of some 1,500 supervisors and supervisees showed that the group conference was the principal context for supervision for about 15 percent of the respondents. For about 60 percent of the respondents the individual conference was the main context for supervision, supplemented by group conferences held once or twice a month. For about 25 percent of the respondents the individual conference was the sole context for supervision (Kadushin 1973). Group supervision was much more frequently a supplement to individual supervision than was individual supervision a supplement to group supervision.

Group supervision may be the preferred modality for the supervision of social workers involved in group work. Interactions in group supervision can be used for illustration and discussion of problems and approaches that might be employed in working with groups of clients. What happens in group supervision can be used to foster understanding of the interactions in client groups.

Definition

Group supervision is distinguishable from other procedures which employ a group setting to achieve agency administrative purposes. Staff meetings, in-service training sessions, agency institutes, seminars, and workshops all use the group setting as context for conducting agency business and for the purpose of educating staff. However, the term "group supervision" is here defined as the use of a group setting to implement the responsibilites of supervision. In group supervision the supervisor, given educational, administrative, and supportive responsibility for the activites of a specific number of workers, meets with them as a group to discharge these responsibilities. In group supervision the agency mandate to the supervisor is implemented in the group and through the group.

The supervisory conference group is a formed group. It is a structured group with a task and an agenda. Membership in the group is defined as a consequence of being a supervisee of a particular group leader-supervisor. These groups are organized under agency administrative auspices. They are formed with the expectation that certain objectives will be achieved; they have a designated place in the formal structure of the agency and have a designated leader in the unit supervisor.

This definition of group supervision solves some of the decisional problems regarding group formation. How large the group should be and whether it should be heterogeneous or homogeneous in composition are questions answered by the definition. The size of the group is determined by the number of supervisees for whom the supervisor has administrative responsibility, generally four or five. The supervisees assigned to any one supervisor probably have some similarity in education and training, but even more probably are concerned with similar problems and similar service. As a result, the group is likely to be homogeneous with regard to significant factors that determine group interests and concerns.

The fact that members of the group share concern about the same social problems and the same group of services suggests that they have high interaction potential. Sharing significant concerns, they have much to talk about, and much of what they have to talk about is mutually understandable. Since they are all social workers in the same agency, they share a common frame of reference. These factors make for considerable mutual predictability, enhancing group members' trust and confidence in each other.

The primary ultimate objective of group supervision is the same as the ultimate objective of all supervision: more effective and efficient service to agency clients. Unlike group therapy or sensitivity training groups, group supervision is not directed toward the personal development of the supervisee, personal problem-solving, or satisfaction derived from group activities and interaction.

While the group explicitly meets to work on job-related concerns, the group meetings may have social and therapeutic pay-offs for supervisees. But these, like the therapeutic effects of educational supervision that relate to self-awareness, are not the intent, objective, or obligation of group supervision.

An agency introducing group supervision as a substitute for, or a supplement to, individual supervision needs to prepare its workers for the change. This modification of supervision should be introduced only with the concurrence of staff, with whom the reasons for the change have been discussed. The specifics of how group supervision will operate should be clearly interpreted following the acceptance of the desirability of the change. There are distinct advantages and disadvantages to group supervision that can be made explicit.

Advantages of Group Supervision

One clear advantage of group supervision is economy of administrative time and effort. Administrative communications regarding standardized policies and procedures can be communicated once to all the supervisees in a unit. Matters that are of common concern can be most economically communicated to individuals as members of a group. Kaslow (1972) has confirmed the fact that there are financial savings to an agency that moves from individual supervision to group supervision, since the latter involves less expenditure of supervisory personnel's time. Group supervision is currently being recommended in redesigning supervision to lower costs in response to budget cuts.

Group conferences make possible the efficient utilization of a wider variety of teaching-learning experiences. A presentation by a specialist can be scheduled, a film can be shown, a tape recording can be played, a role-playing session can be organized, a panel presentation can be arranged. Such learning experiences are designed primarily for the group context.

Group supervision provides the opportunity for supervisees to share their experiences with similar problems encountered on the job and possible solutions which each has formulated in response. "All of us are smarter than any one of us." However similar the assignments, the aggregate of all the caseloads (which is the total pool for discussion in the group) provides a greater variety of experiences than is available in any one worker's caseload. Consequently the sources for learning are richer and more varied than in the individual conference. Different members of the group can further provide a greater variety of points of view for learning. "The right explanation of behavior (one's own!) yields to the possibility of multi-dimensional understanding. The one right treatment approach (one's own!) bears reexamination" (Judd, Kohn, and Shulman 1962, p. 102).

The sharing of relevant experiences in the group supervisory conference is illustrated in the following excerpt. This conference of psychiatric social workers in a mental hospital setting is concerned with "factors affecting casework movements with psychiatric patients." One supervisee, Mr. N, reported that his client

> had regressed since his admission to the hospital. The patient's wife had noticed this further withdrawal and had discussed with Mr. N her concern about this observation. Mr. N pointed out that he felt he had been able to help the patient's wife understand that regressions during psychotic episodes occurred frequently.
>
> Addressing the group, the supervisor pointed out that Mr. N had helped the relative to anticipate what so commonly happens during the course of mental illness and its treatment: that there were frequent vacillations in reality anchorage and in observable responses to treatment. The supervisor wondered if the others hadn't observed examples of these swings in their case assignments.
>
> Miss Delmar said she had a patient who had recently been taken off of ECT and had regressed immediately afterward. Mr. Drake explained that he had a case like Miss D's and also one like Mr. N's. So far, most of Miss Gleeson's patients had been responding very well to treatment; however, when discharge plans had been mobilized with one of her cases, the patient had regressed, showing worse symptoms than had been shown on admission to hospital. The reversal had been sudden.
>
> The group expressed its opinion that temporary regression at the time of discharge or termination is a common reaction among clients. (Abrahamson 1959, pp. 89–90)

Members of the group also act as a source of emotional support. Group members console, sympathize with, and praise each other during the course of group meetings. The group not only provides the opportunity for lateral teaching—peer to peer—but provides opportunitites of mutual aid of various kinds. This opportunity for a supervisee to share her knowledge and to give emotional support to peers is a gratifying, morale-building experience that reinforces a feeling of belonging to the group.

In the following passage, Cohen (1972) notes the mutually reinforcing aspects of interaction in group supervision—for better and for worse. The setting is a geriatric center and the supervisor is reporting.

> Vividly I can remember the day that the first client in the unit caseload had died. The [worker] rushed into my office, tears streaming down her face, sobbing "Mrs. H died and I wasn't there and I didn't know anything about it." Intuitively the three other [workers] in the unit came out of their offices and the four of them sat with me for the next hour as we talked about their own feelings about dying and death. Real comfort was derived for each of them, and for me too, as in a very poignant manner we lent support to each other.
>
> The reverse side of the coin of mutual support can be one [worker's] negativism or pessimism feeding into others. During a [group] meeting one [worker] began with "If this is what it's like to grow old who wants it. It's terrible." Whereupon each [worker] began to share the depressed, upset, gloomy feelings that had been accumulating. (p. 175)

Group supervision facilitates an attitude of mutuality among members of the unit which carries over into the interaction outside the group session (Joelson 1982). The opportunity for the sharing of common problems encountered on the job is, in itself, a therapeutically reassuring contribution to individual morale. In the interchange made possible through group supervision, a worker often becomes aware that his problems are not unique, that his failures and difficulties are not the result of his own particular ineptitude, that all the other workers seem to be equally disturbed by some clients and equally frustrated by some situations. The group context permits a living experience with the supportive technique of universalization. The worker is given a keen appreciation of the fact that these are "our problems" rather than "my problems." It decreases the tendency to personalize problems and increases the likelihood of objectifying them.

For some workers the group situation is the most comfortable learning environment. For some, the one-to-one tutorial conference is too intense a relationship. They need a more diffuse relationship with the supervisor to feel sufficiently comfortable to devote all their energies to learning; they need the give and take of the group interaction. It is easier for some workers to accept criticism, suggestions, and advice from peers than from parental surrogates such as the supervisor. For some supervisees, then, the group context has the advantage of meeting their idiosyncratic educational needs.

The group context provides the safety in numbers which individual supervisees may need in order to challenge the supervisor. In the highly personalized, isolated context of the individual conference, the supervisee may be afraid to articulate his questions and objections to what the supervisor is saying. "In the individual conference . . . there are only two opinions available and in case of disagreement the supervisor's opinion will usually prevail" (Pointer and Fishman 1968, p. 19). Given the support of potential allies, the supervisee may find the courage to present his differing opinions in the protected setting of the group conference.

Workers find it difficult to assess their comparative competence because they perform their tasks in private and discuss their performance in the privacy of the individual supervisory conference. Group supervision gives workers an opportunity to "see" the work of others and provides them with a basis for comparison. A worker can develop a clear sense of how he is doing as compared with other workers of comparable education and experience. Not only does the worker get a different perspective on his colleagues and their work through group supervision, he also gets a less threatening perspective of the supervisor. "The supervisor seems less the personalized judge, jury and evaluator as he is seen functioning in relation to the cases of others" (Judd, Kohn, and Shulman 1962, p. 102).

Through group conferences the individual supervisee develops a sense of belonging to a unit in the agency, a sense of group and professonal identity, of group cohesion. It is true that supervisees working in close proximity in a common enterprise develop some sense of solidarity through informal interaction. Group life is inevitable in any agency and is fostered by coffee breaks, lunching together, and working together on the job. The group supervisory conference supplements and reinforces what happens naturally and ensures that feelings of affiliation and commitment will, in fact, develop. Furthermore, formal group interaction in supervisory sessions feeds back to intensify and improve informal staff interaction outside these sessions.

The group conference provides the supervisor with the opportunity of observing the supervisee in a different kind of relationship. Individual conferences permit the supervisor to understand how a supervisee reacts in a dyadic relationship; the group conference shows the supervisee in action in a group. It provides the supervisor with an additional perspective of how the supervisee functions. As a consequence the supervisor may be in a better position to supervise the worker more effectively in the individual conference. This result is illustrated in the following vignette:

> Mrs. D is a kindly middle-aged worker who does a fine job with her clients but tends to overprotect the underdogs to the extent of denying them room for growth. Mr. L, her supervisor, has been unsuccessful in handling this with Mrs. D in individual supervision. In group supervision Mrs. D assumes the same role, becomes protector of Miss T, the soft-spoken new worker. With direct observation of this interaction, Mr. L is able to assess with Mrs. D how needful Miss T is of this protection, how Miss T might be allowed to try coping with criticism on her own at future meetings, perhaps even considering how needful Mrs. D is of this role. (S. Moore 1979, p. 19)

Group supervision permits an advantageous specialization of function. Any ongoing system, individual conference or group supervisory conference, requires the implementation of both expressive and instrumental roles. Some things need to be done to see that the system is kept operating harmoniously, and successfully completes its assigned task. In the individual conference the supervisor has to perform both roles, to see that the work gets done while maintaining a harmonious relationship between supervisor and supervisee. The instrumental demands may at times be antithetical to expressive needs. To insist that expectations be met, to confront in order to get the work done, conflicts with the need to comfort and reassure. The supervisor has to be simultaneously both the "good" and the "bad" parent.

Group supervision permits the separation of these sometimes conflicting role responsibilities. While the supervisor is communicating support to some member of the group, the group may communicate expectations. While the supervisor is acting to confront, members of the group may act to reassure. Because the group situation allows delegation of different functions to different people, the task of the supervisor is in some ways simplified. He can let the group carry the instrumental tasks, confronting, demanding, raising uncomfortable questions, while he devotes his attention to supportive interventions. At other times the supervisor can do the needling, counting on the group to be supportive.

It may be easier for the supervisor to achieve modification of a supervisee's behavior through the medium of the group conference than in an individual conference. If members of the peer group indicate, in the group discussions, an acceptance of the supervisor's point of view, the individual supervisee may be less resistive to change. Learning from peers with whom one feels identified can be easier than learning from a supervisor. Learning from peers is free of the feelings of dependency and authority that complicate learning from the supervisor. Taking advantage of these benefits of the group conference, the supervisor consciously uses them to influence workers toward desirable changes in their behavior.

Blau and Scott (1962) studied workers in a public welfare agency and found that the attitude of the group was a significant determinant of individual worker behavior (p. 101). Despite differences in commitment to the desirability of service to the client, those workers who were assigned to a group where a pro-client attitude was dominant were more likely to offer service than workers in an anti-service-oriented group.

As Moore (1971) notes, "Norms formulated in the group through peer interaction are more readily internalized by workers than are the standards handed down from the supervisor as an authority figure. Workers are more apt to incorporate peer-formulated standards into improved work performance (p. 5)." This process is illustrated in the following extract:

> Shortly after the group supervisory meeting opened, Mr. L, a caseworker, complained that the meetings were dealing with material that was "too elementary," and they should move on to getting more "advanced" help with their cases. The supervisor, Mr. W, had anticipated this complaint and was prepared to answer; but he kept silent a moment and his patience was soon rewarded when Mr. M and Miss C came to his defense, itemizing instances where the so-called elemen-

tary material helped them with clients. Further, they suggested that some of the problems workers were having (the shoe seemed to fit Mr. L) were because they ignored elementary techniques and wanted to be self-styled psychiatrists. The force of the remarks at this point was greatly enhanced by having come from workers rather than the supervisor. (Moore 1971, p. 5)

Just as the group conference permits the supervisor to observe the supervisee in a somewhat different set of relationships, it permits the supervisee to observe the supervisor under different conditions. This setting provides the supervisee with the opportunity for using the supervisor as a model in learning group-interaction skills. Through the individual conference the worker learns something about dyadic interaction; through group supervision the worker learns something about group interaction. With the growing acceptance of multimethod responsibilities for all workers, and the increasing use of group approaches by caseworkers, there is a clear advantage to learning about group interaction through group supervision.

Group supervision provides a gradual step toward independence from supervision. The movement is from dependence on the supervisor, to a lesser measure of dependence on peers, to autonomous self-dependence. Group supervision offers an effective medium for power sharing and power equalization between supervisors and supervisees. Consequently it can serve as a half-way house in the movement toward independent functioning (Weinberg 1960).

I have emphasized that the agency, and particularly the supervisory personnel, should move in the direction of actively encouraging the development of greater independence in functioning by all workers. For the worker who comes to the job with professional qualifications, such as a master's degree in social work, the move should be toward rapid and nearly total relinquishment of supervisory controls. For the worker who comes without any prior knowledge of social work, the tempo is less rapid and the relinquishment less total. The direction is the same for all workers, toward a decline in the amount and extent of supervision, although the rapidity with which the change is accomplished varies.

Group supervision requires active participation of the worker in lateral teaching of peers, by peers. Such sharing among colleagues emphasizes a greater measure of practice independence than is true for individual supervision. Not only does the supervisor share with supervisees responsibility for teaching in the group conference, the power of the supervisor is also shared. The supervisees have a greater measure of control and a greater responsibility for the initiative in the group conference. Even responsibility for evaluation is shared. What is evaluation in the individual conference becomes feedback from peers in the group conference. Hence, if at the beginning there is much individual supervision and only a limited amount of group supervision, the movement toward independent, responsible practice should see a change in this balance. Gradually there should be less individual supervision and a greater measure of group supervision. In line with this idea, some agencies have used group supervision in explicit recognition of its potential as a vehicle for fostering independence and autonomy from supervision. Judd, Kohn, and Shulman (1962) have reported on their agency's use of group supervision "in helping the worker achieve greater independence and thereby accelerate his professional development" (p. 96).

Disadvantages of Group Supervision

The great advantage of the individual conference is that teaching and learning can be explicitly individualized to meet the needs of a particular supervisee. The group conference has to be directed toward the general, common needs of all the supervisees and the special, particular needs of none. As a consequence, the interest in group activity may be highly variable for the individual supervisee. At one moment the group may be concerned with something of vital interest to a particular worker; a half-hour later the matter under discussion may be boring or repetitious and of no concern. The principal disadvantage of the group conference is that it cannot easily provide specific application of learning to the worker's own caseload.

If the supervisee can learn more easily in a group conference through identification with peers, unencumbered by feelings of dependency and hostility toward the authority of the supervisor, the group presents its own impediments to learning. The group situation stimulates sibling rivalry and peer competition. Each supervisee may be concerned that another will say the smart thing first, will get more of the attention, approval, and affection of the supervisor. Each may be anxious about how well he compares with others in the group.

This problem was noted by Apaka, Hirsch, and Kleidman (1967) in describing the introduction of group supervision in a hospital social-work department. "There was hostility and competitiveness among workers that previously had been concealed effectively. It became clear that the group process was potent in underscoring and bringing out all the previously underscored or unacknowledged subtleties of staff interrelationships" (p. 58).

It is more difficult to incorporate a new appointee into a supervisory group than to provide the same appointee with individual supervision. A group with any continuity develops a group identity, a pattern of interpersonal relationships, an allocation of roles, development of cliques and subgroups, a set of shared understandings. The newcomer, a stranger to all of this, threatens the established equilibrium and is apt to be resented. Group supervision thus imposes a particular problem for new appointees.

The individual conference forces the supervisee to come up with his own answers, his own decisions regarding the problem he faces. The group context permits the supervisee to abdicate such responsibility and to accept group solutions and decisions. He is forced to participate and respond in the individual conference; he can hide in the safety of numbers provided by the group.

If a group offers a larger pool of possible sources of insight and support, it also offers more sources of critical feedback. It is easier to expose your feelings to one supervisor in the privacy of an individual conference than to present somewhat inadequate work publicly to a group of four or five peers. If a worker is seeking and can accept critical feedback, the number of participants is an advantage of group supervision; if she is hesitant and anxious about critical feedback, it can be a disadvantage. There is a similar risk for the supervisor. The threat to self-esteem and narcissism from saying something stupid in front of a group is greater than the risk of a similar failure in the individual conference. Supervisory ineptitude is exposed simultaneously to many rather than to one.

Operating with confidence as a group leader requires more self-assurance than does successfully conducting an individual conference. The group context is more complex and demanding. The complexity of interaction increases geometrically as the number in the group increases arithmetically. Four times as many people makes a 16-fold increase in possibilities for interaction. In any group there are simultaneous interactions between (1) individual group members, (2) individual group members and the supervisor, (3) the group as a whole and individual members, (4) the group as a whole and the supervisor, (5) a subgroup and individual members of subgroups and the supervisor. There is therefore a greater diversity of informational cues and pressures to which the supervisor has to adjust and accommodate as compared with the less complex, more manageable, individual supervisory conference.

Communcation within a group risks a higher probability of failure than in the dyadic interaction. In the dyad the communicator can select his ideas and choose his words with regard for what may be specially required to ensure accurate reception by his one partner. In facing a group of people, each of whom requires a somewhat different approach to the idea, a somewhat different vocabulary for best understanding, the supervisor must compromise. He must select his message and his words so that they can be received with reasonable accuracy by all, but they may fail to meet the particular needs of any one.

An intervention that meets the needs of one person may at the same time create a problem for someone else. A complimentary comment to one member may seem like a rejecting comment to another member if the two are in intense rivalry for the supervisor's acceptance. On the other hand, the group context is an advantage as well. It permits the supervisor to indirectly target a comment to B while responding to A.

The safety of numbers which allows the supervisee to raise critical questions and comments also presents a danger that the peer group may organize against the supervisor in the group conference. The supervisor may feel more comfortable in the individual conference, where there is a greater likelihood that she can control the interaction. There is a greater threat to such control in the group situation. Consequently some supervisors might be uneasy about employing group supervision.

In group supervision the supervisor risks loss of control of the meeting. Stimulating, encouraging, and supporting more active participation by the group and granting a larger measure of responsibility for interaction to the group are acts of control by the supervisor. She consciously decides to encourage such activity because she feels that it is desirable. But the group may decide to do some things the supervisor does not feel are desirable. Having encouraged maximum participation and fuller responsibility for action on the part of the group, the supervisor may find that the group has taken the play out of her hands. In the individual conference, when something comparable to this occurs the supervisor can reassert control. In the group situation, she is outnumbered. Faced with the solidarity of a group in opposition to her, the supervisor may find it difficult to regain control of the situation. Because of the risk in sharing control of the supervisory conference with the group, the need for personal security on the part of the supervisor is greater.

Accepting the responsibility for group supervision requires additional learning and a reorientation of focus for many casework supervisors. They have to learn about, or at least refresh their knowledge of, group interaction, group dynamics, and the psychology of individual behavior in the group context. They have to move from an accustomed focus on the individual as the center of interest to perceiving the group entity as the center of concern. If a supervisor cannot successfully reorient her focus, she may find herself engaged in an individual supervisory conference in the presence of others. Her tendency might be to respond to a collection of individuals rather than to the group.

There is, of course, a need to focus simultaneously on both the individual and the group; each member is concerned with his own problems as well as group problems and may, in fact, be working on his individual problem by working on group problems. The worker has to travel the narrow path between aiding the group at the expense of any one member and aiding one member at the expense of the group. But the group is first among equals in priority for the supervisor's attention.

The situation for the interviewer is inevitably more difficult as a consequence of a need for a dual focus. The supervisor has to develop and maintain a relationship and a productive pattern of communication between himself and each supervisee. In addition, he has to develop and maintain relationships and communication patterns between each group member and all the others.

Competent leadership in the individual conference requires a knowledge and understanding of social work, the educational process, and individual behavior. Competent leadership of the group requires all of these plus a knowledge and understanding of group dynamics and group process. The fact that group supervision does require special competence for its effective implementation is a disadvantage that limits its use.

The more cohesive a group is, the more the individual member feels identified with the group, the greater are the felt pressures to conform to group thinking and group attitudes. This cohesion is both a strength and a weakness of group supervision. It operates as an advantage in influencing individual supervisees to accept agency procedures and professionally desirable approaches in interaction with clients. On the other hand, it tends to stifle individuality and creativity. Considerable strength and conviction are needed to express ideas and attitudes that run counter to those held by the group. Sometimes these atypical ideas may be valid and helpful to the group in more effectively implementing its tasks. The supervisor, as group leader, needs to act so as to preserve group cohesion but mitigate group tyranny. In achieving this aim, the supervisor supports the expression of atypical attitudes and ideas, is sensitive to a supervisee's ambivalence about expressing them, and establishes as a norm for group interaction the accepting encouragement of such contributions to group discussion.

Research on the Value of Group Supervision

The question of the advantages and disadvantages of group supervision has been the subject of some empirical research. Looking at the experience in supervision of 671 supervisees and 109 supervisors, Shulman (1982) found that group sessions were held on an average of twice a month and that "holding regularly scheduled group sessions correlated positively with a good working relationship" (p. 261) between supervisor and supervisee.

The University of Michigan School of Social Work conducted an experiment in which a sample of students assigned to a group supervision in fieldwork was compared with a sample of students assigned to individual supervision (Sales and Navarre 1970). Comparisons were made in terms of student satisfaction with mode of supervision, content of supervisory conferences, time expended in supervision, the general level and quality of participation in conferences, and evaluation of practice skills as the outcome of training. In general the experiment indicated that "students performed equally well under each mode of supervision when supervisors' ratings of student practice skills were compared." However, "field instructors using individual supervision spent substantially more time per student in supervisory activities than those who employed group supervision." Since both "modes of supervision result in equivalent overall student performance" and since the difference in time expended "unequivocally favors group supervision," "the time factor may become pivotal to a choice" (Sales and Navarre 1970, pp. 39–41).

In addition to the greater efficiency in time expended in group supervision, the study further confirms some of the other hypothesized advantages of the approach. "Students in group supervision felt greater freedom to communicate dissatisfaction with field instruction to their supervisors and greater freedom to differ with them about professional ideas"; "students in group supervision most liked the varying ideas, experiences, and cases made possible by this mode of supervision" (p. 40). On the other hand, confirming the individualizing advantage of individual supervision, "students in individual supervision most liked the specific help, the help in specific problem areas provided by this method" (p. 40).

An experiment that tested the two supervisory procedures in training counselors arrived at similar conclusions. The group of trainees were randomly assigned to individual supervision and group supervision. The data regarding training outcomes

> suggest that the individual method is not significantly different from the group method in producing some desirable outcomes. It is reasonable, therefore, to use group supervision at least as an adjunct to individual supervision until further research suggests that a different method is obviously superior. (Lanning 1971, p. 405)

Because both individual and group supervision provide special advantages and disadvantages, because both are more or less appropriate in response to different conditions and different needs, it is desirable to employ them as planned, complementary procedures.

Frequently the agenda for group conferences derives from recurrent problems discussed in individual conferences; frequently the group discussions are subsequently referred to in individual conferences on individual supervisee case situations. The flow is circular, from individual conferences to group conferences to individual conferences. Since the same supervisor is generally responsible for both the individual and group conferences, the two different procedures can have unity and continuity. The supervisor has the responsibility of determining how each approach can best be used to further the learning needs of individual supervisees.

> The decision as to what should be taught on an individual basis and what should be taught through the group must be based diagnostically on the educational needs of the learner. For example the staff member whose own personal deprivation in early childhood makes it difficult for him to accept placement of children away from their own homes will require considerable help and support in understanding how his own emotional experience influences the way he works with clients. For such a worker, learning would have to have an internal focus where, on a case-by-case basis, he could be helped to change his attitudes toward inadequate parents. The same staff member, however, could also profit from group consideration of this problem. He may discover, for example, that [other staff members] feel this way about such parents and that disapproving attitudes can stem from what is conceived to be a violation of our social values as well as from judgments growing out of individual developmental experiences. In a group the individual may get a different perspective which enables him to grapple more successfully with his own attitudes. This, in turn, may help him to feel less guilt as he works on the problem more introspecitvely in individual supervision. (Blackey 1957, pp. 62–63)

Group Supervision—Process

Many considerations to which we might call attention regarding the process of group supervision are not particular or unique to the group supervisory situation. They are generally true for any circumstance in which a group is used as the vehicle for achieving the desired objective. Consequently, social workers familiar with the different uses of groups in providing agency service already know much that is applicable to the use of the group in supervision. This is true not only for group-service social workers but for caseworkers who have employed group approaches in adoption, foster care, protective service, public assistance, corrections, and family therapy, and for community organizers who operate in a group context. Awareness of the procedures that are most productive, the recurrent problems in group interaction that are likely to be encountered, is applicable, with some adaptation, to the group supervisory situation. The objective in this section is to review some of these considerations, translating the generally applicable material to the special context of group supervision.

1. Group Setting

Physical arrangement is a determinant of group interaction and needs to be given careful attention by the supervisor in preparing for a group supervisory conference. A circle of chairs in a room of moderate dimensions for the size of the group is perhaps the most desirable arrangement. Too large a room makes the group feel insignificant and lost; too small a room may produce a cramped, uncomfortable feeling and may require too great a closeness and intimacy between members. A circular arrangement permits everybody to look at and talk to everybody else. Being able to look at, as well as listen to, everyone else permits easier perception of nonverbal communication messages. A circle, furthermore, has no identifiable status position, no front-of-group position. The supervisor can melt into the group by taking his place unobtrusively anywhere in the circle. While the circle does not entirely neutralize the supervisor's dominant status in the group, it helps to mute it somewhat. Freedom from competing noises and from interruptions are other components of desirable physical arrangement.

A schedule specifying the hour and day for meetings should be clearly established and adhered to with some regularity. It helps give the group continuity and becomes a necessary part of group structure. It shows respect for the workers' time and permits them to schedule other appointments in advance with assurance that there will not be a conflict. In general it might be good to avoid scheduling group supervisory meetings early in the afternoon. The lethargy that follows lunch tends to dampen group interaction.

While perhaps responsible for the initial series of meetings, the supervisor may subsequently delegate responsibility for calling and chairing the meeting to members of the group.

2. Purpose

The group meeting like the individual conference, needs to have a clearly defined purpose. Formed by the agency to achieve agency purposes, the group is not entirely free to determine its own purposes. Group and individual supervision have the same ultimate objectives, and group conferences are required to have purposive outcomes that further these objectives. A considerable amount of expensive agency-personnel time is invested in each group supervisory conference. A meeting of eight people for an hour and a half costs more than a day's pay for one worker. The supervisor consequently has some responsibility to attempt to direct the group interaction so that purposes congruent with the general objectives of supervision are selected and so that such purposes are more or less achieved.

Group members are also personally investing their own limited time and energy. If the group meeting serves no productive, useful purpose, they have every right to feel disappointed and resentful. In a study of social work students' reactions to group supervision, a major dissatisfaction was "time wasted in tedious, irrelevant discussions" (Sales and Navarre 1970, p. 40).

3. Leadership and Planning

In group supervision, group interaction is employed as a "method used toward a specified end and group supervisory discussions are bounded discussions," bounded by the objectives of supervision (Perlman 1950, p. 335). Consequently the supervisor in the group conference is a leader in the explicit sense of having "the authority and the obligation to guide and to direct and often to require. . . . He must take responsibility both for stimulating discussion and for controlling it; both for releasing the (supervisees') energies and for insistently directing them to the task for which they have been freed. He is responsible not only to promote movement but literally to 'steer the course' so that direction is not lost. He must not only keep the [group] going but help it to arrive" (ibid.).

However egalitarian his approach, the supervisor cannot entirely shed the mantle of group leadership. His status in the agency hierarchy and his position inevitably give him a special status in the social system of the group. This status is reinforced by his education and experience, which give him some special knowledge and skill that he is responsible for using, and is expected to use, in behalf of the group.

An egalitarian stance on the part of the supervisor ("I am just another member of the group"; "We are all the same here") is seen as false by some and as an abdication of responsibility by others. The very fact that the supervisor has the authority to define his position as not having authority is, in and of itself, proof of his authority.

Since the supervisor, as designated leader, has authority not from the group but from agency administration and is reponsible to agency administration for what the group does, the group is not a democratic group. The supervisor, in some instances, may have to determine what decision will be made, what procedures will need to be accepted by the group.

The group is not free to develop its own solutions but needs to recognize constraints imposed by agency budgets, legislative regulations, or agency policy. The supervisor has the responsibility of being knowledgeable about such constraints and sharing this knowledge with the group. Groups which formulate recommendations that cannot be implemented feel futile and discouraged.

Although leadership of the group is primarily the responsibility of the supervisor, it is not his responsibility alone. The group itself has considerable responsibility for the many decisions that relate to group purpose and functioning. The supervisor is here, as in the individual conference, only as the first among equals. Furthermore, it is clear that rigid, insistent adherence to an approach that emphasizes supervisory control is self-defeating and counterproductive. Supervisees can be required by the agency to attend group meetings, but there is no way to compel their participation. While physically present, supervisees can absent themselves psychologically and emotionally and hence defeat the purposes of group supervision. The purpose of the meeting and the nature of group interaction have to meet, in some measure, not only the needs of the agency but also the needs of the supervisees themselves.

The amount of leadership exercised by the supervisor should be the minimum necessary to assure that the group can do its job. As in the individual conference, the supervisor, as group leader, faces the dilemma of leading without imposing, directing without controlling, suggesting without dictating. Over a period of time in the history of the group, the supervisor should be progressively less active, and an increasing proportion of the initiative, responsibility, control, direction, and activity should pass over to the group itself. The supervisor has to be flexible and comfortable enough to share this responsibility. Some roles are most effectively enacted by a member of the group rather than the supervisor. Leadership is then diffused rather than focused in the supervisor.

If the supervisor is invested with the responsibility for defining and implementing, however tentatively, however gently, the aim and objectives of the group, adequate preparation for group meetings is mandatory. The supervisor has to have a clear idea of what she will propose for group consideration, however experimentally. She must decide the points that need to be raised for discussion, the content that needs to be communicated and taught. The supervisor needs to think out the answers to some of the more difficult questions that can be anticipated. She needs to clarify for herself which points will encounter greatest resistance and which may require repeated emphasis. In effect, she needs to imagine the general scenario of the meeting as it might, in actuality, unfold.

Some plan—flexible, subject to change and if necessary to abandonment—is desirable. Having an outline of how the group meeting is likely to go is, in itself, reassuring. However, a plan is advantageous only if used as a guide. If it becomes a crutch, the supervisor will resist deviating from it even when that appears necessary to follow the legitimate interests of the group, since she is psychologically dependent on it. The supervisor's preparation also involves bringing in the supporting books, pamphlets, articles, forms, and directives that are pertinent to the content of the meeting.

The general purpose of group supervision may be clear, but since it is often stated in a very global way the supervisor has to help translate it into specific, clearly identifiable objectives for each particular meeting. "Learning to offer more effective and efficient service" does not answer the question of what the group will actually do when it meets next Tuesday morning from 9:00 to 10:30. The supervisor, whose experience and perspective give her a clear idea of what supervisees need to know, to do, and to be, should be in a position to derive from the general purpose the topics for a series of meetings. However, while it would be helpful for the supervisor, as group leader, to propose specific topics for group meetings, it would be best if these were advanced tentatively as suggestions for consideration rather than as requirements for acceptance. The group itself may have suggestions for relevant and significant topics that have greater priority and interest for the members. However, achieving a shared purpose is not easy. Often the purpose that interests one subgroup is of little or no interest to others in the group. The objectives on which the supervisor is administratively required to focus may be accepted with reluctance or covert resistance.

A clearly stated purpose that has group understanding and acceptance is one of the best guarantees against overcontrol and overdirection of group activities by the supervisor. The group rather than the supervisor gives direction and meaning to group interaction, determines the relevance of contributions, and structures group activity. Knowing what to do and being motivated to do it permit the group to exercise self-direction.

Consideration needs to be given not only to the plan for a particular meeting but also to the way this meeting relates to the meeting that precedes and follows it. To what extent and in what ways does this specific meeting fit into some overall plan for group supervision?

Planning should include consideration of the most advantageous format for the kind of content with which the meeting is concerned. Sometimes a case presentation might be best, sometimes a movie, a role-playing session, or a panel presentation. Different kinds of presentation procedures involve different levels of participation, involvement, and preparation from different members of the group.

4. Content and Method

The content of group supervisory meetings includes matters of general concern to social workers in any agency—recording, interviewing, referral procedures, psychological tests, caseload management, worker-client interaction, use of consultation, and so on. Often it is specific to the clientele served by a particular agency—understanding the delinquent, the adoptive child, the patient with a terminal illness, the unmarried mother. Sometimes it is concerned with procedures, forms, and reports that are particular to a given agency, with communications to workers from administration, or with problems identified by workers which they are anxious to communicate to administration. It may also be concerned with the particular community in which the agency operates—community composition, community problems, agency resources in the community, and the nature of the relationship between this agency and other agencies.

Group supervision may, by deliberate choice, become individual supervision in a group setting. The group of supervisees might decide to conduct sessions in which the work of a particular member of the group is singled out for discussion. Rather than discussing matters that are of general concern, each meeting is devoted to the particular concerns of some individual member through case presentations.

On occasion, general agency situations determine agenda items: If the agency is concerned with formulating a budget, this might be the opportune time to discuss budgeting matters as they relate to the unit's operations; if a state case-audit is scheduled, it makes reviews of some related content relevant; if evaluations for unit members are scheduled for the immediate future, the evaluaton form and associated questions might be discussed. Agenda items for group meetings are frequently, and most desirably, derived from interests and problems recurrently identified in individual supervisory conferences as common to a number of different workers.

Traditionally, clinical case material is the most frequently used stimulus for group supervisory discussions. Such material vicariously replicates actual situations with which group members are grappling, making it vivid and interesting, and motivating group involvement. For most productive use, case material needs to be carefully selected and prepared. Its very richness permits all sorts of digressions that have little real yield. Consequently, selection of case material should be in line with clearly defined objectives of the group meeting. In preparing the material for distribution, the supervisor may profitably condense and paraphrase so as to sharpen the focus for teaching. Often a section of dramatic interaction may be excerpted from a longer case record for group discussion purposes.

Although case material by definition is concerned with some individual instance, the focus of the discussion cannot remain tied to the individual case situation if learning is to be generalized and transferred. At some point the group (and if not the group, the supervisor) needs to determine what the particular case situation offers for learning about such situations in general.

When a group member presents his own material for discussion, there are additional problems. The supervisor may work with the supervisee toward selecting a case for presentation that is likely to have greatest value for both the supervisee and the group. The supervisee may need help in preparing the case for group presentation; he may also need the supervisor's support in coping with the anxiety that case presentation arouses and help in clarifying what group reactions he is likely to encounter. Because this is a case situation in which the agency has ongoing contact, the presentation may run the risk of group supervision of the worker which parallels the individual supervisory conference in deciding on specific planning for the case. The more appropriate use of the case situation in the group context would, again, be a general focus that permits group members to apply learning from this case to situations in their own caseloads.

Role playing is a procedure often used in group conferences. It can be improvised readily and offers a dramatic episode for discussion. The outlines of the proposed role play have to be clearly presented to the group—what is the nature of the problem to be acted out, and who are the participants? Situations for role playing could include an application interview at a department of public welfare, a welfare rights advocate's meeting with an agency director, a rejection interview with an adoptive applicant, an interview with an unmarried mother struggling to decide whether to surrender a child, a first interview with a parolee after his return to the community, an interview with a daughter concerned about institutionalization for her aged mother. Beyond the definition of the situation and identification of participants, the approach of the worker can also be defined. The worker can be asked to play the role in Rogerian terms or behavioral terms, punitively or acceptingly.

Willingness to participate in role playing requires a considerable sense of security in the group. Particularly in early meetings, obtaining volunteers may be difficult. It is easier if initially the supervisor volunteers to play the worker—the more difficult role. Her playing the worker may inhibit spontaneous critical comment but this depends partially on the freedom to criticize which the supervisor communicates to the group. Using the role-playing names of the participants helps to depersonalize the discussion afterward. It is not "Mr. P" (the actual name of the supervisor whose work the group is discussing) but rather "Mr. Smith," the name the supervisor used in the role play.

The group can move into role playing through the use of brief playlets. In the midst of some discussion, the supervisor can suggest that, for the moment, she play the client they have been talking about. "As the client, I have just said to the worker, 'I got so mad and discouraged that I sometimes feel like I just want to get away and never see the kids again.' How would you, as a worker, respond to that? Let's play it for a minute." Frequent use of such role-playlets provides a good group introduction to role playing.

Role-play participation enables the workers to understand more clearly, through vicarious identification, how an assistance applicant, an unmarried mother, an adoptive parent, or a parolee feels about his situation. However, like a thematic apperception test, role playing permits and encourages self-revelation. Without realizing it, we tend to act ourselves and expose to the group some parts of ourselves that were previously hidden. Consequently, role playing makes participants vulnerable. The supervisor has to be sensitive to the need to protect participants from destructive criticism. There is also a possibility that a role-playing session which generates strong feelings may become a group therapy session.

Films and audio and video tapes are appropriately used as the basis for group discussions. Adequate preparation is invariably necessary. Showing a film without previewing it can often be disappointing and time wasting. The description in the film catalogue may be only remotely related to the film itself. Familiarity with the equipment and with the room used for showing is also necessary. Countless groups have been frustrated because an extension cord was not long enough to meet an outlet, because there were not blinds to darken the room, because nobody could thread the film correctly and it kept fluttering or the sound track was garbled.

Checking the equipment and the material to be used is equally important for audio and video tapes. Audio tapes are often difficult to understand, and the strain of listening to unclear, disembodied voices can leave the group without energy for discussion. If possible, written transcripts of the tapes should be made available to the group. They not only permit people to follow what is said but make subsequent discussion easier as people refer to the transcript in making a point.

5. Process in the Group Conference

Just as the supervisor has inducted supervisees into the social system of the individual conference and has interpreted the respective, differentiated responsibilities of supervisor and supervisee in that system, she similarly inducts supervisees into their role as members of the group supervisory conference. The nature of reciprocal group-membership role expectations and obligations should be clearly outlined. Supervisees are given to understand that they have some responsibility for preparing for the meetings, for reading any relevant material that is distributed in advance. They have responsibility for contributing to group interaction and keeping such contributions pertinent to the discussion; they have responsibility for listening to others with respect and attention and should refrain from making interventions that will create unproductive conflict and tension, and should help in dealing with such conflicts and tensions as do arise. They need to indicate respect for other members of the group, to display a willingness to accept them as resources for learning and demonstrate some commitment to help achieve group goals.

Early on in the group process the supervisor needs to make an explicit attempt to establish, with the group, some group norms. The norms, if accepted and repeatedly implemented, help to regulate the behavior of group members. Agreed upon norms of productive group supervision might include the following:

1. To allow everyone to have his say without undue interruption.
2. To listen carefully and attentively to what others are saying.
3. To respond to what others have said.
4. To keep one's contribution and response reasonably relevant to the focus of what is being discussed. Group membership re-

quires a measure of deindividuation, some setting aside of one's own preferences in order to maintain the integrity of the group.
5. To share material and experiences that might contribute to more effective professional practice.

Most of the principles of learning that are applicable to the individual conference are equally applicable to the group conference. As in the individual conference, the supervisor is responsible for establishing a context that facilitates learning.

The supervisor, as group leader, engages in many of the same kinds of behavior he manifests in individual conferences—asking questions, soliciting and supporting the expression of ideas, attitudes, and feelings, requesting amplification of supervisees' points of view, restating and clarifying supervisees' ideas and feelings, summarizing, recapitulating, enabling, expediting, facilitating, focusing and redirecting, resolving conflicts, making suggestions and offering information and advice, supporting and reassuring, while also challenging and communicating agency expectations. The supervisor, as group leader, raises the provocative suggestion, acts as devil's advocate, calls attention to what has been missed, stimulates productive conflict to enhance instruction, acts as a traffic cop to the interaction. She acts as catalyst, mentor, arbiter, and resource person.

The supervisor orchestrates the activities of the individuals who make up the group. She maximizes individual contributions, coordinates and synthesizes them, weaves them together into a pattern. "The discussion leader must be able to focus discussion so that, for all its diversity, it maintains an essential wholeness, a basic unity. . . . Periodically the discussion leader 'pulls together' related points of the discussion. If discussion is visualized as the spokes of a wheel radiating from the hub, the leader may be said to 'rim the wheel'" (Perlman 1950, p. 336).

Discussion, in and of itself, is not a particularly efficient procedure for learning, problem-solving, or decision-making. Discussion has been known to confuse and confound rather than to systematize and clarify thinking. As Towle (1954) said, discussion which is not focused through the direction of a leader and organized and reorganized through intermittent summarization can become a flight into purposeless activity—"activity which, in not attaining its aims, often breaks down into noisy fragments or sinks into silence. . . . For just as the client's unburdening will not necessarily reeducate or heal, just as the caseworker must direct him to talk to a purpose and help him focus and relate his production toward activity in the solution of his problem" (p. 359), so the supervisor as group leader must take some responsibility for purpose and focus of group discussion.

Groups, like individuals, resist the often difficult, unpleasant, uncomfortable tasks that need to be worked on if productive purposes are to be achieved. Groups manifest ambivalence and resistance by irrelevant digressions, unproductive silences, fruitless argumentation, and side conversations among subgroups. The supervisor has the responsibility of holding the group to its purpose, of stimulating and rewarding the kind of group interaction that will optimally help the group achieve its purpose.

At the same time the supervisor delays disclosure of her own views in order to prevent premature closure of discussion. Ultimately, of course, she is obligated to share them with the group, clearly and explicitly. But if, as in the individual conference, she indicated early in the discussion what she thought, this would act as a constraint on free exchange and would relieve supervisees of the stimulus and responsibility in finding their own answers. If challenged with "well what do *you* think?" the supervisor can legitimately say, "I'll be glad to share that with you later but at this point I think you all have some thoughts about this that we can profitably share with one another."

The pattern of informal group interaction which takes place in the agency outside the group meetings is brought into the group supervision meetings. Some people like each other, some dislike each other, some are indifferent to each other. Workers play out these feelings in the way they relate to each other during the total work time. The supervisor needs to be aware of these patterns of relationship and how they might influence subgroup formation and reactions to what a particular individual says in the group. A knowledge of individual needs and the pattern of informal interaction outside the group helps the supervisor identify the nature of "hidden agendas" that help explain otherwise inexplicable in-group behavior. The supervisor knows a great deal about the individuals who make up the group and actively uses this knowledge in evaluating and understanding group interaction.

As Shulman (1982) points out, however, a deviant member of the group can be of considerable assistance to the supervisor as a catalyst in getting difficult work done. Shulman illustrates this by detailing a group supervisory meeting concerned with discussion of "how to make do with less" because of agency cutbacks and "still maintain service." After the supervisor introduced the problem

> A few people asked some questions, there was some silence, then Lou made a suggestion for a minor cutback in his area. I said I thought that was a helpful start. Frank jumped in and said he thought the discussion was a waste of time. I was angry at his cutting off what I thought was a beginning at a hard job. I said: "I'm sorry you feel that way, Frank. It's not a very constructive attitude. I don't think you are being helpful, and I am sure the others in the department feel the same way". . . . Frank was quiet for the remainder of the discussion. (p. 239)

The supervisor's reaction made it difficult for other members of the group to express their strong feelings about the cutback. Recognizing this the supervisor at the next meeting used Frank's remark to reopen the discussion.

> "I began by saying . . . that when Frank said the discussion was a waste of time, I felt on the spot, so I put him off. I didn't admit how uncomfortable the whole idea of talking to you about the cuts had made me. I suspect many of you probably agreed with Frank. Is that true?"
>
> Lorraine said she thought across-the-board cuts were unfair. The fact is, many other departments had fat in them, we all knew it, and yet each department was being treated equally in the cuts. I was surprised by how strongly she said this, obviously very upset. (p. 240)

This was followed by similar expressions of dissatisfaction from other members of the group. Rather than planning on how to reformulate service delivery to accommodate the cuts, the group, as a result of this discussion of their feelings, planned on a meeting with the administrator to protest the cuts.

Each supervisee brings to the group meeting his own needs and anxieties, which eventually find expression in the way he behaves in the group. The supervisor has the problem of responding to individual behavior in a way that furthers the purposes of the group and at the same time meets the individual's needs. Often the best that can be achieved is some compromise between individual need and group need. Reconciliation of conflicting group and individual needs is sometimes impossible, and the supervisor, giving priority to group needs, may have to ignore or actually deny the satisfaction of individual need. The persistent disrupter who seeks to use the group for satisfaction of insatiable attention-getting needs may have to be suppressed; the time allotted to monopolizers of group discussion may have to be firmly limited; the cynical demolisher of group morale may have to be resolutely moderated; the consistently passive supervisee may need to be prodded out of his lethargy. To keep all the group interested and motivated the supervisor must, without guilt, limit his concern for any one person in the group. Needs of the group, as a group, have priority.

The supervisor's responsibility denies him the flexibility of accepting any contribution as subjectively correct for the person advancing it. If our claim to being a profession has substance, it means that we have established some procedures, practice principles, and approaches that are objectively more correct, more desirable, more efficacious than others. It is these responses that the supervisor is helping the group to learn and accept. Consequently some contributions from the group need to be challenged and rejected by the supervisor. Since the hurt of rejection in the presence of a group is sharper than in the individual conference, the supervisor has to be even more sensitive and compassionate here.

The group-supervision equivalent of "reject the sin but not the sinner" is to "reject the comment but not the commentator." The supervisor does this subtly and understandingly: "I see you have given this considerable thought but if we did it this way what negative consequences could result?" "It's easy to get confused about this. The point you are making is based on somewhat outmoded information. Actually the average assistance payment for a family of four is currently. . . ." "I know that what you say is a point of view held by many people, but studies relating to this show that. . . ." Sometimes the supervisor can accept part of the comment and by reinterpretation or change of emphasis convert it into an acceptable contribution. "It may be, as you say, that the social system rather than the client needs changing, but how can we help Mrs. F, for whom something has to be done this afternoon?"

It would be best, of course, if the group itself takes the responsibility for correcting, rejecting, or amending erroneous information and approaches that might do a disservice to the client. But the group is not always aware of what needs correcting, and the supervisor cannot abdicate her responsibility for this. Since members of the group are frequently on the same level in terms of education and experience, the nature of the error is not as readily evident to them. In addition, they identify as peers with other group members, and they are understandably reluctant to confront them. Reluctance to criticize also derives from hesitancy about creating friction in the group. Refraining from necessary criticism in order to maintain group harmony is one of the weaknesses of group supervision. Maintenance of a good group relationship may take precedence over the desirability of engaging in some difficult activities necessary for the optimum achievement of the group's objective. Expressive needs prevent fulfillment of instrumental tasks. Furthermore, because the supervisor has administrative responsibility for the work of every individual member of the group, there is hesitancy about intruding on her responsibility. Group members may feel limited responsibility to critique the work of a peer since this responsibility is formally invested in the individual supervisor-supervisee relationship.

For a number of different reasons, then, willingness to be openly critical develops slowly in most groups. In reporting on her own experience as a group supervisor, Smith notes that "for the first dozen sessions we were very supportive and encouraging towards the other participants, and few challenging or critical comments were made during the early reticent stage. Since then, workers have become more clear, direct and specific with their observations and thoughts" (Smith 1972, p. 15).

When necessary expressive functons—group maintenance functions—are not performed by members of the group, the supervisor performs them. She mediates between conflicting subgroups; she prevents, or tempers, scapegoating; she offers help and support to group members who are fearful or reticent about participating; she tries to influence the monopolizer to accept a more quiescent role. Good discussion leadership does not necessarily imply that everyone participates equally, only that everyone has the opportunity for equal participation.

The supervisor attempts to protect individual members from the hostile reaction of the group and protects the group from its own self-destructive, divisive tendencies. While protecting the weak from the assaults of the strong, the supervisor has to act in a non-condemning manner, redirecting or redefining the hostile intervention so that only the comment is rejected.

In implementing the expressive-system maintenance responsibilities, the supervisor is friendly, warm, encouraging and accepting in his interaction with the group, is sensitive to emerging feelings which may be disruptive to group interaction and moves to harmonize and resolve them, and exercises a gate-keeping function so that each member will have a safe opportunity to share her thoughts and feelings. The supervisor has to be ready to find compromises for serious disagreements and in doing so be able to distinguish disabling disagreements from helpful differences of opinion.

The supervisor is responsible for keeping the tension at a level of optimum group productivity, heightening it by stimulation and/or confrontation when necessary, reducing it by reassuring, encouraging, tension-releasing humor when it gets too high.

As in the individual conference the supervisor must seek to establish and maintain an emotional atmosphere that will foster the achievement of goals. He seeks to establish a climate that will enable people to learn freely, to consider freely all alternatives to a decision, to risk change, to communicate freely and openly. The kinds of relationships between supervisor and supervisee which are helpful in the conference are similarly helpful in the group meeting. The responses of the supervisor demonstrate to group members a model of tolerance, acceptance, and good patterns of communication. Research on the outcome of group experiences indicates that positive outcomes are associated with warm, caring group leaders who provide a cognitive framework for group interaction.

Task and group-maintenance problems are interrelated. The group that is effective in accomplishing its tasks is likely to have better morale and a greater sense of cohesion. A group that seems to accomplish little, that never gets anywhere, is more likely to encounter expressions of dissatisfaction and divisiveness. The supervisor who effectively aids the group in accomplishing acceptable objectives is also, at the same time, helping to develop more positive patterns of interaction among group members.

In ending the group supervisory meeting, the supervisor summarizes the main points covered in the meeting, relates them, if possible, to conclusions of previous meetings, and ties them in with the topic of the next meeting. Material for the next meeting is distributed, and the group is reminded of specific responsibilities previously contracted for by individual members for the next meeting. If such continuity has not been previously established, the leader needs to reserve a block of time before the end of the meeting for a firm decision on what the group will be doing the next time it meets.

Whereas the frequency of participation on the part of the supervisor decreases (as it should) as the group continues to meet, the nature of her interventions remains rather constant. Most often the supervisor's interventions are concerned with direct teaching, e.g., giving technical information about agency procedures; explaining agency policy; explaining social work theory, or questioning to stimulate further discussion, get clarification of thinking, elicit negative and positive feeling reactions, get further information from the group. In addition, interventions offer support to the group or to some individual member, clarify the nature and direction of group discussion, provide active leadership to the group (i.e., initiating and terminating group activity) and summarizing. See table 8.1.

Table 8.1 Activity of the Supervisor in 25 Consecutive Weekly Fieldwork Group-Supervisory Sessions

	Supervisor responses during:			
Activity	Weekly sessions no. 1–8	Weekly sessions no. 9–17	Weekly sessions no. 18–25	Total responses
Direct Teaching	21	26	12	59
Support	16	7	9	32
Helping to express negative feelings	2	0	0	2
Active leadership	24	7	8	39
Clarification and Mediation	10	6	7	23
Questioning	23	16	10	49
Total	96	62	46	204

Source: Adapted from Lawrence E. Cooper, Raymond C. Every, Alice L. Garvey, and Margaret E. Morris, "A Study of Group Supervision in a Field Work Placement," Master of Social Work group research project, Graduate School of Social Work, University of Washington, 1957, as reprinted by Abrahamson (1959, p. 56).

Illustration of Group Supervision

The following long extract is from the supervisor's report of a group supervisory meeting of a protective-service unit in a county public welfare agency. It illustrates some aspects of the process of group supervision. The group consists of the seven workers who are assigned to the unit. Five of them have a master's degree in social work. All have at least one year of experience in the unit. The group meetings, scheduled for one and a half hours every two weeks, supplement individual conferences held once a week. The supervisor is responsible for scheduling and conducting the meetings. The meetings are held in the agency conference room around a large, boat-shaped table. The first 30 to 40 minutes of this meeting were devoted to some general announcements followed by a discussion of techniques in helping abusive parents to make changes in their behavior.

> George had been, as usual, a rather inactive participant. I observed that he had taken some notes, had nodded his head in apparent agreement with others at different times and had leaned forward at other times in apparent interest in what was being said. However, he himself had contributed little to the discussion. At this point, however, his nonverbal activity seemed to increase in intensity. He crossed and uncrossed his legs, leaned forward and back in his chair, and rubbed the back of his neck. I interpreted this to suggest that he might respond to a direct invitation to participate so I chanced it and, taking advantage of a slight pause in the discussion, I said, "George, I wonder if you would care to share your reactions to what has been said?" I tried to make the invitation tentative and general so that he would not feel an obligation to respond to any particular point made in the discussion but could feel free to respond to anything that had been said. I attempted to make the tone of my invitation light rather than peremptory so as to suggest that it would be all right if he declined my invitation to participate. I tried to catch his eye as I said this, pausing a little after calling his name. He, however, kept looking at his notebook.
>
> There was a moment of silence which increased the pressure on George to respond. Having initiated the invitation out of a conviction that George, like any other member of the group, had an obligation to contribute his fair share to the discussion, I wasn't going to rescue George too early by breaking the silence without waiting a while. He shifted in his chair but continued to look down. He said, "Well," and then paused. Then, looking at the wall, avoiding eye contact with any member of the group, he started up again, saying, "I guess the whole

discussion kind of pisses me off. Here we are trying to figure out how to be nice and understanding and accepting of these lousy parents who crack skulls and belt a defenseless infant around. I say to hell with them. They had their chance to care for the kid adequately and they didn't. Out of protection to the kids we ought to petition the courts for termination [of parental rights] and place them. And then take legal action against the parents for abuse. That's the only way to discourage this sort of behavior and this is the way to protect other children from this sort of thing."

The more he talked, the more vehement he became. When he finished there was a kind of dead silence. I recognized that he had articulated a strongly felt, but often suppressed, attitude that was generally characterized as "unprofessional," a component of the protective social worker's ambivalence that was rarely openly expressed— at least in officially sponsored meetings (it is frequently said by one worker to another in informal contacts in the washroom, coffee breaks, etc.). Consequently, after a short pause, but not giving anybody else a real chance to respond, I said, "Well, there is something to what you say. It's understandable that social workers concerned with child abuse might get to feel this way. What do others in the group feel about this?"

I was deliberate in taking the initiative because I wanted to protect George from any direct criticism from others, which would be easy to do, because he was expressing an "unfashionable" opinion. Secondly, some members of the group might be threatened by what George had said because it was a feeling that they themselves were struggling to control and [they might be] prompted to attack him in an effort to protect their own equilibrium. Thirdly, I wanted to give official sanction to George's comments—not as a correct point of view but one which was acceptable for open discussion. Fourthly, I suspected that many in the group had hostile feelings toward abusive parents (you would have to be either pretty callous or pretty saintly not to, after some of the things we had all seen) and might welcome a chance to discuss it now that it was brought out in the open. Consequently, I was more directive than usual in taking the initiative here but did it consciously and deliberately for the reasons cited.

In saying what I said, to focus the discussion on the point of view raised, I tried to depersonalize it and universalize the comment. Not "What do you think about what George has said?" but "Social workers might feel this way. What do you think?" Having said what I said I sat back, physically withdrawing, my intent being to give the initiative back to the group and suggest that they were once again in control and responsible for the proceedings.

It didn't work. George's comment was too threatening or too tempting. Perhaps some felt that once they started expressing hostility to the abusive parents, they might not be able to control themselves. I really don't know what was operating internally in members of the group. I do know that nobody responded to what I had said and the continuing silence was growing more oppressive. Something needed to be done and I, as the one officially in charge of the group (the leader?), had the responsibility for doing it.

After a silence which seemed eternal (but was really only about 7–10 seconds) I intervened again. I was also pressured by the fact that I was conscious that George, for all the vehemence with which he had said what he had said, was now growing more and more uncomfortable about being responsible for getting us into this impasse—so I felt an obligation to protect him again. My intervention this time was designed to deliberately sanction negative feelings toward abusive parents and consequently to make acceptable the open expression of such feelings in the group.

Very briefly I told the group about a call I had made in response to a report about a baby crying continuously, apparently uncared for. The apartment was in a rundown rooming house, and the baby, in a crib, had apparently not been fed for some time. It was covered with sores and the diaper had not been changed for days. Feces and urine had dribbled down the child's legs and covered the bottom of the crib. In addition, the child's face was bruised as a result of a beating. The mother was lying on a bed in a drugged or drunken stupor. As I stood there taking in the situation I kept saying to myself openly but in a low voice, "You shit. You lousy bastard"—because that's the way I felt at the moment.

Having finished, I sat back again. I shared this with the group in giving further sanction to expression of negative feelings. Assuming that some in the group identified with me, openly sharing my own reactions might prompt a response.

I had, during the 7–10 second silence, briefly considered, and then rejected, an alternative intervention. I knew from our individual conference meetings that Sandra had strong negative feelings about abusive parents. I was tempted to use this knowledge and call on Sandra to share her feelings with the group. However, I felt that would be a breach of confidentiality which Sandra might resent. It might also make the others anxious about my use of any information they had confided in the individual conference.

An uneasy silence followed what I said and then Paul (bless him) said that as he thought about it this reminded him of his reaction with the "R" family. (Paul, 27, who did a 2-year stint with the Peace Corps in Guatemala, is the indigenous leader of the group.) Paul's comment started a general discussion which lasted for about 35 minutes during which I said nothing. The initiative and control remained with the group throughout. All I did was nod and "mmm-mmm" on occasion and in general indicated I was an active, interested, accepting listener.

Paul's comment, focused on his hostile feelings toward some parents, was followed by similar expressions of feeling by Ann, Cathy, Bill, and George again. As each one took the ball in turn, there was less hesitancy and stronger feelings expressed. The sense of group contagion was almost palpable. There was, particularly at first, a good deal of embarrassment, tension-relieving laughter—the kind one hears in middle-aged, middle-class groups when sex is discussed. Neither Lillian nor Ruth said anything, but they listened avidly and reacted, nonverbally, with approval to what was said. They really enjoyed hearing the group tear into abusive parents. It was clear (at least to me) that the effect was cathartic (and needed) by the group— and was not as likely to have happened in the individual conference where each member of the group reacted in isolation.

After a time, however, this expression of such previously suppressed feelings kind of ran its course. Once again, Paul initiated a change in direction of the group discussion. He said something to the effect that that's all well and good but how does that help the kids. Perhaps it was satisfying to feel punitive toward the parents, but we all knew that in most instances the courts would not terminate parental rights even if we petitioned for it and furthermore, in most instances, we would be abusing the child if we opted for removal and placement. He used the "R" case, once again, to discuss that fact that even though, sure, he felt hostile toward the parents, his job was to do what was best for the kid and even here he felt that preserving the home for the kid by helping the parents change was the best thing he could do to protect the child.

This changed the direction of the discussion. It returned to the earlier focus—how does one help the abusive parent to change, but with a difference. There was a conviction that this was a necessary and correct approach in helping the child and that, while hostility toward the parents was an understandable and acceptable reaction, it got us nowhere. We needed to control our feelings because if we all responded punitively toward the parents, this would get in our way in trying to establish a therapeutic relationship with them. If we were going to keep the child in the home by changing the parents, we would kill our chances by communicating hostility toward them.

Once again the discussion with regard to this question was pretty general and for the most part I stayed out of it completely. Members of the group used their own caseload (as did Paul with the "R" case) and their own experience to illustrate the futility of hostility toward parents if your aim was to help the child.

The meeting went about 10 minutes beyond scheduled time. At the official end-time the discussion was still pretty active so I let it run for a while. When it began to slow down and get somewhat repetitious I intervened to sum up and recapitulate. I rapidly reviewed the course the meeting had taken from general discussion on approaches in helping abusive parents to change, to a cathartic expression of hostility, to a discussion of the pragmatic need to control negative feelings if we were going to do our job effectively.

I was conscious of the need to do this rapidly (3–5 min.), because once the scheduled time is past some people stop listening and get restive ("overtime" is an imposition), others get anxious because they may have interviews scheduled. But I was also conscious of the need for closure and for a transition to the next meeting. Consequently I kept the group a moment longer and said that, while we had established a pragmatic reason for self-discipline of feelings, perhaps we could discuss what makes abusive parents act this way. Perhaps we could come to the desirability of self-discipline of hostile feelings through understanding. I threw in the old "to understand is to forgive," first in French (pandering a bit to my narcissism—a venal sin). I proposed that we think about this as the focus for our next group meeting, and if the group thought that this would be helpful to discuss, to let me know before next Tuesday (meetings are on Thursday afternoon).

The supervisor has acted consciously and deliberately to help the group move productively toward the achievement of some significant learning related to their work. Each intervention he makes is the result of a disciplined assessment of the needs of the group at that moment. The exercise of direction is not restrictive but tends to enhance group participation. The supervisor tries to limit his interventions to those necessary to expedite the work of the group, giving direction and control back to the group as soon as possible.

He shows a sensitivity to verbal and nonverbal reactions of individual members of the group as well as perceptiveness to the general climate of the group as a whole.

At every point the supervisor is faced with a series of possibilities. For instance, when the group was silent the supervisor might have chosen to focus on group dynamics or steer the discussion in a direction which developed greater group awareness of group-dynamics interaction: "I wonder what prompts the silence; perhaps it might be productive to discuss how each of us is feeling now." This would have encouraged a transition away from the question of dealing with abusive parents and it would have led to teaching regarding group process. By focusing group attention, by his interventions on one or another aspect of the situation, the supervisor can narrow, widen, or change the focus of discussion.

The "Effective" Supervisor

At various points in the text, reference has been made in passing to factors which characterize "good" supervision. Our objective at this point is to pull together and highlight these factors in a systematic way. The recapitulation is based on reviews of the supervision research literature, empirical studies of effective and ineffective supervision, studies of supervision associated with supervisees' positive and negative responses to supervisors, and studies which define the kind of supervision that has the highest possibility of achieving the objectives of supervision (Hansen and Warner 1971; Nash 1975; Mayer and Rosenblatt 1975; Hansen, Pound and Petro 1976; Herrick 1977; Thingpen 1979; Ford 1979; Blumberg 1980; Lambert 1980; Hansen, Robins and Grimes 1982; Shulman 1982; Kaplan 1983).

What Tolstoy said about families can be said about supervision. He noted that all happy families are happy in the same way but unhappy families are unhappy in many different ways. Ineffective supervision is not the neat obverse of "good," "effective" supervision. There are a limited number of ways to be a "good" supervisor; there are many more different ways to be an "ineffective" supervisor. But conspicuous violation of many of the characteristics of "good" supervision is a reasonably certain prescription for "ineffective" supervision.

The following listing presents a composite picture of the effective supervisor. The effective supervisor:

1. establishes full and free reciprocal communication with the supervisee in an atmosphere that not only permits but encourages the expression of authentic feeling;

2. projects an attitude of confidence and trust toward the supervisee, resulting in optimization of supervisee autonomy and discretion;

3. has a problem-solving orientation toward the work of the agency, based on consensus and cooperation derived from democratic participation rather than power-centered techniques;

4. values a consultative-leadership relationship in supervision rather than a subordinate-superordinate relationship;

5. establishes benign relationships with supervisees characterized by a sense of psychological safety—accepting, warm, empathic, respectful, interested, supportive, flexible, genuine;

6. displays technical professional competence in helping supervisees with their work as well as competence in interpersonal human relations with supervisees;

7. makes active efforts to integrate agency's need for production with the socio-emotional needs of the workers, balancing agency output objectives with worker's morale, making task demands with concern for employees, balancing instrumental tasks with expressive needs;

8. accepts, is comfortable with, and appropriately implements the administrative authority and power inherent in the position, in a nonauthoritarian manner; holds workers accountable for assigned work and sensitively but determinedly evaluates supervisee's practice; balances support and clear expectations of work in conformity with clearly defined performance standards;

9. provides clearly structured procedures and constructive feedback for workers in their relation to the agency and their clinical practice;

10. balances the agency's need for stability with need to change; and is ready to advocate for validated change;

11. communicates effectively up as well as down the hierarchical communication ladder, vigorously representing worker's messages for administration consideration;

12. is generally physically available as well as psychologically accessible and approachable;

13. is unobtrusive in her supervision, so that supervisees know that they are being supervised but are not consciously and

explicitly aware of this; availability without continuous presence is manifested;

14. actively prepares for conferences and group supervisory meetings; preparation involves review of knowledge of supervisees as well as knowledge of content;

15. is ready, willing, and able to share expertise, effectively teach her practice in a way which optimally facilitates learning; sharing involves readiness to engage in appropriate self-disclosure;

16. is comfortable in nondefensively considering negative feedback and countertransferance reaction and is tolerant of constructive criticism;

17. makes continuing efforts to learn and grow with changes in the field;

18. has a positive, forward-looking attitude toward social work and its mandate; displays a solidarity with and commitment to the profession; embodies the values of the profession in his behavior.

But the contribution of the effective supervisor to the supervisor-supervisee interaction is only one factor in the equation. A detailed analysis of 94 supervisory experiences based on structured interviews found that supervisees also made a contribution to the kind of relationship that developed. While supervisors were more or less inclined to be permissive or controlling, directive or nondirective, egalitarian or distant, accepting or disparaging, these tendencies were muted or intensified by the supervisees' own characteristic way of relating.

> In order for a supervisor to be collaborative, the supervisee must be someone he can collaborate with; [supervises] who have a collaborative approach to supervision themselves most probably elicit collaborative behavior from their supervisors. . . . In many cases a supervisor's coercive style may be the result of the [supervisee's] continually challenging or resisting his authority. . . . The exercise of coercive power is not necessarily attributable to the intrapsychic dynamics of the supervisor but may be the result of the supervisory interaction. (Nash 1975, p. 26)

Some supervisors were described by some supervisees as their most preferred supervisor while the same supervisor was described by others as their least preferred supervisor.

The configuration of effective and ineffective supervision which emerges is then in the nature of a generalization. This implies that an approach to supervision that mirrors the "good" supervisor configuration is more apt to lead to effective supervision. But like all generalizations, it suggests that this is not invariably the case. The complexity of bidirectional interaction between supervisee and supervisor precludes any such statement. A contingency model which takes into consideration the uniqueness of the relationship between these factors comes closer to the truth. It argues for a best-fit decision on the part of the individual supervisor in contact with a particular supervisee working in a particular agency offering service to a specific client in an idiosyncratic, problematic situation. But a generalization is useful. It suggests that among the myriad of possibilities, the relevant literature shows the approaches listed above should be given priority for consideration because the research indicates they have been shown to be effective for many supervisors in many instances.

Summary

Group supervision is the use of the group setting to implement the administrative, educational, and supportive functions of supervision. It is most frequently used as a supplement for, rather than a substitute for, individual supervision.

Among the advantages of the use of the group setting for supervision are: it ensures economical use of administrative time and effort; it ensures efficient utilization of a wider variety of teaching-learning experiences; it provides a forum for discussion of problems and experiences common to group members which not only aids in the formulation of possible solutions but also provides a wider variety of experiences to each worker; it provides emotional support; it provides an opportunity for the supervisees to share their own knowledge and give support to others; it aids in the maintenance of morale; it provides a comfortable learning environment, one that is potentially less threatening than the individual supervisory conference; it provides an opportunity for the supervisees to confront the supervisor with some degree of safety; it provides each worker with an opportunity to compare his work with that of the other supervisees; it gives the supervisees a chance to feel more involved with and a part of the agency as a whole; it provides the supervisor with the chance to see the supervisees in a different light; it allows the sharing of supervisory functions between the supervisor and the group; it facilitates modification of the supervisees' behavior through giving them a chance to learn from peers; it allows the supervisees to see the supervisor in a different light; and it permits the development of greater supervisee autonomy.

Among the disadvantages of the use of the group setting for supervision are: group-learning needs take precedence over individual learning needs; it fosters peer competition; the supervisee can abdicate responsibility for developing his own work-problem solutions; it threatens the loss of the supervisor's group control; group pressures to conform may stifle individual creativity; it demands considerable group-work skills from supervisors.

The basic principles of group process and dynamics and the general principles of learning are applicable to group supervision. The supervisor as group leader shares with the group the responsibility for stimulating and focusing group interaction.

CHAPTER NINE
Problems and Innovations

A T DIFFERENT points in the earlier chapters, I have alluded to persistent problems that confront supervisors in social work. Some relate to inadequacies in current procedures for supervision; some are more basic and relate to the desirability of, and the justification for, supervision per se. The first series of problems is primarily technological in nature; the second series deals with professional policy issues. The intent in this chapter is to pull together and make explicit the different sets of problems and to review the innovative methods and procedures that have been proposed to deal with them.

Observation of Performance

The supervisor faces a technical problem related to access to the supervisee's performance. If the supervisor is to be administratively accountable for the worker's performance and if she is to help the worker learn to perform his work more effectively, the supervisor needs to have clear knowledge of what the worker is doing. However, the supervisor most often cannot directly observe the worker's performance. This is particularly true in casework. The caseworker-client contact is a private performance, deliberately screened from public viewing. Concealment of what takes place in the physically isolated encounter is reinforced and justified by dictates of "good" practice and professional ethics. Protecting the privacy of the encounter guarantees the client his right to confidentiality and guards against the disturbances to the worker-client relationship which, it is thought, would result from intrusion of an observer. What Freud said of analysis is applied to the social work interview: "The dialogue which constitutes the analysis will permit of no audience; the process cannot be demonstrated."

Although most of the interview is private, some aspects may be open to supervisory observation if the performance takes place on agency grounds: meeting the client in the waiting room, accompanying her to the door on termination. The worker who contacts a client in the field is shielded from even this limited opportunity for supervisory observation.

The group worker's performance is more open to observation. Miller (1960) points out that "what goes on between the worker and the group is directly visible to many people"—to group members, to other workers, and to supervisors (p. 72). However, "observations of a worker's activity take place . . . on an informal, not a deliberatley planned, basis" (p. 75).

While the community worker's activities also seem to be open to observation, this openness is more apparent than real. As Brager and Specht (1973) note,

> Community organization practice is at once more visible and more private than casework. Although it takes place in the open forums of the community, where higher authorities may be present, this is usually only on ceremonial occasions. Surveillance of the workers' *informal* activities is another matter. The real business of community workers is less likely to occur within the physical domain of higher ranking participants than the activities of other workers. Thus the community worker has ample opportunity, if he wishes, to withhold or distort information. (p. 240)

Many of the community organizer's activities are highly informal and unstructured. "Whereas casework interviews can be scheduled and group workers conduct meetings on some scheduled basis, the activities of community workers defy regulation and schedule. Much time is absorbed with informal telephone conversations, attending meetings in which they may have no formal role, talking to other professionals and other difficult-to-specify activities" (Brager and Specht 1973, p. 242).

By far the most common source of information used by supervisors in learning about a worker's performance is the written case-record material supplemented by a verbal report prepared and presented by the supervisee (Kadushin 1974). Thus, in most instances, the supervisor "observes" the work of the supervisee at second hand, mediated through the supervisee's perception and recording of it. Discussing the supervision of psychiatric residents, Wolberg (1977) says:

A professional coach who sends his players out to complete a number of practice games with instructions on what to do and who asks them to provide him at intervals with a verbal description of how they had played and what they intend to do next would probably last no more than one season. Yet this is the way much of the teaching in psychotherapy is done. What is lacking is a systematic critique of actual performances as observed by peers or supervisors. (p. 37)

The traditional, and current, heavy dependence on record material and verbal reports for information regarding workers' performance necessitates some evaluation of these sources. Studies by social workers (Armstrong, Huffman, and Spain 1959; Wilkie 1963) as well as other professionals (Covner 1943; Froehlich 1958; Muslin et al. 1967) indicate that case records present a selective and often distorted view of worker performance.

Distortions in reporting are self-protective measures against the possibility of criticism and rejection by the supervisor. They are also an effort to obtain approval and approbation for work seemingly well done. It needs to be remembered that approval and criticism are intensified by inevitable transference elements in the relationship with the supervisor.

Comparisons of process recordings with tape recordings of the same contacts indicated that workers failed to hear and remember significant, recurrent patterns of interaction. Workers do not perceive and report important failings in their approach to the client. This omission is not necessarily intentional falsification of the record in order to make the worker look good, although that does happen. It is, rather, the result of selective perception in the service of the ego's attempt to maintain self-esteem. Fifty years ago Elon Moore (1934) wrote an article entitled "How Accurate Are Case Records?" The question, which he answered negatively, is still pertinent today. Supervision based on written records supplemented by verbal reports is supervision based on "retrospective reconstructions which are subject to serious distortions" on the part of the supervisee (Ward 1962, p. 1128). A supervisee writes candidly:

The tendency in writing process notes is to sort of gloss over things that you found embarrassing or that you found difficult. I think there are times when I've made super boo-boos that I've left out purposely. And my reason for leaving out super mistakes is that I don't feel like being embarrassed. And if I know it's a mistake, why do I have to present it to the supervisor? (Nash 1975, p. 67)

Seeking approval through selective reporting, another supervisee says:

> If I'm concerned about my supervisor writing down in his evaluation that I tend to ignore transference phenonema, then, even if I don't believe it, I'll make sure to include material that shows transference phenomena, because he happens to be interested in that. (Nash 1975, p. 68)

This difficulty regarding recording is sometimes viewed not as a hindrance but as an aid in educational supervision. The "process record may distort the actual events that transpire between therapist and patient but it will more faithfully record the way the therapist sees his experience and wishes to communicate it to the supervisor for the purpose of making particular use of supervision" (Ekstein and Wallerstein 1972, p. 276). The worker then reveals himself to the perceptive supervisor through the nature of his selective perception in the recording. "The assumption is that the supervisor's- insight and experience, especially when augmented by discussion with the worker, enable him to fill in the missing pieces" not available in the written record (Leader 1968, p. 288). While Hallowitz (1962) concedes that "all case records inevitably contain some distortions and fail to capture important subtleties in the feelings of the client and the worker," he goes on to say that "it is mainly in the supervisory conferences that these distortions are clarified and subtleties of feelings come to light." The skill of the supervisor in correcting distortion "is analogous to that employed by the worker in the clinical interview" (p. 291). The very omissions and distortions become the content for supervisory teaching and the source of supervisee learning about self. Distorted recording is a form of communication. The supervisor is required, in this view, to be perceptive enough to be aware of the nature of the deficiencies in the recording and to discuss these with the supervisee. The supervisor must also accurately extrapolate from the behavior of the supervisee in the supervisory conference to his likely behavior in the interview with the client. These are very difficult tasks, and it is questionable how often they are successfully accomplished. An empirical test of this indicates that the supervisor usually is not successful in ex post facto reconstruction of what actually took place between worker and client (Muslin et al. 1967).

Stein et al. (1975) compared the psychiatric evaluations of patients made under two conditions. In one condition the psychiatric resident described the patient in a supervisory conference and the supervisor completed an evaluation statement. In the second condition, supervisors directly observed the interview between the psychiatric resident and the same patient and on the basis of this observation completed an evaluation. "The results of the study supported the hypothesis that a supervisor who does not see the patient is handicapped in his evaluation of the patient's psychopathology (p. 267). . . . Indirect supervision results in decreased accuracy" (p. 268).

Differences between reports provided supervisors and the assessments of the situation by observers of the same interaction was again confirmed in a study of intake interviews (Spitzer et al. 1982).

Even if this were a valid procedure for educational supervision, it would be a hazard for evaluation. Valid evaluation requires that we know what the worker actually did, not what he thinks he did or what he says he did. If we apply what we know about human behavior to the supervisee reporting on his own performance, we recognize the inadequacies of such a procedure as a basis for either good teaching or valid evaluation. As a consequence of anxiety, self-defense, inattention, and ignorance of what he should look for, the worker is not aware of much that takes place in the encounter in which he is an active participant; some of what he is aware of he may fail to recall; if he is aware of it and does recall it, he may not report it. The comment by two supervisors of child-psychotherapy trainees is applicable to social workers:

> In supervision of child psychotherapists over the year the authors have become impressed with . . . the unexpected degree to which direct observation of the trainee's psychotherapeutic hours reveals important and often flagrant errors in the trainee's functioning—errors which are somehow missed during supervision which is not supplemented by direct observation. This seems to be the case despite the trainee's attempt to be as honest as possible in talking with his supervisors, his use of the most detailed and complete process notes or his attempt to associate freely about the case without looking at his notes. (Ables and Aug 1972, p. 340)

This clinical observation is confirmed in an empirical study by Muslin, Turnblad, and Meschel (1981). They systematically compared the actual interview material as recorded on videotape with an audiotape of the reports of these interviews to supervisors. The interviews were conducted by medical students during their psychiatric clerkship. They found that less than half of the material was actually reported to the supervisor and some degree of distortion was present in 54 percent of the interview reports. The four clinicians who independently studied the actual videotaped interviews and the reports to supervisors also made a judgment on the significance of the interview material that was not reported to supervisors. Forty-four percent of the material that the judges felt would "totally alter the evaluation" of the patient was omitted and 9 percent of such material was distorted. "These results indicate that to proceed in supervision *as if* [emphasis in original] an adequate data base were present is misleading" (p. 824; see also Wolfson and Sampson 1976).

Direct Observation

Sitting In

In response to these difficulties, various innovations have been proposed to give the supervisor more direct access to the worker's performance. The simplest procedure is direct observation of the interview, either by unobtrusively sitting in on the interview or through a one-way screen. The client's permission is needed, of course, for this and any other procedure that opens the client-worker contact to outside observation.

Kadushin (1956a,b; 1957) tested the feasibility of sitting in on an interview in both a family-service agency and a public-assistance agency. Very few clients objected to the introduction of an observer. Postinterview discussion with both the worker and the client, supplemented by some objective measures of interview contamination attributable to observation, indicated that an unobtrusive observer had little effect on the interview.

Schuster and his colleagues utilized this procedure in the supervision of psychiatric residents. "We decided on a simple direct approach to the matter. We decided to have the supervisor sit with each new patient and the resident, as a third party, relatively inactive and inconspicuous but present. . . . In very few instances did our presence seem to interfere significantly with either the resident or the patient" (Schuster, Sandt, and Thaler 1972, p. 155). Duncan (1963), Kohn (1971), and Leader (1968) have also reported on the successful use of direct observation of worker performance in supervision and training.

One-Way Mirrors

The one-way-vision screen permits observation without the risk, or necessity, of participation and minimizes the observer intrusion on the interview or group session (Fleischmann 1955). The supervisor can see and hear the interview without himself being seen or heard. Peer-group observation of the interview or group session is also possible. One-way viewing requires a special room, and it has its own hazards. Gruenberg, Liston, and Wayne (1969) note that "the physical setting of the one-way mirror arrangement has been less than conducive to continuous alertness in the supervisor. The darkened room is more often conducive to languor than attentiveness" (p. 96; see also Adler and Levy 1981).

Co-Therapy Supervision

The supervisor-observer, sitting in on an interview, can easily move to a new role, that of co-worker or co-therapist (Van Atta 1969a). Co-therapy has also been termed multiple therapy and, in group work, co-leadership. If supervision through co-therapy is offered, it is generally provided as a supplement to, rather than a substitute for, individual supervision.

One of the principal advantages of co-therapy is that the supervisor is, as an active participant in the supervisee's performance, in a position to witness first-hand the behavior of the supervisee. Having initiated co-therapy, a supervisor notes that he became immediately aware of a supervisee's problematic approach to the client—a problem that "had not been clear to me during the few months of traditional supervision we had had" (Rosenberg, Rubin, and Finzi 1968, p. 284). In analyzing the experience over a 6-month period of co-therapy between a supervising psychotherapist and students, Rosenberg, Rubin, and Finzi note that "the direct observation of the student did away with retrospective falsification in the student's traditional role in reporting his work to the supervisor" (p. 293).

Manifestations of countertransference are more open to the supervisor as he observes this first-hand. Co-therapy then makes more information and more valid information available to the supervisor. Consequently, it is an innovation that helps resolve the problem regarding the information needed by the supervisor for effective supervision.

During the co-therapy sesson, it is advisable for the supervisor to allow the supervisee to take primary responsibility for the interaction. The supervisor intervenes only when the supervisee is experiencing some difficulty, when the supervisee signals a request for intervention, or when the supervisor sees a clear opportunity of modeling behavior that she is anxious to teach.

Protected by the presence of the supervisor, the supervisee can venture to attempt interventions and procedures that he might have otherwise been hesitant to risk. The opportunity to model desirable social work behavior in the actual living worker-client context is a second principal advantage of co-therapy supervision.

As an active participant in co-therapy supervision the supervisee has "a first-hand opportunity to observe and participate in the work of a more experienced practitioner" and it provides "a means of ongoing supervision within the context of a directly shared situation" (Schlenoff and Busa 1981, p. 30).

The use of co-therapy for educational supervision does present a problem, however. Successful use of the co-therapy arrangements indicates that it works best with co-leadership of equal status, and co-therapy using a supervisor and supervisee violates this caveat. In attempting to equalize the inherently unequal relationship, the supervisor arranges the seating so the supervisee does not sit side-by-side, but assumes a position which gives her an independent identity. The supervisor encourages and supports active participation by the supervisee. There is conscious use of the pronoun "we" in reference to the co-therapist pair.

After initial contacts have been established, the supervisor may deliberately absent herself from an occasional session, reinforcing, if warranted, her communication of confidence in the supervisee's competence. Rather than always signaling the beginning and the end of the session, as the prerogative of seniority, the supervisor might share the initiation of these procedures with the supervisees. The use of these procedures tend to diminish, if not completely eradicate, the inequality in the supervisor-supervisee co-therapy relationship.

When the supervisor moves from passive observation of the worker's performance to active participation as a co-worker, conflicting roles may present a problem. The supervisor is simultaneously a co-worker and a teacher-observer-supervisor. Problems of control of the proceedings, initiative in making interventions, and clear acceptance of shared responsibility need to be worked out. In one report of supervisor-supervisee co-therapy responsibility for a group, the ending of the sessions illustrated this conflict. The end of the group meetings was "almost always initiated by the senior co-therapist nodding to the [psychiatric] resident co-therapist who then follow[ed] the senior therapist's initiative in standing up and leaving the room" (Anderson, Pine, and Mee-lee 1972, p. 193).

Productive use of co-therapy for purposes of supervision "requires a conscious effort by the supervisor to modify what tendency he might have to take over and be the expert and for the [supervisee] to resist a tendency to sit back and be an observer" (Siddall and Bosma 1976, p. 210).

Those reporting on the use of the co-therapy procedure in supervision cite the dangers of too direct imitation of the supervisor by the worker and the fact that the worker may feel unable to participate freely and equally in the interview (Rosen and Bartemeier 1967). The threat and consequent strain of a threatening-dominating co-leadership experience is graphically described by Waldman (1980). However, Ryan (1964), who has used this procedure in social work supervision, notes that while supervisees are cautious at first, playing "the part of a passive observer during most of the first interview," by the third interview they are "comfortable enough to become more active and from then on the process is well under way" (p. 473).

Co-therapy is threatening to the supervisor in that she is called upon actually to enact effective social work skills rather than talk about such skills. While a very skilled performance on the part of the supervisor provides the worker with a model for identification, it can be discouraging to the supervisee and he may be disheartened by a feeling that he can never achieve such a level of perfection. A poor performance on the part of the supervisor may help the supervisee go from a possibly idealized to a more realistic estimation of the supervisor's capabilities.

Co-therapy provides the supervisee not only with an opportunity for direct observation of the work of a skilled practitioner, but also with a stimulating basis for joint discussions. "The supervisory conference takes on new meaning as the [supervisor] evaluates for the [supervisee's] benefit not only the [supervisee's] performance, but also his own" (Ryan 1964, p. 473). The co-therapy experience is most productive if prepared for carefully and if followed, as soon as possible, by a joint discussion of the experience.

The fact that supervisor and supervisee share the experience enhances a feeling of mutuality and collaboration between the two. The fact that both are party to the same information directly experienced makes the subsequent supervisory discussion more stimulating.

As Bernard, Babineau, and Schwartz (1980) note, "Supervisory discussion immediately following co-therapy sessions has a lively quality and is often more productive than the traditional supervisory format because of the freshness of the data and the shared experience" (p. 141).

A modification of the co-therapy arrangement is alternate therapy. Supervisor and supervisee share the responsibility for service. For one session the supervisee meets with the individual client or group while the supervisor acts as an observer through a one-way mirror; the following session the responsibilities are reversed (Jarvis and Esty 1968). Although this pattern risks discontinuity in the worker-client relationship, client confusion and resentment, rivalry between supervisor and supervisee in the relationship with clients, and the clients' manipulation of one worker against the other, these difficulties did not seem to develop to any serious extent when the procedure was used.

Observation Via Tapes

Dependence on retrospective written and verbal reports of the worker-client interaction means that the experience as it actually occurred is lost forever. Similarly, direct interview observation and observation through a one-way screen leave no record for retrieval, study, and discussion. To meet this deficiency some attempts have been made to obtain movie recordings of interviews. The expense, technical difficulties, and delay in making the recording available have inhibited such efforts. Far more feasible, and hence more frequently used, are audio-tape records of interviews. They allow retrieval of the vocal-verbal components of interaction even if visual, nonverbal aspects are missing. The development of videotape has made possible the retrieval of both visual and aural cues.

As quality, convenience, ease of operation, and stability of performance of the available equipment increase, and as bulk and expense (beyond initial outlay) decrease, the use of such procedures is becoming widespread in human service professions generally, despite its current limited use in social work. The importance of such technical aids for supervision is that their use enables us to "reenact the unobservable."

Video taping is done through an unobtrusive port from an adjoining control room containing the equipment. The lens "sees" through a one-way mirror. The simplest procedure is to turn the equipment on at the beginning of the interaction and off at the end. However, in agencies with more elaborate equipment, additional cameras are used, and wide-angle shots, zoom closeups, superimpositions, and split-screen images are edited by personnel in the control room to determine what actually goes on the final tape. One of the disadvantages in the use of these procedures for supervision is that the supervisor has to develop some technical competence—the minimum requirement being a knowledge of how to turn the equipment on and off. Group meetings and conferences require special wide-angle cameras and omnidirectional or multiple microphones.

The client is informed in advance of the taping, and a signed release is obtained. The client also is given the option of specifying that the tape be erased after use in supervision. Videotaping through camera ports in the wall rather than inside the interview or conference room is designed primarily to reduce distraction, not to hide the fact of taping from the clients.

Video and audio taping provide considerable advantages for teaching and evaluation besides the more complete, reliable, and vivid information regarding the worker's performance. The availability of recordings "retrieves" the client for the supervisory conference.

The supervisor who knows the client only from the supervisee's written record and verbal reports may have difficulty in holding the client as the focus of attention of the conference. The client is a disembodied, dehumanized abstraction. Audio or video tape makes the client's presence immediate and vivid. This increases the certainty that the client is not "forgotten" during the supervisory conference, that clinical supervision remains truly triadic, including the supervisor, supervisee, and client.

Audio and video tapes allow the supervisor to discuss the client in a way which makes more vivid what he says to the supervisee. To be told is not as effective as to be shown. But to see for ourselves, which tapes make possible, is perhaps the most insightful method of learning (Hirsh and Freed 1970, p. 46). The supervisee, through tape replay, faces himself in his own performance rather than the supervisor's definition of him. One rather cocksure resident denied feeling much anxiety in the interview situation. On a replay of his videotape, however, he saw himself light cigarettes and eagerly puff away at them during several tense moments during the hour. In the discussion of his behavior, he was able to recall the tension and consider the possibilities of its origin (Hirsh and Freed 1970, p. 45).

The disjunction between a supervisee's mental image of his behavior and the actuality becomes undeniably clear on tape replay. One student said, "You get an idea of what you really look like and project to the [client] but often this is not what you intended" (Suess 1970, p. 275). The experience of self-discovery which follows video playback has been aptly described as "self-awkwardness." One worker said, "I discovered by watching the tape that I was too halting in my speech and that there was not enough continuity in what I was saying. Without videotape it might have taken months for a [supervisor] to convince me of this" (Benschoter, Eaton, and Smith 1965, p. 1160).

Tape playback involves confrontation with self, by self, not, as so often is the case, confrontation by reflection from others. "A therapist was shocked when she saw and heard herself making cumbersome and convoluted interpretations of such semantic complexity that *she* could barely understand them while later viewing the tape. However, months of reporting had given her supervisor the impression that her interventions were precise and articulate." Another "recognized while watching a tape that he gratuitously mumbled 'uh huh' throughout the session regardless of the patient's words" (Rubenstein and Hammond 1982, pp. 149–50).

Audio-visual playback permits considerable self-learning. It thus encourages the development of self-supervision and independence from supervision. The supervisee has the "opportunity of distinguishing between the model he has of his own behavior and the reality of his behavior" (Gruenberg, Liston, and Wayne 1969, p. 49). He has a chance for a second look at what he did, an opportunity to "integrate multi-level messages" he might have missed in the heat of the interaction. Playback provides a less pressured, more neutral opportunity to detect missed interventions or formulate what might have been more appropriate ones. As a supervisor said in pointing to the advantages for self-instruction in video tape, "Sometimes there is no need to point out a mistake. The tape speaks for itself" (Benschoter, Eaton, and Smith 1965, p. 1160).

As a participant-observer in the interview, group meeting, or conference, the supervisee can devote only part of his time and energy to self-observation and introspective self-analysis. He must devote most of his time and energy to focusing on client needs and client reactions. Furthermore, much of his behavior is beyond self-observation. He cannot see himself smile, grimace, arch his eyebrows, or frown. Retrieving the interaction on tape, the supervisee can give his undivided attention to the role of self-observer. Videotape comes close to implementing Robert Burns' wish "to see ourselves as others see us."

The supervisee can play the tape when he is more relaxed and less emotionally involved, and can therefore examine his behavior somewhat more objectively. At the same time, repeating his contact with the full imagery of the event as it took place tends to evoke some of the same feelings that he felt then. The tape allows the supervisee-observer to relive the experience with some of the associated affect.

Viewing themselves on videotape or listening to themselves on audio tape may be ego-supportive for supervisees. For many, their self-image is reinforced positively by what they see and hear. Supervisees said, in response to the playback experience, "I look better, sound better than I thought"; "I did better than I realized." Adjectives used to describe themselves, elicited after playback, were similar to, and as positive as, those elicited before playback (Walz and

Johnston 1963, p. 233). The direction of the limited change that had taken place was toward a more objective view of their performance. It was a humbling rather than a humiliating experience. Without supervisory intervention, but as a consequence of the playback alone, supervisees' perception of their work tended to become more congruent with the supervisor's perceptions (Walz and Johnston 1963, p. 235). Seeing oneself engaged in behaving competently, intervening in ways that are helpful, tends to reinforce such behavior. Replay not only helps correct errors, it helps to reinforce learning.

The nature of tape technology permits considerable flexibility in how it might be used in supervision. The opportunity for repeated replaying of the interactional event permits supervisor and supervisee to focus exclusively on a single aspect each time. At one time they can focus on the client; another time they can focus on the worker. The same one or two minutes of interaction can be played repeatedly to focus on worker-client interchange. Shutting off the sound on videotape permits exclusive concentration on nonverbal behavior; shutting off the visual image permits exclusive attention to verbal content.

Tapes do not diminish the desirability of supervision even though they do provide the supervisee with a rich opportunity for critical, retrospective self-examination of his work. Seeing and hearing this material in the presence of a supervisor who asks the right provocative questions and calls attention to what otherwise might be missed, provides the supervisee with greater opportunities for learning. The procedure has been institutionalized in counselor training by Norman Kagan and his associates (Kagan, Krathwohl, and Miller 1963) in what they term Interpersonal Process Recall (IPR). The supervisee watches a playback of his videotaped interview in the presence of a trained counselor. The counselor encourages the supervisee, through sensitive questioning, to describe the feelings he experienced during the interview, to translate body movements, to reconstruct the thinking that led him to do and say the particular things he did and said at specific points in the interview.

Self-defensive activity by the supervisee is just as probable in playback observation as during the interview itself. The use of tapes is optimally productive only when there is a supervisor available who can gently, but insistently, call attention to what the supervisee would rather not hear or see. Mark Twain once said that "you can't depend on your eyes when your imagination is out of focus." The supervisor, watching or listening to the tape alongside the supervisee, helps keep imagination in focus.

Video tapes are employed in group supervision as a stimulus for discussion. Chodoff (1972) played tapes of interviews in group supervisory meetings, stopping the tape at various points in an interview to elicit comments from supervisees as to how they would have handled the situation at that point if they were the interviewer and to speculate on what would happen next in the interview.

Supervisor evaluation feedback is likely to have greater effect under conditions of high visibility of worker performance. Any assessment is likely to be easily dismissed by the worker if she has little confidence in the supervisor's evaluation because of limited opportunity to observe performance. Taped material can be used in evaluation to demonstrate, or validate, patterns of changing performance over a period of time. An interview, or group session, taped at one point in time can be compared with a similar interview or group session taped several months or a year later.

Tapes can also be used, as records are currently, to induct new staff. A library of audio and video tapes can be developed which give the new worker a clear and vivid idea of the work the agency does.

There are some disadvantages, however, in the use of audio and video tapes. Conscious of the fact that their entire performance is being recorded, with no possibility of change or revision, the supervisees may be somewhat more guarded and less spontaneous in their behavior. They may tend to take more seriously La Rochefoucauld's maxim, "It is better to remain silent and be thought a fool, than to speak and remove all doubt."

The worker is more likely than the client to feel anxious, "since the therapist can feel himself being examined while the [client] sees himself as being helped" (Kornfeld and Kolb 1964, p. 457). For most supervisees, the gains from taping their performance appear to offset the risks. Itzin (1960) found that supervisees who taped their interviews for supervision were very much in favor of the procedure. They felt it introduced a desirable objectivity into supervision and helped them overcome evasions, distortions, and other defenses manifested in written reports of their work. One supervisee said, "I feel certain that the supervisor was able to pin down my problems quite early—and understood me much better than he could have had I been able to hide behind process recording" (p. 198). Another commented, "It gave [the supervisor] a much more accurate account of what went on during the interview. When reporting happenings we tend to flavor them with our own thoughts, feelings and needs. I fail to see how it could be otherwise. He knew what we were doing rather than what we said we were doing" (p. 198). One student said, "I can read a thousand books on theory but when I actually saw what was happening it was a great awakening" (Ryan 1969, p. 128).

One of the principal advantages of the use of tapes for supervision is, at the same time, one of its principal disadvantages. Audio and video tapes are complete and indiscriminate. The supervisor faces an embarrassment of riches and may be overwhelmed by the detail available. The problem is clearly exemplified by a detailed analysis of the first five minutes of a tape-recorded psychotherapeutic interview, which yielded a book of over 350 pages exclusively devoted to an analysis of what took place during this limited period (Pittenger, Hockett, and Danehy 1960). A video tape would, of course, have made available even more material; a similarly detailed analysis of the first five minutes of a video-taped interview would have resulted in a much larger book. Perhaps because enough is enough and beyond the point of satiation further additions have little significant incremental effect, some of the studies comparing audio-tape supervision with videotape supervison show audio tape, with more limited cues available, to be equally effective (English and Jelenevsky 1971). It is possible to avoid the danger of being overwhelmed, however, by selecting limited sections for viewing, judiciously sampling the interaction, and taking an "audio-visual biopsy."

The time involved in using the videotape for supervision can be reduced by asking the supervisee to select the points on the tape that he wants to discuss and identify the counter numbers where this interaction appears on the tape, giving this information to the supervisor in advance. Rather than reviewing the entire hour-long tape, the supervisor can merely spot-check and then focus on those interactions that the supervisee would like to discuss.

In response to the fact that listening to supervisee tapes is both time-consuming and possibly overwhelming, Hewer (1974) has devised a recording form as a supervisor ad. The form, adaptable for social work, provides the supervisor with a procedure for organizing his response in listening to tapes. The disadvantage of increased demand on supervisory time in "observing" through one or another of these devices is compensated for by the savings in time otherwise spent in reading records or listening to a lengthy rehashing of the worker-client contact.

An additional disadvantage of tapes for supervision is that, because of their specificity and concreteness, audio and videotape tends to focus attention on the manifest content of the interviews. There is so much of a manifest nature available for discussion that intrapersonal and interactional feeling elements may be slighted (Goldberg 1983).

Taping procedures present a possibly hazardous challenge to the supervisor. If the supervisor can observe the supervisee's performance through use of these procedures, the supervisee can likewise have access to the supervisor's performance. There is an implied invitation to have the supervisor conduct an interview or lead a group so that the supervisee can observe how it should be done. The supervisee who is dependent solely on hearing the supervisor talk about social work has to extrapolate from the supervisor's behavior in the conference how he might actually behave with clients. The role model available to the supervisee is largely imaginary. Direct observation of the supervisor in action would make available a more vivid, authentic, and realistic role model for emulation.

Videotaping of interviews by the supervisor with clients allows the worker to "see their teachers at work removed from the unrealistic vacuum of didactic pontification. In seeing their supervisor's sessions firsthand, warts and all, the [supervisees] not only see their supervisor's skills and learn from them but may also be given the chance to renounce the previous idealization of the supervisor" (Rubinstein and Hammond 1982, p. 159).

Supervisors as well as supervisees can profit from taping and reviewing their work. There is no reported use of such procedures in social work, but supervisors in education have tape-recorded their conferences for self-study. Goldhammer (1969) says:

> Procedurally the most useful device we have found for self-supervision is to tape-record supervision conferences and, along with whatever notes are taken in the process, to use such tapes as an object of

analysis (p. 274). . . . Although it is possible to perform a post mortem
without having tape-recorded the supervision, it is generally clear that
to do so is more difficult, less efficient and less trustworthy than with
the analysis of tapes. (p. 278)

There is a persistent question of the distortion of the worker-
client interaction resulting from the use of all observational procedures, and the threat to confidentiality. We inevitably face such
risks. The requirement that the interview be written up for supervisory discussion breaches confidentiality and is an intrusion on the
interview itself. The client's confidences are shared with the supervisor (and sometimes other staff) without his full knowledge and
permission. Note-taking to aid recall tends to have an intrusive
effect. For the supervisee the interview room is always inhabited by
the image of the supervisor. Often the supervisee says or does something in response to what the supervisor might say or feel about it
rather than in response to the needs of the client. What is done is
done for the benefit of the supervisor to whom the event will be
reported. Consequently, even the most benign, least contaminating
procedure has intrusive effects.

Reports by psychologists, psychiatrists, and social workers who
have used audio and video tape in recording individual or group
interviews are almost unanimous in testifying that no serious distortions of interaction had taken place. With considerable consistency, professionals state that very few clients object to the use of
these devices; that whatever inhibiting effects these devices have
on client communication are transient; that clients are less disturbed than the workers, who are anxious about exposing their
performance so openly to the evaluation of others; and that workers
take longer to adapt comfortably to this situation than do clients.

The subjective reports of those who have used audio or video tape
for service, research, and supervision are consistently supported by
systematic research on the effects of such procedures. Some years
ago Kogan (1950) found that the use of an audio tape recorder had
no significant intrusive effect on social casework interviews. Subsequent studies (Harper and Hudson 1952; Lamb and Mahl 1956;
Poling 1968; Roberts and Renzaglia 1965) confirm this conclusion.

That is not to say that such procedures have no effects. Any
change makes for some change. The important question is whether
the effects are significant, whether the intrusive consequences are
sufficiently deleterious to offset the clear advantages in the use of

tapes. The answer clearly seems to be that there are no serious deleterious effects.

The use of tapes cannot be careless or indiscriminate. There are some clients for whom the effects are greater than for others (Gelso 1972; Gelso and Tanney 1972; Van Atta 1969b), and particularly with paranoid clients these procedures would be contraindicated. Niland and co-workers (1971) have observed some of the inhibitory consequences of the use of tape recordings; they emphasize the need for sensitivity to the supervisee's "index of readiness" to utilize audio and video recording.

Supervision During the Interview

Even if the supervisor can observe the work of the supervisee more fully and directly, she is still denied the possibility of teaching at the moment when such intervention is likely to be most effective. Whether she sits in on the interview, observes through a one-way mirror, or listens to and sees the work of the supervisee on audio and video tape, her discussion of the worker's performance is retro- spective. It comes after the interview, at a point in time removed from the most intense affective involvement of the worker in the problem situation, when he might be most amenable to teaching. The advantages of immediacy and heightened receptivity to sugges- tion while under stress are lost. Consequently there have been a number of attempts to use modern technology to permit the super- visor to supervise while the worker is actually engaged in an inter- view.

The main thrust of live supervision is to move supervisory inter- action closer to where the action is taking place, to increase the immediacy and spontaneity of the supervisor's teaching. Live su- pervision also permits the supervisee to immediately test his ability to implement the supervisor's suggestions and to ascertain immedi- ately the client's response to suggested interventions. This sup- posedly has a potent impact on learning.

Bug-in-the-Ear

A miniaturized transmitter used by the supervisor and a receiving apparatus worn as a small, unobtrusive, lightweight, behind-the-ear hearing aid, allow the supervisor to communicate with the supervisee during the course of the interview or group meeting. Watching and listening behind a one-way mirror or through a video camera pickup, the supervisor can make suggestions which only the supervisee can hear. The communication is in the nature of a space-limited broadcast, and there are no wires impeding the movements of the supervisee.

Korner and Brown (1952) first reported the use of such a procedure over thirty years ago, calling it "the mechanical third ear." Ward (1960, 1962) and Boylston and Tuma (1972) have reported on the use of this device in psychiatric training in medical schools; Montalvo (1973) detailed use of a similar procedure in a child guidance clinic; and Levine and Tikler (1974) describe the use of the device in supervision of behavior modification clinicians.

By 1975, devices for such explicit purposes in supervision were being sold commercially and were electronically very sophisticated. One company that sells a variety of such instruments for "direct use in therapy and training" in psychiatry, psychology, social work, and counseling and guidance, advertises it as a "Bug-in-the-Ear—a private prompting device, an electronic aid in training." "The supervisor can point out errors in psychotherapeutic technique at the moment they are being committed and redirect the course of therapy into more productive channels. The trainee can immediately see the appropriateness of the supervisor's guidance and is not left to speculate about what really would have happened if he had done things differently" (Farrall Instrument Company n.d.). Appealing to the behaviorally oriented supervisor, the brochure claims that the "Bug-in-ther-Ear is a most excellent reinforcer. Worn unobtrusively by the individual whose behavior is to be modified, verbal reinforcements can be administered instantaneously whenever an appropriate behavior arises. Thus the reinforcement comes immediately following the desired behavior and therefore can be expected to be maximally effective."

For a beginning worker, such a device may help lower "his initial encounter anxiety, thus allowing him more freedom to focus on the patient's anxieties. The fact that a supervisor is immediately available provides significant support so that the therapist is able to be more relaxed, spontaneous, and communicative" (Boylston and Tuma 1972, p. 93).

In defense of directive intrusions by the supervisor during the therapy, Lowenstein and Reder (1982) state that for the beginning therapist, "There is a feeling of gratitude for the 'powerful voice' which offers generous help in moments of stagnation, perplexity, and chaos." They note further that the supervisor does or should know better than the supervisee and directivity is not antithetical to development of creativity since "it is only reasonable to expect that creativity will be developed *after* [emphasis in original] fundamental techniques are mastered" (p. 121).

The supervisor can call attention to nonverbal comunication which is often missed, to the latent meaning of communication to which the worker fails to respond, to significant areas for exploration that have been ignored. As Montalvo (1973) notes, "This arrangement assumes that you do not have to wait until the damage is done to attempt to repair events" (p. 345). Becoming aware of these considerations on the spot promotes immediate learning and helps to offer the client more effective service. Boylston and Tuma (1972) illustrate the use of the bug device. A nine-year-old was very late for his interview, and the therapist was annoyed and upset. When the boy came in,

> he was obviously anxious. He looked at the therapist and stated that the therapist looked different—his hair was "all messed up." Misunderstanding the communication, the therapist commented on his hair. When it was pointed out to the therapist (via the bug) that the boy recognized his more curt voice, the therapist was able to comment on the boy's fear that perhaps the therapist was angry at him for being late. The interpretation of the boy's fears of the therapist's anger led to the patient's being able to relax and promoted further psychotherapeutic intervention. (p. 94)

Such a procedure enables the supervisor to directly evaluate the supervisee's effectiveness in using supervision. It has an additional advantage for the supervisor, in that he is in a better position to deter possible legal action against himself by stopping the supervisee if there is any danger of harm to the client. The procedure combines client protection with enhancing the professional growth of the supervisees.

Clients rarely ask about the hearing aid, "maybe because the earpiece has achieved the status of eyeglasses, which are rarely looked upon with suspicion" (Korner and Brown 1952, p. 83). If a client asks, however, he is told frankly about the use of the device. There is nothing in the reports which suggests that use of the hearing aid has a deleterious effect as far as the client is concerned.

Korner and Brown (1952) report that students felt that "the third-ear experience was worthwhile—were appreciative of the help received through immediate supervision and agreed it was an excellent learning experience" (p. 84). Ward (1962) comments that "to our surprise we found this electronic device to be remarkably ego-syntonic. . . . During the past two years we have systematically surveyed student reaction to direct electronic preceptoring and find that about 80 percent of the students react favorably to it" (p. 1129). Levine and Tickler (1974) note that "many trainees made positive remarks about the use of such procedures," and that they "encountered only minor problems" with it (p. 184; see also McClure and Vriend [1976], and Tentoni and Robb [1977]). As Baum (1976) notes in describing the use of the bug-in-the-ear in training psychometerists, "The system permits the instructor to provide both corrective feedback and reinforcement at the moment it is likely to be most effective" (p. 310).

Such supervision permits "mid-course alteration of sessions gone awry" and correction of "therapist errors at the point at which they occurred." It makes available the "supervisor's support and skills to be used at the moment that they are most required—during the conduct of a session" (Liddle and Schwartz 1983, p. 488).

Certain dangers associated with the use of the device are clearly recognized. These include the possibility of confusing and disconcerting the worker by too frequent interventions, the possibility of addictive dependence on outside help, the possibility of interference with the worker's autonomy and his opportunity for developing his own individual style. To meet these disadvantages, the approach suggested by those who have used the device is for the supervisor to "broadcast" only during silences or when the worker is making notes; to limit such interventions to clearly important points in the interaction, when the worker is seriously in error or in difficulty; and to make suggestions that are phrased in general terms, "leaving the actual dialogue and action pattern" to the students. "Most trainees point to the fact that the real value for them lies in interpretations of general themes in the psychotherapy process rather than in specific interpretive remarks" (Boylston and Tuma 1972, p. 95).

Further, supervisor and supervisee might agree in advance that if the supervisor's interventions are at any point confusing or not helpful, the supervisee can take the bug out of the ear using some agreed-upon signal. In general, though, the bug-in-the-ear is the least intrusive of the direct supervisory approaches. Sometimes, for that very reason, messages from the supervisor can be ignored. Supervision that involves entering the actual space of the interview, or stopping the interview and supervising in person on the spot, is the most intrusive of the direct supervision procedures.

Live Supervision

The family therapy field has pioneered in radical departures in supervision. Basic elements in their approach involve (1) direct observation of the work of the supervisee either through a one-way mirror or sitting in on the interview with the supervisee and family; (2) directly intervening during the course of the interview, either through use of a device such as a bug-in-the-ear, a telephone contact with the supervisee, calling the supervisee out of the interview for a brief consultation or entering the interview space, or stopping the interview and discussing the interaction in the presence of the family. These procedures, involving supervisory guidance of the supervisee while he works, are discussed, explained, and defended in a series of articles edited by Whiffen and Byng-Hall (1982).

Given the fact that "family therapy has always been defined as a public event encouraging direct observation of the family therapist at work" (Breunlin and Cade 1981, p. 453), it may not be surprising that family therapy supervision has moved in the direction of increasing the supervisor's direct activity in, and responsibility for, the therapy session. Furthermore, supervision based on retrospective supervisee reports are more difficult in family therapy because the complexity of interaction increases the probability that the reports will have less validity.

In offering criteria for determining when personal contact with the supervisor is necessary and when a phone call will suffice, Berger and Damman (1982) say:

we find it helpful to call the therapist out of the room to talk with the supervisor when changes in strategy are proposed. . . . It is difficult for the therapist to comprehend a change in strategy while in the presence of the family. Once a joint strategy is developed, however, phone calls from the supervisor to the therapist suggesting changes in tactics (e.g., "Have the therapist persuade his wife to go along with" or "tell the family you must explain the tasks further") are very useful. (pp. 340–41)

Family therapy supervisors are less hesitant and less apologetic about being openly directive and acknowledge that such procedures clearly reflect the hierarchical nature and structure of their supervisor-supervisee relationship. Their comments might be peremptory instructions, telling the supervisee to do this or that: "Explore the parents, conflicts on discipline; confront father with his failure to respond to son; get mother to negotiate with daughter on homework; include grandmother in the discussion." More often their supervisory comments tend to be suggestive: "Think about——; if you have a chance——; see if you can——; it might help to try——." Or their comments may be supportive: "That was good; keep it up; fine intervention." Or suggestive: "Perhaps a short role play might help at this point."

Some family therapist supervisors not only share their instructions and suggestions to the supervisee openly with the family during the family therapy session itself, but further include the family in a postinterview supervisory conference with the supervisee. It is claimed that as a consequence the supervisee learns not only from the supervisor but also from the family's critique of the experience (Pegg and Manocchio 1982, p. 65).

Implementing live supervision requires development of new skills on the part of the supervisee. The supervisee needs to learn judicious, nondisruptive, "withdrawal"-skills etiquette, so he can feel comfortable in leaving the family to consult with the supervisor. The supervisee also has to learn skills in coping with the interruptions to therapy that come with communication via bug or telephone. These procedures increase the number of configurations which the supervisee has to monitor and to which he has to respond.

In addition to the family system interaction and the therapist-family system interaction, direct supervision further includes the supervisor-supervisee system interaction. These multiple inputs might overload the supervisee. Live supervision inputs from the supervisor tend to distract the supervisee's concentrated focus on family interaction, requiring a momentary digression in attention. And an overly active supervisor may abort the worker's initiative by making a suggestion that the supervisee might have formulated himself if given the time.

The supposition that direct supervision inevitably leads to the supervisee becoming dependent on the supervisor, merely parroting what has been suggested, is rejected by those who have experienced live supervision. One supervisee said:

> It meant a great deal to me. In a sense it was taking a risk. You do something you would never have done without someone suggesting it specifically. But now that you've done it, it's yours. Even though the words were suggested to me, I owned them—it was something I did. It's funny because you would think, theoretically, that I might negate the whole experience. I might say, I was just parroting her. But it had none of that at all. Somehow in the process of translating it, putting it into my own words, dealing with the family's reactions and mine, it gave me something very special. It gave me the ability to use it again, and relate that way. (McGoldrick 1982, p. 36)

Montalvo's (1973, p. 345) concern that the supervisee "may feel as if he is under remote control" may not be valid. Supervisees have testified to the value of these more direct interventive procedures for their professional growth and development (Gershenson and Cohen 1978).

There are some costs associated with live supervision. Like the use of tapes, live supervision requires a considerable investment of supervisory time. And since the supervisor has to be available for observation during the time the supervisee is conducting the session, scheduling may present a problem. Also, in the use of all of these procedures—video recorders, one-way mirrors, phones, "bugs," etc.—equipment availability is a perennial problem.

In evaluating their experience with various formats that might be used for supervising family therapists, Markowski and Cain (1983) note that "live supervision along with videotaping is the most beneficial format. Audiotaping is recommended only when either live supervision or videotaping is not possible. Discussion using case notes is the least helpful format" (p. 45).

Observing Worker Performance—a Recapitulation

Case-record material supplemented by the supervisee's verbal report has served a long and useful purpose in social work supervision despite its deficiencies. There is nothing to suggest that it should be discarded. There is much to indicate that it does require selective supplementation through more frequent use of the other procedures discussed in this chapter. Despite the availability and clear utility of such procedures in meeting some of the problems of supervision, social workers, by and large, have made very limited use of them. (Barth and Gambrill 1984)

In contrast, a study of clinical-psychology training conducted some 20 years ago reported that "use of some form of observing or recording devices in the supervision of interns seems to be a fairly standard procedure" (American Psychological Association 1954, p. 762). A questionnaire study indicated that 60 percent of the clinical-psychology internship programs responding used television as part of the training (Zimny et al. 1972).

Admittedly, the use of videotape does require large initial expense for an agency, consultation in the selection of equipment from the bewildering array available, and some technical knowledge in the use of the equipment. These considerations may act as deterrents. However, audio tape equipment of high quality requires little expense, minimal knowledge for use, is light and unobtrusive, and its use is familiar to most clients. Observation through one–way mirrors and through sitting in on an occasional interview requires even less imposition. There seems little justification for the neglect of these various methods for direct supervisory access to worker performance.

The Problem of Interminable Supervision

The innovative procedures I have been discussing are all intended to provide the supervisor with more open, more complete access to the worker's performance. Another series of innovations has been proposed in response to the serious controversy regarding the continued need for supervision of professionally competent workers. In 1950 the Census Bureau questioned the advisability of listing social work as a profession, "since its members apparently never arrived at a place where they were responsible and accountable for their own acts" (Stevens and Hutchinson 1956, p. 51). Kennedy and Keitner (1970) note that "there is no other profession where self-determination applies to the client and not the worker" (p. 51).

Arguments about autonomy derive more often from considerations regarding the professional status of social work than from the demands of direct service workers. The limitations on autonomy implied in a system of supervision is perceived as an insult to the professional status of social work. A worker says: "Supervision creates a poor image of social work in relation to other professions. As a mature, experienced, professional social worker, I am embarrassed to refer to someone as 'my supervisor.'"

The literature reverberates with charges that supervision "perpetuates dependency," "inhibits self-development," "violates the worker's right to autonomy," and "detracts from professional status." Reynolds, in 1936, complained of supervision as cultivating "perpetual childhood" in workers: "Much of the time, one must admit, supervision is a necessary evil and it becomes more evil as it becomes less necessary" (p. 103). Judd, Kohn, and Shulman (1962) write that, through supervision "workers are caught up in a stage of interminable dependency, . . . that the close, personalized relationship in individual supervision, characteristic of social work, contributes to infantilizing the worker" (p. 96).

The debate and suggestions for dealing with the problem has been going on for a long time. In *Social Diagnosis*, published in 1917, Mary Richmond gives suggestions for self-supervison by workers, outlining the kinds of questions that they might ask themselves about their work (pp. 449–53). And, in describing the process of supervision over fifty years ago, Williamson (1931) noted that the "degree of supervision over workers who are no longer new to the organization is likely to be in inverse ratio to their length of service and capacity. With an experienced case worker whose ability and judgment have been demonstrated, the relationship is often cooperative rather than supervisory" (p. 154).

Fifty years ago, social workers were arguing that "as soon as the worker has passed his probationary period, his internship, and is ready to assume full responsibility, he needs to be made independent in all matters of case work procedure and held fully account-able for the results he obtains in these cases" (C.D. 1938, p. 15). By the late 1960's the concern with the harmful personal consequences of prolonged supervision was reinforced by other, quite different considerations. The civil rights movement, women's liberation, gay activism, the student revolt, and the zeitgeist of the counterculture both reflect and support a general orientation that views encroach-ment on personal freedoms as progressively more suspect and un-acceptable. Supervision on the job—any job—has come under examination as part of this general change in ideological climate. The greater concern with "job conditions" in recent union contract negotiations includes a reevaluation of the justifications for super-visory controls.

Mandell (1973) notes that the "equality revolution," which tends toward a reduction in social distance between all professionals and clients, reinforces the already strong press toward an equalization of the supervisor-supervisee relationship. It had always been inap-propriate for a person aspiring to full professional status to have his autonomy limited by subordination to a supervisor. Now it is not only professionally inappropriate but also violates the tenets of egalitarian participatory democracy.

The discussion regarding autonomy and freedom from supervi-sion, previously debated with reference to the MSW worker, has received recent additional impetus with the legitimation of the Bachelor in Social Work as the first professional degree. Some stan-dard-setting documents indicate that the practice of such profes-sionals should be "under supervision" or "using social work supervision" or with supervision "readily and consistently avail-able." The need for supervision of such workers is, however, clearly rejected by others who regard this as an infringement on the auton-omy of the worker in his self-directing, self-responsible practice and a derogation of his competence.

Most of the assertions with regard to "interminable" supervision are perhaps just that—assertions based on limited evidence. Al-though there are early complaints about "interminable" supervi-sion, real concern does not appear to have developed until the early 1950's, when reports by Babcock (1951) and Schour (1951) indi-cated that some social workers were personally troubled about pro-longed supervision. Babcock, a psychiatrist, treated some 60 social workers, some of whom complained of dissatisfaction with unduly prolonged supervision.

Beyond this clinical material, there is little factual data available which would permit us to know how many social workers are supervised for how long, and whether supervison is, in fact, "interminable" for any sizable number of professionally trained workers. There are contrary complaints that trained social workers move into supervisory and administrative positions too soon after graduation, that it is atypical for a trained social worker to be employed in direct practice and supervised five years after graduation. Such claims (or boasts) are made even more frequently for the trained group worker and community organizer. The fact that most entry-level positions in supervision require only one or two years of post-master's-degree experience would imply that few professionally qualified practitioners are themselves supervised by the time they reach their sixth year of practice. Studies of the allocation of supervisor's time indicates that there is a relationship between an increasing shift from supervision to consultation and increasing levels of education and experience of workers (Shulman 1982, p. 24).

It is not altogether true that graduate social workers with practice experience are the only professionals who are supervised. Professionally accredited teachers, engineers, and nurses continue to be responsible to supervisory personnel after years of practice. A study of professionals in industry shows that "industrial laboratories tend not to grant autonomy to scientists regardless of their academic training until after they have proved themselves over a period of time" (Abrahamson 1967, p. 107). Furthermore, the highly independent professions of medicine and law are facing increasing supervision as more of their members find employment in organizational settings. The determining factor seems to be the complexity of the organizational context in which the professional is employed.

In the Daree case, involving a medical researcher who published 100 reports the bulk of which were faked, neither the peer review nor the journal referee system was sufficiently effective to guard against falsification. In retrospect the editor of the *New England Journal of Medicine*, which had published some of the reports, felt that "rather than relying in the self-policing system *closer supervision* and more contact among researchers is the best way to prevent and detect fraud" (*N.Y. Times,* June 14, 1983).

There is an additional point of controversy regarding the question of interminable supervision. At the same time that the contention is made that social workers are supervised too much and too long, there is the argument that social workers are unsupervised and have too much autonomy and discretion. While social workers, regarding themselves as professionals, have pressed for more autonomy, more discretion, and fewer administrative controls over their action, client advocates and civil libertarians, acting in defense of clients' rights, have been pressing for greater restrictions on worker discretion (Handler 1973, 1979; Grammer 1979; Shnit 1978).

There is limited information on the extent to which social work supervisors actually limit supervisee discretion regarding work decisions. A study of the actions taken by public welfare social workers regarding 35 different significant decisions indicated that more than two-thirds were made "independent of higher authority" (Kettner 1973). These ranged from deciding "which cases should have priority of attention," through "which cases should be closed or referred," to "whether or not to act as client's advocate with landlord, utility company, credit agency." The worker was free to engage in such activities as acting as client advocate or advising clients to use the Welfare Rights Organization as a resource. The decisions most commonly indicated as requiring higher approval focused on assignment of worker's time and money matters. In both instances, we are dealing with scarce, or limited, resources. Thus, prior supervisory approval was more often required regarding cases the worker might accept or refuse, setting up a group for clients with similar needs or problems, deciding which of the client's economic needs could be met, and whether or not to offer a service when an addtional cost to the agency was involved.

The overall conclusion of Kettner's (1973) research was that "while some policy clarification with regard to individual freedom to make decisions may be helpful, most public welfare employees seemed to agree that considerable leeway has already been delegated the worker in making decisions relating to work with clients" (p. 183).

Analyzing the foster care delivery system in California, Gambrill and Wiltse (1974) found

a wide discretionary component in worker behavior in relation to what decisions are made and on what basis; how workers organize their time, what they do within working time, and their pace of activity. The overall absence of organizational sanctions for desirable and undesirable worker behavior contributes to the maintenance of this discretionary component. The problem of too great a discretionary component is heightened by the impossibility of adequate supervision under the current system. (p. 18)

A majority of 97 social workers surveyed in a detailed study of job satisfaction among rural social workers indicated that the majority did not feel deprived of automony (Kim, Boo, and Wheeler 1979, p. 56). And, in studying over 200 supervisees in child welfare agencies, Shapiro (1976) asked about the "extent to which supervisors were involved in the [worker's] case decisions. The largest group of respondents (50 percent) felt that decisions were made jointly while 31 percent thought they made most decisions themselves. Only 19 percent felt that the supervisors were the real decision makers" (p. 138).

The detailed studies by Prottas (1979) and Lipsky (1980) of the actual decision-making procedures of "street-level bureaucrats"— their term for the direct service worker—confirms a picture of very considerable discretionary behavior on the part of such workers. Lipsky (1980) concluded that two characteristic interrelated aspects of the direct service position in the human service profession were the "relatively high degree of discretion and relative autonomy from organizational authority" (p. 13).

Reviewing the research regarding the balance betwen autonomy and control of direct service workers in public welfare agencies, Prottas (1979) notes that the research shows the "balance surprisingly tilted toward autonomy" (p. 286). They are not independent actors but they do have considerable independence of action (p. 287). "There is a surprisingly large degree of autonomy and self-direction displayed in the behavior" of the direct service worker (p. 388).

In his observation and interview study on the day-to-day activities of over 60 public welfare direct service workers, Prottas (1979) notes that the workers are successful in capturing the autonomy they need to "respond to a complex and unpredictable" situation (p. 7). While the amount of discretion formally allocated to the direct service public welfare worker is modest, the study indicated "that considerable discretion is in fact exercised" (p. 18). This had been noted previously by Handler (1973; 1979), who pointed to the considerable autonomy exercised by social workers in making day-to-day decisions.

A detailed study of the work of a public child welfare agency through participant observation and extended interviews with 40 workers over a two-year period led the researcher to conclude that the workers "were treated by and large as responsible professionals—accountable to their senior, but able to plan their time and priorities themselves" (Satyamurti 1981, p. 12).

In an English study of the practice of over 300 social workers the researchers report that "most social workers in our study chose how to work with clients in their caseload and when to close cases without either being required or choosing to have discussion with their seniors" (Parsloe and Stevenson 1975, p. 211). "The vast majority of workers interviewed . . . said that they were free to make their own decisions if they so wished, while at the same time acknowledging some agency constraints" (p. 80).

A national study of social work in England conducted under the auspices of the National Institute of Social Work found that "discretion already exists de facto in the hands of front-line social workers—some of our evidence indeed suggested that too much freedom is given to inexperienced social workers rather than too little" (Barclay Report 1982, p. 131).

These accounts of the nature of supervisory control and of worker autonomy differ from the general picture presented by the literature, which, most often, suggests limited worker autonomy in a controlling agency bureaucracy (Zischka and Fox 1983).

The charge of interminable supervision may be factually dubious and yet psychologically correct. This paradox results from the lack of any formalized procedure for termination of supervision. The physician is supervised for a prolonged period after graduation, but there is a clearly understood and accepted date of termination for the period of internship. The social work profession might well consider adopting a formal, institutionalized prodedure for termination of educational supervision after a given period.

Studies of attitudes of both supervisors and supervisees regarding this question indicate considerable agreement about the desirability of diminishing supervision with the worker's increasing competence. An NASW chaper study of opinions on supervision found "that most social workers believed supervision should change gradually and flexibly according to the needs of the person supervised, from a phase of direction and teaching to one of more permissive consultation." However, "not one suggested that supervisors should not have administrative responsibilities" (Cruser 1958, p. 25).

In a study of a random sample of some 400 supervisees, most of whom were professionally trained, 75 percent indicated that "as the worker develops professional competence, supervision should change to a consultation relationship to be used when and how the supervisee decides." Only 5 percent of the respondents felt that "supervision should continue on the same basis since professional development is a continuous process." Responses from 470 supervisors were almost identical (Kadushin 1974).

There have been cogent defenses of extended supervision (Eisenberg 1956a, b; Levy 1960). Eisenberg (1956a) points to the continuing supportive needs of the supervisee: "It would be an extraordinary worker who did not, at times, experience some burden and some guilt, some anger and some despair—even a mature and experienced practitioner [does] . . . . In all of this the supervisor stands as helper of the caseworker for the agency; the worker is not alone" (p. 49). The argument is also made that supervision of even the most experienced worker is necessary because help is always needed in objectifying the complex interpersonal relationships in which the worker is involved. However, others might note that while the availability of such objectivity and support is a functional necessity even for the most experienced worker, these can be made available through consultation initiated by the worker when he feels a need for assistance, rather than through supervision.

We might see continuing supervision not as a training device but as a procedure to help the worker to continue to improve and upgrade his practice. This is a professional obligation which has no termination. Even the skill of the most advanced practitioners can stand improvement. Such a perspective justifies continuation of supervision. Even the most renowned concert pianists continue to practice and profit from critical feedback. We all are in the process of becoming; none of us have ever fully arrived.

There is some disagreement about the time needed to achieve freedom from supervision and what aspects of supervision might need to continue to operate. Despite efforts to clarify the criteria of readiness for worker emancipation from supervision (Henry 1955; Lindenberg 1957), they are still very ambiguous. Time in practice is often given as a criterion, but the recommendations vary from one year in practice following graduation from a school of social work (Stevens and Hutchinson 1956, p. 52) to three years (Leader 1957, p. 464) to "four to six years" (Hollis 1964, p. 272).

Wax (1963) reports on one agency's use of "time limited" supervision for master's-degree social workers, permitting them to move toward independent practice within a period of two years in the agency. Supervision is followed by formal and informal peer consultation, and "social pressure from the colleague group replaces the pressure of the parent surrogate supervisor" (p. 41).

In one highly professionalized agency, the procedure in 1982 was to have "regularly scheduled supervision" with new staff members "until the worker and supervisor agree that it was no longer needed. Generally this is six months to one year after hiring. Supervision in group continues beyond this" (Dublin 1982, p. 234).

The National Association of Social Workers statement on *Standards for the Classification of Social Work Practice* (Washington, D.C., NASW, 1981) requires "at least two years of post master's experience under appropriate professional supervision" (p. 9) before achieving the level of Independent Professional Practice.

Others regard time in practice to be an artificial criterion that denies differences in the tempo at which workers move toward readiness for independent practice.

The principal dissatisfaction with continued supervision seems to lie with prolonging educational supervision. Continuing obligatory educational supervision suggests that the worker does not know enough, is not fully competent, is incapable of autonomous practice. As Toren (1972) says, "trained social workers are willing to concede administrative authority to their supervisors as part of the limitations imposed by the organizational framework; however, they resent and resist the teaching function of the supervisor which they perceive as encroaching upon their professional judgment, responsibility and competence" (p. 79).

In contrast to the opposition to prolonged educational supervision, there is a readier acceptance of the necessity for continued administrative supervision. One of the earliest advocates of freedom from supervision believed that since social workers "work in agencies that are accountable for the performance of each staff member," autonomous practice would still require "that agencies continue to maintain structural channels for enabling staff to be most effectively accountable to administration" (Henry 1955, p. 40). As Leyendecker (1959) notes, freedom from authority of others in autonomous practice does "not seem to be truly appplicable to the operation of a social agency requiring, as it does, an organizational structure in which responsibility and accountability are clearly defined and allocated" (p. 56). The recognition that someone in the hierarchical agency structure must continue to perform the functions of administrative supervision has been echoed and reechoed by those who have advocated greater independence from supervision (Aptekar 1959, p. 9; Austin 1961, p. 189; Leader 1957, p. 407; Lindenberg 1957, p. 43).

Even if all the workers were well trained, were objectively self-critical, and had developed a level of self-awareness that eliminated the need for educational supervision, even if all workers were so highly motivated, so self-assured, so rich in inner resources that they felt no need for supervisory support, administrative supervision would continue to be necessary as long as the workers were employees of an agency.

The guarantee of autonomy to the worker protects the worker from unwarranted interference by the organization. The question is, then, who protects the client from the worker? Only the most optimistic and charitable assessment of worker behavior would suggest that all decisions are made in the best interests of the client. It is probable that some decisions are prompted by the worker's needs—for survival on a difficult job, for convenience, in self-protection, for self-aggrandizement, etc. The exercise of a grant of discretion and autonomy may be used in response neither to the needs of the organization nor to the needs of the client, but in response to the needs of the worker. The cause and effect relationship between worker behavior and case outcome is generally so ambiguous that very many decisions made by the worker for the worker can be rationalized and justified as ostensibly serving the needs of the client. Administrative supervision functions to protect the client from possible abuse of worker autonomy. The possibility that the worker's real power may be used in oppressive, arbitrary, or inequitable ways argues for the need for some procedural controls (Wilding 1982).

Handler (1979) notes that good supervision serves the same function as a fair hearings appeal on the part of the client. Both serve to check discriminatory practices and failure to comply with rules and regulations—matters which can have an adverse effect on client rights and interests (pp. 101–2).

Other professions, including medicine, have adopted similar procedures in dealing with the conflict between professional autonomy and the need for conformity to organizational requirements (Goss 1961; W. Moore 1970). In organizations such as hospitals and clinics, a distinction is made between supervision concerned with administrative detail, the maintenance of orderly routines in the interest of the collectivity, such as scheduling, assignments, coordination of work, allocation of space and organizational resources, and supervision concerned with the content and procedure of the physician's actual work with the patient. Compliance with supervisory directives is expected with regard to administrative detail. While advice may be offered by supervisory personnel with regard to the physician's professional activity, the ultimate decision remains with the physician in contact with the patient.

In moving toward greater worker autonomy, the social work supervisor retains her administrative responsibilities vis-à-vis the supervisee, and the hierarchial relationship remains essentially the same. But even administrative supervision becomes progressively more perfunctory and automatic as supervisors develop greater confidence in the decisions of more experienced workers. While sanction by supervisors of some worker decisions may be administratively required, such actions with experienced and skilled workers become automatic "rubber stamp" operations. With regard to the educational component, however, the supervisee moves from required supervision to optional consultation, sought at the initiative of the worker. The spirit of the contact changes accordingly. The supervisor accepts the worker as a colleague of nearly equal status as far as knowledge and skill are concerned.

Innovations Toward Worker Autonomy

There is a general recognition of the need for a structured approach to granting the experienced professional worker progressively increasing freedom from supervision. What innovations have been reported in social work which seek to achieve this goal?

Peer Supervision

I noted in chapter 8 that group supervision can offer the worker a greater measure of autonomy than that permitted through individual supervision. Peer-group supervision is an extension of this procedure in the direction of still greater independence. As distinguished from group supervision, peer-group supervision invests the peer group with control of group meetings; the supervisor, if he sits in at all, is just another member of the group. It has been defined as a process by which "a group of professionals in the same agency meet regularly to review cases and treatment approaches without a leader, share expertise and take responsibility for their own and each other's professional development and for maintaining standards of [agency] service" (Hare and Frankena 1972, p. 527). In such peer supervision, more properly termed peer consultation, each member of the group feels a responsibility for the practice of the others and for helping them to improve their practice. What a worker does with the suggestions and advice offered by his peers is his own responsibility.

Peer-group supervision symbolizes the capacity for greater independence of the worker; it also allows greater spontaneity and freedom in the absence of an authority figure. Nonetheless it presents its own difficulties. Rivalry for leadership and control is often present (Brugger, Ceasor, and Martz 1962), and unless the group is composed of workers with somewhat equal education and experience some staff members may be reluctant to participate, feeling that they cannot learn much from "peers" who know less than they do.

One report of peer-group supervision indicated that the "major disadvantage . . . for the [agency] was the difficulty of administrative decision-making in the area of salary increments and professional advancement." The author suggested that this could be handled by a "core supervisor being exposed to the individual [supervisee's] work at stated intervals by means of direct observations and case reviews" (Hare and Frankena 1972, p. 529).

Another disadvantage concerns work demands. The supervisor has the positional authority to make demands regarding work, but the peer supervisor is not formally granted this authority so peers are much more hesitant and more apologetic about enforcing necessary work demands on each other.

A less authority-bound version of peer-group supervision is peer consultation. Peer consultation can be organized in the context of the individual conference. For example, Fizdale (1958) discusses a worker in her agency who had

> done considerable interviewing of both partners together in marital counseling cases. She had, therefore, developed a special skill in handling these "joint" interviews and had special knowledge about when they can be productive. It is quite usual for any staff member to consult with her about the value of a joint interview in a particular case or to get her help in preparing for such an interview or in reviewing the results. (p. 446)

The process of peer consultation can result in some feedback which makes its operation time-limited. The system works best with a group of peers of equal competence and status in the group who consult with one another. In such reciprocal consultation, while all members incur obligations as consultees, they repay these obligations when they act in the role of consultants. The peer consultant who is repeatedly asked for advice is faced with a diminishing gain and increasing cost. "As he is increasingly often asked for advice, the value [utility] of the respect implicit in being once more consulted by his colleagues declines, and the cost of the time needed for consultation increases for him. Hence he would become more and more reluctant to give further advice" (Blau 1963, p. 137). The less competent worker, who is more frequently asking for advice, incurs an ever greater obligation to the other consultant-peers, which he finds difficult to discharge. He wears out his welcome and attempts to make restitution by becoming more deferential. The more often he asks for consultation, the more threatening it becomes for his status in the group. At some point it becomes more painful to ask than to go without the necessary help. Either that or he turns to a less competent peer whom he had not previously consulted and to whom he is not, consequently, obligated.

The worker who consistently makes demands on peers for help and support without reciprocating soon begins to develop the image of a quasi-client in the minds of his peers. Satyamurti (1981) noted these effects in an intensive observational study of social workers:

> In general, being in the position of needing more support and help from colleagues than one was able to give was experienced as uncomfortable. . . . New staff were expected to receive more than they gave

and more experienced workers were usually ungrudging of their time [but] if this went on too long, there tended to be a lasting effect on people's image of the person concerned: [he came to be] seen as a passenger. (pp. 61–62)

As reflected in the material presented above, the term "peer-group supervision" as used in the literature is a very loosely defined term. In one sense it is an extension of the infomal kind of consultation that goes on in "bull sessions" between workers in any agency as they talk with each other about their clinical experiences. In another sense, it applies to a program of continuing education organized by peers employing their own case material as the basis for group discussion (Allen 1976; Schreiber and Frank 1983). It is often difficult to distinguish peer supervision from more traditional group supervision except for the fact that the designated leader is someone other than the supervisor (Bardill 1978). While these procedures encourage greater autonomy and independence in the examination of clinical practice, peer supervision as reported does not attempt to take responsibility for the necessary administrative functions of supervision. At best, peer supervision is an adjunct to and supplement to traditional supervision, not a substitute for it.

"Interminable" Supervision and Debureaucratization

Other proposals for dealing with the negative reactions to continuing supervision concern alterations in administrative structure or in administrative relationships.

Suggestions for changes in the administrative structure involve a redistribution of power and responsibility so that a greater measure of both is given to worker peer groups (Kahle 1969; Rice 1973; Weber and Polm 1974). Instead of an agency whose administrative structure is sharply pyramidal—large numbers of workers at the base, supervised by a more limited number of middle managers, topped by an administrator—the suggested shape is somewhere between pyramidal and rectangular. Instead of an agency with a hierarchical orientation, the suggested orientation is more egalitarian.

Intensified implementation of participatory management procedure tends to enhance the autonomy of the worker. Deliberate efforts have been made in some agencies to actively involve direct-service workers in the determination of significant policy decisions and in formulation of operating procedures (Fallon 1974; Weber and Polm 1974).

Participatory management is one way of attempting to debureaucratize the agency and reallocate power. Other efforts at debureaucratization, or at least diluted hierarchy, have involved attempts to "eliminate" supervision by redistributing supervisory responsibilities to training specialists, to staff-performance specialists (responsible for evaluation), to operation and program specialists, and to the workers themselves. The reports of such efforts indicate increases in worker autonomy but tend to show problems related to equitable task allocation and other dissatisfactions not previously experienced (Weber and Polm 1974).

One agency has experimented with giving workers greater control over the supervisory process by instituting a contract system (Fox 1974). The supervisee negotiates a contract with the supervisor, specifying the kinds of things he feels he needs to learn within a specific period of time. Similar efforts have involved application of the principles of management by objectives (MBO) to supervision (Wiehe 1973; Raider 1975).

Management by objectives (or, more appropriately, supervision by objectives) is an effort to establish a procedure of control which is acceptable and measurable. With the participation and cooperation of the supervisee, definite objectives are formulated for achievement in each case. These objectives are stated in precise and explicit terms which lend themselves to observation and measurement. Once objectives have been formulated in conferences between worker and supervisor and measurable outcome criteria have been defined, a time limit is established for achievement of objectives, and the different objectives are ranked in priority. The process is monitored by the supervisor with active worker participation (Granvold 1978; Fox and Zischka 1982; Fox 1983). Work efforts are evaluated by establishing the extent to which such objectives are achieved in each case. Bloom (1978) presented a practitioner's critical view of MBO. He noted that "too often many workers simply developed plans and presented them to their supervisor for perfunctory review" (p. 485).

Another innovation involves team service delivery (Brieland, Briggs, and Leuenberger 1973; Rowley and Faux 1966). A team of workers, working together as a unit, is given responsibility for supervision. The "supervisor" is merely one of the team members, although somewhat more equal than the others. He acts as a consultant, coordinator, and resource person to team members and, when necessary, as team leader. However, the responsibility for work assignments, monitoring quantity and quality of team member's work, and meeting educational needs of team members is invested in the group.

Supervisory functions still need to be performed in team service delivery. They can be differently allocated and distributed, but such functions cannot be eliminated or ignored (Brill 1976, pp. 92–96). Team service delivery takes group supervision one step further as a procedure for augmenting worker autonomy. It gives administrative mandate to the peer group to perform the main functions previously performed by the supervisor. The team can, as a team, engage in much significant decision making, but the imperatives of organizational life still have to be implemented. Final decisions have to be validated by the supervisor, who has ultimate administrative responsibility for team performance. More recent studies of team delivery in England tend to confirm the persistence with which traditional supervisory functions continue to be performed by team supervisors (Olsen 1975; Parsloe and Stevenson 1978).

The problems of organizational coordination and communication may even be intensified with team service delivery, making the functions of supervision especially important. Since different members of the team may be involved with the same family at different times, this approach requires having up-to-date record and reporting material available. It also requires constant coordination to see that team members are not falling over each other in offering service to the family.

Watson (1973) proposes an eclectic approach to supervision, one that would counter the "restrictive, infantilizing" effects of "traditional supervision." He suggests that a variety of supervisory procedures be available—individual tutorial, case consultation, supervisory group, peer group, tandem and team supervision—to be used differentially as needed. Having experimented with a variety of approaches to supervision in the large voluntary child-welfare agency with which he is associated, Watson noted that whatever system is used needs to be supplemented

to provide externally those elements that are missing or not emphasized. For instance, in those models in which the teaching component is secondary (such as the team) the agency must make available additional formal teaching opportunities to the staff served by such a model. In those systems in which accountability is not part of the primary unit of contact (such as the peer group model) there must be a designated representative of agency administration to whom group members are accountable and formal procedures must be established to make sure this administrative function is performed. (Watson 1973, p. 87)

Watson thus confirms the fact that while the functions of supervision can be redistributed and reassigned in a variety of different ways, to a variety of different people in the agency, these functions ultimately need to be performed if the agency is to get its work done effectively.

Agency Debureaucratization Experiences

No information is available which would enable us to know how many agencies have adopted any of these proposed changes or what percentage of social work supervisees is currently being supervised in accordance with such innovative procedures. My guess is that relatively few workers are affected. This may be only partially in response to inertia and the normal resistance to change encountered by any innovation. It may also be a consequence of the fact that some of the proposed innovations present difficult problems in implementation and the fact that their application is feasible only if certain conditions are met.

Generally the reports of peer supervision and consultation describe workers who were professionally trained, had considerable practice experience and, in addition, often had advanced training. Agency administration had confidence that the workers were sufficiently competent, committed, and self-disciplined to operate autonomously without harm to clients.

Agencies reporting successful efforts to reduce or eliminate supervision recognize that these innovative efforts were made possible by virtue of special staff and structural qualities. Stevens and Hutchinson (1956), reporting on their substitution of consultation for supervision for workers with one year of agency experience, say "we recognize that the plan as we are using it is geared to an agency where all members are professionally trained and experienced. Our agency is small. . . . There are fewer rules and regulations necessary in an agency such as this" (p. 54). In an updated report of the Stevens and Hutchinson innovation, Parsons (1976) likewise noted that a collegial administrative model "beyond bureaucracy" requires an experienced, professionalized, homogeneously oriented staff.

Kahle (1969) reported on a successful use of the team-unit approach and said that the "modified pyramidal-collegial structure, with its emphasis on unit supervision, is possible only when the majority of the staff have high-level skills" (p. 25).

Reporting on debureaucratization of a professional voluntary child welfare agency, Taylor (1980) noted the agency's success in eliminating some supervisory positions and in assigning cases on a peer level. Success of the innovation was explained in part by the fact that peers "were comparable in experience and skill" at a high level. The agency, however, was still struggling with the problem of "how evaluations of caseworker performance will be done" (p. 587). Weatherley (1983) notes that efforts at increasing worker participation in a large, turbulent, complex public agency whose activities have considerable political implications were less successful.

The success of increasing autonomy through agency debureaucratization, increased participation in decision making on the part of the workers, and increased responsibility of supervisory task performance by workers is largely predicated on conditions that obtain in only a minority of agencies. A collegial model requires a highly trained and experienced staff, with a consensual commitment to clearly understood objectives and a mutual sense of trust and regard—conditions not easy to achieve.

We noted previously the research by Lipsky (1980), Prottas (1979), Handler (1973, 1979), Pawlak (1976), Pearson (1975) indicating that workers are granted, or have arrogated, a considerable amount of autonomy and discretion. Consequential decision making at the lowest levels of the hierarchy is a fact. Eliminating or reducing the number and power of subexecutives such as the supervisor would, some suggest, merely be a formal recognition of the current informal structure of service delivery (Palfrey 1981).

There are contradictory trends in regard to increasing the autonomy of the work force and debureaucratization of organizations. The orientation toward debureaucratization gets support and increased impetus from the ferment in American industry generally around "worker participation" (Kanter 1983), "quality circles," "matrix structure," "theory Z" (Ouchi 1981), "managing without managers" (Martin 1983), and "job enrichment." But it needs to be remembered that much of this is in regard to activities in industry which have been previously tightly controlled and where supervision is close.

Given the concern with accountability and protection of client's rights, the movement in the human services areas, where administrative controls have traditionally been more permissive and democratic, is in the opposite direction. In the human services over the past decade, there has been "a distinct increase in pressure toward strengthening administrative power" (Freidson 1975, p. 10).

The two contradictory trends exist side by side but apply to different groups in the work force. The pressure for greater organizational democratization applies most appropriately to industrial workers and white collar workers who have had far less control over their work situation than they desired or could effectively use. Expansion of worker power in this sector is understandable. Professionals, however, have always had a considerable amount of autonomy. Currently the concern is with limiting the possible abuse of this autonomy by requiring more organizational procedures. Social workers, while appealing to the trend developing out of problems in industrial organizations, are more likely to be affected by the trend relating to professional organizations.

Procedures which have been proposed, and in some cases implemented, as substitutes for or as alternatives to the supervisory control system present problems. Attempts by professional peers to police themselves so as to ensure their clients are protected and community accountability demands adequately met have not been notably successful. Professional organizations rarely and reluctantly discipline professional colleagues. The National Association of Social Workers has very infrequently taken such action. Colleagues within a professional organization, when aware of dereliction by peers, present a variety of explanations to excuse taking action (Freidson 1975). The legally required peer review systems (PSRO), utilization reviews, quality assurance programs, and sophisticated management information systems have been met with something less than enthusiastic response. Social workers in general have many questons and considerable uneasiness about such procedures (Sung 1982; Chernesky 1981; Weirich 1980).

The innovations outlined above are expressions of a series of fundamental and related problems. These concern the place of the professional in an organization, the distribution of power in the organization, and the prerogatives of worker autonomy. Such questions are of particular relevance to the focus of this text since they get played out in the organization most explicitly at the supervisory level.

Problem: The Professional and the Bureaucracy

The problem of professional worker autonomy in a bureaucratic context raises once again the central question encountered earlier in the chapter on Administrative Supervision (p. 59). It speaks to the strain between the requirements for worker discretion dictated by the nature of social work practice and the need to accommodate to the requirements that have to do with working in an organization (Glastonbury, Cooper, and Hawkins 1980). This tension is mediated by the supervisor, who represents both the worker and the organization.

Social workers have always conceded, however grudgingly, the need for some sort of control structure in order to accomplish the work of the agency. But the clearly preferred control structure was that of the profession rather than that of the bureaucracy. The orientation of a profession and that of a bureaucracy are, supposedly, inherently in conflict. The needs of the bureaucracy for standardization, uniformity, role specificity, efficiency, impersonality, and rule adherence are antithetical to the needs of the professional for flexibility, maximum discretion and autonomy, sensitivity to the uniqueness of individual situations, and a primary concern with client needs. What is professionally correct is more important than what is organizationally desirable. There is recognition that a complex organization requires the performance of certain tasks, but the basis for obtaining conformity to organizational needs, for ensuring coordination, and for limiting individual, idiosyncratic behavior lies not in hierarchically delegated authority but in professional self-discipline, in voluntary adherence to professional norms and peer governance. The essential difference between these control structures is outlined by Toren (1972):

> The distinctive control structure of the professions . . . is fundamentally different from bureaucratic control exercised in administrative organizations. Professional control is characterized as being exercised from "within" by an internalized code of ethics and special knowledge acquired during a long period of training and by a group of peers which is alone qualified to make professional judgments. This type of authority differs greatly from bureaucratic authority which emanates from a hierarchical position. (p. 51).

The difference lies in the basis of the legitimated authority which supports the differing control systems, one based on expertise which prompts voluntary compliance, the other based on power vested in a position which obligates compliance. The professional control structure recognizes colleagues as having equal authority and power rather than supervisor and supervisee with differing amounts.

The strain between the professionals' preference for self- and peer-government and the bureaucratic-hierarchical control structure encountered in working in complex organizations such as social agencies is the subject of very considerable discussion (Abrahamson 1967; Billingsley 1964a, b; Miller and Podell 1970). However, with the "bureaucratization of the professions" and the "professionalization of bureaucracies," there has been increasing accommodation between the two control systems. "Organizations are increasingly governed by professional standards and professions are increasingly subject to bureaucratic controls" (Kornhauser 1962, p. 7). The basis for accommodation efforts lies in the fact that the professional needs the organization almost as much as the organization needs the professional.

There has been some rethinking generally about the inevitability of conflict between professionals and the bureaucracy. An analysis of professional-bureaucratic relationships leads Finch (1976) to question whether it is true that bureaucracy threatens professional autonomy. Kogan (1971), Rowbottom (1973), Brown (1975), Hall (1968), and Engle (1970), analyzing different possible administrative organizational structures, conclude that hierarchical organization is not necessarily antithetical to professional autonomy.

There is greater current acceptance of the idea, first proposed by Harris-Jenkins (1970), that "The contemporary professional who works in an organizational setting is quite likely to feel at home and at ease there because professions and organizations are fused into a new social form" (Blankenship 1977, p. 38). And a questionnaire study of 267 professional social workers in health and welfare agencies found that bureaucratic and professional value orientations were not necessarily in conflict. The two sets of values were perceived as separate, rather than polar opposites on one continuum (Wilson, Voth, and Hudson 1980). "The findings clearly indicate that while social workers may value autonomy, flexibility, and innovation in their work situations they may at the same time value bureaucratic organizational arrangements. Assertions that bureaucratic values, which guide the policies and procedures of organizations, are antithetical to the professional values of workers are highly questionable" (p. 29).

Reviewing the empirical findings regarding organizational infringement on professional autonomy, Bar-Oren (1977) concludes that "the findings are far from supporting the logically derived conflict approach conclusively, and furthermore there is evidence suggesting that organizational employment of professionals does not curtail their autonomy and in fact provides them with professional facilities that can enhance the provision of service delivery" (p. 56).

Research by Orgon and Greene (1981) points to the fact that professionalism and bureaucracy are not necessarily inherently antithetical concepts. While the professionals' press for individual autonomy does conflict with the organizational imperative for standardization and coordination, bureaucracy can expedite the work of professionals and provide the resources which increase the effectiveness of their work.

Bureaucratic formalization reduces the problems associated with role ambiguity. "By providing the professional with a greater scope and clearer context for self-expression in work, formalization may prevent self-estrangement." Their research with engineers and scientists in organizations showed compensatory effects balancing some of the disadvantages of bureaucracy. They conclude that "conflict between formalization of organizational context and professional job involvement is neither omnipresent nor inevitable" (p. 252). Heraud (1981) notes that the relationship between bureaucracy and the profession is not, as is frequently depicted, in all cases one of conflict and in social work in particular there is considerable congruence between bureaucratic and professional criteria. Concepts such as organizational professionalism or bureau-professionalism have been developed to express this relationship. Bureaucracy and professionalism have, for example, both been seen as subtypes of a wider category, that of rational administration. (p. 135)

Thus it might be concluded that while there is a dynamic tension between the needs of the professional and the needs of the organization, these differences are reconcilable, that bureaucratization does not necessarily result in deprofessionalization, that identification with the organization does not necessarily occur at the expense of identification with the profession. Supervision and professionalism are not necessarily antithetical concepts.

Not only might there be less conflict than supposed between the professional and the bureaucracy, but, as mentioned above, there are significant advantages for the professional in operating in an organizational context. Through the agency the professional is provided with community and legal sanction and support for the work he is doing. The organization provides the professional with clients so that he does not need to expend energy in developing a clientele. The agency provides resources that assist the professional in task performance—clerical and financial help, technical materials, paraprofessional assistance, insurance coverage, specialized consultation. The organization provides the stimulation that derives from immediate, close contact with other professionals, the emotional support that comes from an immediately accessible peer group, and the technical advisement that comes from good supervision. Within the context of a complex organization, the professional has available a rich network of related specialists with whom he can coordinate his own activities.

The advantage of a bureaucratic context for work is noted by Farber and Heifetz (1981) in studying the stresses encountered by psychotherapists in private practice. They note that the "insular nature of private practice, though beneficial in some regards, impedes the formation of collegial support systems that serve to attenuate the personally depleting aspects of therapeutic work" (p. 629).

If bureaucratic controls limit the worker's discretion and autonomy, they make for reliable, predictable, nondiscriminating decision making. The statement that may come closest to reality is that
professionalism and bureaucracy, being multidimensional, may be
in conflict with regard to some considerations, but congruent and
mutually supportive with regard to others (Anderson and Martin
1982).

Administrative and Educational Supervision—the Problem of Separation

A problem that has received considerable attention and debate in
the literature on social work supervision is the desirability of separating the administrative and educational functions of supervision.
Such a change is designed to reduce the conflict between teaching
and evaluation; to reduce the excessive concentration of power in
the hands of the person (generally the supervisor) who is simultaneously responsible for both these significant functions; and to
reduce the burden which responsibility for both these functions
imposes on the supervisor, making effective implementation of
each difficult.

The argument for separation of the two functions is also based on
the contention that the knowledge, skills, and aptitudes required
for competent administration are different from those required for
effective teaching. Combining the two functions means that the
supervisor would have to be a good administrator as well as a good
teacher. Separation permits specialization in performance of these
different tasks.

Originally advocated by Austin (1956, 1960, 1961), the suggestion
for separation of functions receives support from Devis (1965),
Hanlan (1972), and Schwartz and Sample (1972). They suggest
that while both responsibilities are complementary, they are also
antithetical. The bureaucratic review, control, and evaluation functions of supervision establish a relationship between supervisor and
supervisee that makes difficult, if not impossible, the development
of the desirable teacher-learner relationship. Conversely, the question is raised whether the requirements of receptivity and psychological freedom necessary for the good learning situation do not
conflict with the exercise of authority in administrative supervision.

Toren (1969) notes this: "The personal-expressive relationship of teacher-learner infringes upon the maintenance of bureaucratic controls by the supervisor" (p. 174).

In their study of supervision in public welfare, Schwartz and Sample (1972) found supervisors to be excessivly burdened by the demands of both functions:

> In the public assistance agencies the staff development functions of the supervisor tend to be honored more in the breach than in the observance. Among the reasons for this failure are the inability of some supervisors to carry out this function because of the press of administrative work; their lack of knowledge, skills, or personal aptitude; or other incapacities for staff development. A specialized in-service training and staff development program represents one kind of response by public assistance agencies to the need to supplement and strengthen supervisors' contributions in this area. (p. 168)

Here the need for specialized competence for effective discharge of the responsibilities of educational supervision is explicitly raised.

Studies of rehabilitation supervision have also advocated separation of supervisory functions and allocation to different areas of administration. Emener (1978) notes that it is suggested that rehabilitation counselors have supervisors "available to them who can function as casework supervisors and not be burdened with administrative responsibility" (p. 47).

Chase (1978), however, has argued against single-role supervisors. He notes that such separation "can result in confusion among rehabilitation counselors and some managers as to which supervising figure has ultimate authority in casework-related activities" (p. 56).

Harris and Allison (1982) describe successful separation of educational and administrative supervisory functions in a large centralized department of social work in a teaching hospital and both Austin and Schwartz recommend assignment of a supervisee to different supervisors for administrative supervision and educational supervision.

It might be noted that contamination of the educational relationship by the administrative relationship is faced in all of education. Every educator in every educational institution faces the problem of establishing an effective teacher-learner relationship while carrying the burden of evaluating the work of the learner. But there is no substantial empirical evidence that learning seriously suffers as a result, nor is there any good evidence that learning substantially improves when the educator is absolved of the responsibility for evaluating and grading.

A certain level of anxiety is conducive to learning. Consequently the anxiety that relates to evaluation may be necessary, rather than antithetical, to learning. Nor would separating educational and administrative supervision eliminate anxiety. It may eliminate the anxiety of the formal aspects of evaluation. However, the worker would still be anxious about the personal, informal evaluation of her work by the educational supervisor who had no formal administrative-evaluation responsibilities.

The recommended cure may create greater problems than the supposed disease. The learning needs of the individual worker can be best discerned by the administrative supervisor who is responsible for careful review of the worker's performance. That person is in the most advantageous position to provide the necessary corrective feedback that advances learning. Control over selection and assignment of work responsibilities toward attainment of learning objectives also rests with the administrative supervisor. Consequently it would seem desirable that the adminstrative supervisor also be responsible for educational supervision.

Although the literature of social work supervision continues to debate the problem, it does not seem to be much of a problem for supervisors. Kledaras (1971) studied role conflict in supervision among 40 supervisors who "indicated that teaching and administration did not pose conflicting demands on their job" (p. 145). Olyan (1972) asked 228 supervisors from a variety of settings to respond to the statement that "the administrative and educational components of a supervisor's job are too much for any one person to do effectively." Fully three-quarters of the supervisors either disagreed or disagreed strongly with the statement (p. 153). In another study, 74 percent of 470 supervisors polled indicated that they felt no conflict between the two responsibilities (Kadushin 1974). An earlier study, which asked a similar question, found that 78 percent of the supervisors saw no conflict (Cruser 1958).

A study of 1,660 workers in 31 social welfare and rehabilitation agencies showed that 56 percent of the supervisees and 66 percent of the supervisors who were asked about this matter felt that administrative supervision and educational supervision should not be separated. Seventy-seven percent of the supervisors felt that they could do an "adequate job when [they try] to coach and train workers and at the same time take care of routine supervision" (Olmstead and Christensen 1973, p. 205). However, the researchers note that, while the majority opinion is against separation, "enough people experience difficulty in performing the dual roles for serious thought to be given to the question of whether supervisory effectiveness might not be enhanced if training and supervision were separated, despite the long tradition to the contrary in social work" (p. 206).

Ethical Dilemmas in Supervision

Advances in medical technology, changes in the sexual mores, and a broadening conception of rights and entitlements more frequently now pose ethical questions for supervisors for which no ready answers are available.

In addition to providing opportunities for discussion for clarification and catharsis, workers might legitimately feel that the supervisor should provide some direction, some suggestion for resolving the ethical question. The problem is that neither the profession nor the community has formulated clear-cut answers to many of the ethical questions that have confronted workers with greater frequency recently. Supervisors consequently often find that they only have themselves to look to in offering guidance to supervisees faced with such problems.

A single woman elects to conceive through artificial insemination and is applying for AFDC to support herself and the child. A parent has been told that the newborn has a number of serious congenital abnormalities, needs an operation to survive, and is faced with the question of consenting to the operation or allowing the child to die. A pregnant 15-year-old seeks the help of the social worker in obtaining an abortion and does not want either her parents or the father of the child notified of her decision. A man asks for medicaid support for a sex change operation and feels that unless he can become a woman, he is at high risk for suicide. A pregnant woman has been informed that an amneocyntesis examination shows that the child will have Downs Syndrome and is faced with the decision to abort or carry the child to term. A client at a community mental health center, with whom the worker has a very good relationship, has confided to the worker that he has physically abused his 5-year-old son, a fact that the worker is under legal obligation to report to protective services. A virginal 32-year-old man seeks the help of the worker for a referral to a sexual surrogate to overcome his inhibitions and for agency financial support for the procedure. A terminally ill cancer patient requests the help of the worker as an advocate in persuading the medical staff to withhold life supports so that she might die. A stable gay couple have applied to the agency to adopt a young nonhandicapped child. A borderline schizophrenic client has refused medication, exercising his right to refuse treatment; during two brief psychiatric interludes that might have been controlled by medication, he abused a 6-year-old boy and frightened women by exposing himself in a crowded department store; the local papers have raised questions about his social worker's responsibilities.

Recent procedures make it possible to know the sex of the fetus. What ethical problems need to be resolved by the workers faced with a request for abortion of a female fetus by a family that has four girls and very much wants a boy?

The recent growing development of transplant surgery raises complex ethical questions of allocation of resources in short supply. What are the defensible guidelines for deciding who gets a heart or kidney or bone marrow transplant in situations where there are more applicants than organs available?

In response to each of these questions the general orientation is that the clients have the right and the obligation to make the decision for themselves, the worker's responsibility being to help the clients come to a decision. But with regard to the situations cited above, and other equally difficult questions, the worker is involved in helping the client implement the decision. Community funds and agency resources often need to be allocated in support of the decision. Conflicts can arise between client rights and public interest. Consequently, the worker, and through the worker the supervisor, find it difficult to be entirely neutral in response to the decision the client selects. Which way do they lean, or should they lean, in response to these situations? The problem for supervision is that many of these situations pose ethical dilemmas which are, as yet, unresolved (Hoot 1979; Rabow and Manos 1980; Levy 1982; Reamer 1982; Yelaja 1982; Edelwich and Brodsky 1982).

A social worker in a maximum security state prison says,

> Over the course of about a year, I had developed a very close relation-ship with Donald, who was serving a 10-year sentence for manslaugh-ter. During a recent interview, he shared with me the information that he had taken a spoon from the mess hall and sharpened and shaped it into a knife. Donald, who was black, was continually harassed by a white prisoner with racist tendencies. Emphasizing confidentiality, Donald told me that he planned to knife the white prisoner. He seemed deadly serious and completely unwilling to consider alterna-tives. For days I anxiously lived the dilemma of adhering to confiden-tiality at the risk of serious injury to a prisoner, or violating confidenti-ality in protection of life and losing my relationship with Donald and any chance of being helpful to him. I would have appreciated the opportunity of talking this over with a supervisor—but I was not su-pervised. In the end, I chose protection of life over confidentiality and my relationship with Donald—but I sure was unhappy with the deci-sion and still don't know if I did the right thing.

It is still an open question as to whether or not client informed consent involves explicitly sharing with the client the fact that the worker is supervised and that the content of worker-client interac-tion is discussed with the supervisor. Does informed consent re-quire that the supervisor meet with the client if the client wants to see the person supervising her worker?

Many questions faced by the worker do not yield to technical solutions because they are primarily ethical rather than technical questions. No amount of technical skill can help a worker answer a question regarding situations where confidentiality might need to be set aside to protect threatened people, where agency rules and regulations might need to be "bent" to accommodate highly individ-ualized client needs, or where a "white lie" might be considered to mitigate a client's pain or suffering. In instances of difficult ethical decisions between one "good" and another conflicting "good," the worker might find that the opportunity to talk things over with a supervisor provides relief and a sense of direction—provided that the supervisor has formulated a sense of direction.

Sexism and Social Work Administration

Sexism is defined as discrimination based on gender. There is a problem in social work relating to equitable access of females to administrative positions. The term social work administration covers a variety of levels from the lowest supervisory position to agency executive director. For both men and women, supervisor is the entry-level position to the administrative hierarchy.

While the majority of social workers are women, the administrative enclave in many social work agencies is disproportionately male (Szakacs 1977; Chernesky 1980).

Females are at a disadvantage both for recruitment and selection of managerial positions and as staff members for promotion to such positions. A study of a sample of MSW family agency staff throughout Michigan found that "fewer females were hired initially at the supervisory level . . . were promoted at a slower rate than males, and there was a significant relationship between sex and position level" (Knapman 1977, p. 463).

Ezell and Odewhan (1980) studied beliefs relating to difficulties facing women in moving into managerial positions as expressed by 360 men and women managers in state public welfare agencies. The results indicated that agency environment and recruiting and selecting practices had negatively affected the likelihood of women moving into managerial positions in the agency. While both male and female respondents agreed there were no pervasive patterns of difference between men and women which would limit the capability of women to perform effectively as managers, women felt at a disadvantage for promotion in that they were not part of the informal male communication and administrative network that had the power to make decisions regarding selection for administrative offerings.

Whatever the realities of promotional possibilities to supervisory positions, there is a difference between men and women social workers in their perception of the opportunities for such advancement. A questionnaire study of 160 NASW members in California indicated that 68 percent of the women respondents agreed with the statement that "men have a better chance to become supervisors in my agency than women" (Zietz and Erlien 1976, p. 436). And whatever the reasons, the research does tend to show a greater hesitancy and ambivalence about administrative aspirations on the part of women in general as compared with men in general.

In a study by Brager and Michael (1969) female social workers showed a "greater commitment to a practice role than to a policy-making one" (p. 599). Valentich and Gripton (1978) found a strong relationship between sex and career orientation. A significantly greater percentage of male respondents than female respondents in a NASW survey indicated an interest in administration.

A mail questionnaire study of some 1,600 NASW members in Pennsylvania found a "significant relationship between career goals and sex, confirming that females were not striving for administrative positions to the same degree as males" (Sutton 1982, p. 215). While the finding was applicable to top administration as an ultimate career goal, this was not true of aspirations toward supervision. More women than men respondents had supervision as the ultimate career goal.

In studying the careers of graduates of a school of social work, Jennings and Daley (1979) found that male and female graduates had "differential preferences for administrative and direct service positions" (p. 20). Males were much more likely than females to have majored in administration and to have selected jobs with possibilities in mind for movement into administration.

A study of students in a graduate social work program indicated that "significantly more men than women reported that they planned to leave the field for at least six months and then return" and "more women than men said it was 'not likely' that they would be supervisors following graduation" (Kravatz and Jones 1982, pp. 80–81).

However, the research also shows that when women are assigned and accept administrative jobs, they do as well and sometimes better than men. Women in managerial positions can, and do, manifest the leadership style and behavior, managerial capabilities and managerial performance, organizational cooperation and competition, and problem-solving capacity necessary for successful enactment of the managerial role (Ezell, Odewahn, and Sherman 1982; Cullen and Perrewe 1981).

A review of some 32 female leadership studies concluded that "even though the traditional sex stereotyping is pervasive, the widely held belief that women make inferior leaders seems to give way in actual work situations" (Brown 1979). And studies of male and female social work supervisors found no difference between men and women in the level of competence with which they performed their work (Bartol and Wortman 1975; Munson 1979a).

A study of a large sample of female employees of "federally funded social service organizations in 23 states" found that women in supervisory positions saw themselves as equally competent as men (Snyder and Bruning 1979). And where women hold administrative jobs in social work, they report a high level of satisfaction with the position, equal to the level felt by men administrators (Jayaratne and Chess 1983).

Some of the negative perception of women's motivation toward and potential competence in managerial positions derives from limited information about and experience with women as managers. Studies which control for actual experience with women managers tend to show that traditional cultural prejudices toward women managers are eroded as a consequence of such experiential exposure (Ezell, Odewhan, and Sherman 1981, p. 297).

As Terborg et al. (1977) note, "given these results, it appears untenable to conclude that differential treatment of women vis-à-vis management positions is justified, using behavioral criteria" (p. 90).

At this point, there is a need for a corrective statement. While the above discussion relates to administrative positions generally, there is a need to be more specific in delineating the extent of gender discrimination for the various levels of administrative positions.

While men are clearly overrepresented in top social work administrative positions, this is less true at the middle-management supervisory level. At this level the disproportion is much more modest and the gender gap moves toward closure. Studies of positional distribution of men and women social workers which provide information for specific levels of administration confirm this (see Sutton 1982, tables 1 and 2, p. 15; Jennings and Daley 1979, table 4, p. 20; Knapman 1977, table 2, p. 463). In each instance, for the limited sample of social workers studied, the number of men at the different administrative levels is disproportionately higher at the top administrative level, but not at the supervisory level.

The 1982 NASW Data Bank Survey of 60,000 members provides

the most extensive data on this question available.* At the "management/administration" level, 49 percent of the respondents were male; 51 percent female. At the "supervisory" level, however, 33.6 percent of the respondents were male, 66.4 percent were female. At the supervisory level, the distribution of male and female position holders almost exactly reflects the distribution of men and women in social work generally. At this level, gender discrimination appears to be very much attenuated. Furthermore studies tend to indicate that having more women as supervisors will result in increasing the number of women supervisors. A study of managers in a large state social service organization found that being supervised by a woman had affected both male and female supervisors' perception of women's managerial competence. "Those respondents who have been supervised by a woman at some point in their career held more positive views of the managerial skills, abilities, and motivations of women as managers" (Ezell, Odewhan, and Sherman 1982, p. 25).

What the data appears to show overall, however, is that for men supervision is a way station to higher levels of administration, for women supervision is more often a terminal step in career advancement.

The Problem of Education for Supervision

We have noted above that lack of training is one of the problems encountered by direct service workers making the transition to supervision. Education for supervision is a problem for the profession as well.

Over a decade ago Olmstead and Christiansen (1973), in concluding a national study of social work personnel problems, called attention to the need for formal and explicit training for supervision. "There appears to be a pressing need for supervisory training. The function of supervision is too critical to leave to trial-and-error learning. Systematic instruction in the fundamentals of supervision warrants a high place on any list of training requirements" (Report no. 2, p. 6).

* Myles Johnson, 1983. Letter dated July 25, 1983, providing preliminary information on the 1982 NASW Data Bank Survey.

Educating supervisors to supervise remains a problem today. Relatively few supervisors have had any extended systematic education in supervision. Aiken and Weil (1981) note that "role adoption" (learning to do the job after being assigned the title) and "emulation or modeling" (imitating supervisors previously encountered) are the principal ways of learning to supervise.

Researching social work graduate school offerings in the area of social work supervision, Munson (1983) found that only 13 percent of the schools required a course in supervision (p. 13). Twenty-eight percent of the schools did not have a course in supervision, 58 percent offering such a course as an elective (p. 15). The 1983 curriculum policy statement of the Council on Social Work Education does not require schools to offer a course in supervision.

Some suggestions for supplementing such training have appeared in the literature. A training program for supervisors might include the supervisor-trainee engaging in co-supervision sessions with a more experienced supervisor (Davis and Arvey 1978). Peer group supervision of, by, and for supervisors has been reported as a procedure for upgrading the skills of supervisors (Hamlin and Timberlake 1982). "A group of supervisors come together to share and examine personal supervisory practices" (p. 85). Videotape of supervision can be used in training new supervisors. Granet, Kalman, and Socks (1980) have employed such tapes for "the supervision of supervision." "Supervisors can view the tape and discuss the process in addition to suggesting alternatives that might improve the supervision" (p. 1445).

The Problem of Computerization of Service

An incipient problem not as yet clearly addressed in the social work supervision literature relates to the supervisor and the computer. There is growing interest in the use of computers in human service agencies. A network of some 400 dues-paying members of CUSS (Computer Use in Social Services), an organization of people experimenting with the use of computers, testifies to this growing concern. A special issue of *Administration in Social Work* was devoted to applying computers in social services and mental health agencies (1982). Ultimately direct service workers will need to use computers to store and retrieve information about their caseloads and ultimately supervisors will need to be knowledgable about how computers might be programmed and used.

Supervisors may have to come to terms with their feelings about computers. For older supervisors, they may be mystifying and unfamiliar objects that create anxiety. They may have misgivings about their ability to master the operations required in the use of computers. Computers may be a threat for all supervisors since they could give administrators easy access to the specifics of their unit's operation.

It might be noted that the use of computers can provide all kinds of additional information to the supervisor about performance of the work unit. However, there is little evidence that the wealth of information made available by the computer has been imaginatively or productively used by agency supervisors or administrators. Information is occasionally distributed and discussed with subordinates but rarely is it used to determine administrative decisions (Rapp 1984).

The Problems of Research and a Theory of Social Work Supervision

We have earlier noted (pp. 27–28) the fact that, given the multidimensional nature of supervision and the different sets of theories associated with each aspect of it, the formulation of a "theory of social work supervision" is an unlikely undertaking.

The problem in building a theory that is unique to social work supervision and that speaks to all the different aspects of social work supervision lies in the paucity of research regarding social work supervision. The preponderance of research available on supervision in the human services lies outside social work in related disciplines—psychiatry, psychology, counseling, rehabilitation, speech and hearing therapy, and pastoral counseling (Hansen and Warner 1971; Hansen, Pound, and Petro 1976; Hansen, Robins, and Grimes 1982; Lambert 1980; Ford 1979). But aside from supervision in rehabilitation (Emener 1982), which is most clearly analogous to supervision in social work, the research in the other fields reflects a very constricted definition of supervision. It is applied almost exclusively to the training-educational preparation of students, trainees, residents, interns. And almost all of the research has students of the profession as its research subject population.

Supervision in almost all of the sibling human service disciplines is defined as a teaching-learning process primarily. The research on supervision in counseling, psychiatry, clinical psychology, and speech and hearing therapy, for instance, is focused on the supervision of students in training, on training procedures, training approaches, training outcomes. Aside from some research on supervision in rehabilitation, there is almost no research in related disciplines on ongoing supervision of paid staff. One cannot, therefore, validly apply the findings of such research, which is in itself limited, to building a "theory of social work supervision."

The research on social work supervision per se is very limited. While there is sizable literature on social work supervision available, most of it is anecdotal, idiosyncratic, nonquantifiable, speculative "theorizing." A variety of "conceptual models" are available, each standing alone and relatively nonintegratable with each other.

Such material is largely descriptive—based on practice wisdom and supervisory experience. Even contributions regarded as benchmarks, such as the work by Robinson and Towle, contain little research material in support of the presentation.

After critically reviewing 136 articles concerned with agency management published between 1978 and 1980 in social work journals, Rapp et al. (1983) pointed to the "idiosyncratic and weak nature of much of the management research reviewed for the study" (p. 99).

Social work supervision is clearly an art, a function which has as yet a very limited empirical base. We are, in the 1980s, somewhat further ahead than in the 1960s when Briar (1966) called attention to the lack of research on social work supervision and in the 1970s when he (1971) reiterated the need for such research. Essentially, however, we are at square one in theory building, without a clear descriptive knowledge of what supervisors do, how they do it, how what they do affects the worker, much less how it affects the client. The bulk of this text, in retrospect, is based, to a considerable extent, on what it is thought should be done in supervision by supervisors. A search for substantiation in practice of perscriptive statements very often yielded zero findings. Given the problem related to the paucity of necessary research, it seems clear that developing a "theory of social work supervision" is currently premature.

A Perspective

Focusing on the problems of supervision tends to obscure the very real contribution made by supervision to the effective operation of social work agencies, and the general satisfaction with current supervisory procedures.

Burns (1958) calls attention to the possibility of exaggerating the extent of dissatisfaction with supervision. In summarizing her history of social supervision, she notes that

> despite the evident and intense dissatisfaction with supervision as it has been practiced, it would be easy to overestimate the extent of the problem. Scrutiny of the literature reveals that the negative response to traditional supervisory practice has been evoked, for the most part, in those private agencies where the social work job has been one of relatively low volume, where staff members have been professionally trained, where there has been less turnover of personnel, and where consultation with other disciplines has been available. Agencies handling a large volume of work, with personnel less well trained, with heavy work loads and less available consulation service, apparently have not found the same problem. The extent of dissatisfaction, therefore, has been limited. Its limitation does not decry its importance. (p. 162)

Despite some dissatisfaction, agency supervision is, for the most part, doing the job it is charged with doing. A nationwide sample of approximately 400 professionally trained supervisees anonymously answered the following question: "In general, how satisfied do you feel with the relationship you now have with your supervisor?" Responses were in terms of a five-point scale ranging from "I am extremely satisfied" to "I am extremely dissatisfied." Some 28 percent of the respondents indicated extreme satisfaction and an additional 32 percent indicated that they were "fairly satisfied"—a total of 60 percent of respondents expressing a reasonable degree of satisfaction in the supervisory experience. Only 15 percent were "fairly dissatisfied" or "extremely dissatisfied" (Kadushin 1974).

Olmstead and Christensen's study of 1,660 workers throughout the country showed that, overall, 77 percent were "satisfied" with the supervision they were receiving. The fact that 78 percent of the respondents answered "no" to the question "would you prefer a different type of supervision than you get?" further confirms the generally positive attitude of these workers toward supervision (1973, p. 205). The study found that mean satisfaction with supervision was higher than the global score for satisfaction and higher than the scores on 6 of the 8 sources of work satisfaction studied. On a six-point scale, the mean for global satisfaction in public welfare agencies was 3.84; satisfaction with supervisor rated 4.51. Workers in voluntary agencies rated global satisfaction at 4.8 but satisfaction with supervision had a mean rating of 5.1 (Olmstead and Christensen, report no. 2, 1973, table 91, pp. 283–84). Other studies available also tend to indicate considerable satisfaction with social work supervision (Galambos and Wiggens 1970, p. 18; Greenleigh Associates 1960, p. 132; Scott 1969, p. 95).

The level of satisfaction with supervision reported by social workers responding to standardized job satisfaction questionnaires is close to the level reported for a normative sample of workers (Harrison 1980, p. 38; see also Cherniss and Egnatios 1978). Parsloe and Stevenson (1978), in a detailed interview study of over 300 British social workers, found that, rather than being antagonistic or resistive to supervision, "most social workers expected and wanted supervision" (p. 205).

Munson's (1960) study of 65 supervisees from a variety of agencies indicated that satisfaction scores with supervision are "fairly high, indicating that there is overall satisfaction with supervision" (p. 7). A survey of the job satisfactions of some 370 workers in mental health settings found that "respondents tended to be most satisfied with their supervision, followed closely by satisfaction with co-workers and with their work" (Webb et al. 1980).

In a study of the experience with supervision of 222 workers in child welfare agencies, Shapiro (1976) says "respondents' evaluation of the quality of their supervision was more likely to be positive than negative." Sixty-three percent thought their supervisors were always or usually helpful, 26 percent found their supervisors only occasionally or rarely helpful, and the remainder indicated that helpfulness varied with the case discussed. The most commonly named areas of helpfulness were "implementing casework skills and adding to the worker's general knowledge of the field" (pp. 137–38).

At a state human services agency, 636 supervisees rated their supervisors on 7 dimensions reflecting their attitudes toward supervisees. The dimensions included such aspects as communication, unit management, personnel policies, personnel evaluations. Overall the supervisors rated a mean of 3.27 on a five-point scale from 2 ("not at all") to 5 ("very well"), indicating a reasonable level of satisfaction with supervisors on the part of the 636 supervisees (Russell, Lankford, and Grinnell 1984, table 1).

Forty caseworkers employed by a department of human resources were asked to assess the factors that they perceived as hindering their efficiency and effectiveness. Of the variety of factors rated, supervision was marked as being least significant as a hindrance (Grinnell and Hill 1979, p. 121).

Olmstead and Christensen's nationwide study concluded that good supervision is an important determinant of agency effectiveness. "The data are conclusive. High agency scores on the supervision variable were accompanied by greater employee satisfaction, better individual performance, less absenteeism, better agency performance, and higher agency competence" (1973, p. 304). Consequently, to improve agency effectiveness, greater time and attention need to be devoted to improving current supervisory practice. Many of the complaints about supervision are not the result of problems in supervision as such, but rather of the improper application of supervisory procedures.

The functions of supervision can be performed in a manner that respects the integrity of the worker, permitting areas of worker autonomy in an atmosphere of trust and shared concern. The functions can be implemented in a manner that provides assistance as well as assessment and facilitates the optimum performance of the worker while holding her accountable for her performance.

It is not supervision as such that encourages "infantilizing dependency," but rather poor supervision; it is not supervision as such that restricts and inhibits worker autonomy, but rather poor supervision. The profession might seriously consider, as a partial solution to the problems posed by supervision, a more active program of explicit, formal training for social work supervision in order to increase the number of better supervisors doing good supervision.

There is some research support for the contention that workers supervised by more professionally competent supervisors were less critical of supervision than those workers who experienced less adequate supervision (Scott 1965, p. 81). Supervisors who hold an MSW degree appear to be more effective than non-MSW supervisors in enabling their supervisees to use their knowledge and skills. In testing students entering a graduate school of social work after having worked in the field, Torre (1974) found that "the professional background of the supervisors" was one of only two factors related to how well the students performed. Students who, as workers, had been supervised by professionally trained supervisors did statistically better than those who had been supervised by non-MSW supervisors.

A detailed study of supervision in a county department of public welfare showed that

> professionally oriented supervisors were seen as less likely to adhere closely to agency rules and policies and to be generally more permissive and nonautocratic in their relations with workers. Professionally oriented supervisors were also more likely to be described by their subordinates as self-confident and willing to back workers in conflicts with clients; they were less likely to be described as impatient or as reluctant to make decisions which were theirs to make than the less professionally oriented supervisors. In summary, the data suggests that . . . those supervisors with more graduate training adhered more closely to the professional model of the supervisor—that of permissive educator who allows caseworkers a greater measure of autonomy. It is also important to note that caseworkers in the county agency apparently preferred the style of supervision offered by the more professionally oriented supervisors. (Scott 1969, pp. 99–100, reprinted with permission of Macmillan Publishing Co.)

Further data "contain at least the suggestion that professionally oriented supervisors were the more effective group in motivating workers to perform as measured by agency criteria" (p. 101).

Ultimately, however, even with the best of training and the most adequate preparation, supervisors cannot resolve some of the persistent difficulties of supervision. The most significant problems of supervision reflect the significant problems of the profession. They cannot be solved in supervision, by supervisors, but need to be solved by the profession.

498

PROBLEMS AND INNOVATIONS

Good supervision requires a clear conception of the profession's objectives. Only the profession itself can supply this, and the matter is currently open to debate. At this point the profession of social work seems to have little functional specificity, its claims are pluralistic and diffuse, its objectives are ambiguous, and its image is blurred. Traditionally accepted goals have been challenged, underlying assumptions have been questioned, previously accredited practice is discounted as ineffective or misdirected. In recognition of this reality, the Publications Committee of the NASW called attention in 1974 to the need for another Milford Conference. That historic conference, held in 1929, was a successful effort to develop a consensus on the definition of social work, its function and purpose. In indicating the need for another such conference in the 1970s, the Publications Committee noted that at this time "there appears to be no agreement within the social work profession on a common conceptual framework for viewing social work functions and practice."

Since 1974, there have been two national meetings of social work leaders, researchers, and theorists to answer the question, "Is there a common conceptual framework for the social work profession?" Summarizing the results of the first meeting held in Madison, Wisconsin, in 1976, Scott Briar (1977) said, "the seemingly inescapable conclusion is that at this time in the history of social work, there is not a widespread consensus about the profession's mission and purpose." The second conference in 1979 did not resolve the issue any more satisfactorily.

The supervisory cadre lacks the needed support which derives from membership in, and affiliation with, a clearly defined profession whose objectives and functions are sharply specified and whose hegemony over some significant social problem areas has clear community acceptance and legitimation. The conscientious supervisor finds his task made more difficult by the conceptual heterogeneity, if not the conceptual disarray, which currently characterizes the approach to social work objectives and functions, and by the community's ambivalent sanction of social work.

Good supervision further requires an effective practice technology, and only the profession and allied sciences can supply it. Good supervision requires a consensually accepted practice theory and adequate procedures for measuring outcomes, and only the profession can supply them. In many respects the essential problems of supervision derive from the unsolved questions facing the profession. What Mosher and Purpel (1972) say about supervision in education is equally applicable to social work.

> The difficulty of defining supervision in relation to education . . . stems, in large part, from unresolved theoretical problems about teaching. Quite simply, we lack sufficient understanding of the process of teaching. Our theories of learning are inadequate, the criteria for measuring teaching effectiveness are imprecise, and deep disagreement exists about what knowledge . . . is most valuable to teach. There is no generally agreed-upon definition of what teaching is or how to measure its effects. When we have achieved more understanding of what and how to teach and [what are the] special effects on students, we will be much less vague about the supervision of these processes. (p. 3)

Social work supervision essentially faces the same dilemmas.

The present situation is one of transition and crisis. It has the advantage, at least, of making the problems faced by the profession clear and explicit. Determined efforts are being made to resolve these issues, and the result is likely to be a more unified, strengthened profession with a clearer conception of its direction. Social work supervisors will profit from the change and can effectively contribute to achieving it.

Summary

The lack of direct access to supervisees' performance is a problem for supervisors. Workers' reports of their activities often suffer from significant omissions and distortions. Procedures such as direct observation, audio and video tapes, and co-therapy supervision are being used in response to this problem. Tapes provide the supervisor with a complete, reliable view of the worker's performance and provide the worker with the opportunity for self-supervision.

Peer supervision and time-limited supervision have been proposed in response to the problem of prolonged supervision. There is agreement that the supervisory relationship should yield to consultation, although some administrative supervision will continue to be required.

The antithetical components of administrative and educational supervision are not a problem for most supervisors but are sufficiently troublesome that active consideration has been given to separating these responsibilities.

A variety of procedures are being tried to debureaucratize the agency and redistribute managerial decision-making power. These include team service delivery, participatory management, and a supervisory contract system.

Studies show that most supervisees express satisfaction with the supervision they are receiving and that supervisors do a more effective job as a result of formal training.

BIBLIOGRAPHY

Abels, Paul A. 1977. *The New Practice of Supervision and Staff Development*. New York, Association Press.
Aber, J. Lawrence. 1982. "Social Policy Issues in Prevention of Burn-out: A Case Study." In *Stress and Burn-out in the Helping Professions,* ed. Barry A. Farber. New York, Pergamon Press.
Ables, Billie S., and Aug, Robert G. 1972. "Pitfalls Encountered by Beginning and Child Psychotherapists." *Psychotherapy: Theory, Research and Practice* 9:340–45.
Abrahamson, Arthur C. 1959. *Group Methods in Supervision and Staff Development*. New York, Harper.
Abrahamson, Mark. 1967. *The Professional in the Organization*. Chicago, Rand McNally.
Abramczyk, Lois W. 1980. "The New M.S.W. Supervisor: Problems of Role Transition." *Social Casework* 61:83–89.
Abramowitz, Stephan I., and Abramowitz, Christine V. 1976. "Sex Role Psychodynamics in Psychotherapy Supervision." *American Journal of Psychotherapy* 30:583–92.
Abramson, Marcia. 1981. "Ethical Dilemmas for Social Workers in Discharge Planning." *Social Work in Health Care* 6:33–42.
Adler, Jacqueling, and Levy, Carmela. 1981. "The Impact of the One Way Screen: Its Uses as a Teaching Aid." *Contemporary Social Work Education* 4(1):66–74.
Aiken, Wilbur J.; Smits, Stanley S.; and Lollar, Donald J. 1972. "Leadership Behavior and Job Satisfaction in State Rehabilitation Agencies." *Personnel Psychology* 25:65–73.
Akin, Gib, and Weil, Marie. 1981. "The Prior Question: How Do Supervisors Learn to Supervise?" *Social Casework* 62:472–79.
Alexander, Leslie B. 1972. "Social Work's Freudian Deluge: Myth or Reality?" *Social Service Review* 46:517–38.
Allen, James D. 1976. "Peer Group Supervision in Family Therapy." *Child Welfare* 55:183–88.
Alonson, Anne, and Scott, Rutan J. 1978. "Cross-Sex Supervision for Cross-Sex Therapy." *American Journal of Psychiatry* 135(8):928–31.
Amacher, Kloh-Ann. 1971. "Explorations into the Dynamics of Learning in Field Work." D.S.W. dissertation, Smith College School of Social Work.
American Psychological Association. 1954. "Internship in Clinical Psychology." *American Psychologist* 9:760–64.
Anderson, Bruce N.; Pine, Irving; and Mee-lee, Denis. 1972. "Resident

Training in Co-Therapy Groups." *International Journal of Psychotherapy* 22:192–98.

Anderson, William A., and Martin, Patricia Y. 1982. "Bureaucracy and Professionalism in the Social Services—A Multi-Dimensional Approach to the Analysis of Conflict and Congruity." *Journal of Social Service Research* 5(3/4):33–51.

Apaka, Tusencko, K.; Hirsch, Sidney; and Kleidman, Sylvia. 1967. "Establishing Group Supervision in a Hospital Social Work Deparment." *Social Work* 12:54–60.

Aptekar, Herbert H. 1959. "The Continued Education of Experienced Workers." *Child Welfare* 38:7–12.

Arlow, Jacob A. 1963. "The Supervisory Situation." *Journal of the American Psychoanalytic Association* 11:576–94.

Armstrong, Katherine. 1979. "How to Avoid Burn-out: A Study of the Relationship between Burn-out and Worker, Organizational and Management Characteristics in Eleven Child Abuse and Neglect Projects." *Child Abuse and Neglect* 3:145–49.

Armstrong, Margaret; Huffman, Margaret; and Spain, Marianne. "The Use of Process and Tape Recordings as Tools in Learning Casework." M.A. Thesis, State University of Iowa.

Arndt, Hilda. 1973. "Effective Supervision in a Public Welfare Setting." *Public Welfare* 31:50–54.

Austin, Lucille. 1956. "An Evaluation of Supervision." *Social Casework* 37:375–82.

Austin, Lucille. 1960. "Supervision in Social Work." *Social Work Year Book, 1960,* pp. 579–86.

Austin, Lucille. 1961. "The Changing Role of Supervisor." *Smith College Studies in Social Work* 31:179–95.

Austin, Michael. 1977. *An Exploratory Study of the Burn-out Syndrome in the Social Work Profession.* Kalamazoo, Western Michigan University.

Austin, Michael. 1978. *Professionals and Paraprofessionals.* New York, Human Services Press.

Austin, Michael. 1981. *Supervisory Management for the Human Services.* Englewood Cliffs, N.J., Prentice-Hall.

Babcock, Charlotte G. 1953. "Social Work as Work." *Social Casework* 36:415–22.

Barclay Report. 1982. *Social Workers: Their Roles and Tasks.* Published for the National Institute for Social Work by Bedford Square Press, London.

Bardill, D. R. 1978. "The Peer Group Model for Supervision." *Social Thought* 4(4):3–14.

Barker, Robert L. 1972. "Conclusion: Research Findings Related to the Education of Baccalaureate Social Workers." In *Manpower Research on the Utilization of Baccalaureate Social Workers: Implications for Education,* ed. Robert L. Barker and Thomas L. Briggs, pp. 89–96. Washington, D.C., U.S. Govt. Printing Office.

Barnard, Chester. 1938. *The Functions of the Executive.* Cambridge, Mass., Harvard University Press.

Bar-Oren, Yachiel. 1976. *The Impact of Professional and Bureaucratic Norms on Social Workers: Perceptions of Their Work Autonomy, Orientation, and Performance in Social Welfare Agencies.* Ph.D. dissertation, Brandeis University.

Barr, Sherman. 1967. "Some Observations on the Practice of Indigenous Non-Professionals." In *Personnel in Anti-poverty Programs: Implications for Social Work Education,* pp. 51–62. New York, Council on Social Work Education.

Barth, Richard, and Gambrill, Eileen D. 1984. "Learning to Interview: The Quality of Training Opportunities." *The Clinical Supervisor* 2:3–14.

Bartlett, Willis E.; Goodyear, Rodney K.; and Bradley, Fred O. 1983. "Special Issue on Supervision." *The Counseling Psychologist* 11.

Bartol, K. M., and Wortman, M. S. 1975. "Male Versus Female Leaders: Effects of Perceived Leaders' Behavior and Satisfaction in a Hospital." *Personnel Psychology* 28:533–47.

Bar-Yosef, Rivka, and Schild, Erling. 1966. "Pressure and Defenses in Bureaucratic Rules." *American Journal of Sociology* 71:665–73.

Baum, Dale D. 1976. "An Application of the Bug-in-the-Ear Communication System for Training Psychometrists." *Counselor Education and Supervision* 15:309–10.

Bauman, William F. 1972. "Games Counselor Trainees Play: Dealing with Trainee Resistance." *Counselor Education and Supervision* 12:251–57.

Becker, Dorothy G. 1963. "Early Adventures in Social Casework: The Charity Agent 1880–1910." *Social Casework* 44:253–261.

Behling, John; Curtis, Cartetta; and Foster, Sara A. 1982. "Impact of Sex Role Combination on Student Performance in Field Instruction." *Journal of Education for Social Work* 18(2):93–97.

Beiser, Helen. 1966. "Self-Listening during Supervision of Psychotherapy." *Archives of General Psychiatry* 15:135–39.

Beitman, Bernard D. 1983. "The Demographics of American Psychotherapists." *American Journal of Psychotherapy* 37(1):37–48.

Bell, Joanne I. n.d. *Staff Development and Practice Supervision: Criteria and Guidelines for Determining Their Appropriate Function.* Washington, D.C., U.S. Department of Health, Education and Welfare, Social and Rehabilitation Service, Assistance Payments Administration.

Benschoter, R. A.; Eaton, M. T.; and Smith, D. 1965. "Use of Videotape to Provide Individual Instruction in Techniques of Psychotherapy." *Journal of Medical Education* 40:1159–61.

Berengarten, Sidney. 1957. "Identifying Learning Patterns of Individual Students: An Exploratory Study." *Social Serivce Review* 31:407–17.

Berger, Michael, and Dammann, Cassell. 1982. "Live Supervision as Contest in Treatment and Training." *Family Process* 21(3):337–44.

Berger, Milton M. 1978. *Videotape Techniques in Psychiatric Training and Treatment.* Revised ed. New York, Bruner-Mazel.

Berkeley Planning Associates. 1977. *Project Management and Worker Burnout Report*. Berkeley, California, Berkeley Planning Associates.

Berliner, Arthur. 1971. "Some Pitfalls in Administrative Behavior." *Social Casework* 52:562–66.

Bernard, Harold S.; Babineau, Raymond; and Schwartz, Allen J. 1980. "Supervisor-Trainee Co-Therapy as a Method for Individual Psychotherapy Training." *Psychiatry* 43:138–45.

Bernstein, Howard A., 1981. "Survey of Threats and Assaults Directed Toward Psychotherapists." *American Journal of Psychotherapy* 35(4):542–49.

Billingsley, Andrew. 1964a. "Bureaucratic and Professional Orientation Patterns in Social Casework." *Social Service Review* 38:400–7.

Billingsley, Andrew. 1964b. *The Role of the Social Worker in a Child Protective Agency: A Comparative Analysis*. Boston, Society for Prevention of Cruelty to Children.

Birchler, Gary R. 1975. "Live Supervision and Instant Feedback in Marriage and Family Therapy." *Journal of Marriage and Family Counseling* 1:331–42.

Bishop, J. B. 1971. "Another Look at Counselor, Client and Supervisor Ratings of Counselor Effectiveness." *Counselor Education and Supervision* 10:310–23.

Bishop, Maxine H. 1969. *Dynamic Supervision: Problems and Opportunities*. New York, American Management Association.

Blackey, Eileen. 1957. *Group Leadership in Staff Training*. Bureau of Public Assistance, H.E.W. Report no. 29. Washington, D.C., U.S. Govt. Printing Office.

Blake, R. R., and Mouton, S. S. 1961. *The Managerial Grid*. Houston, Gulf.

Blane, Stephen M. 1968. "Immediate Effect of Supervisory Experiences on Counselor Candidates." *Counselor Education DD& Supervision* 8:39–44.

Blankenship, Ralph L. 1977. *Colleagues in Organization—The Social Construction of Professional Work*. New York, John Wiley.

Blau, Peter M. 1960. "Orientation toward Clients in a Public Welfare Agency." *Administrative Science Quarterly* 5:341–61.

Blau, Peter M. 1963. *The Dynamics of Bureaucracy*. Revised ed. Chicago, University of Chicago Press.

Blau, Peter M. and Scott, Richard W. 1962. *Formal Organizations*. San Francisco, Chandler.

Bloom, Allan A. 1978. "Pitfalls of a Managerial Approach to Supervision in a Public Welfare Agency." *Administration in Social Work* 2:482–87.

Bloom, Leonard, and Herman, Cherie. 1958. "A Problem of Relationship in Supervision." *Journal of Social Casework* 39:402–6.

Blumberg, Arthur. 1980. *Supervisors and Teachers: A Private Cold War*, 2nd ed. Berkeley, California, McCuthan.

Blumenfield, Michael, ed. 1982. *Applied Supervision in Psychotherapy*. New York, Grune and Stratton.

Boyd, John D. 1978. *Counselor Supervision: Approaches, Preparation, Practice.* Muncie, Indiana, Accelerated Development Inc.

Boylston, William H., and Tuma, June M. 1972. "Training of Mental Health Professonals Through the Use of the 'Bug in the Ear.'" *American Journal of Psychiatry* 129:92–95.

Brackett, Jeffrey. 1904. *Education and Supervision in Social Work.* New York, Macmillan.

Bradshaw, Walter H. 1982. "Supervision in Black and White: Race as a Factor in Supervision." In *Applied Supervision in Psychotherapy,* ed. Michael Blumenfield, pp. 199–220. New York, Grune and Stratton.

Brady, Carol A.; Kinnaird, Keri; and Fredrick, William. 1980. "Job Satisfaction and Perception of Social Climate in a Mental Health Facility." *Perceptual and Motor Skills* 51:559–64.

Brager, George, and Michael, John A. 1969. "The Sex Distribution in Social Work: Causes and Consequences." *Social Casework* 50:595–601.

Brager, George, and Specht, Harry. 1973. *Community Organizing.* New York, Columbia University Press.

Bramford, Terry. 1978. "The Gulf Between Managers and Practitioners." *Social Work Today* 10.

Brandon, Joan, and Davies, Martin. 1979. "The Limits of Competence in Social Work: The Assessment of Marginal Students in Social Work Education." *British Journal of Social Work* 9:297–347.

Brearley, Paul C. 1982. *Risk and Social Work.* Boston, Routledge and Kegan Paul.

Brennan, E. Clifford; Arkava, Morton L.; Cummins, David E.; and Wicks, Leona K. 1976. "Expectations for Baccalaureate Social Workers." *Public Welfare* 34:19–23.

Brennan, E. Clifford. 1982. "Evaluation of Field Teaching and Learning." In *Quality Field Instruction in Social Work,* ed. Bradford W. Sheafer and Louise E. Jenkins, pp. 76–97. New York, Longmans.

Breunlin, D., and Cade, B. W. 1981. "Intervention in Family Systems with Observer Messages." *Journal of Marital and Family Therapy* 7:453–60.

Briar, Scott. 1966. "Family Services." In *Five Fields of Social Services: Reviews of the Literature,* ed. Henry Maas, pp. 9–50. New York, National Association of Social Workers.

Briar, Scott. 1971. "Family Services and Casework." In *Research in the Social Services: A Five Year Review,* ed. Henry Maas, pp. 108–25. New York, National Association of Social Workers.

Briar, Scott. 1977. "In Summary." Special Issue on Conceptual Frameworks. *Social Work* 22(1):145.

Brieland, Donald. 1959. *An Experimental Study of Adoptive Parents at Intake.* New York, Child Welfare League of America.

Brieland, Donald; Briggs, Thomas L.; and Leuenberger, Paul. 1973. *The Team Model of Social Work Practice.* Syracuse, N.Y., Syracuse University School of Social Work.

Briggs, Thomas. 1973. "Social Work Manpower: Development and Dilemmas of the 1970s." In *Educating MSW Students to Work with Other Social Welfare Personnel*, ed. Margaret Purvine, pp. 4–31. New York, Council on Social Work Education.

Brill, Naomi. 1976. *Teamwork: Working Together with Human Services.* New York, J. B. Lippincott.

Brintnall, Michael. 1981. "Caseloads, Performance and Street-Level Bureaucracy." *Urban Affairs Quarterly* 16:281–98.

Briscoe, Catherine, and Thomas, David. 1977. *Community Work: Learning and Supervision.* London, Allen and Unwin.

Brodsky, Annette M. 1980. "Sex Role Issues in the Supervision of Therapy." In *Psychotherapy Supervision: Theory, Research, and Practice*, ed. Allen K. Hess, pp. 509–22. New York, John Wiley.

Brodsky, A., and Edelwich, J. 1980. *Burn-out: Stages of Disillusionment in the Helping Professions.* New York, Human Sciences Press.

Bromberg, Phillip. 1982. "The Supervisory Process and the Parallel Psychoanalysis." *Contemporary Psychoanalysis* 18(1):92–111.

Brown, Edwin G. 1970. "Selection of Adoptive Parents: A Videotape Study." Ph.D. dissertation, School of Social Service Administration, University of Chicago.

Brown, R. S. G. 1975. *The Management of Welfare.* London, Robertson.

Brown, Stephen. 1979. "Male versus Female Leaders: A Comparison of Empirical Studies." *Sex Roles* 5(5):595–611.

Bruck, Max. 1963. "The Relationship Between Student Anxiety, Self-Awareness and Self-Concept, and Competence in Casework." *Social Casework* 44:125–31.

Brugger, T.; Ceasor, G.; Frank, A.; and Martz, S. 1962. "Peer Supervision as a Method of Learning Psychotherapy." *Comprehensive Psychiatry* 3:47–53.

Bruner, Jerome S. 1971. *Toward a Theory of Instruction.* Cambridge, Mass., Harvard University Press.

Burke, Donald, and Wilcox, Douglas S. 1971. "Basis of Supervisory Power and Subordinate Job Satisfactions." *Canadian Journal of Behavioral Science* 3:184–93.

Burns, Mary E. 1958. "The Historical Development of the Process of Casework Supervision as Seen in the Professional Literature of Social Work." Ph.D. dissertation, School of Social Service Administration, University of Chicago.

Bush, James. 1977. "The Minority Administrator: Implications for Social Work Education." *Journal of Education for Social Work* 13(1)15–22.

Calligor, Leopold. 1981. "Parallel and Reciprocal Process in Psychoanalytic Supervision." *Contemporary Psychoanalysis* 17(1):1–27.

Caplow, Theodore. 1954. *The Sociology of Work.* Minneapolis, University of Minnesota Press.

Caragonne, Penelope A. 1979. "Implementation Structures in Community Support Programs: Manpower Implications of Case Management Systems" (May 1979). Reprinted in *Selected Readings on the Enhancement of Social Service Management Systems,* DHHS Publication No. (OHDS) 80-30273. Washington, D.C., U.S. Govt. Printing Office, 1980.

Caron, Cheryl, et al. 1983. "Intrapersonal Correlates of Burn-out: The Role of Locus of Control in Burn-out and Self Esteem." *The Clinical Supervisor* 1:53–62.

"Casework Notebook: Dynamic Aspects of Role of Supervisor." 1939. *Social Work Today* 6:41–42.

C. D. 1938. "The Role of the Casework Supervisor Re-Examined." *Social Work Techniques* 3:12–16.

Chafetz, Janet S. 1972. "Women in Social Work." *Social Work* 17(5):12–18.

Chase, P. 1978. "Comments on the Emener Theory Article." *Journal of Rehabilitation Administration* 2:55–56.

Chatterjee, Pranab. 1972. "Commitment to Work Among Public Welfare Workers." *Public Welfare* 30:53–58.

Chernesky, Roslyn H. 1980. "Women Administrators in Social Work." In *Women's Issues and Social Work Practice,* ed. Elaine Norman and Arlene Mancuso, pp. 241–61. Itasca, Illinois, Peacock Press.

Chernesky, Roslyn H. 1981. "Attitudes of Social Workers Toward Peer Review." *Health and Social Work* 6(2):67–73.

Chernesky, Roslyn H. 1983. "The Sex Dimension of Organizational Processes: Its Impact on Women Managers." *Administration in Social Work* 7:133–43.

Cherniss, Cary. 1977. "Styles of Clerical Supervision in Community Mental Health Programs." *Journal of Counseling and Clinical Psychology* 45(6):1195–96.

Cherniss, Cary. 1980. *Professional Burn-out in Human Service Organizations.* New York, Praeger.

Cherniss, Cary, and Egnatios, E. 1978. "Clinical Supervision in Community Mental Health." *Social Work* 23(3):219–23.

Chevron, Eve, and Rounsaville, Bruce J. 1983. "Evaluating the Clinical Skills of Psychotherapists—A Comparison of Techniques." *Archives of General Psychiatry* 40:1129–32.

Chodoff, Paul. 1972. "Supervision of Psychotherapy with Videotape: Pros and Cons." *American Journal of Psychiatry* 128:819–23.

Cohen, Neil and Rhodes, Gary B. 1977. "A View Toward Leadership Style and Job Orientation in Education and Practice." *Administration in Social Work* 1(3):281–91.

Cohen, Ronald J. 1979. *Malpractice: A Guide for Mental Health Professionals.* New York, Free Press.

Cohen, Ruth. 1972. "Student Training in a Geriatric Center." In *Issues in Human Services,* ed. Florence W. Kaslow and associates, pp. 168–84. San Francisco, Jossey-Bass.

Compton, Beulah, and Galaway, Burt. 1975. *Social Work Processes.* Homewood, Illinois, Dorsey Press.

Conte, Jon R., et al. 1981. *A Qualitative Evaluation of Citizen's Review of Boards in Four States,* p. 40. Chicago, University of Illinois Center for

Policy and Research.

Conyngton, Mary. 1909. *How to Help: A Manual of Practical Charity Designed for the Use of Nonprofessional Workers Among the Poor.* New York, Macmillan.

Cope, Ronald. 1982. "Concurrent Validity of a Written Test for Entry Level Social Workers." *Educational and Psychological Measurement* 42(4):1181–88.

Cormier, L. Sherilyn, and Bernard, Janine M. 1982. "Ethical and Legal Responsibilities of Clinical Supervisors." *The Personnel and Guidance Journal,* 60:486–91.

Cornwell, Max, and Pearson, Rosemary. 1981. "Co-Therapy Teams and One-Way Screen in Family Therapy Practice and Training." *Family Process* 20:199–209.

Cournoyer, Barry B. 1983. "Assertiveness Among MSW Students." *Journal of Education for Social Work* 19:24–30.

Covner, B. S. 1943. "Studies in the Phonographic Recorders of Verbal Material: III. The Completeness and Accuracy of Counselor Interview Reports." *Journal of General Psychology* 30:181–203.

Cross, Darryl, and Brown, David. 1983. "Counselor Supervision as a Function of Trainee Experience: An Analysis of Specific Behaviors." *Counselor Education and Supervision* 22:333–40.

Cruser, Robert W. 1958. "Opinions on Supervision: A Chapter Study." *Social Work* 3:18–25.

Culatta, Richard, and Seltzer, Herbert. 1976. "Content and Sequence Analysis of the Supervisory Session." *ASHA Social Work*18:8–12.

Culatta, Richard, and Seltzer, Herbert. 1977. "Content and Sequence of the Supervisory Session: A Report of the Clinical Use." *ASHA* 19:523–26.

Culatta, Richard, and Helmick, Joseph. 1981. "Clinical Supervision: The State of the Art." *ASHA* 23:21–31.

Cullen, John, and Perrewe, Pamela. 1981. "Superior and Subordinates Gender; Does It Really Matter?" *Psychological Reports* 48:435–38.

Dailey, Dennis M. 1983. "Androgyny, Sex Role Stereotypes, and Clinical Judgement." *Social Work Research and Abstracts* 19(1):20–24.

Davidson, Terrence N., and Emmer, Edmund T. 1966. "Immediate Effect of Supportive and Nonsupportive Supervisor Behavior on Counselor Candidates' Focus of Concern." *Counselor Education and Supervision* 6:27–31.

Davis, Edward W., and Barrett, Marjie C. 1981. "Supervision for Management of Worker Stress." *Administration in Social Work* 5:55–64.

Davis, Kathleen L., and Arvey, Harriet H. 1978. "Dual Supervision: A Model for Counseling and Supervision." *Counselor Education and Supervision,* 18:294–99.

Dawson, John B. 1926. "The Case Supervisor in a Family Agency." *Family* 6:293–95.

De la Torre, Jorge. 1974. "Use and Misuse of Cliches in Clinical Supervision." *Archives of General Psychiatry* 31:302–6.

Delbeeg, Andre, and Ladbrook, Dennis. 1979. "Administrative Feedback on the Behavior of Subordinates." *Administration in Social Work* 3:15B1.

Demos, George. 1964. "Suggested Uses of Tape Recordings in Counseling Supervision." *Personnel and Guidance Journal* 42(7):704–5.

Devine, Edward. 1901. *The Practice of Charity.* New York, Handbook for Practical Workers.

Devis, Donald A. 1965. "Teaching and Administrative Functions in Supervision." *Social Work* 46:83–89.

Dimock, Hedley S., and Trecker, Harleigh B. 1949. *The Supervisor of Group Work and Recreation.* New York, Association Press.

Doehrman, Margery. 1976. "Parallel Processes in Supervision and Psychotherapy." *Bulletin of the Menninger Clinic* 40:3–104.

Dornbusch, Sanford M., and Scott, Richard W. 1975. *Evaluation and the Exercise of Authority.* San Francisco, Jossey-Bass.

Douds, Alexander F., and Collingwood, Thomas R. 1978. "Management by Objectives, A Successful Application." *Child Welfare* 57(3):181–85.

Dublin, Richard A. 1982. "Supervision as an Orienting and Integrating Process." *Social Casework* 63:233–36.

Duncan, Mina G. 1963. "An Experiment in Applying New Methods in Field Work." *Social Casework* 44:179–84.

Durlak, J. A. 1979. "Comparative Effectiveness of Paraprofessional and Professional Helpers." *Psychological Bulletin* 86:80–92.

Edelwich, Jerry and Brodsky, Archie. 1980. *Burn-out—Stages of Disillusionment in the Helping Professions.* New York, Human Sciences Press.

Edelwich, Jerry, and Brodsky, Archie. 1982. *Sexual Dilemmas for the Helping Professional.* New York, Bruner-Mazel.

Educational Testing Service. 1973. *Summary of Research Proposals Submitted to ACSW.* Princeton, N.J.

Eisenberg, Sidney. 1956a. *Supervision in the Changing Field of Social Work.* Philadelphia, Jewish Family Service of Philadelphia.

Eisenberg, Sidney. 1956b. "Supervision as an Agency Need." *Social Casework* 37:233–37.

Ekstein, Rudolf, and Wallenstein, Robert S. 1972. *The Teaching and Learning of Psychotherapy.* 2d ed. New York, International Universities Press.

Emener, W. G. 1978. "Clinical Supervision in Rehabilitation Settings." *Journal of Rehabilitation Administration* 2:44–58.

Emener, William; Luck, Richard; and Smits, Stanley. 1981. *Rehabilitation: Administration and Supervision.* Baltimore, University Park Press.

Emerson, Richard M. 1962. "Power-Dependence Relations." *American Sociological Review* 27:31–41.

Engel, Gloria J. 1970. "Professional Autonomy and Bureaucratic Organization." *Administrative Science Quaterly* 15:12–21.

English, R. William, and Jelenevsky, Serge. 1971. "Counselor Behavior as Judged under Audio, Visual, and Audiovisual Communication Conditions." *Journal of Counseling Psychology* 18:509–13.

Epstein, Irwin. 1970. "Professionalization, Professionalism, and Social Worker Radicalism." *Journal of Health and Social Behavior* 11:67–77.

Etzioni, Amitai. 1961. *A Comparative Analysis of Complex Organizations.* New York, Free Press.

Ewalt, Patricia L. 1980. "From Clinician to Manager." In *New Directions for Mental Health Servies–Middle Management in Mental Health,* ed. Stephan White, pp. 1–10. San Francisco, Jossey-Bass.

Ezell, Hazel F., and Odewahn, Charles A. 1980. "An Empirical Inquiry of Variables Impacting on Women in Management in Public Social Service Organizations." *Administration in Social Work* 4(4):53–70.

Ezell, Hazel F.; Odewhan, C. A.; and Sherman, J. D. 1982. "Women Entering Management: Differences in Perception of Factors Influencing Integration." *Group and Organizational Studies* 7(2):243–53.

Fallon, Kenneth P. 1974. "Participatory Management: An Alternative in Human Service Delivery Systems." *Child Welfare* 53:555–62.

Family Service Association of America. 1957. *A Guide to Classification of Professional Positions and Evaluation Outlines in a Family Service Agency.* New York.

Farber, Barry A., and Heifetz, Louis J. 1981. "The Satisfactions and Stresses of Psychotherapeutic Work: A Factor Analytic Study." *Professional Psychology* 12(5):621–29.

Farber, Barry A., and Heifetz, Louis J. 1982. "The Process and Dimensions of Burn-out in Psychotherapists." *Professional Psychology* 13(2): 293–301.

Farrall Instrument Co. n.d. "Bug-in-the-Ear" advertising brochure. Grand Island, Nebr.

Feldman, Yonata; Sponitz, Hyman; and Nagelberg, Leo. 1953. "One Aspect of Casework Training through Supervision." *Social Casework* 34: 150–56.

Fiedler, Fred E. 1967. *A Theory of Leadership Effectiveness.* New York, McGraw.

Fields, Mrs. James T. 1885. *How to Help the Poor.* Boston, Houghton.

Finch, Wilbur. 1976. "Social Workers versus Bureaucracy." *Social Work* 21:370–75.

Fizdale, Ruth. 1958. "Peer Group Supervision." *Social Casework* 39:443–50.

Fleischmann, O. 1955. "A Method of Teaching Psychotherapy: One-Way-Vision Room Technique." *Bulletin of the Menninger Clinic* 19:160–72.

Fleming, Joan, and Benedek, Therese. 1966. *Psychoanalytic Supervision.* New York, Grune.

Ford, Julian D. 1979. "Research on Training Counselors and Clinicians." *Review of Educational Research* 49:87–130.

Foren, Robert, and Bailey, Royston. 1968. *Authority in Social Casework.* New York, Pergamon.

Fox, Raymond. 1974. "Supervision by Contract." *Social Casework* 55:247–51.

Fox, Raymond. 1983. "Contracting in Supervision: A Goal Oriented Process." *The Clinical Supervisor* 1:37–49.

Fox, Raymond, and Zischka, Pauline C. 1982. "Using Goal Focused Contracts in Supervision." *Social Work in Education* 4(3):16–27.

Frances, A. and Clarkin, J. 1981. "Parallel Techniques in Supervision and Treatment." *Psychiatric Quarterly* 53:242–48.

Freidson, Eliot. 1975. *Doctoring Together: A Study of Professional Social Control.* Chicago, University of Chicago Press.

Freidson, Eliot, and Rhea, Buford. 1965. "Knowledge and Judgment in Professional Evaluations." *Administrative Science Quarterly* 10:107–24.

French, John R. P., Jr., and Raven, Bertram. 1960. "The Bases of Social Power." In *Group Dynamics,* ed. D. Cartwright and A. Zander, pp. 607–23. Evanston, Ill., Row, Peterson.

Freudenberger, Herbert. 1980. *Burn-out.* New York, Anchor Press.

Friedlander, G. 1983. "Trainees' Expectations for the Supervision Proseminar." *Counselor Education and Supervision* 22:342–48.

Friesen, Deloss D., and Dunning, G. B. 1973. "Peer Evaluation and Practicuum Supervision." *Counselor Education and Supervision* 13:229–35.

Froehlich, Clifford P. 1958. "The Completeness and Accuracy of Counseling Inverview Reports." *Journal of General Psychology* 58:81–96.

Galambos, Eva C., and Wiggens, Xenia R. 1970. *After Graduation: Experiences of College Graduates in Locating and Working in Social Welfare Positions.* Atlanta, Southern Regional Education Board.

Gale, Melvin. 1978. "Resident Perception of Psychiatry Supervision." *Comprehensive Psychiatry* 17:191–94.

Galm, Sharon. 1972. *Issues in Welfare Administration: Welfare—An Administrative Nightmare.* Subcommittee on Fiscal Policy of the Joint Economic Committee, U.S. Congress. Washington, D.C., U.S. Govt. Printing Office.

Gambrill, Eileen, and Wiltse, Kermit. 1974. "Foster Care Plans and Activities." *Public Welfare* 32:12–21.

Gasiorowicz, Nina. 1982. "The Parallel Process Supervision and Psychotherapy—An Empirical Study." *Smith College Studies in Social Work* 53:67.

Geer, Blanche. 1966. "Occupational Commitment and the Teaching Profession." *School Review* 74:31–47.

Geideman, H. 1980. "The Parallelism Phenomenon in Psychoanalysis and Supervision." *Psychoanalytic Quarterly* 49(2):234–55.

Gelso, Charles. 1972. "Inhibition Due to Recording and Clients' Evaluation of Counseling." *Psychological Reports* 31:67577.

Gelso, Charles, and Tanney, Mary F. 1972. "Client Personality as a Mediator of the Effects of Recording." *Counselor Education and Supervision* 12:109–14.

Gershenson, Judith, and Cohen, Martin B. 1978. "Through the Looking Glass: The Experience of Two Family Therapy Trainees with Live Supervision." *Family Process* 17:225–30.

Getzels, Jacob W., and Guba, E. G. 1957. "Social Behavior and Administrative Process." *School Review* 65:423–41.

Gillespie, David F., and Cohen, Susan. 1984. "Causes of Worker Burn-out."

Children and Youth Services Review 6:115–24.

Gitterman, Alex. 1972. "Comparison of Educational Models and Their Influence on Supervision." In *Issues in Human Services,* ed. Florence W. Kaslow and associates, pp. 18–38. San Francisco, Jossey-Bass.

Gitterman, Alex, and Gitterman, Naomi P. 1979. "Social Work Student Evaluation Format and Method." *Journal of Education for Social Work* 15:103–8.

Gizynski, M. 1978. "Self Awareness of the Supervisee in Supervision." *Clinical Social Work Journal* 6(3):202–10.

Gladstone, Bernard. 1967. *Supervisory Practice and Social Service in the Neighborhood Center.* New York, United Neighborhood Homes.

Glastonbury, Bryan; Cooper, David M.; and Hawkins, Pearl. 1980. *Social Work in Conflict—The Practitioner and the Bureaucrat.* London, Croom Helm.

Glendenning, John M. 1923. "Supervision through Conferences on Specific Cases." *Family* 4:7–10.

Gockel, Galen. 1967. "Social Work as a Career Choice." In *Manpower and Social Welfare: Research Perspectives,* ed. Edward Schwartz, pp. 89–98. New York, National Association of Social Workers.

Goffman Erving. 1952. "On Cooling the Mark Out: Some Aspects of Adaptation to Failure." *Psychiatry* 15:451–63.

Goffman, Erving. 1959. *The Presentation of Self in Everyday Life.* Garden City, N.Y., Doubleday, Anchor.

Goin, Marcia K., and Kline, Frank M. 1974. "Supervision Observed." *Journal of Nervous and Mental Disease* 158:208–13.

Goin, Marcia K., and Kline, Frank. 1976. "Countertransference: A Neglected Subject in Clinical Supervision." *American Journal of Psychiatry* 133(1):41–44.

Goldberg, David. 1983. "Resistance to the Use of Video in Individual Psychotherapy Training." *American Journal of Psychiatry* 140:1172–76.

Goldhammer, Robert. 1969. *Clinical Supervision: Special Methods for the Supervision of Teachers.* New York, Holt.

Goldstein, Arnold P.; Heller, Kenneth; and Sechrest, Lee B. 1966. *Psychotherapy and the Psychology of Behavior Change.* New York, Wiley.

Goss, Mary W. E. 1961. "Influence and Authority among Physicians in an Outpatient Clinic." *American Sociological Review* 26:39–50.

Gouldner, Alvin. 1954. *Patterns of Industrial Democracy.* New York, Free Press.

Granet, Roger B.; Kalman, Thomas P.; and Socks, Michael H. 1980. "From Supervisee to Supervisor: An Unexplored Aspect of the Psychotreatment Education." *American Journal of Psychotherapy* 137:1443–45.

Granvold, Donald K. 1977. "Supervisory Style and Educational Preparation of Public Welfare Supervisors." *Administration in Social Work* 1(1): 79–87.

Granvold, Donald K. 1978a. "Training Social Work Supervisors to Meet Organizational and Worker Objectives." *Journal of Education for Social Work* (14(2):38–46.

Granvold, Donald K. 1978b. "Supervision by Objectives." *Administration in Social Work* 2(2):199–209.

Green, A. D. 1966. "The Professional Social Worker in the Bureaucracy." *Social Service Review* 40:71–83.

Green, Solomon H. 1972. "Educational Assessments of Student Learning through Practice in Field Instruction." *Social Work Education Reporter* 20:48–54.

Greenleigh Associates. 1960. *Addenda to Facts, Fallacies, and Future: A Study of the AFDC Program, Cook County, Ill.* New York.

Grinnell, Richard M., and Hill, Linda Sue. 1979. "The Perceived Effectiveness and Efficiency of DHR Employees." *Social Service Review* 53: 116–122.

Grossbard, Hyman. 1954. "Methodology for Developing Self-Awareness." *Social Casework* 35:380–85.

Grotjohn, M. 1945. "The Role of Identification in Psychiatric and Psychoanalytic Training." *Psychiatry* 12:141–45.

Gruenberg, Peter B.; Liston, Edward H., Jr.; and Wayne, George J. 1969. "Intensive Supervision of Psychotherapy with Videotape Recording." *American Journal of Psychotherapy* 23:95–105.

Gummer, Burton. 1979. "On Helping and Helplessness: The Structure of Discretion in the American Welfare System." *Social Service Review* 53:215–28.

Gurk, M. D., and Wicas, E. D. 1979. "Generic Models of Counseling, Supervision, Counseling Instruction, Dichotomy and Consultation Metamodel." *The Personnel and Guidance Journal* 57:407–9.

Gurteen, Humphrey S. 1882. *A Handbook of Charity Organizations.* Buffalo, N.Y., privately published.

Gutheil, T. G. 1981. "Patients' Viewing of Videotaped Psychotherapy: Part III, Aspects of Supervision." *Psychiatric Quarterly* 54:227–33.

Gutowski, Michael F., and Koshel, Jeffrey J. 1982. "Social Services." In *The Regan Experiment*, ed. John L. Palmer and Isabel V. Sawhill, pp. 307–28. Washington, D.C., Urban Institute Press.

Hage, Jerald, and Aiken, Michael. 1967. "Relationship of Centralization to Other Structural Properties." *Administrative Science Quarterly* 12:72–91.

Haley, Jay. 1977. *Problem Solving Therapy.* San Francisco, Jossey-Bass.

Hall, Richard H. 1968. "Professionalization and Bureaucratization." *American Sociological Review* 33:92–104.

Hallowitz, David. 1962. "The Supervisor as Practitioner." *Social Casework* 63:82–88.

Handler, Joel F. 1973. *The Coercive Social Worker.* Chicago, Rand McNally.

Handler, Joel F. 1979. *Protecting the Social Service Client—Legal and Structural Controls on Official Discretion.* New York, Academic Press.

Handler, Joel F., and Hollinsworth, Ellen Jane. 1971. *The Deserving Poor.* Chicago, Markham.

Hanlan, Archie. 1972. "Changing Functions and Structures." In *Issues in Human Services,* ed. Florence W. Kaslow and associates, pp. 39–50.

514

San Francisco, Jossey-Bass.

Hansen, James, and Warner, Richard W. 1971. "Review of Research on Practicum Supervision." *Counselor Education and Supervision* 11:261–72.

Hansen, James; Pound, Ronald; and Petro, C. 1976. "Review of Research on Practicum Supervision." *Counselor Education and Supervision* 16: 107–16.

Hansen, James; Robins, Terri H.; and Grimes, John. 1982. "Review of Research on Practicum Supervision." *Counselor Education and Supervision* 15:15–24.

Hare, Rachel T., and Frankena, Susan T. 1972. "Peer Group Supervision." *American Journal of Orthopsychiatry* 42:527–29.

Hargie, Owen D., and Saunders, Christine Y. 1983. "Training Professional Skills." In *Using Video*, ed. P. W. Dowrick and S. J. Briggs, pp. 150–66. New York, John Wiley.

Haring, Barbara. 1974. *Workload Measurement in Child Welfare: A Report of CWLA Member Agencies, Activities, and Interests*. New York, Child Welfare League of America.

Harper, Robert A., and Hudson, John W. 1952. "The Use of Recordings in Marriage Counseling: A Preliminary Empirical Investigation." *Marriage and Family Living* 14:332–34.

Harris, D. V., and Allison, E. K. 1982. "Performance Management and Professional Development as Separate Functions of Supervision." *Health and Social Work* 7(4):283–91.

Harris, Patrick. 1977. "Staff Supervision in Community Work." In *Community Work: Learning and Supervision*, ed. Catherine Briscoe and David N. Thomas, pp. 33–42. London, Allen and Unwin.

Harris-Jenkins, G. 1970. "Professionals in Organizations." In *Professions and Professionalization*, ed. J. A. Jackson, pp. 55–108. Cambridge University Press.

Harrison, W. David. 1980. "Role Strain and Burn-out in Child-Protective Service Workers." *Social Service Review* 54:31–44.

Harshbarger, Dwight. 1973. "The Individual and the Social Order: Notes on the Management of Heresy and Deviance in Complex Organizations." *Human Relations* 26:251–70.

Hart, Gordon M. 1982. *The Process of Clinical Supervision*. Baltimore, Maryland, University Park Press.

Harvey, Sally H., and Raider, Melvyn C. 1984. "Administrator Burnout." *Administration in Social Work* 8:81–90.

Hasenfeld, Yeshkel. 1983. *Human Service Organizations*. Englewood Cliffs, N.J., Prentice-Hall.

Hathway, Marion. 1943. "Utilizing Available and New Personnel." *Compas* 24:41–42.

Hawthorne, Lillian. 1975. "Games Supervisors Play." *Social Work* 20: 179–83.

Hayward, Christine. 1979. *A Fair Assessment—Issues in Evaluating Counselors*. London, Central Council for Education and Training in Social Work.

H. C. D. 1949. "Through Supervision with Gun and Camera: The Personal Account of a Beginning Supervisor." *Social Work Journal* 30:161–63.

Hegarty, W. H. 1974. "Using Subordinate Ratings to Elicit Behavioral Changes in Supervisors." *Journal of Applied Psychology* 59:764–66.

Henry, Charlotte S. 1955. "Criteria for Determining Readiness of Staff to Function without Supervision." In *Administrative, Supervision and Consultation,* pp. 34–45. New York, Family Service Association of America.

Henry, William E.; Sims, John H.; and Spray, Lee S. 1971. *The Fifth Profession.* San Francisco, Jossey-Bass.

Heppner, Paul P., and Roehike, Helen J. 1984. "Differences Among Supervisees at Different Levels of Training: Implications for a Developmental Model of Supervision." *Journal of Counseling Psychology* 31:70–90.

Heppner, Paul P., and Handley, Patrick G. 1981. "A Study of Interpersonal Influence Process in Supervision." *Journal of Counseling Psychology* 28(5):437–44.

Heraud, Brian. 1970. *Sociology and Social Work.* New York, Pergamon Press.

Heraud, Brian. 1981. *Training for Uncertainty—A Sociological Approach to Social Work Education.* Boston, Routledge and Kegan Paul.

Herrick, Christine D. 1977. *A Phenomenological Study of Supervisees' Positive and Negtive Experiences in Supervision.* Ph.D. diss., University of Pittsburgh.

Herzberg, Frederick. 1968. "One More Time—How Do You Motivate Employees?" *Harvard Business Review* 46:220–38.

Herzberg, Frederick; Mausner, B.; and Snyderman, B. B. 1959. *The Motivation to Work.* 2d ed. New York, Wiley.

Herzlinger, Regina E. 1981. "Management Control Systems in Human Serivce Organizations." In *Organization and the Human Services Cross Disciplinary Reflections,* ed. Herman D. Stein, pp. 205–32. Philadelphia, Temple University Press.

Hess, Allen K., ed. 1980. *Psychotherapy Supervision—Theory, Research, Practice.* New York, John Wiley.

Hewer, Vivian. 1974. "An Aid to Supervision in Practicuum." *Journal of Counseling Psychology* 21:66–70.

Hirsh, Herman, and Freed, Herbert. 1970. "Pattern Sensitization in Psychotherapy Supervision by Means of Video Tape Recording." In *Videotape Technique in Psychiatric Training and Treatment,* ed. Milton M. Berger. New York, Bruner-Mazel.

Hogan, R. A. 1964. "Issues and Approaches to Supervision." *Psychotherapy—Theory, Research, and Practice* 2:139–41.

Hollis, Florence. 1964. *Casework, a Psycho-Social Therapy.* New York, Random House.

Holloway, Stephen. 1980. "Up the Hierarchy: From Clinician to Administrator." *Administration in Social Work* 4:2.

Holtzman, Reva Fine. 1966. "Major Teaching Methods in Field Instruction in Casework." D.S.W. dissertation, Columbia University School of Social Work.

Hoot, John. 1979. *Social Work and Sexual Conduct.* Boston, Routledge and Kegan-Paul.

Horner, Matina. 1969. "A Bright Woman is Caught in a Double Bind." *Psychology Today* (November).

Howe, E. 1980. "Public Professions and the Private Model of Professionalism." *Social Work* 25:179–91.

Hunt, Winslow. 1981. "The Use of Countertransference in Psychotherapy Supervision." *Journal of the American Academy of Psychoanalysis* 9(3):361–73.

Itzin, Frank. 1960. "The Use of Tape Recording in Field Work." *Social Casework* 41:197–202.

Jacobs, Jerry. 1969. "Symbolic Bureaucracy: A Case Study of a Social Welfare Agency." *Social Forces* 47:513–22.

Janeway, Elizabeth. 1980. *Power of the Weak.* New York, Knopf.

Jarvis, Paul E., and Esty, Jonathan F. 1968. "The Alternative-Therapist-Observer Technique in Group Therapy Training." *International Journal of Group Psychotherapy* 18:95–99.

Jay, Anthony. 1967. *Management and Machiavelli.* New York, Bantam Books.

Jayaratne, Srinika, and Chess, Wayne A. 1982–83. "Some Correlates of Jobs Satisfaction Among Social Workers." *The Journal of Applied Social Sciences* 7(1):1–17.

Jayaratne, Srinika, and Chess, Wayne A. 1983. "Job Satisfaction and Turnover Among Social Work Administrators." *Administration in Social Work* 7(2):11–22.

Jayaratne, Srinika; Tripode, Tony; and Chess, Wayne A. 1983. "Perceptions of Emotional Support, Stress and Strain by Male and Female Social Workers." *Social Work Research and Abstracts* 19(2):19–29.

Jennings, Peter L., and Daley, Michael. 1979. "Sex Discrimination in Social Work Careers." *Social Work Research and Abstracts* 15:17–21.

Jewish Community Center. 1949. "Principles and Practices of Supervision in the Jewish Center." *Jewish Center Worker,* p. 44.

Joelson, J. 1982. "Friday Afternoon at the Board—Group Supervision in School Practice." *Social Work in Education* 4(4):26–34.

Jones, Mary Ann, and Noore, Anne. 1983. *Annual Salary Study and Survey of Selected Personnel Issues.* New York, Child Welfare League of America.

Judd, Jawiga; Kohn, Regina E.; and Shulman, Gerda L. 1962. "Group Supervision: A Vehicle for Professional Development." *Social Work* 7(1): 96–102.

Kadushin, Alfred. 1956a. "Interview Observation as a Teaching Device." *Social Casework* 37:334–41.

Kadushin, Alfred. 1956b. "The Effects of Interview Observation on the Interviewer." *Journal of Counseling Psychology* 3:130–35.

Kadushin, Alfred. 1957. "The Effect on the Client of Interview Observation at Intake." *Social Service Review* 31:22–38.

Kadushin, Alfred. 1968. "Games People Play in Supervision." *Social Work* 13(3):23–32.

Kadusin, Alfred. 1973. *Supervisor-Supervisee: A Questionnaire Study.* Madison, Wisconsin, School of Social Work, University of Wisconsin.

Kadushin, Alfred. 1974. "Supervisor-Supervisee: A Survey." *Social Work* 19:288–98.

Kagan, Morris. 1963. "The Field Instructor's Evaluation of Student Performance: Between Fact and Fiction." *Social Worker* 3:15–26.

Kagan, Norman; Krathwohl, David R.; and Miller, Ralph. 1963. "Stimulated Recall in Therapy Using Video-Tape: A Case Study." *Journal of Counseling Psychology* 10:237–43.

Kagle, Jill D. 1979. "Evaluating Social Work Practice." *Social Work* 24:292–96.

Kahle, Joseph H. 1969. "Structuring and Administering a Modern Voluntary Agency." *Social Work* 14(4):21–28.

Kahn, Eva. 1979. "The Parallel Process in Social Work Treatment and Supervision." *Social Casework* 60:520–28.

Kahn, Robert L. 1964. *Organizational Stress.* New York, Wiley.

Kallegian, Verne: Brown, Paula, and Wechsler, Irving. 1954. "The Impact of Interpersonal Relations on Ratings of Performance." *Public Personnel Review* 15:166–70.

Kanter, Rosabeth M. 1983. *The Charge Masters: Innovation for Productivity in the American Corporation.* New York, Simon and Schuster.

Kaplan, David M. 1983. "Current Trends in Practicum Supervision Research." *Counselor Education and Supervision* 22:215–26.

Kaslow, F. W. 1972. "Group Supervision." In *Issues in Human Services,* ed. Florence W. Kaslow and associates, pp. 115–41. San Francisco, Jossey-Bass.

Kaslow, F. W., et al., eds. 1977. *Supervision, Consultation, and Staff Training in the Helping Professions.* San Francisco, Jossey-Bass.

Katz, Fred E. 1968. *Autonomy and Organization.* New York, Random House.

Kaufman, Herbert. 1960. *The Forest Ranger.* Baltimore, Johns Hopkins University Press.

Kaufman, Herbert. 1973. *Administrative Feedback: Monitoring Subordinate Behavior.* Washington, D.C., Brookings Institution.

Kavanagh, Michael J. 1975. "Expected Supervisor Behavior, Interpersonal Trust and Environmental Preferences: Some Relationships Based on a Dyadic Model of Supervision." *Organizational Behavior and Human Performance* 13:17–30.

Kennedy, A. J., and Ferra, K. 1935. *Social Settlements in New York City.* New York, Columbia University Press.

Kennedy, Miriam, and Keitner, Lydia. 1970. "What is Supervision: The Need for a Redefinition." *Social Worker* 38:51–52.

Kermish, Irving, and Kushin, Frank. 1969. "'Why High Turnover?': Social Work Staff Losses in a County Welfare Agency." *Public Welfare* 27:134–37.

Kettner, Peter M. 1973. "Some Factors Affecting Use of Professional Knowledge and Skill by the Social Worker in Public Welfare Agencies." D.S.W. dissertation, University of Southern California, School of Social Work.

Kettner, Peter M. 1979. "A Conceptual Framework for Developing Learning Modules for Field Education." *Journal of Education for Social Work* 15:51–58.

Kim, Dong I; Boo, Sung L.; and Wheeler, Allan. 1979. "Professional Competency, Autonomy, and Job Satisfaction Among Social Workers in an Appalachian Rural Area." *Social Thought* 5:47–59.

Kledaras, Constantine G. 1971. "A Study of Role Conflict in Supervision." D.S.W. dissertation, Catholic University of America.

Kleinman, L. S., and Lounsbury, J. W. 1978. "Validating Procedures for Selecting Social Work Personnel." *Social Work* 23:481–88.

Klienman, Sherryl. 1981. "Making Professionals 'Into Persons'—Discrepancies in Traditional and Humanistic Expectations of Professional Identity." *Sociology of Work and Occupations* 8:41–87.

Knapman, N. S. 1977. "Sex Discrimination in Family Agencies." *Social Work* 22:461–65.

Knowles, Malcom. 1971. "Innovations in Teaching Styles and Approaches Based upon Learning." *Journal of Education for Social Work* 7(3):32–59.

Kogan, Leonard S. 1950. "The Electrical Recording of Social Casework Interviews." *Social Casework* 31:371–78.

Kohn, Regina. 1971. "Differential Use of Observed Interview in Student Training." *Social Work Education Reporter* 19:45–46.

Kolb, David A. 1981. "Learning Styles and Disciplinary Differences." In *The Modern American College,* ed. Arthur A. Chickering and Associates, pp. 232–55. San Francisco, Jossey-Bass.

Kolevson, Michael. 1978. "Evaluating the Supervisory Relationship in Field Placements." *Social Work* 24(3):241–44.

Konrad, George. 1969. *The Caseworker.* New York, Harcourt Brace Jovanovich.

Korner, Ija N., and Brown, William H. 1952. "The Mechanical Third Ear." *Journal of Consulting Psychology* 16:81–84.

Kornfeld, D. S., and Kolb, L. C. 1964. "The Use of Closed Circuit Television in the Teaching of Psychiatry." *Journal of Nervous and Mental Diseases* 138:452–59.

Kornhauser, William. 1962. *Scientists in Industry: Conflict and Accommodation.* Berkeley, University of California Press.

Kravetz, Diane, and Jones, Linda E. 1982. "Career Orientation of Female Social Work Students: An Examination of Sex Differences." *Journal of Education for Social Work* 18(3):77–84.

Kugel, Linda, and Riggs, R. Thomas. 1981. "Practitioner to Administration." *Social Casework* 62:241.

Kupius, Dewayne, and Baker, Ronald. 1977. "The Supervision Process: Analysis and Synthesis." In *Supervision and Applied Training—A Com-*

parative Review, ed. D.J. Kupius, R.D. Baker, and J.D. Thomas, pp. 225–60. Westport, Conn., Greenwood Press.

Kurzmann, Paul A. 1977. "Rules and Regulations in Large Scale Organizations: A Theoretical Approach to the Problem." *Administration in Social Work* 14:421–31.

Kutzik, Alfred. 1977. "The Social Work Field." In *Supervision Consultation and Staff Training in the Helping Professions,* ed. Florence W. Kaslow and Associates, pp. 25–60. San Francisco, Jossey-Bass.

Lamb, Richard, and Mahl, George. 1956. "Manifest Reactions of Patients and Interviewers to the Use of Sound Recording in the Psychiatric Interview." *American Journal of Psychiatry* 112:733–35.

Lambert, M.J. 1980. "Research and the Supervisory Process." In *Psychotherapy Supervision: Theory, Research and Practice,* ed. A.K. Hess, pp. 423–50. New York, Wiley.

Lambert, M. S., and Beier, E. G. 1974. "Supervisory and Counseling Process: A Comparative Study." *Counselor Education and Supervision* 14:54–60.

Landy, Frank, and Farr, Jane. 1980. "Performance Rating." *Psychological Bulletin* 87(1):72–110.

Langs, Robert. 1979. *The Supervisory Experience.* New York, Jason Aronson.

Lanning, Wayne L. 1971. "A Study of the Relation between Group and Individual Counseling Supervision and Three Relationship Measures." *Journal of Counseling Psychology* 18:401–6.

Lauderdale, Michael. 1981. *Burn-out.* Austin, Texas, Learning Concepts.

Lazerson, Alan M. 1972. "The Learning Alliance and Its Relation to Psychiatric Teaching." *Psychiatry in Medicine* 3:81–91.

Leader, Arthur L. 1957. "New Directions in Supervision." *Social Casework* 38:462–68.

Leader, Arthur L. 1968. "Supervision and Consultations through Observed Interviewing." *Social Casework* 49:288–93.

Lechnyr, Ronald J. 1975. "Evaluation of Student Effectiveness." *Social Work* 20(2):148–50.

Lee, Porter. 1923. "A Study of Social Treatment." *Family* 4:191–99.

Levine, F.M., and Tikler, H.A. 1974. "A Behavior Modification Approach to Supervision of Psychotherapy." *Psychotherapy: Theory, Research, and Practice* 11(2):182–88.

Levinson, Daniel, and Klerman, Gerald. 1967. "The Clinician—Executive." *Psychiatry* 30:13–15.

Levinson, Daniel, and Klerman, Gerald. 1972. "The Clinician-Executive Revisited." *Administration in Mental Health* 6:53–67.

Levy, Charles S. 1960. "In Defense of Supervision." *Journal of Jewish Communal Service* 37:194–201.

Levy, Charles. 1982. *Guide to Ethical Decisions and Action for Social Science Administrators—A Handbook for Managerial Personnel.* New York, Haworth Press.

Levy, Gerald. 1970. "Acute Workers in a Welfare Bureaucracy." In *Social Problems and Social Policy*, ed. Deborah Offenbacher and Constance Poster, pp. 168–75. New York, Appleton.

Leyendecker, Gertrude. 1959. "A Critique of Current Trends in Supervision." In *Casework Papers, National Conference on Social Welfare, 1959*. New York, Family Service Association of America.

Liddle, Howard A. 1982. "Family Therapy Training: Current Issues, Future Trends." *International Journal of Family Therapy* 4:81–95.

Liddle, Howard A., and Halpin, Richard J. 1978. "Family Therapy Training and Supervision Literature: A Comparative Review." *Journal of Marriage and Family Counseling* 4:77–98.

Liddle, Howard A., and Schwartz, Richard C. 1983. "Live Supervision/Consultation: Conceptual and Pragmatic Guidelines for Family Therapy Trainers." *Family Process* 22:477–90.

Lieberman, S. 1956. "The Effects of Change in Roles on the Attitudes of Role Occupants." *Human Relations* 9:385–402.

Likert, Rensis. 1967. *The Human Organization: Its Management and Value.* New York, McGraw.

Lindenberg, R. 1957. "Changing Traditional Patterns of Supervision." *Social Work* 2:42–46.

Lindenberg, Sidney. 1939. *Supervision in Social Group Work.* New York, Association Press.

Lipsky, Michael. 1980. *Street Level Bureaucracy—Dilemmas of the Individual in Public Services.* New York: Russell Sage Foundation.

Liston, Edward; Yager, Joel; and Strauss, Gordon D. 1981. "Assessment of Psychotherapy Skills: The Problem of Interrater Agreement." *American Journal of Psychiatry* 138(8):1069–74.

Littrell, J. M., et al. 1979. "A Developmental Framework for Counseling Supervision." *Counselor Education and Supervision* 19:129–36.

Litwak, Eugene. 1964. "Models of Bureaucracy Which Permit Conflict." *American Journal of Sociology* 67:177–84.

Loganbill, Carol. 1982. "Supervision—A Conceptual Model." *The Counseling Psychologist* 10(1):49–52.

Lowenberg, Frank M. 1972. *Time and Quality in Graduate Social Work Education: Report of the Special Committee to Study the Length of Graduate Social Work Education.* New York, Council on Social Work Education.

Lowenstein, Sophie, and Reder, Peter. 1982. "The Consumer Response: Trainees' Discussion of the Experience of Live Supervision." In *Family Therapy Supervision—Recent Developments in Practice*, ed. Rosemary Whiffen and John Byng-Hall, pp. 115–30. New York: Grune and Stratton.

Lutz, Werner A. 1956. *Student Evaluation: Workshop Report, 1956.* Annual Program Meeting of the CSWE, Buffalo, N.Y. New York, Council on Social Work Education.

McClure, W. J., and Vriend, J. 1976. "Training Counselors Using Absentee-calling Systems." *Canadian Counselor* 10:120–26.

Maccoby, 1976. *The Gamesman*. New York, Simon and Schuster.

McCune, Shirleyk D. 1966. "An Exploratory Study of the Measured Behavioral Styles of Students in Five Schools of Social Work." Ph.D. dissertaton, School of Social Service, Catholic University of America.

McGoldrick, M. 1982. "Through the Looking Glass: Supervision of a Trainee 'Trigger' Family." In *Family Therapy Supervision—Recent Developments in Practice,* ed. Rosemary Whiffen and John Byng-hall, pp. 17–37. New York, Academic Press.

MacGuffie, Robert; Janzen, Frederick V.; and McPhee, William M. 1970. "The Expression and Perception of Feelings between Students and Supervisors in a Practicum Setting." *Counselor Education and Supervision* 10:263–71.

Mandell, Betty. 1973. "The 'Equality' Revolution and Supervision." *Journal of Education for Social Work* 9:43–54.

Marcus, Grace. 1927. "How Casework Training May Be Adapted to Meet Workers' Personal Problems." In *Proceedings of the National Conference of Social Work, 1927.* Chicago, University of Chicago Press.

Markowski, Edward M., and Cain, Harry. 1983. "Live Marital and Family Therapy Supervision: A Model for Community Mental Health Centers." *The Clinical Supervisor* 1:37–46.

Marohn, Richard C. 1969. "The Similarity of Therapy and Supervisory Themes." *International Journal of Group Psychotherapy* 19:176–84.

Martin, Shan. 1983. *Managing without Managers*. Beverly Hills, Sage Publications.

Maslach, Christina. 1982. *Burn-out—The Cost of Caring*. Englewood Cliffs, N.J., Prentice-Hall.

Matorin, Susan. 1979. "Dimensions of Student Supervision—A Point of View." *Social Casework* 60:150–56.

Mattinson, Janet. 1975. *The Reflection Process in Casework Supervision*. Washington, D.C., National Association of Social Workers.

Mayer, John E., and Rosenblatt, Aaron. 1973a. "Sources of Stress among Student Practitioners in Social Work: A Sociological Review." Paper read at the annual meeting, Council on Social Work Education, San Francisco, January 1973.

Mayer, John E., and Rosenblatt, Aaron. 1973b. "Strains between Social Work Students and Their Supervisors: A Preliminary Report." Paper read at the National Conference on Social Welfare, Atlantic City, N.J., May 1973.

Mayer, John E., and Rosenblatt, Aaron. 1974. "Sources of Stress among Student Practitioners in Social Work: A Sociological View." *Journal of Education for Social Work* 10:56–66.

Mayer, John E., and Rosenblatt, Aaron. 1975a. "Encounters with Danger—Social Workers in the Ghetto." *Sociology of Work and Occupations* 2:227–45.

Mayer, John E., and Rosenblatt, Aaron. 1975b. "Objectionable Supervisory Styles: Students' Views." *Social Work* 20:184–89.

Maypole, Donald, and Skaine, Rosemarie. 1982. "Sexual Harassment of

Blue Collar Workers." *Journal of Sociology and Social Welfare* 9:682–95.

Maypole, Donald. 1983. "Sexual Harassment of Social Workers at Work: Injustice Within." Cedar Falls, Iowa, University of Northern Iowa. Mimeo, 22 pp.

Mead, E., and Crane, D. R. 1978. "An Empirical Approach to Supervision and Training of Relationship Therapists." *Journal of Marriage and Family Counseling* 4:67–75.

Mechanic, David. 1964. "Sources of Power of Lower Participants in Complex Organizations." In *New Perspectives in Organizational Research*, ed. W. W. Cooper, M. W. Shelly, and H. J. Leavitt, pp. 136–49. New York, Wiley.

Megargee, Edwin I. 1969. "Influence of Sex Roles on the Manifestation of Leadership." *Journal of Applied Psychology* 53(2):27–34.

Melichercik, John. 1973. "Social Work Education and Social Work Practice." *Social Worker* 41:22–27.

Merton, Robert. 1957. *Social Theory and Social Structure*. Revised ed. New York, Free Press.

Meyer, Carol H. 1966. *Staff Development in Public Welfare Agencies*. New York, Columbia University Press.

Meyer, Herbert A.; Kay, Emanual; and French, John R. P. 1965. "Split Roles in Performance Appraisal." *Harvard Business Review* 43:123–29.

Miars, Russel D. 1983. "Variations in Supervision Process Across Trainee Experience Levels." *Journal of Counseling Psychology* 30:403–12.

Middleman, Ruth R. 1984. "The Quality Circle: Fad, Fix, Fiction?" *Administration in Social Work* 8:31–44.

Milford Conference Report. 1929. *Social Work: Generic and Specific*. New York, American Association of Social Workers.

Miller, C. Dean, and Oetting, E. R. 1966. "Students React to Supervision." *Counselor Education and Supervision* 6:73–74.

Miller, Harry L.; Milick, Sidney; and Miller, Marilyn. 1973. *Cases in Administration of Mental Health and Human Service Agencies*. New York, Institute for Child Mental Health.

Miller, Irving. 1960. "Distinctive Characteristics of Supervision in Group Work." *Social Work* 5(1):69–76.

Miller, Ronald, and Podell, Lawrence. 1970. *Role Conflict in Public Social Services*. New York, State of New York Office of Community Affairs, Division of Research and Innovation.

Miller, Samuel O. 1970. "Components of Job Satisfaction for Beginning Social Workers." Mimeographed. School of Social Work, Western Michigan University, Kalamazoo.

Miringoff, Marc L. 1980. *Management in Human Service Organizations*. New York, MacMillan.

Moffatt, Ronald. 1977. "Using the Task Centered Model as an Introduction to Casework in Student Supervision." *Contemporary Social Work Education* 1(1):24–36.

Montalva, Braulio. 1973. "Aspects of Live Supervision." *Family Process* 12: 343–59.

Moore, Elon H. 1934. "How Accurate Are Base Records?" *Social Forces* 12:501.

Moore, Stewart. 1970. "Group Supervision: Forerunner or Trend Reflector: Part I—Trends and Duties in Group Supervision." *Social Worker* 38:16–20.

Moore, Stewart. 1971. "Group Supervision: Forerunner or Trend Reflector: Part II—Advantages and Disadvantages." *Social Worker* 39:3–7.

Moore, Wilbert E. 1970. *The Professions: Rules and Roles.* New York, Russell Sage.

Morton, Thomas D., and Kurtz, P. David. 1980. "Educational Supervision: A Learning Theory Approach." *Social Casework* 61:240–46.

Mosher, Ralph L., and Purpel, David E. 1972. *Supervision: The Reluctant Profession.* Boston, Houghton.

Mueller, William S., and Kell, Bill L. 1972. *Coping with Conflict: Supervisory Counselors and Psychotherapists.* New York, Appleton.

Munson, Carlton. 1979a. "Evaluation of Male and Female Supervisors." *Social Work* 24:104–10.

Munson, Carlton. 1979b. "An Empirical Study of Structure and Authority in Social Work Supervision." In *Social Work Supervision—Classic Statements and Critical Issues,* ed. Carlton E. Munson, pp. 286–96. New York, Free Press.

Munson, Carlton. 1979c. "Authority and Social Work Supervision: An Emerging Model." In *Social Work Supervision—Classic Statements and Critical Issues,* ed. Carlton Munson, pp. 336–45. New York, Free Press.

Munson, Carlton. 1980. "Differential Impact of Structure and Authority in Supervision." *Arete* 6:3–15.

Munson, Carlton. 1981. "Style and Structure in Supervision." *Journal of Education for Social Work* 17(1):66–72.

Munson, Carlton. 1983. *An Introduction to Clinical Social Work Supervision.* New York: Haworth Press.

Muslin, Hyman; Burstein, Alvin G.; Gedo, John E.; and Sadow, Leo. 1967. "Research on the Supervisory Process. I. Supervisor's Appraisal of the Interview Data." *Archives of General Psychiatry* 16:427–31.

Musling, Hyman; Turnblad, Robert J.; and Meschel, George. 1981. "The Fate of the Clinical Interview: An Observational Study." *American Journal of Psychiatry* 138(6):822–25.

Nadelson, Carol, and Maikan, Notman. 1977. "Psychotherapy Supervision: The Problem of Conflicting Values." *American Journal of Psychotherapy* 31:275–83.

Nader, Ralph; Petkas, Peter J.; and Blackwell, Kate, eds. 1974. *Whistle Blowing: Report of the Conference on Professional Responsibility.* New York, Grossman Publishers.

Nash, V.C. 1975. *The Clinical Supervisor of Psychotherapy.* Ph.D. dissertaton, Yale University.

Nathanson, Theresa. 1962. "Self-Awareness in the Educative Process." *Social Casework* 43:31–38.

National Association of Social Workers. n.d. *Reference for Candidates for Admission to the Academy of Certified Social Workers.* Washington, D.C., Academy of Certified Social Workers, National Association of Social Workers.

National Association of Social Workers. 1971. *NASW Standards for Social Work Personnel Practices: Professional Standards.* Washington, D.C.

National Association of Social Workers. 1981. *Special Issue—Conceptual Frameworks* 22:339–444.

National Social Welfare Assembly. 1961. *Salaries and Working Conditions of Social Welfare Manpower, 1960.* New York.

Nelsen, Judith C. 1973. "Early Communication Between Field Instructors and Casework Student." D.S.W. dissertation, Columbia University School of Social Work.

Nelsen, Judith C. 1974. "Relationship Communication in Early Fieldwork Conferences. Part I–II." *Social Casework* 55:237–43.

Nelson, G.L. 1978. "Psychotherapy Supervision from the Trainee's Point of View: A Survey of Preferences." *Professional Psychology* 9:539–50.

Newman, Edward, and Delaplaine, John W. 1974. *Social Work Manpower in the Seventies.* Washington, D.C., Linton, Mields, and Coston.

Nichols, Margo, and Cheers, Judy. 1980. "The Evaluation of the Practicuum." *Contemporary Social Work Education* 3(1):54–71.

Niland, Thomas M.; Duling, John; Allen, Jada; and Panther, Edward. 1971. "Student Counselors' Perception of Videotaping." *Counselor Education and Supervision* 11:97–101.

O'Connor, Robert, and Spence, Larry. 1976. "Communication Disturbances in a Welfare Bureaucracy: A Case for Self Management." *Journal of Sociology and Social Welfare* 4(2):178–204.

Olmstead, Joseph A. 1973. *Organizational Structure and Climate: Implications for Agencies.* National Study of Social Welfare and Rehabilitation Workers, Work and Organizational Contexts, Working Paper no. 2, Washington, D.C., U.S. Govt. Printing Office.

Olmstead, Joseph, and Christensen, Harold E. 1973. *Effects of Agency Work Contexts: An Intensive Field Study.* Research Report no. 2. Washington, D.C., Department of Health, Education, and Welfare, Social and Rehabilitation Service.

Olsen, Rolf, ed. 1975. *Management in the Social Services—The Team Leader's Task.* Bangor, Wales, University College of North Wales.

Olyan, Sidney D. 1972. "An Explanatory Study of Supervision in Jewish Community Centers as Compared to Other Welfare Settings." Ph.D. dissertation, University of Pittsburgh.

Orchard, Bernice. 1965. "The Use of Authority in Supervision." *Public Welfare* 23:32–40.

Orgon, D.W., and Green, C.N. 1981. "The Effects of Formalization on Profes-
    sional Involvement: A Compensatory Problem Approach." *Administra-
    tion Science Quarterly* 26(12):237–52.
Ouchi, W., 1981. *Theory Z: How American Business Can Meet the Japanese
    Challenge.* New York, Addison Wesley.
Paige, Clara P. 1927. "Supervising Casework in a District Office." *Family*
    8:307–9.
Paine, Whiton S. 1982. *Job Stress and Burn-out—Research Theory and
    Intervention Perspectives.* Beverly Hills, Sage Publications.
Palfrey, Colin F. 1981. "Management Training Needs in Social Services De-
    partments." *Social Policy and Administration* 15(2):125–37.
Parsloe, Phyllida, and Stevenson, Olive. 1978. *Social Service Teams: The
    Practitioner's View.* London, Her Majesty's Stationery Office.
Parsons, Jack R. 1976. "Collegial Administration as a Model for Social Agen-
    cies." *Social Casework* 57:104–10.
Patti, Rino, J. 1974a. "Organizational Resistance and Change: The View
    from Below." *Social Service Review* 48:367–83.
Patti, Rino J. 1974b. "Limitations and Prospects of Internal Advocacy."
    Social Casework 55:537–45.
Patti, Rino J. 1977. "Patterns of Management's Activity in Social Welfare
    Agencies." *Administration in Social Work* 1(1):5–18.
Patti, Rino J. 1983. *Social Welfare Administration: Managing Social Pro-
    grams in a Developmental Context.* Englewood Cliffs, N.J., Prentice-
    Hall.
Patti, Rino J. 1984. "Who Leads the Human Services—The Prospects for
    Social Work Leadership in the Age of Political Conservatism." *Admin-
    istration in Social Work* 8:17–30.
Patti, Rino J., and Maynard, Charles. 1978. "Qualifying for Managerial Jobs
    in Public Welfare." *Social Work* 23:288–94.
Patti, Rino J., and Rauch, Ronald. 1978. "Social Work Administration Gradu-
    ates on the Job Market: An Analysis of Managers' Hiring Preferences.
    Social Service Review 52:567–82.
Patti, Rino J., and Resnick, Herman. 1972. "Changing the Agency from
    Within." *Social Work* 17(4):48–57.
Patti, Rino J., et al. 1979. "From Direct Service to Administration: A Study of
    Social Workers' Transitions to Clinical to Management Roles."
    Administration in Social Work 3:131–51.
Pawlak, Edward J. 1976. "Organizational Tinkering." *Social Work*
    21:376–80.
Payne, Paul A.; Winter, Donna E.; and Bell, Glenn E. 1972. "Effects of
    Supervisor Style on the Learning of Empathy in a Supervision Ana-
    logue." *Counselor Education and Supervision* 11:262–69.
Peabody, Robert L. 1964. *Organizational Authority: Superior-Subordinate
    Relationships in Three Public Service Organizations.* New York, Ather-
    ton.

Pearson, Geoffrey. 1975. "Making Social Workers." In *Radical Social Work*, ed. Roy Bailey and Mike Brake, pp. 18–45. New York, Pantheon Books.

Pegg, P. E., and Manocchio, A. J. 1982. "In the Act." In *Family Therapy Supervision—Recent Developments in Practice*, ed. Rosemary Whiffon and John Byng-Hall, pp. 57–68. New York, Grune and Stratton.

Pelz, Donald. 1952. "Influence: A Key to Effective Leadership in the First Line Supervisor." *Personnel* 29:209–17.

Perlman, Helen H. 1947. "Content in Basic Social Casework." *Social Service Review* 21:76–84.

Perlman, Helen H. 1940. "Teaching Casework by the Discussion Method." *Social Service Review* 24:334–46.

Peters, Charles, and Branch, Taylor. 1972. *Blowing the Whistle: Dissent in the Public Interest*. New York, Praeger.

Pettes, Dorothy E. 1967. *Supervision in Social Work*. London, George Allen.

Pettes, Dorothy E. *Staff and Student Supervision—A Task Centered Approach*. London, Allen and Unwin, 1979.

Pines, Ayala; Aronson, Elliot; and Kafry, Ditsa. 1981. *Burn-out—From Tedium to Personal Growth*. New York, The Free Press.

Pines, Ayala. 1982. "On Burn-out and the Buffering Effects of Social Support." In *Stress and Burn-out in Human Service Professions*, ed. Barry A. Farber, pp. 155–169. New York, Pergamon Press.

Pines, A. and Maslach, C. 1978. "Characteristics of Staff Burn-out in Mental Health Settings." *Hospital and Community Psychiatry* 29:233–37.

Pittenger, Robert E.; Hockett, Charles F.; and Danehy, John J. 1960. *The First Five Minutes: A Sample of Microscopic Interview Analyses*. Ithaca, N.Y., Martineau.

Piven, Herman, and Pappenfort, Donald. 1960. "Strain between Administrator and Worker: A View from the Field of Corrections." *Social Work* 5:37–45.

Podell, Lawrence. 1967. "Examination Grades and New Workers." *Welfare in Review* 5:37–45.

Poertner, John, and Rapp, Charles A. 1983. "What is Social Work Supervision?" *Journal of Clinical Supervision* 1:53–67.

Pope, Kenneth; Levenson, Hanna; and Schover, Leslie R. 1979. "Sexual Intimacy in Psychology Training—Results and Implications of a National Survey." *American Psychologist* 34(8):682–89.

Powell, David J. 1980. *Clinical Supervision: Skills for Substance Abuse Counselors*. New York, Human Sciences Press.

Presthus, Robert. 1962. *The Organizational Society*. New York, Knopf.

Pretzer, Clarence A. 1929. "Significant Facts Regarding the Turnover of Case Workers in Family Welfare Agencies during 1927 and 1928." *Family* 10:163–73.

Prottas, Jeffrey. 1978. "The Power of the Street-level Bureaucrat in Public Service Bureaucracies." *Urban Affairs Quarterly* 13(3):285–311.

Prottas, Jeffrey. 1979. *People Processing—The Street Level Bureaucrat in Public Service Bureaucracies*. Lexington, Mass., Lexington Books.

Purvis, Lurline C. 1972. "Self-Awareness: A Proposal for Supervision." *Journal of Contemporary Psychotherapy* 4:107–12.
Rabow, Jerome, and Manos, Jorja J. 1980. "Values in Psychotherapy." *Humboldt Journal of Social Relations* 7(2):31–50.
Raider, Melvyn C. 1975. "An Evaluation of Management by Objectives." *Social Casework* 57:523–28.
Raider, Melvin C. 1977. "Installing Management by Objectives in Social Agencies." *Administration in Social Work* 1(3):235–44.
Ralph, Norbert. 1980. "Learning Psychotherapy: A Developmental Perspective." *Psychiatry* 43:243–50.
Rapoport, Lydia. 1954. "The Use of Supervision as a Tool in Professional Development." *British Journal of Psychiatric Social Work* 2:66–74.
Rapp, Charles A. 1984. "Information, Performance and the Human Service Manager of the 1980's—Beyond 'Housekeeping.'" *Administration in Social Work* 8:69–80.
Rapp, Charles A.; Hardcastle, David A.; Rosenzweig, Julie; and Poertner, John. 1983. "The Status of Research in Social Service Management." *Administration in Social Work* 7:89–100.
Reamer, Frederic G. 1982. *Ethical Dilemmas in Social Service.* New York, Columbia University Press.
Reich, Charles A. 1970. *The Greening of America.* New York, Random House.
Reid, William S. 1967. "Social Work and Motherhood: Competitors for Womenpower." *Personnel Information: NASW* 10:44–47.
Reising, Gregory, and Daniels, M. Harry. 1983. "A Study of Hogan's Model of Counselor Development and Supervision." *Journal of Counseling Psychology* 30:235–44.
Reiter, Laura. 1980. "Professional Morale and Social Work Training: A Study." *Clinical Social Work Journal* 8(3):198–205.
Resnick, Herman, and Patti, Rino J. 1980. *Change from Within: Humanizing Social Welfare Organizations.* Philadelphia, Temple University Press.
Reynolds, Bertha C. 1936. "Art of Supervision." *Family* 17:103–7.
Reynolds, Bertha C. 1942. *Learning and Teaching in the Practice of Social Work.* New York, Farrar.
Rhim, Bonnie. 1976. "The Uses of Videotape in Social Work Agencies." *Social Casework* 57:644–50.
Rice, Robert. 1973. "Organizing to Innovate in Social Work." *Social Casework* 54:20–26.
Richmond, Mary. 1897. "The Need for a Training School in Applied Philanthropy." In *Proceedings of the National Conference of Social Welfare, 1897.*
Richmond, Mary. 1889. *Friendly Visiting Among the Poor: A Handbook for Charity Workers.* New York, Macmillan.
Rickert, Veron C., and Turner, John E. 1978. "Through the Looking Glass: Supervision in Family Therapy." *Social Casework* 59:131–37.

Roberts, Ralph R., and Renzaglia, G. A. 1965. "The Influence of Tape Recording on Counseling." *Journal of Counseling Psychology* 12:10–15.

Robinson, Virginia 1949. *The Dynamics of Supervision under Functional Controls*. Philadelphia, University of Philadelphia Press.

Rose, Sheldon. 1970. "A Behavioral Model for Field Instruction." In *Current Patterns in Field Instruction in Graduate Social Work Education*, ed. Betty L. Jones, pp. 125–34. New York, Council on Social Work Education.

Rosen, Benson, and Jerdee, Thomas H. 1978. "Perceived Sex Differences in Managerially Relevant Characteristics." *Sex Roles* 4(6):837–43.

Rosen, Harold, and Bartemeier, Leo H. 1967. "The Psychiatric Resident as Participant Therapist." *American Journal of Psychiatry* 123:1371–78.

Rosenberg, Louis M.; Rubin, Sam S.; and Finzi, Hilda. 1968. "Participatn Supervision—The Teaching of Psychotherapy." *American Journal of Psychotherapy* 22, 280–95.

Rosenberg, Morris. 1957. *Occupations and Values*. New York, Free Press.

Rothman, Beulah. 1973. "Perspectives on Learning and Teaching in Continuing Education." *Journal of Education for Social Work* 9:39–52.

Rothman, Jack. 1974. *Planning and Organizing for Social Change: Action Principles from Social Science Research*. New York, Columbia University Press.

Rowbottom, R. 1973. "Organizing Social Service Hierarchies." *Public Administration* 15:291–305.

Rowbottom, Ralph; Hay, Anthea; and Billis, David. 1976. *Social Service Departments—Developing Patterns of Work and Organization*. London, Heinemann.

Rowley, Carl M., and Faux, Eugene. 1966. "The Team Approach to Supervision." *Mental Hygiene* 50:60–65.

Royster, Eugene C. 1972. "Black Supervisors: Problems of Race and Role." In *Issues in Human Services*, ed. Forence W. Kaslow and associates, pp. 72–84. San Francisco, Jossey-Bass.

Rubinstein, Mark, and Hammond, David. 1982. "The Use of Video Tape in Psychotherapy Supervision." In *Applied Supervision in Psychotherapy*, ed. Michael Blumenfield, pp. 143–63. New York, Grune and Stratton.

Russell, Pamela A.; Lankford, Michael M.; and Grinnell, Richard M. 1984. "Administrative Styles of Social Work Supervision in a Human Service Agency." *Administration in Social Work* 8(1):1–16.

Russell, Pamela A.; Lankford, Michael W.; and Grinnell, Richard M. 1983. "Attitudes Toward Supervisors in a Human Service Agency." *The Clinical Supervisor* 1(3):57–72.

Ryan, C. 1969. "Video Aids in Practicuum Supervision." *Counselor Education and Supervision* 8:125–29.

Ryan, Francis. 1964. "Joint Interviewing by Field Instructor and Student." *Social Casework* 45:471–74.

Sachs, D. M., and Shapiro, S. H. 1976. "On Parallel Process in Therapy and Teaching." *Psychoanalytic Quarterly* 45:394–415.

Sales, Esther, and Navarre, Elizabeth. 1970. *Individual and Group Supervision in Field Instruction: A Research Report.* Ann Arbor, Mich., School of Social Work, University of Michigan.

Satyamurti, Carole. 1981. *Occupational Survival.* Oxford: Basil Blackwell.

Schein, Edgar H. 1970. *Organizational Psychology.* 2d ed. Englewood Cliffs, N.J., Prentice-Hall.

Scher, Maryonda. 1981. "Gender Issues in Psychiatric Supervision." *Comprehensive Psychiatry* 22(2):179–83.

Schilit, Warran K., and Locke, Edwin. 1982. "A Study of Upward Influence in Organizations." *Administrative Science Quarterly* 27:304–15.

Schlenoff, Marjorie, and Busa, Sandra H. 1981. "Student and Field Instructor as Group Co-therapists—Equalizing an Unequal Relationship." *Journal of Education for Social Work* 17:29–35.

Schmidt, Frances, and Perry, Martha. 1940. "Values and Limitations of the Evaluation Process. I: As Seen by the Supervisor. II: As Seen by the Worker." In *Proceedings of the National Conference of Social Work,* pp. 629–47. New York, Columbia University Press.

Schmidt, James P. 1979. "Supervision: A Cognitive Behavioral Model." *Professional Psychology* 10(3):278–84.

Schour, Esther. 1951. "Helping Social Workers Handle Work Stresses." *Social Casework* 25:423–28.

Schreiber, Pamela, and Frank, Elaine. 1983. "The Use of a Peer Supervision Group by Social Work Clinicians." *The Clinical Supervisor* 1(1):29–36.

Schubert, G., and Nelson, J. 1976. "An Analysis of Verbal Behaviors Occurring in Speech Pathology Supervisory Sessions." *The Journal of the National Student Speech and Hearing Association* 4:17–26.

Schubert, Margaret. 1960. "Field Work Performance: Repetition of a Study." *Social Service Review* 34:286–99.

Schultz, Virginia M. 1970. "Employment Trends of Recent Graduates." *Personnel Information* 16:15.

Schur, Edith. 1979. "The Use of the Co-Worker Approach as a Teaching Model in Graduate Student Field Education." *Journal of Education for Social Work* 15:72–79.

Schuster, Daniel B.; Sandt, John J.; and Thaler, Otto F. 1972. *Clinical Supervision of the Psychiatric Resident.* New York, Brunner/Mazel.

Schutz, Benjamin M. 1982. *Legal Liability in Psychotherapy.* San Francisco, Jossey-Bass.

Scott, W. Richard. 1965. "Reactions to Supervision in a Heteronomous Professional Organization." *Administrative Science Quarterly* 10:65–81.

Scott, W. Richard. 1969. "Professional Employees in a Bureaucratic Structure." In *The Semiprofessions and Their Organization,* ed. Amitai Etzioni, pp. 82–140. New York, Free Press.

Scurfield, Raymond, M. 1981. "Clinician to Administrator: Difficult Role Transition?" *Social Work* 26:495–501.

Searles, Harold F. 1955. "The Informational Value of the Supervisor's Emotional Experiences." *Psychiatry* 18:135–46.

Sennett, Richard. 1981. *Authority*. New York, Vintage Books.

Shaefor, Bradford, and Jenkins, Lowell. 1982. *Quality Field Instruction in Social Work*. New York, Longman.

Shapiro, Constance H. 1982. "Creative Supervision—An Underutilized Antidote." In *Job Stress and Burn-out: Research, Theory, and Intervention Perspectives*, ed. Whiton S. Paine. Beverly Hills, Sage Publications.

Shapiro, Deborah. 1976. *Agencies and Foster Children*. New York, Columbia University Press.

Sherwood, David A., and Daley, Michael R. 1979. "Curriculum Directions for an MSW: Administration for Everyone." *Journal of Education for Social Work* 15(2):65–72.

Shinn, Marybeth, and Morch, Hanne. 1982. "A Tripartite Model of Coping with Burn-out." In *Stress and Burn-out in the Human Service Professions*, ed. Barry A. Farber, pp. 227–38. New York, Pergamon Press.

Shnit, Dan. 1978. "Professional Discretion in Social Welfare Administration." *Administration in Social Work* 2(4):439–50.

Shriberg, L., et al. 1975. "The Wisconsin Procedures for Appraisal of Clinical Competence." *ASHA* 17:158–65.

Shulman, Lawrence. 1982. *Skills of Supervision and Staff Management*. Itasca, Illinois, Peacock Publishers.

Shyne, Ann W. 1980. "Who Are the Children? A National Overview of Services." *Social Work and Abstracts*.

Shyne, Ann W., and Schroeder, Anita. 1978. *National Study of Social Services to Children and Their Families—Overview*. Rockville, Md., Westat.

Sidall, Lawrence B., and Bosma, Barbara J. 1976. "Co-therapy as a Training Process." *Psychotherapy: Theory, Research Practice* 13(3):209–13.

Simon, Herbert A. 1957. *Administrative Behavior: A Study of Decision-Making Processes in Administrative Organization*, 2d ed. New York, Free Press, 1976.

Simpson, Richard L., and Simpson, Ida H. 1969. "Women and Bureaucracy in the Semiprofessions." In *The Semiprofessions and Their Organization*, ed. Amitai Etzioni, pp. 196–265. New York, Free Press.

Slovenko, Ralph. 1980. "Legal Issues in Psychotherapy Supervision." In *Psychotherapy Supervision-Theory Research and Practice*, ed. Allen K. Hess, pp. 453–73. New York, John Wiley.

Smith, Donald M. 1972. "Group Supervision: An Experience." *Social Work Today* (London) 3:13–15.

Smith, Zilpha D. 1884. "Volunteer Visiting, The Organization Necessary to Make it Effective." In *Proceedings of The National Conference of Charities and Corrections*. Boston, Geo. H. Ellis.

Smith, Zilpha D. 1887. "How to Get and Keep Visitors." In *Proceedings of the National Conference of Charities and Corrections*, pp. 156–62. Boston, Geo. H. Ellis.

Smith, Zilpha D. 1892. "The Education of the Friendly Visitor." *The Charities Review* 2(1):48–58.

Smith, Zilpha D. 1901a. "Friendly Visitors." *Charities* 7:159–60.

Smith, Zilpha D. 1901b. "How to Win and How to Train Charity Visitors." *Charities* 7:46–47.

Snyder, Robert A., and Bruning, Nealia S. 1979. "Sex Differences in Perceived Competence." *Administration in Social Work* 3(3):349–57.

Social Work. 1981. *Conceptual Frameworks II: Second Special Issue on Conceptual Frameworks.* 26(1).

Solnit, A. 1970. "Learning from Psychoanalytic Supervision." *International Journal of Psychoanalysis* 51:359.

Spellman, Dorothea. 1946. "Improving the Quality of Social Group Work Practice through Individual Supervisory Conferences." In *Toward Professional Standards.* New York, Association Press.

Spergel, Irving. 1966. *Street Gang Work: Theory and Practice.* Reading, Mass., Addison-Wesley.

Spitzer, Robert, et al. 1982. "Supervising Intake Diagnosis." *Archives of General Psychiatry* 39:1297–1305.

Star, Barbara. 1979. "Exploring the Boundries of Videotape Self-Confrontation." *Journal of Education for Social Work* 15(1):87–94.

Star, Barbara. 1984. "Patient Violence—Therapist Safety." *Social Work* 29:255–30.

Steggert, Frank X. 1970. "Organization Theory: Bureaucratic Influences and the Social Welfare Task." In *Social Work Administration: A Resource Book,* ed. Harry A. Schatz, pp. 43–56. New York, Council on Social Work Education.

Stein, Herman. 1961. "Administrative Implications of Bureaucratic Theory," *Social Work* 6(3):14–21.

Stein, Herman. 1965. "Administration." In *Encyclopedia of Social Work,* ed. Robert Morris. New York, National Association of Social Workers.

Stein, Stafan P., et al. 1975. "Supervision or the Initial Interview—A Study of Two Methods." *Archives of General Psychiatry* 32:265–68.

Steiner, Richard. 1977. *Managing the Human Service Organization—From Survival to Achievement.* Beverly Hills, California, Sage Publications.

Stelling, Joan, and Bucher, Rue. 1973. "Vocabularies of Realism in Professional Socialization." *Social Science and Medicine* 7:661–75.

Stevens, Ruth N., and Hutchinson, Fred A. 1956. "A New Concept of Supervision is Tested." *Social Work* 1(3):50–55.

Stewart, Rosemary. 1972. *The Reality of Organizations.* New York, Doubleday, Anchor.

Stiles, Evelyn. 1963. "Supervision in Perspective." *Social Casework* 44: 19–25.

Stodgill, R. M., and Coons, A. E. 1957. *Leader Behavior: Its Description and Measurement.* Columbus, Ohio, Bureau of Business Research, Ohio State University.

Stoltenberg, Carl. 1981. "Approaching Supervision from a Developmental Perspective: The Counselor Complexity-model." *Journal of Counseling Psychology* 28(1):59–65.

Strauss, Anselm L. 1964. *Psychiatric Ideologies and Institutions.* New York, Free Press.

Streepy, Joan. 1981. "Direct Service Providers and Burn-out." *Social Casework* 62:352–61.

Studt, Elliot. 1954. "An Outline for Study of Social Authority Factors in Casework." *Social Casework* 35:231–38.

Studt, Elliot. 1959. "Worker Client Authority Relationships in Social Work." *Social Work* 4:18–28.

Suess, James F. 1970. "Self-confrontation of Videotaped Psychotherapy as a Teaching Device for Psychiatric Students." *Journal of Medical Education* 45:271–82.

Sung, Kyu-Taik. 1982. "Working Under the Accountability System: A Study of the Recreation of Social Workers." *Administration in Social Work.* 6(4):15–29.

Sutton, Jacquelyn A. 1982. "Sex Discrimination Among Social Workers." *Social Work* 27:211–17.

Swanson, Al, and Brown, John A. 1982. "Racism, Supervision, and Organizational Environment." *Administration in Social Work* 5(2):59–67.

Switzer, Elaine. 1973. "Chicago Settlement, 1972: An Overview." *Social Service Review* 47:581–92.

Szakacs, J. 1977. "Survey Indicates Women Losing Ground in Leadership." *NASW News* 22:12.

Tannenbaum, Arnold A. 1968. *Control in Organizations.* New York, McGraw.

Taylor, Joseph L. 1980. "A Practice Note on Staff Reorganization." *Child Welfare* 59(9):583–87.

Tentoni, S. C., and Robb, G. P. 1977. "Improving the Counseling Practicum Through Immediate Radio Feedback." *College Student Journal* 12:279–83.

Terborg, James R., et al. 1977. "Organizational and Personal Correlates of Attitudes Toward Women as Managers." *Academy of Management Journal* 20:89–100.

Thing, Pen. 1979. "Perceptual Differences in the Supervision of Paraprofessional Mental Health Workers." *Community Mental Health Journal* 15:139–48.

Thomas, David N., and Warburton, William. 1978. "Staff Development in Community Workers in Social Service Departments." In *Community Work: Learnng Supervision,* ed. C. Briscoe and D. Thomas, pp. 22–32. London, Allen and Unwin.

Thomas, George, and LaCavera, Anthony. 1979. *Evaluation of the South Carolina Department of Social Services Child Protective Services Certification Training Program.* Thesis, Georgia Regional Institute of Social Welfare Research.

Toren, Nina. 1969. "Semiprofessionalism and Social Work: A Theoretical Perspective." In *The Semiprofessions and Their Organization,* ed.

Amitai Etzioni, pp. 141–95. New York, Free Press.

Toren, Nina. 1972. *Social Work: The Case of a Semiprofession*. Beverly Hills, Sage Publications.

Torre, Elizabeth. 1974. "Student Performance in Solving Social Work Problems and Work Experience Prior to Entering the MSW Program." *Journal of Education for Social Work* 10:114–17.

Tosi, Henry, et al. 1976. "How Real Are Changes Induced by Management-by-Objectives?" *Administrative Science Quarterly* 21:275–306.

Towle, Charlotte. 1945. *Common Human Needs*. Washington, D.C., U.S. Govt. Printing Office.

Towle, Charlotte. 1954. *The Learner in Education for the Professions: As Seen in Education for Social Work*. Chicago, University of Chicago Press.

Towle, Charlotte. 1962. "Role of Supervision in the Union of Cause and Function in Social Work." *Social Service Review* 36:396–411.

Tropman, John E. 1968. "The Married Professional Social Worker." *Journal of Marriage and the Family* 30:661–65.

Tucker, Bernice; Hart, Gordon; and Liddle, Howard A. 1976. "Supervision in Family Therapy: A Developmental Perspective." *Journal of Marriage and Family Counseling* 2:269–76.

Tyler, Ralph W. 1971. *Basic Principles of Curriculum and Instruction*. Chicago, University of Chicago Press.

U.S. Civil Service Commission. 1955. *Leadership and Supervision: A Survey of Research Findings*. U.S. Civil Service Commission, Personnel Management Series no. 9. Washington, D.C.

U.S. Department of Health, Education and Welfare, Social Rehabilitation Service. 1975. *Public Welfare Personnel Annual Statistical Data: June 1973*. Washington, D.C., National Center for Social Statistics.

U.S. Department of Health, Education and Welfare. 1978. *Systems of Social Services for Children and Families: Detailed Design*. Washington, D.C., U.S. Govt. Printing Office. DHEW Publication no. (OHDS) 73-30131.

Valentich, M., and Gripton, J. 1978. "Sexism and Sex Differences in Career Management of Social Workers." *Social Science Journal* 15(2):101–11.

Van Atta, R. E. 1969a. "Co-Therapy as a Supervisory Process." *Psychotherapy: Theory, Research and Practice* 6:137–39.

Van Atta, R. E. 1969b. "Excitory and Inhibitory Effect of Various Modes of Observation in Counseling." *Journal of Counseling Psychology* 16:433–39.

Vargus, Ione D. 1980. "The Minority Administrator." In *Leadership in Social Administration*, ed. Simon Slavin and Felice D. Perlmutter, pp. 216–29. Philadelphia, Temple University Press.

Vinokur, Diane K. 1983. *The View from the Agency: Supervisors and Workers Look at In-Service Training for Child Welfare*. Ann Arbor, Mich., National Child Welfare Training Center, University of Michigan School of Social Work.

Vinter, Robert D. 1959. "The Social Structure of Service." In *Issues in American Social Work*, ed. Alfred J. Kahn, pp. 242–69. New York, Columbia University Press.

Wahba, S. P. 1976. "Women in Libraries." *Law Library Journal* 69:223–31.

Waldman, Ellen. 1980. "Co-leadership as a Method of Training." *Social Work with Groups* 3(1):51–58.

Walker, Sydnor H. 1928. *Social Work and the Training of Social Workers.* Chapel Hill, N.C., University of North Carolina Press.

Walton, Mary. 1967. "Rats in the Crib, Roaches in the Food." *Village Voice*, May 11.

Walz, G. R., and Johnston, J. A. 1963. "Counselors Look at Themselves on Video Tape." *Journal of Counseling Psychology* 10:232–36.

Walz, Thomas. 1971. "A New Breed of Social Workers: Fact or Fantasy?" *Public Welfare* 29:19–23.

Wanous, J. P. 1975. "A Job Preview Makes Recruiting More Effective." *Harvard Business Review* 53:166–68.

Ward, C. H. 1960. "An Electronic Aide for Teaching Inverviewing Techniques." *Archives of General Psychiatry* 3:357–58.

Ward, C. H. 1962. "Electronic Preceptoring in Teaching Beginning Psychotherapy." *Journal of Medical Education* 37:1128–29.

Warren, D. I. 1968. "Power, Visibility and Conformity in Formal Organizations." *American Sociological Review* 6:951–70.

Wasserman, Harry. 1970. "Early Careers of Professional Social Workers in a Public Child Welfare Agency." *Social Work* 15(3):93–101.

Wasserman, Harry. 1971. "The Professional Social Worker in a Bureaucracy." *Social Work* 16(1):89–95.

Watson, Kenneth W. 1973. "Differential Supervision." *Social Work* 8(3): 37–43.

Weatherly, Richard, et al. 1980. "Accountability of Social Serivce Workers at the Front Line." *Social Service Review* 54:556–71.

Weatherley, Richard. 1983. "Participatory Management in Public Welfare: What Are the Prospects?" *Administration in Social Work* 7(1):39–49.

Webb, Linda, et al. 1980. "Employees' Satisfaction Among Workers in Mental Health Settings." *Psychological Reports* 47:30.

Weber, Max. 1946. *Essays in Sociology*, trans. and ed. H. H. Gerth and C. Wright Mills. New York, Oxford University Press.

Weber, Shirley, and Polm, Donald. 1974. "Participatory Management in Public Welfare." *Social Casework* 55:297–306.

Weinbach, Robert W. 1984. "Implementing Change: Insights and Strategies for the Supervisor." *Social Work* 29:282–86.

Weinberg, Gladys. 1960. "Dynamics and Content of Group Supervision." *Child Welfare* 39:1–6.

Weirich, Thomas W. 1980. "The Design of Information Systems." In *Leadership in Social Administration—Perspectives for the 1980s*, ed. F. D. Perlmutter and S. Slavin, pp. 142–56. Philadelphia, Temple University Press.

Weissman, Harold H. 1973. *Overcoming Mismanagement in the Human Service Professions*. San Francisco, Jossey-Bass.

Westheimer, Ilse J. 1977. *The Practice of Supervision in Social Work: A Guide for Staff Supervisors*. London, Ward Lock Educational.

Whiffen, Rosemary, and Byng-Hall, John. 1982. *Family Therapy Supervision-Recruit Developments in Practice*. New York, Grune and Stratten.

White, William A. 1978. *A Systems Response to Staff Burn-out*. Rockville, Maryland, ITCS Inc., p. 15.

Wiehe, Vernon. 1973. "Management by Objectives in a Family Service Agency." *Social Casework* 54:142–46.

Wiehe, Vernon. 1975. "Performance Appraisal of Staff." *Journal of Social Welfare* 2(1):15–22.

Wiehe, Vernon. 1980. "Current Practices in Performance Appraisal." *Administration in Social Work* 4(3):1–11.

Wilding, Paul. 1982. *Professional Power and Social Welfare*. Boston, Routledge and Kegan Paul.

Wilkie, Charlotte H. 1963. "A Study of Distortions in Recording Interviews." *Social Work* 8:31–36.

Williamson, Margaretta. 1931. *The Social Worker in Child Care and Protection*. New York, Harper and Brothers.

Williamson, Margaret. 1961. *Supervision: New Patterns and Processes*. New York, Association Press.

Wilson, Gertrude, and Ryland, Gladys. 1949. *Social Group Work Practice*. Boston, Houghton.

Wilson, Paul A.; Voth, Victor; and Hudson, Walter A. 1980. "Professionals and the Bureaucracy: Measuring the Orientations of Social Workers." *Journal of Social Service Research* 4(1):15–30.

Wilson, Suanna J. 1981. *Field Instruction: Techniques for Supervisors*. New York, The Free Press.

Winstead, D.K.; Bonovitz, J.S.; Gale, M.S.; and Evans, J.W. 1974. "Resident Peer Supervision of Psychotherapy." *American Journal of Psychiatry* 131:318–21.

Wisconsin Department of Health and Social Services. 1977. *A Study in the Job Tasks and Associated Knowledge Areas of the Supervisor I Position in Wisconsin*. Milwaukee, School of Social Welfare—Center for Advanced Studies in the Human Services, University of Wisconsin.

Wolberg, Lewis R. 1977. *The Techniques of Psychotherapy*. 3d ed., part 2. New York, Grune and Stratton.

Wolfson, Abby, and Sampson, Harold. 1976. "A Comparison of Process Notes and Tape Recordings." *Archives of General Psychiatry* 33:558–63.

Woodcock, G. D. C. 1967. "A Study of Beginning Supervision." *British Journal of Psychiatric Social Work* 9:66–74.

Worthington, E. L., and Roehlke, H. J. 1979. "Effective Supervisor as Perceived for Beginning Counselors' Training." *Journal of Counseling Psychology* 26:64–73.

Yelaja, Shankar A., ed. 1971. *Authority and Social Work: Concept and Use*.

Toronto, University of Toronto Press.

Yelaja, Shankar A., ed. 1982. *Ethical Issues in Social Work*. Springfield, Illinois, C.G. Thomas.

Yodefet, Yona; Yaakovson, Yoheved; Pinto, Meir. 1978. "The Relationship Between the Social Worker and His Supervisor: Dependence or Independence." *Society and Welfare: Quarterly for Social Work Ministry of Labour and Social Affairs*. Jerusalem-Israel.

York, Reginald O. 1977. "Can Change be Effectively Managed?" *Administration in Social Work* 1(2):187–97.

Zander, Alvin. *Groups at Work*. San Francisco, Jossey-Bass, 1977.

Zetzel, E. 1953. "The Dynamic Basis of Supervision." *Social Casework* 34:143–49.

Zietz, D. and Erlich, J. L. 1976. "Sexism in Social Agencies: Practitioners' Perspectives." *Social Work* 21:434–39.

Zimny, George H.; Brown, Joseph E.; Ellis, Joanna J.; and Sorenson, James C. 1972. "Use of Television in the Clinical Internship Programs." *Professional Psychology* 3:271–76.

Zischka, Pauline C., and Fox, Raymond. 1973. "Burn-out and the Catalytic Role of the Supervisor." *The Clinical Supervisor* 1(2):43–52.

INDEX

Absenteeism, of supervisee: occurrences of, 1, 63; supervision reduces, 1, 276; as sign of noncompliance, 134; low morale causes, 230; symptomatic of burn-out, 233

Accountability: of social agency to the community, 31–32, 33, 76, 332; influences work delegation, 61; related to evaluations, 322; of worker to agency, 332

Administration: focus of, in social work, 23; tasks related to, 24–25; defined, 47; of bureaucratic organization, 47–48

Administrative supervision: recent emphasis on, 15–16; group supervisors' stress, 17; objectives of, 21, 227; short-range objectives of, 22; priority of, among supervisors, 24–25, 27, 293; theory of, 27; in a host setting, 61; communication in, 69, 71–72, 72–73; as supportive, 75, 236, 262; vicarious liability in, 82–84; problems of power in, 85–97 *passim;* reward power in, 88–89, 228; coercive power in, 89–90; legitimate power in, 90; referent power in, 90–91; expert power in, 91–92; authority in, 99–102, 107–11; and caseload pressures, 110–11; agency rules and, 117–23; and worker noncompliance, 123–32; relationship to educational supervision, 141–42; as source of worker tension, 236; evaluations important to, 333; extended, 466–67; protects client, 467; separation of, from educational supervision, 481–84

——tasks of: general, 24–25; staff recruitment, 48–49; inducting the worker, 49–52; work planning, 52–53; work assignment, 53–58; work delegation, 58–62; worker evaluation, 62–64; inspectional, 62–64; work coordina-

tion, 64–66; handling worker conflicts, 65–66; facilitating intra-agency communication, 67–74 *passim;* managing client complaints, 74–75; protecting worker, 75; defending agency policies, 76–78; reformulating agency policy, 78–79; *see also* Supervision; Supervisor: Administrative

Age differences, supervisor-supervisee, 310–11

Agency, social service: bureaucratic structure of, 22–23, 30–31, 47; hierarchy of, 22–23, 30–31, 65, 67; as central to social work, 30–31; public accountability of, 31–32, 33, 61, 76, 132; as heteronomous organizations, 32–33; as affecting public policy, 33; as nonstandardized, 34; clients captive to, 35–36, 244–45; personnel recruitment in, 48–49, 333; placing the worker in, 49–52; work planning in, 52–53; work assignment in, 53–58; work delegation in, 61; supervisor as representing, 63; work coordination in, 64–66; conflicts within, 65–66, 144; communication in, 67–74 *passim;* supervisor as buffer in, 74–77; deviance in, 75–76; self-preservation of, 76; supervisor defends, 76–77; worker conflicts with, 76–77, 79–80, 124–31, 254; innovations in, 78, 80; administrative authority needed in, 85; conformity in, 86, 93–94; limited reward power of, 89; as supporting supervisor's authority, 101; ambiguous objectives of, 107–8, 250, 253–54; supervisor constrained by, 107–11, 115–16; supervisor in conflict with, 121–22; excessive demands on, 125; and staff development, 139–40; in-service training in, 140; loyalty to,

and growth of paid staff, 8; and first professional conferences, 9; and growth of training programs, 9; and growth of periodical literature, 9–10; and development of a knowledge base, 10; and early schools of social work, 11–12; and changing conceptions of supervision, 13–20 *passim;* and origins of casework, 14, 17; and rise of educational supervision, 15; and reaction against supervision, 15–16; and rise of administrative supervision, 15–16; *see also* Administrative supervision; Educational supervision; Extended supervision; Group supervision; Supportive supervision

Supervisor: historical predecessors of, 4–7, 12; changing orientation of, 13–20; definition of, 20, 24; educational functions of, 20, 24, 25–26, 40, 139, 140–41; administrative functions of, 21, 24–25, 26, 40; supportive functions of, 21, 24, 26; objectives of, 21–22, 24, 180–81; hierarchical position of, 22–23; provides indirect service, 23; sequential activities of, 23; primary tasks of, 24–27; percentage of social workers employed as, 28–29; demography of, 28–30; educational background of, 29; income of, 30; caseload of, 30, 110–11; in bureaucratic organizations, 47; functional power of, 92–93; authority of, 103–5, 107–11; supervisory responsibilities avoided by, 103–7; educational supervision satisfying for, 140–41; role ambiguity of, 182–84, 304, 308; as directive, 208–9; and job-related stress, 225, 306–11; as task centered, 225–26; expressive orientation of, 225–26, 227, 293–94; as parent surrogate, 239, 240; conflicts with supervisee, 241–43, 308–9; accessibility of, 262, 429; supervisee's manipulation of, 282–91 *passim;* source of power of, 285; counters supervisee's games, 291–93; ranked low on instrumental functions, 294; autonomy of, 307, 310; limitations of, 307–8; as agency mediator, 309; conference stressful for, 309; role conflicts of, 309, 310; ex-

pressive needs of, met by supervisee, 309–10; as lacking resources, 310; younger than supervisee, 310–11; white, with black supervisee, 311–12; black, 313–15; female, 315–17; and sexual contact with supervisee, 317–19; supportive resources available to, 320, 322; dissatisfaction of, 321–22; burn-out of, 323; develop own vocabularies of realism, 323; indifference of, 323–24; games of, 324–28; rank satisfactions in supervision, 325; agency rules selectively enforced by, 327; double-talk by, 327; value of evaluations for, 334–35; evaluations disliked by, 336–40; leniency bias of, 337–39, 347, 353, 355–56; productive evaluation by, 340–45; evaluation errors of, 346–57 *passim;* evaluation of, 380–83; validity of evaluations by, 385–89; encourages worker autonomy, 399–428 *passim;* successful, characteristics of, 428–43 *passim;* problems of, in observing worker's performance, 433–38; sits in on interview, 438–39; co-therapy supervision used by, 439–42; taping of worker by, 443–50; in team service delivery, 472–73; ethical dilemmas of, 484–86; success of, related to training, 497

——administrative: responsibilities of, 47–48; staff recruitment by, 48–49; worker induction by, 49–52; work planning by, 52–53; work assignment by, 53–58, 56–58; inspectional tasks of, 62–64; work evaluations of, 64; work coordination by, 64–66; hierarchical position of, 65, 67; adjudicates work conflicts, 65–66; resources needed by, 66; communication functions of, 67–74 *passim;* represents supervisee's interests, 69–70, 75; credibility of, 72; handles client complaints, 74–75; as administrative buffer, 74–77, 79; defends agency policy, 75–77, 117–18; conflicts with agency, 77; as change agent, 78–80; as community liaison, 80–81; malpractice suits against, 82–84; as responsible for supervisee's actions, 82–84; power of, 85–91, 92–96; authority of,

264–73; effective implementation of, 272–73, 293; limitations of, 273–74; positive consequences of, 275–77; peer group used in, 280–81; *see also* Supervision; Supervisor: supportive

Tardiness: of supervisee, 63; as non-compliance, 134; low morale causes, 230; symptomatic of burn-out, 233–34
Task-centered, supervision as, 225–26
Teaching, *see* Education; Learning; Educational supervision
Team service delivery: enhances worker autonomy, 472–73; supervisor's role in, 472–73; disadvantages of, 473
Tension: in social work, 225; causes burn-out, 232, 233; supportive supervision concerned with, 227; of clients, 242; indifference, as response to, 323–24; in group supervision, 421
——sources of: learning as, 148–53; 222, 236–37; administrative supervision as, 236; social work training as, 237–38; transference as, 239–40; supervisor-supervisee relationship as, 239–42; client as, 242–47; therapeutic failure as, 245, 247; worker's responsibilities as, 246–47; worker's work setting as, 248, 255; social work tasks as, 248–53; worker's sense of impotence as, 249–50; worker's role ambiguity as, 250–51, 253–54; worker's role conflicts as, 254; public perception of social work as, 256–58; promotion to supervisor as, 296–305 *passim;* supervisor's authority as, 300; supervisor's job demands as, 306–11; supervisor's outmoded knowledge as, 308; supervisor's role ambiguity as, 308; supervisory conference as, 309; racial differences as, 312–15; gender differences as, 315–19; evaluations as, 337, 341–42
——means of reducing: supportive supervision as, 229–30, 276; and educational supervision, 238; through supervisor's help, 264–73 *passim;* job enrichment as, 264; environment modification as, 264; flexible work assignment as, 264–65; sharing feelings as, 265–66; vocabularies of realism as,

268–69; resolving role conflicts as, 269; clients help as, 277–78; peer group's support as, 278–81; humor as, 281; psychological games as, 282–91, 324–28; evaluations as, 331, 335; audio transmitter as, 452–53
Termination: choosing point of, 206; of educational supervision conference, 206; steps involved in, 206; of evaluation conference, 350; of group conference, 422
Therapy: differentiated from educational supervision, 174–82, 211; objectives of, 175–76; patient-therapist relationship in, 178; effective, conditions of, 179; transference in, 179; interactional orientation of, 180; supervision confused with, 241; supervisor's use of, 284; group, distinguished from group supervision, 392–93
Time limited supervision, in social agency, 466
Transference: distorts worker's perception, of client, 162–63; avoided in supervision, 179; in supervisor-supervisee relationship, 239, 240

Veto power, of supervisees, 112–13
Vicarious liability: problem of, for supervisor, 82–84; documented cases of, 83–84
Videotaping: in group supervision, 414, 447; frequency of, in social work, 443; technical procedures of, 443; advantages of, for teaching and evaluation, 443–46; used to induct staff, 447; supervisors favor, 447–48; disadvantages of, in supervision, 447–51; of supervisor, 449–50; intrusive effects of, 450; as effective technique, 457; costs of, 458
Vocabularies of realism: defined, 268; need for, in social work, 268; stress reduced by, 268–69; for supervisors, 274, 323

Wisconsin Department of Health and Social Services, 24
Women: prevalence of, in social work, 42; professional commitment of, 42; as students, sexism a problem for,